McDougal Littell

CALIFORNIA

Science

FOCUS ON PHYSICAL SCIENCES

Space
Science

Chemical
Interactions

The Structure
of Matter

Motion
and Forces

Science Content Standards for California Public Schools reproduced by permission, California Department of Education, CDE Press, 1430 N Street, Suite 3207, Sacramento, CA 95814.

Printed in the U.S.A.

ISBN 13: 978-0-618-64096-6
ISBN 10: 0-618-64096-7   1 2 3 4 5 6 7 8 VJM 09 08 07 06

Internet Web Site: http://www.mcdougallittell.com

Science Consultants

Chief Science Consultant

James Trefil, Ph.D. is the Clarence J. Robinson Professor of Physics at George Mason University. He is the author or co-author of more than 25 books, including *Science Matters* and *The Nature of Science.* Dr. Trefil is a member of the American Association for the Advancement of Science's Committee on the Public Understanding of Science and Technology. He is also a fellow of the World Economic Forum and a frequent contributor to *Smithsonian* magazine.

Rita Ann Calvo, Ph.D. is Senior Lecturer in Molecular Biology and Genetics at Cornell University, where for 12 years she also directed the Cornell Institute for Biology Teachers. Dr. Calvo is the 1999 recipient of the College and University Teaching Award from the National Association of Biology Teachers.

Kenneth Cutler, M.S. is the Education Coordinator for the Julius L. Chambers Biomedical Biotechnology Research Institute at North Carolina Central University. A former middle school and high school science teacher, he received a 1999 Presidential Award for Excellence in Science Teaching.

Instructional Design Consultants

Douglas Carnine, Ph.D. is Professor of Education and Director of the National Center for Improving the Tools of Educators at the University of Oregon. He is the author of seven books and over 100 other scholarly publications, primarily in the areas of instructional design and effective instructional strategies and tools for diverse learners. Dr. Carnine also serves as a member of the National Institute for Literacy Advisory Board.

Linda Carnine, Ph.D. consults with school districts on curriculum development and effective instruction for students struggling academically. A former teacher and school administrator, Dr. Carnine also co-authored a popular remedial reading program.

Donald Steely, Ph.D. serves as principal investigator at the Oregon Center for Applied Science (ORCAS) on federal grants for science and language arts programs. His background also includes teaching and authoring of print and multimedia programs in science, mathematics, history, and spelling.

Sam Miller, Ph.D. is a middle school science teacher and the Teacher Development Liaison for the Eugene, Oregon, Public Schools. He is the author of curricula for teaching science, mathematics, computer skills, and language arts.

Vicky Vachon, Ph.D. consults with school districts throughout the United States and Canada on improving overall academic achievement with a focus on literacy. She is also co-author of a widely used program for remedial readers.

Content Reviewers

John Beaver, Ph.D.
Ecology
Professor, Director of Science Education Center
College of Education and Human Services
Western Illinois University
Macomb, IL

Donald J. DeCoste, Ph.D.
Matter and Energy, Chemical Interactions
Chemistry Instructor
University of Illinois
Urbana-Champaign, IL

Dorothy Ann Fallows, Ph.D., MSc
Diversity of Living Things, Microbiology
Partners in Health
Boston, MA

Michael Foote, Ph.D.
The Changing Earth, Life Over Time
Associate Professor
Department of the Geophysical Sciences
The University of Chicago
Chicago, IL

Lucy Fortson, Ph.D.
Space Science
Director of Astronomy
Adler Planetarium and Astronomy Museum
Chicago, IL

Elizabeth Godrick, Ph.D.
Human Biology
Professor, CAS Biology
Boston University
Boston, MA

Isabelle Sacramento Grilo, M.S.
The Changing Earth
Lecturer, Department of the Geological Sciences
San Diego State University
San Diego, CA

David Harbster, MSc
Diversity of Living Things
Professor of Biology
Paradise Valley Community College
Phoenix, AZ

Richard D. Norris, Ph.D.
Earth's Waters
Professor of Paleobiology
Scripps Institution of Oceanography
University of California, San Diego
La Jolla, CA

Donald B. Peck, M.S.
*Motion and Forces; Waves, Sound, and Light;
  Electricity and Magnetism*
Director of the Center for Science Education (retired)
Fairleigh Dickinson University
Madison, NJ

Javier Penalosa, Ph.D.
Diversity of Living Things, Plants
Associate Professor, Biology Department
Buffalo State College
Buffalo, NY

Raymond T. Pierrehumbert, Ph.D.
Earth's Atmosphere
Professor in Geophysical Sciences (Atmospheric Science)
The University of Chicago
Chicago, IL

Brian J. Skinner, Ph.D.
Earth's Surface
Eugene Higgins Professor of Geology and Geophysics
Yale University
New Haven, CT

Nancy E. Spaulding, M.S.
Earth's Surface, The Changing Earth, Earth's Waters
Earth Science Teacher (retired)
Elmira Free Academy
Elmira, NY

Steven S. Zumdahl, Ph.D.
Matter and Energy, Chemical Interactions
Professor Emeritus of Chemistry
University of Illinois
Urbana-Champaign, IL

Susan L. Zumdahl, M.S.
Matter and Energy, Chemical Interactions
Chemistry Education Specialist
University of Illinois
Urbana-Champaign, IL

Safety Consultant

Juliana Texley, Ph.D.
Former K–12 Science Teacher and School Superintendent
Boca Raton, FL

English Language Advisor

Judy Lewis, M.A.
Director, State and Federal Programs for reading proficiency
and high risk populations
Rancho Cordova, CA

California Teacher Reviewers

Bill Bruce
Tenaya Middle School
Fresno, CA

Mark J. Handwerker, Ph.D.
Erle Stanley Gardner Middle School
Temecula, CA

Jack Castro
William Sheppard Middle School
San Jose, CA

Sandy Steinburg
Winston Churchill Middle School
Carmichael, CA

Bernice Filerman, Ph.D.
Bell Gardens High School
Bell Gardens, CA

California Panel Members and Lab Evaluators

Al Brofman
Tehipite Middle School,
Fresno, CA

Jenifer Cox
Sylvan Middle School,
Citrus Heights, CA

Ann Marie Lynn
Amelia Earhart Middle School,
Riverside, CA

Barbara Newell
Charles Evans Hughes Middle School,
Long Beach, CA

Greg Pirolo
Golden Valley Middle School,
San Bernardino, CA

Nancy Stubbs
Sweetwater Union Unified
School District,
Chula Vista, CA

Lori Walker
Audubon Middle School &
Magnet Center,
Los Angeles, CA

Teacher Panel Members

Carol Arbour
Tallmadge Middle School,
Tallmadge, OH

Patty Belcher
Goodrich Middle School,
Akron, OH

Gwen Broestl
Luis Munoz Marin Middle School,
Cleveland, OH

John Cockrell
Clinton Middle School,
Columbus, OH

Linda Culpepper
Martin Middle School,
Charlotte, NC

Melvin Figueroa
New River Middle School,
Ft. Lauderdale, FL

Doretha Grier
Kannapolis Middle School,
Kannapolis, NC

Robert Hood
Alexander Hamilton Middle School,
Cleveland, OH

Scott Hudson
Covedale Elementary School,
Cincinnati, OH

Loretta Langdon
Princeton Middle School,
Princeton, NC

Carlyn Little
Glades Middle School,
Miami, FL

James Minogue
Lowe's Grove Middle School,
Durham, NC

Kathleen Montagnino-DeMatteo
Jefferson Davis Middle School,
West Palm Beach, FL

Joann Myers
Buchanan Middle School,
Tampa, FL

Anita Parker
Kannapolis Middle School,
Kannapolis, NC

Laura Pottmyer
Apex Middle School,
Apex, NC

Lynn Prichard
Williams Middle Magnet School,
Tampa, FL

Jacque Quick
Walter Williams High School,
Burlington, NC

Robert Glenn Reynolds
Hillman Middle School,
Youngstown, OH

Stacy Rinehart
Lufkin Road Middle School,
Apex, NC

Theresa Short
Abbott Middle School,
Fayetteville, NC

Rita Slivka
Alexander Hamilton Middle School,
Cleveland, OH

Marie Sofsak
B F Stanton Middle School,
Alliance, OH

Sharon Stull
Quail Hollow Middle School,
Charlotte, NC

Donna Taylor
Bak Middle School of the Arts,
West Palm Beach, FL

Sandi Thompson
Harding Middle School,
Lakewood, OH

Teacher Lab Evaluators

Andrew Boy
W.E.B. DuBois Academy,
Cincinnati, OH

Jill Brimm-Byrne
Albany Park Academy,
Chicago, IL

Gwen Broestl
Luis Munoz Marin Middle School,
Cleveland, OH

Michael A. Burstein
The Rashi School,
Newton, MA

Trudi Coutts
Madison Middle School,
Naperville, IL

Larry Cwik
Madison Middle School,
Naperville, IL

Jennifer Donatelli
Kennedy Junior High School,
Lisle, IL

Melissa Dupree
Lakeside Middle School,
Evans, GA

Carl Fechko
Luis Munoz Marin Middle School,
Cleveland, OH

Paige Fullhart
Highland Middle School,
Libertyville, IL

Sue Hood
Glen Crest Middle School,
Glen Ellyn, IL

William Luzader
Plymouth Community Intermediate School,
Plymouth, MA

Ann Min
Beardsley Middle School,
Crystal Lake, IL

Aileen Mueller
Kennedy Junior High School,
Lisle, IL

Nancy Nega
Churchville Middle School,
Elmhurst, IL

Oscar Newman
Sumner Math and Science Academy,
Chicago, IL

Lynn Prichard
Willimas Middle Magnet School,
Tampa, FL

Jacque Quick
Walter Williams High School,
Burlington, NC

Stacy Rinehart
Lufkin Road Middle School,
Apex, NC

Seth Robey
Gwendolyn Brooks Middle School,
Oak Park, IL

Kevin Steele
Grissom Middle School,
Tinley Park, IL

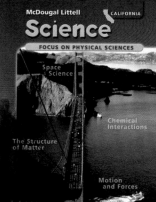

MCDOUGAL LITTELL SCIENCE
Focus on Physical Sciences

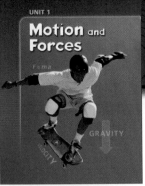

UNIT 1
Motion and Forces

eEdition

Unit Features

1 Motion   6

2 Forces   38

What must happen for a team to win this tug of war? page 38

What forces are acting on this snowboarder? on the snow? page 68

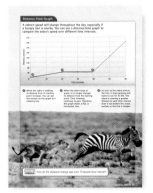

Visual Highlights

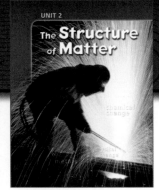

UNIT 2

The Structure of Matter

eEdition

UNIT 2
The Structure of Matter

How would you describe the matter in this photo? page 162

You can't zoom in any closer than this! The picture is an extremely close-up view of nickel. How do things look different the closer you get to them? page 196

Visual Highlights

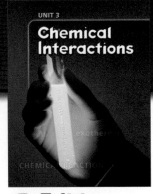

UNIT 3
Chemical Interactions

eEdition

UNIT 3
Chemical Interactions

Unit Features

What changes are happening in this chemical reaction? page 268

*What chemistry
important for living
things is shown in this
picture? page 336*

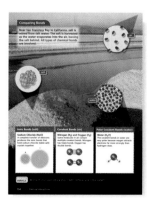

Visual Highlights

UNIT 4
Space Science

eEdition

Unit Features

12 Earth, Moon, and Sun 372

the **BIG** idea

Earth and the Moon move in predictable ways as they orbit the Sun.

13 Our Solar System 410

the **BIG** idea

Planets and other objects form a system around our Sun.

This image shows Jupiter with one of its large moons. How big are these objects compared with Earth? page 410

What could be present in the light and dark areas in this galaxy? page 450

14 Stars, Galaxies, and the Universe 450

Visual Highlights

Features

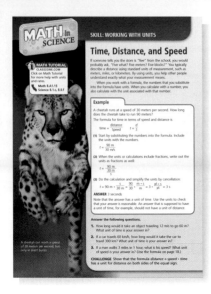

Math in Science

Think Science

Science on the Job

Extreme Science

Connecting Sciences

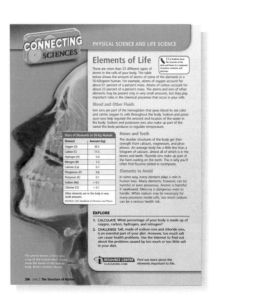

California Close-Up

Frontiers in Science

Timelines in Science

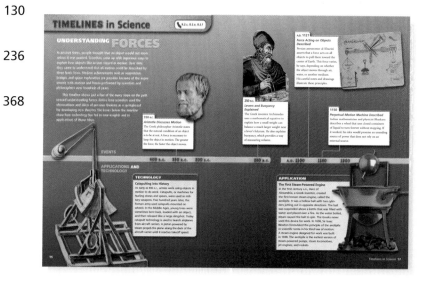

Internet Resources @ ClassZone.com

Simulations

Visualizations

Career Centers

Resource Centers

MOTION AND FORCES
Resources for the following topics may be found at ClassZone.com: *Finding Position; Acceleration; Inertia; Moving Rocks; Newton's Laws of Motion; Gravity; Friction, Forces, and Surfaces; Force and Motion Research; Density; Bouyancy.*

THE STRUCTURE OF MATTER
Resources for the following topics may be found at ClassZone.com: *Scale Views of Matter; Scanning Tunneling Microscope Images; Mixtures; Chemical Properties of Matter; Temperature and Temperature Scales; Melting Points and Boiling Points; New Elements; Periodic Table; The Atom; Elements Important to Life.*

CHEMICAL INTERACTIONS
Resources for the following topics may be found at ClassZone.com: *Chemical Formulas; Properties of Ionic and Covalent Compounds; Balancing Chemical Equations; Catalysts in Living Things; Atomic Research; Acids and Bases; Polymers; Carbohydrates, Lipids, Proteins, and Nucleic Acids.*

SPACE SCIENCE
Resources for the following topics may be found at ClassZone.com: *Seasons; Tides; Impact Craters; Moons of Giant Planets; Advances in Astronomy; Life Cycles of Stars; Galaxies; Galaxy Collisions.*

Math Tutorials

NSTA SciLinks

Codes for use with the NSTA SciLinks site may be found on every chapter opener.

Content Reviews

There is content review for every chapter at ClassZone.com.

Test Practice

There is test practice for every chapter at ClassZone.com.

Explore the Big Idea

Chapter Opening Inquiry

Each chapter opens with hands-on explorations that introduce the chapter's Big Idea.

Chapter Investigations

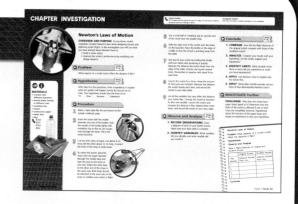

Full-Period Labs

The Chapter Investigations are in-depth labs that let you form and test a hypothesis, build a model, or sometimes design your own investigation.

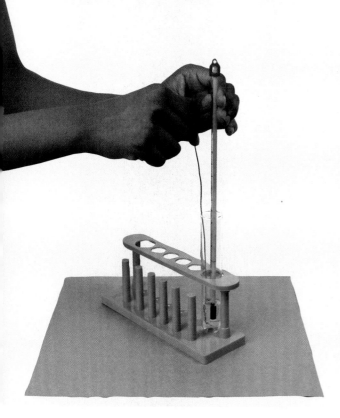

Explore

Introductory Inquiry Activities

Most sections begin with a simple activity that lets you explore the Key Concept before you read the section.

Motion and Forces

The Structure of Matter

Chemical Interactions

Space Science

Investigate

Skill Labs

Each Investigate activity gives you a chance to practice a specific science skill related to the content that you're studying.

California Science Standards

As you read and study your science book this year, you'll be learning many of the ideas described in the California Science Standards. The standards that you will concentrate on are listed here.

Following each standard is an explanation of what it means and how you will learn about it. References to chapters tell you where you'll begin to study the content in the standard. Many standards refer to several chapters. That's because you will read and study information presented in several chapters in order to understand a standard fully. By the end of the year, you will have learned the content of these California Science Standards.

Focus on Physical Science

Motion

Standard 8.1: The velocity of an object is the rate of change of its position.

Standard 8.1.a	What It Means to You
Students know position is defined in relation to some choice of a standard reference point and a set of reference directions.	The position of an object can only be measured by comparing its location to the location of a reference point. A position can be described using a distance and a direction from the reference point. A position can also be given in terms of two directions instead of one, such as in the longitude and latitude system. You will learn how to describe positions in terms of reference points, distances, and directions. **(Chapter 1)**

Standard 8.1.b	What It Means to You
Students know that average speed is the total distance traveled divided by the total time elapsed and that the speed of an object along the path traveled can vary.	When an object moves, the distance it travels in a certain amount of time depends on its speed, or how fast it moves. The speed of an object can change as it moves. You will learn that the average speed over a certain amount of time can be found by dividing the total distance the object moved by the time it took to go that distance. **(Chapter 1)**

Standard 8.1.c	What It Means to You
Students know how to solve problems involving distance, time, and average speed.	The average speed of an object can be written as the mathematical formula speed = distance / time. You will learn to use this formula to solve problems about average speed. **(Chapter 1)**

Standard 8.1.d	What It Means to You
Students know the velocity of an object must be described by specifying both the direction and the speed of the object.	Velocity is speed in a specific direction. The value for velocity includes the speed of an object as well as the direction in which it is moving. You will learn that some measurements, like velocity, need a direction as well as a number value. **(Chapter 1)**

Standard 8.1.e	What It Means to You
Students know changes in velocity may be due to changes in speed, direction, or both.	Velocity includes both a speed and direction. If an object's speed changes, its velocity will change, since velocity includes speed. If an object's direction changes, its velocity will change because velocity includes direction as well. A change in speed, direction, or both produces a change in velocity. **(Chapter 1)**

Standard 8.1.f	What It Means to You
Students know how to interpret graphs of position versus time and graphs of speed versus time for motion in a single direction.	Scientists often make graphs that show how an object changes position in time, or how its speed changes with time. These graphs can be used to understand the object's motion. You will learn how to interpret both distance-time graphs and velocity-time graphs. **(Chapter 1)**

Forces

Standard 8.2: Unbalanced forces cause changes in velocity.

Standard 8.2.a	What It Means to You
Students know a force has both direction and magnitude.	The effect of a force depends not only on the magnitude, or how large the force is, but also on the direction of the force. You will learn how to describe the size and direction of a force. **(Chapter 2)**

Standard 8.2.b	What It Means to You
Students know when an object is subject to two or more forces at once, the result is the cumulative effect of all the forces.	When more than one force acts on an object, the effects of the different forces combine. The overall result of the different forces depends on how both the sizes and directions of the individual forces combine. You will learn about the effects of combining more than one force. **(Chapter 2)**

Standard 8.2.c	What It Means to You
Students know when the forces on an object are balanced, the motion of the object does not change.	Two or more forces can combine in such a way that the result is the same as if there were no force on the object at all. These combinations are called balanced forces. **(Chapter 2)**

Standard 8.2.d	What It Means to You
Students know how to identify separately the two or more forces that are acting on a single static object, including gravity, elastic forces due to tension or compression in matter, and friction.	When an object is not moving, the forces on it are balanced and cancel each other out. You will learn about the common forces acting on objects, including gravity, which gives an object weight; elastic forces, which prevent objects from changing shape; and friction, which opposes the sliding motion between two surfaces. **(Chapters 2 and 3)**

Standard 8.2.e	What It Means to You
Students know that when the forces on an object are unbalanced, the object will change its velocity (that is, it will speed up, slow down, or change direction).	When an object's motion changes, there must be an unbalanced force acting on the object. Newton's first law of motion states that the velocity of an object cannot change unless an unbalanced force acts on it to change its speed or its direction. **(Chapter 2)**

Standard 8.2.f

Standard 8.2.f	What It Means to You
Students know the greater the mass of an object, the more force is needed to achieve the same rate of change in motion.	An unbalanced force changes the velocity of an object. How quickly the velocity changes depends on the force and the mass of the object. Suppose the same force acts on two objects with different masses. The less massive object will change velocity more quickly than the one with greater mass. **(Chapter 2)**

Standard 8.2.g	What It Means to You
Students know the role of gravity in forming and maintaining the shapes of planets, stars, and the solar system.	Objects throughout the universe apply an attractive force on each other because of their mass. This force is gravity. Gas and dust particles attract one another to form stars, planets, solar systems, and other structures we observe throughout the universe. Gravity keeps planets in orbit around stars, and stars in orbit around galaxies. It is also responsible for the shapes of the objects we observe. **(Chapter 3, 12, and 13)**

Structure of Matter

Standard 8.3: Each of the more than 100 elements of matter has distinct properties and a distinct atomic structure. All forms of matter are composed of one or more of the elements.

Standard 8.3.a	What It Means to You
Students know the structure of the atom and know it is composed of protons, neutrons, and electrons.	Atoms are made of three smaller particles: the proton, the neutron, and the electron. Protons and neutrons are at the center of the atom in the nucleus. Electrons are much smaller than protons and neutrons and move about the nucleus in the electron cloud. **(Chapter 7)**

Standard 8.3.b	What It Means to You
Students know that compounds are formed by combining two or more different elements and that compounds have properties that are different from their constituent elements.	The atoms of two or more elements can combine to form compounds. Compounds often have traits that are very different from the elements that make them. For example, water is made of atoms of hydrogen and oxygen. At room temperature, in their pure form, oxygen and hydrogen are gases. When they combine to form water, the water is liquid at room temperature. **(Chapters 5 and 8)**

Standard 8.3.c	What It Means to You
Students know atoms and molecules form solids by building up repeating patterns, such as the crystal structure of NaCl or long-chain polymers.	The properties of a substance are influenced by the structures of their molecules. For example, nylon is stretchable and nylon's molecules resemble long chains. **(Chapters 5, 8, and 11)**

Standard 8.3.d	What It Means to You
Students know the states of matter (solid, liquid, gas) depend on molecular motion.	The atoms and molecules that make up matter are in constant motion. When you increase the temperature of matter, you increase the motion of these particles. Think of ice as an example. As the temperature rises, the molecules move faster and faster. As they move more quickly, they become a liquid and eventually a gas. **(Chapter 6)**

Standard 8.3.e	What It Means to You
Students know that in solids the atoms are closely locked in position and can only vibrate; in liquids the atoms and molecules are more loosely connected and can collide with and move past one another; and in gases the atoms and molecules are free to move independently, colliding frequently.	Solids are hard and keep their shape. The particles that make them up do not move very much. The particles of a liquid can bump into and slide by one another. The particles of a gas move very freely and often bump into one another and the sides of their container. **(Chapter 6)**

Standard 8.3.f	What It Means to You
Students know how to use the periodic table to identify elements in simple compounds.	Each square of the periodic table contains information about an element, such as its name and symbol. For example, H is the symbol for hydrogen and O is symbol for oxygen. When you see the chemical formula for a compound, you can identify the names of the elements by looking for their symbols in the periodic table. **(Chapters 7 and 8)**

Earth in the Solar System (Earth Sciences)

Standard 8.4: The structure and composition of the universe can be learned from studying stars and galaxies and their evolution.

Standard 8.4.a	What It Means to You
Students know galaxies are clusters of billions of stars and may have different shapes.	Billions of stars that are bound together by gravity make up a single galaxy. Galaxies have different sizes and shapes. Two common shapes that large galaxies have are spiral and elliptical. Spiral galaxies, like our own Milky Way galaxy, have flat disks surrounding a central bulge. Elliptical galaxies are galaxies shaped like flattened spheres. **(Chapter 14)**

Standard 8.4.b	What It Means to You
Students know that the Sun is one of many stars in the Milky Way galaxy and that stars may differ in size, temperature, and color.	Our Sun is a star, a hot ball of glowing gas. The Sun is one of the several billion stars that make up the Milky Way galaxy. Stars have different sizes and masses. The color of a star depends on its temperature and can range from a red color to a bluish-white color. The Sun is an average size for a star, and yellow in color. **(Chapter 14)**

Standard 8.4.c	What It Means to You
Students know how to use astronomical units and light years as measures of distances between the Sun, stars, and Earth.	Distances in space are very large compared with distances on Earth. Measuring the distance to another star in meters would be like measuring the distance between two cities in millimeters. Astronomers use astronomical units, the average distance between Earth and the Sun, to measure distances in the solar system. For distances beyond the solar system, light-years are used. A light-year is the distance light travels in one year. **(Chapters 13 and 14)**

Standard 8.4.d	What It Means to You
Students know that stars are the source of light for all bright objects in outer space and that the Moon and planets shine by reflected sunlight, not by their own light.	Stars and planets appear as bright dots in the nighttime sky. Stars produce their own light by fusing hydrogen into helium. Planets and moons do not produce their own visible light. Planets and moons, including our own Moon, are bright because they reflect sunlight. **(Chapters 12, 13, and 14)**

Standard 8.4.e	What It Means to You
Students know the appearance, general composition, relative position and size, and motion of objects in the solar system, including planets, planetary satellites, comets, and asteroids.	By studying the properties and orbits of planets, moons, and other solar system objects, scientists have developed theories about how the solar system formed. The most current theory explains the difference between the rocky inner planets and the gaseous giant outer planets, as well as why planets and moons mostly orbit in the same direction. **(Chapters 12 and 13)**

Reactions

Standard 8.5: Chemical reactions are processes in which atoms are rearranged into different combinations of molecules.

Standard 8.5.a	What It Means to You
Students know reactant atoms and molecules interact to form products with different chemical properties.	After a chemical reaction, a new substance is formed. During a chemical reaction, atoms change places with other atoms to form other compounds. Because atoms are then arranged in a different way, the new compounds have traits that often are not like those of the original compounds. **(Chapter 9)**

Standard 8.5.b	What It Means to You
Students know the idea of atoms explains the conservation of matter: In chemical reactions the number of atoms stays the same no matter how they are arranged, so their total mass stays the same.	Atoms are rearranged in chemical reactions. The number of atoms does not change. The number of atoms present before a chemical reaction is the same number present after a chemical reaction. This is known as the law of the conservation of mass **(Chapter 9)**

Standard 8.5.c	What It Means to You
Students know chemical reactions usually liberate heat or absorb heat.	Some chemical reactions raise the temperature of their surroundings. Other chemical reactions decrease the temperature of their surroundings. **(Chapter 9)**

Standard 8.5.d	What It Means to You
Students know physical processes include freezing and boiling, in which a material changes form with no chemical reaction.	You have seen a physical change each time you have left a glass of ice sit on a table. Eventually, ice melts and turns into water. Ice and water are the same substance. You can easily turn water back to ice simply by placing it in a freezer. When you boil water on a stove to make soup or tea, however, it may seem as if some of the water disappears into thin air. It really does not. It only has become a gas and mixed with the air. **(Chapter 6)**

Standard 8.5.e	What It Means to You
Students know how to determine whether a solution is acidic, basic, or neutral.	Acids and bases are two types of solution. One way to tell the difference between an acid and a base is by using litmus paper. Acids will turn blue litmus paper red. Bases turn red litmus paper blue. A solution that is neutral is neither an acid or a base. **(Chapter 10)**

Chemistry of Living Systems

Standard 8.6: Principles of chemistry underlie the functioning of biological systems.

Standard 8.6.a	What It Means to You
Students know that carbon, because of its ability to combine in many ways with itself and other elements, has a central role in the chemistry of living organisms.	Carbon can form four chemical bonds. These bonds may be either with another carbon atom or different atoms. This ability makes it possible for carbon to form many large molecules having a variety of shapes. Life on Earth is often called "carbon-based" because most of the large, complex molecules in living things contain carbon. **(Chapter 11)**

Standard 8.6.b	What It Means to You
Students know that living organisms are made of molecules consisting largely of carbon, hydrogen, nitrogen, oxygen, phosphorus, and sulfur.	Living things contain many large, complex molecules. The most important atoms of the elements that make up these molecules are carbon, hydrogen, nitrogen, oxygen, phosphorus, and sulfur. Atoms of these six elements can combine in many ways to form the molecules necessary to carry out the complex processes in living things. **(Chapter 11)**

Standard 8.6.c	What It Means to You
Students know that living organisms have many different kinds of molecules, including small ones, such as water and salt, and very large ones, such as carbohydrates, fats, proteins, and DNA.	The molecules that make up organisms and control the processes inside of them are often very complex. For example, DNA molecules are very long and contain all the information necessary to make copies of cells. However, not all important molecules are so complex. Water contains only three atoms: two hydrogen atoms and one oxygen atom. Not many processes inside the cells could happen without water. **(Chapter 11)**

Periodic Table

Standard 8.7: The organization of the periodic table is based on the properties of the elements and reflects the structure of atoms.

Standard 8.7.a	What It Means to You
Students know how to identify regions corresponding to metals, nonmetals, and inert gases.	Elements in the same region of the periodic table have similar properties. Metals are at the left and in the center of the periodic table. Nonmetals are to the right. The inert gases are in the last column at the right of the periodic table. Most periodic tables you will see will indicate the locations of the metals and nonmetals. **(Chapter 7)**

Standard 8.7.b	What It Means to You
Students know each element has a specific number of protons in the nucleus (the atomic number) and each isotope of the element has a different but specific number of neutrons in the nucleus.	The atoms of different elements have a different number of protons in their nuclei. The number of protons is called that element's atomic number. For example, atoms of silver have 47 protons in their nucleus. However, not all atoms of silver have the same number of neutrons in their nuclei. Some silver atoms have 60 neutrons in their nucleus. Other silver atoms have 62 neutrons in their nucleus. These variations are called isotopes of silver. **(Chapter 7)**

Standard 8.7.c

Standard 8.7.c	What It Means to You
Students know substances can be classified by their properties, including their melting temperature, density, hardness, and thermal and electrical conductivity.	An element's position on the periodic table can tell you a lot about its properties. For example, the metals at the left of the table are good thermal and electrical conductors and have high melting and boiling points. The elements at the middle of the table are the most dense. There are many ways to classify substances. **(Chapters 5 and 7)**

Density and Buoyancy
Standard 8.8: All objects experience a buoyant force when immersed in a fluid.

Standard 8.8.a	What It Means to You
Students know density is mass per unit volume.	The density of an object describes how closely packed its matter is. If two objects have the same volume but different masses, the more massive object will have a greater density. Density is found by dividing the mass of the object by its volume. **(Chapter 4)**

Standard 8.8.b	What It Means to You
Students know how to calculate the density of substances (regular and irregular solids and liquids) from measurements of mass and volume.	The formula for density is given as density = mass / volume. Volume can be calculated for regular solids using length measurements and the appropriate formula. If a solid does not have a regular shape, its volume can be found by placing it in a water tank and measuring the volume of the displaced water. **(Chapter 4)**

Standard 8.8.c	What It Means to You
Students know the buoyant force on an object in a fluid is an upward force equal to the weight of the fluid the object has displaced.	When an object is put into a fluid, a force called the buoyant force acts to push the object upward. When placed into the fluid, the object displaces a certain amount of that fluid. The weight of the displaced fluid is equal to the upward buoyant force. **(Chapter 4)**

Standard 8.8.d	What It Means to You
Students know how to predict whether an object will float or sink.	An object in a fluid has an upward force, the buoyant force, acting on it. If the buoyant force is greater than the weight of the object, the object will float. If the buoyant force is less than the weight of the object, the object will sink. This depends on the relative densities of the object and the fluid. **(Chapter 4)**

Investigation and Experimentation
Standard 8.9: Scientific progress is made by asking meaningful questions and conducting careful investigations.

Standard 8.9.a	What It Means to You
Plan and conduct a scientific investigation to test a hypothesis.	A hypothesis is a proposed explanation for why something occurs. In Design Your Own investigations, you will plan and do your own experiments, and use your results to test your hypothesis. In other investigations, you will write your own hypotheses. **(Investigations throughout)**

Standard 8.9.b	What It Means to You
Evaluate the accuracy and reproducibility of data.	Scientists take multiple trials when making observations to determine how accurate their results are. They also perform experiments that other scientists have done to make sure they get the same results. When you take multiple trials in an experiment, you are determining if your data are accurate and reproducible. **(Investigations throughout)**

Standard 8.9.c	What It Means to You
Distinguish between variable and controlled parameters in a test.	Scientists often want to see what happens when changes are made in an experiment. To do this, they change one factor and keep the other factors the same. The one factor they change is called a variable. The factors they keep the same are the controlled parameters, or constants. In some experiments you will have to recognize what the variables are, and what the controlled parameters are. **(Investigations throughout)**

Standard 8.9.d	What It Means to You
Recognize the slope of the linear graph as the constant in the relationship $y = kx$ and apply this principle in interpreting graphs constructed from data.	Graphs can show relationships between two things. If a graph is a straight line, the relationship between the two variables x and y can be represented by $y = kx$, where k is the slope, or steepness. Often the slope of such a line contains information about how the variables are related. **(Chapter 1)**

Standard 8.9.e	What It Means to You
Construct appropriate graphs from data and develop quantitative statements about the relationships between variables.	Some types of data are best represented by a particular graph type. When graphing data, you need to decide if you are making a line graph, a scatter plot, a bar graph, or some other type of graph. Other times you will be asked to describe the relationship between variables in words. **(Investigations throughout)**

Standard 8.9.f	What It Means to You
Apply simple mathematic relationships to determine a missing quantity in a mathematic expression, given the two remaining terms (including speed = distance/time, density = mass/volume, force = pressure × area, volume = area × height).	Many concepts in physics can be expressed as mathematical relationships. The formulas you will learn in this book show the relationships among three variables. If you know the value for two of the terms, you can always arrange the formula to find the value for the missing term. **(Chapters 1, 2, and 4)**

Standard 8.9.g	What It Means to You
Distinguish between linear and non-linear relationships on a graph of data.	When you graph two variables, the graph may not always produce a straight line. Instead, the relationship may be some type of curve, or a nonlinear relationship. As you plot graphs of your data, look at the results carefully to determine the type of relationship the variables have. **(Chapter 1)**

Introducing Science

Scientists are curious. Since ancient times, they have been asking and answering questions about the world around them. Scientists are also very suspicious of the answers they get. They carefully collect evidence and test their answers many times before accepting an idea as correct.

In this book you will see how scientific knowledge keeps growing and changing as scientists ask new questions and rethink what was known before. The following sections will help you get started.

What Is Science?

Science is the systematic study of all of nature, from particles too small to see to the human body to the entire universe. However, no individual scientist can study all of nature. Therefore science is divided into many different fields. For example, some scientists are biologists, others are geologists, and still others are chemists or astronomers.

All the different scientific fields can be grouped into three broad categories: physical science, earth science, and life science.

- Physical science focuses on the study of what things are made of and how they change; it includes the fields of chemistry and physics.
- Earth science focuses on the study of our planet and its place in the universe; it includes the fields of geology, oceanography, meteorology, and astronomy.
- Life science focuses on the study of living things; it includes the fields of cell biology, botany, ecology, zoology, and human biology.

McDougal Littell Science, Focus on Physical Sciences

McDougal Littell Science, Focus on Physical Sciences, explains how things move and work, and what they are made of. It includes some earth/space science and life science as well. In this book you will learn how the principles of motion and forces work in air, on land, and in water. You will learn what things are made of—matter, atoms, and elements—and how they are put together. You will learn some chemistry and understand how chemical reactions work. Finally, you'll study space science to understand how planets like Earth, stars like the Sun, and huge galaxies like the Milky Way fit into the universe.

Unifying Principles

As you learn, it helps to have a big picture of science as a framework for new information. *McDougal Littell Science* has identified unifying principles from each of the three broad categories of science: physical science, earth science, and life science. These unifying principles are described on the following pages. However, keep in mind that the broad categories of science do not have fixed borders. Physical science shades into earth science, which shades into life science, which shades back into physical science.

On the next few pages, look for the four unifying principles of physical science:

- Matter is made of particles too small to see.
- Matter changes form and moves from place to place.
- Energy changes from one form to another, but it cannot be created or destroyed.
- Physical forces affect the movement of all matter on Earth and throughout the universe.

> ### the **BIG** idea
> Each chapter begins with a big idea. Keep in mind that each big idea relates to one or more of the unifying principles.

What is Physical Science?

Physical science is the study of what things are made of and how they change. It combines the studies of both physics and chemistry. Physics is the science of matter, energy, and forces. It includes the study of topics such as motion, light, and electricity and magnetism. Chemistry is the study of the structure and properties of matter. It especially focuses on how substances change into different substances.

Like the tiles that make up this picture, the particles that make up all substances combine to make structures that we can see. Unlike these tiles, the individual particles themselves are too small to see.

UNIFYING PRINCIPLES of Physical Science

Matter is made of particles too small to see.

Objects you can see and touch are all around you. The materials that these objects are made of are called **matter**. All living things—even you—are also matter; the air around you is matter too. Matter is anything that has mass and takes up space. **Mass** is a measure of the amount of matter in an object. **Volume** is the amount of space an object or substance takes up.

The tiny particles that make up all matter are called **atoms**. Atoms are so tiny that they are far too small to see even through a powerful microscope. In fact, an atom is more than a million times smaller than the period at the end of this sentence. There are more than 100 basic kinds of matter called **elements**.

For example, iron, gold, and oxygen are three common elements. Each element has its own unique kind of atom. The atoms of any element are all alike but different from the atoms of any other element.

Many familiar materials are made of particles called molecules. In a **molecule**, two or more atoms stick together to form a larger particle. For example, a water molecule is made of two atoms of hydrogen and one atom of oxygen.

Matter changes form and moves from place to place.

You see objects moving and changing all around you. All changes in matter are the results of atoms moving and combining in different ways. Regardless of how much matter may change, however, under ordinary conditions it is never created or destroyed. Matter that seems to disappear merely changes into another form of matter.

For example, a block of ice is hard like a rock. Leave the ice out in sunlight, however, and it changes into a puddle of water. That puddle of water can eventually change into water vapor and disappear into the air. The water vapor in air can become raindrops, and the cycle goes on. Even when matter changes form, its total mass does not change.

You see matter change form every day. You see the ice in your glass of juice disappear without a trace. You see a black metal gate slowly develop a flaky, orange coating. Matter is constantly changing and moving.

UNIFYING PRINCIPLES of Physical Science,

Energy changes from one form to another, but it cannot be created or destroyed.

All the changes you see around you depend on energy. **Energy**, in fact, means the ability to cause change. Using energy means changing energy. For example, you have seen electric energy changing into light, heat, sound, and mechanical energy in household appliances. Fuels like wood, coal, and oil contain chemical energy that produces heat when burned.

Energy can be converted into forms that can be used for specific purposes. During the conversion, some of the original energy is converted into unwanted or unusable forms. For example, when a power plant converts energy of falling water into electricity, some of the energy is lost to friction and sound. But energy is never created or destroyed, no matter how often it changes form. This fact is known as the **law of conservation of energy**.

Physical forces affect the movement of all matter on Earth and throughout the universe.

A **force** is a push or a pull. Every time you push or pull an object, you are applying a force to that object, whether or not the object moves. There are several forces—several pushes or pulls—acting on you right now. All these forces are necessary for you to do the things you do, even sitting and reading.

- **Gravity** is the force of attraction between two objects. Gravity keeps you on the ground. It keeps the Moon moving around Earth, and Earth moving around the Sun.

- **Friction** is the force that opposes motion. The friction between the bottoms of your shoes and the floor makes it possible for you to walk without slipping.

- Other forces at work include a magnetic force, and electrical forces operating between particles and between objects.

What is Earth Science?

Earth science is the study of Earth's interior, its rocks and soil, its atmosphere, its oceans, and outer space. For many years scientists studied each of these topics separately. Recently, however, they have started to look more and more at the connections among the different parts of Earth—its oceans, atmosphere, living things, rocks and soil, even other planets in the solar system and stars and galaxies far away. Through these studies scientists have learned more about Earth and its place in the universe.

The universe is everything that exists, and everything in the universe is governed by the same physical laws. The same laws govern the stars shown in this picture and the page on which the picture is printed.

UNIFYING PRINCIPLES of Earth Science

Heat energy inside Earth and radiation from the Sun provide energy for Earth's processes.

Energy is the ability to cause change. All of Earth's processes need energy to occur. Earth's interior is very hot. This heat energy moves up to Earth's surface, where it provides the energy to build mountains, cause earthquakes, and make volcanoes erupt. Earth also receives energy from the Sun as **radiation**—energy that travels across distances in the form of certain types of waves. Energy from the Sun causes winds to blow, ocean currents to flow, and water to move from the ground to the atmosphere and back again.

Physical forces, such as gravity, affect the movement of all matter on Earth and throughout the universe.

What do the stars in a galaxy, the planet Earth, and your body have in common? For one thing, they are all made of matter. **Matter** is anything that has mass and takes up space. Rocks are matter. You are matter. Even the air around you is matter. Everything in the universe is also affected by the same physical forces. A **force** is a push or a pull. Forces affect how matter moves everywhere in the universe.

Matter and energy move among Earth's rocks and soil, atmosphere, waters, and living things.

Think of Earth as a huge system, or an organized group of parts that work together. Within this system, matter and energy move among the different parts. The four major parts of Earth's system are the

- **atmosphere**, which includes all the air surrounding the solid planet
- **geosphere**, which includes all of Earth's rocks and minerals, as well as Earth's interior
- **hydrosphere**, which includes oceans, rivers, lakes, and every drop of water on or under Earth's surface
- **biosphere**, which includes all the living things on Earth

Earth has changed over time and continues to change.

Events are always changing Earth's surface. Some events, such as the building or wearing away of mountains, occur over millions of years. Others, such as earthquakes, occur within seconds. A change can affect a small area or an entire continent, such as North America.

What is Life Science?

Life science is the study of living things. As you study life science, you will observe and read about a variety of organisms, from huge redwood trees to the tiny bacteria that cause sore throats. But Life science is not simply about learning the names of millions of organisms. It includes big ideas to help us understand how all these living things interact with their environment. Life science is the study of characteristics and needs that all living things have in common. It's also a study of changes, both daily changes and changes that take place over millions of years. It's the study of how living things depend on Earth and its resources.

What do you need to stay alive? What does an animal like a fish or a coral need to stay alive? All living things have common needs.

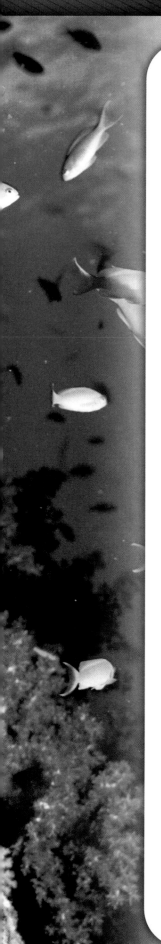

UNIFYING PRINCIPLES of Life Science

All living things share common characteristics.

Despite the variety of living things on Earth, there are certain characteristics common to all. The basic unit of life is the **cell**. Any living thing, whether it has one cell or many, is described as an **organism**. All organisms are characterized by

- organization—the way the organism's body is arranged
- growth—the way that an organism grows and develops over its lifetime
- reproduction—the way that an organism produces offspring like itself
- response—the ways an organism interacts with its surroundings

All living things share common needs.

All living things have three basic needs: energy, materials, and living space. These needs must be met for the organism to stay alive. Energy enables an organism to carry out all the activities of life. The body of every organism needs water and other materials. Water is important because most of the chemical reactions in a cell take place in water. Organisms also require other materials. Plants, for example, need carbon dioxide to make energy-rich sugars, and most living things need oxygen. Living space is the environment in which an organism gets the energy and materials it needs.

Living things meet their needs through interactions with the environment.

The **environment** is everything that surrounds a living thing. This includes other organisms as well as nonliving factors, such as rainfall, sunlight, and soil.

Any exchange of energy or materials between the living and nonliving parts of the environment is an interaction. Plants interact with the environment by capturing energy from sunlight and changing that energy into chemical energy that is stored in sugar. Animals can interact with plants by eating the plants and getting energy from the sugars that plants have made.

The types and numbers of living things change over time.

A **species** is a group of living things so closely related that they can produce offspring together that can also reproduce. Scientists have named about 1.4 million different species. The great variety of species on Earth today is called **biodiversity**. Different species have different characteristics, or **adaptations**, that allow the members of that species to get their needs met in a particular environment. Over the millions of years that life has existed on Earth, new species have come into being and others have disappeared. The disappearance of a species is called **extinction**. Studying fossils of extinct organisms is one way that scientists have of seeing how living things have changed over time.

You may think of science as a body of knowledge or a collection of facts. More important, however, science is an active process that involves certain ways of looking at the world.

Scientific Habits of Mind

Scientists are curious. They are always asking questions. Scientists have asked questions such as, "What is the smallest form of matter?" and "How do the smallest particles behave?" These and other important questions are being investigated by scientists around the world.

Scientists are observant. They are always looking closely at the world around them. Scientists once thought the smallest parts of atoms were protons, neutrons, and electrons. Later, protons and neutrons were found to be made of even smaller particles called quarks.

Scientists are creative. They draw on what they know to form possible explanations for a pattern, an event, or an interesting phenomenon that they have observed. Then scientists create a plan for testing their ideas.

Scientists are skeptical. Scientists don't accept an explanation or answer unless it is based on evidence and logical reasoning. They continually question their own conclusions and the conclusions suggested by other scientists. Scientists trust only evidence that is confirmed by other people or methods.

Scientists cannot always make observations with their own eyes. They have developed technology, such as this particle detector, to help them gather information about the smallest particles of matter.

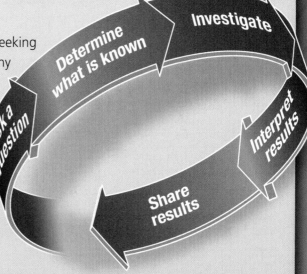

Scientists ask questions about the physical world and seek answers through carefully controlled procedures. Here a researcher works with supercooled magnets.

Science Processes at Work

You can think of science as a continuous cycle of asking and seeking answers to questions about the world. Although there are many processes that scientists use, scientists typically do each of the following:

- Observe and ask a question
- Determine what is known
- Investigate
- Interpret results
- Share results

Observe and Ask a Question

It may surprise you that asking questions is an important skill. A scientific process may start when a scientist asks a question. Perhaps scientists observe an event or a process that they don't understand, or perhaps answering one question leads to another.

Determine What Is Known

When beginning an inquiry, scientists find out what is already known about a question. They study results from other scientific investigations, read journals, and talk with other scientists. A scientist working on subatomic particles is most likely a member of a large team using sophisticated equipment. Before beginning original research, the team analyzes results from previous studies.

Investigate

Investigating is the process of collecting evidence. Two important ways of investigating are observing and experimenting.

Observing is the act of noting and recording an event, a characteristic, or anything else detected with an instrument or with the senses. A researcher may study the properties of a substance by handling it, finding its mass, warming or cooling it, stretching it, and so on. For information about the behavior of subatomic particles, however, a researcher may rely on technology such as scanning tunneling microscopes, which produce images of structures that cannot be seen with the eye.

An **experiment** is an organized procedure to study something under controlled conditions. In order to study the effect of wing shape on the motion of a glider, for instance, a researcher would need to conduct controlled studies in which gliders made of the same materials and with the same masses differed only in the shape of their wings.

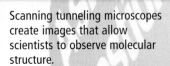

Scanning tunneling microscopes create images that allow scientists to observe molecular structure.

Physical chemists have found a way to observe chemical reactions at the atomic level. Using lasers, they can watch bonds breaking and new bonds forming.

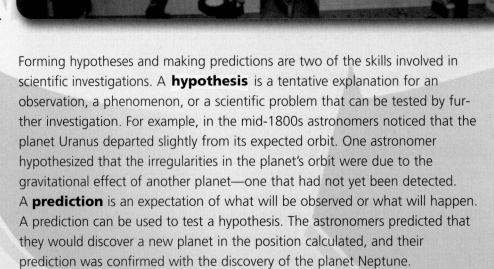

Forming hypotheses and making predictions are two of the skills involved in scientific investigations. A **hypothesis** is a tentative explanation for an observation, a phenomenon, or a scientific problem that can be tested by further investigation. For example, in the mid-1800s astronomers noticed that the planet Uranus departed slightly from its expected orbit. One astronomer hypothesized that the irregularities in the planet's orbit were due to the gravitational effect of another planet—one that had not yet been detected. A **prediction** is an expectation of what will be observed or what will happen. A prediction can be used to test a hypothesis. The astronomers predicted that they would discover a new planet in the position calculated, and their prediction was confirmed with the discovery of the planet Neptune.

Interpret Results

As scientists investigate, they analyze their evidence, or data, and begin to draw conclusions. **Analyzing data** involves looking at the evidence gathered through observations or experiments and trying to identify any patterns that might exist in the data. Scientists often need to make additional observations or perform more experiments before they are sure of their conclusions. Many times scientists make new predictions or revise their hypotheses.

Often scientists use computers to help them analyze data. Computers reveal patterns that might otherwise be missed.

Scientists use computers to create models of objects or processes they are studying. This model shows carbon atoms forming a sphere.

Share Results

An important part of scientific investigation is sharing results of experiments. Scientists read and publish in journals and attend conferences to communicate with other scientists around the world. Sharing data and procedures gives them a way to test one another's results. They also share results with the public through newspapers, television, and other media.

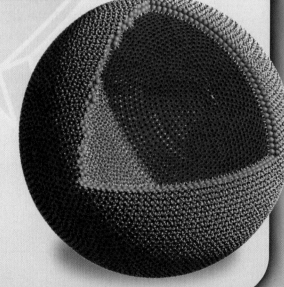

The Nature of Technology

When you think of technology, you may think of cars, computers, and cell phones, as well as refrigerators, radios, and bicycles. Technology is not only the machines and devices that make modern lives easier, however. It is also a process in which new methods and devices are created. Technology makes use of scientific knowledge to design solutions to real-world problems.

Science and Technology

Science and technology go hand in hand. Each depends upon the other. Even designing a device as simple as a toaster requires knowledge of how heat flows and which materials are the best conductors of heat. Just as technology based on scientific knowledge makes our lives easier, some technology is used to advance scientific inquiry itself. For example, researchers use a number of specialized instruments to help them collect data. Microscopes, telescopes, spectrographs, and computers are just a few of the tools that help scientists learn more about the world. The more information these tools provide, the more devices can be developed to aid scientific research and to improve modern lives.

The Process of Technological Design

The process of technology involves many choices. For example, how does an automobile engineer design a better car? Is a better car faster? safer? cheaper? Before designing any new machine, the engineer must decide exactly what he or she wants the machine to do as well as what may be given up for the machine to do it. A faster car may get people to their destinations more quickly, but it may cost more and be less safe. As you study the techno-logical process, think about all the choices that were made to build the technologies you use.

Identify a Need

Successful technology fills a need; it helps us perform a task we need or want to do. For example, as more cars appear on the road, noise and air pollution become serious threats to the environment and to people's health. Gas consumption also depletes precious petroleum resources. There is a need to find a fuel source for a car that will not pollute the air and that will never run out.

Design and Develop

Hydrogen fuel cells are a potential solution to this need. These cells combine hydrogen and oxygen into water, producing electricity in the process. Engineers have found a way to make fuel cells small enough to fit into a car, yet able to produce enough electricity to power an electric motor. Before arriving at this final design, engineers tried many others.

Test and Improve

Just because a technology works doesn't mean it cannot be improved. A fuel-cell-powered car has been driven from San Francisco to Washington, D.C., but it probably will be a while before it's in dealer showrooms. Engineers won't know how these cars will perform until they're driven in real-world conditions. Engineers also won't know if the average driver will be able to handle the necessary maintenance on the car until the car is made available to ordinary drivers. Improvements in the future may well bring cars powered by fuel cells into garages everywhere.

Using the Tools of Science

You can learn about science by doing it. Doing science includes trying experiments or making observations so that you see for yourself what happens. For example, activities such as growing plants, measuring acid in rainwater, looking at live cells under a microscope, and trying to make an object fly are the exciting parts of science. These are the reasons people become scientists.

Safety First!

apron   goggles   disposal

electrical   chemical   fire
safety   safety   safety

sharp   heating   fumes
objects   safety

poison   gloves

To do any experiments, think safety first! You may think it is unnecessary to wear goggles or plastic gloves—and sometimes it is unnecessary. But beakers break and spill, even if the materials are not dangerous. Why take a chance? You can prevent injuries or ruined clothes by taking simple precautions. Remember, we never plan for things to go wrong, but accidents happen!

The investigations and explorations in this book have safety symbols next to them when needed. Some have to do with what you wear—goggles, apron, gloves. Some warn of fire and heat dangers; some concern safety when working with electricity. Others caution you about chemicals, sharp objects, disposing of materials, or working with animals. Look at the safety rules and symbols on page R10. Become familiar with them. Look for them before you do an activity, and take the necessary precautions.

Measuring

Scientists use the International System (SI) for measurements of length, volume, mass, and temperature. The units in the SI system are metric, based on multiples of ten. These are different from the units we use in the United States, but most countries and all scientists use them. Once you learn the SI system, you will become part of the international community.

Measuring Length In science, meters and centimeters, not yards, feet, and inches, are used to measure length. A meter is about a yard. Within the metric system you change units by multiplying or dividing by powers of 10. For example,

1 centimeter (cm) = .01 meter (m), or 1/100 of a meter

1 millimeter (mm) = .001 meter (m), or 1/1000 of a meter

The prefix tells you how large or small each measurement is. You can easily change units to and from the SI units. See page R20 for help in changing units of the metric system.

cm 1   2   3   4   5   6   7   8   9

Measuring Volume The metric system measures volume in liters, not gallons. If you buy a 2 liter bottle of soda, it is about half a gallon in U.S. units. In a lab, it is more precise to measure 20 milliliters than to measure 1 teaspoon. Remember that 1 liter (L) = 1000 milliliters (mL). The prefix *milli-* means "one thousandth." When you measure the volume of a liquid, use a graduated cylinder and read the volume in mL, or milliliters. Each milliliter equals 1 cm^3.

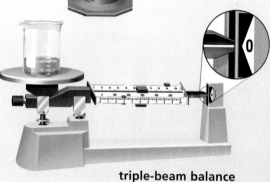

graduated cylinder

Measuring Mass Mass is measured in grams, not pounds. By now you can guess that 1 kilogram (kg) = 1000 grams (g). A pound is a measure of weight, and weight is not the same as mass. In SI units, weight is measured in newtons. To measure mass, you use a double-pan balance or a triple-beam balance.

triple-beam balance

Measuring Temperature There are three systems of temperature measurement in the International System: Kelvin, Celsius, and Fahrenheit. Usually in science class you will use Celsius, not Fahrenheit or Kelvin. The Celsius system uses one hundred degrees between the freezing and the boiling point of water, 0–100° C. The Fahrenheit system, which we commonly use in the United States, goes from 32° to 212° F freezing to boiling point. Again, since it's based on 10's, the Celsius scale is easier to use.

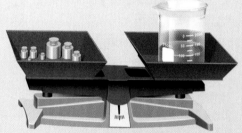

double-pan balance

Why Bother?

Why do all scientists need to use standard tools and measurements? They do this so that others can reproduce their experiments. Remember that scientists are a skeptical bunch—they don't believe what they hear until they try it themselves. To try an experiment that someone else has done, you have to have exact measurements. One drop more of a solution can make a huge difference in the results! One temperature degree higher and the whole experiment might fail!

Reproducibility is the only way scientists accept each other's work. Hypotheses have to be tested over and over again. If the results are different every time the experiment is done, then the hypothesis is not supported.

You need to use the scientific method every time you do an investigation. The scientific method varies according to the kind of investigation you're doing. The next two pages walk you through a lab. How do you make a hypothesis? How do you set up a test for it? How do you interpret your results? **Turn the page to find out.**

Conducting an Investigation

The fun part of science is "doing" science. You "do" science when you conduct your own investigations, collect your own data, and reach your own conclusions. You will practice using scientific methods whenever you do an investigation. Your method will change depending on what you are investigating. Sometimes you will observe and collect data. Sometimes you make a model to see how things work. Sometimes you will conduct an experiment; sometimes you will design your own experiments.

CHAPTER INVESTIGATION

Acceleration and Slope

OVERVIEW AND PURPOSE When a downhill skier glides down a mountain without using her ski poles, her velocity increases and she experiences acceleration. How would gliding down a hill with a greater slope affect her acceleration? In this investigation you will
- calculate the acceleration of an object rolling down two ramps of different slopes
- determine how the slope of the ramp affects the acceleration of the object

▶ Problem   Write It Up

How does the slope of a ramp affect the acceleration of an object rolling down the ramp?

▶ Hypothesize   Write It Up

Write a hypothesis to explain how changing the slope of the ramp will affect acceleration. Your hypothesis should take the form of an "If . . . , then . . . , because . . ." statement.

▶ Procedure

1. Make a data table like the one shown on the sample notebook page.

2. Make a ramp by laying two meter sticks side by side. Leave a small gap between the meter sticks.

3. Use masking tape as shown in the photograph to join the meter sticks. The marble should be able to roll freely along the groove.

4. Set up your ramp on a smooth, even surface, such as a tabletop. Raise one end of the ramp on top of one of the books. The other end of the ramp should remain on the table.

5. Make a finish line by putting a piece of tape on the tabletop 30 cm from the bottom of the ramp. Place a ruler just beyond the finish line to keep your marble from rolling beyond your work area.

Problem

Make sure you understand the purpose of your investigation. What are you trying to find out?

Hypothesis

A hypothesis is your prediction of what will happen and why it may happen. You base your hypothesis on what you know and a bit of educated guessing. You might not be right, but you test it to see. Set it up as a 3-part **if-then-because** statement:

1. **If** I roll a marble down a ramp that has a steeper slope than another, (What you'll do)
2. **then** the marble on the steeper ramp will have greater acceleration, (Your prediction)
3. **because** there is a stronger downward pull on the marble. (Your reason)

Procedure

Read the entire procedure before you begin. Then follow it step by step, recording data accurately as you gather it.

Content Standard
8.1.e Students know changes in velocity may be due to changes in speed, direction, or both.

Investigation Standard
8.9.c Distinguish between variable and controlled parameters in a test.

6. Test your ramp by releasing the marble from the top of the ramp. Make sure that the marble rolls freely. Do not push on the marble.

7. Release the marble and measure the time it takes for it to roll from the release point to the end of the ramp. Record this time under Column A for trial 1.

8. Release the marble again from the same point, and record the time it takes the marble to roll from the end of the ramp to the finish line. Record this time in Column B for trial 1. Repeat and record three more trials.

9. Raise the height of the ramp by propping it up with both paperback books. Repeat steps 7 and 8.

Observe and Analyze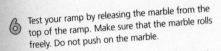

1. **RECORD OBSERVATIONS** Draw the setup of your procedures. Be sure your data table is complete.

2. **IDENTIFY VARIABLES AND CONSTANTS** Identify the variables and constants in the experiment. List them in your notebook.

3. **CALCULATE**

   Average Time For ramps 1 and 2, calculate and record the average time it took for the marble to travel from the end of the ramp to the finish line.

   Final Velocity For ramps 1 and 2, calculate and record v_{final} using the formula below.

   $$v_{final} = \frac{\text{distance from end of ramp to finish line}}{\text{average time from end of ramp to finish line}}$$

   Acceleration For ramps 1 and 2, calculate and record acceleration using the formula below. (**Hint:** Speed at the release of the

Conclude

1. **COMPARE** How did the acceleration of the marble on ramp 1 compare with the acceleration of the marble on ramp 2?

2. **INTERPRET** Answer the question posed in the problem.

3. **ANALYZE** Compare your results with your hypothesis. Do your data support your hypothesis?

4. **EVALUATE** Why was it necessary to measure how fast the marble traveled from the end of the ramp to the finish line?

5. **IDENTIFY LIMITS** What possible limitations or sources of error could have affected your results? Why was it important to perform four trials for each measurement of speed?

INVESTIGATE Further

CHALLENGE Design your own experiment to determine how the marble's mass affects its acceleration down a ramp.

Analyze

Look again at the problem and your hypothesis. Was your prediction correct? Do your results support your hypothesis? If your hypothesis is not supported, you have learned something and can try another.

Identify Limits

Evaluate how accurate your measurements were. If others reproduced this experiment, would they get the results you got? Are all people measuring the same way?

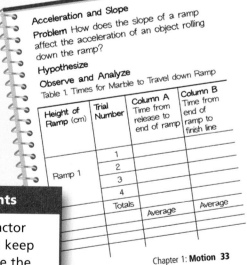

Acceleration and Slope

Problem How does the slope of a ramp affect the acceleration of an object rolling down the ramp?

Hypothesize

Observe and Analyze

Table 1. Times for Marble to Travel down Ramp

Height of Ramp (cm)	Trial Number	Column A Time from release to end of ramp	Column B Time from end of ramp to finish line
Ramp 1	1		
	2		
	3		
	4		
	Totals	Average	Average

Chapter 1: **Motion 33**

Identify Variables and Constants

The **independent variable** is the factor you change in an experiment. You keep all other things the same—they are the **constants** (or controlled parameters). The **dependent variable** is what you measure—it depends on the independent variable.

UNIT 1

Motion and Forces

$F = ma$

VELOCITY

GRAVITY

Contents Overview

ROBOTS on Mars

If you could design a robot to explore Mars, what would you want it to be able to do?

California Content Standards

8.1.b Students know that average speed is the total distance traveled divided by the total time elapsed and that the speed of an object along the path traveled can vary.

8.2.a Students know a force has both direction and magnitude.

SCIENTIFIC AMERICAN FRONTIERS

Watch the video segment "Teetering to Victory" to learn about a competition that challenges students to use their knowledge of motion and forces to design a machine.

The surface of Mars looks rocky and barren today, but scientists have long wondered if life might have existed on Mars long ago. That would have been possible only if Mars once had water, which is necessary for all forms of life.

Searching for Water

We know that Mars is now a cold, dry world, but was that always true? Images from spacecraft in orbit around Mars show land formations that seem to be dried-up lakes and riverbeds. Was Mars more like Earth in the past, warmer and wetter than it is today? We know water is a necessary ingredient for life on Earth. Could a warmer and wetter Mars have also supported life? To answer these questions, in 2003 NASA launched two robotic rovers. They would take six months to reach Mars. The first rover, named *Spirit*, was sent to a crater that looked like a dried-up lake. The second rover, named *Opportunity*, was launched about a month later. *Opportunity*'s landing site was chosen because it contained the mineral hematite, which usually forms in water.

Robot Geologists

To discover the history of water on Mars, *Spirit* and *Opportunity* would have to do the work of a human geologist. They were well equipped to navigate Mars and find interesting spots. Each rover has eight cameras which are used to avoid rocks and make detailed color images of its surroundings. Six-wheel drive gives them solid traction in the sandy Martian soil. Once a rover spots an interesting rock, it can analyze the rock using its RAT (rock abrasion tool) to grind away the rock's surface. The rover can then take a closer look with its microscopic imager, or use its other scientific instruments to see what the rock is made of.

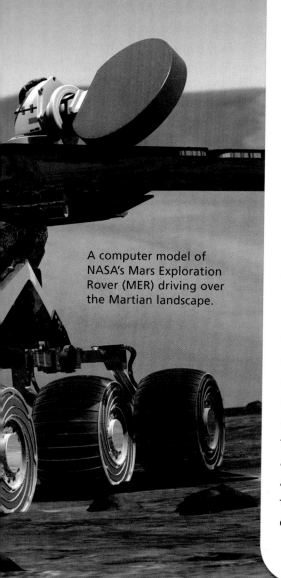

A computer model of NASA's Mars Exploration Rover (MER) driving over the Martian landscape.

Spirit's Mission

Spirit landed safely on Mars in January 2004. Based on the orbital images, it looked as if the landing site might once have been a lake. *Spirit* soon determined that this could not have been the case. The soil contained volcanic minerals that are destroyed even by small amounts of water. There could not have been a significant amount of water at this spot for a very long time. Perhaps the rocks at a different location would tell a different story. The most promising location was a geologic feature named Columbia Hills, but it was 2.7 kilometers away.

Could the rover drive that far? On average, *Spirit* was able to drive 60 meters each sol. A sol is a Martian day, about 40 minutes longer than an Earth day. The time the rover would take to reach the hills can be found by dividing the distance by the average speed—2700 meters divided by 60 meters per sol, which equals 45 sols. The distance was within the rover's range, and *Spirit* accomplished the journey. Once there, *Spirit* found older rocks with a different history. These rocks did indeed show evidence that there had been some liquid water in the past—but not very large amounts.

This rock, nicknamed El Capitan, shows rippled layering and embedded "blueberries." El Capitan provided evidence that Mars contained an ancient sea.

Opportunity's Mission

In an incredible stroke of luck, *Opportunity* landed in a small crater that was only 22 meters across. Craters form when a meteorite crashes into the surface of a planet. The resulting hole exposes layers of rock that would normally be hard to reach. When *Opportunity*'s first images were transmitted back to Earth, it became clear just how lucky the landing was. The images showed layered rocks and small round pebbles. The scientists called these round rocks blueberries.

View the "Teetering to Victory" segment of your Scientific American Frontiers video to learn how some students solved a robotic design challenge.

IN THIS SCENE FROM THE VIDEO ▶ MIT students prepare to test their machines.

BATTLE OF MACHINES Each year more than 100 engineering students at the Massachusetts Institute of Technology (MIT) compete in a contest to see who can design and build the best machine. The challenge this time is to build a machine that starts out sitting on a teeter-totter beam and within 45 seconds manages to tilt its end down against an opponent trying to do the same thing.

Just as the Mars rover designers had to consider the constraints of space travel and Mars' harsh environment, the students had constraints on their designs. They all started with the same kit of materials, and their finished machines had to weigh less than 10 pounds as well as fit inside the box the materials came in. Within these constraints, the student designers came up with an amazing variety of solutions.

Upon closer examination, scientists saw ripples in the rock layers. After a month of exploration, it was determined that the layered rocks, the blueberries, and the large amount of salts in the rocks all meant that this spot had once been a salty sea. *Opportunity* had made the discovery that it had been sent to Mars to make. Mars did have liquid water in the past.

Having made that discovery, *Opportunity* still had more work to do. Unfortunately, it failed in its first attempt to drive out of the crater. It is hard for the rovers to drive up a steep crater wall. When a surface is flat, gravity pushes the rover against the surface, which gives the tires a better grip on the surface. When the crater is steep, however, the rover must use its own force to balance the downward pull of gravity. Also, the tires are more likely to slip. On its second try, *Opportunity* followed a shallower route out of the crater and was successful in climbing out.

They Keep Going and Going . . .

Spirit and *Opportunity* had been designed to last only 90 sols, but they were still going as late as December 2005. In addition to exploring hills and craters, they provided data for movies of dust devils, found a small iron meteorite, and investigated parts of the spacecraft discarded during landing. The more the rovers explore, the more their information prepares us for the day when explorers on Mars will include not only robots but people as well.

UNANSWERED Questions

As scientists learn more and more about Mars, new questions always arise.

- What role, if any, did water, wind, or volcanoes play in shaping the landscape of Mars?

- Were the conditions necessary to support life ever present on Mars?

- Could there be bacteria-like life forms surviving below the surface of Mars today?

UNIT PROJECTS

As you study this unit, work alone or with a group on one of these projects.

Build a Mechanical Arm (8.2.b)

Design and build a mechanical arm to perform a simple task.

- Plan and sketch an arm that could lift a pencil from the floor at a distance of one meter.

- Collect materials and assemble your arm.

- Conduct trials and improve your design.

Multimedia Presentation (8.2.g)

Create an informative program on the forces involved in remote exploration.

- Collect information about the Mars rover mission or a similar expedition.

- Learn how engineers use air resistance, gravity, and rocket thrusters to maneuver the orbiter close to the planet and its moons.

- Give a presentation describing what you learned, using mixed media, such as a computer slide show and a model.

Design an Experiment (8.2.a)

Design an experiment to determine the pressure needed to crush a small object.

- Select a small object, such as a vitamin C tablet, to use in your experiment.

- Collect other materials of your choosing.

- Plan and conduct a procedure to test the pressure required to crush the object. Vary the procedure until you can crush the object using the least amount of force.

CAREER CENTER
CLASSZONE.COM

Learn more about careers in physics and engineering.

CHAPTER

Motion

the **BIG** idea

The motion of an object can be described and predicted.

Where will these people be in a few seconds? How do you know?

Key Concepts

SECTION 1
An object in motion changes position.
Learn about measuring position from reference points, and about relative motion.

SECTION 2
Speed measures how fast position changes.
Learn to calculate speed and how velocity depends on speed and direction.

SECTION 3
Acceleration measures how fast velocity changes.
Learn about acceleration and how to calculate it.

California ClassZone

CLASSZONE.COM

Chapter 1 online resources: Content Review, Simulation, two Resource Centers, Math Tutorial, Test Practice

EXPLORE (the **BIG** idea)

Off the Wall

> **8.1.b** Students know that average speed is the total distance traveled divided by the total time elapsed and that the speed of an object along the path traveled can vary.

Mark a starting line on the floor near a wall using a piece of masking tape. Roll a rubber ball toward the wall. Record the time from the starting line to the wall. Change the distance between the wall and the starting line. Adjust the speed at which you roll the ball until it takes the same amount of time to hit the wall as before.

Observe and Think How did the speed of the ball over the longer distance compare with the speed over the shorter distance?

Rolling Along

> **8.1.e** Students know changes in velocity may be due to changes in speed, direction, or both.

Make a ramp by leaning the edge of one book on two other books. Roll a marble up the ramp. Repeat several times and notice what happens each time. Change the height of the ramp by adding or removing books, and repeat the activity.

Observe and Think How does the speed of the marble change? At what point does its direction of motion change? How did the height of the ramp affect your observations?

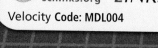

NSTA scilinks.org **SCILINKS**

Velocity **Code: MDL004**

Getting Ready to Learn

◀ CONCEPT REVIEW

- Objects can move at different speeds and in different directions.
- Pushing or pulling on an object will change how it moves.

◀ VOCABULARY REVIEW

See Glossary for definitions.

horizontal

meter

second

vertical

CONTENT REVIEW
CLASSZONE.COM

Review concepts and vocabulary.

▶ TAKING NOTES

OUTLINE

As you read, copy the headings onto your paper in the form of an outline. Then add notes in your own words that summarize what you read.

VOCABULARY STRATEGY

Place each new vocabulary term at the center of a **description wheel** diagram. As you read about the term, write some words on the spokes describing the term.

See the Note-Taking Handbook on pages R45–R51.

SCIENCE NOTEBOOK

OUTLINE

I. Position describes the location of an object.

   A. Describing a position

      1. A position is compared to a reference point.

      2. Position can be described using distance and direction.

can change with time | MOTION | is a change in position

1.1

KEY CONCEPT

An object in motion changes position.

BEFORE, you learned

- Objects can move in different ways
- An object's position can change

NOW, you will learn

- How to describe an object's position
- How to describe an object's motion

VOCABULARY

position p. 9
reference point p. 10
motion p. 12

EXPLORE Location (8.1.a)

How do you describe the location of an object?

PROCEDURE

1. Choose an object in the classroom that is easy to see.

2. Without pointing to, describing, or naming the object, give directions to a classmate for finding it.

3. Ask your classmate to identify the object using your directions. If your classmate does not correctly identify the object, try giving directions in a different way. Continue until your classmate has located the object.

WHAT DO YOU THINK?
What kinds of information must you give another person when you are trying to describe a location?

Position describes the location of an object.

VOCABULARY
Make a description wheel diagram in your notebook for *position*.

Have you ever gotten lost while looking for a specific place? If so, you probably know that accurately describing where a place is can be very important. The **position** of a place or an object is the location of that place or object. Often you describe where something is by comparing its position with where you currently are. You might say, for example, that a classmate sitting next to you is about a meter to your right, or that a mailbox is two blocks south of where you live. Each time you identify the position of an object, you are comparing the location of the object with the location of another object or place.

CHECK YOUR READING Why do you need to discuss two locations to describe the position of an object?

Describing a Position

RESOURCE CENTER
CLASSZONE.COM

Learn more about how people find and describe position.

You might describe the position of a city based on the location of another city. A location to which you compare other locations is called a **reference point.** You can describe where Santiago, Chile, is from the reference point of the city Brasília, Brazil, by saying that Santiago is about 3000 kilometers (1860 mi) southwest of Brasília.

You can also describe a position using a method that is similar to describing where a point on a graph is located. For example, in the longitude and latitude system, locations are given by two numbers—longitude and latitude. Longitude describes how many degrees east or west a location is from the prime meridian, an imaginary line running north-south through Greenwich, England. Latitude describes how many degrees north or south a location is from the equator, the imaginary circle that separates the northern and southern hemispheres. Having a standard way of describing location, such as longitude and latitude, makes it easier for people to compare locations.

Describing Position

There are several different ways to describe a position. The way you choose may depend on your reference point.

① **Reference Point: Brasília**

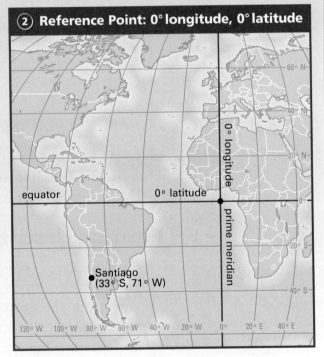

② **Reference Point: 0° longitude, 0° latitude**

To describe where Santiago is, using Brasília as a reference point, you would need to know how far Santiago is from Brasília and in what direction it is.

In the longitude and latitude system, a location is described by how many degrees north or south it is from the equator and how many degrees east or west it is from the prime meridian.

READING VISUALS Compare and contrast the two ways of describing the location of Santiago as shown here.

Measuring Distance

If you were to travel from Brasília to Santiago, you would end up about 3000 kilometers from where you started. The actual distance you traveled, however, would depend on the exact path you took. If you took a route that had many curves, the distance you traveled would be greater than 3000 kilometers.

The way you measure distance depends on the information you want. Sometimes you want to know the straight-line distance between two positions. Sometimes, however, you might need to know the total length of a certain path between those positions. During a hike, you are probably more interested in how far you have walked than in how far you are from your starting point.

When measuring either the straight-line distance between two points or the length of a path between those points, scientists use a standard unit of measurement. The standard unit of length is the meter (m), which is 3.3 feet. Longer distances can be measured in kilometers (km), and shorter distances in centimeters (cm).

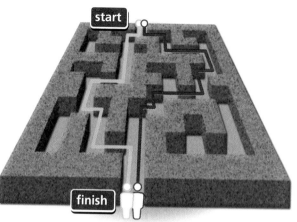

COMPARE How does the distance each person has walked compare with the distance each is from the start of the maze?

INVESTIGATE Changing Position

How are changes in position observed?

PROCEDURE

1. Begin walking while tossing a ball straight up and catching it as it falls back down toward your hand. Observe the changes in the position of the ball as you toss it while walking a distance of about 4 m.

2. Make a sketch showing how the position of the ball changed as you walked. Use your own position as a reference point for the ball's position.

3. Watch while a classmate walks and tosses the ball. Observe the changes in the position of the ball using your own position as a reference point. Make a sketch showing how the ball moved based on your new point of view.

WHAT DO YOU THINK?

- Compare your two sketches. How was the change in position of the ball you tossed different from the change in position of the ball that your partner tossed?

- How did your reference point affect what you observed? Explain.

CHALLENGE How would the change in position of the ball appear to a person standing 4 m directly in front of you?

SKILL FOCUS
Observing (8.1.a)

MATERIALS
- small ball
- paper
- pencil

TIME
20 minutes

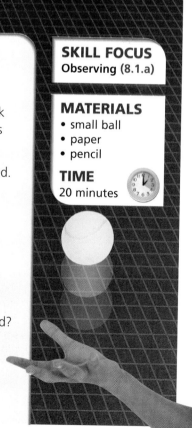

Motion is a change in position.

REMINDER

Horizontal and *vertical* describe directions, as shown.

vertical

horizontal

The illustration below shows an athlete at several positions during a long jump. If you were to watch her jump, you would see that she is in motion. **Motion** is the change of position over time. As she jumps, both her horizontal and vertical positions change. If you missed the motion of the jump, you would still know that motion occurred because of the distance between her starting and ending positions. A change in position is evidence that motion happened.

starting position

ending position

Describing Motion

It is easy to describe motion if it takes place in a straight line. An object's position can be described by showing how its distance from the reference point changes with time. However, many things do not move in a straight line. The jumper above moves in a curved path. Both her horizontal and vertical positions change over time.

You can think of the jumper as having two motions—a horizontal motion and a vertical motion. You can describe how high the jumper is off the ground throughout the jump. You can also describe how far forward the jumper is from her starting position. Suppose the jumper moved sideways and landed on the grass. You could also describe how far to the side she moved.

APPLY Describe the different directions in which the raft is moving.

Relative Motion

If you sit still in a chair, you are not moving. Or are you? The answer depends on the position and motion of the person observing you. You do not notice your position changing compared with the room and the objects in it. But if an observer could leave Earth and look at you from outer space, he could see that you are moving along with Earth as it travels around the Sun. How an observer sees your motion depends on how it compares with his own motion. Just as position is described by using a reference point, motion is described by using a frame of reference. You can think of a frame of reference as the location of an observer, who may be in motion.

Consider a student sitting behind the driver of a moving bus. The bus passes another student waiting at a street sign to cross the street.

1 To the observer on the bus, the driver is not changing his position compared with the inside of the bus. The street sign, however, moves past the observer's window. From this observer's point of view, the driver is not moving, but the street sign is.

2 To the observer on the sidewalk, the driver is changing position along with the bus. The street sign, on the other hand, is not changing position. From this observer's point of view, the street sign is not moving, but the driver is.

OUTLINE

Add relative motion to your outline, along with supporting details.

I. Main idea
  A. Supporting idea
    1. Detail
    2. Detail
  B. Supporting idea

Relative Motion

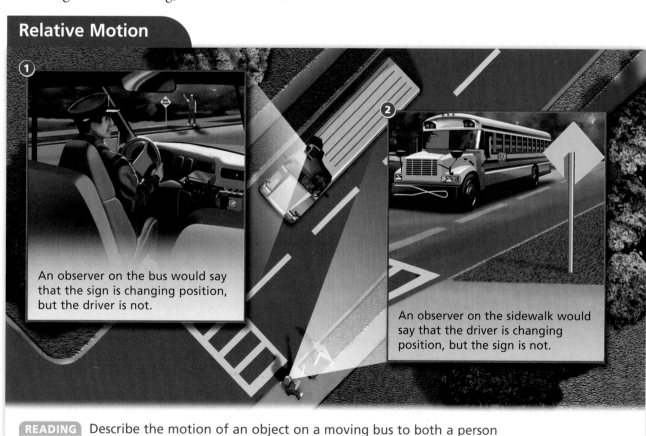

An observer on the bus would say that the sign is changing position, but the driver is not.

An observer on the sidewalk would say that the driver is changing position, but the sign is not.

READING VISUALS Describe the motion of an object on a moving bus to both a person on the bus and a person on the sidewalk.

APPLY In the top picture, the train is moving compared with the camera and the ground. Describe the relative motion of the train, camera, and ground in the bottom picture.

When you ride in a train, a bus, or an airplane, you think of yourself as moving and the ground as standing still. That is, you usually consider the ground as the frame of reference for your motion. If you traveled between two cities, you would say that you had moved, not that the ground had moved under you in the opposite direction.

If you cannot see the ground or objects on it, it is sometimes difficult to tell if a train you are riding in is moving. If the ride is very smooth and you do not look out the window at the scenery, you might never realize you are moving at all.

Suppose you are in a train, and you cannot tell if you are stopped or moving. Outside the window, another train is slowly moving forward. Could you tell which of the following situations is happening?

- Your train is stopped, and the other train is moving slowly forward.
- The other train is stopped, and your train is moving slowly backward.
- Both trains are moving forward, with the other train moving a little faster.
- Your train is moving very slowly backward, and the other train is moving very slowly forward.

Actually, all four of these possibilities would look exactly the same to you. Unless you compared the motion to the motion of something outside the train, such as the ground, you could not tell the difference between these situations.

CHECK YOUR READING   How does your observation of motion depend on your own motion?

Review

KEY CONCEPTS

1. What information do you need to describe an object's location? (8.1.a)

2. Describe how your position changes as you jump over an object. (8.1.a)

3. Give an example of how the apparent motion of an object depends on the observer's motion. (8.1.a)

CRITICAL THINKING

4. **Infer** Kyle walks 3 blocks south from his home to school, and Jana walks 2 blocks north from her home to Kyle's home. How far and in what direction is the school from Jana's home?

5. **Predict** If you sit on a moving bus and toss a coin straight up into the air, where will it land?

○ CHALLENGE

6. **Infer** Jamal is in a car going north. He looks out his window and thinks that the northbound traffic is moving very slowly. Ellen is in a car going south. She thinks the northbound traffic is moving quickly. Explain why Jamal and Ellen have different ideas about the motion of the traffic.

COAST GUARD RESCUE

Rescue!

8.1.a Students know position is defined in relation to some choice of a standard reference point and a set of reference directions.

A rescue operation is often difficult and risky because the person in trouble is in a dangerous situation. As a rescue ship or helicopter approaches a stranded boat, the team must get close enough to help but avoid making the problem worse by colliding with the boat. At the same time, wind, waves, and currents cause changes in the motion of both crafts.

Finding the Problem

A stranded boater fires a flare to indicate his location. The observer on the Coast Guard ship tracks the motion of the flare to its source.

U.S. COAST GUARD

U.S. COAST GUARD

Avoiding Collision

As the boats move closer together, the captain assesses their motion relative to each other. The speeds of the boats must match, and the boats must be close enough that a rope can be thrown across the gap. If the sea is rough, both boats will move up and down, making the proper positioning even more difficult.

Rescue from Above

The helicopter pilot determines where to hover so that the rescue basket lands on target. A mistake could be disastrous for the rescuers as well as the people being rescued.

EXPLORE

1. **PREDICT** Tie a washer to a 30 cm piece of string. Using your hand as a helicopter, lower the rescue washer to a mark on the floor. Turn on a fan to create wind. Predict where you will need to hold the string to land the washer on the mark. Place the fan at a different location and try again. How accurate was your prediction? Does your accuracy improve with practice?

2. **CHALLENGE** Have a partner throw a baseball into the air from behind the corner of a wall. Using the motion of the ball, try to determine the position from which it was thrown. When is it easier—when the ball is thrown in a high arc or lower one?

1.2 Speed measures how fast position changes.

CALIFORNIA
Content Standards

8.1.b Students know that average speed is the total distance traveled divided by the total time elapsed and that the speed of an object along the path traveled can vary.

8.1.d Students know the velocity of an object must be described by specifying both the direction and the speed of the object.

8.1.f Students know how to interpret graphs of position versus time and graphs of speed versus time for motion in a single direction.

VOCABULARY

speed p. 16
velocity p. 22
vector p. 22

◀ BEFORE, you learned

- An object's position is measured from a reference point
- To describe the position of an object, you can use distance and direction
- An object in motion changes position with time

▶ NOW, you will learn

- How to calculate an object's speed
- How to describe an object's velocity

EXPLORE Speed (8.1.b)

How can you measure speed?

PROCEDURE

1. Place a piece of tape on the floor. Measure a distance on the floor 2 m away from the tape. Mark this distance with a second piece of tape.

2. Roll a tennis ball from one piece of tape to the other, timing how long it takes to travel the 2 m.

3. Roll the ball again so that it travels the same distance in less time. Then roll the ball so that it takes more time to travel that distance than it did the first time.

MATERIALS
- tape
- meter stick
- tennis ball
- stopwatch

WHAT DO YOU THINK?
- How did you change the time it took the ball to travel 2 m?
- How did changing the time affect the motion of the ball?

Position can change at different rates.

VOCABULARY
Make a description wheel diagram in your notebook for *speed*.

When someone asks you how far it is to the library, you can answer in terms of distance or time. You can say it is several blocks, or you can say it is a five-minute walk. When you give a time instead of a distance, you are basing your time estimate on the distance to the library and the person's speed. **Speed** is a measure of how fast something moves, or the distance it moves in a given amount of time. The greater the speed an object has, the faster it changes position.

CHECK YOUR READING How are speed and position related?

The way in which one quantity changes compared to another quantity is called a rate. Speed is the rate at which the distance an object moves changes compared to time. If you are riding a bike to a movie, and you think you might be late, you increase the rate at which your distance changes by pedaling harder. In other words, you increase your speed.

Calculating Speed

To calculate speed, you need to know both distance and time measurements. Consider the two bike riders below.

1 The two bikes pass the same point at the same time.

2 After one second, the first bike has traveled four meters, while the second has traveled only two meters. Because the first bike has traveled four meters in one second, it has a speed of four meters per second. The second bike has a speed of two meters per second.

3 If each bike continues moving at the same speed as before, then after two seconds the first rider will have traveled eight meters, while the second one will have traveled only four meters.

Comparing Speed

Objects that travel at different speeds move different distances in the same amount of time.

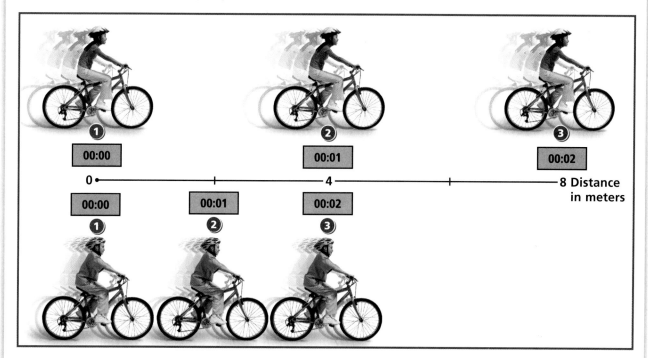

READING VISUALS How far will each rider travel in five seconds?

Racing wheelchairs are specially designed to reach higher speeds than regular wheelchairs.

Speed can be calculated by dividing the distance an object travels by the time it takes to cover the distance. The formula for finding average speed is

$$\textbf{Average Speed} = \frac{\textbf{distance}}{\textbf{time}} \qquad S = \frac{d}{t}$$

Speed is shown in the formula as the letter S, distance as the letter d, and time as the letter t. The formula shows how distance, time, and speed are related. If two objects travel the same distance, the object that took a shorter amount of time will have the greater speed. Similarly, an object with a greater speed will travel a longer distance in the same amount of time than an object with a lower speed will.

The standard unit for speed is meters per second (m/s). Speed is also given in kilometers per hour (km/h). In the United States, where the English system of measurement is still used, speeds are often given in miles per hour (mi/h or mph). One mile per hour is equal to 0.45 m/s.

The man participating in the wheelchair race, at left, will win if his speed is greater than the speed of the other racers. You can use the formula to calculate his speed.

 CHECK YOUR READING If two runners cover the same distance in different amounts of time, how do their average speeds compare?

Calculating Speed

▶ Sample Problem

A wheelchair racer completes a 100-meter course in 20 seconds. What is his average speed?

What do you know? distance = 100 m, time = 20 s

What do you want to find out? average speed

Write the formula: $S = \dfrac{d}{t}$

Substitute into the formula: $S = \dfrac{100 \text{ m}}{20 \text{ s}}$

Calculate and simplify: $S = 5$ m/s

Check that your units agree: Unit is m/s.
Unit of speed is m/s. Units agree.

Answer: $S = 5$ m/s

▶ Practice the Math

1. A man runs 200 m in 25 s. What is his average speed?
2. If you travel 100 m in 50 s, what is your average speed?

Average Speed

Speed is not constant. When you run, you might slow down to pace yourself, or speed up to win a race. At each point as you are running, you have a specific speed. This moment-to-moment speed is called your instantaneous speed. Your instantaneous speed can be difficult to measure; however, it is easier to calculate your average speed over a distance.

READING TiP

The root of *instantaneous* is *instant,* meaning "moment."

In a long race, runners often want to know their times for each lap so that they can pace themselves. For example, an excellent middle school runner might have the following times for the four laps of a 1600-meter race: 83 seconds, 81 seconds, 79 seconds, 77 seconds. The lap times show the runner is gradually increasing her speed throughout the race.

The total time for the four laps can be used to calculate the runner's average speed for the entire race. The total time is 320 seconds (5 min 20 s) for the entire distance of 1600 meters. The runner's average speed is 1600 meters divided by 320 seconds, or 5.0 meters per second.

INVESTIGATE Speed and Distance

How does design affect speed?

Cars are built in different shapes. How does the shape of the car affect the way it moves? Design your own car, and see how fast it can go.

DESIGN —YOUR OWN— EXPERIMENT

PROCEDURE

1. Use the clay, film container lids, and toothpicks to design a car that rolls when it is pushed. The car should have a total mass of 150 g or less.

2. Using any or all of the other materials, design an experiment to measure and compare the speed of your car with the speed of someone else's car. Your experiment should be designed so that the design of the car is the only variable being tested. Write up your procedure.

3. Perform the experiment using your car and another student's car. Record the data you need to calculate the speed of both cars.

4. Calculate the speed of each car, and record which car went faster.

WHAT DO YOU THINK?

- What were the constants in your experiment?
- How would you improve your design if you were to repeat the experiment?

SKILL FOCUS
Designing experiments (8.1.c)

MATERIALS
- clay
- film container lids
- toothpicks
- beam balance
- board
- books
- string
- straw
- scissors
- stopwatch

TIME
20 minutes

Distance-Time Graphs

A convenient way to show the motion of an object is by using a graph that plots the distance the object has traveled against time. This type of graph, called a distance-time graph, shows how speed relates to distance and time. You can use a distance-time graph to see how both distance and speed change with time.

The distance-time graph on page 21 tracks the changing motion of a zebra. At first the zebra looks for a spot to graze. Its meal is interrupted by a lion, and the zebra starts running to escape.

In a distance-time graph, time is on the horizontal axis, or *x*-axis, and distance is on the vertical axis, or *y*-axis.

1 As an object moves, the distance it travels increases with time. This can be seen as a climbing, or rising, line on the graph.

2 A flat, or horizontal, line shows an interval of time where the speed is zero meters per second.

3 Steeper lines show intervals where the speed is greater than intervals with less steep lines.

You can use the steepness, or slope, of a line in a distance-time graph to determine the speed of an object if speed is constant. The slope of the line is calculated by dividing the change in distance by the change in time for that time interval.

▼ REMINDER

The *x*-axis and *y*-axis are arranged as shown:

The line shown can be written as *y* = *kx*, where *k* is a constant and the slope of the line. In a distance-time graph, the slope of a straight line equals the constant speed of the object.

Calculating Speed from a Graph

▶ **Sample Problem**

How fast is the zebra walking during the first 20 seconds?

What do you know? Reading from the graph:
At time = 0 s, distance = 0 m.
At time = 20 s, distance = 40 m.

What do you want to find out? speed

Write the formula: $S = \dfrac{d}{t}$

Substitute into the formula: $S = \dfrac{40 \text{ m} - 0 \text{ m}}{20 \text{ s} - 0 \text{ s}}$

Calculate and simplify: $S = \dfrac{40 \text{ m}}{20 \text{ s}} = 2 \text{ m/s}$

Check that your units agree: Unit is m/s.
Unit of speed is m/s. Units agree.

Answer: S = 2 m/s

▶ **Practice the Math**

1. What is the speed of the zebra during the 20 s to 40 s time interval?
2. What is the speed of the zebra during the 40 s to 60 s interval?

Distance-Time Graph

A zebra's speed will change throughout the day, especially if a hungry lion is nearby. You can use a distance-time graph to compare the zebra's speed over different time intervals.

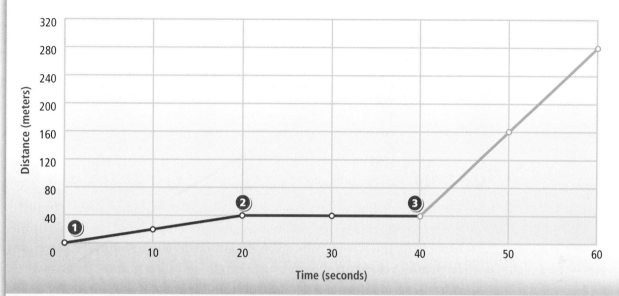

① When the zebra is walking, its distance from its starting point increases. You can see this motion on the graph as a climbing line.

② When the zebra stops to graze, it no longer changes its distance from the starting point. Time, however, continues to pass. Therefore, the graph shows a flat, or horizontal, line.

③ As soon as the zebra notices the lion, it stops grazing and starts to run for its life. The zebra is covering a greater distance in each time interval than it was before the chase started, so the line is steeper.

READING VISUALS How do the distances change over each 10-second time interval?

Velocity includes speed and direction.

CALIFORNIA
Focus

In Valencia, California, there is an amusement park ride that drops riders straight downward. The velocity of the dropping car increases to a maximum velocity of 100 mph straight down. The car then slows to a stop. The size of the velocity changes during the ride, but the direction does not.

Sometimes the direction of motion is as important as its speed. In large crowds, for example, you probably always try to walk in the same direction the crowd is moving and at the same speed. If you walk in even a slightly different direction, you can bump into other people. In a crowd, in other words, you try to walk with the same velocity as the people around you. **Velocity** is a speed in a specific direction. If you say you are walking east at a speed of three meters per second, you are describing your velocity. A person walking north with a speed of three meters per second would have the same speed as you do, but not the same velocity.

 CHECK YOUR READING What is velocity? Give an example of a velocity.

Velocity

The picture below shows several ants as they carry leaves along a branch. Each ant's direction of motion changes as it walks along the bends of the branch. As the arrows indicate, each ant is moving in a specific direction. Each ant's velocity is shown by the length and direction of the arrow. A longer arrow means a greater speed in the direction the arrow is pointing. In this picture, for example, the ant moving up the branch is traveling more slowly than the ant moving down the branch.

To determine the velocity of an ant as it carries a leaf, you need to know both its speed and its direction. A change in either speed or direction results in a change in velocity. For example, the velocity of an ant changes if it slows down but continues moving in the same direction. Velocity also changes if the ant continues moving at the same speed but changes direction.

Velocity is an example of a vector. A **vector** is a quantity that has both size and direction. Speed is not a vector because speed is a measure of how fast or slow an object moves, not which direction it moves in. Velocity, however, has a size—the speed—and a direction, so it is a vector quantity.

READING TiP

Green arrows show velocity.

A longer arrow indicates a faster speed than a shorter arrow. The direction of the arrow indicates the direction of motion.

ant moving
slowly upward

ant moving
quickly downward

INFER How does this ant's velocity compare with those of the other ants?

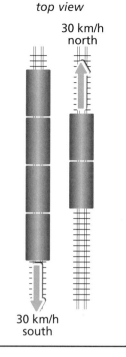

top view

30 km/h
north

30 km/h
south

INFER How do the speeds and velocities of these trains compare?

Velocity Versus Speed

Because velocity includes direction, it is possible for two objects to have the same speed but different velocities. If you traveled by train to visit a friend, you might go 30 kilometers per hour (km/h) north on the way there and 30 km/h south on the way back. Your speed is the same both going and coming back, but your velocity is different because your direction of motion has changed.

Another difference between speed and velocity is the way the average is calculated. Your average speed depends on the total distance you have traveled. The average velocity depends on the total distance you are from where you started. Going north, your average speed would be 30 km/h, and your average velocity would be 30 km/h north. After the round-trip ride, your average traveling speed would still be 30 km/h. Your average velocity, however, would be 0 km/h because you ended up exactly where you started.

 Use a Venn diagram to compare and contrast speed and velocity.

1.2 Review

KEY CONCEPTS

1. How is speed related to distance and time? (8.1.b)

2. How would decreasing the time it takes you to run a certain distance affect your speed? (8.1.b)

3. What two things do you need to know to describe the velocity of an object? (8.1.d)

CRITICAL THINKING

4. **Compare** Amy and Ellie left school at the same time. Amy lives farther away than Ellie, but she and Ellie arrived at their homes at the same time. Compare the girls' speeds.

5. **Calculate** Carlos lives 100 m away from his friend's home. What is his average speed if he reaches his friend's home in 50 s?

CHALLENGE

6. **Synthesize** If you watch a train go by at 20 m/s, at what speed will the people sitting on the train be moving relative to you? Would someone walking toward the back of the train have a greater or lesser speed relative to you? Explain.

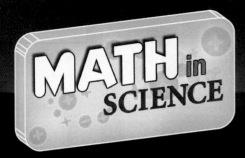

 MATH TUTORIAL
CLASSZONE.COM
Click on Math Tutorial
for more help with units
and rates.

Math 8.A1.15
Science 8.1.c, 8.9.f

A cheetah can reach a speed
of 30 meters per second, but
only in short bursts.

Time, Distance, and Speed

If someone tells you the store is "five" from the school, you would probably ask, "Five what? Five meters? Five blocks?" You typically describe a distance using standard units of measurement, such as meters, miles, or kilometers. By using units, you help other people understand exactly what your measurement means.

When you work with a formula, the numbers that you substitute into the formula have units. When you calculate with a number, you also calculate with the unit associated with that number.

Example

A cheetah runs at a speed of 30 meters per second. How long does the cheetah take to run 90 meters?

The formula for time in terms of speed and distance is

$$\text{time} = \frac{\text{distance}}{\text{Speed}} \qquad t = \frac{d}{S}$$

(1) Start by substituting the numbers into the formula. Include the units with the numbers.

$$t = \frac{90 \text{ m}}{30 \text{ m/s}}$$

(2) When the units or calculations include fractions, write out the units as fractions as well:

$$t = \frac{90 \text{ m}}{\frac{30 \text{ m}}{\text{s}}}$$

(3) Do the calculation and simplify the units by cancellation:

$$t = 90 \text{ m} \cdot \frac{\text{s}}{30 \text{ m}} = \frac{90}{30} \cdot \frac{\text{m} \cdot \text{s}}{\text{m}} = 3 \cdot \frac{\cancel{\text{m}} \cdot \text{s}}{\cancel{\text{m}}} = 3 \text{ s}$$

ANSWER 3 seconds

Note that the answer has a unit of time. Use the units to check that your answer is reasonable. An answer that is supposed to have a unit of time, for example, should not have a unit of distance.

Answer the following questions.

1. How long would it take an object traveling 12 m/s to go 60 m? What unit of time is your answer in?

2. If a car travels 60 km/h, how long would it take the car to travel 300 km? What unit of time is your answer in?

3. If a man walks 3 miles in 1 hour, what is his speed? What unit of speed is your answer in? (Use the formula on page 18.)

CHALLENGE Show that the formula *distance = speed · time* has a unit for distance on both sides of the equal sign.

1.3 Acceleration measures how fast velocity changes.

8.1.e Students know changes in velocity may be due to changes in speed, direction, or both.

8.1.f Students know how to interpret graphs of position versus time and graphs of speed versus time for motion in a single direction.

8.9.g Distinguish between linear and nonlinear relationships on a graph of data.

VOCABULARY

acceleration p. 25

◁ BEFORE, you learned

- Speed describes how far an object travels in a given time
- Velocity is a measure of the speed and direction of motion

▷ NOW, you will learn

- How acceleration is related to velocity
- How to calculate acceleration

OUTLINE

Remember to use the blue and red headings in this chapter to help you make notes on acceleration.

I. Main idea
   A. Supporting idea
      1. Detail
      2. Detail
   B. Supporting idea

THINK ABOUT

How does velocity change?

The photograph at right shows the path that a bouncing ball takes. The time between each image of the ball is the same during the entire bounce. Is the ball moving the same distance in each time interval? Is the ball moving the same direction in each time interval?

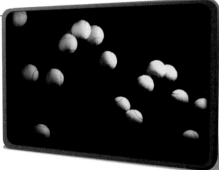

Speed and direction can change with time.

When you throw a ball into the air, it leaves your hand at a certain speed. As the ball rises, it slows down. Then, as the ball falls back toward the ground, it speeds up again. When the ball hits the ground, its direction of motion changes and it bounces back up into the air. The speed and direction of the ball do not stay the same as the ball moves. The ball's velocity keeps changing.

You can find out how much an object's position changes during a certain amount of time if you know its velocity. In a similar way, you can measure how an object's velocity changes with time. The rate at which velocity changes with time is called **acceleration.** Acceleration is a measure of how quickly the velocity is changing. If velocity does not change, there is no acceleration.

 What is the relationship between velocity and acceleration?

The word *acceleration* is commonly used to mean "speeding up." In physics, however, acceleration refers to any change in velocity. A driver slowing down to stop at a light is accelerating. A runner turning a corner at a constant speed is also accelerating because the direction of her velocity is changing as she turns.

Like velocity, acceleration is a vector, which means it has both size and direction. The direction of the acceleration determines whether an object will slow down, speed up, or turn.

READING TIP

Orange arrows are used to show acceleration.

Remember that green arrows show velocity.

A longer arrow means greater acceleration or velocity.

1 Acceleration in the Same Direction as Motion When the acceleration is in the same direction as the object is moving, the speed of the object increases. The car speeds up.

2 Acceleration in the Opposite Direction of Motion When the acceleration is opposite to the motion, the speed of the object decreases. The car slows down. Slowing down is also called negative acceleration.

3 Acceleration at a Right Angle to Motion When the acceleration is at a right angle to the motion, the direction of motion changes. The car changes the direction in which it is moving by some angle, but its speed does not change.

CHECK YOUR READING How does acceleration affect velocity? Give examples.

INVESTIGATE Acceleration

When does an object accelerate?

PROCEDURE

1. Use the template and materials to construct an acceleration measuring tool.

2. Hold the tool in your right hand so that the string falls over the 0 m/s² mark. Move the tool in the direction of the arrow. Try to produce both positive and negative acceleration without changing the direction of motion.

3. With the arrow pointing ahead of you, start to walk. Observe the motion of the string while you increase your speed.

4. Repeat step 3, but this time observe the string while slowing down.

5. Repeat step 3 again, but observe the string while walking at a steady speed.

WHAT DO YOU THINK?

- When could you measure an acceleration?
- What was the largest acceleration (positive or negative) that you measured?

CHALLENGE If you moved the acceleration measuring tool backward, how would the measuring scale change?

Acceleration can be calculated from velocity and time.

Suppose you are racing a classmate. In one second, you go from standing still to running at six meters per second. In the same time, your classmate goes from standing still to running at three meters per second. How does your acceleration compare with your classmate's acceleration? To measure acceleration, you need to know how velocity changes with time.

- The change in velocity can be found by comparing the initial velocity and the final velocity of the moving object.
- The time interval over which the velocity changed can be measured.

In one second, you increase your velocity by six meters per second, and your friend increases her velocity by three meters per second. Because your velocity changes more, you have a greater acceleration during that second of time than your friend does. Remember that acceleration measures the change in velocity, not velocity itself. As long as your classmate increases her current velocity by three meters per second, her acceleration will be the same whether she is going from zero to three meters per second or from three to six meters per second.

Calculating Acceleration

If you know the starting velocity of an object, the final velocity, and the time interval during which the object changed velocity, you can calculate the acceleration of the object. The formula for acceleration is shown below.

$$\text{acceleration} = \frac{\text{final velocity} - \text{initial velocity}}{\text{time}}$$

$$a = \frac{v_{final} - v_{initial}}{t}$$

Remember that velocity is expressed in units of meters per second. The standard units for acceleration, therefore, are meters per second over time, or meters per second per second. This is simplified to meters per second squared, which is written as m/s^2.

As the girl in the photograph at left sleds down the sandy hill, what happens to her velocity? At the bottom of the hill, her velocity will be greater than it was at the top. You can calculate her average acceleration down the hill if you know her starting and ending velocities and how long it took her to get to the bottom. This calculation is shown in the sample problem below.

REMINDER

Remember that velocity is the speed of the object in a particular direction.

Calculating Acceleration

▶ Sample Problem

Ama starts sliding with a velocity of 1 m/s. After 3 s, her velocity is 7 m/s. What is Ama's acceleration?

What do you know?   initial velocity = 1 m/s, final velocity = 7 m/s, time = 3 s

What do you want to find out?   acceleration

Write the formula: $a = \dfrac{v_{final} - v_{initial}}{t}$

Substitute into the formula: $a = \dfrac{7 \text{ m/s} - 1 \text{ m/s}}{3 \text{ s}}$

Calculate and simplify: $a = \dfrac{6 \text{ m/s}}{3 \text{ s}} = 2 \dfrac{\text{m/s}}{\text{s}} = 2 \text{ m/s}^2$

Check that your units agree: $\dfrac{\text{m/s}}{\text{s}} = \dfrac{\text{m}}{\text{s}} \cdot \dfrac{1}{\text{s}} = \dfrac{\text{m}}{\text{s}^2}$ Unit is m/s^2.

Unit of acceleration is m/s^2. Units agree.

Answer: $a = 2 \text{ m/s}^2$

▶ Practice the Math

1. A man walking at 0.5 m/s accelerates to a velocity of 0.6 m/s in 1 s. What is his acceleration?

2. A train traveling at 10 m/s slows down to a complete stop in 20 s. What is the acceleration of the train?

The sledder's final velocity was greater than her initial velocity. If an object is slowing down, on the other hand, the final velocity is less than the initial velocity. Suppose a car going 10 meters per second takes 2 seconds to stop for a red light. In this case, the initial velocity is 10 m/s and the final velocity is 0 m/s. The formula for acceleration gives a negative answer, -5 m/s^2. The negative sign indicates a negative acceleration—that is, an acceleration that decreases the velocity.

RESOURCE CENTER
CLASSZONE.COM
Learn more about acceleration.

 CHECK YOUR READING What would be true of the values for initial velocity and final velocity if the acceleration were zero?

Acceleration over Time

Even a very small positive acceleration can lead to great speeds if an object accelerates for a long enough period. In 1998, NASA launched the *Deep Space 1* spacecraft. This spacecraft tested a new type of engine—one that gave the spacecraft an extremely small acceleration. The new engine required less fuel than previous spacecraft engines. However, the spacecraft needed a great deal of time to reach its target velocity.

The acceleration of the *Deep Space 1* spacecraft is less than 2/10,000 of a meter per second per second (0.0002 m/s^2). That may not seem like much, but over 20 months, the spacecraft could increase its speed by 4500 meters per second (10,000 mi/h).

By carefully adjusting both the amount and the direction of the acceleration of *Deep Space 1*, scientists were able to control its flight path. In 2001, the spacecraft successfully flew by a comet, sending back images from about 230 million kilometers (140 million mi) away.

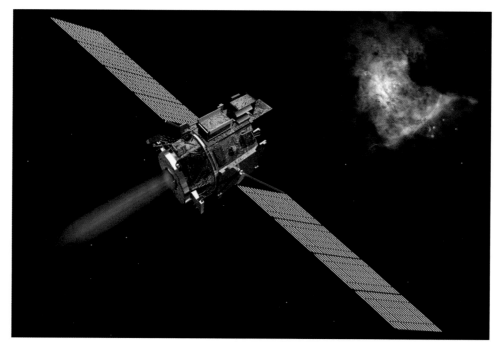

APPLY What makes the new engine technology used by *Deep Space 1* more useful for long-term missions than for short-term ones?

Velocity-Time Graphs

Velocity-time graphs and distance-time graphs are related. This is because the distance an object travels depends on its velocity. Compare the velocity-time graph on the right with the distance-time graph below it.

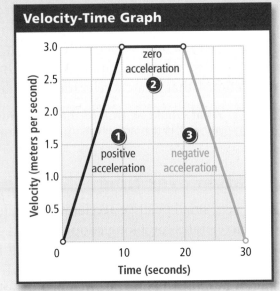

Velocity-Time Graph

zero acceleration ②

positive acceleration ①

negative acceleration ③

Velocity (meters per second)

Time (seconds)

① As the student starts to push the scooter, his velocity increases. His acceleration is positive, so he moves forward a greater distance with each second that passes.

② He coasts at a constant velocity. Because his velocity does not change, he has no acceleration, and he continues to move forward the same distance each second.

③ As he slows down, his velocity decreases. His acceleration is negative, and he moves forward a smaller distance with each passing second until he finally stops.

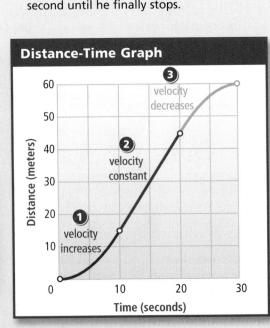

Distance-Time Graph

③ velocity decreases

② velocity constant

① velocity increases

Distance (meters)

Time (seconds)

READING VISUALS What velocity does the student have after five seconds? About how far has he moved in that time?

Velocity-Time Graphs

Acceleration, like position and velocity, can change with time. Just as you can use a distance-time graph to understand velocity, you can use a velocity-time graph to understand acceleration. Both graphs tell you how something is changing over time. In a velocity-time graph, time is on the horizontal axis, or *x*-axis, and velocity is on the vertical axis, or *y*-axis.

Explore how changing the acceleration of an object changes its motion.

The two graphs on page 30 show a velocity-time graph and a distance-time graph of a student riding on a scooter. He first starts moving and speeds up. He coasts, and then he slows down to a stop.

① The rising line on the velocity-time graph shows where the acceleration is positive. The steeper the line, the greater the acceleration. The distance-time graph for the same interval is curving upward more and more steeply as the velocity increases. The curve shows that the relationship is non-linear.

② The flat line on the velocity-time graph shows an interval of no acceleration. The distance-time graph has a straight line, or linear relationship, during this time, since the velocity is not changing.

③ The falling line on the velocity-time graph shows where the acceleration is negative. The same interval on the distance-time graph shows a curve, or non-linear relationship, that becomes less and less steep as the velocity decreases. Notice that the overall distance still increases.

Velocity-time graphs and distance-time graphs can provide useful information. For example, scientists who study earthquakes create these graphs in order to study the up-and-down and side-to-side movement of the ground during an earthquake. They produce the graphs from instruments that measure the acceleration of the ground.

 CHECK YOUR READING What does a flat line on a velocity-time graph represent?

1.3 Review

KEY CONCEPTS

1. What measurements or observations tell you that a car is accelerating? (8.1.e)

2. If an object accelerates in the same direction in which it is moving, how is its speed affected? (8.1.f)

3. What measurements do you need in order to calculate acceleration? (8.1.e)

CRITICAL THINKING

4. **Calculate** A car goes from 20 m/s to 30 m/s in 10 seconds. What is its acceleration?

5. **Infer** Two runners start a race. After 2 seconds, they both have the same velocity. If they both started at the same time, how do their average accelerations compare?

CHALLENGE

6. **Analyze** Is it possible for an object that has a constant negative acceleration to change the direction in which it is moving? Explain why or why not.

CHAPTER INVESTIGATION

Acceleration and Slope

OVERVIEW AND PURPOSE When a downhill skier glides down a mountain without using her ski poles, her velocity increases and she experiences acceleration. How would gliding down a hill with a greater slope affect her acceleration? In this investigation you will

- calculate the acceleration of an object rolling down two ramps of different slopes
- determine how the slope of the ramp affects the acceleration of the object

▶ Problem

How does the slope of a ramp affect the acceleration of an object rolling down the ramp?

▶ Hypothesize

Write a hypothesis to explain how changing the slope of the ramp will affect acceleration. Your hypothesis should take the form of an "If . . . , then . . . , because . . ." statement.

▶ Procedure

1. Make a data table like the one shown on the sample notebook page.

2. Make a ramp by laying two meter sticks side by side. Leave a small gap between the meter sticks.

3. Use masking tape as shown in the photograph to join the meter sticks. The marble should be able to roll freely along the groove.

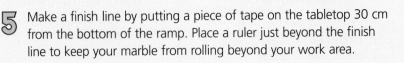

4. Set up your ramp on a smooth, even surface, such as a tabletop. Raise one end of the ramp on top of one of the books. The other end of the ramp should remain on the table.

5. Make a finish line by putting a piece of tape on the tabletop 30 cm from the bottom of the ramp. Place a ruler just beyond the finish line to keep your marble from rolling beyond your work area.

MATERIALS
- 2 meter sticks
- masking tape
- marble
- 2 paperback books
- ruler
- stopwatch
- calculator

8.1.e, 8.9.a, 8.9.b, 8.9.c

Content Standard
8.1.e Students know changes in velocity may be due to changes in speed, direction, or both.

Investigation Standard
8.9.c Distinguish between variable and controlled parameters in a test.

6 Test your ramp by releasing the marble from the top of the ramp. Make sure that the marble rolls freely. Do not push on the marble.

7 Release the marble and measure the time it takes for it to roll from the release point to the end of the ramp. Record this time under Column A for trial 1.

8 Release the marble again from the same point, and record the time it takes the marble to roll from the end of the ramp to the finish line. Record this time in Column B for trial 1. Repeat and record three more trials.

9 Raise the height of the ramp by propping it up with both paperback books. Repeat steps 7 and 8.

▶ Observe and Analyze
Write It Up

1. **RECORD OBSERVATIONS** Draw the setup of your procedures. Be sure your data table is complete.

2. **IDENTIFY VARIABLES AND CONSTANTS** Identify the variables and constants in the experiment. List them in your notebook.

3. **CALCULATE**

   Average Time For ramps 1 and 2, calculate and record the average time it took for the marble to travel from the end of the ramp to the finish line.

   Final Velocity For ramps 1 and 2, calculate and record v_{final} using the formula below.

   $$v_{final} = \frac{\text{distance from end of ramp to finish line}}{\text{average time from end of ramp to finish line}}$$

   Acceleration For ramps 1 and 2, calculate and record acceleration using the formula below. (**Hint:** Speed at the release of the marble is 0 m/s.)

   $$a = \frac{v_{final} - v_{initial} \text{ (speed at release)}}{\text{average time from release to bottom of ramp}}$$

▶ Conclude

Write It Up

1. **COMPARE** How did the acceleration of the marble on ramp 1 compare with the acceleration of the marble on ramp 2?

2. **INTERPRET** Answer the question posed in the problem.

3. **ANALYZE** Compare your results with your hypothesis. Do your data support your hypothesis?

4. **EVALUATE** Why was it necessary to measure how fast the marble traveled from the end of the ramp to the finish line?

5. **IDENTIFY LIMITS** What possible limitations or sources of error could have affected your results? Why was it important to perform four trials for each measurement of speed?

▶ INVESTIGATE Further

CHALLENGE Design your own experiment to determine how the marble's mass affects its acceleration down a ramp.

Acceleration and Slope

Problem How does the slope of a ramp affect the acceleration of an object rolling down the ramp?

Hypothesize

Observe and Analyze

Table 1. Times for Marble to Travel down Ramp

Height of Ramp (cm)	Trial Number	Column A Time from release to end of ramp	Column B Time from end of ramp to finish line
Ramp 1	1		
	2		
	3		
	4		
	Totals		
		Average	Average

Chapter Review

the BIG idea

The motion of an object can be described and predicted.

CONTENT REVIEW
CLASSZONE.COM

◀ KEY CONCEPTS SUMMARY

---

1 An object in motion changes position.

Position is measured from a reference point.

Motion is measured relative to an observer.

start   finish

VOCABULARY
position p. 9
reference point p. 10
motion p. 12

---

2 Speed measures how fast position changes.

- Speed is how fast positions change with time.
- Velocity is speed in a specific direction.

00:00 $\text{Speed} = \dfrac{\text{distance}}{\text{time}}$ 00:02
time

distance

VOCABULARY
speed p. 16
velocity p. 22
vector p. 22

---

3 Acceleration measures how fast velocity changes.

$$\text{acceleration} = \frac{\text{final velocity} - \text{initial velocity}}{\text{time}}$$

initial velocity   acceleration   final velocity

VOCABULARY
acceleration p. 25

Reviewing Vocabulary

Copy and complete the chart below. If the left column is blank, give the correct term. If the right column is blank, give a brief description.

Term	Description
1.	speed in a specific direction
2.	a change of position over time
3. speed	
4.	an object's location
5. reference point	
6.	the rate at which velocity changes over time
7.	a quantity that has both size and direction

Reviewing Key Concepts

Multiple Choice *Choose the letter of the best answer.*

8. A position describes an object's location compared to (8.1.a)
   a. its motion
   b. a reference point
   c. its average speed
   d. a vector

9. Maria walked 2 km in half an hour. What was her average speed during her walk? (8.1.b)
   a. 1 km/h
   b. 2 km/
   c. 4 km/h
   d. 6 km/h

10. A vector is a quantity that has (8.1.d)
    a. speed
    b. acceleration
    c. size and direction
    d. position and distance

11. Mary and Keisha run with the same constant speed but in opposite directions. The girls have (8.1.e)
    a. the same position
    b. different accelerations
    c. different speeds
    d. different velocities

12. A swimmer increases her speed as she approaches the end of the pool. Her acceleration is (8.1.e)
    a. in the same direction as her motion
    b. in the opposite direction of her motion
    c. at right angles to her motion
    d. zero

13. A cheetah can go from 0 m/s to 20 m/s in 2 s. What is the cheetah's acceleration? (8.1.f)
    a. 5 m/s^2
    b. 10 m/s^2
    c. 20 m/s^2
    d. 40 m/s^2

14. Jon walks for a few minutes, then runs for a few minutes. During this time, his average speed is (8.1.b)
    a. the same as his final speed
    b. greater than his final speed
    c. less than his final speed
    d. zero

15. A car traveling at 40 m/s slows down to 20 m/s. During this time, the car has (8.1.e)
    a. no acceleration
    b. positive acceleration
    c. negative acceleration
    d. constant velocity

Short Answer *Write a short answer to each question.*

16. Suppose you are biking with a friend. How would your friend describe your relative motion as he passes you? (8.1.a)

17. Describe a situation where an object has a changing velocity but constant speed. (8.1.e)

18. Give two examples of an accelerating object. (8.1.e)

Thinking Critically

Use the following graph to answer the next three questions.

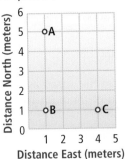

19. OBSERVE Describe the location of point A. Explain what you used as a reference point for your location. (8.1.a)

20. COMPARE Copy the graph into your notebook. Draw two different paths an object could take when moving from point B to point C. How do the lengths of these two paths compare? (8.1.a)

21. ANALYZE An object moves from point A to point C in the same amount of time that another object moves from point B to point C. If both objects traveled in a straight line, which one had the greater speed? (8.1.c)

Read the following paragraph and use the information to answer the next three questions.

In Aesop's fable of the tortoise and the hare, a slow-moving tortoise races a fast-moving hare. The hare, certain it can win, stops to take a long nap. Meanwhile, the tortoise continues to move toward the finish line at a slow but steady speed. When the hare wakes up, it runs as fast as it can. Just as the hare is about to catch up to the tortoise, however, the tortoise wins the race.

22. ANALYZE How does the race between the tortoise and the hare show the difference between average speed and instantaneous speed? (8.1.b)

23. MODEL Assume the racetrack was 100 meters long and the race took 40 minutes. Create a possible distance-time graph for both the tortoise and the hare. (8.1.f)

24. COMPARE If the racetrack were circular, how would the tortoise's speed be different from its velocity? (8.1.e)

25. APPLY How might a person use a floating stick to measure the speed at which a river flows? (8.1.b)

26. CONNECT Describe a frame of reference other than the ground that you might use to measure motion. When would you use it? (8.1.a)

Using Math Skills in Science

27. José skated 50 m in 10 s. What was his speed? (8.1.b)

28. Use the information in the photograph below to calculate the speed of the ant as it moves down the branch. (8.1.b)

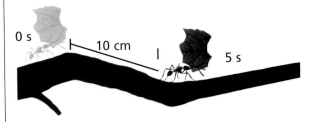

29. While riding her bicycle, Jamie accelerated from 7 m/s to 2 m/s in 5 s. What was her acceleration? (8.1.f)

the BIG idea

30. PREDICT Look back at the picture at the beginning of the chapter on pages 6–7. Predict how the velocity of the roller coaster will change in the next moment. (8.1.d)

31. WRITE A car is traveling east at 40 km/h. Use this information to predict where the car will be in one hour. Discuss the assumptions you made to reach your conclusion and the factors that might affect it. (8.1.c)

UNIT PROJECTS

If you are doing a unit project, make a folder for your project. Include in your folder a list of the resources you will need, the date on which the project is due, and a schedule to keep track of your progress. Begin gathering data.

Standards-Based Assessment

Interpreting Graphs

8.1.c, 8.1.f

The graph below is a distance-time graph showing a 50-meter race.

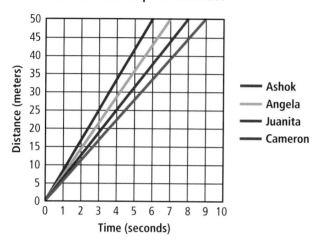

Distance-Time Graph of Foot Race

Study the graph and then answer the questions that follow.

1. Which runner reached the finish line first?
- **a.** Ashok
- **b.** Angela
- **c.** Juanita
- **d.** Cameron

2. How far did Juanita run in the first 4 seconds of the race?
- **a.** 5 m
- **b.** 15 m
- **c.** 25 m
- **d.** 35 m

3. How much time passed between the time Angela finished the race and Cameron finished the race?
- **a.** 1 s
- **b.** 2 s
- **c.** 3 s
- **d.** 4 s

4. Which of the following setups would you use to calculate Angela's average speed during the race?
- **a.** $\dfrac{7\text{ m}}{50\text{ s}}$
- **b.** $\dfrac{7\text{ s}}{50\text{ m}}$
- **c.** $\dfrac{50\text{ m}}{6\text{ s}}$
- **d.** $\dfrac{50\text{ m}}{7\text{ s}}$

5. What can you say about the speed of all of the runners?
- **a.** They ran at the same speed.
- **b.** They ran at a steady pace but at different speeds.
- **c.** They sped up as they reached the finish line.
- **d.** They slowed down as they reached the finish line.

Extended Response

Answer the two questions below in detail.

6. Suppose you are biking. What is the difference between your speed at any given moment during your bike ride and your average speed for the entire ride? Which is easier to measure? Why?

7. Suppose you are riding your bike along a path that is also used by in-line skaters. You pass a skater, and another biker passes you, both going in the same direction you're going. You pass a family having a picnic on the grass. Describe your motion from the points of view of the skater, the other biker, and the family.

CHAPTER 2 Forces

the **BIG** idea

Forces change the motion of objects in predictable ways.

What must happen for a team to win this tug of war?

Key Concepts

SECTION

1 Forces change motion.
Learn about inertia and Newton's first law of motion.

SECTION

2 Force and mass determine acceleration.
Learn to calculate force through Newton's second law of motion.

SECTION

3 Forces act in pairs.
Learn about action forces and reaction forces through Newton's third law of motion.

 California ClassZone

CLASSZONE.COM

Chapter 2 online resources: Content Review, two Simulations, three Resource Centers, Math Tutorial, Test Practice

EXPLORE (the BIG idea)

Popping Ping-Pong Balls

> **8.2.f** Students know the greater the mass of an object, the more force is needed to achieve the same rate of change in motion.

Place a Ping-Pong ball in front of a flexible ruler. Carefully bend the ruler back and then release it. Repeat with a golf ball or another heavier ball. Be sure to bend the ruler back to the same spot each time. Predict which ball will go farther.

Observe and Think
Which ball went farther? Why?

Internet Activity: Forces

> **8.2.b** Students know when an object is subject to two or more forces at once, the result is the cumulative effect of all the forces.

Go to **ClassZone.com** to change the sizes and directions of forces on an object. Predict how the object will move, and then run the simulation to see if you were right.

Observe and Think
What happens if two forces are applied to the object in the same direction? in opposite directions? Why?

NSTA
scilinks.org
SCI LINKS

Forces Code: MDL005

CHAPTER 2
Getting Ready to Learn

◀ CONCEPT REVIEW

- All motion is relative to the position and motion of an observer.
- An object's motion is described by position, direction, speed, and acceleration.
- Velocity and acceleration can be measured.

◀ VOCABULARY REVIEW

velocity p. 22

vector p. 22

acceleration p. 25

mass *See Glossary.*

CONTENT REVIEW
CLASSZONE.COM

Review concepts and vocabulary.

▶ TAKING NOTES

COMBINATION NOTES

When you read about a concept for the first time, take notes in two ways. First, make an outline of the information. Then make a sketch to help you understand and remember the concept. Use arrows to show the direction of forces.

VOCABULARY STRATEGY

Think about a vocabulary term as a **magnet word** diagram. Write the other terms or ideas related to that term around it.

See the Note-Taking Handbook on pages R45–R51.

SCIENCE NOTEBOOK

NOTES

Types of forces
- contact force
- gravity
- friction

forces on a box being pushed

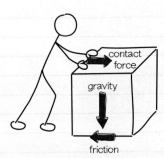

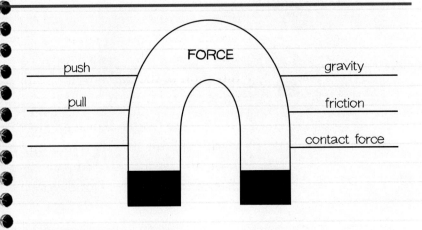

FORCE

push   gravity

pull   friction

      contact force

Forces change motion.

VOCABULARY

force p. 41
net force p. 43
Newton's first law p. 45
inertia p. 46

▷ **BEFORE,** you learned

• The velocity of an object is its change in position over time
• The acceleration of an object is its change in velocity over time

▷ **NOW,** you will learn

• What a force is
• How unbalanced forces change an object's motion
• How Newton's first law allows you to predict motion

EXPLORE Changing Motion (8.2.e)

How can you change an object's motion?

PROCEDURE

① Choose an object from the materials list and change its motion in several ways, from
  • not moving to moving
  • moving to not moving
  • moving to moving faster
  • moving to moving in a different direction

② Describe the actions used to change the motion.

③ Experiment again with another object. First, decide what you will do; then predict how the motion of the object will change.

MATERIALS
• quarter
• book
• tennis ball
• cup
• feather

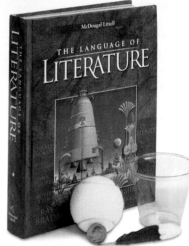

WHAT DO YOU THINK?
In step 3, how were you able to predict the motion of the object?

A force is a push or a pull.

> **REMINDER**
>
> Motion is a change in position over time.

Think about what happens during an exciting moment at the ballpark. The pitcher throws the ball across the plate, and the batter hits it high up into the stands. A fan in the stands catches the home-run ball. In this example, the pitcher sets the ball in motion, the batter changes the direction of the ball's motion, and the fan stops the ball's motion. To do so, each must use a **force,** or a push or a pull.

You use forces all day long to change the motion of objects in your world. You use a force to pick up your backpack, to open or close a car door, and even to move a pencil across your desktop. Any time you change the motion of an object, you use a force.

Types of Forces

A variety of forces are always affecting the motion of objects around you. For example, take a look at how three kinds of forces affect the skater in the photograph on the left.

❶ Contact Force When one object pushes or pulls another object by touching it, the first object is applying a contact force to the second. The skater applies a contact force as she pushes against the ground. The ground applies a contact force that pushes the skater forward.

❷ Gravity Gravity is the force of attraction between two masses. Earth's gravity is pulling on the skater, holding her to the ground. The strength of the gravitational force between two objects depends on their masses. For example, the pull between you and Earth is much greater than the pull between you and a book.

❸ Friction Friction is a force that resists motion between two surfaces that are pressed together. Friction between the surface of the ground and the wheels of the skates exerts a force that resists the skater's forward motion.

You will learn more about gravity and friction in Chapter 3. In this chapter, most of the examples involve contact forces. You use contact forces constantly. Turning a page, pulling a chair, using a pencil to write, pushing your hair away from your eyes—all involve contact forces.

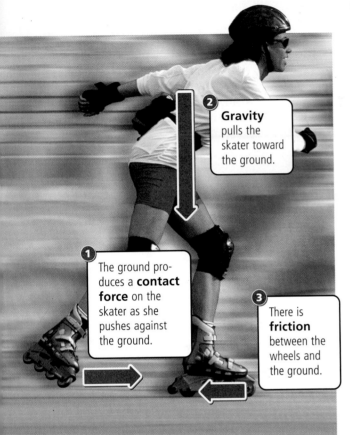

❷ **Gravity** pulls the skater toward the ground.

❶ The ground produces a **contact force** on the skater as she pushes against the ground.

❸ There is **friction** between the wheels and the ground.

⬥ **CHECK YOUR READING** What is a contact force? Give an example of a contact force.

Size and Direction of Forces

Like velocity, force is a vector. That means that force has both size and direction. For example, think about what happens when you try to make a shot in basketball. To get the ball through the hoop, you must apply the right amount of force to the ball and aim the force in the right direction. If you use too little force, the ball will not reach the basket. If you use too much force, the ball may bounce off the backboard and into your opponent's hands.

In the illustrations in this book, red arrows represent forces. The direction of an arrow shows the direction of the force, and the length of the arrow indicates the amount, or size, of the force. A blue box represents mass.

READING TIP

Red arrows are used to show force.

Blue boxes show mass.

◼

Balanced and Unbalanced Forces

Considering the size and the direction of all the forces acting on an object allows you to predict changes in the object's motion. When more than one force acts on an object, the result is a cumulative effect of all those forces. The overall force acting on an object when all the forces are combined is called the **net force.**

If the net force on an object is zero, the forces acting on the object are balanced. Balanced forces have the same effect as no force at all. That is, the motion of the object does not change. For example, think about the forces on the basketball when one player attempts a shot and another blocks it. In the photograph below on the left, the players are pushing on the ball with equal force but from opposite directions. The forces on the ball are balanced, and so the ball does not move.

Only an unbalanced force can change the motion of an object. If one of the basketball players pushes with greater force than the other player, the ball will move in the direction that player is pushing. The motion of the ball changes because the forces on the ball become unbalanced. Even if the ball is already moving, only an unbalanced force will change the ball's motion.

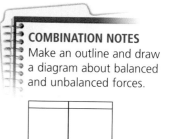

COMBINATION NOTES
Make an outline and draw a diagram about balanced and unbalanced forces.

balanced forces

unbalanced forces

READING VISUALS **COMPARE** Compare the net force on the balls in these two photographs. Which photograph shows a net force of zero?

Forces on Moving Objects

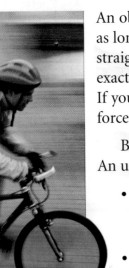

An object with forces acting on it can be moving at a constant velocity as long as those forces are balanced. For example, if you ride a bike straight ahead at a constant speed, the force moving the bike forward exactly balances the forces of friction that would slow the bike down. If you stop pedaling, the forces are no longer balanced, and frictional forces slow you down until you eventually stop.

Balanced forces cannot change an object's speed or its direction. An unbalanced force is needed to change an object's motion.

- To increase the speed of your bike, you may exert more forward force by pedaling harder or changing gears. The net force moves the bike ahead faster.
- To turn your bike, you apply an unbalanced force by leaning to one side and turning the handlebars.
- To stop the bike, you use the extra force of friction that your bike brakes provide.

CHECK YOUR READING What happens to a moving object if all the forces on it are balanced? Which sentence above tells you?

Newton's first law relates force and motion.

In the mid-1600s, the English scientist Sir Isaac Newton studied the effects of forces on objects. He formulated three laws of motion that are still helping people describe and predict the motions of objects today. Newton's ideas were built on those of other scientists, in particular the Italian scientist Galileo Galilei (gal-uh-LEE-oh gal-uh-LAY). Both Galileo and Newton overturned thinking that had been accepted since the times of the ancient Greek philosophers.

The ancient Greeks had concluded that it was necessary to apply a continuous force to keep an object in motion. For example, if you set a book on a table and give the book a quick push, the book slides a short way and then stops. To keep the book moving, you need to keep pushing it. The Greeks reasoned that the book stops moving because you stop pushing it.

Galileo's Thought Experiment

In the early 1600s, Galileo suggested a different way of interpreting such observations. He imagined a world without friction and conducted a thought experiment in this ideal world. He concluded that, in the absence of friction, a moving object will continue moving even if there is no force acting on it. In other words, it does not take a force to keep an object moving; it takes a force—friction—to stop an object that is already moving.

READING TiP

Contrast the last sentence of this paragraph with the last sentence of the previous paragraph.

Objects at rest and objects in motion both resist changes in motion. That is, objects at rest tend to stay at rest, and objects that are moving tend to continue moving unless a force acts on them. Galileo reasoned there was no real difference between an object that is moving at a constant velocity and an object that is standing still. An object at rest is simply an object with zero velocity.

 CHECK YOUR READING How were Galileo's ideas about objects in motion different from the ideas of the ancient Greeks?

Newton's First Law

Newton restated Galileo's conclusions as his first law of motion. **Newton's first law** states that objects at rest remain at rest, and objects in motion remain in motion with the same velocity, unless acted upon by an unbalanced force. You can easily observe the effects of unbalanced forces, both on the ball at rest and the ball in motion, in the pictures below.

Newton's First Law

Objects at rest remain at rest, and objects in motion remain in motion with the same velocity, unless acted upon by an unbalanced force.

An Object at Rest

An object at rest (the ball) remains at rest unless acted upon by an unbalanced force (from the foot).

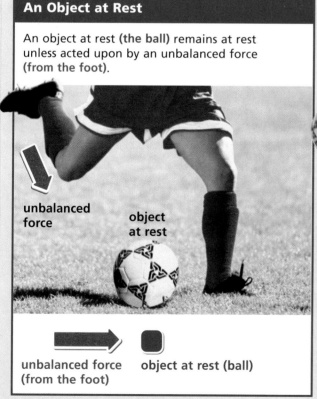

unbalanced force

object at rest

unbalanced force (from the foot)   object at rest (ball)

An Object in Motion

An object in motion (the ball) remains in motion with the same velocity, unless acted upon by an unbalanced force (from the hand).

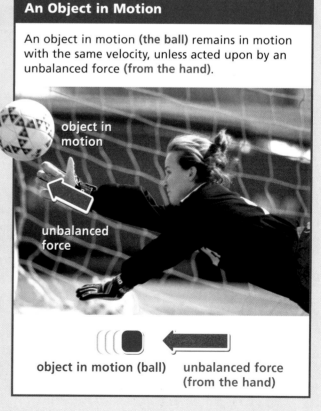

object in motion

unbalanced force

object in motion (ball)   unbalanced force (from the hand)

READING VISUALS What will happen to the ball's motion in each picture? Why?

You will find many examples of Newton's first law around you. For instance, if you throw a stick for a dog to catch, you are changing the motion of the stick. The dog changes the motion of the stick by catching it and by dropping it at your feet. You change the motion of a volleyball when you spike it, a tennis racket when you swing it, a paintbrush when you make a brush stroke, and an oboe when you pick it up to play or set it down after playing. In each of these examples, you apply a force that changes the motion of the object.

Inertia

Inertia (ih-NUR-shuh) is the resistance of an object to a change in the speed or the direction of its motion. Newton's first law, which describes the tendency of objects to resist changes in motion, is also called the law of inertia. Inertia is closely related to mass. When you measure the mass of an object, you are also measuring its inertia. You know from experience that it is easier to push or pull an empty box than it is to push or pull the same box when it is full of books. Likewise, it is easier to stop or to turn an empty wagon than to stop or turn a wagon full of sand. In both of these cases, it is harder to change the motion of the object that has more mass.

INVESTIGATE Inertia

Which ball has more inertia?

Two balls have different masses and therefore different amounts of inertia. Use what you know about force and inertia to design an experiment that shows which ball has more inertia. Your procedure cannot include lifting the balls, weighing the balls, or touching the balls with your hands.

DESIGN
— YOUR OWN —
EXPERIMENT

PROCEDURE

(1) Figure out how to use the meter stick or other materials to compare the inertia of the two balls.

(2) Write up your procedure.

(3) Test your procedure.

WHAT DO YOU THINK?

- What were the results of your experiment? Did it work? Why or why not?
- What was the variable? What were the constants?
- How does your experiment demonstrate the property of inertia?

SKILL FOCUS
Designing experiments (8.2.f)

MATERIALS
- 2 balls of unknown masses
- string
- block
- meter stick

TIME
30 minutes

Inertia is the reason that people in cars need to wear seat belts. A moving car has inertia, and so do the riders inside it. When the driver applies the brakes, an unbalanced force is applied to the car. Normally, the bottom of the seat applies an unbalanced force—friction—which slows the riders down as the car slows. If the driver stops the car suddenly, however, this force is not exerted over enough time to stop the motion of the riders. Instead, the riders continue moving forward with most of their original speed because of their inertia.

CLASSZONE.COM
Find out more about inertia.

1 As a car moves forward, the driver—shown here as a crash-test dummy—moves forward with the same velocity as the car.

2 When the driver hits the brakes, the car stops. If the stop is sudden and the driver is not wearing a seat belt, the driver keeps moving forward.

3 Finally, the windshield applies an unbalanced force that stops the driver's forward motion.

If the driver is wearing a seat belt, the seat belt rather than the windshield applies the unbalanced force that stops the driver's forward motion. The force from the seat belt is applied over a longer time, so the force causes less damage. In a collision, seat belts alone are sometimes not enough to stop the motion of drivers or passengers. Air bags further cushion people from the effects of inertia in an accident.

CHECK YOUR READING If a car makes a sudden stop, what happens to a passenger riding in the back seat who is not wearing a seat belt?

2.1 Review

KEY CONCEPTS

1. Explain the difference between balanced and unbalanced forces. (8.2.c)
2. What is the relationship between force and motion described by Newton's first law? (8.2.c)
3. What is inertia? How is the inertia of an object related to its mass? (8.2.e)

CRITICAL THINKING

4. **Infer** Once a baseball has been hit into the air, what forces are acting upon it? How can you tell that any forces are acting upon the ball?
5. **Predict** A ball is at rest on the floor of a car moving at a constant velocity. What will happen to the ball if the car swerves suddenly to the left?

○ CHALLENGE

6. **Synthesize** What can the changes in an object's position tell you about the forces acting on that object? Describe an example from everyday life that shows how forces affect the position of an object.

Chapter 2: **Forces** 47

Think SCIENCE

Rocks Slide

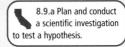
8.9.a Plan and conduct a scientific investigation to test a hypothesis.

In Death Valley, California, there is a dry lakebed known as Racetrack Playa. Rocks are mysteriously moving across the ground there, leaving tracks in the clay. These rocks can have masses as great as 320 kilograms (corresponding to 700 lb). No one has ever observed the rocks sliding, even though scientists have studied their tracks for more than 50 years. What force moves these rocks? Scientists do not yet know.

A playa was once a shallow lake. The water in it evaporated, leaving a dry lakebed.

❿ Observations

Scientists made these observations.

> a. Some rocks left trails that are almost parallel.
> b. Some rocks left trails that took abrupt turns.
> c. Sometimes a small rock moved while a larger rock did not.
> d. Most of the trails are on level surfaces. Some trails run slightly uphill.
> e. The temperature in that area sometimes drops below freezing.

This rock made a U-turn.

❿ Hypotheses

Scientists formed these hypotheses about how the rocks move.

> • When the lakebed gets wet, it becomes so slippery that gravity causes the rocks to slide.
> • When the lakebed gets wet, it becomes so slippery that strong winds can move the rocks.
> • When the lakebed gets wet and cold, a sheet of ice forms and traps the rocks. Strong winds move both the ice sheet and the trapped rocks.

❿ Evaluate Each Hypothesis

On Your Own Think about whether all the observations support each hypothesis. Some facts may rule out some hypotheses. Some facts may neither support nor contradict a particular hypothesis.

As a Group Decide which hypotheses are reasonable. Discuss your thinking and conclusions in a small group, and list the reasonable hypotheses.

CHALLENGE What further observations would you make to test any of these hypotheses? What information would each observation add?

i RESOURCE CENTER Learn more about the
CLASSZONE.COM moving rocks.

2.2 Force and mass determine acceleration.

CALIFORNIA
Content Standards

8.2.e Students know that when the forces on an object are unbalanced, the object will change its velocity (that is, it will speed up, slow down, or change direction).

8.2.f Students know the greater the mass of an object, the more force is needed to achieve the same rate of change in motion.

8.9.f Apply simple mathematic relation-ships to determine a missing quantity in a mathematic expres-sion, given the two remaining terms (including speed = distance / time, density = mass / volume, force = pressure × area, vol-ume = area × height).

BEFORE, you learned

- Mass is a measure of inertia
- The motion of an object will not change unless the object is acted upon by an unbalanced force

NOW, you will learn

- How Newton's second law relates force, mass, and acceleration
- How force works in circular motion

EXPLORE Acceleration (8.2.f)

How are force and acceleration related?

PROCEDURE

MATERIALS
- paper clips
- string

1. Tie a paper clip to each end of a long string. Hook two more paper clips to one end.

2. Hold the single paper clip in the middle of a smooth table; hang the other end of the string over the edge. Let go and observe.

3. Add one more paper clip to the hanging end and repeat the experiment. Observe what happens. Repeat.

WHAT DO YOU THINK?
- What happened each time that you let go of the single paper clip?
- Explain the relationship between the number of hanging paper clips and the motion of the paper clip on the table.

VOCABULARY

Newton's second law p. 50
centripetal force p. 54

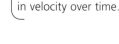

Acceleration is a change in velocity over time.

Newton's second law relates force, mass, and acceleration.

Suppose you are eating lunch with a friend and she asks you to pass the milk container. You decide to slide it across the table to her. How much force would you use to get the container moving? You would probably use a different force if the container were full than if the container were empty.

If you want to give two objects with different masses the same acceleration, you have to apply different forces to them. You must push a full milk container harder than an empty one to slide it over to your friend in the same amount of time.

 What three concepts are involved in Newton's second law?

Newton's Second Law

SIMULATION
CLASSZONE.COM

Explore Newton's second law.

Newton studied how objects move, and he noticed some patterns. He observed that the acceleration of an object depends on the mass of the object and the size of the force applied to it. **Newton's second law** states that the acceleration of an object increases with increased force and decreases with increased mass. The law also states that the direction in which an object accelerates is the same as the direction of the force.

The photographs below show Newton's second law at work in a supermarket. The acceleration of each shopping cart depends upon two things:

- the size of the force applied to the shopping cart
- the mass of the shopping cart

In the left-hand photograph, the force on the cart changes, while the mass of the cart stays the same. In the right-hand photograph, the force on the cart stays the same, while the mass of the cart varies. Notice how mass and force affect acceleration.

Newton's Second Law

The acceleration of an object increases with increased force, decreases with increased mass, and is in the same direction as the force.

Increasing Force Increases Acceleration

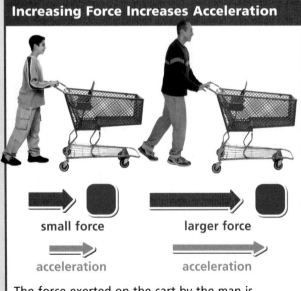

small force   larger force

acceleration   acceleration

The force exerted on the cart by the man is greater than the force exerted on the same cart by the boy, so the acceleration is greater.

Increasing Mass Decreases Acceleration

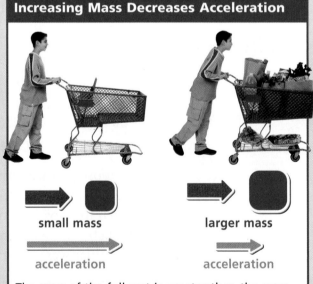

small mass   larger mass

acceleration   acceleration

The mass of the full cart is greater than the mass of the empty cart, and the boy is pushing with the same force, so the acceleration is less.

READING VISUALS What do the arrows in these diagrams show?

Force Equals Mass Times Acceleration

Newton was able to describe the relationship of force, mass, and acceleration mathematically. You can calculate the force, the mass, or the acceleration if you know two of the three factors. The mathematical form of Newton's second law, stated as a formula, is

Force = mass · acceleration
$$F = ma$$

To use this formula, you need to understand the unit used to measure force. In honor of Newton's contribution to our understanding of force and motion, the standard unit of force is called the newton (N). Because force equals mass times acceleration, force is measured in units of mass (kilograms) times units of acceleration (meters per second per second). A newton is defined as the amount of force that it takes to accelerate one kilogram (1 kg) of mass one meter per second per second (1 m/s^2). So 1 N is the same as 1 kg · m/s^2.

REMINDER

Meters per second per second is the same as *m/s^2*, which can be read "meters per second squared."

CHECK YOUR READING If the same force is applied to two objects of different mass, which object will have the greater acceleration?

The mathematical relationship of force, mass, and acceleration allow you to solve problems about how objects move. If you know the mass of an object and the acceleration you want to achieve, you can use the formula to find the force you need to exert to produce that acceleration. Use Newton's second law to find the force that is needed to accelerate the shopping cart in the sample problem.

Calculating Force

Sample Problem

What force is needed to accelerate a 10 kg shopping cart 3 m/s^2?

What do you know?	mass = 10 kg, acceleration = 3 m/s^2
What do you want to find out?	Force
Write the formula:	$F = ma$
Substitute into the formula:	$F = 10 \text{ kg} \cdot 3 \text{ m/s}^2$
Calculate and simplify:	$F = 10 \text{ kg} \cdot \dfrac{3m}{s^2} = 30 \text{ kg} \cdot \text{m/s}^2$
Check that your units agree:	Unit is kg · m/s^2. Unit of force is newton, which is also kg · m/s^2. Units agree.
Answer:	$F = 30$ N

Practice the Math

1. If a 5 kg ball is accelerating 1.2 m/s^2, what is the force on it?
2. A person on a scooter is accelerating 2 m/s^2. If the person has a mass of 50 kg, how much force is acting on that person?

This team of 20 people pulled a 72,000-kilogram (159,000 lb) airplane 3.7 meters (12 ft) in 6.74 seconds.

The photograph above shows people who are combining forces to pull an airplane. Suppose you knew the mass of the plane and how hard the people were pulling. How much would the plane accelerate? The sample problem below shows how Newton's second law helps you calculate the acceleration.

Calculating Acceleration

Sample Problem

If a team pulls with a combined force of 9000 N on an airplane with a mass of 30,000 kg, what is the acceleration of the airplane?

What do you know? mass = 30,000 kg, force = 9000 N

What do you want to find out? acceleration

Rearrange the formula: $a = \dfrac{F}{m}$

Substitute into the formula: $a = \dfrac{9000 \text{ N}}{30,000 \text{ kg}}$

Calculate and simplify: $a = \dfrac{9000 \text{ N}}{30,000 \text{ kg}} = \dfrac{9000 \text{ kg} \cdot \text{m/s}^2}{30,000 \text{ kg}} = 0.3 \text{ m/s}^2$

Check that your units agree: Unit is m/s^2.
Unit for acceleration is m/s^2.
Units agree.

Answer: $a = 0.3 \text{ m/s}^2$

Practice the Math

1. Half the people on the team decide not to pull the airplane. The combined force of those left is 4500 N, while the airplane's mass is still 30,000 kg. What will be the acceleration?

2. A girl pulls a wheeled backpack with a force of 3 N. If the backpack has a mass of 6 kg, what is its acceleration?

Mass and Acceleration

Mass is also a variable in Newton's second law. If the same force acts on two objects, the object with less mass will have the greater acceleration. For instance, if you push a soccer ball and a bowling ball with equal force, the soccer ball will have a greater acceleration.

If objects lose mass, they can gain acceleration if the force remains the same. When a rocket is first launched, most of its mass is the fuel it carries. As the rocket burns fuel, it loses mass. As the mass continually decreases, the acceleration continually increases.

APPLY This NASA launch rocket accelerates with enough force to lift about 45 cars off the ground. As the rocket loses fuel, will it accelerate more or less? Why?

Calculating Mass

Sample Problem

A model rocket is accelerating at 2 m/s². The force on it is 1 N. What is the mass of the rocket?

What do you know?	acceleration = 2 m/s², force = 1 N
What do you want to find out?	mass
Rearrange the formula:	$m = \dfrac{F}{a}$
Substitute into the formula:	$m = \dfrac{1 \text{ N}}{2 \text{ m/s}^2}$
Calculate and simplify:	$m = \dfrac{1 \text{ N}}{2 \text{ m/s}^2} = \dfrac{1 \text{ kg} \cdot \text{m/s}^2}{2 \text{ m/s}^2} = 0.5 \text{ kg}$
Check that your units agree:	Unit is kg. Unit of mass is kg. Units agree.
Answer:	$m = 0.5$ kg

Practice the Math

1. Another model rocket is accelerating at a rate of 3 m/s² with a force of 1 N. What is the mass of the rocket?
2. A boy pushes a shopping cart with a force of 10 N, and the cart accelerates 1 m/s². What is the mass of the cart?

Forces can change the direction of motion.

Usually, we think of a force as either speeding up or slowing down the motion of an object, but force can also make an object change direction. If an object changes direction, it is accelerating. Newton's second law says that if you apply a force to an object, the direction in which the object accelerates is the same as the direction of the force. You can change the direction of an object without changing its speed. For example, a good soccer player can control the motion of a soccer ball by applying a force that changes the ball's direction but not its speed.

 CHECK YOUR READING How can an object accelerate when it does not change speed?

INVESTIGATE Motion and Force

What affects circular motion?

PROCEDURE

① Spread newspaper over your work surface. Place the paper plate down on the newspaper.

② Practice rolling the marble around the edge of the plate until you can roll it around completely at least once.

③ Cut out a one-quarter slice of the paper plate. Put a dab of paint on the edge of the plate where the

marble will leave it. Place the plate back down on the newspaper.

④ Hypothesize: How will the marble move once it rolls off the plate? Why?

⑤ Roll the marble all the way around the paper plate into the cut-away section and observe the resulting motion as shown by the trail of paint.

WHAT DO YOU THINK?

- Did your observations support your hypothesis?
- What forces affected the marble's motion after it left the plate?

CHALLENGE How will changing the speed at which you roll the marble change your results? Repeat the activity to test your prediction.

SKILL FOCUS
Hypothesizing
(8.2.e)

MATERIALS
- newspaper
- paper plate
- marble
- scissors
- poster paint
- paintbrush

TIME
15 minutes

Centripetal Force

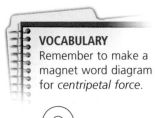

VOCABULARY
Remember to make a magnet word diagram for *centripetal force*.

You have learned that a force causes a mass to accelerate. The direction of the acceleration is the same as the direction of the force. Suppose a force is applied at a right angle to the direction in which an object is moving. The acceleration is also at a right angle to the motion, so the object turns. Sometimes the direction of the force changes as the object moves so that the force stays at a right angle to the motion. In this case, the object keeps turning—it moves in a circle.

Any force that keeps an object moving in a circle is known as a **centripetal force** (sehn-TRIHP-ih-tuhl). This force points toward the center of the circle. Without the centripetal force, the object would go flying off in a straight line. When you whirl a ball on a string, what keeps the ball moving in a circle? The force of the string turns the ball, changing the ball's direction of motion. When the string turns, so does the ball. As the string changes direction, the force from the string also changes direction. The force is always pointing along the string toward your hand, the center of the circle. The centripetal force on the whirling ball is the pull from the string. If you let go of the string, the ball would fly off in the direction it was headed when you let go.

CHECK YOUR READING How does centripetal force change the motion of an object?

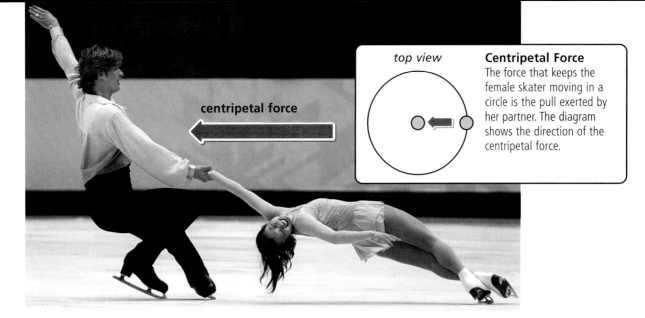

centripetal force

top view

Centripetal Force
The force that keeps the female skater moving in a circle is the pull exerted by her partner. The diagram shows the direction of the centripetal force.

Circular Motion and Newton's Second Law

Suppose the male skater shown above spins his partner faster. Her direction changes more quickly than before, so she accelerates more. To get more acceleration, he must apply more force. The same idea holds for a ball you whirl on a string. You have to pull harder on the string when you whirl the ball faster, because it takes more centripetal force to keep the ball moving at the greater speed.

You can apply the formula for Newton's second law even to an object moving in a circle. If you know the size of the centripetal force acting upon the object, you can find its acceleration. A greater acceleration requires a greater centripetal force. A more massive object requires a greater centripetal force to have the same circular speed as a less massive object. But no matter what the mass of an object is, if it moves in a circle, its force and acceleration are directed toward the center of the circle.

 CHECK YOUR READING How does increasing the centripetal force on an object affect its acceleration?

2.2 Review

KEY CONCEPTS

1. If the force acting upon an object is increased, what happens to the object's acceleration? (8.2.e)

2. How does the mass of an object affect its acceleration? (8.2.f)

3. What force keeps an object moving in a circle? In what direction does this force act?

CRITICAL THINKING

4. **Infer** Use Newton's second law to determine how much force is being applied to an object that is traveling at a constant velocity.

5. **Calculate** What force is needed to accelerate an object 5 m/s² if the object has a mass of 10 kg?

CHALLENGE

6. **Synthesize** Carlos pushes a 3 kg box with a force of 9 N. The force of friction on the box is 3 N in the opposite direction. What is the acceleration of the box? **Hint:** Combine forces to find the net force.

MATH in SCIENCE

MATH TUTORIAL
CLASSZONE.COM
Click on Math Tutorial
for more help with
rounding decimals.
Math 7.MG.1.1
Science 8.2.f

Meaningful Numbers

A student doing a science report on artificial hearts reads that a certain artificial heart weighs about 2 pounds. The student then writes that the mass of the artificial heart is 0.907185 kilograms. Someone reading this report might think that the student knows the mass to a high precision, when actually he knows it only to one meaningful number.

When you make calculations, the number of digits to include in your answer depends in part on the number of meaningful digits, or significant figures, in the numbers you are working with.

Example

In an experiment to find acceleration, a scientist might record the following data.

Force = 3.1 N   mass = 1.450 kg

In this example, force is given to two significant figures, and mass is given to four significant figures.

(1) Use a calculator and the formula $a = F/m$ to find the acceleration. The display on the calculator shows

2.1379310345

(2) To determine how many of the digits in this answer are really meaningful, look at the measurement with the least number of significant figures. In this example, force is given to two significant figures. Therefore, the answer is meaningful only to two significant figures.

(3) Round the calculated number to two digits.

ANSWER acceleration = 2.1 m/s²

The AbioCor artificial heart, which has a mass of about 0.9 kg, is designed to fit entirely inside the human body.

Answer the following questions.

For each pair of measurements, calculate the acceleration to the appropriate number of digits.

1. Force = 3.100 N   mass = 3.1 kg

2. Force = 2 N   mass = 4.2 kg

3. Force = 1.21 N   mass = 1.1000 kg

CHALLENGE Suppose a scientist measures a force of 3.25 N and a mass of 3.3 kg. She could round the force to two significant figures and then divide, or she could divide and then round the answer. Compare these two methods. Which method do you think is more accurate?

Forces act in pairs.

CALIFORNIA
Content Standard

Extension of 8.2.d
Students know how to identify separately the two or more forces that are acting on a single static object, including gravity, elastic forces due to tension or compression in matter, and friction.

BEFORE, you learned

- A force is a push or a pull
- Increasing the force on an object increases the acceleration
- The acceleration of an object depends on its mass and the force applied to it

NOW, you will learn

- How Newton's third law relates action/reaction pairs of forces
- How Newton's laws work together

VOCABULARY

Newton's third law p. 57

THINK ABOUT

How do jellyfish move?

Jellyfish do not have much control over their movements. They drift with the current in the ocean. However, jellyfish do have some control over their up-and-down motion. By squeezing water out of

its umbrella-like body, the jellyfish shown here applies a force in one direction to move in the opposite direction. If the water is forced downward, the jellyfish moves upward. How can a person or an object move in one direction by exerting a force in the opposite direction?

Newton's third law relates action and reaction forces.

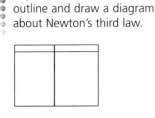

COMBINATION NOTES
In your notebook, make an outline and draw a diagram about Newton's third law.

Newton made an important observation that explains the motion of the jellyfish. He noticed that forces always act in pairs. **Newton's third law** states that every time one object exerts a force on another object, the second object exerts a force that is equal in size and opposite in direction back on the first object. As the jellyfish contracts its body, it applies a downward force on the water. The water applies an equal force back on the jellyfish. It is this equal and opposite force on the jellyfish that pushes it up. This is similar to what happens when a blown-up balloon is released. The balloon pushes air out the end, and the air pushes back on the balloon and moves it forward.

CHECK YOUR READING What moves the jellyfish through the water?

Action and Reaction Pairs

CALIFORNIA Focus

Action and reaction forces are even at work on the historic cable cars in San Francisco! For example, as the cable pulls the car up the hill (action force), the car exerts an equal force on the cable (reaction force).

The force that is exerted on an object and the force that the object exerts back are known together as an action/reaction force pair. One force in the pair is called the action force, and the other is called the reaction force. For instance, if the jellyfish pushing on the water is the action force, the water pushing back on the jellyfish is the reaction force. Likewise, if the balloon pushing the air backward is the action force, the air pushing the balloon forward is the reaction force.

You can see many examples of action and reaction forces in the world around you. Here are three:

- You may have watched the liftoffs of the space shuttle on television. When the booster rockets carrying the space shuttle take off, their engines push fuel exhaust downward. The exhaust pushes back on the rockets, sending them upward.

- When you bang your toe into the leg of a table, the same amount of force that you exert on the table is exerted back on your toe.

- Action and reaction forces do not always result in motion. For example, if you press down on a table, the table resists the push with the same amount of force, even though nothing moves.

CHECK YOUR READING Identify the action/reaction forces in each example described above.

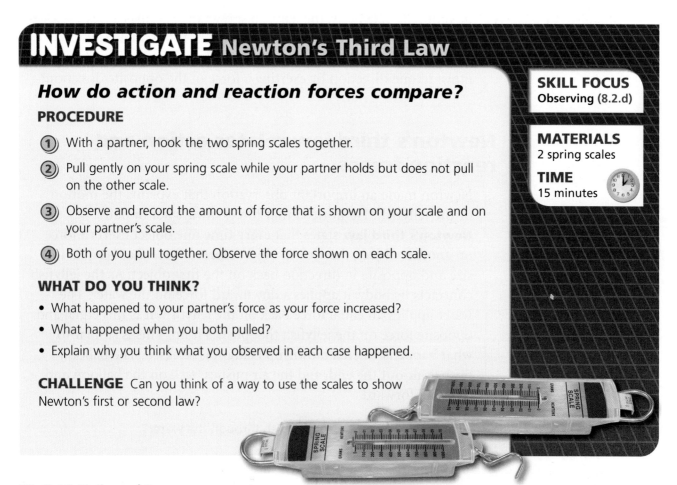

INVESTIGATE Newton's Third Law

How do action and reaction forces compare?

PROCEDURE

1. With a partner, hook the two spring scales together.

2. Pull gently on your spring scale while your partner holds but does not pull on the other scale.

3. Observe and record the amount of force that is shown on your scale and on your partner's scale.

4. Both of you pull together. Observe the force shown on each scale.

WHAT DO YOU THINK?

- What happened to your partner's force as your force increased?
- What happened when you both pulled?
- Explain why you think what you observed in each case happened.

CHALLENGE Can you think of a way to use the scales to show Newton's first or second law?

SKILL FOCUS
Observing (8.2.d)

MATERIALS
2 spring scales

TIME
15 minutes

Action and Reaction Forces Versus Balanced Forces

Because action and reaction forces are equal and opposite, they may be confused with balanced forces. Keep in mind that balanced forces act on a single object, while action and reaction forces act on different objects.

Balanced Forces If you and a friend pull on opposite sides of a backpack with the same amount of force, the backpack doesn't move, because the forces acting on it are balanced. In this case, both forces are exerted on one object—the backpack.

Action and Reaction As you drag a heavy backpack across a floor, you can feel the backpack pulling on you with an equal amount of force. The action force and the reaction force are acting on two different things—one is acting on the backpack, and the other is acting on you.

The illustration below summarizes Newton's third law. The girl exerts an action force on the boy by pushing him. Even though the boy is not trying to push the girl, an equal and opposite reaction force acts upon the girl, causing her to move as well.

Newton's Third Law

When one object exerts a force on another object, the second object exerts an equal and opposite force on the first object.

① One Skater Pushes

reaction force   action force

The action force from the girl sets the boy in motion.

② Both Skaters Move

Even though the boy does not do anything, the reaction force from him sets the girl in motion as well.

 READING VISUALS How does the direction of the force on the girl relate to her motion?

Newton's Three Laws of Motion

All three of Newton's laws work together to help describe how an object will move.

Newton's First Law

force of gravity

This kangaroo has jumped, setting itself in motion. If no other forces acted on it, the kangaroo would continue to move through the air with the same motion. Instead, the force of gravity will bring this kangaroo back to the ground.

Newton's Second Law

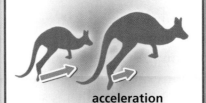

acceleration

The large kangaroo does not have as much acceleration as a less massive kangaroo would if it used the same force to jump. However, the more massive kangaroo can increase its acceleration by increasing the force of its jump.

Newton's Third Law

action force   reaction force

A kangaroo applies an action force on the ground with its powerful back legs. The reaction force from the ground can send the kangaroo as far as 8 meters (26 ft) through the air.

READING VISUALS What forces are involved in a kangaroo jump?

Common Name: Red kangaroo
Scientific Name: *Macropus rufus*
Home: Australia
Top Speed: 65 km/h (40 mi/h)
Maximum Leap: 8 m (26 ft)

AUSTRALIA

Newton's three laws describe and predict motion.

Newton's three laws can explain the motion of almost any object, including the motion of animals. The illustrations on page 60 show how all three of Newton's laws can be used to describe how kangaroos move. The three laws are not independent of one another; they are used together to explain the motion of objects.

You can use the laws of motion to explain how other animals move as well. For example, Newton's laws explain why a squid moves forward while squirting water out behind it. These laws also explain that a bird is exerting force when it speeds up to fly away or when it changes its direction in the air.

You can also use Newton's laws to make predictions about motion. If you know the force acting upon an object, then you can predict how that object's motion will change. For example, if you want to send a spacecraft to Mars, you must be able to predict exactly where Mars will be by the time the spacecraft reaches it. You must also be able to control the force on your spacecraft so that it will arrive at the right place at the right time.

Knowing how Newton's three laws work together can also help you win a canoe race. In order to start the canoe moving, you need to apply a force to overcome its inertia. Newton's second law might affect your choice of canoes, because a less massive canoe is easier to accelerate than a more massive one. You can also predict the best position for your paddle in the water. If you want to move straight ahead, you push backward on the paddle so that the canoe moves forward. Together, Newton's laws can help you explain and predict how the canoe, or any object, will move.

Find out more about Newton's laws of motion.

COMBINATION NOTES
Make an outline and draw a diagram showing how all three of Newton's laws apply to the motion of one object.

2.3 Review

KEY CONCEPTS

1. Identify the action/reaction force pair involved when you catch a ball. (8.2.d)

2. Describe the difference between balanced forces and action/reaction forces. (8.2.d)

3. How do Newton's laws of motion apply to the motion of an animal, such as a cat that is running? (8.2.d)

CRITICAL THINKING

4. **Apply** A man pushes on a wall with a force of 50 N. What are the size and the direction of the force that the wall exerts on the man?

5. **Evaluate** Jim will not help push a heavy box. He says, "My force will produce an opposite force and cancel my effort." Evaluate Jim's statement.

⚫ CHALLENGE

6. **Calculate** Suppose you are holding a basketball while standing still on a skateboard. You and the skateboard have a mass of 50 kg. You throw the basketball with a force of 10 N. What is your acceleration before and after you throw the ball?

CHAPTER INVESTIGATION

Newton's Laws of Motion

OVERVIEW AND PURPOSE As you know, rocket engineers consider Newton's laws when designing rockets and planning rocket flights. In this investigation you will use what you have learned about Newton's laws to

- build a straw rocket
- improve the rocket's performance by modifying one design element

▶ Problem

Write It Up

What aspects of a model rocket affect the distance it flies?

▶ Hypothesize

Write It Up

After step 8 in the procedure, write a hypothesis to explain what you predict will happen during the second set of trials. Your hypothesis should take the form of an "If . . . , then . . . , because . . ." statement.

▶ Procedure

MATERIALS
- 2 straws with different diameters
- several plastic bottles, in different sizes
- modeling clay
- scissors
- construction paper
- meter stick
- tape

  8.2.d,
  8.2.f,
  8.9.a,
  8.9.c

1. Make a data table like the one shown on the sample notebook page.

2. Insert the straw with the smaller diameter into one of the bottles. Seal the mouth of the bottle tightly with modeling clay so that air can escape only through the straw. This is the rocket launcher.

straw clay

3. Cut two thin strips of paper, one about 8 cm long and the other about 12 cm long. Connect the ends of the strips to make loops.

4. To create the rocket, place the straw with the larger diameter through the smaller loop and tape the loop to the straw at one end. Attach the other loop to the other end of the straw in the same way. Both loops should be attached to the same side of the straw to stabilize your rocket in flight.

loops clay

Content Standard
8.2.f Students know the greater the mass of an object, the more force is needed to achieve the same rate of change in motion.

Investigation Standard
8.9.a Plan and conduct a scientific investigation to test a hypothesis.

5 Use a small ball of modeling clay to seal the end of the straw near the smaller loop.

6 Slide the open end of the rocket over the straw on the launcher. Place the bottle on the edge of a table so that the rocket is pointing away from the table.

7 Test launch your rocket by holding the bottle with two hands and squeezing it quickly. Measure the distance the rocket lands from the edge of the table. Practice the launch several times. Remember to squeeze with equal force each time.

8 Launch the rocket four times. Keep the amount of force you use constant. Measure the distance the rocket travels each time, and record the results in your data table.

9 List all the variables that may affect the distance your rocket flies. Change the rocket or launcher to alter one variable. Launch the rocket and measure the distance it flies. Repeat three more times, and record the results in your data table.

▶ Observe and Analyze
Write It Up

1. **RECORD OBSERVATIONS** Draw a diagram of both of your bottle rockets. Make sure your data table is complete.

2. **IDENTIFY VARIABLES** What variables did you identify, and what variable did you modify?

▶ Conclude
Write It Up

1. **COMPARE** How did the flight distances of the original rocket compare with those of the modified rocket?

2. **ANALYZE** Compare your results with your hypothesis. Do the results support your hypothesis?

3. **IDENTIFY LIMITS** What possible limitations or errors did you experience or could you have experienced?

4. **APPLY** Use Newton's laws to explain why the rocket flies.

5. **APPLY** What other real-life example can you think of that demonstrates Newton's laws?

▶ INVESTIGATE Further

CHALLENGE Why does the rocket have paper loops taped to it? Determine how the flight of the rocket is affected if one or both loops are completely removed. Hypothesize about the function of the paper loops and design an experiment to test your hypothesis.

Newton's Laws of Motion

Problem What aspects of a model rocket affect the distance it flies?

Hypothesize

Observe and Analyze

Table 1. Flight Distances of Original and Modified Rocket

Trial Number	Original Rocket Distance Rocket Flew (cm)	Modified Rocket Distance Rocket Flew (cm)
1		
2		
3		
4		

Conclude

2 Chapter Review

the BIG idea

Forces change the motion of objects in predictable ways.

CONTENT REVIEW
CLASSZONE.COM

◀ KEY CONCEPTS SUMMARY

1 Forces change motion.

Newton's first law
Objects at rest remain at rest, and objects in motion remain in motion with the same velocity, unless acted upon by an unbalanced force.

unbalanced   object at rest
force

object in   unbalanced
motion   force

VOCABULARY
force p. 41
net force p. 43
Newton's first law
 p. 45
inertia p. 46

---

2 Force and mass determine acceleration.

Newton's second law
The acceleration of an object increases with increased force and decreases with increased mass, and is in the same direction as the force.

small force   larger force   small mass   larger mass

same mass, larger force = increased acceleration   larger mass, same force = decreased acceleration

VOCABULARY
Newton's second law
 p. 50
centripetal force
 p. 54

---

3 Forces act in pairs.

Newton's third law
When one object exerts a force on another object, the second object exerts an equal and opposite force on the first object.

reaction force   action force

VOCABULARY
Newton's third law
 p. 57

Reviewing Vocabulary

Copy and complete the chart below. If the left column is blank, give the correct term. If the right column is blank, give an example from real life.

Term	Example from Real Life
1. acceleration	
2. velocity	
3. centripetal force	
4.	The pull of a handle on a wagon
5. inertia	
6. mass	
7. net force	
8. Newton's first law	
9. Newton's second law	
10.	When you're walking, you push backward on the ground, and the ground pushes you forward with equal force.

Reviewing Key Concepts

Multiple Choice *Choose the letter of the best answer.*

11. Newton's second law states that to increase acceleration, you (8.2.f)

a. increase force   **c.** increase mass

b. decrease force   **d.** increase inertia

12. What units are used to measure force? (8.2.a)

a. kilograms   **c.** newtons

b. meters   **d.** seconds

13. A wagon is pulled down a hill with a constant velocity. All the forces on the wagon are (8.2.c)

a. balanced   **c.** increasing

b. unbalanced   **d.** decreasing

14. An action force and its reaction force are (8.2.d)

a. equal in size and direction

b. equal in size and opposite in direction

c. different in size but in the same direction

d. different in size and in direction

15. John pulls a box with a force of 4 N, and Jason pulls the box from the opposite side with a force of 3 N. Ignore friction. Which of the following statements is true? (8.2.d)

a. The box moves toward John.

b. The box moves toward Jason.

c. The box does not move.

d. There is not enough information to determine if the box moves.

16. Which law states that objects at rest remain at rest, and objects in motion remain in motion, unless acted upon by an unbalanced force? (8.2.c)

a. Newton's third law

b. Newton's second law

c. Newton's first law

d. law of reflection

Short Answer *Write a short answer to each question.*

17. List the following objects in order, from the object with the least inertia to the object with the most inertia: feather, large rock, pencil, book. Explain your reasoning. (8.2.e)

18. You pull a half bale of straw and a full bale of straw from one side of the barn to the other using the same force. Use Newton's Second Law to explain the differences in acceleration of each object. (8.2.f)

19. Explain how an object can have forces acting on it but not be accelerating. (8.2.c)

20. A sea scallop moves by shooting jets of water out of its shell. Explain how this works. (8.2.e)

Thinking Critically

Use the information in the photographs below to answer the next four questions.

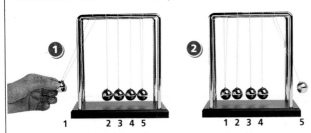

The photographs above show a toy called Newton's Cradle. In the first picture (1), ball 1 is lifted and is being held in place.

21. Are the forces on ball 1 balanced? How do you know? (8.2.c)

22. Draw a diagram showing the forces acting on ball 2. Are these forces balanced? (8.2.d)

In the second picture (2), ball 1 has been let go.

23. Ball 1 swung down, hit ball 2, and stopped. Use Newton's laws to explain why ball 1 stopped. (8.2.e)

24. Using Newton's laws, predict what will happen to ball 5 when it falls down and strikes ball 4. (8.2.e)

Copy the chart below. Write what will happen to the object in each case. (8.2.c)

Cause	Effect
25. Balanced forces act on an object.	
26. Unbalanced forces act on an object.	
27. No force acts on an object.	

28. INFER A baseball is three times more massive than a tennis ball. If the baseball and the tennis ball are accelerating equally, what can you determine about the net force on each? (8.2.f)

Using Math Skills in Science

Complete the following calculations.

29. What force should Lori apply to a 5 kg box to give it an acceleration of 2 m/s^2? (8.2.f)

30. If a 10 N force accelerates an object 5 m/s^2, how massive is the object? (8.2.f)

31. Ravi applies a force of 5 N to a wagon with a mass of 10 kg. What is the wagon's acceleration? (8.2.f)

32. Joey needs to accelerate a 40 kg cart of groceries at 1.5 m/s^2. What amount of force should he apply? (8.2.f)

acceleration = 1.5 m/s

mass = 40 kg

the **BIG** idea

33. PREDICT Look again at the tug of war pictured on pages 38–39. Describe what information you need to know to predict the outcome of the game. How would you use that information and Newton's laws to make your prediction? (8.2.e)

34. WRITE Pick an activity you enjoy, such as running or riding a scooter, and describe how Newton's laws apply to that activity. (8.2.e)

35. SYNTHESIZE Think of a question you have about Newton's laws that is still unanswered. What information do you need in order to answer the question? How might you find the information?

UNIT PROJECTS

If you need to do an experiment for your unit project, gather the materials. Be sure to allow enough time to observe results before the project is due.

Standards-Based Assessment

Analyzing Data

8.2.c, 8.2.e, 8.2.f

To test Newton's second law, Jodie accelerates blocks of ice across a smooth, flat surface. The table shows her results. (For this experiment, you can ignore the effects of friction.)

Accelerating Blocks of Ice							
Mass (kg)	1.0	1.5	2.0	2.5	3.0	3.5	4.0
Acceleration (m/s²)	4.0	2.7	2.0	1.6	1.3	1.1	1.0

Study the data table and then answer the questions that follow.

1. The data show that as mass becomes greater, acceleration
  a. increases
  b. decreases
  c. stays the same
  d. cannot be predicted

2. From the data, you can tell that Jodie was applying a force of
  a. 1 N   **c.** 3 N
  b. 2 N   **d.** 4 N

3. If Jodie applied less force to the ice blocks, the accelerations would be
  a. greater   **c.** the same
  b. less   **d.** inconsistent

4. If Jodie applied a force of 6 N to the 2 kg block of ice, the acceleration would be
  a. 2 m/s²   **c.** 3 m/s²
  b. 4 m/s²   **d.** 5 m/s²

5. The average mass of the ice blocks she pushed was
  a. 1.5 kg   **c.** 3 kg
  b. 2.5 kg   **d.** 4 kg

6. If Jodie used a 3.25 kg block in her experiment, the force would accelerate the block somewhere between
  a. 1.0 and 1.1 m/s²
  b. 1.1 and 1.3 m/s²
  c. 1.3 and 1.6 m/s²
  d. 1.6 and 2.0 m/s²

Extended Response

Answer the two questions in detail. Include some of the terms shown in the word box. Underline each term you use in your answer.

Newton's second law	velocity
mass	inertia
gravity	balanced forces
centripetal force	unbalanced forces

7. Tracy ties a ball to a string and starts to swing the ball around her head. What forces are acting on the ball? What happens if the string breaks?

8. Luis is trying to pull a wagon loaded with rocks. What can he do to increase the wagon's acceleration?

CHAPTER

3

Gravity, Elastic Forces, and Friction

the **BIG** idea

Newton's laws apply to all forces.

Key Concepts

SECTION

1 **Gravity is a force exerted by masses.**
Learn about gravity, weight, and orbits.

SECTION

2 **Elastic forces resist stretching and pressing.**
Learn about elastic forces, compression, and tension.

SECTION

3 **Friction is a force that opposes motion.**
Learn about friction and air resistance.

California ClassZone

CLASSZONE.COM
Chapter 3 online resources:
Content Review, Simulation,
Visualization, two Resource
Centers, Math Tutorial,
Test Practice

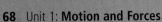

EXPLORE (the BIG idea)

> **What forces are acting on this snowboarder? What forces are acting on the snow?**

Let It Slide

> **8.2.d** Students know how to identify separately the two or more forces that are acting on a single static object, including gravity, elastic forces due to tension or compression in matter, and friction.

Make a ramp using a board and some books. Slide an object down the ramp. Change the surface of the ramp using various materials, such as sandpaper.

Observe and Think
What effects did different surfaces have on the motion of the object? What may have caused these effects?

Internet Activity: Gravity

> **8.2.g** Students know the role of gravity in forming and maintaining the shapes of planets, stars, and the solar system.

Go to **ClassZone.com** to explore gravity. Learn more about the force of gravity and its effect on you, other objects on Earth, and the orbits of planets and satellites. Explore how gravity determines weight, and find out how your weight would be different on other planets.

Observe and Think
What would you weigh on Mars? What would you weigh on Neptune?

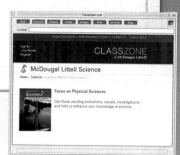

NSTA
scilinks.org

SCiLINKS

Elastic forces **Code: MDL074**

Getting Ready to Learn

CONCEPT REVIEW

- The motion of an object will not change unless the object is acted upon by an unbalanced force.
- The acceleration of an object depends on force and mass.
- For every action force there is an equal and opposite reaction.

VOCABULARY REVIEW

force p. 41

Newton's first law p. 45

Newton's second law p. 50

Newton's third law p. 57

CONTENT REVIEW
CLASSZONE.COM

Review concepts and vocabulary.

TAKING NOTES

SUPPORTING MAIN IDEAS

Make a chart to show main ideas and the information that supports them. Copy the main ideas. Below each main idea, add supporting information, such as reasons, explanations, and examples.

VOCABULARY STRATEGY

Write each new vocabulary term in the center of a **four square** diagram. Write notes in the squares around each term. Include a definition, some characteristics, and some examples of the term. If possible, write some things that are not examples of the term.

See the Note-Taking Handbook on pages R45–R51.

SCIENCE NOTEBOOK

Masses attract each other.

→ More mass = more gravitational force

→ More distance = less gravitational force

Definition	Characteristics
force of gravity acting on an object	• changes if gravity changes • measured in newtons

WEIGHT

Examples	Nonexamples
A 4 kg bowling ball weighs 39 N.	Mass in kg is not a weight.

3.1

KEY CONCEPT

Gravity is a force exerted by masses.

CALIFORNIA
Content Standards

8.2.d Students know how to identify separately the two or more forces that are acting on a single static object, including gravity, elastic forces due to tension or compression in matter, and friction.

8.2.g Students know the role of gravity in forming and maintaining the shapes of the planets, stars, and the solar system.

VOCABULARY

gravity p. 71
weight p. 73
orbit p. 74

BEFORE, you learned

- Every action force has an equal and opposite reaction force
- Newton's laws are used to describe the motions of objects
- Mass is the amount of matter an object contains

NOW, you will learn

- How mass and distance affect gravity
- What keeps objects in orbit

EXPLORE Downward Acceleration (8.2.d)

How do the accelerations of two falling objects compare?

PROCEDURE

① Make a prediction: Which ball will fall faster?

② Drop both balls from the same height at the same time.

③ Observe the balls as they hit the ground.

WHAT DO YOU THINK?

- Were the results what you had expected?
- How did the times it took the two balls to hit the ground compare?

MATERIALS
- golf ball
- Ping-Pong ball

VOCABULARY
Create a four square diagram for *gravity* in your notebook.

Masses attract each other.

When you drop any object—such as a pen, a book, or a football—it falls to the ground. As the object falls, it moves faster and faster. The fact that the object accelerates means there must be a force acting on it. The downward pull on the object is due to gravity. **Gravity** is the force that objects exert on each other because of their masses. You are familiar with the force of gravity between Earth and objects on Earth.

Gravity is present not only between objects and Earth, however. Gravity is considered a universal force because it acts between any two masses anywhere in the universe. For example, there is a gravitational pull between the Sun and the Moon. Even small masses attract one another. The force of gravity between dust and gas particles in space helped form the solar system.

 Why is gravity considered a universal force?

The Force of Gravity

If there is a force between all masses, why are you not pulled toward your desk by the desk's gravity when you walk away from it? Remember that the net force on you determines how your motion changes. The force of gravity between you and the desk is extremely small compared with other forces constantly acting on you, such as friction, the force from your muscles, Earth's gravity, and the gravitational pull from many other objects. The strength of the gravitational force between two objects depends on two factors, mass and distance.

The Mass of the Objects The more mass two objects have, the greater the force of gravity the masses exert on each other. If one of the masses is doubled, the force of gravity between the objects is doubled.

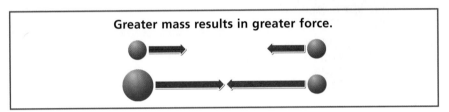

Greater mass results in greater force.

The Distance Between the Objects As distance between the objects increases, the force of gravity decreases. If the distance is doubled, the force of gravity is one-fourth as strong as before.

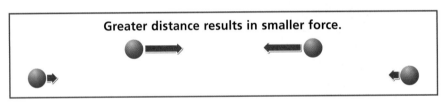

Greater distance results in smaller force.

 CHECK YOUR READING How do mass and distance affect the force of gravity?

Gravity on Earth

SUPPORTING MAIN IDEAS
Support the main ideas about gravity on Earth with details and examples.

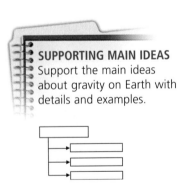

The force of gravity acts on both masses equally, even though the effects on both masses may be very different. Earth's gravity exerts a downward pull on a dropped coin. Remember that every action force has an equal and opposite reaction force. The coin exerts an equal upward force on Earth. Because the coin has an extremely small mass compared with Earth, the coin can be easily accelerated. Earth's acceleration due to the force of the coin is far too small to notice because of Earth's large mass.

The acceleration due to Earth's gravity is called g and is equal to 9.8 m/s^2 at Earth's surface. You can calculate the force of Earth's gravity on an object at Earth's surface using the object's mass and this acceleration. The formula that expresses Newton's second law is $F = ma$. If you use g as the acceleration, the formula for calculating the force due to gravity on a mass close to Earth's surface becomes $F = mg$.

Acceleration Due to Gravity

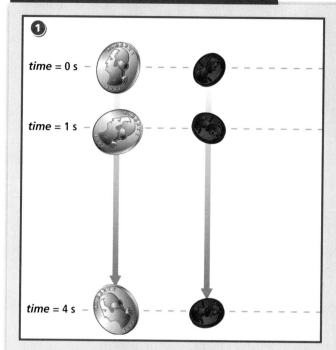

If any two objects are dropped from the same height in a vacuum, they fall at the same rate even if they have different masses.

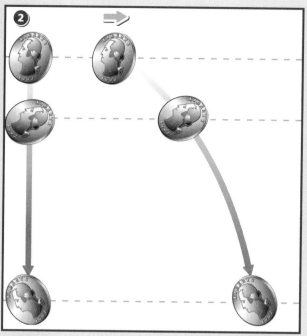

If an object has a velocity in the horizontal direction when it falls, the horizontal velocity does not change its downward acceleration.

In a vacuum—that is, where there is no air—all falling objects have the same acceleration. Look at the diagram above.

❶ Objects with different masses fall with the same acceleration. The quarter falls at the same rate as the penny when they are dropped together. Because the quarter has more mass, gravity exerts more force on it. But greater mass also means more inertia, so the greater force does not produce a larger acceleration.

❷ Horizontal velocity does not affect acceleration due to gravity. A coin that is dropped falls at the same rate as one that is thrown forward. Because gravity is directed downward, it changes only the downward velocity of the coin, not its forward velocity.

VISUALIZATION
CLASSZONE.COM
Explore how objects fall at the same rate in a vacuum.

 CHECK YOUR READING Compare the times it takes two objects with different masses to fall from the same height.

Weight and Mass

While weight and mass are related, they are not the same properties. Mass is a measure of how much matter an object contains. **Weight** is the force of gravity on an object. Mass is a property that an object has no matter where it is located. Weight, on the other hand, depends on the force of gravity acting on that object.

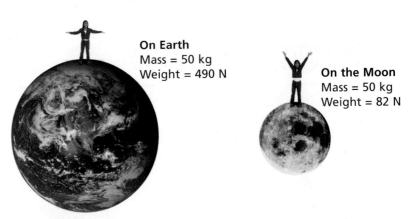

On Earth
Mass = 50 kg
Weight = 490 N

On the Moon
Mass = 50 kg
Weight = 82 N

When you use a balance, you are measuring the mass of an object. A person with a mass of 50 kilograms will balance another mass of 50 kilograms whether she is on Earth or on the Moon. Traveling to the Moon would not change how much matter a person is made of. When you use a spring scale, such as a bathroom scale, to measure the weight of an object, however, you are measuring how hard gravity is pulling on an object. The Moon is less massive than Earth, and its gravitational pull is one-sixth that of Earth's. A spring scale would show that a person who has a weight of 490 newtons (110 lb) on Earth would have a weight of 82 newtons (18 lb) on the Moon.

Gravity keeps objects in orbit.

READING TiP

An elliptical path is a path shaped like an ellipse, as shown below. A circle is a special type of ellipse.

Sir Isaac Newton hypothesized that the force that pulls objects to the ground—gravity—also pulls the Moon in its orbit around Earth. An **orbit** is the elliptical path one body, such as the Moon, follows around another body, such as Earth, due to the influence of gravity. The centripetal force keeping one object in orbit around another object is due to the gravitational pull between the two objects. In the case of the Moon's orbit, the centripetal force is the gravitational pull between the Moon and Earth. Similarly, Earth is pulled around the Sun by the gravitational force between Earth and the Sun.

You can think of an object orbiting Earth as an object that is falling around Earth rather than falling to the ground. Consider what happens to the ball in the illustration on page 75. A dropped ball will fall about five meters during the first second it falls. Throwing the ball straight ahead will not change that falling time. What happens as you throw faster and faster?

Earth is curved. This fact is noticeable only over very long distances. For every 8000 meters you travel, Earth curves downward about 5 meters. If you could throw a ball at 8000 meters per second, it would fall to Earth in such a way that its path would curve the same amount that Earth curves. Since the ball would fall along the curve of Earth, the ball would never actually land on the ground. The ball would be in orbit.

Orbits

An object in orbit, like an object falling to the ground, is pulled toward Earth's center. If the object moves far enough forward as it falls, it orbits around Earth instead of hitting the ground.

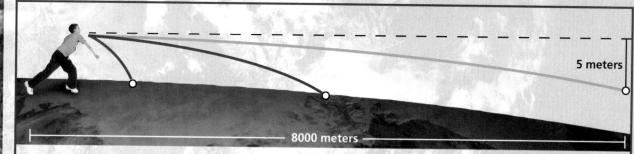

5 meters

8000 meters

If a ball is thrown straight ahead from a 5-meter height, it will drop 5 meters in the first second it falls. At low speeds, the ball will hit the ground after 1 second.

If the ball is going fast enough, the curvature of Earth becomes important. While the ball still drops 5 meters in the first second, it must fall farther than 5 meters to hit the ground.

If the ball is going fast enough to travel 8000 meters forward as it drops downward 5 meters, it follows the curvature of Earth. The ball will fall around Earth, not into it.

A ball thrown horizontally at 8000 m/s will not hit Earth during its fall. Gravity acts as a centripetal force, continually pulling the ball toward Earth's center. The ball circles Earth in an orbit.

Real-World Application
A satellite is launched upward until it is above Earth's atmosphere. The engine then gives the satellite a horizontal speed great enough to keep it in orbit.

 = force

 = velocity

READING VISUALS Compare the direction of the velocity with the direction of the force for an object in a circular orbit.

INVESTIGATE Gravity and Speed

How do different forces affect falling objects?

PROCEDURE

1. Place a coin at the corner of a flat table. Position a ruler next to the coin so that about 10 cm of the ruler is extending out past the edge of the table. Place a coin on the edge of the ruler that is extended out over the floor.

2. Quickly swing the ruler so that it strikes the coin on the table. The coin on the ruler should drop at the same time the coin on the table falls from the edge.

3. Carefully listen to determine which coin hits the ground first.

4. Try swinging the ruler so that the coin on the table has different speeds as it falls. Does the speed change the time it takes the coin to fall?

WHAT DO YOU THINK?

- Identify the forces that acted on both coins to change their motions.
- How did the different forces affect the motion of each coin?

CHALLENGE Why did the coin on the ruler drop closer to the desk than the coin that was hit?

SKILL FOCUS
Inferring (8.2.d)

MATERIALS
- two identical coins
- ruler

TIME
15 minutes

Spacecraft in Orbit

CALIFORNIA Focus

NASA's spacecraft *Gravity Probe B* was launched from the Vandenberg Air Force Base in California in 2004. *Gravity Probe B* was designed to test some unverified predictions of Albert Einstein's theory about the nature of gravity.

The minimum speed needed to send an object into orbit is approximately 8000 meters per second. At this speed, the path of a falling object matches the curve of Earth's surface. If you launch a spacecraft or a satellite at a slower speed, it will eventually fall to the ground.

A spacecraft launched at a greater speed can reach a higher orbit than one launched at a lower speed. The higher the orbit, the greater the distance from Earth and the weaker the force from Earth's gravity. The force of gravity is still very strong, however. If a craft is in a low orbit, about 300 kilometers (190 mi), Earth's gravitational pull is about 91 percent of what it is at Earth's surface. The extra distance makes a difference in the force of only about 9 percent.

If a spacecraft is launched with a speed of 11,000 meters per second or more, it is moving too fast to go into an orbit. Instead, the spacecraft will ultimately escape the pull of Earth's gravity altogether. The speed that a spacecraft needs to escape the gravitational pull of an object such as a planet or a star is called the escape velocity. A spacecraft that escapes Earth's gravity will go into orbit around the Sun unless it is also going fast enough to escape the Sun's gravity.

CHECK YOUR READING Did any facts in the text above surprise you? If so, which surprised you and why?

People in Orbit

When an elevator you are riding in accelerates downward, you may feel lighter for a short time. If you were standing on a scale during the downward acceleration, the scale would show that you weighed less than usual. Your mass would not have changed, nor would the pull of gravity. What would cause the apparent weight loss?

When the elevator is still, the entire force of your weight presses against the scale. When the elevator accelerates downward, you are not pressing as hard on the scale, because the scale is also moving downward. Since the scale measures how hard you are pushing on it, you appear to weigh less. If you and the scale were in free fall—a fall due entirely to gravity—the scale would fall as fast as you did. You would not press against the scale at all, so you would appear to be weightless.

Astronaut Mae Jemison is shown here working in a microgravity environment.

A spacecraft in orbit is in free fall. Gravity is acting on the astronauts and on the ship—without gravity, there could be no orbit. However, the ship and the astronauts are falling around Earth at the same rate. While astronauts are in orbit, their weight does not press against the floor of the spacecraft. The result is an environment, called a microgravity environment, in which objects behave as if there were no gravity. People and objects simply float as if they were weightless.

 CHECK YOUR READING Why do astronauts float when they are in orbit?

3.1 Review

KEY CONCEPTS

1. What effect would increasing the mass of two objects have on the gravitational attraction between them? (8.2.d)

2. What effect would decreasing the distance between objects have on their gravitational attraction to each other? (8.2.d)

3. How does gravity keep the Moon in orbit around Earth? (8.2.g)

CRITICAL THINKING

4. **Compare** How does the size of the force exerted by Earth's gravity on a car compare with the size of the force the car exerts on Earth?

5. **Apply** What would be the effect on the mass and the weight of an object if the object were taken to a planet with twice the gravity of Earth?

◢ CHALLENGE

6. **Synthesize** Precision measurements of the acceleration due to gravity show that the acceleration is slightly different in different locations on Earth. Explain why the force of gravity is not exactly the same everywhere on Earth's surface. **Hint:** Think about the details of Earth's surface.

Kicked Around the Galaxy

8.2.g Students know the role of gravity in forming and maintaining the shapes of planets, stars, and the solar system.

For over forty years, the Jet Propulsion Laboratory (JPL) in Pasadena, California, has made space probes and robots for NASA. JPL spacecraft have explored every known planet except Pluto, and a few have looked out into the universe.

JPL engineers wondered at first how they could send spacecraft on long flights without using giant rockets and a lot of fuel. In the 1960s, two scientists at JPL suggested a method to give the spacecraft extra energy. This method is called gravity assist.

Scientists at JPL celebrate *Cassini*'s successful launch.

How It Works

As a spacecraft approaches a planet, the planet's gravity pulls on the craft with more and more force. But the force of gravity works both ways—the spacecraft also pulls on the planet. Because the planet is huge, the force from the spacecraft does not affect the planet's motion in a noticeable way. But it does affect the planet a little bit. The planet gives up some energy to the spacecraft. The planet slows down a very tiny bit, and the spacecraft speeds up a lot. This extra speed helps the spacecraft go farther.

Voyager 2 was launched by NASA in 1977. It used gravity assist, also called a planet swingby, to hop between planets until it traveled beyond Neptune and out of the solar system. *Cassini* was launched in 1997 to explore Saturn. *Cassini*'s mission depended on the gravity assist method. It took two boosts from Venus, one from Earth, and another from Jupiter for *Cassini* to reach Saturn.

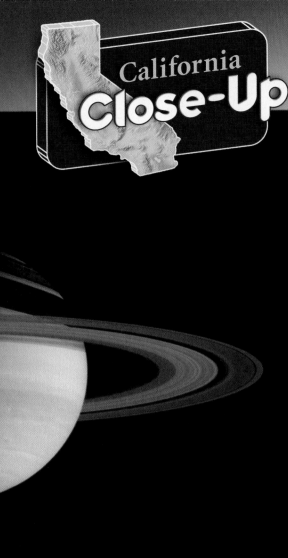

Cassini Trajectory

Second Venus Swingby
June 24, 1999

Saturn
July 1, 2004

Earth Orbit

Jupiter Orbit

Saturn Orbit

Launch
October 15, 1997

Jupiter Swingby
December 30, 2000

Earth Swingby
August 18, 1999

First Venus Swingby
April 26, 1998

Launch to 1st Venus Swingby
1st Venus Swingby to 2nd Venus Swingby
2nd Venus Swingby to Earth Swingby,
Past Jupiter to Saturn

WRITING ABOUT SCIENCE

Choose one of JPL's NASA space probes to research. Write about the probe's mission, and describe some of its discoveries. Explain how the probe used gravity assist to travel through space. Also explain how it will continue to travel on its mission.

3.2 Elastic forces resist stretching and pressing.

CALIFORNIA
Content Standard

8.2.d Students know how to identify separately the two or more forces that are acting on a single static object, including gravity, elastic forces due to tension or compression in matter, and friction.

BEFORE, you learned

- Forces act in pairs
- Gravity is the attractive force masses exert on each other
- Gravity is the force that keeps objects in orbit

NOW, you will learn

- About forces that stretch or press objects
- How objects transfer a force
- How forces affect strings and springs

VOCABULARY

elastic force p. 79
tension p. 80
compression p. 81

EXPLORE Elastic Forces (8.2.d)

How does a force affect shape?

PROCEDURE

① Try to change the shape of the sponge by applying different forces to it. For example, try stretching, squeezing, or gently twisting the sponge. For each force, describe the force and record your observations about the shape of the sponge.

② Repeat step 1 using a lump of clay. Try to use the same forces as you used on the sponge. Write down your observations about the shape of the clay.

MATERIALS
- sponge
- clay

WHAT DO YOU THINK?
Compare your observations about the sponge and the clay. Which observations were similar? Which were different?

Objects resist changing shape.

VOCABULARY
Create a four square diagram for *elastic force* in your notebook.

You have read how forces can affect an object's motion. Forces can also affect an object's shape. For example, if you pull on a rubber band, the rubber band stretches and becomes longer. You can change the shape of a lump of clay by pulling it or by squeezing it.

When you apply a force to an object by pressing or stretching it, the object resists changing shape. You know from Newton's third law that as you pull on a rubber band, the rubber band pulls back on you. Where does the force from the rubber band come from? As you try to stretch the particles in the rubber band apart, the forces between the particles try to pull the rubber band back to its original position. The force in an object that resists stretching or pressing is called the **elastic force**.

Forces can be transferred through materials.

If you push on one side of a wooden block, the whole block moves. The force you apply to the particles on the side of the block is transferred to the other particles in the block through elastic forces. If you push the block against a wall, the force you apply to the block is transferred through the block and to the wall. Similarly, if you pull on a string, your force is transferred through the string. The end of the string can then exert a force on anything it is attached to.

Tension

Suppose you tie a piece of string to a ring stand and hang a mass off the end of it. You know that the force of gravity is pulling the mass downward. However, the mass is not falling as it would if there were no string to hold it up. When objects are static, or not moving, the forces on them must be balanced. Remember Newton's first law—an object at rest won't move if the forces on it are balanced. Since gravity is acting downward, the string must be applying an upward force that balances the weight of the mass. This upward force is the elastic force in the string.

The force that stretches a string or similar object is called **tension.** Tension also refers to the elastic force transmitted through a stretched object. Tension acts along the direction of the string. Tension is present only if an object is stretched. A loose rope is not being stretched and therefore has no tension. You can change the direction of the force by changing the direction of the string.

The tension on the cables of this fire-fighting helicopter balances the weight of the water bucket.

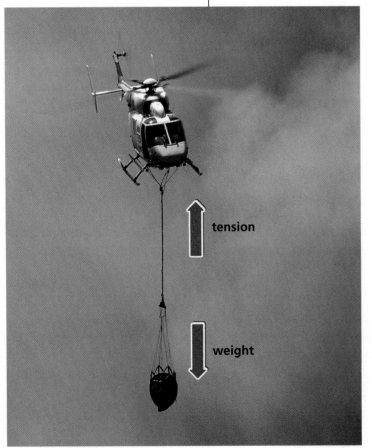

The tension in a string or rope can support the weight of a hanging object. Look at the fire-fighting helicopter in the photograph on the left. If the helicopter is hovering so the water container is not moving, the force from the cables must be equal to the weight of the water bucket. There is a limit to how much elastic force an object can produce, however. If the tension is too great, the cable will break.

Ropes and strings are not the only objects that can have tension. Any object that experiences stretching forces has tension. If a friend tugs at your arm, for instance, you can feel the tension stretching your arm.

Compression

When you push the ends of a foam block together, the particles in the block are pushed closer together. The process of pushing the particles of a material closer together is called **compression.** If you compress a spring between your fingers, you can feel the elastic force of the spring pushing back against your compressive force.

 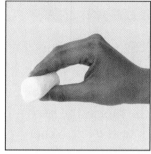 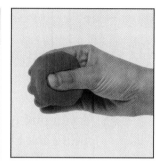

Materials and objects differ in how they respond to compression. A wooden cube will not compress easily. You need a large force to overcome the elastic forces in wood. A marshmallow is easy to compress. A marshmallow will also return to its original shape when you remove the force that is compressing it. If, however, you press the marshmallow too much, you can change its shape permanently. Some materials, such as clay, will change their shape permanently with any compressive force. Elastic forces in clay are not strong enough for it to hold its shape.

 CHECK YOUR READING   Compare and contrast tension and compression.

Elastic forces can cause repeated tension and compression.

In some objects, the size of the elastic force depends on how much an object is stretched or compressed. Think about what happens as you stretch a rubber band or a spring. As you stretch its ends farther apart, you can feel the inward force becoming stronger. A similar thing happens when you compress a spring. The more you compress the spring, the greater the elastic force becomes.

Some springs both compress and stretch easily. If one of these springs is stretched and then let go, the elastic force will pull the spring back, causing it to compress. The compressed spring will push out, causing stretching. A cycle of repeated stretching and compressing occurs.

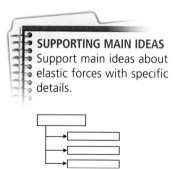

SUPPORTING MAIN IDEAS
Support main ideas about elastic forces with specific details.

Suppose you have a block attached to a spring like the one in the diagram. If you pull the block out, you create tension in the spring. What happens when you let the block go? Consider how the forces on the spring change:

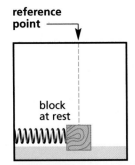

reference point

block at rest

elastic force

force from hand

①

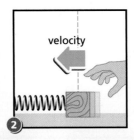

velocity

②

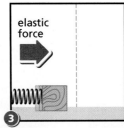

elastic force

③

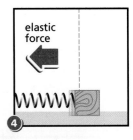

elastic force

④

SIMULATION
CLASSZONE.COM

Explore elastic forces.

① As you pull on the block, the spring increases the elastic force pulling the block to the left. When you let go of the block, this force pulls the block to the left.

② When the block reaches its original position, there is no net force on it. However, the block is moving, so it keeps on moving. The block begins to compress the spring.

③ As the spring compresses, it produces an elastic force pushing on the block to the right. This force slows the block until it has no velocity, then pushes the block back to the right.

④ The block moves to the right, stretching the spring again. This creates a force acting to the left. The block bounces back and forth repeatedly as the cycle continues.

APPLY How do gravity and the elastic force of the springs in the pogo sticks help these jumpers bounce repeatedly?

Some reaction forces are elastic forces.

When you stand on the floor or sit on a chair, gravity acts to pull you downward. Your weight presses on the floor or the chair. You are not moving downward, so there must be a reaction force from the floor or chair pushing upward on you. The particles that make up a surface such as a floor or chair are pushed together by your weight. There is a limit to how closely particles can be pushed together in any material. The elastic force of the surface pushes back on you. Reaction forces that develop when you press on a surface or an object are usually due to the elastic force of the material.

The elastic force that a surface exerts when something is pressing on it is called the normal force. In mathematics, two lines are normal to each other if they are at right angles. The normal force gets its name from the fact that it always acts at a right angle to the surface that is being pressed.

The term *elastic force* is most often used to refer to the force exerted by objects such as springs or rubber bands. However, elastic forces are actually everywhere. As you have seen, different materials respond differently to tension and compression. These different responses help people determine what uses the material can have. For example, a bridge would need to be made of a material that can resist the large compressive forces of the bridge's weight and the load on it.

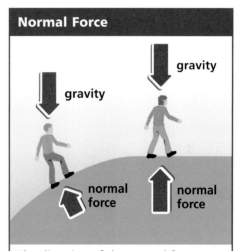

Normal Force

The direction of the normal force depends on the angle of the surface. The normal force from a slope is less than that from a flat surface because less weight presses on the surface.

  What is the normal force?

3.2 Review

KEY CONCEPTS

1. A book is on a table. Gravity acts to pull it downward. Why doesn't the book move? (8.2.d)

2. Give an example of a situation in which a rope has tension. (8.2.d)

3. A mass is hanging from a spring. What forces are acting on the mass? (8.2.d)

CRITICAL THINKING

4. **Infer** A 570 N tire is tied to a tree branch with a rope. What force does the rope exert on the branch?

5. **Analyze** Rope is rated by its break strength, the maximum tension on the rope before it breaks. Why will a rope break if the tension is greater than the break strength?

○ CHALLENGE

6. Synthesize Two books rest on a table. One is twice as heavy as the other, and neither book is moving. Does each book experience the same elastic force? Explain your answer. (**Hint:** Think about Newton's third law.)

CHAPTER INVESTIGATION

Measuring Elastic Forces

OVERVIEW AND PURPOSE As you hang a mass off the hook of a spring scale, the spring extends. When the mass hangs without moving, the elastic force of the spring equals the weight of the mass. How is the elastic force of the spring related to the increased length of the spring that you see reading the spring scale? In this investigation you will

- measure and compare the increased length created by different masses on a spring
- infer the relationship between the elastic force and the increased length in a spring

► Problem

How does an increase in the mass of an object suspended on a spring affect the extension of the spring and the amount of the elastic force acting on the object?

► Hypothesize

Write a hypothesis describing your prediction about how additional masses suspended on a spring scale will affect the extension of the spring and the amount of elastic force acting on each mass. Your hypothesis should take the form of an "If . . . , then . . . , because . . . ," statement.

► Procedure

MATERIALS
- spring
- ring stand and ring
- 100 g mass
- 200 g mass
- 500 g mass
- metric ruler

8.2.d, 8.9.e

1. Make a data table like the one shown on the next page.

2. Hook the spring to the ring on the ring stand. Measure and record the length of the spring.

3. Attach the 100 g mass to the bottom of the spring so that it extends the spring. Measure the new length of the spring.

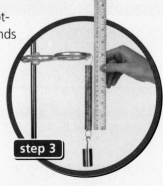

step 3

Content Standard
8.2.d Students know how to identify separately the two or more forces that are acting on a single static object, including gravity, elastic forces due to tension or compression in matter, and friction.

Investigation Standard
8.9.e Students will construct appropriate graphs from data and develop quantitative statements about the relationships between variables.

4 Find the increase in length of the spring by subtracting the extended length from the original length. This is the extension.

5 Repeat step 2 using the 200 g object and the 500 g object.

Observe and Analyze 〈Write It Up〉

1. **RECORD** Complete your data table and record all of your measurements.

2. **COMPARE** How did the length of the spring when the 100 g object was attached compare with the length of the spring when the 500 g object was attached? How did the extensions compare?

Conclude 〈Write It Up〉

1. **IDENTIFY VARIABLES** What forces were acting on the suspended object during your experiment? In what directions were these forces acting?

2. **INTERPRET** Draw a diagram of the forces acting on the 200 g object. Label your forces.

3. **ANALYZE** Compare your results with your hypothesis. Do your data support your hypothesis?

4. **ANALYZE** Make a graph of your data. Choose a type of graph that would display your data most effectively. See pages R24–R27 for ideas.

5. **DRAW CONCLUSIONS** How did the addition of more mass affect the amount of elastic force supplied by the spring scale?

6. **APPLY** How does a spring scale work? Would a spring scale work properly if the spring did not return to its original length each time it was used?

INVESTIGATE Further

CHALLENGE Use your data to find a mathematical formula that relates the extension of the spring to the mass hanging from it.

Measuring Elastic Forces
Problem How are increased mass and spring extension related?
Hypothesize

Observe and Analyze
Original length of spring:_____cm

Table 1: Mass and Spring Extension

Mass of Object (g)	Spring Length (cm)	Extension of Spring (cm)
100		
200		
500		

Conclude

3.3 Friction is a force that opposes motion.

CALIFORNIA
Content Standard

8.2.d Students know how to identify separately the two or more forces that are acting on a single static object, including gravity, elastic forces due to tension or compression in matter, and friction.

VOCABULARY

friction p. 86
fluid p. 89
air resistance p. 90

BEFORE, you learned

- Gravity is the attractive force masses exert on each other
- Gravity increases with greater mass and decreases with greater distance
- Gravity is the centripetal force keeping objects in orbit

NOW, you will learn

- How friction affects motion
- About factors that affect friction
- About air resistance

THINK ABOUT

What forces help you to walk?

As you walk, you exert a backward force on the ground. A reaction force moves you forward. But some surfaces are harder to walk on than others. Ice, for example, is harder to walk on than a dry surface because ice is slippery. How can different surfaces affect your ability to walk?

Friction occurs when surfaces slide against each other.

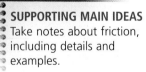

SUPPORTING MAIN IDEAS
Take notes about friction, including details and examples.

Have you ever pushed a heavy box across the floor? You probably noticed that it is easier to push the box over some surfaces than over others. You must apply a certain amount of force to the box to keep it moving. The force that acts against your pushing force is called friction. **Friction** is a force that resists the motion between two surfaces in contact.

When you try to slide two surfaces across each other, the force of friction resists the sliding motion. If there were no friction, the box would move as soon as you applied any force to it. Although friction can make some tasks more difficult, most activities, including walking, would be impossible without it. Friction between your feet and the ground is what provides the action and reaction forces that enable you to walk.

Forces and Surfaces

If you look down from a great height, such as from the window of an airplane, a flat field appears to be smooth. If you were to walk in the field, however, you would see that the ground has many bumps and holes. In the same way, a flat surface such as a piece of plastic may look and feel smooth. However, if you look at the plastic through a strong microscope, you see that it has tiny bumps and ridges. Friction depends on how these bumps and ridges on one surface interact with and stick to the bumps and ridges on other surfaces. There are several factors that determine the friction between two surfaces.

Types of Surfaces Friction between two surfaces depends on the materials that make up the surfaces. Different combinations of surfaces produce different frictional forces. A rubber hockey puck sliding across ice has a smaller frictional force on it than the same puck sliding across a wooden floor. The friction between rubber and ice is less than the friction between rubber and wood.

Motion of the Surfaces You need a larger force to start something moving than you do to keep something moving. If you have ever tried to push a heavy chair, you may have noticed that you had to push harder and harder until the chair suddenly accelerated forward.

As you apply a force to push a chair or any other object that is not moving, the frictional force keeping it from sliding increases so the forces stay balanced. However, the frictional force has an upper limit.

RESOURCE CENTER
CLASSZONE.COM

Learn more about friction, forces, and surfaces.

REMINDER

Remember that balanced forces on an object do not change the object's motion.

Friction and Motion

Before Object Moves

applied force

friction

When an object is standing still, there is a maximum force needed to overcome friction and start it moving. Any force less than this will be exactly balanced by the force of friction, and the object will not move.

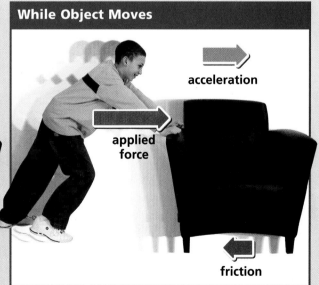

While Object Moves

acceleration

applied force

friction

Once the object is moving, the frictional force remains constant. This constant force is less than the maximum force needed to start the object moving.

When your force is greater than this limit, the forces on the chair are no longer balanced, and the chair moves. The frictional force remains at a new lower level once the chair is moving.

Force Pressing the Surfaces Together The harder two surfaces are pushed together, the more difficult it is for the surfaces to slide over each other. When an object is placed on a surface, the weight of the object presses on that surface. The surface exerts an equal and opposite reaction force on the object. This reaction force, the normal force, is one of the factors that determines how much friction there is.

If you push a chair across the floor, there will be a certain amount of friction between the chair and the floor. Increasing the weight of the chair increases the normal force. The force of friction between the chair and the floor is greater when a person is sitting in it than when the chair was empty.

Friction depends on the total force pressing the surfaces together, not on how much area this force acts over. Consider a rectangular cardboard box. It can rest with its smaller or larger side on the floor. The box will have the same force from friction regardless of which side sits on the floor. The larger side has more area in contact with the floor than the smaller side, but the weight of the box is more spread out on the larger side.

 CHECK YOUR READING What factors influence frictional force? Give two examples.

Friction and Weight

Less Weight

applied force

weight

friction

The force of friction depends on the total force pushing the surfaces together. Here the weight of the chair is the force pressing the surfaces together.

More Weight

applied force

weight

friction

The weight of the chair increases when someone sits in it. The force of friction is now greater than when the chair was empty.

INVESTIGATE Friction

How does the friction created by different surfaces compare?

PROCEDURE

1. Hook the spring scale to the mass and slowly but steadily pull the mass across the flat surface of your desk or worktable. Measure and record the force on the mass as you pulled it across the desk.

2. Tape a sheet of sandpaper on a flat surface. Pull the mass across the sandpaper. Measure and record the force on the mass as you pull steadily.

3. Repeat step 2 using aluminum foil, and again using the sheet of paper.

WHAT DO YOU THINK?

- Which surface caused the mass to have the greatest force? the least force?
- What is the relationship between the amount of force you measured on the spring scale and the amount of friction created by each surface?

CHALLENGE Watch the spring scale as you pull on the mass before it starts moving. What is the maximum force you apply before the mass moves? How does this force compare to the force you measured after the mass was moving?

SKILL FOCUS
Measuring (8.2.a)

MATERIALS
- 500-g hooked mass
- spring scale
- medium grain sandpaper
- aluminum foil
- sheet of paper
- masking tape

TIME
25 minutes

Friction and Heat

Friction between surfaces produces heat. You feel heat produced by friction when you rub your hands together. As you rub, friction causes the individual molecules on the surface of your hands to move faster. As the individual molecules in an object move faster, the temperature of the object increases. The increased speed of the molecules on the surface of your hands produces the warmth that you feel.

The heat produced by friction can be intense. The friction that results from striking a match against a rough surface produces enough heat to ignite the flammable substance on the head of the match. In some machines, such as a car engine, too much heat from friction can cause serious damage. Substances such as oil are often used to reduce friction between moving parts in machines. Without motor oil, a car's engine parts would overheat and stop working.

Motion through fluids produces friction.

As you have seen, two objects in a vacuum fall with the same acceleration. Objects falling through air, however, may have different accelerations. This difference occurs because air causes friction. Air is a fluid. A **fluid** is a substance that can flow easily. Gases and liquids are fluids.

Friction produces sparks between a match head and a rough surface. The heat from friction lights the match.

air resistance | gravity

When the force of air resistance equals the force from gravity, a skydiver falls at a constant speed.

When an object moves through a fluid, it pushes the molecules of the fluid out of the way. At the same time, the molecules of the fluid exert an equal and opposite force on the object that slows it down. This force resisting motion through a fluid is a type of friction that is often called drag. Friction in fluids depends on the shape of the moving object. Objects can be designed either to increase or reduce the friction caused by a fluid. Airplane designs, for example, improve as engineers find ways to reduce drag.

The friction due to air is often called **air resistance.** Air resistance differs from the friction between solid surfaces. Air resistance depends on surface area and the speed of an object in the following ways:

- An object with a larger surface area comes into contact with more molecules as it moves than an object with a smaller surface area does. This increases the air resistance.

- The faster an object moves through air, the more molecules it comes into contact with in a given amount of time. As the speed of the object increases, air resistance increases.

When a skydiver jumps out of a plane, gravity causes the skydiver to accelerate toward the ground. As the skydiver falls, his body pushes against the air. The air pushes back—with the force of air resistance. As the skydiver's speed increases, his air resistance increases. Eventually, air resistance balances gravity, and the skydiver reaches terminal velocity. Terminal velocity is the final, maximum velocity of a falling object. When the skydiver opens his parachute, air resistance increases still further, and he reaches a new, slower terminal velocity that enables him to land safely.

 CHECK YOUR READING How do speed and surface area affect air resistance?

3.3 Review

KEY CONCEPTS

1. How does friction affect forward motion? Give an example. (8.2)

2. Describe two ways to change the frictional force between two solid surfaces. (8.2.d)

3. How does air resistance affect the velocity of a falling object? (8.2.d)

CRITICAL THINKING

4. Infer What two sources of friction do you have to overcome when you are walking?

5. Synthesize If you push a chair across the floor at a constant velocity, how does the force of friction compare with the force you exert? Explain.

CHALLENGE

6. Synthesize If you push a book against a wall hard enough, it will not slide down even though gravity is pulling it. Use what you know about friction and Newton's laws of motion to explain why the book does not fall.

SKILL: CREATING A LINE GRAPH

Smoke Jumpers in Action

Scientists often use graphs as a way to present data. Sometimes information is easier to understand when it is presented in graphic form.

Smoke jumpers parachute into burning forests in order to contain the flames.

Example

Smoke jumpers are firefighters who parachute down into a forest that is on fire. Suppose you measured how the velocity of a smoke jumper changed as he was free-falling, and recorded the following data.

Time (s)	0	2	4	6	8	10	12	14	16	18
Velocity (m/s)	0	18	29	33	35	36	36	36	36	36

Follow these steps to make a line graph of the data in the table.

(1) For both variables, decide the scale that each box on your graph will represent and what range you will show for each variable. For the above time data you might choose a range of 0 to 18 s, with each interval representing 2 s. For velocity, a range of 0 to 40 m/s with intervals of 5 m/s each is reasonable.

ANSWER

(2) Determine the dependent and independent variables. In this example, the velocity depends on the falling time, so velocity is the dependent variable.

(3) Plot the independent variable along the horizontal axis, or x-axis. Plot the dependent variable along the vertical axis, or y-axis. Connect the points with a smooth line.

Use the data below to answer the following questions.

Suppose a smoke jumper varied the mass of his equipment over 5 jumps, and you measured his different terminal velocities as follows:

Extra Mass (kg)	0	5	10	15	20
Terminal Velocity (m/s)	36	37	38	39	40

1. Identify the independent and dependent variables.

2. Choose the scales and intervals you would use to graph the data. **Hint:** Your velocity range does not have to start at 0 m/s.

3. Plot your graph.

CHALLENGE How do different scales give different impressions of the data? Try comparing several different scales for the same data.

the **BIG** idea

Newton's laws apply to all forces.

CONTENT REVIEW
CLASSZONE.COM

◀ KEY CONCEPTS SUMMARY

1 Gravity is a force exerted by masses.

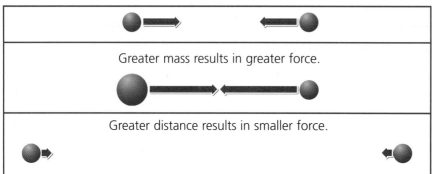

Greater mass results in greater force.

Greater distance results in smaller force.

VOCABULARY
gravity p. 71
weight p. 73
orbit p. 74

2 Elastic forces resist stretching and pressing.

elastic force | force from hand

Tension creates an elastic force that resists stretching.

Compression creates an elastic force that resists pressing.

VOCABULARY
elastic force p. 79
tension p. 80
compression p. 81

3 Friction is a force that opposes motion.

Frictional force depends on—

• types of surfaces
• motion of surfaces
• force pressing surfaces together

Air resistance is a type of friction.

friction

VOCABULARY
friction p. 86
fluid p. 89
air resistance p. 90

Reviewing Vocabulary

Write a sentence describing the relationship between the terms in each pair.

1. gravity, weight

2. gravity, orbit

3. tension, elastic force

4. compression, tension

5. surface, friction

6. force, friction

Reviewing Key Concepts

Multiple Choice *Choose the letter of the best answer.*

7. Which force keeps Venus in orbit around the Sun? (8.2.g)

  a. gravity   **c.** hydraulic force

  b. friction   **d.** buoyancy

8. You and a classmate are one meter apart. If you move farther away, how does the gravitational force between you and your classmate change? (8.2.g)

  a. It increases.

  b. It decreases.

  c. It stays the same.

  d. It disappears.

9. You kick a ball on a level sidewalk. It rolls to a stop because (8.2.e)

  a. there is no force on the ball

  b. gravity slows the ball down

  c. the forces on the ball are balanced

  d. friction slows the ball down

10. You push a chair at a constant velocity using a force of 5 N to overcome friction. You stop to rest, then push again. To start the chair moving again, you must use a force that is (8.2.d)

  a. greater than 5 N

  b. equal to 5 N

  c. greater than 0 N but less than 5 N

  d. 0 N

11. How could you place an empty bottle on a table so that it produces the greatest amount of friction when it is pushed? (8.2.d)

  a. position 1

  b. position 2

  c. position 3

  d. All positions produce the same friction.

12. As you stretch a spring, the elastic force in the spring (8.2.d)

  a. resists the stretching force

  b. adds to the stretching force

  c. pushes your hand away from the spring

  d. compresses the spring

13. Joseph jumps down on a trampoline. Why does he move up into the air? (8.2.e)

  a. Gravity pushes him upward.

  b. Friction between him and the trampoline prevents him from moving downward.

  c. The elastic force of the trampoline pushes him upward.

  d. Air resistance pushes him upward.

Short Answer *Write a short answer to each question.*

14. Why doesn't gravity pull a book downward if the book is on a table? (8.2.d)

15. Explain why a satellite in orbit around Earth does not crash into Earth. (8.2.g)

16. You are pushing a dresser with drawers filled with clothing. What could you do to reduce the friction between the dresser and the floor?

17. If you pull down on a mass that hangs from a spring, it will bounce up and down for a while before stopping. Why does the mass bounce?

18. Suppose you press a basketball against a wall. What happens to the basketball while you are pressing it? (8.2.d)

19. **APPLY** Why is it important for mountain climbers to know the maximum tension they can put on a climbing rope? (8.2.e)

20. **COMPARE** How does the friction between solid surfaces compare with the friction between a moving object and a fluid?

21. **APPLY** Explain why a block of wood gets warm when it is rubbed with sandpaper.

22. **PREDICT** The Moon's orbit is gradually increasing. Each year the Moon is about 3.8 cm farther from Earth than the year before. How does this change affect the force of gravity between Earth and the Moon? (8.2.g)

23. **APPLY** The Moon has one-sixth the gravity of Earth. Why would it be easier to launch spacecraft into orbit around the Moon than around Earth? (8.2.g)

Use the photograph below to answer the next three questions.

24. **APPLY** A skydiver jumps out of a plane. After he reaches terminal velocity, he opens his parachute. Draw a sketch showing the forces of air resistance and gravity on the skydiver after the parachute opens. Use a longer arrow for a greater force. (8.2.e)

25. **SYNTHESIZE** Why does the skydiver fall down toward Earth rather than going into orbit? (8.2.g)

26. **INFER** The Moon has no atmosphere. Would it be safe to skydive on the Moon? Why or why not?

27. **INFER** A person weighing 500 N climbs on a rope. What is the tension on the rope? (8.2.d)

28. **COMPARE** Trisha hangs a mass from a spring as shown in the picture. The mass is not moving. Sketch a diagram showing the forces acting on the spring. (8.2.d)

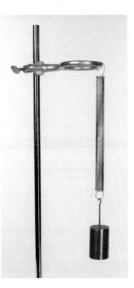

Using Math Skills in Science

Complete the following calculations.

29. How much force does a 10 kg block exert on the ground? (8.2.d)

30. A 6 kg box is placed on a flat surface. What is the weight of the box in newtons? What is the normal force acting on the box? (8.2.d)

the BIG idea

31. **ANALYZE** Look again at the picture on pages 68–69. What forces are acting on the snowboarder? on the snow?

32. **SYNTHESIZE** Choose two concepts discussed in this chapter, and describe how Newton's laws relate to those concepts.

UNIT PROJECTS

Check your schedule for your unit project. How are you doing? Be sure that you have placed data or notes from your research into your project folder.

Interpreting Graphs

8.2.g

The gravitational force on a person above Earth's surface depends on how far the person is from Earth's center. Standing at the surface, a person is about 6400 km from Earth's center. The graph shows the gravitational force exerted by Earth on a 50 kg person traveling away from Earth's surface.

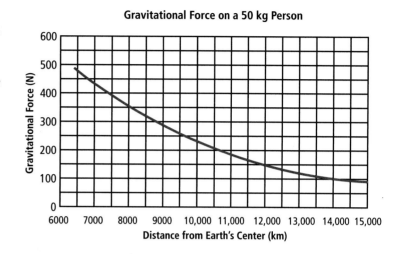

Gravitational Force on a 50 kg Person

Use the graph to answer the questions.

1. What is the force exerted by Earth on a person standing on the surface? (distance = 6400 km)
   - **a.** about 325 N
   - **b.** about 400 N
   - **c.** about 490 N
   - **d.** about 565 N

2. What is the force exerted on Earth by a person standing on the surface? (distance = 6400 km)
   - **a.** less than 10 N
   - **b.** about 325 N
   - **c.** about 400 N
   - **d.** about 490 N

3. The International Space Station (ISS) orbits Earth at a distance of 350 km above its surface. What is the gravitational force between the Earth and a 50 km person aboard the ISS?
   - **a.** about 225 N
   - **b.** about 330 N
   - **c.** about 440 N
   - **d.** about 500 N

4. How does the gravitational force at 12,800 km compare to that at 6400 km?
   - **a.** about one-fourth
   - **b.** about half
   - **c.** about double
   - **d.** about four times as large

5. How does the gravitational force at 14,000 km compare to that at 7000 km?
   - **a.** about one-fourth
   - **b.** about half
   - **c.** about double
   - **d.** about four times as large

Extended response

Answer the two questions below in detail.

6. Every time you double the distance between two objects, the gravitational force is reduced by a factor of four. As two objects are separated farther and farther, do you think that the gravitational force between them will ever reach zero? Why or why not?

7. We know that Earth rotates around the Sun. The gravitational force of Earth on the Sun is the same as the gravitational force of the Sun on Earth. Why does the force from the Sun move Earth so much more than the force from Earth moves the Sun?

UNDERSTANDING FORCES

In ancient times, people thought that an object would not move unless it was pushed. Scientists came up with ingenious ways to explain how objects like arrows stayed in motion. Over time, they came to understand that all motion could be described by three basic laws. Modern achievements such as suspension bridges and space exploration are possible because of the experiments with motion and forces performed by scientists and philosophers over hundreds of years.

This timeline shows just a few of the many steps on the path toward understanding forces. Notice how scientists used the observations and ideas of previous thinkers as a springboard for developing new theories. The boxes below the timeline show how technology has led to new insights and to applications of those ideas.

350 B.C.
Aristotle Discusses Motion
The Greek philosopher Aristotle states that the natural condition of an object is to be at rest. A force is necessary to keep the object in motion. The greater the force, the faster the object moves.

EVENTS

400 B.C.   **350 B.C.**   **300 B.C.**

APPLICATIONS AND TECHNOLOGY

TECHNOLOGY
Catapulting into History

As early as 400 B.C., armies were using objects in motion to do work. Catapults, or machines for hurling stones and spears, were used as military weapons. Five hundred years later, the Roman army used catapults mounted on wheels. In the Middle Ages, young trees were sometimes bent back, loaded with an object, and then released like a large slingshot. Today catapult technology is used to launch airplanes from aircraft carriers. A piston powered by steam propels the plane along the deck of the aircraft carrier until it reaches takeoff speed.

A.D. 1121

Force Acting on Objects Described

Persian astronomer al-Khazini asserts that a force acts on all objects to pull them toward the center of Earth. This force varies, he says, depending on whether the object moves through air, water, or another medium. His careful notes and drawings illustrate these principles.

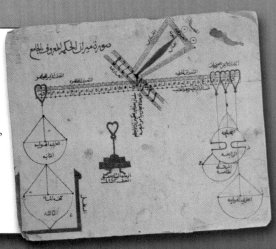

250 B.C.

Levers and Buoyancy Explained

The Greek inventor Archimedes uses a mathematical equation to explain how a small weight can balance a much larger weight near a lever's fulcrum. He also explains buoyancy, which provides a way of measuring volume.

1150

Perpetual-Motion Machine Described

Indian mathematician and physicist Bhaskara describes a wheel that uses closed containers of liquid to turn forever without stopping. If it worked, his idea would promise an unending source of power that does not rely on an external source.

250 B.C.   **A.D. 1100**   **1150**   **1200**

APPLICATION

The First Steam-Powered Engine

In the first century A.D., Hero of Alexandria, a Greek inventor, created the first known steam engine, called the aeolipile. It was a hollow ball with two cylinders jutting out in opposite directions. The ball was suspended above a kettle that was filled with water and placed over a fire. As the water boiled, steam caused the ball to spin. The Greeks never used this device for work. In 1690, Sir Isaac Newton formulated the principle of the aeolipile in scientific terms in his third law of motion. A steam engine designed for work was built in 1698. The aeolipile is the earliest version of steam-powered pumps, steam locomotives, jet engines, and rockets.

1638
Objects Need No Force to Keep Moving

Italian astronomer Galileo Galilei says that an object's natural state is either in constant motion or at rest. Having observed the motion of objects on ramps, he concludes that an object in motion will slow down or speed up only if a force is exerted on it. He also claims that all objects dropped near the surface of Earth fall with the same acceleration due to the force of gravity.

1494
Perpetual-Motion Machine Impossible

Italian painter and engineer Leonardo da Vinci proves that it is impossible to build a perpetual-motion machine that works. He states that the force of friction keeps a wheel from turning forever without more force being applied.

1687
An Object's Motion Can Be Predicted

English scientist Sir Isaac Newton publishes his three laws of motion, which use Galileo's ideas as a foundation. He concludes that Earth exerts a gravitational force on objects on its surface and that Earth's gravity keeps the Moon in orbit.

1500   1550   1600   1650   1700   1750   1800

APPLICATION

A New and Improved Steam Engine

Scottish scientist James Watt designed steam engines that were much more efficient, and much smaller, than older models. About 500 of Watt's engines were in use by 1800. His pump engines drew water out of coal mines, and his rotating engines were used in factories and cotton mills. Watt's steam engines opened the way to the Industrial Revolution. They were used in major industries such as textile manufacturing, railroad transportation, and mining. Watt's steam technology also opened up new areas of research in heat, kinetic energy, and motion.

1919

Gravity Bends Light

A solar eclipse confirms German-American physicist Albert Einstein's modification of Newton's laws. Einstein's theory states that the path of a light beam will be affected by nearby massive objects. During the eclipse, the stars appear to shift slightly away from one another because their light has been bent by the Sun's gravity.

2001

Supercomputers Model Strong Force

Scientists have been using supercomputers to model the force that holds particles in the nucleus of an atom together. This force, called the strong force, cannot be measured directly in the same way that gravity and other forces can. Instead, computer models allow scientists to make predictions that are then compared with experimental results.

RESOURCE CENTER
CLASSZONE.COM

Get current research on force and motion.

1850   1900   1950   2000

TECHNOLOGY

Science Propels Exploration of Outer Space

An increased understanding of forces made space exploration possible. In 1926 American scientist Robert H. Goddard constructed and tested the first liquid-propelled rocket. A replica of Goddard's rocket can be seen at the National Air and Space Museum in Washington, D.C. In 1929 Goddard launched a rocket that carried the first scientific payload, a barometer and a camera.

Many later achievements—including the 1969 walk on the Moon—are a direct result of Goddard's trail-blazing space research.

SPOTLIGHT on
CLAUDIA ALEXANDER

Claudia Alexander is a space plasma scientist at NASA's Jet Propulsion Laboratory (JPL) at the California Institute of Technology in Pasadena. She studies comets and other solid, icy bodies in the solar system.

Alexander was the seventh and final project manager of NASA's *Galileo* mission to Jupiter. *Galileo* was an unmanned spacecraft launched from the space shuttle *Atlantis* in 1989. By the end of the mission, *Galileo* had discovered evidence of water on three of Jupiter's moons. The spacecraft sent back spectacular photos from outer space. *Galileo* was programmed to crash into Jupiter at the end of its mission in 2003. Alexander reported that *Galileo* collected valuable data about the planet's environment up until the very end.

ACTIVITIES

Reliving History

Bhaskara's design for a perpetual-motion machine involved a wheel with containers of mercury around the rim. As the wheel turned, the mercury would move in such a way that the wheel would always be heavier on one side—and stay in motion. Now we know that this theory goes against the laws of physics. Observe a wheel, a pendulum, or a swing. Think about why it cannot stay in motion forever.

Writing About Science

Suppose you won a trip to outer space. Write a letter accepting or refusing the prize. Give your reasons.

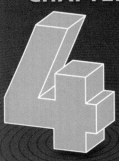

CHAPTER 4

Density and Buoyancy

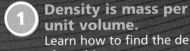

Forces act in fluids.

Key Concepts

SECTION

1 **Density is mass per unit volume.**
Learn how to find the density of an object.

SECTION

2 **Pressure in a fluid varies with depth.**
Learn how particles produce forces in fluids.

SECTION

3 **The buoyant force acts on objects in fluids.**
Learn about the buoyant force and why objects float or sink.

 California ClassZone

CLASSZONE.COM

Chapter 4 online resources:
Content Review,
Visualization, two Resource
Centers, Math Tutorial,
Test Practice

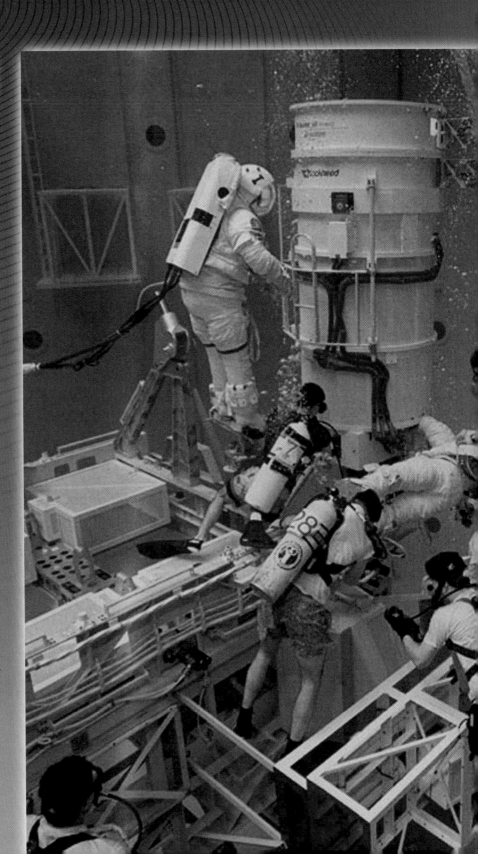

Why do astronauts practice space maneuvers underwater?

EXPLORE (the BIG idea)

What Has Changed?

 8.8.a Students know density is mass per unit volume.

Blow up a balloon. Use a felt-tipped marker to draw a line around its thickest part. Let the air out of the balloon slowly. Observe what happens to the line.

Observe and Think How did the length of the line change with the size of the balloon? Did the amount of material that makes up the balloon change? Did the amount of air inside the balloon change? How did the amount of air inside the balloon affect the size of the balloon?

Will It Float?

 8.8.d Students know how to predict whether an object will float or sink.

Form a piece of clay into a solid ball or cube. Place it in a bowl of water. Notice if it floats or sinks. Then mold the clay into a boatlike shape. Notice if this new object floats or sinks.

Observe and Think What did you change about the clay? What didn't you change? What would happen if you filled the boat with water?

NSTA scilinks.org SCiLINKS

Pressure **Code: MDL006**

Getting Ready to Learn

◀ CONCEPT REVIEW

- The motion of an object does not change if the forces on it are balanced.
- Gravity is an attractive force that depends on mass and distance.
- Weight is the force of gravity on an object.

◀ VOCABULARY REVIEW

force p. 41

net force p. 43

gravity p. 71

fluid p. 89

mass *see glossary*

CONTENT REVIEW
CLASSZONE.COM

Review concepts and vocabulary.

▶ TAKING NOTES

MAIN IDEA WEB

Write each new main idea in a box. Then write notes in boxes around it that give important terms and details about that main idea.

VOCABULARY STRATEGY

Take notes about new vocabulary terms using one or more of the strategies from earlier chapters—**description wheel, magnet word,** or **four square.** Feel free to mix and match the strategies or use a different strategy.

See the Note-Taking Handbook on pages R45–R51.

SCIENCE NOTEBOOK

Mass is how much matter something has.	Objects have different masses.

Objects have mass and volume.

Volume is the amount of space something takes up.	

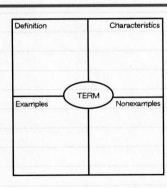

Density is mass per unit volume.

CALIFORNIA
Content Standards

8.8.a Students know density is mass per unit volume.

8.8.b Students know how to calculate the density of substances (regular and irregular solids and liquids) from measurements of mass and volume.

8.7.c Students know substances can be classified by their properties, including their melting temperature, **density**, hardness, and thermal and electrical conductivity.

VOCABULARY

volume p. 103
density p. 105

BEFORE, you learned

• The gravitational force an object can exert depends on the object's mass
• Weight is defined as the force gravity exerts on an object
• Weight depends on mass

NOW, you will learn

• How to measure mass and volume
• How mass, volume, and density are related
• How to calculate density

EXPLORE Similar Objects (8.8.a)

How can two similar objects differ?

PROCEDURE

(1) Look at the two balls but do not pick them up. Compare their sizes and shapes. Record your observations.

(2) Pick up each ball. Compare the way the balls feel in your hands. Record your observations.

MATERIALS
2 balls of different sizes

WHAT DO YOU THINK?
How would your observation be different if the larger ball were made of foam?

VOCABULARY
You might want to make a magnet word diagram for *volume*.

Objects have mass and volume.

All objects are made up of matter. Matter can be defined as anything that has mass and takes up space. Mass is the measure of the amount of matter an object contains. Different objects contain different amounts of matter. An elephant has more mass than a mouse. A metal fork has more mass than a plastic fork.

Matter also has volume. **Volume** is the measure of the amount of space an object takes up. An elephant has a greater volume than a mouse because the elephant takes up more space. A metal fork and a plastic fork might take up the same amount of space. In this case, the two forks would have the same volume although they have different masses. Often the volume of an object includes other substances inside the object. For example, the volume of a basketball is the volume the whole sphere takes up. The volume of the outside material is only a part of this. Most of the volume is taken up by air.

 What is mass? What is volume?

Measuring Mass

Objects of similar size, or volume, may differ greatly in mass. A bowling ball has more mass than a basketball even when both are the same volume. To find out how much more massive a bowling ball is than a basketball, you can measure their masses. Measuring mass involves comparing the mass of a particular object with a standard unit of mass. For example, you can find the mass of a bowling ball and a basketball using a pan balance like the one below.

One pan holds the ball. The other pan holds metal blocks that all have the same mass. When the mass of blocks equals the mass of the ball, the pan balances. A beam balance works in a similar way. However, instead of placing blocks on a pan, you slide a standard mass along a beam. When the beam is level, you read the mass on the beam.

In science, the standard unit of mass is the kilogram (kg). A bowling ball has a mass of about 5 kilograms. A basketball has a mass of just over 0.5 kilogram. The mass of a basketball can easily be given in smaller units—grams. There are 1000 grams in a kilogram. So a basketball has a mass of about 500 grams. In comparison, a penny has a mass of between two and three grams.

For more details on using a triple-beam balance, see page R18.

 CHECK YOUR READING What is the standard unit of mass?

Measuring Volume by Formula

Bowling balls, boxes, and many other objects have regular, defined shapes. It is easy to calculate the volume by substituting values you measure into a mathematical formula. To find the volume of a rectangular solid, you measure the length, the width, and the height. Then you substitute these values into the formula for a rectangular solid.

Volume = length • width • height

$$V = lwh$$

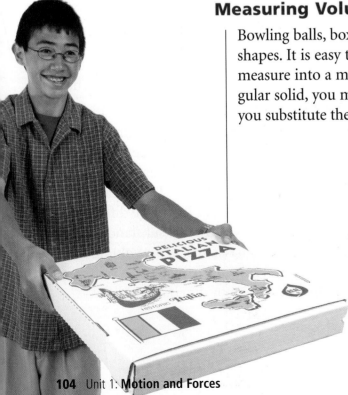

Suppose you had a pizza box that had a length of 40 cm, a width of 40 cm, and a height of 8 cm. To find the volume multiply the length, width, and height together. The pizza box has a volume of 40 cm • 40 cm • 8 cm = 12,800 cubic centimeters (cm^3). You can also find the volume of a rectangular solid or a regular prism by multiplying the area times the height ($V = A • h$).

Formulas help you find the volume of other regular shapes, such as spheres and cylinders. All the measurements used in a volume formula must be made in the same length units. The units for volume are often expressed in terms of cubic units, that is, a length to the third power, such as meters or centimeters cubed.

Measuring Volume by Displacement

Not all objects have a regular shape. There is no simple formula for calculating the volume of something with an irregular shape. Instead, you can make use of a simple fact: two objects cannot take up the same space at the same time. This method of measuring is called displacement. That is because the object being measured displaces, or takes the place of, liquid in a container during the measurement process. The process is described below.

❶ Add water to a graduated cylinder. Note the volume.

❷ Submerge the object in the water. The water level goes up. Note the new volume of the water with the object in it.

❸ Subtract the volume of the water before the object was added (found in step 1) from the volume of the water and the object together (found in step 2). The difference is the volume of the object. The object displaces a volume of water equal to the volume of the object.

The volume of a liquid is often measured in milliliters (mL). One milliliter of water has a volume of one cubic centimeter. Milliliters and cubic centimeters are equivalent. In other words, $1 \text{ mL} = 1 \text{ cm}^3$.

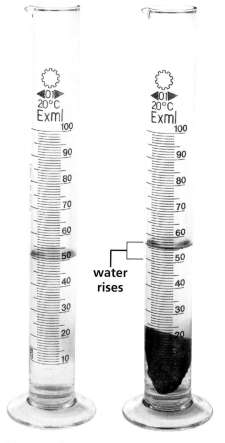

water rises

Measure the volume of water without the rock.

Measure the volume of water with the rock in it.

Density is mass divided by volume.

As discussed earlier, a bowling ball and a basketball are about the same size. But the bowling ball has a much greater mass. This example can help you understand the concept of density. **Density** is a measure of the amount of matter present in a given volume of a substance. Density describes how closely packed matter is. The bowling ball is much denser than the basketball.

Density depends on both the mass and the volume of an object. If you cut a bar of gold in half, you would have two bars with half the mass of the original bar. However, each bar would also have half the volume of the original bar. The density of gold does not change. The density of a substance does not depend on how much of it you have. A bar of gold and a nugget of gold have the same density.

RESOURCE CENTER
CLASSZONE.COM

Learn more about density.

Calculating Density

MAIN IDEA WEB
Use a main idea web to take notes on how mass, volume, and density are related.

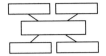

The density of any substance or object can be found in the same way: divide the total mass of the object by the total volume of the object. Although you might need to use different methods to find the volume or the mass of different substances, you would calculate the density in the same way using this formula:

$$\textbf{Density} = \frac{\textbf{mass}}{\textbf{Volume}} \qquad D = \frac{m}{V}$$

How would you find the density of a metal fork?

1 Measure the mass of the fork. Using a pan balance, you find that this particular fork has a mass of 41 grams.

2 Find the volume of the fork. You submerge the fork in water and measure the displacement as 5.2 milliliters. This means the fork has a volume of 5.2 cubic centimeters.

3 Calculate the density using the mass and the volume you measured. The metal fork has a density of 41 g divided by 5.2 cm^3, or 7.9 g/cm^3.

Notice that the units are grams per centimeter cubed, or g/cm^3. Density is often measured in these units.

Calculating Density

▶ Sample Problem

A plastic fork has a mass of 5 g and a volume of 5.2 cm^3. What is the density of the plastic fork?

What do you know?	mass = 5 g; volume = 5.2 cm^3
What do you want to find out?	Density
Write the formula:	$D = \dfrac{m}{V}$
Substitute into the formula:	$D = \dfrac{5\ g}{5.2\ cm^3}$
Calculate and simplify:	$D = 0.96$ g/cm^3
Check that your units agree:	Unit is g/cm^3.
	Unit of density is g/cm^3. Units agree.
Answer:	$D = 0.96$ g/cm^3.

▶ Practice the Math

1. A lead sinker has a mass of 227 g and a volume of 20 cm^3. What is the density of lead?

2. A glass of milk has a volume of 100 cm^3 and a mass of 103 g. What is the density of this type of milk?

Comparing Densities

The table lists densities of some common substances. At any given temperature, the density of a substance remains constant. For this reason, scientists can use density to identify particular substances.

Note that the density of a substance does not depend on the amount of the substance that you have. Suppose you have a sheet of thick aluminum foil. You calculate the density as 2.7 g/cm^3. You cut the aluminum foil equally into three smaller sheets. Each sheet has a third the volume but also has a third the mass. The density, which depends on both the volume and the mass, does not change. The density of each of the smaller sheets of aluminum foil is still 2.7 g/cm^3. No matter how you divide the aluminum foil, a smaller sheet will have the same density as the original sheet.

Densities of Common Substances	
Substance	**Density (g/cm³)**
Mercury	13.60
Lead	11.34
Aluminum	2.70
Bone	1.85
Milk (whole)	1.03
Seawater	1.03
Water	1.00
Ice	0.92
Gasoline	0.73
Cork	0.24

Aerogel, shown here floating on soap bubbles, is about 330 times less dense than water and only 2.5 times denser than air.

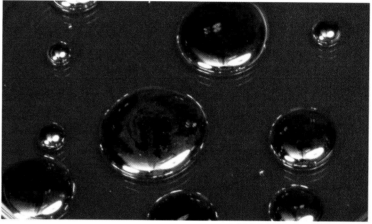

Mercury is 13.6 times denser than water.

4.1 Review

KEY CONCEPTS

1. Describe a way to measure mass and a way to measure volume. (8.8.a)

2. How are mass and volume related to density? (8.8.a)

3. An object is made of a single substance. How can knowing the density of the object help you identify what the object is made of? (8.8.a)

CRITICAL THINKING

4. **Infer** A metal fork has a density of 7.8 g/cm^3. Is this fork made of aluminum? Explain your answer.

5. **Calculate** A glass marble has a volume of 5 cm^3 and a mass of 13 g. What is the density of the marble?

○ CHALLENGE

6. **Analyze** You have a bucket half full of ice. You find that the ice has a density of 0.92 g/cm^3. You fill the bucket completely with ice. What will happen to the density of the ice? What will happen to the density of the substance when the ice melts?

CHAPTER INVESTIGATION

Density

OVERVIEW AND PURPOSE In order for scientists around the world to communicate with one another about calculations in their research, they use a common system of measurement called the metric system. Scientists use the same tools and methods for the measurement of length, mass, and volume. In this investigation you will

- use a ruler, a graduated cylinder, and a balance to measure the mass, volume, and density of different objects
- determine which method is best for measuring the volume of the objects

MATERIALS
- small rock
- 5 pennies
- rectangular sponge
- tissue box
- beam balance
- large graduated cylinder
- water
- ruler

8.8.a, 8.8.b, 8.9.f

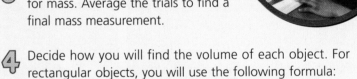

▶ **Procedure**

1. Make a data table like the one shown on the sample notebook page.

2. Measure the mass of each object: rock, pennies, sponge, and tissue box. Record each mass.

step 2

3. For each object, conduct three trials for mass. Average the trials to find a final mass measurement.

4. Decide how you will find the volume of each object. For rectangular objects, you will use the following formula:

Volume = length · width · height

For irregular objects, you will use the displacement method and the following formula:

Volume of object = volume of water with object – volume of water without object

Content Standard
8.8.b Students know how to calculate the density of substances (regular and irregular solids and liquids) from measurements of mass and volume.

Investigation Standard
8.9.f Apply simple mathematic relationships to determine a missing quantity in a mathematic expression, given the two remaining terms (including speed = distance/time, density = mass/volume, force = pressure • area, volume = area • height).

5 For rectangular objects, use metric units for measuring the length, width, and height. Record the measurements in your data table.

step 5

6 For irregular objects, fill the graduated cylinder about half full with water. Record the exact volume of water in the cylinder. **Note:** The surface of the liquid will be curved in the graduated cylinder. Read the volume of the liquid at the bottom of the curve, called the meniscus.

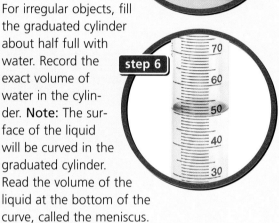
step 6

7 Carefully place the object you are measuring into the cylinder. The object must be completely under the water. Record the exact volume of water in the cylinder containing the object by reading the meniscus.

8 For each object, conduct three trials for measuring volume. Average the trials to find a final volume measurement.

▶ Observe and Analyze
Write It Up

1. **RECORD OBSERVATIONS** Make sure you have filled out your data table completely.

2. **ANALYZE** Using the average mass and average volume for each object, calculate the average density of each object. Record your densities in a table.

3. **INTERPRET** For each object, explain why you chose the particular method for measuring the volume.

4. **INFER** Which objects were the least dense? What did these objects have in common?

▶ Conclude

Write It Up

1. **IDENTIFY LIMITS** Which sources of error might have affected your measurements?

2. **APPLY** How would the density of a wet sponge compare to the density of a dry sponge?

3. **APPLY** If someone wanted to know the density of cardboard, would you give the person your results for the tissue box? Why or why not?

▶ INVESTIGATE Further

CHALLENGE A tablespoon of salt contains both salt and air. How might you find the density of salt alone? Note that the volume of the salt alone cannot be found by displacing water because salt dissolves in water.

Density

Observe and Analyze

Table 1. Masses of Various Objects

| Object | Mass (g) | | | |
	Trial 1	Trial 2	Trial 3	Average
rock				
5 pennies				

Table 2. Volumes of Various Objects

| Object | Method Used | Volume (cm³ or mL) | | | |
		Trial 1	Trial 2	Trial 3	Average
rock					
5 pennies					

Table 3. Densities of Various Objects

Object	Avg. Mass (g)	Avg. Volume (cm³)	Density (g/cm³)
rock			
5 pennies			

KEY CONCEPT

4.2 Pressure in a fluid varies with depth.

CALIFORNIA
Content Standard

Background for
8.8.c Students know the buoyant force on an object in a fluid is an upward force equal to the weight of the fluid the object has displaced.

BEFORE, you learned

- The net force is the sum of all forces acting on an object
- Volume is a measure of the amount of space a material takes up

NOW, you will learn

- How pressure and force are related
- How fluids exert pressure
- How fluid pressure changes with density and depth

VOCABULARY

pressure p. 110
pascal p. 110

THINK ABOUT

Why do your ears pop sometimes?

Imagine you are in a car that is going up and down the hill in the photograph. As you ride over the hill, your ears might hurt a little, or even pop. Why does this happen? The answer has to do with slight changes in air pressure.

Pressure describes how a force is spread over an area.

MAIN IDEA WEB
Use a main idea web to take notes on pressure.

Pressure is a measure of how much force is acting on a certain area. In other words, pressure describes how concentrated a force is. When a cat lies down on your lap, the entire force of the cat's weight is spread out over a large area on your lap. If the cat stands up, however, the entire force of the cat's weight is concentrated at its four paws. The cat exerts more pressure on you.

While the increased pressure may make you feel as if there is more force on you, the size of the force actually remains the same. The force is the cat's weight. When the cat stands up, its weight is simply pressing on a smaller area. You notice the increase in pressure.

Pressure is measured in units called **pascals** (Pa). One pascal is the pressure exerted by one newton (1 N) of force on an area of one square meter (1 m^2). One pascal is equivalent to one newton per square meter, or N/m^2.

Pressure acts in all directions in fluids.

Fluids are made of a large number of very small particles, much too small to see. These particles are in constant, rapid motion. They bump into one another. They bump into the walls of any container that holds them. They bump into objects in the fluid.

As the particles of a fluid bump into an object in the fluid, they apply forces to the object. The forces, acting over the object's surface, exert pressure on the object. When the pressure in a fluid increases, the particles bump together more frequently. This increases the pressure on objects in the fluid.

The pressure a fluid exerts on an object in the fluid is applied in all directions. That is because the particles that make up the fluid can move in any direction. These particles exert forces as they bump into objects in the fluid. The picture shows how water exerts pressure on a diver who is underwater. Notice that the arrows point in different directions. That is because the water is pressing all around the diver, not just from above.

VISUALIZATION
CLASSZONE.COM
Explore how a fluid produces pressure.

 CHECK YOUR READING How does understanding particle motion help you to understand pressure?

Pressure in Fluids

Randomly moving water molecules collide with a diver. The net force from the many collisions produces the pressure on the diver.

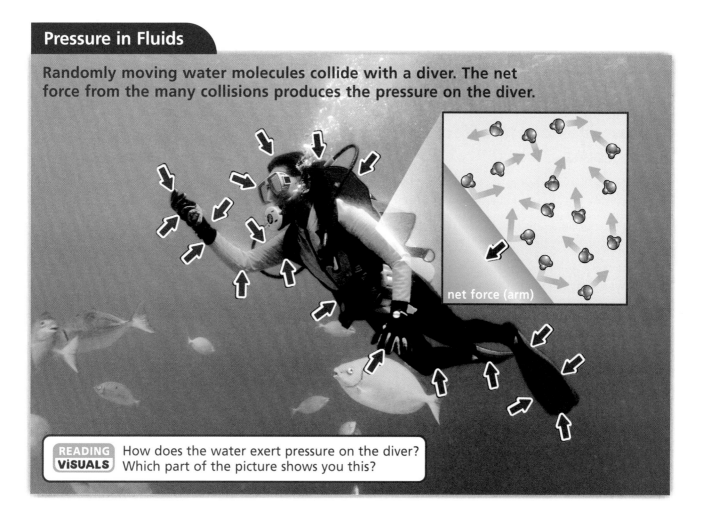

net force (arm)

READING VISUALS How does the water exert pressure on the diver? Which part of the picture shows you this?

Fluid pressure depends on density and depth.

READING TiP

The word *depth* comes from the word *deep*.

The pressure that a fluid exerts depends on the density and the depth of the fluid. Imagine that you have a tall cylinder of water balanced on the palm of your hand. You feel the base of the cylinder exert a pressure on your hand. Now suppose that you start filling the cylinder with water. Almost immediately, you become aware of the increased pressure the cylinder now puts on your hand. As you add more water, the pressure of the cylinder increases even more.

Pressure and Density

Oil is less dense than water. Would you expect the cylinder to exert the same pressure on your hand if you filled it with oil instead of water? How would the height of oil in the cylinder affect the pressure?

Because oil is not as dense as water, a container full of oil weighs less than the same container full of water does. The force causing the pressure is the weight of the fluid. A cylinder full of oil exerts less pressure on your hand than a cylinder full of water does. The denser a fluid is, the more pressure it will exert on objects in it.

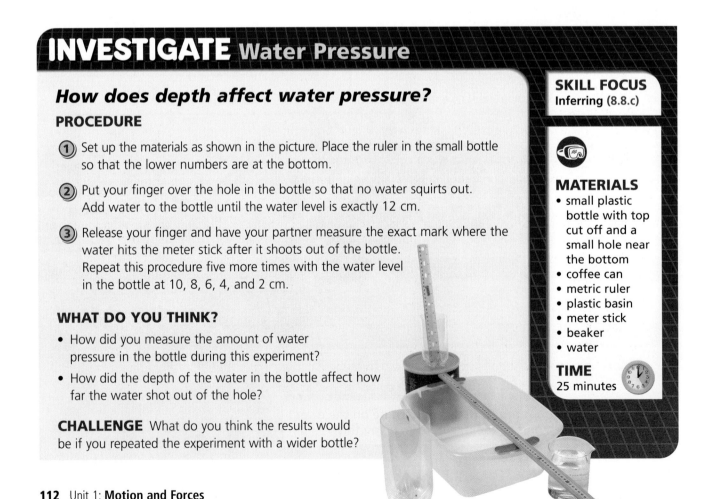

INVESTIGATE Water Pressure

How does depth affect water pressure?

PROCEDURE

1. Set up the materials as shown in the picture. Place the ruler in the small bottle so that the lower numbers are at the bottom.

2. Put your finger over the hole in the bottle so that no water squirts out. Add water to the bottle until the water level is exactly 12 cm.

3. Release your finger and have your partner measure the exact mark where the water hits the meter stick after it shoots out of the bottle. Repeat this procedure five more times with the water level in the bottle at 10, 8, 6, 4, and 2 cm.

WHAT DO YOU THINK?

- How did you measure the amount of water pressure in the bottle during this experiment?

- How did the depth of the water in the bottle affect how far the water shot out of the hole?

CHALLENGE What do you think the results would be if you repeated the experiment with a wider bottle?

SKILL FOCUS
Inferring (8.8.c)

MATERIALS
- small plastic bottle with top cut off and a small hole near the bottom
- coffee can
- metric ruler
- plastic basin
- meter stick
- beaker
- water

TIME
25 minutes

Water Pressure and Depth

Pressure in fluids increases with depth. Think back to the example of the cylinder sitting on the palm of your hand. You slowly pour water into the cylinder. At first, when the water level is very low, you feel very little pressure on your palm. As you add more water, the pressure you feel increases. The more water you add, the stronger the pressure you feel.

If a cylinder of water were resting on your palm, you would feel the pressure of the water pushing down on an area of your hand. The deeper the water column, the greater the pressure. Now imagine going swimming in a deep pool. The pool is just like a large column of water. When you swim, water pressure acts not just on part of your hand, but on your entire body. However, the principle remains the same. The more water that pushes on you from above, the greater the pressure you feel.

At the surface of the pool, you sense very little water pressure. That is because only a very small amount of water pushes down on you there. Suppose you dive under water. The deeper you dive, the more pressure you feel. You are feeling the weight of more and more water pressing on you.

CHECK YOUR READING If you dove to the bottom of a pool, why would you feel more pressure there than near the surface?

A deep-diving whale at 1000 meters (3280 ft) below the surface experiences about 34 times more pressure than a turtle diving to a depth of 20 meters (65 ft).

Water pressure increases with the depth of the water. This is because the weight of the column of water above the object increases. But a large, shallow pond may have more water in it than a small, deep pond. Why doesn't water pressure depend on the volume of water?

Pressure is determined by force and the area over which that force acts. Suppose two ponds are the same depth. One pond has twice the water of the other pond, so it is twice as large in area. The water in the large pond presses on an object with twice the weight of the water in the small pond. However, the large pond applies that force over twice the area. The result is that the pressure is the same at the bottom of a large pond as it is at the bottom of a small pond.

The water pressure at a given depth does not depend on the shape of the container. Suppose you fill a cylinder, a bowl, and a tube with twists and turns in it all to the same height with water. The water pressure at the bottom of each of these containers will be exactly the same. Depth is what determines the pressure for any given fluid.

decreasing pressure

A person at an altitude of 2000 meters experiences approximately 20 percent less pressure than a person at sea level.

Air Pressure and Elevation

Wherever you are on Earth, you are at the bottom of a huge, deep ocean of air. That ocean is the atmosphere. The air in the atmosphere presses down on you all the time. At sea level, it exerts a pressure of about 100,000 pascals.

In air, as in water, pressure varies with depth. Less depth means less pressure. Therefore, as you go up in elevation, or height, air pressure decreases. For example, if you were at the top of a high mountain, you would have less air pushing down on you than you would if you were at sea level. Both air and water are fluids. However, air is different from water because air is a gas. Water particles are very close together. As the pressure on water increases, the particles get a little closer together, but they cannot be squeezed together much. Air, on the other hand, has particles that are very far apart. As the pressure increases, the particles in air are pushed closer together. As the pressure decreases, the particles move farther apart.

When air pressure is lower, as at the top of a mountain, you get less air with each breath you take. At the top of Mount Everest, Earth's highest mountain, air pressure is one-third of what it is at sea level. With air pressure so low, many people have trouble breathing and thinking. That is one reason that many mountaineers breathe oxygen from tanks as they climb high mountains.

Differences in air pressure help explain why your ears might pop as you drive up and down steep hills. The air pressure inside your ears might be higher than the air pressure outside your ears. You feel your ears pop as the pressure inside your ears drops, becoming equal to the pressure outside your ears.

 CHECK YOUR READING   How are air pressure and water pressure similar? How do they differ?

4.2 Review

KEY CONCEPTS

1. How is pressure related to force and to area?
2. Describe the reason a fluid exerts pressure on an object immersed in the fluid.
3. How does changing depth affect water pressure?

CRITICAL THINKING

4. **Interpret** Would water pressure be the same at the same depth in two containers that had very different shapes? Explain.
5. **Infer** What is likely to happen if a balloon that was blown up at a low altitude is brought to a high altitude? Why would this occur?

⬥ CHALLENGE

6. **Synthesize** To explore the deepest parts of the ocean, scientists have to design special underwater vehicles. Why do these vehicles need to be extremely strong?

MATH TUTORIAL
CLASSZONE.COM
Click on Math Tutorial for help with solving for variables in formulas.

Math 7.AF.1
Science 8.9.f

SKILL: USING FORMULAS

Underwater Forces

Because pressure varies with depth, the pressure exerted on a diving dolphin varies. As a dolphin dives down nose first, the water pressure is slightly greater at the dolphin's head than at the dolphin's tail. Suppose you know the pressure on and the area of a surface that is in a fluid. You can then calculate the force acting on it, using the formula **Force = Pressure • Area,** or **F = PA.** You can use this formula to compare the forces acting on the top and bottom of an object.

Example

A cylinder is tied to the bottom of a container as shown. The area of each circular end is 0.25 m². The water pressure at the top of the cylinder is 110,000 N/m². The water pressure at the bottom of the cylinder is 120,000 N/m². How much greater is the force on the bottom than the force on the top?

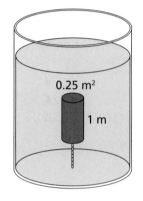

0.25 m²
1 m

(1) In order to find the difference, you must find the force on the top and the force on the bottom. Substitute the values for pressure and area into the equation, and find the two forces.

F (top) = Pressure • Area (top) =
110,000 N/m² • 0.25 m² = 27,500 N
F (bottom) = Pressure • Area (bottom) =
120,000 N/m² • 0.25 m² = 30,000 N

(2) Find the difference between the two forces. Notice that the force on the bottom is larger than the force on the top.

30,000 N − 27,500 N = 2,500 N

ANSWER The force on the bottom of the cylinder is 2500 N greater than the force on the top of the cylinder.

Use the information in each problem to find the difference between the force at the top and bottom of the cylinder above.

1. The cylinder has been placed in oil. The pressure on the top of the cylinder is 109,000 N/m² and the pressure on the bottom of the cylinder is 118,000 N/m².

2. The cylinder is in a liquid called glycerin. The pressure on the top of the cylinder is 112,600 N/m², and the pressure on the bottom of the cylinder is 125,200 N/m².

CHALLENGE In air, the difference in force between the top and the bottom of the cylinder is 0.0003 N. If the pressure at the bottom is 100,000 N/m³, what is the pressure at the top?

4.3 The buoyant force acts on objects in fluids.

CALIFORNIA Content Standards

8.8.c Students know the buoyant force on an object in a fluid is an upward force equal to the weight of the fluid the object has displaced.

8.8.d. Students know how to predict whether an object will float or sink.

VOCABULARY

buoyant force p. 117

BEFORE, you learned

- Objects immersed in water displace some of the water
- Pressure acts in all directions on objects immersed in a fluid and varies with depth
- Density is mass divided by volume

NOW, you will learn

- About the buoyant force
- How fluid displacement relates to buoyant force
- What determines if an object sinks or floats

EXPLORE Forces in Liquid (8.8.c)

How does water affect weight?

PROCEDURE

① Tie a piece of string to the middle of the pencil. Tie 4 paper clips to a string on each end of the pencil as shown.

② Move the middle string along the pencil until the paper clips are balanced and the pencil hangs parallel to the table.

③ While keeping the pencil balanced, slowly lower the paper clips on one end of the pencil into the water. Observe what happens.

MATERIALS
- 3 pieces of string
- pencil
- 8 paper clips
- cup full of water

WHAT DO YOU THINK?
- How did the water affect the balance between the two sets of paper clips?
- Did the water exert a force on the paper clips? Explain.

Fluids exert an upward force on objects.

If you drop an ice cube into a glass of water, the ice cube may sink a little bit at first, but it will quickly rise and float at the surface of the water. Ice isn't the only thing that floats in water. Most people can float in water. Plastic bags, cork, and many types of wood also float.

If you drop an ice cube, a plastic bag, a cork, or a piece of wood in air, each of them will fall quickly to the ground. What causes an object to fall in air but float in water? Gravity acts with the same force whether the object is in air or in water. It pulls all objects downward. When an object floats, a force pushes up on the object. The force acts against the downward force of gravity. It is called the buoyant force.

The Buoyant Force

READING TiP
The verb *buoy* means "to keep afloat." A buoy is a float moored in water to mark a location.

The **buoyant force** is the upward force a fluid exerts on any object in the fluid. This force is also sometimes referred to as buoyancy. All objects in a fluid, whether they float or not, experience a buoyant force. However, an object that is actually floating is called a buoyant object.

The buoyant force exists because of pressure differences in fluids. Remember that in any fluid, pressure varies with depth. The greater the depth, the greater the pressure the fluid exerts.

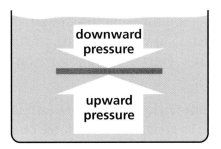
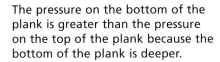

The pressure on the bottom of the plank is greater than the pressure on the top of the plank because the bottom of the plank is deeper.

The difference in pressure produces a net upward force on the plank.

In the diagram above, a thin plank of wood has been pushed underwater. Even a very small difference in pressure between the top and bottom of the plank produces a net upward force on the plank. This is the buoyant force on the plank. If the plank were thicker, there would be a greater difference in depth between the top and the bottom. The greater depth difference would produce a greater buoyant force.

 CHECK YOUR READING Why is the water pressure on the bottom of an object greater than on the top of the object?

Because pressure acts in all directions in a fluid, there is a net upward force no matter what shape the submerged object has. The photograph on the right shows a balloon in a beaker of water. The force due to water pressure acts on the surface of the balloon, as shown by the arrows. As the depth increases, a greater force acts on the surface of the balloon.

The forces due to water pressure are exerted in different directions because of the shape of the surface. It is the net force on the balloon, however, that determines the buoyant force. Notice that the force arrows get longer as the water gets deeper. The length of the arrow represents the size of the force. The sideways forces on the balloon balance and cancel each other out. The upward force on the balloon, however, is greater than the downward force. This difference produces a net upward force—the buoyant force.

Buoyancy in Gases

Seeing ice cubes float in a glass of water is a common experience. You've probably had other experiences with the buoyant force that liquids can exert. These might include swimming, boating, bathing, and even washing dishes by hand.

Like water, air is a fluid. Air also exerts a buoyant force. You are observing the buoyant force in air when you watch a helium balloon float up to the ceiling. When a passenger balloon floats up into the air, the buoyant force is in action as well. All fluids, whether they are liquids or gases, exert a buoyant force on the objects in the fluid.

Generally, we do not notice the buoyant force of air. Air does not produce as great a buoyant force on an object as water does. The buoyant force that air produces on familiar objects is usually far smaller than the weight of the object. Balloons like the one in the photograph can carry passengers because they have a buoyant force acting on them that is greater than the weight of the balloon and the passengers together.

INVESTIGATE Buoyancy

Do fluids experience a buoyant force?

PROCEDURE

1. Carefully pour water into the cup until it is about 2/3 full. Put a few drops of food coloring into the cup of water and stir.

2. Carefully pour the vegetable oil into the cup until there is a thick layer of oil on top of the water. Observe and record what happens to the oil after you pour it in.

3. Use the spoon to sprinkle some salt into the cup. Watch the cup for a short time. Observe and record what happens.

4. Repeat step 3 several times, varying the amount of salt you use. Record your observations.

WHAT DO YOU THINK?

- What happened to the oil when you added the salt?
- What do you think was happening to the salt and the oil during steps 3 and 4?
- What role did buoyant forces play in what happened?

CHALLENGE How might you test your explanation of what was happening?

SKILL FOCUS
Observing (8.8.c)

MATERIALS
- food coloring
- water
- clear plastic cup
- vegetable oil
- plastic spoon
- salt

TIME
20 minutes

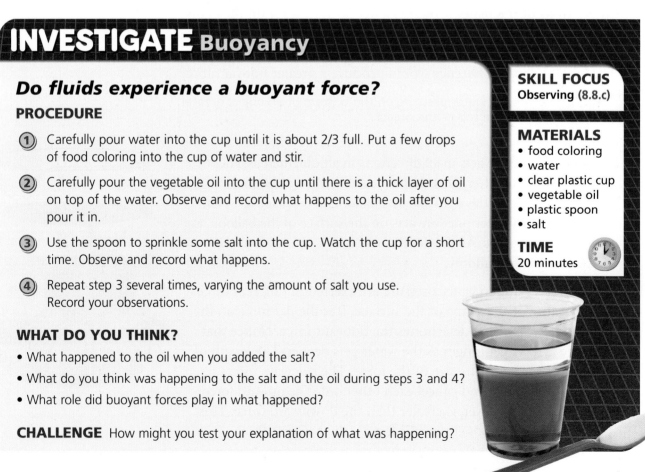

The size of the buoyant force equals the weight of the displaced fluid.

Think back to the method for measuring the volume of an object with an irregular shape. This involves placing the object in a known volume of a liquid, usually water. The level of the liquid rises. By measuring the rise in the liquid level, you can figure out the volume of the submerged object. This method works because the object displaces some of the liquid.

Archimedes' Principle

More than 2000 years ago, a Greek scientist named Archimedes was trying to understand forces that act on objects when they are placed in water. He discovered that there was a connection between the amount of water an object displaced when it was submerged and the buoyant force. The buoyant force is equal to the weight of the displaced water. This fact is often called Archimedes' principle, after its discoverer.

Suppose you fill a beaker to the very top with water. What would happen if you placed a marble into the beaker? Water would spill over the edge of the beaker as the marble displaced the water in the beaker. If you collected the spilled water in a container and weighed it, you would know the buoyant force on the object.

The strength of the buoyant force acting on an object depends in part on the fluid the object is placed into. You can see this easily with Archimedes' principle. Corn syrup is denser than water. If you dropped a marble into a beaker of corn syrup, it would displace the same amount of corn syrup as it would water. However, the displaced corn syrup would weigh more than the same amount of displaced water. The buoyant force due to corn syrup is greater than the buoyant force due to water.

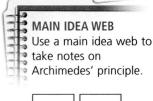

MAIN IDEA WEB
Use a main idea web to take notes on Archimedes' principle.

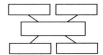

buoyant force (water)

buoyant force (corn syrup)

Floating and Sinking

How can you determine if an object in a fluid will float or sink? You must compare the buoyant force pushing the object upward with the downward force of gravity, or weight of the object. If the two are equal, the object will neither rise nor sink. If the weight is greater, the object will sink. If the buoyant force is greater, the object will rise to the surface and float. An object floating on the surface of a liquid has no net force on it.

CALIFORNIA
Focus

The giant octopus, whose habitat ranges from California to Asia, is a relative of the nautilus. Like the nautilus, it uses jet propulsion to move around.

A sea animal called a nautilus moves mostly by shooting water out in a jet through a part of its body that is like a funnel. In order to move effectively, the nautilus's weight must balance the buoyant force. The nautilus moves best when it does not rise or sink. The nautilus adjusts its buoyancy by changing how much water or gas fills its shell.

1 If the nautilus weighs less than the buoyant force, it tends to float upward. The nautilus can increase its density by sucking water into its shell. This water is transferred to the shell chambers by a tube called the siphuncle.

2 When the nautilus weighs more than the buoyant force, it tends to sink downward. The nautilus decreases its density by removing water from the chambers in its shell.

The buoyant force depends on the volume of an object, and the weight depends on the mass of the object. Recall that density is mass per unit volume. Whether or not an object will float or sink depends on the relative densities of the object and the fluid. If the object is denser than the fluid it is in, it will sink. A glass marble placed in a beaker of water sinks to the bottom of the beaker. The buoyant force, which is equal to the weight of the water the marble displaces, is smaller than the weight of the marble. As a result, there is a net downward force on the marble. That is why the marble sinks.

 How does density determine if an object floats or sinks?

Floating and Sinking

The nautilus moves most effectively when the buoyant force on it equals its weight. It can slowly adjust its density so it does not float or sink.

net force

weight   buoyant force

① If the buoyant force is greater than the weight, the nautilus has a net force upward. In order to balance the forces, the nautilus will take more water into its shell.

Anatomy of a Nautilus

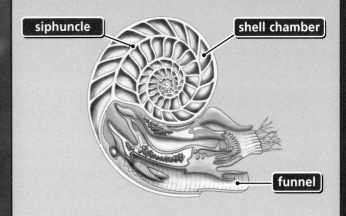

siphuncle   shell chamber

funnel

The nautilus takes water in through the funnel and transfers it to and from the chambers in its shell through the siphuncle.

weight   buoyant force

net force

② If the weight is greater than the buoyant force, the nautilus has a net force downward. To balance the forces, the nautilus will replace water in its shell with gas.

READING VISUALS What would the arrows for the buoyant force and the weight look like if there were no net force on the nautilus?

RESOURCE CENTER
CLASSZONE.COM

Find out more about
buoyancy.

Suppose an object has the same density as the fluid it is placed in. In this case, the weight of the object and the weight of the fluid the object displaces are exactly the same. The buoyant force and weight are balanced, and the object will be neutrally buoyant—it will not move unless it was already moving, or unless a force other than gravity or buoyancy acts on it.

If an object is less dense than the fluid it is in, the object will float. The volume of fluid the object displaces is actually smaller than the volume of the object itself. Therefore, part of the object will rise above the surface of the fluid. Think about an ice cube placed in water. The ice cube floats, and part of it sticks up above the water.

A nautilus changes its density so that it has neutral buoyancy. It does this by changing its mass, as it is not able to change its volume. Another way to change the density of an object is to change its volume. If you put an aluminum bar into water, it will sink because aluminum is denser than water. If, however, the same amount of aluminum is in the shape of a bowl, the bowl will float. The aluminum displaces more water as a bowl because you have increased the space the aluminum takes up. The extra space is filled with air, so the overall density of the bowl is less than the density of water. The bowl will float. This is why an aluminum canoe floats instead of sinking.

Wood (pine)
density =
0.53 g/cm^3

Soybean oil
density =
0.916 g/cm^3

Ice
density =
0.917 g/cm^3

Water
density =
1.00 g/cm^3

Steel
density =
7.9 g/cm^3

4.3 Review

KEY CONCEPTS

1. Why is there an upward force on objects in a fluid? (8.8.c)

2. Restate Archimedes' principle. (8.8.c)

3. An ice cube is dropped into a glass of water. Describe the motion of the ice cube and explain why it moves this way. (8.8.d)

CRITICAL THINKING

4. **Draw Conclusions** What two things determine whether a particular object will float or sink in a particular fluid?

5. **Predict** A graduated cylinder contains three liquids—fresh water, salt water, and gasoline. Predict the order of the liquids, from top to bottom.

CHALLENGE

6. **Synthesize** It is common knowledge that hot air rises. Use what you have learned about density and about why materials float and sink to explain the movement of heated air.

Deep-Sea Diver

> **8.8.c** Students know the buoyant force on an object in a fluid is an upward force equal to the weight of the fluid the object has displaced.

The Monterey Submarine Canyon is one of the deepest underwater canyons in the Pacific Ocean. In some places it is more than 3600 meters (12,000 ft) deep. The region doesn't have much oxygen. The pressure of overhead water is tremendous. The canyon is a pitch-black world whose creatures have never seen sunlight. Scientists know little about some of these mysterious creatures.

Technology Helps Out

Scientists at the Monterey Bay Aquarium Research Institute are eager to learn more about life in the ocean's depths. Getting down to these depths, however, can be a problem. The pressure of the water would crush a person, even if he or she were wearing the best protective gear. Scientists, therefore, use a remotely operated vehicle, or ROV. The Monterey Bay Aquarium's ROV is named *Tiburon*. *Tiburon*'s video and still cameras send back close-up views from the ocean depths. Its remotely controlled arms allow the ROV to collect samples for further study.

A Sneaky ROV

Because motion and noise scare the fish away, *Tiburon* has to be sneaky. It must be able to sit motionless for hours. To do this, *Tiburon* must be able to control its buoyancy. As the ROV rises or sinks to different ocean depths, the water pressure varies. A variable buoyancy system on the ROV measures the changes. The

system quickly adjusts *Tiburon*'s weight so that the sub does not float up or sink down. To add weight, valves let in seawater to fill a chamber. To decrease weight, valves pump water out of the chamber. The buoyancy system is very sensitive. It responds to any slight change in the underwater pressure. Therefore, *Tiburon* can travel to any depth and then sit there quietly, observing its surroundings.

WRITING ABOUT SCIENCE

On the Internet, find out about one underwater creature or life form that was discovered by scientists at the Monterey Bay Aquarium Research Institute. Then write a news story that explains how it was discovered.

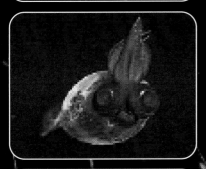
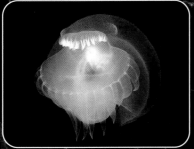

The sea creatures in these photographs are found in the Monterey Submarine Canyon.

4 Chapter Review

the BIG idea

Forces act in fluids.

CONTENT REVIEW
CLASSZONE.COM

KEY CONCEPTS SUMMARY

 Density is mass per unit volume.

- Mass is a measure of how much matter an object contains.
- Volume is a measure of how much space an object takes up.

$$\text{Density} = \frac{\text{mass}}{\text{Volume}} \qquad D = \frac{m}{V}$$

VOCABULARY
volume p. 103
density p. 105

---

2 Pressure in a fluid varies with depth.

- Pressure describes how a force is spread over an area.
- Pressure acts in all directions in fluids.
- Fluid pressure depends on density and depth.
  - Pressure increases with density.
  - Pressure increases with depth.

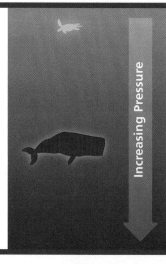

Increasing Pressure

VOCABULARY
pressure p. 110
pascal p. 110

 The buoyant force acts on objects in fluids.

- Fluids exert an upward force on objects.
- The size of the buoyant force equals the weight of the displaced fluid.

weight buoyant force
no net force

weight buoyant force
net force

VOCABULARY
buoyant force p. 117

Reviewing Vocabulary

Copy and complete the chart below.

Term	Description	Units (in metric system)
buoyant force	**1.**	**2.**
3.	mass per unit volume	**4.**
5.	**6.**	kilograms or grams
pressure	**7.**	**8.**
9.	**10.**	cubic centimeters or milliliters

Reviewing Key Concepts

Multiple Choice *Choose the letter of the best answer.*

11. To quantify how much matter a bottle of salad dressing has, you would measure (8.8.a)
  a. mass
  b. density
  c. pressure
  d. volume

12. By pouring salad dressing into a graduated cylinder and reading the markings on the side of the cylinder, you are measuring (8.8.a)
  a. mass
  b. density
  c. pressure
  d. volume

13. You can identify a pure substance if you know its (8.7.c)
  a. mass
  b. weight
  c. density
  d. buoyant force

14. A block of metal has a volume of 10 cm^3 and a mass of 193 g. What is its density? (8.8.b)
  a. 0.052 g/cm^3
  b. 5.2 g/cm^3
  c. 1.93 g/cm^3
  d. 19.3 g/cm^3

15. You are swimming under water in a swimming pool. How does water pressure change as you swim down deeper?
  a. The water starts pressing on you from all directions.
  b. The water stops pressing on you from all directions.
  c. The water pressure increases.
  d. The water pressure decreases.

16. You place two identical objects in two different fluids. One fluid is a liquid. The other fluid is a gas. Which object experiences a larger buoyant force? (8.8.c)
  a. the object in the liquid
  b. the object in the gas
  c. Both experience the same buoyant force.
  d. You can't tell unless you know what the object is.

17. With any object in a fluid, the buoyant force is equal to (8.8.c)
  a. the volume of the object
  b. the weight of the object
  c. the volume of the displaced fluid
  d. the weight of the displaced fluid

18. Ironwood is more dense than water. If you hold a piece of ironwood under water and then let go, it will (8.8.d)
  a. move upward
  b. move downward
  c. move upward then downward
  d. not move

Short Answer *Write a short answer to each question.*

19. What is the relationship between grams and kilograms?

20. Which has a greater density, a bowling ball or a soccer ball? Explain. (8.8.a)

21. Why is air pressure lower at the top of a mountain than at the bottom of a mountain?

22. Why do objects placed in fluids experience a buoyant force? (8.8.c)

Thinking Critically

Use the information in the photograph below to answer the next three questions.

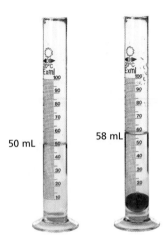

50 mL   58 mL

23. INFER One way to find the volume of a marble is by displacement. To determine a marble's volume, add 50 mL of water to a graduated cylinder. Then, place the marble in the graduated cylinder. Why does the water level change when you add the marble?

24. CALCULATE What is the volume of the marble? (8.8.a)

25. PREDICT If you carefully removed the marble and let all of the water on it drip back into the graduated cylinder, what would the volume of the water be? Explain.

26. COMMUNICATE You have a glass of ice water. You push an ice cube under the surface of the water. Explain what happens to the ice cube, referring to Archimedes' principle. (8.8.c)

27. INTERPRET You have a stick of butter that you cut up into small pieces. How does the density of the original stick of butter compare with the density of the smallest piece? Explain. (8.8.a)

28. ANALYZE Why would a denser fluid exert stronger pressure on an object in the fluid than a less dense fluid would?

29. PREDICT Ebony is a dark wood that has a density of 1.2 g/cm^3. Water has a density of 1.0 g/cm^3. Will a block of ebony float in water? Explain. (8.8.d)

30. INFER Cooking oil floats on water. What can you infer about the density of cooking oil? (8.8.d)

31. COMMUNICATE Concrete blocks help anchor a pier. Use a drawing to help explain why it would be easier to move these blocks when they are under water than when they are on the shore. (8.8.c)

Using Math Skills in Science

Complete the following calculations.

32. What is the volume of an aquarium that is 120 cm long, 60 cm wide, and 100 cm high?

33. You have three pennies. The total mass of the pennies is 6.6 grams and the total volume of the pennies is 0.74 cubic centimeters. Find the density of the pennies. (8.8.b)

34. A piece of balsa has a volume of 30 cm^3 and a mass of 3.6 g. What is the density of balsa? (8.8.b)

the BIG idea

35. SYNTHESIZE Look back at the photograph on pages 100–101. Explain how practicing under water helps astronauts prepare for a space mission.

36. PREDICT Refer to the chart on page 107. Choose one of the liquids listed in the chart. Pick five other substances from the chart. Predict whether each of the five substances would float or sink in the liquid that you chose.

UNIT PROJECTS

Evaluate all of the data, results, and information from your project folder. Prepare to present your project to the class. Be ready to answer questions posed by your classmates about your results.

Analyzing Experiments

8.8.b, 8.9.f

*Read the following description of an experiment together with the chart.
Then answer the questions that follow.*

Archimedes was a Greek mathematician and scientist who lived in the third century B.C. He figured out that any object placed in a liquid displaced a volume of that liquid equal to its own volume. He used this knowledge to solve a problem.

The king of Syracuse had been given a crown of gold. But he was not sure whether the crown was pure gold. Archimedes solved the king's problem by testing the crown's density.

He immersed the crown in water and measured the volume of water it displaced. Archimedes compared the amount of water displaced by the crown with the amount of water displaced by a bar of pure gold with the same mass. The comparison told him whether the crown was all gold or a mixture of gold and another element.

Element	Density (g/cm³)
copper	8.96
gold	19.30
iron	7.87
lead	11.34
silver	10.49
tin	7.31

1. Which problem was Archimedes trying to solve?
   a. what the density of gold was
   b. what the crown was made of
   c. what the mass of the crown was
   d. how much water the crown displaced

2. Archimedes used the method that he did because a crown has an irregular shape and the volume of such an object cannot be measured in any other way. Which one of the following objects would also require this method?
   a. a square wooden box
   b. a cylindrical tin can
   c. a small bronze statue
   d. a rectangular piece of glass

3. Suppose Archimedes found that the crown had a mass of 772 grams and displaced 40 milliliters of water. Using the formula $D = m/V$, what would you determine the crown to be made of?
   a. pure gold
   b. half gold and half another element
   c. some other element with gold plating
   d. cannot be determined from the data

4. Using the formula, compare how much water a gold crown would displace if it had a mass of 579 grams.
   a. 10 mL   **c.** 30 mL
   b. 20 mL   **d.** 193 mL

5. If you had crowns made of each element in the chart that were the same mass, which would displace more water than a gold crown of that mass?
   a. all   **c.** tin only
   b. lead only   **d.** none

Extended Response

Answer the two questions below in detail.

6. Jamal is floating on his back in a pool. When he breathes out, he sinks. When he breathes in, he floats. Explain why.

7. Why might a large, heavy piece of wood float, while a small, light stone sinks?

The Structure of Matter

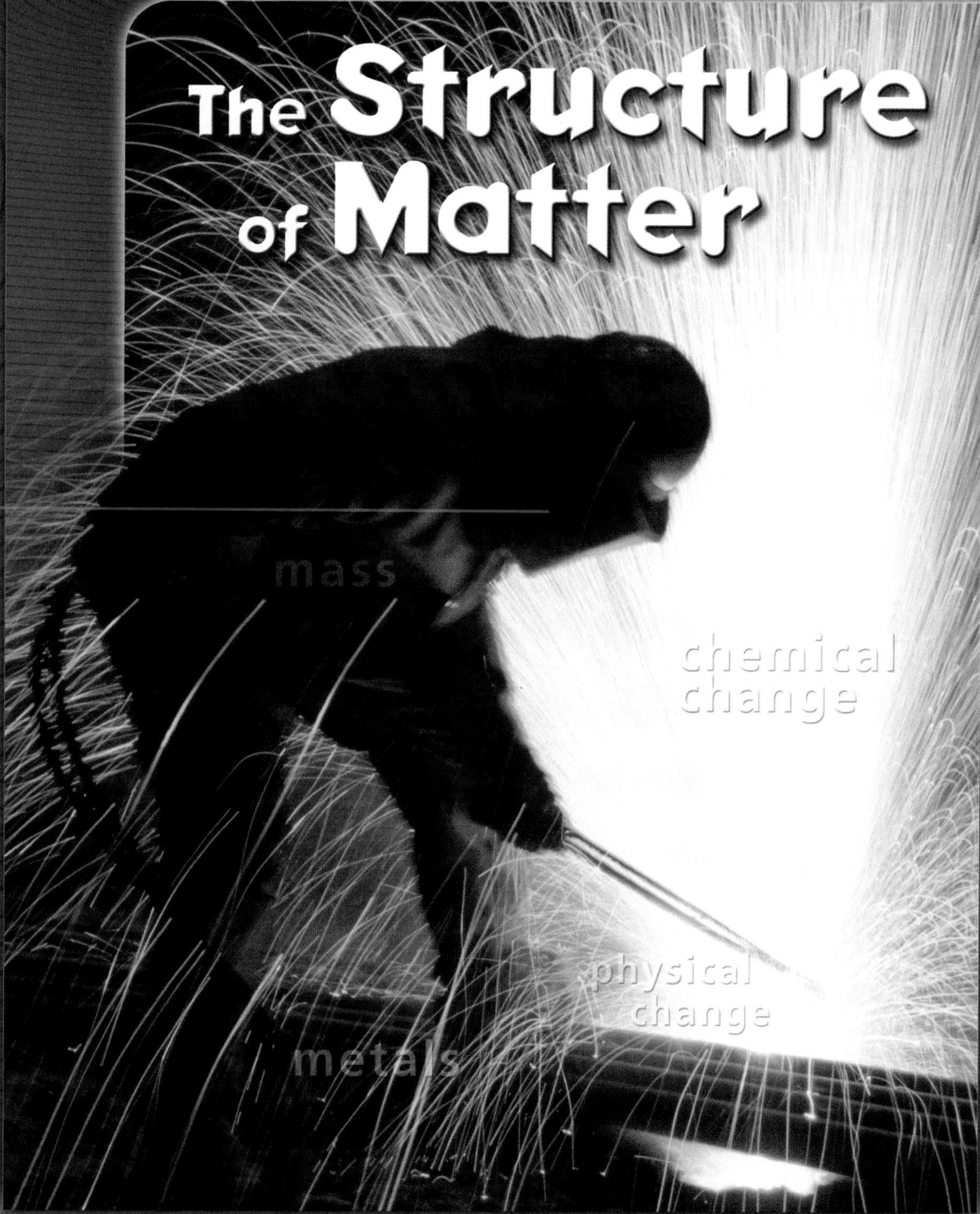

mass

chemical change

physical change

metals

Contents Overview

FUELS of the FUTURE

Where does this spacecraft get its fuel?

California Content Standards

8.2.e Students know that when the forces on an object are unbalanced, the object will change its velocity (that is, it will speed up, slow down, or change direction).

8.5.c Students know chemical reactions usually liberate heat or absorb heat.

SCIENTIFIC AMERICAN FRONTIERS

View the "Sunrayce" segment of your *Scientific American Frontiers* video to learn about a cross-country race in which cars use solar power instead of gasoline.

Deep Space 1 was an experimental design. Its successful mission prepared the way for the development of more ion-propelled spacecraft.

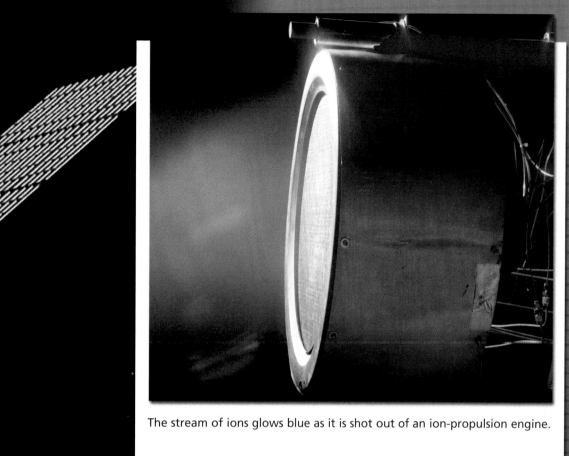

The stream of ions glows blue as it is shot out of an ion-propulsion engine.

Ion Engines for Long Voyages

Rocket engines must provide huge amounts of energy to move spacecraft away from Earth and to keep them in orbit. They get the energy from the chemical changes that occur in the fuels they carry. To get to far-off places, rocket engines need a lot of fuel. Sometimes, the fuel weighs more than the vehicles themselves. That is why scientists and engineers are always looking for more efficient ways to give spacecraft and other vehicles the energy to move.

One method of powering spacecraft uses electrically charged particles called ions. The atoms of a gas—usually xenon—are first made into ions. An electric field is then used to pull these ions out of the engine at a very high speed—faster than 100,000 kilometers per hour (62,000 mi/h). This stream of rapidly moving ions works in the same way as the gases coming out of a jet engine on a plane. They propel the spacecraft in the direction opposite to the ion stream.

An advantage of ion propulsion is that its fuel is much lighter than the chemical fuel used in rockets. Ion propulsion does not provide enough thrust to be used for a rocket launch, but it can be used to move a spacecraft through long distances in outer space. This method of propulsion provides a small force to the spacecraft; however, over time the spacecraft can reach great speeds. The space probe *Deep Space 1* was the first to use an ion engine to travel between planets.

Solar sails will reflect sunlight to move a spacecraft through space.

Running on Sunlight

Solar cells are made of a special material that can convert sunlight to electrical energy. Atoms absorb energy from the sunlight and release it as an electric current. However, once a spacecraft travels far away from the Sun—as far as the outer planets—the amount of solar energy reaching it is very small. The sunlight can be helpful only if solar cells on the vehicle can collect enough of it. One solution is to reflect sunlight. Scientists are developing solar sails that will act like enormous mirrors. The pressure of reflected sunlight on the sails can be used to move a large ship through space—even far from the Sun.

Beaming Energy from Earth

Another possible way to power a spacecraft involves no matter at all but a beam of energy sent from Earth. This idea is called beamed energy propulsion. A beam delivers energy to solar sails on the spacecraft. The energy can be in the form of microwaves—the same form of energy used to heat food in an oven or to deliver calls on a cell phone. Or it can be in the form of laser light, a very concentrated beam of visible light. This method has already been used successfully to power very small vehicles, 10 centimeters (4 in.) long.

Combined Technologies

Some recent space flights have combined common and experimental technologies. For example, the *Cassini* space probe has two regular rocket engines for propulsion. Other energy comes from three generators powered by radioactive decay. This combination of engines allowed *Cassini* to be one of the largest and most complicated spacecraft ever launched. It has sent back important data about the planet Saturn.

SCIENTIFIC AMERICAN FRONTIERS

View the "Sunrayce" segment of your *Scientific American Frontiers* video to see what is involved in solar-car racing.

IN THIS SCENE FROM THE VIDEO ▶ Students from California State University, Los Angeles, work on their solar car.

CATCHING THE SUN'S RAYS Since 1990 teams of college students have built and raced solar-powered cars. The races are held every two years to promote awareness of solar energy and to inspire young people to work in science and engineering.

Solar cells on the cars' bodies convert sunlight into electricity. The goal is to make lightweight cars that convert sunlight efficiently. Today's solar cars can reach speeds of up to 75 miles per hour, but the average racing speed is 25 miles per hour. On cloudy or rainy days, the teams conserve power by traveling more slowly—or risk running down their batteries.

In 2003 the American Solar Challenge took place on historic Route 66 from Chicago to Claremont, California. At 3700 kilometers (2300 mi), the ten-day event was the longest solar-car race in the world.

Alternative Fuels on Earth

Scientists and inventors have long been looking for practical alternative fuels to power vehicles on Earth as well as in outer space. Most vehicle engines on Earth use gasoline or other fossil fuels. These fuels are based on resources, such as petroleum, that are found in underground deposits. Those deposits will not be replaced for millions of years.

Solar energy, by contrast, is endlessly renewable. It may be a promising alternative to nonrenewable fossil fuels. In fact, a group of Dutch students built an outstanding solar powered car in 2001. The *Nuna*, as they called it, used technology once developed for space travel. The car's body was reinforced with Kevlar, a material also used in satellites, space suits, and bulletproof vests. This was one reason why the car was able to race through 3010 kilometers of Australian desert.

Another alternative fuel is hydrogen. Like sunlight, hydrogen is also endlessly renewable. It is, in fact, the most abundant substance in the universe. We have enough hydrogen as long as rain falls to Earth. Water contains hydrogen and oxygen.

But some areas do not receive adequate sunlight. And, while hydrogen is plentiful, we may spend more energy getting it than it will provide. Using alternate fuels also involves changing the way we live. Some changes are obvious and easy to do. Others may not be too clear and will take time to achieve.

UNANSWERED Questions

Even as scientists and inventors solve problems in solar energy and hydrogen fuel, new questions arise.

- Can solar technology be made affordable?
- Is hydrogen fuel practical for large-scale public transportation?
- Are there any hidden costs to the use of alternative fuels?

UNIT PROJECTS

As you study this unit, work alone or with a group on one of these projects.

Build a Solar Oven (8.5.d)

Design and build a solar oven that can boil a quarter cup of water.

- Plan and sketch a design for a solar oven that can reach 100°C.
- Collect materials and assemble your oven. Then conduct trials and improve your design.

Multimedia Presentation (8.7.c)

Create an informative program on solar race cars and the way they work.

- Collect information about solar race cars. Research how they are powered.
- Examine why solar cars are made from specific materials. Emphasize how the properties of the materials enable the car to collect solar energy.
- Give a multimedia presentation describing what you learned.

Design an Experiment (8.5.c)

Design an experiment that compares how well two of the following alternative energy sources move an object: biomass fuel from plant materials, fuel from waste materials, and hydrogen fuel cells.

- Research the energy sources, and pick two types to compare.
- List materials for your experiment. Create a data table and write up your procedure.
- Describe your experiment for the class.

 **CAREER CENTER**
CLASSZONE.COM

Learn more about careers in electrical engineering.

CHAPTER 5

Properties of Matter

the **BIG** idea

Matter is made of atoms and has observable properties.

Key Concepts

SECTION

1 Matter is made of atoms.
Learn about the movement of atoms and molecules.

SECTION

2 Matter combines to form different substances.
Learn how atoms form compounds and mixtures.

SECTION

3 Matter has observable properties.
Learn how to recognize physical and chemical properties.

 California ClassZone

CLASSZONE.COM

Chapter 5 online resources:
Content Review, Simulation,
four Resource Centers,
Math Tutorial, Test Practice

What properties could help you identify this sculpture as sugar?

EXPLORE (the BIG idea)

Where Does the Sugar Go?

> 8.5.d Students know physical processes include freezing and boiling, in which a material changes form with no chemical reaction.

Stir some sugar into a glass of water. Observe what happens. Use water at several different temperatures and observe any differences. Stir some mixtures slowly and others quickly. Observe any differences.

Observe and Think What happened to the sugar as you stirred? Do you think you would be able to separate the sugar from the water? If so, how? Can you draw any conclusions about the effects of water temperature? Can you draw any conclusions about the effects of stirring the mixture more quickly?

Internet Activity: Size of an Atom

> 8.3.a Students know the structure of the atom and know it is composed of protons, neutrons, and electrons.

Go to **ClassZone.com** to explore the smallest units of matter. Start with a faraway view of an object. Then try closer and closer views until you see that object at the atomic level.

Observe and Think Are all objects seen at faraway views made up of the same parts at an atomic level? Are there any similarities between extremely faraway views and extremely close-up views? Explain your answers.

NSTA
scilinks.org
SCiLINKS

Physical Properties of Matter **Code: MDL062**

CHAPTER 5

Getting Ready to Learn

CONCEPT REVIEW

- Matter has mass and volume.
- Each element is made of one kind of atom.

VOCABULARY REVIEW

mass p. 103

density p. 106

See Glossary for definitions.

mass

particle

substance

CONTENT REVIEW
CLASSZONE.COM

Review concepts and vocabulary.

▶ TAKING NOTES

MIND MAP

Write each main idea, or blue heading, in an oval; then write details that relate to each other and to the main idea. Organize the details so that each spoke of the web has notes about one part of the main idea.

VOCABULARY STRATEGY

Place each vocabulary term at the center of a **description wheel.** On the spokes write some words explaining it.

See the Note-Taking Handbook on pages R45–R51.

SCIENCE NOTEBOOK

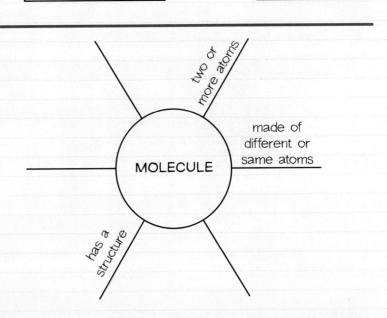

smallest basic unit of matter

basic building blocks

Two or more atoms bond to form a molecule.

Atoms are extremely small.

too small to see

do have mass

Molecule can be made of same or different atoms.

two or more atoms

made of different or same atoms

MOLECULE

has a structure

Matter is made of atoms.

CALIFORNIA
Content Standards

8.3.a Students know the structure of the atom and know it is composed of protons, neutrons, and electrons.

8.3.c Students know atoms and molecules form solids by building up repeating patterns, such as the crystal structure of NaCl or long-chain polymers.

VOCABULARY

atom p. 137
molecule p. 139

BEFORE, you learned

- Matter has mass
- Matter has volume

NOW, you will learn

- About the smallest particles of matter
- How atoms combine into molecules
- How atoms and molecules move

THINK ABOUT

How small is an atom?

All matter is made up of very tiny particles called atoms. It is hard to imagine exactly how small these particles are. Suppose that each of the particles making up the pin shown in the photograph on the right were actually the size of the round head on the pin. How large would the pin be in that case? If you could stick such a pin in the ground, it would cover about 90 square miles—about one-seventh the area of London, England. It would also be about 80 miles high—almost 15 times the height of Mount Everest.

Atoms are extremely small.

How small can things get? If you break a stone wall into smaller and smaller pieces, you would have a pile of smaller stones. If you could break the smaller stones into the smallest pieces possible, you would have a pile of atoms. An **atom** is the smallest basic unit of matter.

The idea that all matter is made of extremely tiny particles dates back to the fifth century B.C., when Greek philosophers proposed the first atomic theory of matter. All matter, they said, was made of only a few different types of tiny particles called atoms. The different arrangements of atoms explained the differences among the substances that make up the world. Although the modern view of the atom is different from the ancient view, the idea of atoms as basic building blocks has been confirmed. Today scientists have identified more than 100 different types of atoms.

VOCABULARY
Add a description wheel diagram for *atom* in your notebook.

CHECK YOUR READING What are atoms? How are they like building blocks?

Atoms

READING TiP

The word *atom* comes from the Greek word *atomos,* meaning "indivisible," or "cannot be divided."

It is hard to imagine that visible matter is composed of particles too tiny to see. Although you cannot see an individual atom, you are constantly seeing large collections of them. You are a collection of atoms. So are your textbook, a desk, and all the other matter around you. Matter is not something that contains atoms; matter is atoms. A desk, for example, is a collection of atoms and the empty space between those atoms. Without the atoms, there would be no desk—just empty space.

Atoms are so small that they cannot be seen even with very strong optical microscopes. Try to imagine the size of an atom by considering that a single teaspoonful of water contains approximately 500,000,000,000,000,000,000,000 atoms. Although atoms are extremely small, they do have a mass. The mass of a single teaspoonful of water is about 5 grams. This mass is equal to the mass of all the atoms that the water is made of added together.

INVESTIGATE Mass

How do you measure the mass of an atom?

PROCEDURE

1. Find the mass of the empty beaker. Record your result.

2. Place 10 pennies into the beaker. Find the mass of the beaker with the pennies in it. Record your result.

3. Subtract the mass of the empty beaker from the mass of the beaker with the pennies. Record your result.

4. Divide the difference in mass by 10. Record your result.

WHAT DO YOU THINK?

- What is the mass of one penny? What assumptions do you make when you answer this question?
- How might scientists use a similar process to find the mass of a single atom?

CHALLENGE All pennies may not be the same. After years of use, some pennies may have had some of their metal rubbed away. Also, the materials that make up pennies have changed. Find the individual mass of several pennies and compare the masses. Do all pennies have exactly the same mass?

SKILL FOCUS
Modeling (8.3.a)

MATERIALS
- beam balance
- beaker
- 10 pennies

TIME
20 minutes

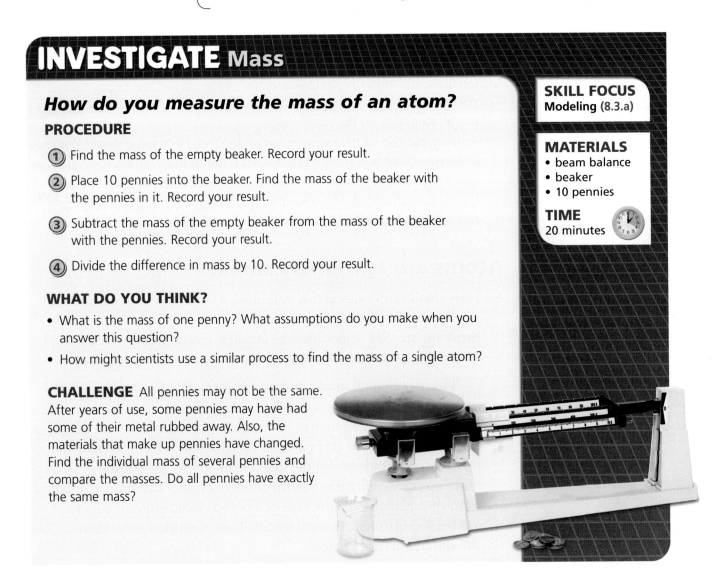

Molecules

When two or more atoms bond together, or combine, they make a particle called a **molecule.** A molecule can be made of atoms that are different or atoms that are alike. A molecule of water, for example, is a combination of different atoms—two hydrogen atoms and one oxygen atom, also written as H_2O. Hydrogen gas molecules are made of the same atom—two hydrogen atoms bonded together.

A molecule is the smallest amount of a substance made of combined atoms that is considered to be that substance. Think about what would happen if you tried to divide water to find its smallest part. Ultimately you would reach a single molecule of water. What would you have if you divided this molecule into its individual atoms of hydrogen and oxygen? If you break up a water molecule, it is no longer water. Instead, you would have hydrogen and oxygen, two different substances.

READING TiP

In this book atoms and molecules are given different colors to make them easier to identify.

CHECK YOUR READING How is a molecule related to an atom?

The droplets of water in this spider web are made of water molecules. Each molecule contains two hydrogen atoms (shown in white) and one oxygen atom (shown in red).

hydrogen — oxygen

water

Molecules can be made up of different numbers of atoms. For example, carbon monoxide is a molecule that is composed of one carbon atom and one oxygen atom. Molecules also can be composed of a large number of atoms. The most common type of vitamin E molecule, for example, contains 29 carbon atoms, 50 hydrogen atoms, and 2 oxygen atoms.

Molecules made of different numbers of the same atom are different substances. For example, an oxygen gas molecule is made of two oxygen atoms bonded together. Ozone is also composed of oxygen atoms, but an ozone molecule is three oxygen atoms bonded together. The extra oxygen atom gives ozone properties that are different from those of oxygen gas.

oxygen   **ozone**

Structure of Molecules

Molecules are very small. Even the largest molecules cannot be seen by an optical microscope. But, a molecule's shape is important. A molecule's shape has an effect on the properties of the substance.

For example, nylon is made from long molecules that look a lot like chains. We call these long-chain molecules polymers. This shape is what makes nylon flexible and stretchable. When you stretch a piece of nylon, you're actually stretching out the long-chain molecules.

The shapes of a substance's molecules also can affect the substance's boiling and melting points. For example, a substance with longer, thinner molecules probably has a higher melting point than a substance with shorter molecules. Longer molecules get tangled like strands of spaghetti. It takes more energy to break them apart.

Long-chain molecules also may make a substance a good lubricant. A lubricant is any substance that reduces friction between two surfaces. Motor oils contain long molecules made mostly of carbon and hydrogen. These molecules easily slip and slide past one another. There is little for them to get stuck on. The long molecules also can slide easily into microscopic places in the surfaces.

Making nylon is easy in the laboratory. Atomic units join together like the links of a chain.

Crystal Structure

Have you ever seen light reflected from a rock? You may have been looking at a crystal. Crystals occur when atoms combine to form repeating patterns.

Common table salt is one type of crystal. Salt contains the elements sodium and chlorine. You can think of a salt crystal as having individual sodium and chlorine units. These units build up like blocks. In the case of salt, each sodium unit attaches to one chlorine unit. The pattern gets repeated. This is what gives salt its square look.

Crystals have many uses. They can bend light waves in certain ways. Some crystals can change electrical energy into mechanical energy. All these properties depend on the crystal structure.

The regular way in which sodium and chlorine units join together is evident in the salt crystals in this photo. Most salt crystals in this photo are oddly shaped because of impurities.

This photograph shows the interior of Grand Central Terminal in New York City. Light from the window reflects off dust particles that are being moved by the motion of the molecules in air.

Atoms and molecules are always in motion.

If you have ever looked at a bright beam of sunlight, you may have seen dust particles floating in the air. If you were to watch carefully, you might notice that the dust does not fall toward the floor but instead seems to dart about in all different directions. Molecules in air are constantly moving and hitting the dust particles. Because the molecules are moving in many directions, they collide with the dust particles from different directions. This action causes the darting motion of the dust that you observe.

Atoms and molecules are always in motion. Sometimes this motion is easy to observe, such as when you see evidence of molecules in air bouncing dust particles around. Water molecules move too. When you place a drop of food coloring into water, the motion of the water molecules eventually causes the food coloring to spread throughout the water.

The motion of individual atoms and molecules is hard to observe in solid objects, such as a table. The atoms and molecules in a table cannot move about freely like the ones in water and air. However, the atoms and molecules in a table are constantly moving—by shaking back and forth, or by twisting—even if they stay in the same place.

Review

KEY CONCEPTS

1. What are atoms? (8.3.a)
2. What is the smallest particle of a substance that is still considered to be that substance? (8.3.a)
3. Why do dust particles in the air appear to be moving in different directions? (8.3.a)

CRITICAL THINKING

4. **Apply** How does tea flavor spread from a tea bag throughout a cup of hot water?
5. **Infer** If a water molecule (H_2O) has two hydrogen atoms and one oxygen atom, how would you describe the make-up of a carbon dioxide molecule (CO_2)?

○ CHALLENGE

6. **Synthesize** Assume that a water balloon has the same number of water molecules as a helium balloon has helium atoms. If the mass of the water is 4.5 times greater than the mass of the helium, how does the mass of a water molecule compare with the mass of a helium atom?

EXTREME SCIENCE

Scientists can manipulate individual atoms to build structures, such as this one made of iron atoms.

Particles Too Small to See

8.3.a Students know the structure of the atom and know it is composed of protons, neutrons, and electrons.

Atoms are so small that you cannot see them through an ordinary microscope. In fact, millions of them could fit in the period at the end of this sentence. Scientists can make images of atoms, however, using an instrument called a scanning tunneling microscope (STM).

Bumps on a Surface

The needle of the scanning tunneling microscope has a very sharp tip that is only one atom wide. The tip is brought close to the surface of the material being observed, and an electric current is applied to the tip. The microscope measures the interaction between the electrically charged needle tip and the nearest atom on the surface of the material. An image of the surface is created by moving the needle just above the surface. The image appears as a series of bumps that shows where the atoms are located. The result is similar to a contour map.

Tiny Pieces of Matter

- Images of atoms did not exist until 1970.
- Atoms are so small that a single raindrop contains more than 500 billion trillion atoms.
- If each atom were the size of a pea, your fingerprint would be larger than Alaska.

needle

material

tip of needle

atoms of material

An STM maps the position of atoms using a needle with a tip that is one atom wide.

Moving Atoms

Scientists also can use the tip of the STM needle to move atoms on a surface. The large image at left is an STM image of a structure made by pushing individual atoms into place on a very smooth metal surface. This structure was designed as a corral to trap individual atoms inside.

EXPLORE

1. **INFER** Why must the tip of a scanning tunneling microscope be only one atom wide to make an image of atoms on a surface?
2. **CHALLENGE** Find out more about images of atoms on the Internet. How are STM images used in research to design better materials?

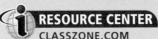

RESOURCE CENTER
CLASSZONE.COM
Find more images from scanning tunneling microscopes.

5.2 Matter combines to form different substances.

CALIFORNIA
Content Standard

8.3.b Students know that compounds are formed by combining two or more different elements and that compounds have properties that are different from their constituent elements.

VOCABULARY

element p. 144
compound p. 145
mixture p. 145

BEFORE, you learned

- Matter is made of tiny particles called atoms
- Atoms combine to form molecules

NOW, you will learn

- How pure matter and mixed matter are different
- How atoms and elements are related
- How atoms form compounds

EXPLORE Mixed Substances (8.3.b)

What happens when substances are mixed?

PROCEDURE

1. Observe and describe a teaspoon of cornstarch and a teaspoon of water.

2. Mix the two substances together in the cup. Observe and describe the result.

WHAT DO YOU THINK?

- After you mixed the substances, could you still see each substance?
- How was the new substance different from the original substances?

MATERIALS
- cornstarch
- water
- small cup
- spoon

MIND MAP
Make a mind map for the first main idea: *Matter can be pure or mixed.*

Matter can be pure or mixed.

Matter can be pure, or it can be two or more substances mixed together. Most of the substances you see around you are mixed, although you can't always tell that by looking at them. For example, the air you breathe is a combination of several substances. Wood, paper, steel, and lemonade are all mixed substances.

You might think that the water that you drink from a bottle or from the tap is a pure substance. However, drinking water has minerals dissolved in it and chemicals added to it that you cannot see. Often the difference between pure and mixed substances is apparent only on the atomic or molecular level.

A pure substance has only one type of component. For example, pure water contains only water molecules. Pure silver contains only silver atoms. Coins and jewelry that look like silver are often made of silver in combination with other metals.

If you could look at the atoms in a bar of pure gold, you would find only gold atoms. If you looked at the atoms in a container of pure water, you would find water molecules, which are a combination of hydrogen and oxygen atoms. Does the presence of two types of atoms mean that water is not really a pure substance after all?

A substance is considered pure if it contains only a single type of atom, such as gold, or a single combination of atoms that are bonded together, such as a water molecule. Because the hydrogen and oxygen atoms are bonded together as molecules, water that has nothing else in it is considered a pure substance.

Elements

One type of pure substance is an element. An **element** is a substance that contains only a single type of atom. The number of atoms is not important as long as all the atoms are of the same type. You cannot separate an element into other substances.

You are probably familiar with many elements, such as silver, oxygen, hydrogen, helium, and aluminum. There are as many elements as there are types of atoms—more than 100. You can see the orderly arrangement of atoms in the element gold, on the left below.

CHECK YOUR READING   Why is an element considered to be a pure substance?

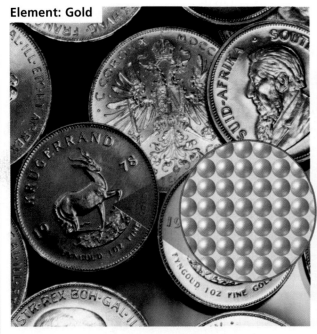

Element: Gold

The atoms in gold are all the same type of atom. Therefore, gold is an element.

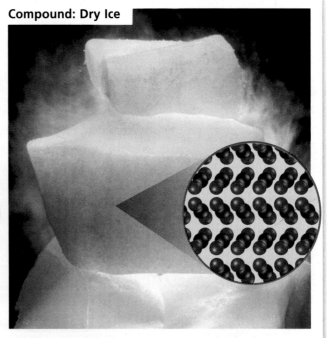

Compound: Dry Ice

Dry ice is frozen carbon dioxide, a compound. Each molecule is made of one carbon atom and two oxygen atoms.

Compounds

A **compound** is a substance that consists of two or more different types of atoms bonded together. A large variety of substances can be made by combining different types of atoms to make different compounds. Some types of compounds are made of molecules, such as water on page 139 and carbon dioxide on page 144. Other compounds are made of atoms that are bonded together in a different way. Table salt is an example.

A compound can have very different properties from the individual elements that make up that compound. Pure table salt is a common compound that is a combination of sodium and chlorine. Although table salt is safe to eat, the individual elements that go into making it—sodium and chlorine—can be poisonous.

 CHECK YOUR READING What is the relationship between atoms and a compound?

VOCABULARY
Add a description wheel diagram for *compound* to your notebook.

Mixtures

Most of the matter around you is a mixture of different substances. Seawater, for instance, contains water, salt, and other minerals mixed together. Your blood is a mixture of blood cells and plasma. Plasma is also a mixture, made up of water, sugar, fat, protein, salts, and minerals.

A **mixture** is a combination of different substances that remain the same individual substances and can be separated by physical means. For example, if you mix apples, oranges, and bananas to make a fruit salad, you do not change the different fruits into a new kind of fruit. Mixtures do not always contain the same amount of the various substances. For example, depending on how the salad is made, the amount of each type of fruit it contains will vary.

CALIFORNIA Focus

In the San Francisco and San Diego Bay areas, salt is harvested from seawater. Wind and sand cause the water to evaporate, leaving the salt behind.

APPLY In what ways can a city population be considered a mixture?

INVESTIGATE Mixtures and Compounds

How do you know a new compound has formed?

PROCEDURE

1. Place a piece of chalk into each beaker. Break the chalk if necessary so it can rest flat at the bottom of the beaker.

2. Using the masking tape, label one beaker *water* and the other beaker *vinegar*.

3. Pour water over the chalk in the beaker marked *water*. Pour vinegar over the chalk in the beaker marked *vinegar*. Be certain the chalk is completely covered in each beaker.

4. Record what happens to the chalk in each beaker.

5. Allow the liquids in both beakers to evaporate. Record your observations of the materials left behind.

MATERIALS
• 2 pieces of chalk
• 2 beakers
• water
• vinegar
• masking tape

TIME
30 minutes

WHAT DO YOU THINK?

• Which beaker contained only a mixture? Which beaker now contains a new compound?

• What might be an indication that a compound was formed?

CHALLENGE Try mixing other substances with vinegar. Can you predict which substances will behave like the chalk?

Comparing Mixtures and Compounds

RESOURCE CENTER
CLASSZONE.COM

Find out more about mixtures.

Although mixtures and compounds may seem similar, they are very different. Consider how mixtures and compounds compare with each other.

• The substances in mixtures remain the same substances. Compounds are new substances formed by atoms that bond together.

• Mixtures can be separated by physical means. Compounds can be separated only by breaking the bonds between atoms.

• The proportions of different substances in a mixture can vary throughout the mixture or from mixture to mixture. The proportions of different substances in a compound are fixed because the type and number of atoms that make up a basic unit of the compound are always the same.

CHECK YOUR READING   How is a mixture different from a compound?

Parts of mixtures can be the same or different throughout.

It is obvious that something is a mixture when you can see the different substances in it. For example, if you scoop up a handful of soil, you might see that it contains dirt, small rocks, leaves, and even insects. You can separate the soil into its different parts.

Exactly what you see depends on what part of the soil you scoop up. One handful of soil might have more pebbles or insects in it than another handful would. There are many mixtures, such as soil, that have different properties in different areas of the mixture. Such a mixture is called a hetero-geneous (HEHT-uhr-uh-JEE-nee-uhs) mixture.

In some types of mixtures, however, you cannot see the individual substances. For example, if you mix sugar into a cup of water and stir it well, the sugar seems to disappear. You can tell that the sugar is still there because the water tastes sweet, but you cannot see the sugar or easily separate it out again.

When substances are evenly spread throughout a mixture, you cannot tell one part of the mixture from another part. For instance, one drop of sugar water will be almost exactly like any other drop. Such a mixture is called a homogeneous (HOH-muh-JEE-nee-uhs) mixture. Homogenized milk is processed so that it becomes a homogeneous mixture of water and milk fat. Milk that has not been homogenized will separate—most of the milk fat will float to the top as cream while leaving the rest of the milk low in fat.

READING TIP

The prefix *hetero* means "different," and the prefix *homo* means "same." The Greek root *genos* means "kind."

5.2 Review

KEY CONCEPTS

1. What is the difference between pure and mixed matter? (8.3.b)

2. How are atoms and elements related? (8.3.b)

3. How are compounds different from mixtures? (8.3.b)

CRITICAL THINKING

4. **Infer** What can you infer about the size of sugar particles that are dissolved in a mixture of sugar and water?

5. **Infer** Why is it easier to remove the ice cubes from cold lemonade than it is to remove the sugar?

○ **CHALLENGE**

6. **Apply** A unit of sulfuric acid is a molecule of 2 atoms of hydrogen, 1 atom of sulfur, and 4 atoms of oxygen. How many of each type of atom are there in 2 molecules of sulfuric acid?

MATH TUTORIAL
CLASSZONE.COM
Click on Math Tutorial for more help with circle graphs.

Math 8.PS.8
Science 8.3.b

A Mixture of Spices

Two different mixtures of spices may contain the exact same ingredients but have very different flavors. For example, a mixture of cumin, nutmeg, and ginger powder can be made using more cumin than ginger, or it can be made using more ginger than cumin.

One way to show how much of each substance a mixture contains is to use a circle graph. A circle graph is a visual way to show how a quantity is divided into different parts. A circle graph represents quantities as parts of a whole.

Example

Make a circle graph to represent a spice mixture that is 1/2 cumin, 1/3 nutmeg, and 1/6 ginger.

(1) To find the angle measure for each sector of the circle graph, multiply each fraction in your mixture by 360°.

Cumin: $\frac{1}{2} \cdot 360° = 180°$

Nutmeg: $\frac{1}{3} \cdot 360° = 120°$

Ginger: $\frac{1}{6} \cdot 360° = 60°$

(2) Use a compass to draw a circle. Use a protractor to draw the angle for each sector.

(3) Label each sector and give your graph a title.

ANSWER

Spice Mixture

Answer the following questions.

1. Draw a circle graph representing a spice mixture that is 1/2 ginger, 1/4 cumin, and 1/4 crushed red pepper.

2. A jeweler creates a ring that is 3/4 gold, 3/16 silver, and 1/16 copper. Draw a circle graph representing the mixture of metals in the ring.

3. Draw a circle graph representing a mixture that is 1/5 sand, 2/5 crushed rock, and 2/5 salt.

CHALLENGE Dry air is a mixture of about 78 percent nitrogen, 21 percent oxygen, and 1 percent other elements. Create a circle graph representing the elements found in air.

5.3 Matter has observable properties.

CALIFORNIA
Content Standards

8.5.c Students know chemical reactions usually liberate heat or absorb heat.

8.5.d Students know physical processes include freezing and boiling, in which a material changes form with no chemical reaction.

8.7.c Students know substances can be classified by their properties, including their melting temperature, density, hardness, and thermal and electrical conductivity.

VOCABULARY

physical property p. 149
physical change p. 151
chemical property p. 154
chemical change p. 154

BEFORE, you learned

- Matter is made of atoms
- Atoms combine to form compounds

NOW, you will learn

- About physical and chemical properties
- About physical changes
- About chemical changes

EXPLORE Physical Properties (8.7.c)

How can a substance be changed?

PROCEDURE

① Observe the clay. Note its physical characteristics, such as color, shape, texture, and size.

② Change the shape of the clay. Note which characteristics changed and which ones stayed the same.

WHAT DO YOU THINK?

- How did reshaping the clay change its physical characteristics?
- How were the mass and the volume of the clay affected?

MATERIAL
rectangular piece of clay

Physical properties describe a substance.

What words would you use to describe a table? a chair? the sandwich you ate for lunch? You would probably say something about the shape, color, and size of each item. Next you might consider whether it is hard or soft, smooth or rough to the touch. Normally, when describing an object, you identify the characteristics of the object that you can observe without changing the identity of the object.

The characteristics of a substance that can be observed without changing the identity of the substance are called **physical properties.** In science, observation can include measuring and handling a substance. All of your senses can be used to detect physical properties. Color, shape, size, texture, volume, and mass are a few of the physical properties you probably have encountered.

MIND MAP
Make a mind map for the first main idea: *Physical properties describe a substance.*

 CHECK YOUR READING Describe some of the physical properties of your desk.

Physical Properties

How do you know which characteristics are physical properties? Just ask yourself whether observing the property involves changing the substance to a different substance. For example, you can stretch a rubber band. Does stretching the rubber band change what it is made of? No. The rubber band is still a rubber band before and after it is stretched. It may look a little different, but it is still a rubber band.

Mass and volume are two physical properties. Measuring these properties does not change the identity of a substance. For example, a lump of clay might have a mass of 200 grams (g) and a volume of 100 cubic centimeters (cm^3). If you were to break the clay in half, you would have two 100 g pieces of clay, each with a volume of 50 cm^3. You can bend and shape the clay too. Even if you were to mold a realistic model of a car out of the clay, it still would be a piece of clay. Although you have changed some of the properties of the object, such as its shape and volume, you have not changed the fact that the substance you are observing is clay.

> **REMINDER**
> Because all formulas for volume involve the multiplication of three measurements, volume has a unit that is cubed (such as cm^3).

CHECK YOUR READING Which physical properties listed above are found by taking measurements? Which are not?

Physical Properties

Physical properties of clay—such as volume, mass, color, texture, and shape—can be observed without changing the fact that the substance is clay.

Block of Clay

Shaped Clay

READING VISUALS COMPARE AND CONTRAST Which physical properties do the two pieces of clay have in common? Which are different?

Physical Properties of Substances

Some physical properties are specific to a substance. It makes no difference how much of the substance you have; the property does not change. Density is one such physical property. Remember, density is mass divided by volume. In the example on page 150, a 200 g piece of clay with a volume of 100 cm³ was broken in half to make two pieces, both with a mass of 100 g and a volume of 50 cm³. Each piece, however, has a density of 2 g/cm³. If you found another piece of clay with a different density, it is probably not the same type of clay.

Another physical property of a substance is color. If you have a red cloth and tear off a piece, it still remains a red cloth. The mass and the volume of the cloth change. The fact that the cloth is red, however, has not changed.

Hardness also does not depend on the amount of the substance present. Diamonds are one of the hardest substances on Earth. Denting or scratching a diamond is very difficult. A smaller diamond is as difficult to scratch as a larger diamond. This is why diamonds are often used in saws designed for precision cutting.

Physical properties such as density and hardness can help you identify substances. Mass and volume cannot. Knowing an object's density, for instance, allows you to eliminate possibilities. If it is a very high density, you would know that the substance is probably not feathers or cloth.

READING TiP

The density of solids is usually measured in grams per cubic centimeter (g/cm³). The density of liquids is usually measured in grams per milliliter (g/mL). Recall that 1 mL = 1 cm³.

Physical Changes

You have read that a physical property is any property that can be observed without changing the identity of the substance. What then would be a physical change? A **physical change** is a change in any physical property of a substance, not in the substance itself. Breaking a piece of clay in half is a physical change because it changes only the size and shape of the clay. Stretching a rubber band is a physical change because the size of the rubber band changes. The color of the rubber band sometimes can change as well when it is stretched. However, the material that the rubber band is made of does not change. The rubber band is still rubber.

What happens when water changes from a liquid into water vapor or ice? Is this a physical change? Remember to ask yourself what has changed about the material. Ice is a solid and water is a liquid, but both are the same substance—both are composed of H_2O molecules. As you will read in more detail in the next chapter, a change in a substance's state of matter is a physical change.

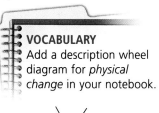

VOCABULARY
Add a description wheel diagram for *physical change* in your notebook.

 CHECK YOUR READING How is a physical change related to a substance's physical properties?

A substance can go through many different physical changes and still remain the same substance. As a matter of fact, physical changes allow us to turn something we can't use into something we can. We can change a substance without losing desirable properties. For example, wool has been used since ancient times because it is a good insulator. Yet, if we could only use it as it is when it comes off the sheep, we couldn't do much with it. Consider the physical changes that happen to wool from the time it is removed from the sheep until it becomes a sweater.

❶ Wool is sheared from the sheep. The wool is then cleaned and placed into a machine that separates the wool fibers from one another. Shearing and separating the fibers are physical changes that change the shape, volume, and texture of the wool.

❷ The wool fibers are spun into yarn. Again, the shape and volume of the wool change. The fibers are twisted so that they are packed more closely together and are intertwined with one another.

❸ The yarn is dyed. The dye changes the color of the wool, but it does not change the wool into another substance. This type of color change is a physical change.

❹ Knitting the yarn into a sweater also does not change the wool into another substance. A wool sweater is still wool, even though it no longer resembles the wool on a sheep.

It can be difficult to determine if a specific change is a physical change or not. Some changes, such as a change in color, also can occur when new substances are formed during the change. When deciding whether a change is a physical change or not, ask yourself whether you have the same substance you started with. If the substance is the same, then the changes it underwent were all physical changes.

 CHECK YOUR READING What physical properties of the wool change when it's spun?

CLASSZONE.COM

Learn about the chemical properties of matter.

Chemical properties describe how substances form new substances.

If you wanted to keep a campfire burning, would you add a piece of wood or a piece of iron? You would add wood, of course, because you know that wood burns but iron does not. Is the ability to burn a physical property of the wood? The ability to burn seems to be quite different from physical properties such as color, density, and shape. More important, after the wood burns, all that is left is a pile of ashes and some new substances in the air. The wood has obviously changed into something else. The ability to burn, therefore, must describe another kind of property that substances have—not a physical property but a chemical property.

Physical Changes

The process of turning wool into a sweater requires that the wool undergo physical changes. Changes in shape, volume, texture, and color occur as raw wool is turned into a colorful sweater.

① Shearing

Preparing the wool produces physical changes. The wool is removed from the sheep and then cleaned before the wool fibers are separated.

② Spinning

Further physical changes occur as a machine twists the wool fibers into a long, thin rope of yarn.

③ Dyeing

Dyeing produces color changes but does not change the basic substance of the wool.

④ The final product, a wool sweater, is still wool.

READING VISUALS How does the yarn in the sweater differ from the wool on the sheep?

Chemical Properties and Changes

Chemical properties describe how substances can form new substances. Combustibility, for example, describes how well an object can burn. Wood burns well and turns into ashes and other substances. Can you think of a chemical property of the metal iron? Iron rusts, especially when left outdoors in wet weather. The ability to rust is a chemical property of iron. The metal silver does not rust, but eventually a darker substance called tarnish forms on its surface.

The chemical properties of copper cause it to become a blue-green color when it is exposed to air. A famous example of tarnished copper is the Statue of Liberty. The chemical properties of bronze are different. Some bronze objects tarnish to a dark brown color.

Chemical properties can be identified by the changes they produce. The change of one substance into another substance is called a **chemical change.** A piece of wood burning, an iron fence rusting, and a silver spoon tarnishing are all examples of chemical changes. A chemical change affects the substances involved in the change. During a chemical change, combinations of atoms in the original substances are rearranged to make new substances. For example, when rust forms on iron, the iron atoms combine with oxygen atoms in the air to form a new substance that is made of both iron and oxygen.

A chemical change is also involved when an antacid tablet is dropped into a glass of water. As the tablet dissolves, bubbles of gas appear. The water and the substances in the tablet react to form new substances. One of these substances is carbon dioxide gas, which forms the bubbles that you see.

Not all chemical changes are as destructive as burning, rusting, or tarnishing. Chemical changes are also involved in cooking. When you boil an egg, for example, the substances in the raw egg change into new substances as energy is added to the egg. When you eat the egg, further chemical changes take place as your body digests the egg. The process forms new molecules that your body then can use to function.

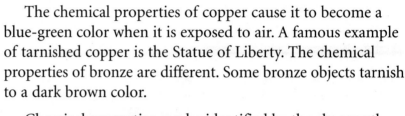

CHECK YOUR READING Give three examples of chemical changes.

The only true indication of a chemical change is that a new substance has been formed. Sometimes, however, it is difficult to tell whether new substances have been formed or not. In many cases you have to judge which type of change has occurred only on the basis of your observations of the change and your previous experience. However, some common signs can suggest that a chemical change has occurred. You can use these signs to guide you as you try to classify a change that you are observing.

INFER The bust of Abraham Lincoln is made of bronze. Why is the nose a different color from the rest of the head?

SIMULATION
CLASSZONE.COM

Explore some physical and chemical changes.

Signs of a Chemical Change

You may not be able to see that any new substances have formed during a change. Below are some signs that a chemical change may have occurred. If you observe two or more of these signs during a change, you most likely are observing a chemical change.

Production of an Odor Some chemical changes produce new smells. The chemical change that occurs when an egg is rotting produces the smell of sulfur. If you go outdoors after a thunderstorm, you may detect an unusual odor in the air. The odor is an indication that lightning has caused a chemical change in the air.

Change in Temperature Chemical changes often are accompanied by a change in temperature. You may have noticed that the temperature is higher near logs burning in a campfire.

Change in Color A change in color is often an indication of a chemical change. For example, fruit may change color when it ripens.

Formation of Bubbles When an antacid tablet makes contact with water, it begins to bubble. The formation of gas bubbles is another indicator that a chemical change may have occurred.

Formation of a Solid When two liquids are combined, a solid called a precipitate can form. The shells of animals such as clams and mussels are precipitates. They are the result of a chemical change involving substances in seawater combining with substances from the creatures.

Carbon dioxide bubbles form as substances in the antacid tablet react with water.

 CHECK YOUR READING Give three signs of chemical changes. Describe one that you have seen recently.

5.3 Review

KEY CONCEPTS

1. What effect does observing a substance's physical properties have on the substance? (8.5.d)
2. Describe how a physical property such as mass or texture can change without causing a change in the substance. (8.5.d)
3. Explain why burning is a chemical change in wood. (8.5.a)

CRITICAL THINKING

4. **Synthesize** Why does the density of a substance remain the same for different amounts of the substance?
5. **Apply** Describe how you would determine if a physical or chemical change had occurred.

CHALLENGE

6. **Infer** Iron can rust when it is exposed to oxygen. What method could be used to prevent iron from rusting?

CHAPTER INVESTIGATION

Chemical and Physical Changes

OVERVIEW AND PURPOSE Changes happen around you every day. You might observe an egg boiling in water, a sheet of paper ripping, or rust forming on the handlebars of your bike. Some of these changes are physical changes, while others are chemical changes. The difference between physical and chemical changes is not always easy to notice. Cotton candy, for example, is simply sugar melted and spun. In this investigation you will

- observe several common changes taking place
- identify physical and chemical changes

▶ Procedure

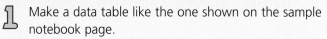

1. Make a data table like the one shown on the sample notebook page.

2. Place an ice cube in a plastic cup and let it sit for 10 minutes. Record your observations.

3. Use the metal spoon to grind a sugar cube into a fine powder. Record how the sugar has changed.

4. Pour a half spoonful of the granular sugar into a test tube. Light the candle and hold the test tube with the holder so the bottom of the test tube is just above the flame for several minutes. Be sure the top of the test tube is pointed away from you. Place the hot test tube in the test-tube rack when done. Record your observations.

5. Pour 50 mL of water into a plastic cup and add 50 mL of vinegar. Record your observations.

6. Pour 50 mL of vinegar into a plastic cup. Add a spoonful of baking soda powder. Record your observations.

MATERIALS
- ice cube
- 3 plastic cups
- metal spoon
- sugar cube
- granular sugar
- 2 test tubes
- wooden matches
- candle
- test-tube holder
- test-tube rack
- 2 50 mL beakers
- water
- vinegar
- baking soda

8.5.c, 8.9.b

Content Standard
8.5.c Students know chemical reactions usually liberate heat or absorb heat.

Investigation Standard
8.9.b Evaluate the accuracy and reproducibility of data.

7 Dispose of the material according to your teacher's instructions.

Observe and Analyze *Write It Up*

1. **RECORD OBSERVATIONS** Record all your observations about each change in your data table.

2. **ANALYZE** Identify observations that you made that would indicate a physical change has occurred.

3. **ANALYZE** Identify observations that you made that would indicate a chemical change has occurred.

4. **CLASSIFY** In your data table, classify each of the changes that you observed as either a physical or chemical change.

Conclude *Write It Up*

1. **IDENTIFY LIMITS** How might it be difficult to know if a physical or a chemical change has occurred?

2. **COMPARE** Compare your observations of the changes in the sugar that was crushed with the changes occurring when the sugar was heated over a flame.

3. **INFER** Make a list of general observations that would indicate that a physical change has occurred.

4. **INFER** Make a list of general observations that would indicate that a chemical change has occurred.

5. **EVALUATE** Look at your lists of observations indicating physical and chemical changes. Can any of these be confused? How can you be certain something like a color change is a physical or a chemical change?

6. **APPLY** What type of change would the burning of wood in a campfire be? What evidence would indicate that the burning wood was that type of change?

INVESTIGATE Further

CHALLENGE Observe five changes that you or your family members cause while preparing food for a family meal. Record your observations about the changes and identify each as either physical or chemical.

Chemical and Physical Changes
Observe and Analyze
Table 1. Observations of Chemical and Physical Changes

Change	Observations	Chemical or Physical Change
Ice melting		
Sugar cube crushed into powder		
Sugar heated over a flame		
Mixing water and vinegar		
Mixing vinegar and baking soda		

Chapter Review

the BIG idea

Matter is made of atoms and has observable properties.

CONTENT REVIEW
CLASSZONE.COM

◄ KEY CONCEPTS SUMMARY

1 **Matter is made of atoms.**

An atom is the smallest basic unit of matter. Two or more atoms bonded together form a molecule. Atoms and molecules are always in motion.

VOCABULARY
atom p. 137
molecule p. 139

2 **Matter combines to form different substances.**

Matter can be pure, such as an element (gold), or a compound (water).

Matter can be a mixture. Mixtures contain two or more pure substances.

VOCABULARY
element p. 144
compound p. 145
mixture p. 145

3 **Matter has observable properties.**

- Physical properties can be observed without changing the substance.
- Physical changes can change some physical properties but do not change the substance.

- Chemical properties describe how substances form new substances.
- Chemical changes create new substances.

VOCABULARY
physical property p. 149
physical change p. 151
chemical property p. 154
chemical change p. 154

Copy and complete the chart below. If the right column is blank, give a brief description or definition. If the left column is blank, give the correct term.

Term	Description
1. physical property	
2.	the smallest basic unit of matter
3.	when one substance changes into another substance
4.	a combination of different substances that remain individual substances
5. physical change	
6.	describes how substances can form new substances
7. element	
8.	a particle made of two or more atoms bonded together
9. compound	

Reviewing Key Concepts

Multiple Choice *Choose the letter of the best answer.*

10. The smallest basic unit of matter is a(n) (8.3.a)
   a. atom
   b. molecule
   c. compound
   d. mixture

11. Breaking a water molecule apart (8.3.b)
   a. makes a smaller amount of water
   b. is impossible because water is an element
   c. yields the elements hydrogen and oxygen
   d. yields the elements carbon and oxygen

12. Molecules can be made of (8.3.b)
   a. only different atoms
   b. only the same atoms
   c. both similar and different atoms
   d. only three different types of atoms

13. Everything on Earth is made of about 100 different types of (8.3.b)
   a. atoms
   b. molecules
   c. crystals
   d. compounds

14. Color, shape, size, and texture are (8.7.c)
   a. physical properties
   b. chemical properties
   c. physical changes
   d. chemical changes

15. Melting sugar is an example of a (8.5.d)
   a. physical change
   b. chemical change
   c. mixture
   d. pressure change

16. An electric current can be used to decompose, or break down, water into oxygen gas and hydrogen gas. This is an example of a (8.5.c)
   a. physical change
   b. chemical change
   c. change in state
   d. pressure change

17. The formation of rust on iron is a chemical change because (8.5.c)
   a. the color and shape have changed
   b. the mass and volume have changed
   c. the substance remains the same
   d. a new substance has been formed

18. Compounds can be separated only by (8.3.b)
   a. breaking the atoms into smaller pieces
   b. breaking the bonds between the atoms
   c. using a magnet to attract certain atoms
   d. evaporating the liquid that contains the atoms

Short Answer *Answer each of the following questions in a sentence or two.*

19. When a sculptor shapes marble to make a statue, is this a physical or a chemical change? Explain your answer. (8.5.d)

20. In bright sunlight, dust particles in the air appear to dart about. What causes this effect? (8.3.a)

21. Describe and identify various physical changes that water can undergo. (8.5.d)

22. Explain what is meant by the term *pure substance*. (8.3.a)

Thinking Critically

23. **CLASSIFY** Write the headings *Element* and *Compound* on your paper. Place each of these terms in the correct category: aluminum, sodium chloride, magnesium, helium, sulfur dioxide, carbon monoxide. (8.3.b)

24. **INFER** If you could break up a carbon dioxide molecule, would you still have carbon dioxide? Explain your answer. (8.3.b)

25. **MODEL** Why is vegetable soup a mixture? Explain your answer. (8.3.b)

26. **INFER** Sharpening a pencil leaves behind pencil shavings. Why is sharpening a pencil a physical change instead of a chemical change? (8.5.d)

27. **COMPARE AND CONTRAST** Create a Venn diagram that shows how mixtures and compounds are alike and different. (8.3.b)

28. **ANALYZE** Whole milk is a mixture. When bacteria in the milk digest part of the mixture, changes occur. Lactic acid is produced, and the milk tastes sour. Explain why this process is a chemical change. (8.5.c)

29. **INFER** You pour powdered lemonade mix into a pitcher of water and stir, producing lemonade. Is the mixture the same throughout the pitcher, or are parts of it different? Explain your answer. (8.3.b)

30. **ANALYZE** Chalk is a compound formed from three elements: calcium, carbon, and oxygen. Explain how the properties of chalk are different from two of the individual elements that make it: carbon and oxygen. (8.3.b)

Use the information in the chart below to answer the next three questions.

Heterogeneous Mixture	Homogeneous Mixture
gravel	cup of coffee
birdseed	engine oil
chili soup	water

31. **ANALYZE** Explain the difference between a heterogeneous mixture and a homogeneous mixture. (8.3.b)

32. **INFER** Why is chili soup a heterogeneous mixture and a cup of coffee is not? (8.3.b)

33. **PREDICT** If a homogeneous mixture of engine oil and a homogeneous mixture of water are mixed, will the resulting mixture be homogeneous? Explain your answer. (8.3.b)

the BIG idea

34. **PREDICT** Look again at the photograph on pages 134–135. The chef has melted sugar to make a sculpture. Describe how the sugar has changed in terms of its physical and chemical properties. Predict what will happen to the sculpture over time. (8.7.c)

35. **RESEARCH** Think of a question you have about the properties of matter that is still unanswered. For example, there may be a specific type of matter about which you are curious. What information do you need in order to answer your question? How might you find the information? (8.3.e)

UNIT PROJECTS

If you are doing a unit project, make a folder for your project. Include in your folder a list of the resources you will need, the date on which the project is due, and a schedule to track your progress. Begin gathering data.

Analyzing Changes

8.5.c, 8.5.d

Read the following paragraphs and answer the questions below.

Many changes occur during food processing and cooking. Some changes are physical changes. Others are chemical changes. A physical change is a change in a substance that does not change the substance. Grinding coffee beans, for example, is a physical change. All that happens is the beans are broken apart. They are still coffee beans. After a chemical change, however, the identity of a substance is different. For example, roasting coffee beans involves many chemical changes. During roasting, starches and sugars in the coffee change into oils. You can detect these chemical changes in the strong odors, colors, and flavors of the roasted beans. Odors, changing colors, and a rise in temperature are often indications of chemical changes.

As another example of the physical and chemical changes that take place during food preparation, consider making tortillas. Tortillas have been made in Mexico since pre-Columbian times. Following is an example:

1. The harvested corn kernels are dried in sunlight.
2. The kernels are soaked and simmered in a lime water solution until the outer skins are softened. The lime water solution contains calcium hydroxide.
3. The softened kernels are then ground and formed into a dough called masa.
4. The masa is then pressed into a round shape and baked on a hot pan known as a comal until it turns golden brown.

1. Drying the corn kernels in sunlight is an example of a
  a. physical change   **c.** mixture of substances
  b. chemical change   **d.** separation of substances

2. In which of the following steps of the tortilla-making process does a chemical change occur?
  a. harvesting of the corn
  b. soaking in the lime water
  c. grinding of the corn kernels
  d. pressing of the masa

3. Cooking often involves reactions that create new substance from the substances in the ingredients. This process is an example of a
  a. chemical change
  b. physical change
  c. mixture of substances
  d. separation of substances

4. The kernels are traditionally ground using a stone tool known as a *metate y mano*. This grinding process is an example of a
  a. chemical change   **c.** mixture of substances
  b. physical change   **d.** separation of substances

Extended Response

Answer the two following questions in detail. Include some of the terms from the list in the box at right. Underline each term that you use in your answer.

element	compound	mixture
physical change	chemical change	atom
molecule		

5. Physical changes do not change a substance, but can all physical changes be undone? Explain your answer.

6. The air we breathe is a mixture of several elements. Oxygen and hydrogen are two of them. Water also contains oxygen and hydrogen. How can both these elements appear so different?

CHAPTER

States of Matter

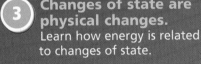

Particles of matter are
in constant motion.

> How would you
> describe the matter
> in this photo?

Key Concepts

SECTION

① **Matter exists in
different physical
states.**
Learn how different states
of matter behave.

SECTION

② **Temperature depends
on particle movement.**
Learn how kinetic energy is
the basis of temperature.

SECTION

③ **Changes of state are
physical changes.**
Learn how energy is related
to changes of state.

 California ClassZone

CLASSZONE.COM

Chapter 6 online resources:
Content Review, two
Simulations, two Resource
Centers, Math Tutorial, Test
Practice

EXPLORE the BIG idea

Moving Colors

> **8.3.e** Students know that in solids the atoms are closely locked in position and can only vibrate; in liquids the atoms and molecules are more loosely connected and can collide with and move past one another; and in gases the atoms and molecules are free to move independently, colliding frequently.

Fill a clear plastic cup halfway with cold water. Fill another cup halfway with hot water. Using an eyedropper, place a drop of food coloring at the very bottom of each cup. Observe. Next, try placing drops at other points in hot and cold water. Observe.

Observe and Think What happened to the drop of food coloring in cold water? in hot water? Why might this have happened? What does this tell you about liquids? about matter in general?

Hot Chocolate

> **8.3.d** Students know the states of matter (solid, liquid, gas) depend on molecular motion.

Place two candy-coated chocolates on a paper towel. Place two more in your hand and close your hand. Wait three minutes. Break open the candies and examine the chocolate.

Observe and Think What happened to the chocolate in your hand? on the towel? What do you think accounts for any differences you see? Try placing the candies in other locations. Can you predict what will happen to them?

NSTA
scilinks.org
SCLINKS

Solids, liquids, and gases **Code: MDL061**

Getting Ready to Learn

CONCEPT REVIEW

- Atoms combine to form molecules.
- Atoms and molecules are in constant motion.

VOCABULARY REVIEW

See Glossary for definitions.

kinetic energy

mass

particle

volume

 **CONTENT REVIEW** CLASSZONE.COM

Review concepts and vocabulary.

TAKING NOTES

OUTLINE

As you read, copy the headings on your paper in the form of an outline. Then add notes in your own words that summarize what you read.

VOCABULARY STRATEGY

Think about a vocabulary term as a **magnet word** diagram. Write related terms and ideas on lines around it.

See the Note-Taking Handbook on pages R45–R51.

SCIENCE NOTEBOOK

OUTLINE

I. Matter exists in different physical states.

  A. Particle arrangement and motion determine the state of matter.

    1.

    2.

    3.

  B. Solid, liquid, and gas are common states of matter.

    1.

    2.

    3.

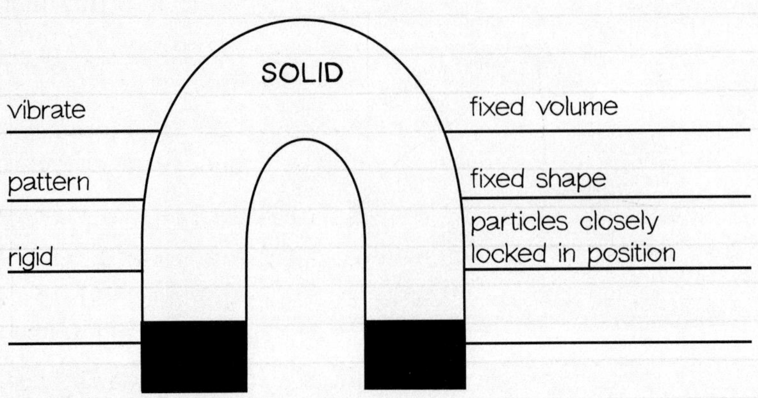

SOLID

vibrate   fixed volume

pattern   fixed shape

          particles closely locked in position

rigid

Matter exists in different physical states.

CALIFORNIA
Content Standards

8.3.d Students know the states of matter (solid, liquid, gas) depend on molecular motion.

8.3.e Students know that in solids the atoms are closely locked in position and can only vibrate; in liquids the atoms and molecules are more loosely connected and can collide with and move past one another; and in gases the atoms and molecules are free to move independently, colliding frequently.

VOCABULARY

states of matter p. 165
solid p. 166
liquid p. 166
gas p. 166

◀ BEFORE, you learned

- Matter has mass
- Matter is made of particles
- Particles in matter are always moving

▶ NOW, you will learn

- About the different states of matter
- How the different states of matter behave

EXPLORE Solids and Liquids (8.3.d)

How do solids and liquids compare?

PROCEDURE

1. Observe the water, ice, and marble. Pick them up and feel them. Can you change their shape? their volume?

2. Record your observations. Compare and contrast each object with the other two.

WHAT DO YOU THINK?

- How are the ice and the water in the cup similar? How are they different?
- How are the ice and the marble similar? How are they different?

MATERIALS
- water in a cup
- ice cube
- marble
- pie tin

Particle arrangement and motion determine the state of matter.

When you put water in a freezer, the water freezes into a solid (ice). When you place an ice cube on a warm plate, the ice melts into liquid water again. If you leave the plate in sunlight, the water becomes water vapor. Ice, water, and water vapor are made of exactly the same type of molecule—a molecule of two hydrogen atoms and one oxygen atom. What, then, makes them different?

Ice, water, and water vapor are different states of water. **States of matter** are the different forms in which matter can exist. The three familiar states are solid, liquid, and gas. When a substance changes from one state to another, the molecules in the substance do not change. However, the arrangement of the molecules does change, giving each state of matter its own characteristics.

VOCABULARY
Make a magnet word diagram for *states of matter* in your notebook.

Solid, liquid, and gas are common states of matter.

OUTLINE

Remember to take notes on this section in outline form.

I. Main idea
   A. Supporting idea
      1. Detail
      2. Detail
   B. Supporting idea

A substance can exist as a solid, a liquid, or a gas. The state of a substance depends on the space between its particles and on the way in which the particles move. The particles in all matter are always in motion.

❶ A **solid** is a substance that has a fixed volume and a fixed shape. In a solid, the particles are close together and may form a regular pattern. Particles in a solid are locked in place, but they vibrate. Because each particle is attached to several others, individual particles cannot move from one location to another, and the solid is rigid.

❷ A **liquid** has a fixed volume but does not have a fixed shape. Liquids take on the shape of the container they are in. The particles in a liquid are attracted to one another and are close together. However, particles in a liquid are not fixed in place. They move freely enough to collide and move past each other.

❸ A **gas** has no fixed volume or shape. A gas can take on both the shape and the volume of a container. Gas particles are not close to one another and can move easily in any direction. They frequently collide. There is much more space between gas particles than there is between particles in a liquid or a solid. The space between gas particles can increase or decrease with changes in temperature and pressure.

 CHECK YOUR READING   Describe two differences between a solid and a gas.

The particles in a solid are usually closer together than the particles in a liquid. For example, the particles in solid steel are closer together than the particles in molten—or melted—steel. However, water is an important exception. The molecules that make up ice actually have more space between them than the molecules in liquid water do.

The fact that the molecules in ice are farther apart than the molecules in liquid water has important consequences for life on Earth. Because there is more space between its molecules, ice floats on liquid water. By contrast, a piece of solid steel would not float in molten steel but would sink to the bottom.

Because ice floats, it remains on the surface of rivers and lakes when they freeze. The ice layer helps insulate the water and slow down the freezing process. Animals living in rivers and lakes can survive in the liquid water layer below the ice layer.

The illustration on page 167 shows how particles behave in the three states of matter. As you can see, the people in the seats can move but only back and forth. Can you name other similarities among the three familiar states of matter and the people in the illustration?

States of Matter

Matter can exist in different states. The state of matter depends on the arrangement and motion of the particles.

① Solid

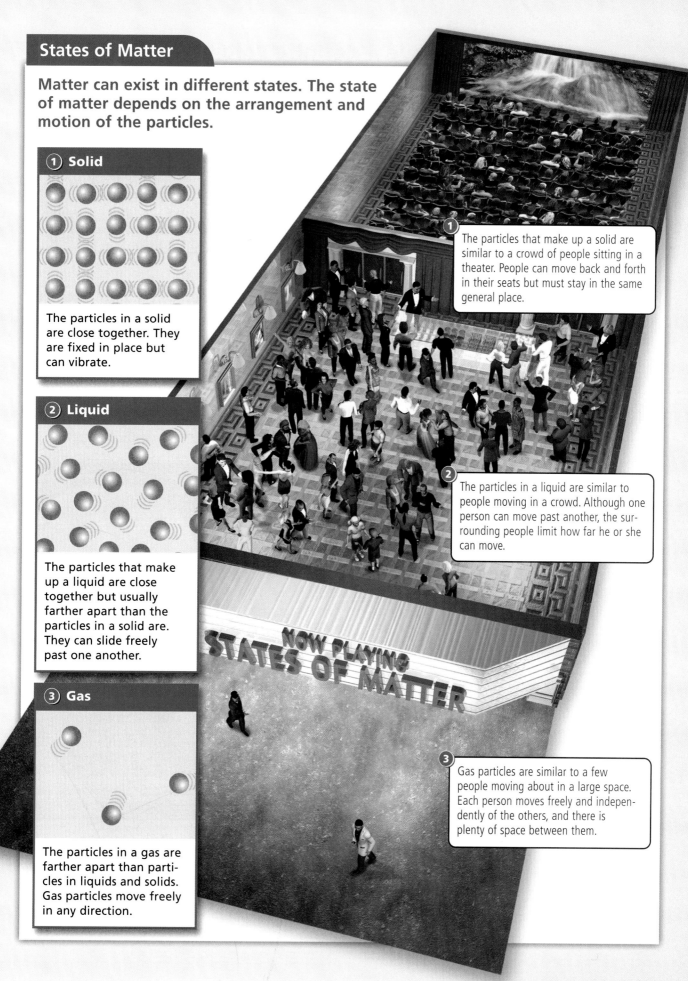

The particles in a solid are close together. They are fixed in place but can vibrate.

② Liquid

The particles that make up a liquid are close together but usually farther apart than the particles in a solid are. They can slide freely past one another.

③ Gas

The particles in a gas are farther apart than particles in liquids and solids. Gas particles move freely in any direction.

① The particles that make up a solid are similar to a crowd of people sitting in a theater. People can move back and forth in their seats but must stay in the same general place.

② The particles in a liquid are similar to people moving in a crowd. Although one person can move past another, the surrounding people limit how far he or she can move.

③ Gas particles are similar to a few people moving about in a large space. Each person moves freely and independently of the others, and there is plenty of space between them.

Solids have a definite volume and shape.

REMINDER

Volume is the amount of space that an object occupies.

A piece of ice, a block of wood, and a ceramic cup are solids. They have shapes that do not change and volumes that can be measured. Any matter that is a solid has a definite shape and a definite volume.

The molecules in a solid are in fixed positions and are close together. Although the molecules can still vibrate, they cannot move from one part of the solid to another part. As a result, a solid does not easily change its shape or its volume. If you force the molecules apart, you can change the shape and the volume of a solid by breaking it into pieces. However, each of those pieces will still be a solid and have its own particular shape and volume.

The particles in some solids, such as ice or table salt, are arranged in a very regular pattern. The pattern of the water molecules in ice, for example, can be seen when you look at a snowflake like the one shown below. The water molecules in a snowflake are arranged in hexagonal shapes that are layered on top of one another. Because the molecular pattern has six sides, snowflakes form with six sides or six points. Salt also has a regular structure; salt crystals have a cubic shape. This shape also is a result of how the particles that make up salt are arranged.

The particles in many solids, such as the water molecules in this snowflake, have a regular pattern.

Not all solids have regular shapes in the same way that ice and salt do, however. Some solids, such as plastic and glass, have particles that are not arranged in a regular pattern.

 CHECK YOUR READING   What two characteristics are needed for a substance to be a solid?

Liquids have a definite volume but no definite shape.

Water, milk, and oil are liquids. A liquid has a definite volume but does not have a definite shape. The volume of a certain amount of oil can be measured, but the shape that the oil takes depends on what container it is in. If the oil is in a tall, thin container, it has a tall, thin shape. If it is in a short, wide container, it has a short, wide shape. Liquids take the shape of their containers.

The molecules in a liquid are close together, but they are not tightly attached to one another as the molecules in a solid are. Instead, molecules in liquids can move independently. As a result, liquids can flow. Instead of having a rigid form, the molecules in a liquid move and fill the bottom of the container they are in.

 CHECK YOUR READING How is a liquid different from a solid?

INVESTIGATE Liquids

How do different liquids behave?

PROCEDURE

1. Using the graduated cylinder, measure 5 mL of colored water. Add it to the test tube.

2. Measure 5 mL of vegetable oil. Pour the oil into the test tube. Record your observations.

3. Pour a small amount of corn syrup directly into the test tube. Record what happens to all three liquids.

4. Add 10 mL more of colored water to the test tube and record what happens.

5. Add 5 mL more of vegetable oil and record what happens.

WHAT DO YOU THINK?

- How did the layers change as more liquid was added?
- What are some behaviors of each of the liquids in this experiment that can be used to tell them apart?
- What would happen if you changed the order in which you added the liquids?

CHALLENGE Think of a liquid you are familiar with that was not used in this experiment. What do you think would happen if you added that liquid to your test tube? Explain.

SKILL FOCUS
Measuring (8.3.d)

MATERIALS
- graduated cylinder
- colored water
- test tube
- test-tube rack
- vegetable oil
- corn syrup

TIME
20 minutes

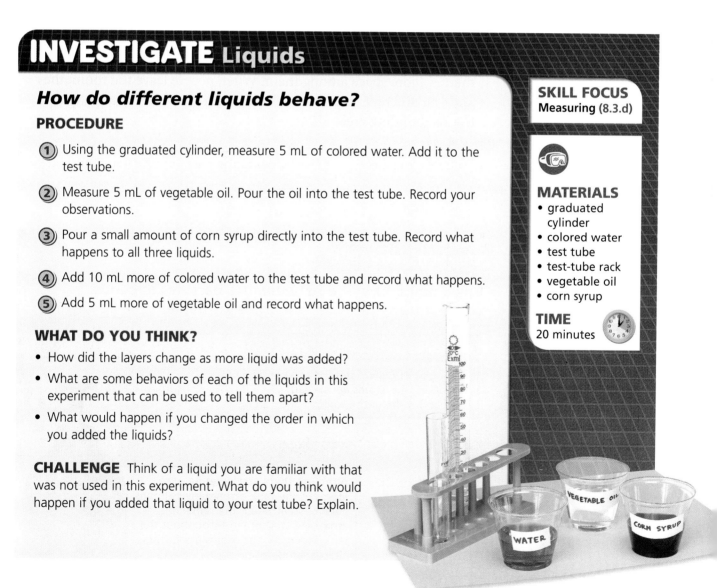

VOCABULARY
Add a magnet word diagram for *gas* to your notebook.

SIMULATION
CLASSZONE.COM

Explore the behavior of a gas.

Gases have no definite volume or shape.

The air that you breathe, the helium in a balloon, and the neon inside the tube in a neon light are gases. A gas is a substance with no definite volume and no definite shape. Solids and liquids have volumes that do not change easily. A gas, on the other hand, has a volume that changes to match the volume of its container.

Gas Composition

The molecules in a gas are very far apart compared with the molecules in a solid or a liquid. The amount of space between the molecules in a gas can change easily. If a rigid container—one that cannot change its shape—has a certain amount of air and more air is pumped in, the volume of the gas does not change. However, there is less space between the molecules than there was before. If the container is opened, the molecules spread out and mix with the air in the atmosphere.

As you saw, gas molecules in a container can be compared to a group of people in a room. If the room is small, there is less space among people. If the room is large, people can spread out so that there is more space among them. When people leave the room, they go in all different directions and mix with all of the other people in the surrounding area.

 CHECK YOUR READING Contrast the amount of space among the particles of a gas with the amount of space among the particles of a liquid or solid.

Gas and Volume

The amount of space between gas particles depends on how many particles are in the container.

Before Use

The atoms of helium gas are constantly in motion. The atoms are spread throughout the entire tank.

After Use

Although there are fewer helium atoms in the tank after many balloons have been inflated, the remaining atoms are still spread throughout the tank. However, the atoms are farther apart than before.

Plasmas

You've learned about the three familiar states of matter—solid, liquid, and gas. But there are other states of matter. You probably don't come into direct contact with them very often. One of them, called plasma, is actually the most common state of matter in the universe. Scientists consider 99 per cent of the known universe to be in the plasma state.

Look up at the stars at night. You're actually seeing glowing balls of plasma. Plasmas are gases whose particles have so much energy that they become electrically charged. The electrical charges in plasmas give them special properties. This is why we consider them to be a separate state of matter.

One naturally occurring plasma on Earth is lightning. Lightning is a discharge of electric charge. The discharge can travel between two clouds or between a cloud and Earth. The heat produced by the discharge causes the air around it to enter the plasma state. This causes a bright flash.

You may be closer to a plasma than you think. If you use a fluorescent light, you're using a plasma. Fluorescent lights contain gas. When an electric current passes through the gas, it becomes a plasma. The plasma particles then cause a special coating on the glass of the bulb to glow.

Engineers have found exciting uses for plasmas. One use you may have heard of is in television displays. A plasma is used to cause many thousands of pixels to light up. You can think of each pixel as a tiny fluorescent light. The pixels are the basic units of the television picture. Computers control which pixels light and when they do. This is what produces the picture you see.

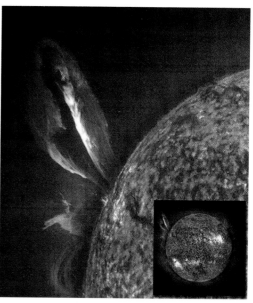

The sun ejects large amounts of plasmas. The inset photo of the whole sun shows how large these plumes can be.

 Review

KEY CONCEPTS

1. What are the characteristics of the three familiar states of matter? (8.3.e)

2. How can you change the shape and volume of a liquid? (8.3.d)

3. What happens to the particles of a gas when there are fewer of them? (8.3.d)

CRITICAL THINKING

4. **Infer** What happens to a liquid that is not in a container?

5. **Infer** What about the behavior of gas particles allows you to blow up a balloon?

⬥ CHALLENGE

6. **Synthesize** Can an oxygen canister ever be half empty? Explain.

Resurfacing the Landscape

8:3.d Students know the states of matter (solid, liquid, gas) depend upon molecular motion.

The landscape of northern California shows evidence of much volcanic activity. It is a place of many different types of rocks formed during various eruptions. Volcanic eruptions can be very violent or very slow. The type of eruption determines the type of rock formed.

Molten and Solid Rock

The history of volcanic eruptions can be told as a story of solids, liquids, and gases. Molten rock below Earth's surface is called magma. Magma is a mixture of liquid rock, solid minerals, and dissolved gases. Liquid rock is less dense than solid rock. Thus, magma tends to rise slowly through the surrounding solid rock. As magma gets closer to the surface, the pressure from the rocks above it becomes lower. The trapped gases expand, increasing the pressure inside the magma. A very rapid expansion of the trapped gases may cause an explosive eruption. Slower expansion causes less violent eruptions.

Magma that reaches the surface is called lava. Molten lava cools to form solid rock again. The chemical composition of the lava—that is, the elements and compounds it is made of—determines the type of rock that is formed. But even lavas of similar composition can result in very different types of rock. Obsidian and pumice, shown on the left, are examples.

Smooth and Foamy Rocks

Obsidian is a glasslike rock that is high in silica (SiO_2). It forms when silica-rich lava cools rapidly. The fast rate of cooling does not give crystals time to form. When obsidian breaks, it forms sharp edges. Native Americans traditionally used obsidian to make tools.

Pumice has a chemical composition that is similar to obsidian, but it looks very different. It is full of holes, like a pile of soap bubbles. These holes make it less dense, so it may even float in water. The holes formed when gases expanded quickly. Then the rock cooled so rapidly that the holes did not have time to collapse. This is one way in which different types of rock form.

WRITING ABOUT SCIENCE

Pumice and obsidian have many uses today. For example, obsidian is used in jewelry, and obsidian blades are even used to make surgical tools. Research some of the uses of pumice or obsidian and describe in a paragraph how the composition and texture of the rocks suit their uses.

The lack of mineral crystals in obsidian is evidence that the rock cooled very quickly.

Pumice is full of holes. The holes formed as expanding bubbles of gas escaped from rapidly cooling lava.

This ground is quite young in geologic terms. The pumice, with its tiny holes, is evidence of violent volcanic eruptions. Notice Mt. Shasta in the background.

KEY CONCEPT

6.2 Temperature depends on particle movement.

CALIFORNIA
Content Standard

8.3.e Students know that in solids the atoms are closely locked in position and can only vibrate; in liquids the atoms and molecules are more loosely connected and can collide with and move past one another; and in gases the atoms and molecules are free to move independently, colliding frequently.

BEFORE, you learned

- All matter is made of particles
- Particles of matter are always moving

NOW, you will learn

- How temperature depends on kinetic energy
- How temperature is measured
- How changes in temperature can affect matter

VOCABULARY

kinetic theory of matter p. 174
temperature p. 175
thermometer p. 177

EXPLORE Temperature (8.3.e)

What can cause a change in temperature?

PROCEDURE

1. Work with a partner. Hold the rubber band with both hands. Without stretching it, hold it to the underside of your partner's wrist.

2. Move the rubber band away, then quickly stretch it once and keep it stretched. Hold it to the underside of your partner's wrist.

3. Move the rubber band away and quickly let it return to its normal size. Hold it to the underside of your partner's wrist.

WHAT DO YOU THINK?
- What effect did stretching the rubber band have on the temperature of the rubber band?
- What may have caused this change to occur?

MATERIALS
large rubber band

All matter is made of moving particles.

OUTLINE

Remember to take notes on this section in outline form.

I. Main idea
  A. Supporting idea
    1. Detail
    2. Detail
  B. Supporting idea

Any object in motion has kinetic energy. Kinetic energy is often called the energy of motion. All the moving objects you see around you—from cars to planes to butterflies—have kinetic energy. Even objects so small that you cannot see them, such as atoms, are in motion and have kinetic energy. An object's kinetic energy depends both on its speed and mass. The more massive and faster moving an object is, the more kinetic energy it has.

You might think that a large unmoving object, such as a house, does not have any kinetic energy. However, all matter is made of atoms, and atoms are always in motion. Atoms are in motion even if the objects themselves do not change their position. The motion of these tiny particles gives the object energy.

The Kinetic Theory of Matter

REMINDER

Kinetic energy is the energy of motion.

The states of matter are the result of how particles of matter behave. The **kinetic theory of matter** states that all of the particles that make up matter are constantly in motion. As a result, all particles in matter have kinetic energy. You have already seen how particles move in the three states of matter. The kinetic theory of matter is what explains the different states of matter—solid, liquid, and gas.

1 The particles in a solid, such as concrete, are not free to move around very much. They vibrate back and forth in the same position and are held tightly together by forces of attraction.

2 The particles in a liquid, such as water in a pool, move much more freely than particles in a solid. They are constantly sliding around and tumbling over each other as they move.

3 In a gas, such as the air around you or in a bubble in water, particles are far apart and move around at high speeds. Particles might collide with one another, but otherwise they do not interact much.

Particles do not always move at the same speed. Within any group of particles, some are moving faster than others. A fast-moving particle might collide with another particle and lose some of its speed. A slow-moving particle might be struck by a faster one and start moving faster. Particles have a wide range of speeds and often change speeds.

READING TiP

In illustrations of particle movement, more motion lines mean a greater speed.

CHECK YOUR READING What is the kinetic theory of matter?

Matter in Motion

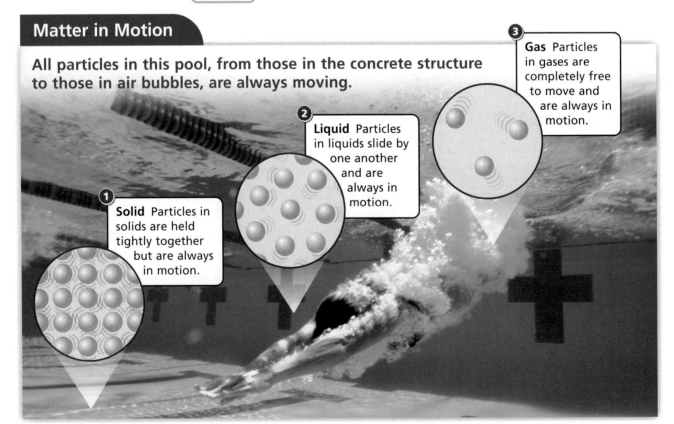

All particles in this pool, from those in the concrete structure to those in air bubbles, are always moving.

1 Solid Particles in solids are held tightly together but are always in motion.

2 Liquid Particles in liquids slide by one another and are always in motion.

3 Gas Particles in gases are completely free to move and are always in motion.

Temperature and Kinetic Energy

Particles of matter moving at different speeds have different kinetic energies. This is because kinetic energy depends on speed. It is not possible to know the kinetic energy of each particle in an object. However, the average kinetic energy of all the particles in an object can be determined.

Temperature is a measure of the average kinetic energy of all the particles in an object. If a liquid, such as hot cocoa, has a high temperature, the particles in the liquid are moving very fast and have a high average kinetic energy. The cocoa feels hot. If a drink, such as a fruit smoothie, has a low temperature, the particles in the liquid are moving more slowly and have a lower average kinetic energy. The smoothie feels cold.

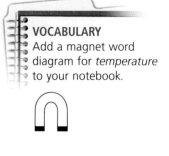

VOCABULARY
Add a magnet word diagram for *temperature* to your notebook.

hot liquid   cold liquid

You experience the connection between temperature and the kinetic energy of particles every day. For example, to raise the temperature of your hands on a cold day, you have to add energy. You perhaps may put your hands near a fire or a hot stove. The added energy makes the particles in your hands move faster. If you let a hot bowl sit on a table for a while, the particles in the bowl slow down. They collide with particles in the air and in the table. The temperature of the bowl decreases, and it becomes cooler.

SIMULATION
CLASSZONE.COM

Examine the effects of temperature and mass on average kinetic energy.

Temperature is the measurement of the average kinetic energy of particles, not just their speed. Kinetic energy depends on mass as well as speed. Particles in a metal doorknob do not move as fast as particles in air. However, the particles in a doorknob have more mass and they can have the same amount of kinetic energy as particles in air. As a result, the doorknob and the air can have equal temperatures.

CHECK YOUR READING How does temperature change when kinetic energy increases?

Temperature can be measured.

RESOURCE CENTER
CLASSZONE.COM

Find out more about temperature and temperature scales.

You have read that a warmer temperature means a greater average kinetic energy. How is temperature measured and what does that measurement mean? Suppose you hear on the radio that the temperature outside is 30 degrees. Do you need to wear a warm coat to spend the day outside? The answer depends on the temperature scale being used. There are two common temperature scales. Both scales measure the average kinetic energy of particles. However, 30 degrees on one scale is quite different from 30 degrees on the other scale.

Temperature Scales

To establish a temperature scale, two known values and the number of units between the values are needed. The freezing and boiling points of pure water are often used as the standard values. These points are always the same under the same conditions and they are easy to reproduce. In the two common scales, temperature is measured in units called degrees (°), which are equally spaced units between two points.

The scale used most commonly in the United States for measuring temperature—in uses ranging from cooking directions to weather reports—is the Fahrenheit (FAR-uhn-HYT) scale (°F). It was developed in the early 1700s by Gabriel Fahrenheit. On the Fahrenheit scale, pure water freezes at 32°F and boils at 212°F. Thus, there are 180 degrees—180 equal units—between the freezing point and the boiling point of water.

During a summer day in Death Valley, California, the temperature can reach 49°C (120°F).

The temperature scale most commonly used in the rest of the world, and also used more often in science, is the Celsius (SEHL-see-uhs) scale (°C). This scale was developed in the 1740s by Anders Celsius. On the Celsius scale, pure water freezes at 0°C and boils at 100°C. There are 100 degrees—100 equal units—between these two temperatures.

Recall the question asked in the first paragraph of this page. If the outside temperature is 30 degrees, do you need to wear a warm coat? If the temperature is 30°F, the answer is yes, because that temperature is colder than the freezing point of water. If the temperature is 30°C, the answer is no—it is a nice warm day (86°F).

 CHECK YOUR READING How are the Fahrenheit and Celsius temperature scales different? How are they similar?

Thermometers

Temperature is measured by using a device called a thermometer. A **thermometer** measures temperature through the regular variation of some physical property of the material inside the thermometer. A liquid thermometer, for example, can measure temperature because the liquid expands or contracts as the temperature changes.

Liquid-filled thermometers measure how much the liquid expands in a narrow tube as the temperature increases. The distances along the tube are marked so that the temperature can be read. At one time, thermometers were filled with liquid mercury because it expands or contracts evenly at both high and low temperatures. This means that mercury expands or contracts by the same amount in response to a given change in temperature. However, mercury is dangerous to handle, so many thermometers today are filled with alcohol instead.

Some thermometers work in a different way. They use a material whose electrical properties change when the temperature changes. These thermometers can be read by computers. Some show the temperature on a display panel. They are often used in cars and in homes.

 CHECK YOUR READING How do liquid-filled thermometers work?

INVESTIGATE Temperature Measurements

How does a thermometer work?

PROCEDURE

1. To make your own thermometer, fill the bottle halfway with the alcohol solution. Add a small amount of food coloring and mix thoroughly.

2. Place the straw into the bottle. Use clay to suspend the straw above the bottom of the bottle and to seal the bottle's mouth completely.

3. Pour ice water into the bowl and place the bottle into the ice water. Record your observations, and then empty the bowl. Allow the bowl to reach room temperature before continuing.

4. Pour hot water into the bowl and place the bottle into the hot water. Record your observations.

WHAT DO YOU THINK?

- What happened to the level of the alcohol solution in the straw when the bottle was put into the ice water? into the hot water?

- Why do you think these changes happened?

CHALLENGE How could you modify your thermometer so that you could use it to measure a temperature?

SKILL FOCUS
Modeling (8.3.e)

MATERIALS
- plastic bottle
- alcohol solution
- food coloring
- clear plastic straw
- clay
- bowl
- ice water
- hot tap water

TIME
30 minutes

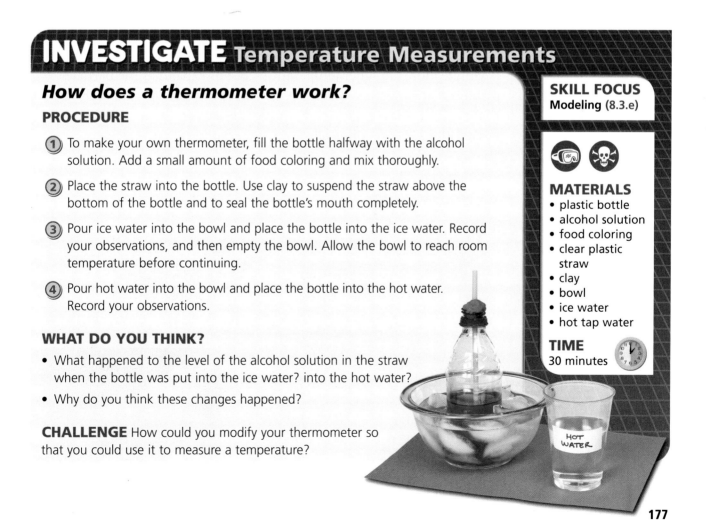

During construction of the Gateway Arch in St. Louis, engineers had to account for thermal expansion.

CALIFORNIA
Focus

The Skyway section of the San Francisco–Oakland Bay Bridge contains steel tubes between each deck segment. The steel tubes allow the segments to slide in response to expansion and contraction caused by changes in temperature.

Thermal Expansion

The property that makes liquid-filled thermometers work is called thermal expansion. Thermal expansion affects many substances, not just alcohol and liquid mercury. All gases, many liquids, and most solids expand when their temperature increases.

Construction engineers often have to take thermal expansion into account because steel and concrete both expand with increasing temperature. An interesting example involves the construction of the Gateway Arch in St. Louis, which is built mostly of steel.

The final piece of the Arch to be put into place was the top segment joining the two legs. The Arch was scheduled to be completed in the middle of the day for its opening ceremony. However, engineers knew that the side of the Arch facing the Sun would get hot and expand due to thermal expansion.

This expansion would narrow the gap between the legs and prevent the last piece from fitting into place. In order to complete the Arch, workers sprayed water on the side facing the Sun. The water helped cool the Arch and decreased the amount of thermal expansion. Once the final segment was in place, engineers made the connection strong enough to withstand the force of the expanding material.

Thermal expansion occurs in solids because the particles of solids vibrate more at higher temperatures. Solids expand as the particles move ever so slightly farther apart. This is why bridges and highways are built in short segments with slight breaks in them, called expansion joints. These joints allow the material to expand safely.

 CHECK YOUR READING Why do solids expand when their temperatures increase?

6.2 Review

KEY CONCEPTS

1. Describe the relationship between temperature and kinetic energy. (8.3.e)
2. Describe the way in which thermometers measure temperature. (8.3.e)
3. How can you explain thermal expansion in terms of kinetic energy? (8.3.e)

CRITICAL THINKING

4. **Synthesize** Suppose a mercury thermometer shows that the air temperature is 22°C (72°F). Do particles in the air have more average kinetic energy than particles in the mercury? Explain.
5. **Infer** If a puddle of water is frozen, do particles in the ice have kinetic energy? Explain.

CHALLENGE

6. **Apply** Why might a sidewalk be built with periodic breaks in it?

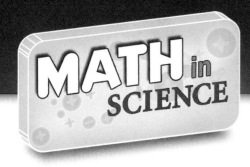

How Hot Is Hot?

Temperatures on Earth can vary greatly, from extremely hot in some deserts to frigid in polar regions. The meaning of a temperature measurement depends on which temperature scale is being used. A very high temperature on the Fahrenheit scale is equal to a much lower temperature on the Celsius scale. The table shows the formulas used to convert temperatures between the two scales.

Conversion	Formula
Fahrenheit to Celsius	$°C = \frac{5}{9}(°F - 32)$
Celsius to Fahrenheit	$°F = \frac{9}{5}°C + 32$

Example

The boiling point of pure water is 212°F. Convert that temperature to a measurement on the Celsius scale.

(1) Use the correct conversion formula.

$$°C = \frac{5}{9}(°F - 32)$$

(2) Substitute the temperature given for the correct variable in the formula.

$$°C = \frac{5}{9}(212 - 32) = \frac{5}{9} \cdot 180 = 100$$

ANSWER °C = 100

Use the information in the table below to answer the questions that follow.

Highest and Lowest Temperatures Recorded on Earth			
Location	Highest Temp. (°F)	Location	Lowest Temp. (°F)
El Azizia, Libya	136	Vostok, Antarctica	−129
Death Valley, California	134	Oimekon, Russia	−90
Tirat Tsvi, Israel	129	Verkhoyansk, Russia	−90
Cloncurry, Australia	128	Northice, Greenland	−87
Seville, Spain	122	Snag, Yukon, Canada	−81

1. What is the highest temperature in °C?

2. What is the temperature difference in °C between the highest and second highest temperatures?

3. What is the difference between the highest and lowest temperatures in °F? in °C?

CHALLENGE The surface of the Sun is approximately 5500°C. What is this temperature in °F?

Temperatures on Earth, ranging from the extremes of frigid polar regions to the hottest deserts, can differ by more than 250°F.

MATH TUTORIAL
CLASSZONE.COM
Click on Math Tutorial for more help with temperature conversions.

Math 7.MG.1.1
Science 8.9.f

6.3 Changes of state are physical changes.

CALIFORNIA
Content Standards

8.5.d Students know physical processes include freezing and boiling, in which a material changes form with no chemical reaction.

8.7.c Students know substances can be classified by their properties, including their melting temperature, density, hardness, and thermal and electrical conductivity.

BEFORE, you learned

- Substances have physical and chemical properties
- Physical changes do not change a substance into a new substance
- Changes in temperature can affect matter

NOW, you will learn

- How liquids can become solids, and solids can become liquids
- How liquids can become gases, and gases can become liquids
- How energy is related to changes of state

VOCABULARY

melting p. 181
melting point p. 181
freezing p. 182
freezing point p. 182
evaporation p. 183
sublimation p. 183
boiling p. 184
boiling point p. 184
condensation p. 185

THINK ABOUT

Where does dew come from?

On a cool morning, droplets of dew cover the grass. Where does this water come from? You might think it had rained recently. However, dew forms even if it has not rained. Air is made of a mixture of different gases, including water vapor. Some of the water vapor condenses—or becomes a liquid—on the cool grass and forms drops of liquid water.

Matter can change from one state to another.

Recall that matter is commonly found in three states: solid, liquid, and gas. A solid has a fixed volume and a fixed shape. A liquid also has a fixed volume but takes the shape of its container. A gas has neither a fixed volume nor a fixed shape. Matter is in a certain state at one time, but it can change from one state to another.

When matter changes from one state to another, the substance itself does not change. Water, ice, and water vapor are all the same basic substance. As water turns into ice or water vapor, the water molecules themselves do not change. What changes is the amount of kinetic energy the molecules have. Changes in state are physical changes because changes in state do not change the basic substance.

 CHECK YOUR READING Why is a change in state a physical change rather than a chemical change?

OUTLINE
Remember to take notes on this section in outline form.

I. Main idea
   A. Supporting idea
      1. Detail
      2. Detail
   B. Supporting idea

Solids can become liquids, and liquids can become solids.

If you leave an ice cube on a kitchen counter, it changes to the liquid form of water. Water changes to the solid form of water, ice, when it is placed in a freezer. In a similar way, if a bar of iron is heated to a high enough temperature, it will become liquid iron. As the liquid iron cools, it becomes solid iron again.

Melting

Melting is the process by which a solid becomes a liquid. Different solids melt at different temperatures. The lowest temperature at which a substance begins to melt is called its **melting point.** Although the melting point of ice is 0°C (32°F), iron must be heated to a much higher temperature before it will melt.

VOCABULARY
Add magnet word diagrams for *melting* and *melting point* to your notebook.

Remember that particles are always in motion, even in a solid. Because the particles in a solid are bound together, they do not move from place to place—but they do vibrate. As a solid heats up, its particles gain kenetic energy and vibrate faster. If the vibrations are fast enough, the particles break loose and slide past one another. In other words, the solid melts and becomes a liquid.

Some substances have a well-defined melting point. If you are melting ice, for example, you can predict that when the temperature reaches 0°C, the ice will start to melt. Substances with an orderly structure start melting when they reach a specific temperature.

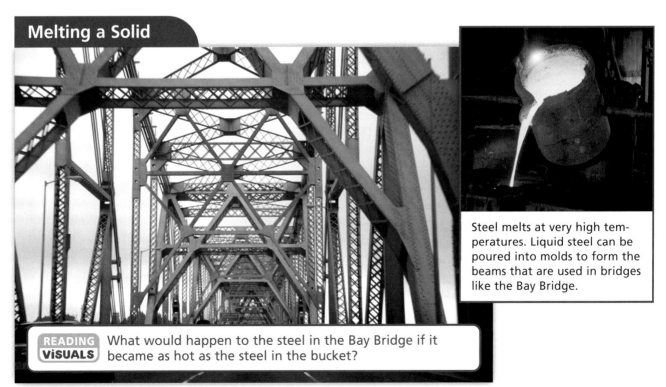

Melting a Solid

Steel melts at very high temperatures. Liquid steel can be poured into molds to form the beams that are used in bridges like the Bay Bridge.

READING VISUALS What would happen to the steel in the Bay Bridge if it became as hot as the steel in the bucket?

Other substances, such as plastic and chocolate, do not have a well-defined melting point. Chocolate becomes soft when the temperature is high enough, but it still maintains its shape. Eventually, the chocolate becomes a liquid, but there is no specific temperature at which you can say the change happened. Instead, the melting happens gradually over a range of temperatures.

CHECK YOUR READING Describe the movement of molecules in a substance that is at its melting point.

Icicles grow as water drips down them, freezes, and sticks to the ice that is already there. On a warm day, the frozen icicles melt again.

Freezing

READING TiP

On the Celsius temperature scale, under normal conditions, water freezes at 0°C and boils at 100°C. On the Fahrenheit scale, water freezes at 32°F and boils at 212°F.

Freezing is the process by which a liquid becomes a solid. Although you may think of cold temperatures when you hear the word *freezing*, many substances are solid, or frozen, at room temperature and above. Think about a soda can and a candle. The can and the candle are frozen at temperatures you would find in a classroom.

As the temperature of a liquid is lowered, its particles lose energy. As a result, the particles move more slowly. Eventually, the particles move slowly enough that the attractions among them cause the liquid to become a solid. The temperature at which a specific liquid becomes a solid is called the **freezing point** of the substance.

The freezing point of a substance is the same as that substance's melting point. At this particular temperature, the substance can exist as either a solid or a liquid. At temperatures below the freezing/melting point, the substance is a solid. At temperatures above the freezing/melting point, the substance is a liquid.

CHECK YOUR READING What is the relationship between a substance's melting point and freezing point?

Liquids can become gases, and gases can become liquids.

Suppose you spill water on a picnic table on a warm day. You might notice that the water eventually disappears from the table. What has happened to the water molecules? The liquid water has become water vapor, a gas. The water vapor mixes with the surrounding air. At the same picnic, you might also notice that a cold can of soda has beads of water forming on it. The water vapor in the air has become the liquid water found on the soda can.

Evaporation

Evaporation is a process by which a liquid becomes a gas. It usually occurs at the surface of a liquid. Although all particles in a liquid move, they do not all move at the same speed. Some particles move faster than others. The fastest moving particles at the surface of the liquid can break away from the liquid and escape to become gas particles.

As the temperature increases, the kinetic energy in the liquid increases. More particles can escape from the surface of the liquid. As a result, the liquid evaporates more quickly. This is why spilled water will evaporate faster in hot weather than in cold weather.

The root of the word *evaporation* is *vapor*, a Latin word meaning "steam."

CHECK YOUR READING Describe the movement of particles in a liquid as it evaporates.

It is interesting to note that under certain conditions, solids can lose particles through a process similar to evaporation. When a solid changes directly to a gas, the process is called **sublimation.** You may have seen dry ice being used in a cooler to keep foods cold. Dry ice is frozen carbon dioxide that sublimates in normal atmospheric conditions.

Evaporation

During evaporation, fast-moving particles escape from the surface of a liquid and become gas particles.

Boiling

RESOURCE CENTER
CLASSZONE.COM

Explore melting points
and boiling points.

Boiling is another process by which a liquid becomes a gas. Unlike evaporation, boiling produces bubbles. If you heat a pot of water on the stove, you will notice that after a while tiny bubbles begin to form. These bubbles contain dissolved air that is escaping from the liquid. As you continue to heat the water, large bubbles suddenly form and rise to the surface. These bubbles contain energetic water molecules that have escaped from the liquid water to form a gas. This process is boiling.

Boiling can occur only when the liquid reaches a certain temperature, called the **boiling point** of the liquid. Liquids evaporate over a wide range of temperatures. Boiling, however, occurs at a specific temperature for each liquid. Water, for example, has a boiling point of 100°C (212°F) at normal atmospheric pressure.

In the mountains, water boils at a temperature lower than 100°C. For example, atop Mount Whitney in Eastern California, which has an elevation of 4418 m (14,494 ft) above sea level, water would boil at about 84°C (184°F). This happens because at high elevations the air pressure is much lower than at sea level. Because less pressure is pushing down on the surface of the water, bubbles can form inside the liquid at a lower temperature. Less energetic water molecules are needed to expand the bubbles under these conditions. The lower boiling point of water means that foods cooked in water, such as pasta, require a longer time to prepare.

Different substances boil at different temperatures. Helium, which is a gas at room temperature, boils at –270°C (–454°F). Aluminum, on the other hand, boils at 2519°C (4566°F). This fact explains why some substances usually are found as gases but others are not.

Boiling

Bubbles of vapor form inside the boiling water.

Tiny droplets of water form on a window as water vapor from the air condenses into liquid water.

Condensation

The process by which a gas changes its state to become a liquid is called **condensation.** You probably have seen an example of condensation when you enjoyed a cold drink on a warm day. The beads of water that formed on the glass or can were water vapor that condensed from the surrounding air.

The cold can or glass cooled the air surrounding it. When you cool a gas, it loses kinetic energy. As the particles move more slowly, the attractions among them cause droplets of liquid to form. Condensed water often forms when warm air containing water vapor comes into contact with a cold surface, such as a glass of ice or ground that has cooled during the night.

As with evaporation, condensation can occur over a wide range of temperatures. Like the particles in liquids, the individual particles in a gas have different average kinetic energies. Slowly moving particles near the cool surface condense as they lose kinetic energy. The faster moving particles also slow down but continue to move too fast to stick to the other particles in the liquid that is forming. However, if you cool a gas to a temperature below its boiling point, almost all of the gas will condense.

READING **TiP**

The root of the word *condensation* is *condense,* which comes from a Latin word meaning "to thicken."

 Review

KEY CONCEPTS

1. Describe three ways in which matter can change from one state to another. (8.7.c)

2. Compare and contrast the processes of evaporation and condensation. (8.7.c)

3. How does adding energy to matter by heating it affect the energy of its particles? (8.7.c)

CRITICAL THINKING

4. **Synthesize** Explain how water can exist as both a solid and a liquid at 0°C.

5. **Apply** Explain how a pat of butter at room temperature can be considered to be frozen.

⬤ CHALLENGE

6. **Infer** You know that water vapor condenses from air when the air temperature is lowered. Should it be possible to condense oxygen from air? What would have to happen?

CHAPTER INVESTIGATION

Freezing Point

OVERVIEW AND PURPOSE Stearic acid is a substance used in making candles. In this experiment you will
- observe melted stearic acid as it changes from a liquid to a solid
- record the freezing point of stearic acid

▶ Problem

What is the freezing point of stearic acid?

▶ Procedure

1. Make a data table like the one shown on the sample notebook page.

2. Use the test-tube tongs to take the test tube of melted stearic acid and place it in the test-tube rack. Keep the test tube in the rack for the entire experiment.

3. Use the wire-loop stirrer and stir the liquid to make sure that it is the same temperature throughout.

4. Place the thermometer into the stearic acid to take a reading. Hold the thermometer so that it does not touch the sides or bottom of the test tube. Wait until the liquid in the thermometer stops rising. Then record the temperature on your data table. Also note whether the stearic acid is a liquid or a solid—or whether both states are present.

5. Take the temperature of the stearic acid every minute, stirring the stearic acid with the stirrer before each reading. To get an accurate reading, place the loop of the stirrer around the thermometer and use an up-and-down motion.

6. Continue taking temperature readings until two minutes after the acid has become totally solid or you are no longer able to stir it.

MATERIALS
- large test tube
- stearic acid
- test-tube tongs
- test-tube rack
- wire-loop stirrer
- thermometer

8.5.d, 8.7.c, 8.9.e

Content Standard
8.5.d Students know physical processes include freezing and boiling, in which a material changes form with no chemical reaction.

Investigation Standard
8.9.e Construct appropriate graphs from data and develop quantitative statements about the relationships between variables.

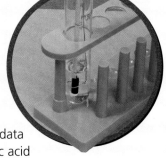

7 Make a note of the temperature on your data table when the first signs of a solid formation appear.

8 Make a note of the temperature on your data table when the stearic acid is completely solid.

9 Leave the thermometer and stirrer in the test tube and carry it carefully in the test-tube rack to your teacher.

▶ Observe and Analyze `Write It Up`

1. **RECORD OBSERVATIONS** Make a line graph showing the freezing curve of stearic acid. Label the vertical axis **Temperature** and the horizontal axis **Time.**

2. **RECORD OBSERVATIONS** Label your graph to show when the stearic acid was a liquid, when it was a solid, and when it was present in both states.

3. **ANALYZE** Explain how your graph tells you the freezing point of stearic acid.

▶ Conclude `Write It Up`

1. **INTERPRET** Answer the question in the problem.

2. **IDENTIFY** How does the freezing point of stearic acid compare with the freezing point of water?

3. **INFER** What happened to the energy of the molecules as the stearic acid changed from a liquid to a solid?

4. **INFER** From your observations, infer the melting point of stearic acid. How is the melting point of stearic acid related to its freezing point?

5. **APPLY** Why do you think stearic acid is used as an ingredient in bar soaps but not in liquid soaps?

▶ INVESTIGATE Further

CHALLENGE What do you think would happen if you mixed in another substance with the stearic acid? How would that affect the freezing point? What experiment would you perform to find the answer?

Freezing Point

Problem What is the freezing point of stearic acid?

Observe and Analyze

Table 1. Freezing Point of Stearic Acid

Time (min)	Temperature (°C)	Liquid	Solid	Both
0.0				
1.0				
2.0				
3.0				
4.0				
5.0				
6.0				
7.0				

Chapter Review

the BIG idea

Particles of matter are in constant motion.

CONTENT REVIEW
CLASSZONE.COM

◀ KEY CONCEPTS SUMMARY

1 **Matter exists in different physical states.**

Solids have a fixed volume and a fixed shape.

Liquids have a fixed volume but no fixed shape.

Gases have no fixed volume and no fixed shape.

VOCABULARY

states of matter p. 165
solid p. 166
liquid p. 166
gas p. 166

---

2 **Temperature depends on particle movement.**
- All particles in matter have kinetic energy.
- Temperature is the measurement of the average kinetic energy of particles in an object.
- Temperature is commonly measured on the Fahrenheit or Celsius scale.

hot liquid   cold liquid

Particles in a warmer substance have a greater average kinetic energy than particles in a cooler substance.

VOCABULARY

kinetic theory of matter p. 174
temperature p. 175
thermometer p. 177

---

3 **Changes of state are physical changes.**
Matter can change from a solid to a liquid and from a liquid to a gas.

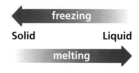

freezing

Solid   Liquid

melting

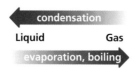

condensation

Liquid   Gas

evaporation, boiling

VOCABULARY

melting p. 181
melting point p. 181
freezing p. 182
freezing point p. 182
evaporation p. 183
sublimation p. 183
boiling p. 184
boiling point p. 184
condensation p. 185

Describe how the terms in the following sets of terms are related.

1. temperature, thermometer

2. states of matter, liquid

3. solid, liquid, gas

4. melting, melting point, freezing point

5. boiling, boiling point

6. evaporation, condensation

7. sublimation, solid

Reviewing Key Concepts

Multiple Choice *Choose the letter of the best answer.*

8. What is the most common state of matter in the universe? (8.3.d)
   a. solid
   b. liquid
   c. gas
   d. plasma

9. Compared to a liquid, the particles in a solid are usually (8.3.e)
   a. closer together
   b. farther apart
   c. the same distance apart
   d. smaller

10. Gases do not have a fixed volume or shape and their particles (8.3.e)
    a. are close together
    b. are fixed in one place
    c. move easily in any direction
    d. form a regular pattern

11. An increase in temperature causes all gases, many liquids, and some solids to become larger through (8.3.e)
    a. thermal expansion
    b. evaporation
    c. freezing
    d. condensation

12. The average kinetic energy of particles in an object can be measured by its (8.3.e)
    a. heat
    b. melting point
    c. boiling point
    d. temperature

13. The process by which a solid becomes a liquid is called (8.5.d)
    a. boiling
    b. freezing
    c. melting
    d. evaporating

14. The process by which a liquid becomes a solid is called (8.5.d)
    a. boiling
    b. freezing
    c. melting
    d. evaporating

15. Two processes by which a liquid can become a gas are (8.5.d)
    a. evaporation and boiling
    b. melting and freezing
    c. sublimation and condensation
    d. evaporation and condensation

Short Answer *Answer each of the following questions in a sentence or two.*

16. Describe the movement of particles in a solid, a liquid, and a gas. (8.3.e)

17. How are kinetic energy and temperature related to each other? (8.3.e)

18. Why does dew often form on grass on a cool morning, even if there has been no rain? (8.3.d)

19. Describe the difference between evaporation and boiling in terms of the movement of the liquid's particles in each case. (8.3.e)

20. What effect does elevation have on the boiling point of water? (8.5.d)

Thinking Critically

21. ANALYZE If you place a solid rubber ball into a box, why doesn't the ball change its shape to fit the container? (8.3.e)

22. COMPARE The electric thermometer on the bank downtown reads 70°F. Based on the thermometer on p. 176, what would the temperature be in degrees Celsius?

23. MODEL In what ways is sand in a bowl like a liquid? In what ways is it different? (8.3.e)

24. INFER If you cut a hole in a basketball, what happens to the gas inside? (8.3.e)

25. MODEL Make a sketch comparing the motions of ice, liquid water, and water vapor particles. How would you compare the particle motion in the three sketches? (8.3.e)

26. INFER It hasn't rained for days, but you find an outdoor picnic table that is wet. Knowing no one has been there before you, what can you suppose has happened? (8.5.d)

27. COMMUNICATE How would you relate a local weather forecast to someone from another country? What distinctions would you be sure to make?

Use the photograph below to answer the next three questions.

28. INFER On what days would the kinetic energy of the water be greater? Explain. (8.3.e)

29. ANALYZE Can water evaporate from this puddle on a cold day? Explain your answer. (8.5.d)

30. PREDICT What would happen to any minerals and salts in the water if the water completely evaporated? (8.5.e)

Use the thermometers below to answer the next four questions.

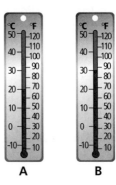

A   **B**

31. How much of a change in temperature occurred between A and B in the Fahrenheit scale? in the Celsius scale?

32. What is a bigger change in temperature, from 0° to 10°C or from 0° to 10°F? Why might this be an important thing to consider when reading temperature changes?

33. Suppose the two thermometers are showing the temperatures of two identical blocks of metal. The particles of which block would have the higher kinetic energy? Why? (8.3.d)

34. At which temperature (A or B) would you expect an ice cube to melt more quickly? Explain this in terms of the kinetic theory. (8.3.d)

the BIG idea

35. SYNTHESIZE Look back at the photograph on pages 162–163. Describe the picture in terms of states of matter. (8.3.d)

36. RESEARCH Make a list of all the matter in a two-meter radius around you. Classify each as a solid, a liquid, or gas. (8.3.e)

UNIT PROJECTS

Check your schedule for your unit project. How are you doing? Be sure that you have placed data or notes from your research in your project folder.

Standards-Based Assessment

Interpreting Graphs

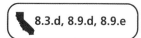
8.3.d, 8.9.d, 8.9.e

The graph below shows the changing volume of a gas as it was slowly heated, with the pressure held constant.

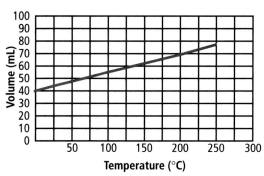

Use the graph to answer the questions.

1. As the temperature of the gas rises, what happens to its volume?

   a. It increases.

   b. It stays the same.

   c. It decreases.

   d. It changes without pattern.

2. What is the volume of the gas at 250°C as compared with the volume at 0°C?

   a. about three times greater

   b. about double

   c. about one-half

   d. about the same

3. What would happen to this gas if it were cooled below 0°C?

   a. The volume would increase.

   b. The volume would continue to decrease.

   c. The volume would remain at 40 mL.

   d. A gas cannot be cooled below 0°C.

4. If you raised the temperature of this gas to 300°C, what would be its approximate volume?

   a. 70 mL   **c.** 80 mL

   b. 75 mL   **d.** 85 mL

5. If the volume of the gas at 0°C was 80 mL instead of 40 mL, what would you expect the volume to be at 200°C?

   a. 35 mL   **c.** 80 mL

   b. 70 mL   **d.** 140 mL

Extended Response

Answer the two questions below in detail. Include some of the terms from the word box. Underline each term you use in your answer.

| temperature | thermometer | boiling point |
| states of matter | degree | |

6. You and your friend both hear that the temperature outside is 30 degrees. You grab a coat. Your friend prepares to go swimming. Who has the right idea? What might be the source of the confusion?

7. Explain how water changes as it moves from a solid to a liquid and then to a gas.

TIMELINES in Science

THE STORY OF ELEMENTS

Scientists once thought there were only four elements: earth, water, air, and fire. Each substance was different, because it contained a different ratio of these four elements. For example, one rock could be lighter than another rock because it had more air in it.

In 1789 a chemist named Antoine Lavoisier made the first modern list of elements. His list had 33 substances. Lavoisier said that there probably were even more elements. Scientists hadn't yet discovered them. In the years that followed, scientists would find that some of Lavoisier's elements weren't really elements. They would, however, add more than 70 elements to Lavoisier's list. They are still identifying more elements.

This timeline shows a few of the more exciting discoveries scientists made while searching for elements. It also shows some of the devices scientists used to identify these elements.

1860

Every Element Has a Spectrum

German chemist Robert Bunsen and physicist Gustav Kirchhoff show that each element emits only certain wavelengths of visible light when heated. A chemist can use a spectroscope to instantly identify an element by observing the spectrum it produces. Bunsen used spectroscopy to identify a new element, cesium (Cs).

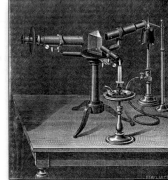

EVENTS

1800	1820	1840

APPLICATIONS AND TECHNOLOGY

TECHNOLOGY

The Color of Matter

The 1860s saw the rise of chemical spectroscopy. Chemists now had an extremely accurate method for identifying substances. All they needed to do was examine the spectral lines produced by a heated element. If they had an unknown substance, obtaining its spectrum would let them know instantly if it was something they'd seen before or something new. Spectroscopy helped chemists identify many elements that had never before been isolated. It has been one of the most important tools chemists have had in studying the elements.

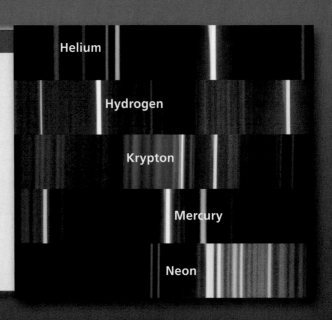

Helium

Hydrogen

Krypton

Mercury

Neon

1868

New Elements in the Sun

English astronomer J. Norman Lockyer and English chemist Edward Franklin notice a line in the Sun's spectrum that doesn't belong to any known element. Lockyer proposes that this line in the spectrum of the Sun is a new element not yet found on Earth. He suggests the name helium for this new element.

1898

Discovery of Polonium

Working at the Sorbonne in Paris, chemists Marie and Pierre Curie find a new element. They name the element polonium, after Marie's native country, Poland. Polonium is the first element to be discovered using radioactivity as a guide. The Curies realize that the high level of radiation they are detecting from their ore samples could not be coming from any known element. The rate of radioactive decay is now another tool chemists have to identify new elements.

1860   **1880**   **1900**

TECHNOLOGY

The Etching Machine

In the 1880s, the manufacture of high quality diffraction gratings greatly assisted the study of spectroscopy. Diffraction gratings are highly polished glass plates etched with thousands of tiny lines. They can produce very detailed spectra of elements. The new gratings allowed scientists to pinpoint the locations of spectral lines very accurately. They could analyze substances as never before and know exactly which elements they contained. American physicist Henry Rowland was a leader in the manufacture of diffraction gratings. His machine could produce diffraction gratings having about 16,000 etched lines per centimeter. This was far better than previous manufacturers could do.

1913

Soddy Says "All Atoms Not Equal."

English chemist Frederick Soddy coins the term *isotope* for atoms of the same element that do not have the same atomic mass. These atoms have all the same physical and chemical properties. The existence of isotopes explains why two apparently identical substances could show different levels of radioactivity.

1940

The First Element Heavier Than Uranium: Neptunium

Edwin McMillan and P. H. Abelson make the first element with an atomic number (93) higher than that of uranium (92). McMillan suggests calling the element neptunium, after the planet Neptune. He chose the name because uranium had been named after the planet Uranus. McMillan and Abelson work in Berkeley, California.

1925

X-Rays Reveal New Element

Using *x*-ray spectroscopy, Walter Noddack, Ida Tacke (pictured), and Otto Berg announce the discovery of the element rhenium (Re). They were able to isolate a small amount of the element from hundreds of kilograms of ore.

1937

Scientists Synthesize Element

Carlo Perrier and Emilio Segrè use the cyclotron to produce the first element to be made artificially. They call the element technetium. Dmitiri Mendeleev had predicted the existence of this element many years before, when he made the first periodic table of the elements. It has the atomic number 43.

1920   **1940**   **1960**

TECHNOLOGY

Mass Spectrometer

In the early decades of the twentieth century, the improvement of the mass spectrometer allowed scientists to separate the atoms of an element into isotopes. For the first time, scientists were able to determine the masses of the different isotopes of an element. The mass spectrometer confirmed that elements have isotopes. The atomic mass measured is an average of all naturally occurring isotopes. The mass spectrometer works by deflecting charged atomic particles in magnetic and electric fields. How far a particle moves depends on its mass. Today's mass spectrometers are very large, complicated machines.

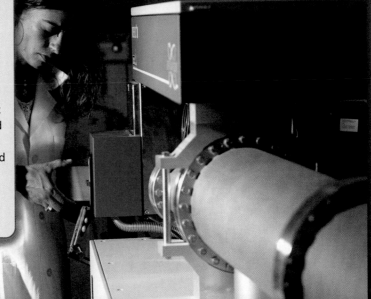

SPOTLIGHT on
ALBERT GHIORSO

Nuclear scientist Albert Ghiorso is best known for helping to discover many new chemical elements on the periodic table. In 2004, he was awarded a Lifetime Achievement Award from the Radiochemistry Society.

Ghiorso was part of a research team at the University of California, Berkeley, whose goal was to expand the number of known elements. From the 1950s to the 1970s, Ghiorso co-discovered elements 95 (americium) through 106 (seaborgium). He and his associates found the radioactive elements 99 (einsteinium) and 100 (fermium) in radioactive debris from a hydrogen bomb test over the Pacific Ocean.

It was proposed in 2000 that the newly discovered element 118 be named ghiorsium to honor Ghiorso's work. However, scientists have so far been unable to duplicate the element.

2004

Element 111 Gets a Name

The International Union of Pure and Applied Chemistry (IUPAC) officially gives element 111 a name, *roentgenium*. The name honors scientist William Roentgen, discoverer of *x*-rays. It often takes years for a new element to get an official name. The scientific community must be sure the element has been produced. For example, roentgenium reportedly was first made ten years before it received an official name.

RESOURCE CENTER
CLASSZONE.COM

Discover the research behind new elements.

1980   2000

APPLICATION

The Place Where Elements Are Made

As of the end of 2005, the famous 88-inch cyclotron is still in operation at the Lawrence Berkeley Laboratory in Berkeley, California. In the cyclotron lighter elements are shot towards one another. The hope is that the nuclei will stick together, making a heavier element. The cyclotron has been the site for the making of some of the heaviest elements. Scientists are still not sure how many more elements can be made. If new elements are made, there's a good chance they will be made in California.

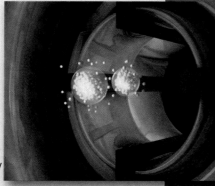

ACTIVITIES

Element Safari

Locate the following objects in your home or in a grocery store: baking soda, vinegar, cereal flakes, and antacid tablets. You may examine other products if you wish. Look at the labels on the products. Can you recognize the names of any elements? Make a list of the names you suspect to be elements. You can use a dictionary to see if the name is that of an element.

Writing About Science

The element lawrencium was named for physicist Ernest O. Lawrence. Research the life and accomplishments of Ernest Lawrence. Write a short report.

7 Atomic Structure and the Periodic Table

the **BIG** idea

A substance's atomic structure determines its physical and chemical properties.

Key Concepts

SECTION

1 Atoms are the smallest form of elements.
Learn about the structure of atoms and how each element's atoms are different.

SECTION

2 Elements make up the periodic table.
Learn how the periodic table of the elements is organized.

SECTION

3 The periodic table is a map of the elements.
Learn more about the groups of elements in the periodic table.

SECTION

4 Patterns exist among the elements.
Learn about the trends in the periodic table.

California ClassZone

CLASSZONE.COM

Chapter 7 online resources: Content Review, Simulation, Visualization, three Resource Centers, Math Tutorial, Test Practice.

You can't zoom in any closer than this! The picture is an extremely close-up view of nickel. How do things look different the closer you get to them?

EXPLORE (the **BIG** idea)

That's Far!

> **8.3.a** Students know the structure of the atom and know it is composed of protons, neutrons, and electrons.

Place a baseball in the middle of a large field. Hold a dime and count off the number of steps from the baseball to the edge of the field. If the baseball were an atom's nucleus and the dime an electron, you would need to go about 6000 steps to walk the distance between the nucleus and the electrons.

Observe and Think
How far were you able to go? How much farther would you need to go to model the pro-portion of an atom? What does this tell you about atomic structure?

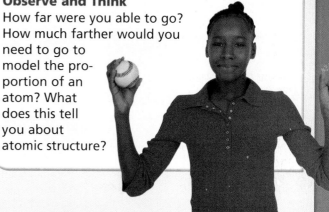

Internet Activity: Periodic Table

> **8.7.b** Students know each element has a specific number of protons in the nucleus (the atomic number) and each isotope of the element has a different but specific number of neutrons in the nucleus.

Go to **ClassZone.com** to explore the periodic table. See different ways to set up the table and learn more about the listed elements.

Observe and Think How do atomic number and mass change as you move across the periodic table?

scilinks.org
Atomic Theory **Code:** MDL022

CHAPTER 7
Getting Ready to Learn

CONCEPT REVIEW

- Matter is made of particles called atoms that are too small to see with the eyes.
- Matter can be an element, a compound, or a mixture.
- Matter can undergo physical and chemical changes.

VOCABULARY REVIEW

atom p. 137
compound p. 145
element p. 144

CONTENT REVIEW
CLASSZONE.COM
Review concepts and vocabulary.

TAKING NOTES

MAIN IDEA WEB

Write each new blue heading in a box. Then write notes in boxes around the center box that give important terms and details about that blue heading.

VOCABULARY STRATEGY

Write each new vocabulary term in the center of a **frame game** diagram. Decide what information to frame it with. Use examples, descriptions, parts, sentences that use the term in context, or pictures. You can change the frame to fit each term.

See the Note-Taking Handbook on pages R45–R51.

SCIENCE NOTEBOOK

Atoms are made of protons, neutrons, and electrons.

The atomic number is the number of protons in the nucleus.

Each element is made of a different atom.

Every element has a certain number of protons in its nucleus.

Central part of atom

contains most of an atom's mass

NUCLEUS

Electrons move about it.

is made of protons and neutrons

Atoms are the smallest form of elements.

CALIFORNIA
Content Standards

8.3.a Students know the structure of the atom and know it is composed of protons, neutrons, and electrons.

8.7.b Students know each element has a specific number of protons in the nucleus (the atomic number) and each isotope of the element has a different but specific number of neutrons in the nucleus.

VOCABULARY

proton p. 201
neutron p. 201
nucleus p. 201
electron p. 201
atomic number p. 202
atomic mass number p. 202
isotope p. 202
ion p. 204

> **READING TIP**
>
> The word *element* is related to *elementary*, which means "basic."

BEFORE, you learned

- All matter is made of atoms
- Elements are the simplest substances

NOW, you will learn

- Where atoms are found and how they are named
- About the structure of atoms
- How ions are formed from atoms

EXPLORE The Size of Atoms (8.3.a)

How small can you cut paper?

PROCEDURE

1. Cut the strip of paper in half. Cut one of these halves in half.

2. Continue cutting one piece of paper in half as many times as you can.

WHAT DO YOU THINK?

- How many cuts were you able to make?
- Do you think you could keep cutting the paper forever? Why or why not?

MATERIALS

- strip of paper about 30 centimeters long
- scissors

All matter is made of atoms.

Think of all the substances you see and touch every day. Are all of these substances the same? Obviously, the substances that make up this book you're reading are quite different from the substances in the air around you. So how many different substances can there be? People have been asking this question for thousands of years.

About 2400 years ago, Greek philosophers proposed that everything on Earth was made of only four basic substances—air, water, fire, and earth. Everything else contained a mixture of these four substances. As time went on, chemists came to realize that there had to be more than four basic substances. Today chemists know that about 100 basic substances, or elements, account for everything we see and touch. Sometimes these elements appear by themselves. Most often, however, these elements appear in combination with other elements in compounds.

Finding Elements

Modern chemistry really began in 1789. In this year, Antoine Lavoisier published his book *An Elementary Treatise on Chemistry*. It was the first modern chemistry textbook. In it, Lavoisier explained many important concepts in chemistry. Lavoisier urged that all elements should be given names everyone could understand and that all chemists could agree on. He then drew up a list of 33 elements and gave them names. His idea was a simple one. If you had a substance that was a combination of other substances, you would include all names of those substances in the name of the combination. He also said that chemists always should try to break down elements into simpler substances.

Zinc is an element often added to other metals to prevent corrosion.

Lithium is found in everything from airplane bodies to medications.

Names and Symbols of Elements

Elements get their names in different ways. Magnesium, for example, was named for the region in Greece known as Magnesia. *Lithium* comes from the Greek word *lithos,* which means "stone." Neptunium was named after the planet Neptune. The elements einsteinium and fermium were named after scientists Albert Einstein and Enrico Fermi.

Each element has its own unique symbol. For some elements, the symbol is simply the first letter of its name.

hydrogen (H)   sulfur (S)   carbon (C)

The symbols for other elements use the first letter plus one other letter of the element's name. Notice that the first letter is capitalized but the second letter is not.

aluminum (Al)   platinum (Pt)   cadmium (Cd)   zinc (Zn)

The origins of some symbols, however, are less obvious. The symbol for gold (Au), for example, doesn't seem to have anything to do with the element's name. The symbol refers instead to gold's name in Latin, *aurum.* Lead (Pb), iron (Fe), and copper (Cu) are a few other elements whose symbols come from Latin names.

Each element is made of a different atom.

In the early 1800s British scientist John Dalton proposed that each element is made of tiny particles called atoms. Dalton stated that all of the atoms of a particular element are identical but are different from atoms of all other elements. Every atom of silver, for example, is similar to every other atom of silver but different from an atom of iron.

How could atoms of elements be the same but different? That was the question that needed to be answered.

The Structure of an Atom

A key discovery leading to the current model of the atom was that atoms contain particles that have electric charges. A particle's charge can be either positive or negative. Particles with the same charge repel each other—they are pushed apart. Particles with different charges attract each other—they are drawn toward each other.

Atoms are composed of three types of particles—protons, neutrons, and electrons. A **proton** is a positively charged particle. A **neutron** is an uncharged particle. The neutron has approximately the same mass as a proton. Protons and neutrons are grouped together in the atom's center. This combination of protons and neutrons is called the **nucleus** of the atom. Because protons are the only particles in the nucleus that have an electric charge, the nucleus is positively charged. **Electrons** are negatively charged particles that move around outside the nucleus.

We can only guess where electrons are at any time. Because we can't locate any one electron with certainty, we say that electrons move about in an electron cloud. We do know that each electron in the electron cloud has a certain amount of energy. This energy keeps it moving about the nucleus. The energy keeps the negative electron from falling into the positive nucleus. We also know that electrons with similar amounts of energy are grouped together in shells. Each shell can hold only a certain number of electrons that have about the same energy. An electron may jump from one shell to the next if enough energy is added to it.

RESOURCE CENTER
CLASSZONE.COM
Learn more about the atom.

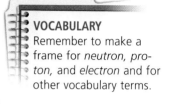

VOCABULARY
Remember to make a frame for *neutron, proton,* and *electron* and for other vocabulary terms.

The Atomic Model

Atoms are made of protons, neutrons, and electrons.

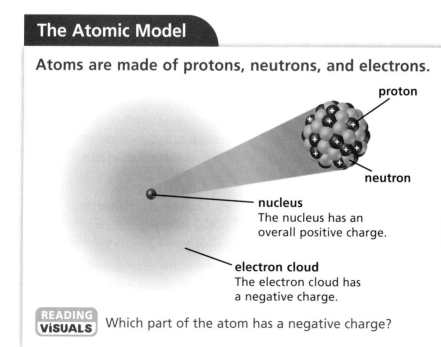

proton

neutron

nucleus
The nucleus has an overall positive charge.

electron cloud
The electron cloud has a negative charge.

Particle Charges and Mass		
Particle	Relative Mass	Relative Charge
Electron	1	−1
Proton	2000	+1
Neutron	2000	0

READING VISUALS Which part of the atom has a negative charge?

The Size of the Atom

Atoms are extremely small, about
0.0000000001 meters in diameter. This means
that you could fit millions of atoms in the
period at the end of this sentence. It would
take you about 500 years to count the number
of atoms in a grain of salt.

Atom Size
⟶ .
Millions of atoms could fit in a space the size of this dot.

Electrons are much less massive than protons or neutrons—about
2000 times less massive. This means almost all of an atom's mass is in
the nucleus. The electron cloud, however, is much larger than the
nucleus. It is about 10,000 times the diameter of the nucleus. The
diagram on page 201, picturing the basic structure of the atom, is
not drawn to scale. If the nucleus were as large as shown, the electron
cloud would extend far beyond your classroom.

The negative electrons stick around the nucleus because they are
attracted to the positively charged protons. Electrical charges that are
alike (such as two negative charges) repel each other. Negative electrons,
therefore, remain spread out in the electron cloud. Neutral atoms have
an equal number of protons and electrons.

Gold atoms have 79 pro-
tons and 79 electrons.

Atomic Numbers

If all atoms are composed of the same particles, how can there be more
than 100 different elements? The identity of an atom is determined
by the number of protons in its nucleus, called the **atomic number.**
Every hydrogen atom—atomic number 1—has exactly one proton in
its nucleus. Every gold atom has 79 protons; the atomic number of
gold is 79.

Atomic Mass Numbers

The total number of protons and neutrons in an atom's nucleus is
called its **atomic mass number.** The atoms of a certain element always
have the same number of protons. They may not, however, always
have the same number of neutrons. Not all atoms of an element,
therefore, have the same atomic mass number.

All chlorine atoms, for instance, have 17 protons. However, some
chlorine atoms have 18 neutrons, while other chlorine atoms have
20 neutrons. Atoms of chlorine with 18 and 20 neutrons are called
chlorine isotopes. **Isotopes** are atoms of the same element that have
a different number of neutrons. Some elements have many naturally
occuring isotopes, while other elements have just a few.

READING TiP

The prefix *iso-* in *isotope*
is from Greek, and it
means "equal."

CHECK YOUR
READING   How is atomic mass number different from atomic number?

Isotopes

Isotopes have different numbers of neutrons.

Chlorine-35
atomic mass number = 35

17 protons
18 neutrons

nucleus   17 electrons

Chlorine-37
atomic mass number = 37

17 protons
20 neutrons

nucleus   17 electrons

An isotope is identified by the name of the element and its atomic mass number. You can find the number of neutrons in an isotope by subtracting the atomic number from the atomic mass number. For example, chlorine-35 indicates the isotope of chlorine that has 18 neutrons (35 minus 17). Chlorine-37 has 20 neutrons (37 minus 17). Every atom of a given element always has the same atomic number, because it has the same number of protons. However, the atomic mass number varies, because the number of neutrons varies.

INVESTIGATE Masses of Atomic Particles

How can you model the relative masses of atomic particles?

PROCEDURE

(1) Use a paper clip to represent an electron. Determine its mass.

(2) Find a substance in the classroom (sand, clay, water) from which you could make a model representing the mass of a proton or neutron. The mass of a proton or neutron is about 2000 times the mass of an electron.

(3) Measure out the substance until you have enough of it to make your model.

WHAT DO YOU THINK?

- What substance did you use to make your model?
- What was the model's mass?
- What do you conclude about the masses of atomic particles?

CHALLENGE The diameter of an electron is approximately 1/2000 that of a proton. What two objects could represent each of these to scale?

SKILL FOCUS
Modeling (8.3.a)

MATERIALS
- balance
- large paper clip
- other items

TIME
20 minutes

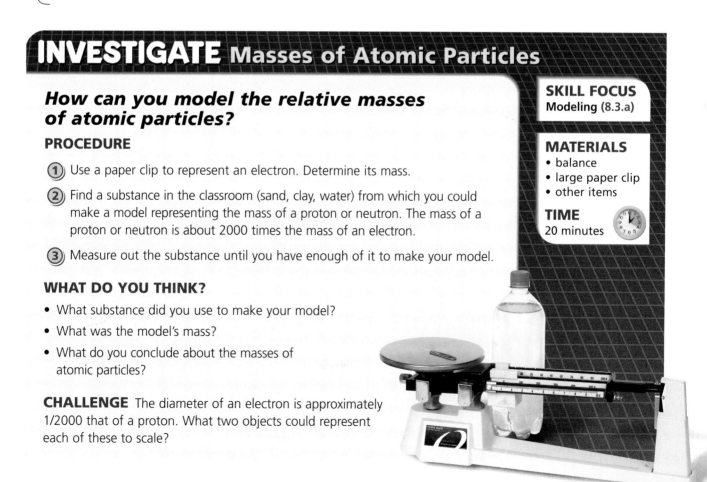

Atoms form ions.

MAIN IDEA WEB
Make a main idea web to organize what you know about ions.

A neutral atom has an equal number of electrons and protons. Since each electron has one negative charge and each proton has one positive charge, atoms have no overall electric charge. An **ion** is formed when an atom loses or gains one or more electrons. Because the number of electrons in an ion is different from the number of protons, an ion does have an overall electric charge.

Formation of Positive Ions

Consider how a positive ion can form from an atom. The left side of the illustration below represents a sodium (Na) atom. Its nucleus contains 11 protons and some neutrons. Because the electron cloud surrounding the nucleus consists of 11 electrons, there is no overall charge on the atom. If the atom loses one electron, however, the charges are no longer balanced. There is now one more proton than there are electrons. The ion formed, therefore, has a positive charge.

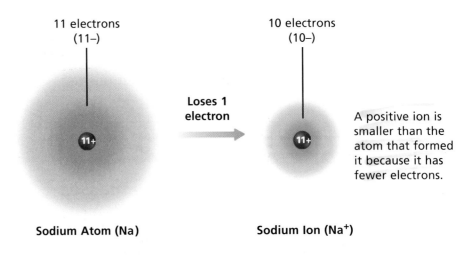

11 electrons
(11–)

Loses 1 electron

10 electrons
(10–)

A positive ion is smaller than the atom that formed it because it has fewer electrons.

Sodium Atom (Na)

Sodium Ion (Na⁺)

Notice the size of the positive ion. It is smaller than the neutral atom. One reason the ion is smaller is because it has one less electron. The electron that was lost is usually the one farthest away from the nucleus. The size of the electron cloud, therefore, is decreased.

Positive ions are represented by the symbol for the element with a raised plus sign to indicate the positive charge. In the above example, the sodium ion is represented as Na^+.

Some atoms form positive ions by losing more than one electron. In those cases, the symbol for the ion also indicates the number of positive charges on the ion. For example, calcium loses two electrons to form an ion Ca^{2+}, and aluminum loses three electrons to form Al^{3+}.

CHECK YOUR READING   What must happen to form a positive ion?

Formation of Negative Ions

The illustration below shows how a negative ion is formed. In this case the atom is chlorine (Cl). The nucleus of a chlorine atom contains 17 protons and some neutrons. The electron cloud has 17 electrons, so the atom has no overall charge. Chlorine has a tendency to gain one electron. When an electron is added to the chlorine atom, a negatively charged ion is formed. Notice that a negative ion is larger than the neutral atom that formed it. An additional electron has been added to the electron cloud. The electron has gone into the space in the electron cloud that is farthest from the nucleus. The electron cloud is, therefore, larger.

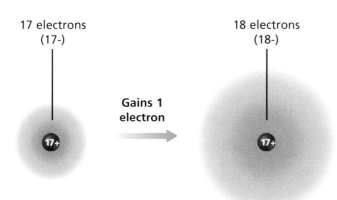

17 electrons
(17-)

18 electrons
(18-)

Gains 1 electron

17+

17+

A negative ion is larger than the atom that formed it because it has more electrons.

Chlorine Atom (Cl)

Chloride Ion (Cl⁻)

Negative ions are represented by placing a minus sign to the right and slightly above the element's symbol. The negative chloride ion in the example, therefore, would be written as Cl^-. If an ion has gained more than one electron, the number of added electrons is shown by a number in front of the minus sign. Oxygen (O), for example, gains two electrons when it forms an ion. Its symbol is O^{2-}.

 Review

KEY CONCEPTS

1. Describe how elements are named. (8.7.b)

2. What determines the identity of an atom? (8.3.a)

3. What happens when an atom forms an ion? (8.3.a)

CRITICAL THINKING

4. **Infer** Magnesium and sodium atoms are about the same size. How does the size of a magnesium ion with a 2+ charge compare with that of a sodium ion with a single + charge?

5. **Compare** The atomic number of potassium is 19. How does potassium-39 differ from potassium-41?

○ CHALLENGE

6. **Analyze** When determining the mass of an atom, the electrons are not considered. Why can scientists disregard the electrons?

Elements of Life

> 8.3.a Students know the structure of the atom and know it is composed of protons, neutrons, and electrons.

There are more than 25 different types of atoms in the cells of your body. The table below shows the amount of atoms of some of the elements in a 50-kilogram human. For example, atoms of oxygen account for about 61 percent of a person's mass. Atoms of carbon account for about 23 percent of a person's mass. The atoms and ions of other elements may be present only in very small amounts, but they play important roles in the chemical processes that occur in your cells.

Blood and Other Fluids

Iron ions are part of the hemoglobin that gives blood its red color and carries oxygen to cells throughout the body. Sodium and potassium ions help regulate the amount and location of the water in the body. Sodium and potassium ions also make up part of the sweat the body produces to regulate temperature.

Bones and Teeth

The sturdier structures of the body get their strength from calcium, magnesium, and phosphorus. An average body has a little less than a kilogram of calcium, almost all of which is in the bones and teeth. Fluoride ions make up part of the hard coating on the teeth. This is why you'll often find fluorine added to toothpaste.

Elements to Avoid

In some way, every element plays a role in human lives. Many elements, however, can be harmful or even poisonous. Arsenic is harmful if swallowed. Mercury is dangerous even to handle. While sodium may be necessary for many processes inside cells, too much sodium can be a serious health risk.

Mass of Elements in 50 kg Human

Element	Amount (kg)
Oxygen (O)	30.5
Carbon (C)	11.5
Hydrogen (H)	5.0
Nitrogen (N)	1.3
Calcium (Ca)	0.7
Phosphorus (P)	0.6
Potassium (K)	0.1
Sodium (Na)	> 0.1
Chlorine (Cl)	> 0.1

Other elements are in the body in very small amounts.

SOURCE: *CRC Handbook of Chemistry and Physics*

EXPLORE

1. **CALCULATE** What percentage of your body is made up of oxygen, carbon, hydrogen, and nitrogen?
2. **CHALLENGE** Salt, made of sodium ions and chloride ions, is an essential part of your diet. However, too much salt can cause health problems. Use the Internet to find out about the problems caused by too much or too little salt in your diet.

RESOURCE CENTER
CLASSZONE.COM

Find out more about the elements important to life.

This photo shows a false-color x-ray of the human skull. X-rays show the bones in the human body. Bones contain calcium.

KEY CONCEPT
7.2 Elements make up the periodic table.

CALIFORNIA
Content Standards

8.3.f Students know how to use the periodic table to identify elements in simple compounds.

8.7.b Students know each element has a specific number of protons in the nucleus (the atomic number) and each isotope of the element has a different but specific number of neutrons in the nucleus.

8.7.c Students know substances can be classified by their properties, including their melting temperature, density, hardness, and thermal and electrical conductivity.

BEFORE, you learned

- Atoms have a structure
- Every element is made from a different type of atom

NOW, you will learn

- How the periodic table is organized
- How properties of elements are shown by the periodic table

VOCABULARY

atomic mass p. 207
periodic table p. 208
group p. 212
period p. 212

EXPLORE Similarities and Differences of Objects (8.7.c)

How can different objects be organized?

PROCEDURE

① With several classmates, organize the buttons into three or more groups.

② Compare your team's organization of the buttons with another team's organization.

WHAT DO YOU THINK?

- What characteristics did you use to organize the buttons?
- In what other ways could you have organized the buttons?

MATERIALS
buttons

Elements can be organized by similarities.

One way of organizing elements is by the masses of their atoms. Finding the masses of atoms was a difficult task for the chemists of the past. They could not place an atom on a pan balance. All they could do was find the mass of a very large number of atoms of a certain element. Then they inferred the mass of a single one of them.

Remember that not all the atoms of an element have the same atomic mass number. Elements have isotopes. When chemists try to measure the mass of an atom, therefore, they are actually finding the average mass of all its isotopes. The **atomic mass** of the atoms of an element is the average mass of all the element's isotopes. Even before scientists knew all the ways in which atoms of different elements differ, they knew atoms had different atomic masses.

Mendeleev's Periodic Table

In the early 1800s several scientists proposed systems to organize the elements based on their properties. None of these suggested methods worked very well. Finally, a Russian chemist named Dmitri Mendeleev (MENH-duh-LAY-uhf) decided to work on the problem.

In the 1860s Mendeleev began thinking about how he could organize the elements based on their physical and chemical properties. He made a set of element cards. Each card contained the atomic mass of an atom of an element and any information about the element's properties. Mendeleev spent hours arranging the cards in various ways. He was looking for a relationship between properties and atomic mass.

The exercise led Mendeleev to list the elements in a chart. In the rows of the chart, he placed those elements showing similar chemical properties. He arranged the rows so the atomic masses increased as one moved down each vertical column. It took Mendeleev quite a bit of thinking and rethinking to get all the relationships correct. In 1869 he produced the first **periodic table** of the elements. We call it the periodic table because it shows a periodic, or repeating, pattern of properties of the elements. Look at the reproduction of Mendeleev's first table shown below. Notice how he placed carbon (C) and silicon (Si), two elements that are similar, in the same row.

CHECK YOUR READING What organizing method did Mendeleev use?

Dmitri Mendeleev (1834–1907) first published a periodic table of the elements in 1869.

— 70 —

ъ ней, мнѣ кажется, уже ясно выражается примѣнимость вы
лемаго мною. начала ко всей совокупности элементовъ, пай
ыхъ извѣстенъ съ достовѣрностію. На этотъ разъ я и желалъ
ущественно найдти общую систему элементовъ. Вотъ этотъ

		Ti=50	Zr=90	?=180.
		V=51	Nb=94	Ta=182.
		Cr=52	Mo=96	W=186.
		Mn=55	Rh=104,4	Pt=197,4
		Fe=56	Ru=104,4	Ir=198.
	Ni=Co=59	Pl=106,6	Os=199.
H=1		Cu=63,4	Ag=108	Hg=200.
Be=9,4	Mg=24	Zn=65,2	Cd=112
B=11	Al=27,4	?=68	Ur=116	Au=197?
C=12	Si=28	?=70	Sn=118
N=14	P=31	As=75	Sb=122	Bi=210
O=16	S=32	Se=79,4	Te=128?

Predicting New Elements

When Mendeleev constructed his table, he left some empty spaces where no known elements fit the pattern. He predicted that new elements that would complete the chart would be discovered. He even described some of the properties of these unknown elements.

At the start, many chemists found it hard to accept Mendeleev's predictions of unknown elements. Only six years after he published the table, however, the first of these elements was discovered. This element was given the name gallium, after the country France (whose ancient name was Gallia) where it was discovered. In the next 20 years, two other elements Mendeleev predicted were discovered.

The periodic table organizes the atoms of the elements by properties and atomic number.

MAIN IDEA WEB
Make a main idea web to summarize the information you can learn from the periodic table.

The modern periodic table on pages 210–211 differs from Mendeleev's table in several ways. For one thing, elements with similar properties are found in columns, not rows. More important, the elements are not arranged by atomic mass but by atomic number.

Reading the Periodic Table

Each square of the periodic table gives particular information about the atoms of an element.

❶ The number at the top of the square is the atomic number. This is the number of protons in the nucleus of an atom of that element.

❷ The chemical symbol is an abbreviation for the element's name. It contains one or two letters. A few elements that have not yet been named are designated by temporary three-letter symbols.

❸ The name of the element is written below the symbol.

❹ The number below the name indicates the average atomic mass of all the isotopes of the element.

The color of the element's symbol indicates the physical state of the element at room temperature. White letters—such as the *H* for hydrogen in the box to the right—indicate a gas. Blue letters indicate a liquid, and black letters indicate a solid. The background colors of the squares show whether the element is a metal, a nonmetal, or a metalloid. These terms will be explained in the next section.

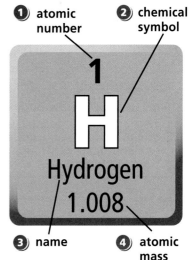

❶ atomic number
❷ chemical symbol

1
H
Hydrogen
1.008

❸ name
❹ atomic mass

The Periodic Table of the Elements

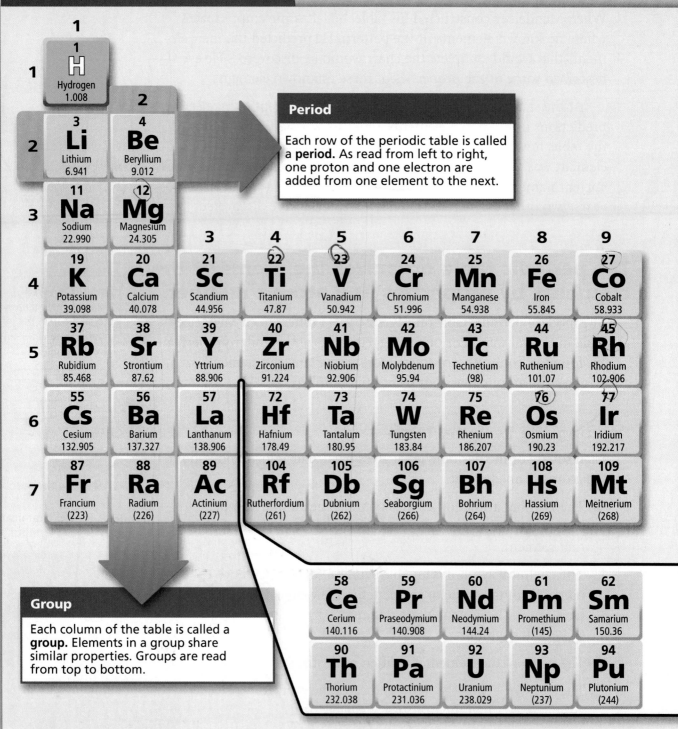

Period

Each row of the periodic table is called a **period**. As read from left to right, one proton and one electron are added from one element to the next.

Group

Each column of the table is called a **group**. Elements in a group share similar properties. Groups are read from top to bottom.

1								
1 **H** Hydrogen 1.008								

2
| 3
Li
Lithium
6.941 | 4
Be
Beryllium
9.012 |
| 11
Na
Sodium
22.990 | 12
Mg
Magnesium
24.305 |

		3	4	5	6	7	8	9
19 **K** Potassium 39.098	20 **Ca** Calcium 40.078	21 **Sc** Scandium 44.956	22 **Ti** Titanium 47.87	23 **V** Vanadium 50.942	24 **Cr** Chromium 51.996	25 **Mn** Manganese 54.938	26 **Fe** Iron 55.845	27 **Co** Cobalt 58.933
37 **Rb** Rubidium 85.468	38 **Sr** Strontium 87.62	39 **Y** Yttrium 88.906	40 **Zr** Zirconium 91.224	41 **Nb** Niobium 92.906	42 **Mo** Molybdenum 95.94	43 **Tc** Technetium (98)	44 **Ru** Ruthenium 101.07	45 **Rh** Rhodium 102.906
55 **Cs** Cesium 132.905	56 **Ba** Barium 137.327	57 **La** Lanthanum 138.906	72 **Hf** Hafnium 178.49	73 **Ta** Tantalum 180.95	74 **W** Tungsten 183.84	75 **Re** Rhenium 186.207	76 **Os** Osmium 190.23	77 **Ir** Iridium 192.217
87 **Fr** Francium (223)	88 **Ra** Radium (226)	89 **Ac** Actinium (227)	104 **Rf** Rutherfordium (261)	105 **Db** Dubnium (262)	106 **Sg** Seaborgium (266)	107 **Bh** Bohrium (264)	108 **Hs** Hassium (269)	109 **Mt** Meitnerium (268)

58 **Ce** Cerium 140.116	59 **Pr** Praseodymium 140.908	60 **Nd** Neodymium 144.24	61 **Pm** Promethium (145)	62 **Sm** Samarium 150.36
90 **Th** Thorium 232.038	91 **Pa** Protactinium 231.036	92 **U** Uranium 238.029	93 **Np** Neptunium (237)	94 **Pu** Plutonium (244)

 Metal   Metalloid   Nonmetal   **Fe** Solid   Liquid   Gas

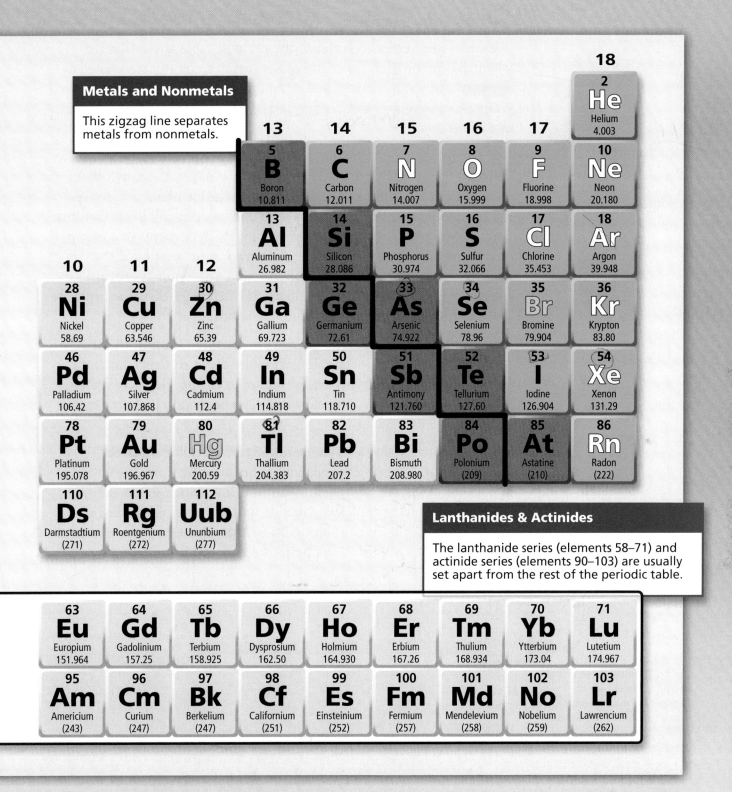

Metals and Nonmetals

This zigzag line separates metals from nonmetals.

							18
							2 **He** Helium 4.003
13	14	15	16	17			
5 **B** Boron 10.811	6 **C** Carbon 12.011	7 **N** Nitrogen 14.007	8 **O** Oxygen 15.999	9 **F** Fluorine 18.998	10 **Ne** Neon 20.180
13 **Al** Aluminum 26.982	14 **Si** Silicon 28.086	15 **P** Phosphorus 30.974	16 **S** Sulfur 32.066	17 **Cl** Chlorine 35.453	18 **Ar** Argon 39.948

10	11	12					
28 **Ni** Nickel 58.69	29 **Cu** Copper 63.546	30 **Zn** Zinc 65.39	31 **Ga** Gallium 69.723	32 **Ge** Germanium 72.61	33 **As** Arsenic 74.922	34 **Se** Selenium 78.96	35 **Br** Bromine 79.904	36 **Kr** Krypton 83.80
46 **Pd** Palladium 106.42	47 **Ag** Silver 107.868	48 **Cd** Cadmium 112.4	49 **In** Indium 114.818	50 **Sn** Tin 118.710	51 **Sb** Antimony 121.760	52 **Te** Tellurium 127.60	53 **I** Iodine 126.904	54 **Xe** Xenon 131.29
78 **Pt** Platinum 195.078	79 **Au** Gold 196.967	80 **Hg** Mercury 200.59	81 **Tl** Thallium 204.383	82 **Pb** Lead 207.2	83 **Bi** Bismuth 208.980	84 **Po** Polonium (209)	85 **At** Astatine (210)	86 **Rn** Radon (222)
110 **Ds** Darmstadtium (271)	111 **Rg** Roentgenium (272)	112 **Uub** Ununbium (277)						

Lanthanides & Actinides

The lanthanide series (elements 58–71) and actinide series (elements 90–103) are usually set apart from the rest of the periodic table.

63 **Eu** Europium 151.964	64 **Gd** Gadolinium 157.25	65 **Tb** Terbium 158.925	66 **Dy** Dysprosium 162.50	67 **Ho** Holmium 164.930	68 **Er** Erbium 167.26	69 **Tm** Thulium 168.934	70 **Yb** Ytterbium 173.04	71 **Lu** Lutetium 174.967
95 **Am** Americium (243)	96 **Cm** Curium (247)	97 **Bk** Berkelium (247)	98 **Cf** Californium (251)	99 **Es** Einsteinium (252)	100 **Fm** Fermium (257)	101 **Md** Mendelevium (258)	102 **No** Nobelium (259)	103 **Lr** Lawrencium (262)

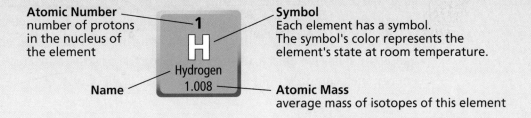

Atomic Number
number of protons in the nucleus of the element

1
H
Hydrogen
1.008

Symbol
Each element has a symbol. The symbol's color represents the element's state at room temperature.

Name

Atomic Mass
average mass of isotopes of this element

Groups and Periods

Elements in a vertical column of the periodic table are similar in chemical and physical properties. Elements in a column are known as a **group.** Each group is identified by a number at the top of the column. Sometimes a group is called a family of elements, because these elements are related.

The illustration at the left shows Group 17, commonly called the halogen group. Halogens tend to combine easily with many other elements and compounds, especially with the elements in Groups 1 and 2. An element that combines with one halogen will likely combine with another halogen. That is one way in which elements in a group are chemically similar. However, the physical properties of the elements in a group are not all the same. Look again at group 17. At room temperature, fluorine and chlorine are gases, while bromine is a liquid, and iodine and astatine are solids.

Lithium, sodium, and potassium are listed in Group 1 on the periodic table. These metals all react violently when they come into contact with water. Copper and silver are in Group 11. These metals do not react with water. Therefore, they can be used to make containers for water.

Each horizontal row in the periodic table is called a **period.** Properties of elements change in a predictable way from one end of a period to the other. In the illustration below, which shows Period 3, the elements on the far left are metals, and the ones on the far right are nonmetals. The chemical properties of the elements show a pattern. Similar patterns appear in the periods above and below this one.

The elements in Group 17, the halogens, show many similarities.

Period 3 contains elements with a wide range of properties. Aluminum (Al) is used to make drink cans, while argon (Ar) is a gas used in light bulbs.

Electron Arrangement

The chemical properties of an element depend on the way the electrons are arranged about the nucleus. Remember, we don't really know for sure where electrons are. We only know that there are regions, called energy shells, in which collections of electrons move. All the electrons in an energy shell have about the same amount of energy. The energy keeps the negative electrons moving about the positive nucleus. Each energy shell can only hold a certain number of electrons.

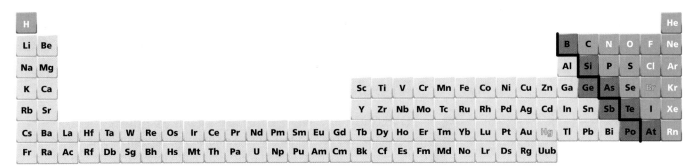

Each period of the periodic table corresponds to one energy shell. Some squares normally get placed below the table to make it shorter.

Look again at the periodic table. Can you guess now when one period ends and another begins? That's right. Energy shells. A period ends when an energy shell gets filled up with electrons. The first energy shell holds two electrons. The second and third energy shells hold eight electrons. The fourth and fifth hold as many as 18 electrons. The sixth and seventh energy shells can hold even more electrons. Placing all these element squares in the same row would make the table very large. This is why the lanthanides and the actinides are placed below the main table.

The way in which electron energy shells fill up gives a clue to why groups have similar chemical properties. For example, lithium, sodium, and potassium are all at the start of a period. They each have one electron added to a new energy shell. On the other hand, chlorine, bromine, and iodine are all near the end of a period. These elements have energy shells that are almost full.

The precise geometry of electron energy shells is complicated. The important point to remember is that the elements in a group have a similar arrangement of electrons. This arrangement gives them their particular properties.

CHECK YOUR READING When does one period end and another begin?

7.2 Review

KEY CONCEPTS

1. How is the modern periodic table organized? (8.7.c)

2. What information about an atom's properties can you read from the periodic table? (8.7.c)

3. How are the relationships of elements in a group different from the relationships of elements in a period? (8.7.c)

CRITICAL THINKING

4. **Infer** Looking at the periodic table would you expect strontium (Sr) to be more like potassium (K) or bromine (Br)? Why?

5. **Predict** One chlorine (Cl) atom combines with one sodium (Na) atom. How many potassium (K) atoms do you think combine with a chlorine atom?

CHALLENGE

6. **Analyze** Explain how chemists can state with certainty that no one will discover an element between sulfur (S) and chlorine (Cl).

CHAPTER INVESTIGATION

Modeling Atomic Masses

OVERVIEW AND PURPOSE Atoms are extremely small. They are so small, in fact, that a single drop of water contains more atoms than you could count in a lifetime! Measuring the masses of atoms to discover the patterns in the periodic table was not an easy task for scientists in the past. This investigation will give you some sense of how scientists determined the masses of atoms. You will

- compare the masses of different film can "atoms"
- predict the number of washers in each film can "atom"

▶ Procedure

1. Create a data table similar to the one shown on the sample notebook page.

2. Find the mass of one empty film can. Record this mass in the second row of the table.

3. Collect the four film cans labeled A, B, C, and D in advance by your teacher. Each can contains a different number of washers and represents a different atom. The washers represent the protons and neutrons in an atom's nucleus.

4. Measure the mass of each of the four film cans. Record the masses of the film can atoms in the first row of your data table.

5. Subtract the mass of an empty film can from the mass of each film can atom. Record the differences under "Mass of washers" in your data table. Think of these masses as the masses of the nuclei.

MATERIALS
- empty film can
- balance
- 4 filled film cans

  8.3.a, 8.3.f, 8.9.e

Content Standard
8.3.a Students know the structure of the atom and know it is composed of protons, neutrons, and electrons.

Investigation Standard
8.9.e Construct appropriate graphs from data and develop quantitative statements about the relationships between variables.

6 Divide the mass of the washers in can B by the mass of the washers in can A. Record the value under "Mass of the washers divided by can A" in the column for can B.

7 Repeat step 6 for film can atoms A, C, and D. Record the values in the appropriate spaces.

8 Round the values you obtained in steps 6 and 7 to the nearest whole number. Record the rounded figures in the next row of the table.

Observe and Analyze
Write It Up

1. **RECORD OBSERVATIONS** Be sure your data table and calculations are complete. Double-check your arithmetic.

2. **ANALYZE DATA** Examine your data table. Do you notice any patterns in how the masses increase? Given that all the washers in the film can atoms have identical masses, what might the ratio of the mass of the washers to the smallest mass tell you?

3. **PREDICT** Assume there is only one washer in can A. Estimate the number of washers in the other cans and record your estimates in the last row of the table.

4. **GRAPH DATA** On a sheet of graph paper, plot the masses (in grams) of the washers in the film can atoms on the y-axis and the number of washers in each can on the x-axis. Connect the points on the graph.

5. **INTERPRET DATA** Compare the masses of your film can atoms with the masses of the first four atoms on the periodic table. Which film can represents which atom?

Conclude
Write It Up

1. **IDENTIFY LIMITS** What can't this activity tell you about the identity of your film can atoms? (**Hint:** Protons and neutrons in real atoms have about the same mass.)

2. **INFER** Hydrogen has only a single proton in its nucleus. If your film can atoms represent the first four elements in the periodic table, what are the numbers of protons and neutrons in each atom?

3. **APPLY** Single atoms are far too small to place on a balance. How do you think scientists determine the masses of real atoms?

INVESTIGATE Further

CHALLENGE Use a periodic table to find the masses of the next two atoms (boron and carbon). How many washers would you need to make film can atom models for each?

Modeling Atomic Masses

Observe and Analyze

Table 1. Masses of Film Can Atoms

	A	B	C	D
Mass of film can atom (g)				
Mass of empty film can (g)				
Mass of washers (g)				
Mass of washers divided by can A				
Value rounded to nearest whole number				
Estimated number of washers in each can				

7.3 The periodic table is a map of the elements.

CALIFORNIA
Content Standards

8.7.a Students know how to identify regions corresponding to metals, nonmetals, and inert gases.

8.7.b Students know each element has a specific number of protons in the nucleus (the atomic number) and each isotope of the element has a different but specific number of neutrons in the nucleus.

BEFORE, you learned

• The periodic table is organized into groups of elements with similar characteristics
• The periodic table shows atomic structure

NOW, you will learn

• How elements are classified as metals, nonmetals, and metalloids
• About different groups of elements
• About radioactive elements

VOCABULARY

reactive p. 216
metal p. 217
nonmetal p. 219
metalloid p. 220
radioactivity p. 220
half-life p. 222

THINK ABOUT

How are elements different?

The photograph shows common uses of the elements copper, aluminum, and argon. Copper is in a penny, aluminum in a pie plate, and argon in a light bulb. Each element is located in a different part of the periodic table, and each has a very different use. Find these elements on the periodic table. What other elements are near these?

The periodic table has distinct regions.

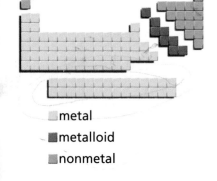

▢ metal
▢ metalloid
▢ nonmetal

The periodic table is a kind of map of the elements. Just as a country's location on the globe gives you information about its climate, an element's position on the periodic table indicates its properties. The periodic table has three main regions. Metals are on the left. Nonmetals (except hydrogen) are on the right. Metalloids are in between the two. The periodic table on pages 210–211 shows these regions with different colors. A yellow box shows a metal; green, a nonmetal; and purple, a metalloid.

An element's position on the table also indicates how reactive it is. **Reactive** means how likely an element is to undergo a chemical change. Most elements are somewhat reactive and combine with other elements. The atoms of the elements in Groups 1 and 17 are the most reactive. On the other hand, the elements of Group 18 are almost completely unreactive.

 CHECK YOUR READING How does the periodic table resemble a map?

Most elements are metals.

You can see from the colors of the squares that most of the elements are metals. In general, **metals** are elements that conduct electric current and heat well and have a shiny appearance. Metals can be shaped easily. They can even be drawn into a long wire. Except for mercury, which is a liquid, metals are solids at room temperature.

Sodium is a metal that is so soft it can be cut with a knife at room temperature.

You probably can name many uses for the metal **copper.**

Aluminum is often used for devices that must be strong and light.

Reactive Metals

The metals in Group 1 of the periodic table are the alkali metals. These metals are very reactive. Sodium and potassium are so reactive that they are often stored in oil to keep them away from air. When exposed to air, these elements react rapidly with oxygen and water vapor. Later, you'll learn how some of these metals are important for living cells.

Group 2 is the alkaline earth metals. These metals are less reactive than the alkali metals. They, however, are still more reactive than most other metals. Calcium ions are an essential part of your diet. Bones and teeth contain calcium ions. Magnesium is a light metal often combined with other metals to make strong lightweight materials. Many airplane frames contain magnesium.

Reactive Metals

Transition Metals

The elements in Groups 3–12 are called the transition metals. These metals are some of the earliest known elements, such as copper, gold, silver, and iron. These metals are generally less reactive than most other metals. For example, gold and silver are easily shaped and do not react easily. For thousands of years these metals have been used to make jewelry and coins. Ancient relics made from transition metals can be found in many museums. They remain relatively unchanged since the time they were made. Today, dimes and quarters are made of copper and nickel. Pennies are made of zinc with a coating of copper. Transition metal ions are even found in the foods you eat.

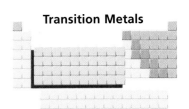

Transition Metals

Transition metals are very important to industry. Iron is the main part of steel. Steel is a material used for bridges and buildings. Most electric wires and many other electrical devices are made of copper. Copper is also used to make water pipes. It would be hard to think of an industry that doesn't make use of transition metals.

Some transition metals may be less familiar, but they are still important for modern technology. The tiny coil of wire inside incandescent light bulbs is made of tungsten. Platinum helps automobile engines burn fuel more cleanly.

Often, two or more metals are combined to form an alloy. Alloys can be stronger, less likely to rust, or easier to shape than pure metals. For example, steel is iron that contains other metals such as nickel, chromium, or manganese. Brass, an alloy of copper and zinc, is stronger than either metal alone. Silver jewelry often contains some copper, making it stronger than pure silver.

Rare Earth Elements

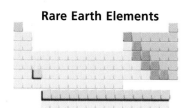

Rare Earth Elements

Two rows of elements are set below the main periodic table. You have read that this was done to save space. The top row is the rare earth elements. These elements are often referred to as lanthanides because they follow the element lanthanum (La) on the table. They are called rare earth elements because scientists once thought that they were available only in tiny amounts in Earth's crust. As mining methods improved, however, the rare earths were found to be not so rare—just hard to isolate in pure form.

More and more uses are being found for the rare earth elements. For example, neodymium (Nd) is useful for making cheap yet very powerful permanent magnets. Cerium (Ce) is used in the walls of self-cleaning ovens to prevent the build up of grime. Most often, however, the rare earths are used to add color to glass. Europium (Eu), for example, is used as a coating for some television tubes. Praseodymium (Pr) provides a protective coating against harmful radiation in the welder's helmet in the photograph.

Nonmetals and metalloids have a wide range of properties.

The elements to the right side of the periodic table are called **nonmetals.** As the name implies, the properties of nonmetals tend to be the opposite of those of metals. Many are gases at room temperature, and only one, bromine (Br), is a liquid. The solid nonmetals often have dull surfaces and and are not easily shaped. Nonmetals are generally poor conductors of heat and electric current.

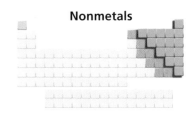
Nonmetals

The properties of nonmetals also tend to vary more from element to element than do the properties of the metals. The main components of the air that you breathe are the nonmetals nitrogen and oxygen. Nitrogen is a fairly unreactive element. Oxygen, however, reacts easily to form compounds with many other elements. Burning and rusting are two processes in which oxygen binds with other elements. Compounds containing carbon are essential to living things. Two forms of the element carbon are graphite, a soft, slippery, black material, and diamond, a hard crystal. Sulfur is a bright yellow powder that can be mined from deposits of the pure element.

Halogens

The elements in Group 17 are known as halogens. This name comes from Greek words meaning "forming salts." Halogens are very reactive nonmetals. They easily form compounds called salts with many metals. Because they are so reactive, halogens are often used to kill harmful microorganisms. For example, the halogen chlorine is used to prevent the growth of algae in swimming pools and to purify drinking water. Solutions containing iodine are often used in hospitals and in doctors' offices to kill germs on skin.

Halogens and Noble Gases

Noble gases produce the light for many signs.

Noble Gases

Group 18 elements are called the noble gases. They almost never react with other elements. For this reason the noble gases are also called the inert gases. *Inert* means "unable to move or act." Most noble gases are found in the atmosphere in small amounts. Argon gas makes up about one percent of the atmosphere. Passing an electric current through a glass tube filled with a noble gas can produce a colorful light, as in the photograph to the right. Argon gas also is placed in tungsten filament light bulbs, because it will not react with the hot filament.

 CHECK YOUR READING Where on Earth can you find noble gases?

Metalloids

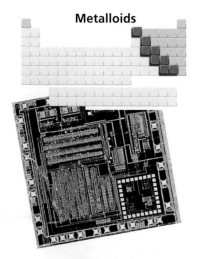

Metalloids

Metalloids have properties of both metals and nonmetals. In the periodic table, they lie on either side of a zigzag line separating metals from nonmetals. The most common metalloid is silicon. Silicon atoms are the second most common atoms in Earth's crust.

Metalloids are used in the semiconductors found in electronic devices. Semiconductors are materials that conduct an electric current under some conditions but not under others. Silicon, gallium, and germanium are three semiconductors used in computer chips.

The metalloid silicon is found in sand and in computer microchips.

Some atoms can change their identity.

Remember that the number of protons in the nucleus determines an element's identity. Chemical changes do not affect the nucleus, so chemical changes cannot change one type of atom into another. The number of protons in a nucleus does change sometimes, however. The identity of the atom, therefore, changes.

Recall that the nucleus of an atom contains protons and neutrons. Attractive forces between these particles hold the nucleus together even though protons repel one another. When the forces in the nucleus are strong enough to keep it together, we say the nucleus is stable.

Radioactive Elements

Each element has isotopes with different numbers of neutrons. The stability of a nucleus depends on the right balance of protons and neutrons. If there are too few or too many neutrons, the nucleus may become unstable. When this happens, particles are produced from the nucleus of the atom. The production of particles restores stability. This change is accompanied by a release of energy.

The production of particles can change the number of protons. The atom is thus transformed into an atom of a different element. In the early 1900s, the physicist Marie Curie named the process by which atoms produce energy and particles **radioactivity.**

Isotopes are radioactive if their nuclei have too many or too few neutrons. Most elements have radioactive isotopes. These isotopes are rare for small atoms. For the heaviest of elements—those beyond bismuth (Bi)—all of the isotopes are radioactive. The nucleus gets too big for the forces to hold it together.

Scientists study radioactivity with a device called a Geiger counter. The Geiger counter detects the particles and energy from the breakup of the atomic nucleus. Audible clicks are heard when an atom changes. More clicks indicate that more particles are being produced.

 CHECK YOUR READING How can an atom of one element change into an atom of a different element?

Uses of Radioactivity in Medicine

Radioactivity is used in hospitals to diagnose and treat patients. Some forms of radiation can be used to destroy harmful tumors inside a person's body without performing an operation. Radiation can also be used to test if the organs in the body are functioning properly. A patient is injected with a solution containing a radioactive isotope. Radioactive isotopes of a given atom move through the body in the same way as non-radioactive isotopes do. Doctors can detect the radiation produced by the isotopes. They can tell, therefore, where and how the body is using the substance.

Although radiation has its benefits, it is harmful to living things in large doses. Radiation can damage or kill cells. The energy from its particles can burn the skin. Extended contact with radiation causes cancer and other health problems.

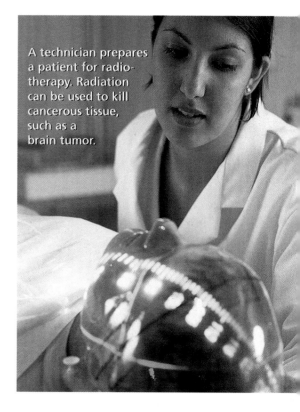

A technician prepares a patient for radiotherapy. Radiation can be used to kill cancerous tissue, such as a brain tumor.

INVESTIGATE Radioactivity

How quickly can atoms change?

PROCEDURE

1. Put 50 pennies in a bag. The pennies represent 50 atoms.

2. Pour out the pennies.

3. Count the number of pennies that landed head side up. These represent atoms whose nuclei changed.

4. Refill the bag with only the pennies that landed tail side up.

5. Repeat steps 2–4 until all of the pennies have landed head side up. Each time you pour out the pennies counts as one turn.

6. Construct a graph with the number of atoms that changed on the *y*-axis and the number of turns on the *x*-axis.

WHAT DO YOU THINK?

- After one turn, how many atoms had changed? had not changed?
- How many turns did it take for all the atoms to change?
- From looking at your graph, what can you conclude about the rate of radioactive change?

CHALLENGE If you used a different number of pennies, would your results be different? In what way?

SKILL FOCUS
Modeling (8.7.b)

MATERIALS
- 50 pennies
- bag
- graph paper

TIME
30 minutes

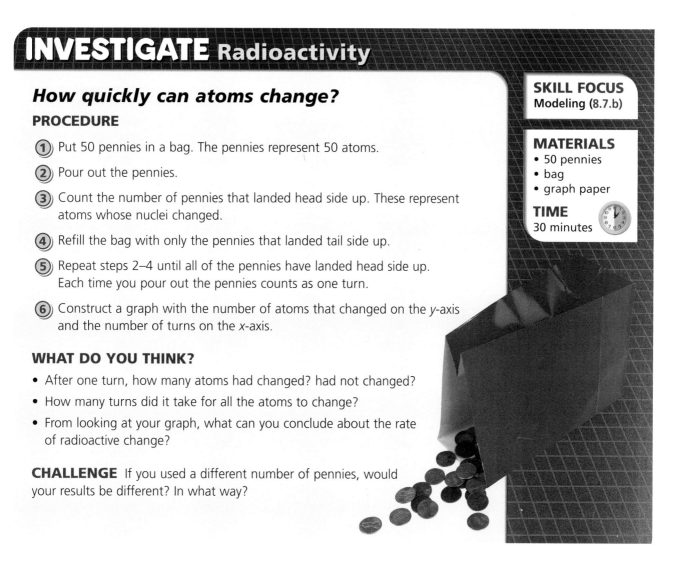

Radioactive Decay

The identities of radioactive atoms change because the numbers of protons in the nuclei changes. This process is known as radioactive decay. Over time, all of the atoms of a radioactive isotope will change into atoms of another element.

Radioactive decay occurs at a steady rate. This rate is characteristic of the particular isotope. The time it takes for one-half of the atoms in a particular sample to decay is called the **half-life** of the isotope. For example, if you had 1000 atoms of a radioactive isotope with a half-life of one year, 500 of the atoms would change into another element over the course of one year. In the next year, 250 more atoms would decay. The illustration to the right shows how the amount of the original isotope would decrease over time.

The half-life is a characteristic of each isotope. It is independent of the amount of material. Half-life is also not affected by such conditions as temperature or pressure. Half-lives of isotopes range from a small fraction of a second to many billions of years. Scientists often date materials by determining the amount of radioactive decay they have undergone.

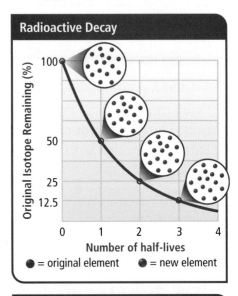

Radioactive Decay

Original Isotope Remaining (%)

Number of half-lives

● = original element   ● = new element

Half-Lives of Selected Elements

Isotope	Half-Life
Uranium-238	4,510,000,000 years
Carbon-14	5,730 years
Radon-222	3.82 days
Lead-214	27 minutes
Polonium-214	.00016 seconds

7.3 Review

KEY CONCEPTS

1. What are the three main classes of elements in the periodic table? (8.7.c)

2. What are the major characteristics of metals? (8.7.c)

3. How can an atom of one element change to an atom of another element? (8.7.a)

CRITICAL THINKING

4. **Compare** Use the periodic table to determine whether a carbon (C) or a fluorine (F) atom would be more reactive.

5. **Calculate** What fraction of a radioactive sample remains after three half-lives?

⊘ CHALLENGE

6. **Analyze** Why do you think the noble gases were among the last of the naturally occurring elements to be discovered?

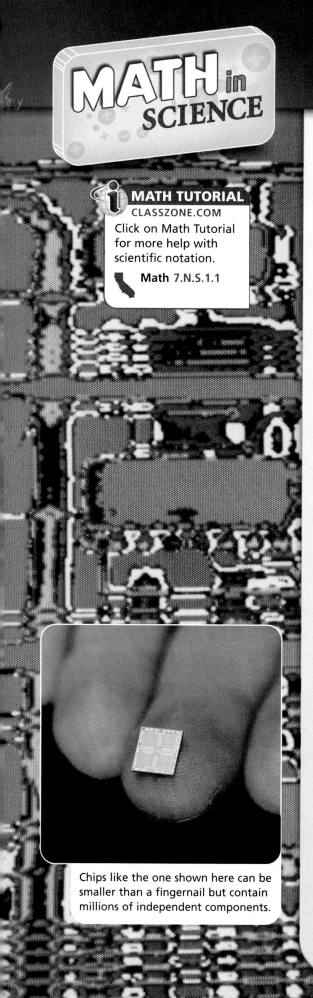

MATH in SCIENCE

MATH TUTORIAL
CLASSZONE.COM
Click on Math Tutorial for more help with scientific notation.

Math 7.N.S.1.1

Chips like the one shown here can be smaller than a fingernail but contain millions of independent components.

SKILL: USING SCIENTIFIC NOTATION

Numbers with Many Zeros

Semiconductor devices are at the heart of the modern personal computer. Today, tiny chips can contain more than 42,000,000 connections and perform about 3,000,000,000 calculations per second. Computers have little problem handling such large numbers. Scientists, however, use a scientific notation as a shorthand way to write large numbers. Scientific notation expresses a very large or very small number as the product of a number between 1 and 10 and a power of 10.

Example

Large Number How would you express the number 6,500,000,000—the approximate population of the world as of July 2005—in scientific notation?

(1) Look at the number and count how many spaces you would need to move the decimal point to get a number between 1 and 10.

$$6, \underset{9}{\frown} 5 \underset{8}{\frown} 0 \underset{7}{\frown} 0, \underset{6}{\frown} 0 \underset{5}{\frown} 0 \underset{4}{\frown} 0, \underset{3}{\frown} 0 \underset{2}{\frown} 0 \underset{1}{\frown} 0$$

(2) Place the decimal point in the space and multiply the number by the appropriate power of 10. The power of 10 will be equivalent to the number of spaces you moved the decimal point.

ANSWER 6.5×10^9

Small Number How would you express 0.0000023 in scientific notation?

(1) Count the number of places you need to move the decimal point to get a number between 1 and 10. This time you move the decimal point to the right, not the left.

$$0, \underset{1}{\frown} 0 \underset{2}{\frown} 0 \underset{3}{\frown} 0 \underset{4}{\frown} 0 \underset{5}{\frown} 0 \underset{6}{\frown} 2 3$$

(2) The power of 10 you need to multiply this number by is still equal to the number of places you moved the decimal point. Place a negative sign in front of it to indicate that you moved the decimal point to the right.

ANSWER 2.3×10^{-6}

Answer the following questions.

1. Express the following numbers in scientific notation:
   (a) 75,000   (b) 54,000,000,000   (c) 0.0000064

2. Express these numbers in decimal form:
   (a) 6.0×10^{24} (b) 7.4×10^{22} (c) 5.7×10^{-10}

CHALLENGE What is 2.2×10^{22} subtracted from 4.6×10^{22}?

Chapter 7: **Atomic Structure and the Periodic Table** 223

Patterns exist among the elements.

CALIFORNIA
Content Standard

8.7.c Students know substances can be classified by their properties, including their melting temperature, density, hardness, and thermal and electrical conductivity.

BEFORE, you learned

- The periodic table organizes elements according to their properties
- Elements are classified as metals, nonmentals, and metalloids

NOW, you will learn

- How the periodic table can be used to make predictions
- How atomic structure relates to physical properties of elements
- How the periodic table shows patterns among properties of elements

VOCABULARY

thermal
   conductivity p.227
electrical
   conductivity p.227

EXPLORE Trends in the Periodic Table (8.7.c)

Are there relationships among the elements?

(1) Find the four elements listed at right on the periodic table.

(2) Arrange them according to their positions in the periodic table.

WHAT DO YOU THINK?

- How are the elements located in relation to one another?
- Can you make a generalization about the densities of elements in a group?

Element	Symbol	Density (G/cm³)
Silicon	Si	2.33
Germanium	Ge	5.32
Carbon	C	2.26
Tin	Sn	7.31

The periodic table is expanding.

CALIFORNIA Focus

Physicist Ernest Lawrence constructed the first cyclotron in January, 1931 in Berkeley, California. It measured only about 11 cm (4.5 inches). Today's cyclotrons can be as much as 18 m (709 inches or 60 ft) in diameter. Particles may travel 45 km (28 mi) before they strike a nucleus.

Before 1940, no one had found an element whose atoms had more than 92 protons in its nucleus. That year at the University of California, Berkely, scientists Edwin McMillan and Philip Abelson thought they might be able to make one. They used a device called a cyclotron. The cyclotron can hurl protons and neutrons towards the nuclei of other atoms. If some of these particles stick to a nucleus, there is a chance a different element can form. McMillan and Abelson used the cyclotron to assemble an element with 93 protons in its nucleus. They decided to call the element neptunium. The next year, Berkeley scientist Glenn Seaborg assembled an element with 94 protons in its nucleus, plutonium.

Scientists study the tracks left behind by particles after they collide in the cyclotron. To an expert, these markings show the masses of the particles.

Seaborg went on to predict the properties of elements with even higher atomic numbers. It wasn't long before all these elements had been produced. Some were first made in labs at Berkeley. Seaborg's predictions turned out to be true. Much as Mendeleev had done almost a century before, Seaborg had made predictions about unknown elements based on their location in the periodic table.

The periodic table shows trends in atomic structure.

Remember, a group is one column of the periodic table. Atoms of the elements in a group have the same number of electrons in their outer energy shells. This gives the elements similar chemical properties. It also gives rise to the trends in the periodic table. Some trends are very evident. Others are not.

The Sizes of Atoms

We measure the size of an atom by the size of its electron cloud. The size of the cloud depends a lot on how many electrons it contains. It also depends on how strongly the protons in the nucleus pull on the electrons. If the nucleus exerts a strong pull on the electrons, the atom is smaller. If the nucleus pulls only weakly on the electrons, the atom is larger.

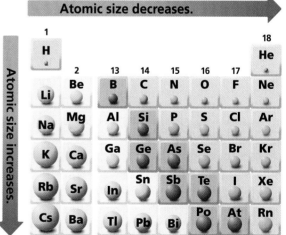

Groups 3 to 12 are not shown here.

The excerpt from the periodic table shows how the sizes of atoms vary within groups and across periods. Notice that within each group, atomic size increases as you read down the periodic table. The electron cloud around the nucleus grows as more energy shells are filled. Notice that as you read from left to right across each period, atomic size decreases. Even though there are more electrons, the nucleus pulls more strongly on these electrons, so the atoms are smaller.

Ability to Form Ions

Reactive Metals

Ions are atoms that have either gained or lost electrons. Atoms that form ions more easily are said to be more reactive. How easily an atom may gain or lose an electron depends on many factors. Two important factors are how the electrons are arranged around the atom, and how strongly the nucleus holds the electrons.

Metals, for example, usually lose electrons to form positive ions. The metals in Group 1 lose one electron easily. As you move from left to right across the periodic table, more energy is required to remove an electron from an atom. However, the farther down a column you go, the less energy is required to remove an electron.

If you go to the other side of the periodic table, you find a similar but opposite pattern. These atoms are mainly nonmetals. Nonmetals tend to gain electrons to form negative ions. Atoms farther to the right of the periodic table gain electrons more easily. Fluorine gains an electron more easily than oxygen, for example.

At the far right side of the periodic table are the noble gases. They form Group 18. The noble gases normally do not form ions at all. This is because their electron shells are filled.

Pure sodium metal reacts violently with water. Atoms of the element sodium form ions easily.

CHECK YOUR READING What is one factor affecting an atom's ability to form ions?

The periodic table reflects physical properties of elements.

Remember a physical property is any property of a substance that can be observed without changing the substance. Density is one example of a physical property. Conductivity of both heat and electric current, melting point, and boiling point are others. The structure of the periodic table displays a few trends in the physical properties of the elements.

Density and Hardness

Density is the mass of a substance per unit volume. It is a measure of how much matter is packed into a particular space. With each group in the periodic table, density increases as you read down the column. With each period, however, the elements at the right and left edges of the row are the least dense. The elements in the middle of the row are the most dense. Study the periodic table on pages 210–211. Note that the elements osmium (Os) and iridium (Ir) are at the center of the table. They are the densest of all the elements.

Dense elements tend to be hard. Hardness means a material can't be scratched or dented easily. Osmium and iridium are often added to other metals to make them harder.

Osmium is one of the densest elements. It is in the middle of the periodic table.

Conductivity and Melting Temperature

Some elements conduct heat and electric current very easily. Others are poor conductors of heat and electric current. Elements on the right side of the periodic table tend to be poor conductors. They are nonmetals. The best conductors of both heat and electric current are the metals, which are on the left side and in the middle of the periodic table. The measure of how well a substance conducts thermal energy is called **thermal conductivity.** The measure of how well a substance conducts electric current is **electrical conductivity.**

Recall that the melting point of a substance is the temperature at which the solid form of the substance becomes a liquid. The boiling point of a substance is the temperature at which the liquid form of the substances becomes a gas. A substance with a high melting point will also have a high boiling point. And a substance with a low melting point will also have a low boiling point.

The periodic table shows broad patterns for melting and boiling points. For example, the nonmetals, which are on the right side of the periodic table, tend to have lower melting and boiling points than the metals, which make up the left and central parts of the table. This helps explain a general pattern in melting points and boiling points across the periods. Also, on the left side of the periodic table, melting points tend to fall as you read down a group. On the right side of the periodic table, melting points rise as you read down a group.

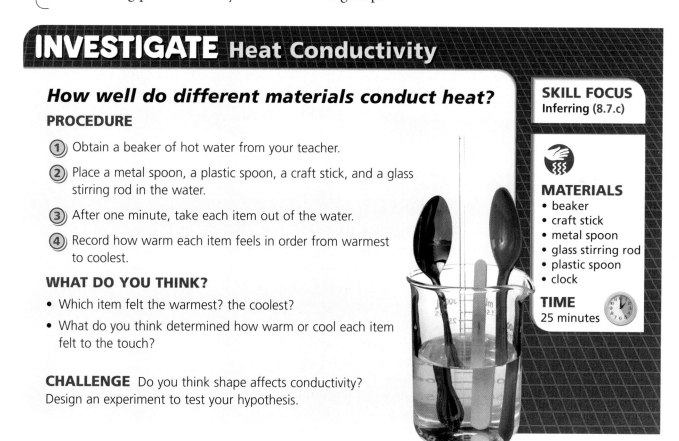

INVESTIGATE Heat Conductivity

How well do different materials conduct heat?

PROCEDURE

1. Obtain a beaker of hot water from your teacher.

2. Place a metal spoon, a plastic spoon, a craft stick, and a glass stirring rod in the water.

3. After one minute, take each item out of the water.

4. Record how warm each item feels in order from warmest to coolest.

WHAT DO YOU THINK?

- Which item felt the warmest? the coolest?

- What do you think determined how warm or cool each item felt to the touch?

CHALLENGE Do you think shape affects conductivity? Design an experiment to test your hypothesis.

SKILL FOCUS
Inferring (8.7.c)

MATERIALS
- beaker
- craft stick
- metal spoon
- glass stirring rod
- plastic spoon
- clock

TIME
25 minutes

Carbon in the form of diamond has one of the highest melting points of any element. It is also one of the hardest substances on Earth.

With only an additional proton in its nucleus, nitrogen is very different from carbon. It is a gas down to –196°C.

Exceptions

We've seen a few trends in the physical properties of the elements in the periodic table. Knowing these trends makes the periodic table a valuable tool. If two elements are close together in the periodic table, you can feel fairly certain you can identify some relationship between them.

Or can you? For example, carbon, which has the atomic number 6, and nitrogen, which has the atomic number 7, could not be more different. Carbon is a solid up to about 3,700°C. Nitrogen, however, is a gas to –196°C. Obviously, the difference of a proton in the atom's nucleus makes a huge difference in the properties of the two elements.

This goes to show that atomic structure is very complex. We can only present a simplified picture of it here. Not even the most knowledgeable scientists, however, know exactly why some atoms behave the way they do. With each question answered, it seems another question arises.

Remember, scientists realized that certain elements had related properties before they knew about atomic structure. The two ideas were separate. They were only later linked. There were many false starts. But each false start brought scientists closer to what they know today.

So, when you look at the periodic table, don't think of it as just a collection of symbols. Think of it as a reflection of the relationships among the elements. Think of it as a map of the elements. Think of it as a reflection of atomic structure.

CHECK YOUR READING Which element has one more proton than carbon?

7.4 Review

KEY CONCEPTS

1. How have scientists used the periodic table in making new discoveries? (8.7.c)

2. Why don't atoms simply get larger as you read across the periodic table? (8.7.c)

3. Which elements in the periodic table are better conductors of heat? (8.7.c)

CRITICAL THINKING

4. **Predict** Barium (Ba) is in Group 2. Recall that atoms in Group 1 lose one electron to form ions with a 1+ charge. What type of ion does barium probably form?

5. **Interpret** Name two elements that are side by side on the periodic table that do not reflect the general trend in melting points for the periods.

○ CHALLENGE

6. **Infer** Long ago, chemists hoped to find a way of turning any element into gold. Do you think this is possible today? Why or why not?

California Close-Up

THE PROPERTIES OF ELEMENTS

The Properties of Gold

> **8.7.c** Students know substances can be classified by their properties, including their melting temperature, density, hardness, and thermal and electrical conductivity.

In January 1848, James Marshall made an unexpected discovery on the American River. He found several pea-sized, shiny nuggets. Could it be gold? He wondered. He had to be sure before he dared to say anything.

Marshall pounded a piece with a rock. It didn't crack, but it did bend. This made sense. Gold is a very soft and easily shaped metal. This property was one reason why gold had been used for centuries to make coins. He next tried boiling a piece in a strong solution of lye. The nugget came out unchanged. This also made sense. Gold does not react with many substances. This property is the reason gold objects made thousands of years ago can look remarkably new today.

Is It Gold?

Marshall took a sample of the substance to James Sutter. Marshall had been helping to build a sawmill for Sutter when he found it. Sutter performed the ultimate test. He made a mixture of the chemicals nitric acid and hydrochloric acid. For centuries, this mixture had been known as *aqua regia,* or royal water. It was called royal water because it was the only known mixture that could dissolve the royal metal, gold. The sample did dissolve. It was gold!

This 7.1 gram (0.25 oz) piece of gold was found in 1848. It is now in the Bancroft Library.

Gold is a very dense metal. This property was good for prospectors. During the gold rush, prospectors panned for gold by shaking river sand in a flat pan in a stream. Because gold is dense, it sank to the bottom. Lighter sediments washed away.

WRITING ABOUT SCIENCE

Write a short story from the point of view of a gold-rush prospector. Describe finding a shiny nugget that you suspect is gold. How could you tell it was gold? Describe at least three tests you will perform to identify the metal.

If gold is in the sand, it stays at the bottom when the pan is shaken.

Even today, people still hope to find gold in the sand.

Chapter Review

the BIG idea

A substance's atomic structure determines its physical and chemical properties.

CONTENT REVIEW
CLASSZONE.COM

◀ KEY CONCEPTS SUMMARY

1 Atoms are the smallest form of elements.

All matter is made of the atoms of approximately 100 elements. Atoms of elements contain protons, neutrons, and electrons.

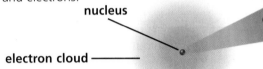

proton   neutron

nucleus

electron cloud

VOCABULARY
proton p. 201
neutron p. 201
nucleus p. 201
electron p. 201
atomic number p. 202
atomic mass number
 p. 202
isotope p. 202
ion p. 204

2 Elements make up the periodic table.

Elements can be organized by similarities.

Groups of elements have similar properties.

Elements in a period have varying properties.

VOCABULARY
atomic mass p. 207
periodic table p. 208
group p. 212
period p. 212

3 The periodic table is a map of the elements.

The periodic table has distinct regions. Three regions are metals, metalloids, and nonmetals.

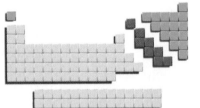

☐ metal ■ metalloid ▨ nonmetal

VOCABULARY
reactive p. 216
metal p. 217
nonmetal p. 219
metalloid p. 220
radioactivity p. 220
half-life p. 222

4 Patterns exist among the elements.

The periodic table has trends. One trend is that atomic size gets smaller as one moves from left to right.

Na Mg Al Si P S Cl Ar

VOCABULARY
thermal conductivity
 p. 227
electrical conductivity
 p. 227

Reviewing Vocabulary

Describe how the vocabulary terms in the following pairs are related to each other. Explain the relationship in a one- or two-sentence answer. Underline each vocabulary term in your answer.

1. isotope, nucleus

2. atomic mass, atomic number

3. electron, proton

4. group, period

5. metals, nonmetals

6. radioactivity, half-life

7. density, hardness

Reviewing Key Concepts

Multiple Choice *Choose the letter of the best answer.*

8. The central part of an atom is called the (8.3.a)
  a. electron   **c.** proton
  b. nucleus   **d.** neutron

9. The electric charge on a proton is (8.3.a)
  a. positive   **c.** neutral
  b. negative   **d.** changing

10. The number of protons in the nucleus is the (8.7.b)
  a. atomic mass   **c.** atomic number
  b. isotope   **d.** half-life

11. Nitrogen's atomic number is 7. An isotope of nitrogen containing seven neutrons would be (8.7.b)
  a. nitrogen-13   **c.** nitrogen-15
  b. nitrogen-14   **d.** nitrogen-16

12. How does the size of a negative ion compare to the size of the atom that formed it? (8.3.a)
  a. It's smaller.
  b. It's larger.
  c. It's the same size.
  d. It varies.

13. The modern periodic table is organized by (8.7.c)
  a. size of atom
  b. atomic mass
  c. number of neutrons
  d. atomic number

14. Elements in a group have (8.7.c)
  a. a wide range of chemical properties
  b. the same atomic radius
  c. similar chemical properties
  d. the same number of protons

15. Elements in a period have (8.7.c)
  a. a wide range of chemical properties
  b. the same atomic radius
  c. similar chemical properties
  d. the same number of protons

16. From left to right in a period, the size of atoms (8.7.c)
  a. increases   **c.** remains the same
  b. decreases   **d.** shows no pattern

17. The elements in Group 1 of the periodic table are commonly called the (8.7.c)
  a. alkali metals   **c.** alkaline earth metals
  b. transition metals   **d.** rare earth metals

18. The isotope nitrogen-13 has a half-life of 10 minutes. If you start with 40 grams of this isotope, how many grams will you have left after 20 minutes? (8.3.a)
  a. 10   **c.** 20
  b. 15   **d.** 30

Short Answer *Write a short answer to each question. You may need to consult a periodic table.*

19. Rubidium forms the ion Rb^+. Is this ion larger or smaller than the neutral atom? Explain. (8.3.a)

20. How can you find the number of neutrons in the isotope nitrogen-16? (8.7.b)

21. Explain how density varies across and up and down the periodic table. (8.7.c)

22. Place these elements in order from least reactive to most reactive: nickel (Ni), xenon (Xe), lithium (Li). How did you determine the order? (8.7.c)

Thinking Critically

The table below lists some properties of six elements. Use this information and your knowledge of the properties of elements to answer the next three questions.

Element	Appearance	Density (g/cm^3)	Conducts Electricity
A	dark purple crystals	4.93	no
B	shiny silvery solid	0.97	yes
C	shiny silvery solid	22.65	yes
D	yellow powder	2.07	no
E	shiny gray solid	5.32	semiconductor
F	shiny bluish solid	8.91	yes

23. **ANALYZE** Use the listed properties to identify each of the elements as a metal, a nonmetal, or a metalloid. (8.7.c)

24. **APPLY** Which would weigh more: a cube of element A or a same-sized cube of element D? (8.7.c)

25. **HYPOTHESIZE** Which element(s) do you think you might find in electronic devices? Why? (8.7.c)

26. **HYPOTHESIZE** The thyroid gland, located in your throat, secretes hormones. In 1924 iodine was added to table salt. As more and more Americans used iodized salt, the number of cases of thyroid diseases decreased. Write a hypothesis that explains the observed decrease in thyroid-related diseases. (8.6.c)

27. **INFER** How does the size of a beryllium (Be) atom compare with the size of an oxygen (O) atom? (8.7.c)

28. **PREDICT** Although noble gases do not naturally react with other elements, xenon and krypton have been made to react with halogens, such as chlorine, in laboratories. Why are the halogens most likely to react with the noble gases? (8.7.c)

Below is an element square from the periodic table. Use it to answer the next two questions.

80
Hg
Mercury
200.59

29. **CALCULATE** One of the more common isotopes of mercury is mercury-200. How many protons and neutrons are in the nucleus of mercury-200? (8.7.b)

30. **INFER** Cadmium occupies the square directly above mercury on the periodic table. Is a cadium atom larger or smaller than a mercury atom? (8.7.c)

31. **CALCULATE** An isotope has a half-life of 40 minutes. How much of a 100-gram sample would remain unchanged after two hours? (8.7.b)

32. **APPLY** When a uranium atom with 92 protons and 146 neutrons undergoes radioactive decay, it produces a particle that consists of two protons and two neutrons from its nucleus. Into which element is the uranium atom transformed? (8.7.b)

the BIG idea

33. **ANALYZE** Look again at the photograph on pages 196–197. Answer the question again, using what you have learned in the chapter.

34. **DRAW CONCLUSIONS** Suppose you've been given the ability to take apart and assemble atoms. How could you turn lead into gold?

35. **ANALYZE** Explain how the structure of an atom determines its place in the periodic table.

UNIT PROJECTS

Evaluate all the data, results, and information from your project folder. Prepare to present your project.

Interpreting Tables

8.3.a, 8.7.c

The table below shows part of the periodic table of elements.

Group

	1			13	14	15	16	17	18
1	1 H	2							2 He
2	3 Li	4 Be		5 B	6 C	7 N	8 O	9 F	10 Ne
3	11 Na	12 Mg		13 Al	14 Si	15 P	16 S	17 Cl	18 Ar
4	19 K	20 Ca		31 Ga	32 Ge	33 As	34 Se	35 Br	36 Kr

(Period — vertical axis label on the left)

Answer the questions based on the information given in the table.

1. What does the number above the symbol for each element represent?

  a. its number of isotopes

  b. its atomic number

  c. its number of neutrons

  d. its atomic mass

2. The atom of what element is in Period 4, Group 13?

  a. Na   **c.** Al

  b. Ga   **d.** K

3. What do the elements on the far right of the table (He, Ne, Ar, and Kr) have in common?

  a. They do not generally react with other elements.

  b. They are liquids under normal conditions.

  c. They are metals that rust easily.

  d. They are very reactive gases.

4. How many electrons does a neutral chlorine (Cl) atom contain?

  a. 16   **c.** 18

  b. 17   **d.** 19

5. If a sodium (Na) atom loses one electron to form a positive ion, how many electrons would lithium (Li) lose to form a positive ion?

  a. 0   **c.** 2

  b. 1   **d.** 3

6. If a fluorine (F) atom gains one electron to form a negative ion, how many electrons would bromine (Br) gain to form a negative ion?

  a. 0   **c.** 2

  b. 1   **d.** 3

Extended Response

Answer the following two questions in detail. Include some of the terms shown in the word box at right. Underline each term you use in your answer.

electron	nucleus	proton
isotope	neutron	radioactivity

7. Democritus was an ancient Greek philosopher who claimed that all matter was made of tiny particles he called atoms. Democritus said that all atoms were made of the same material. The objects of the world differed because each was made of atoms of different sizes and shapes. How does the modern view of atoms differ from this ancient view? How is it similar?

8. Half-life is a measure of the time it takes half of the radioactive atoms in a substance to decay into other atoms. If you know how much radioactive material an object had to begin with, how could you use half-life to determine its age now?

Chemical Interactions

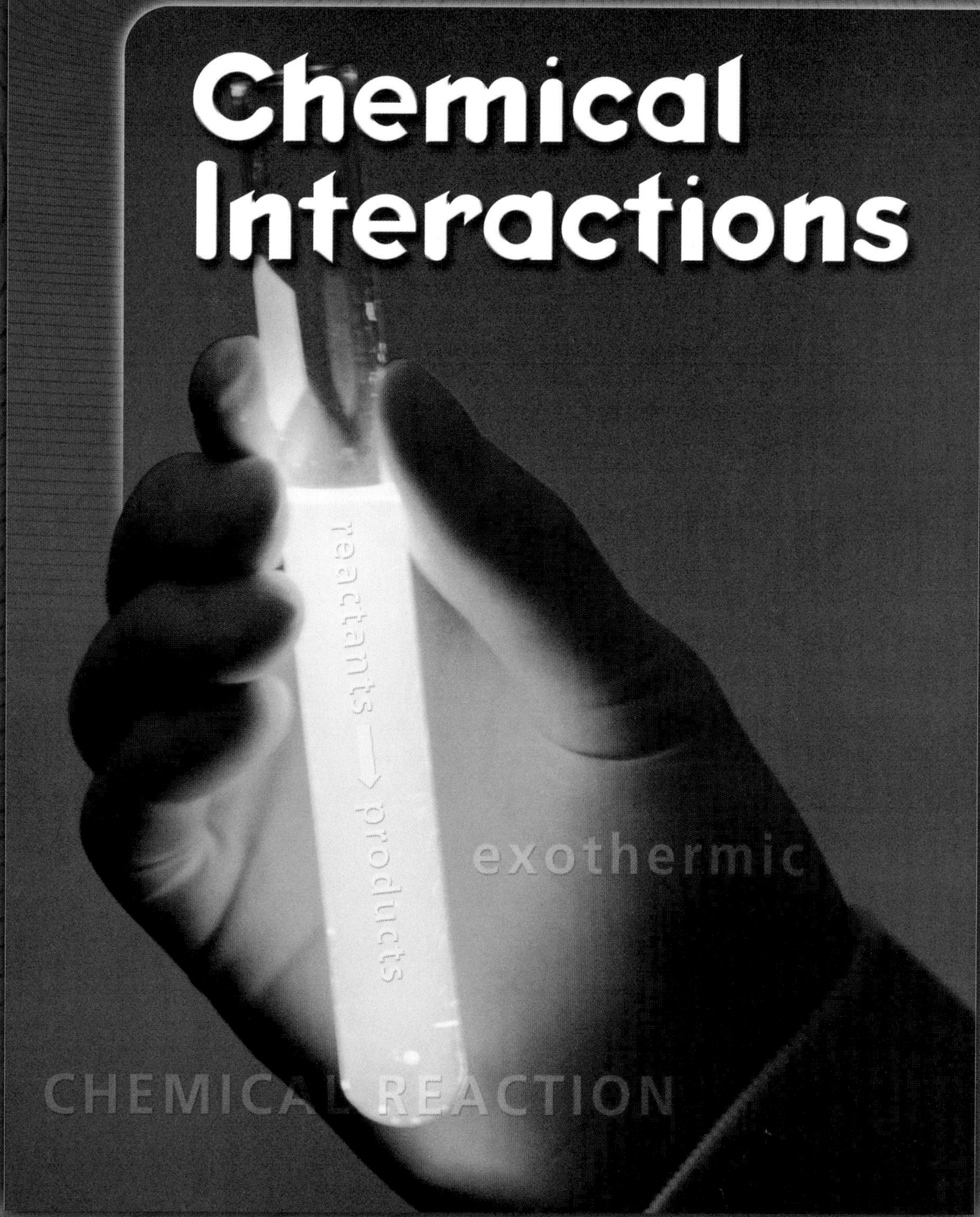

exothermic

reactants → products

CHEMICAL REACTION

Contents Overview

Medicines from Nature

Where have people found medicines?

In Brazil, extracts from plants are used to treat everything from Parkinson's Disease to arthritis.

Finding Natural Remedies

In the 1960s, people were searching for new cancer-fighting agents. Scientists tested over 35,000 compounds. They tried chemicals from plants because they knew that people had been using plants as medicines since ancient times. They tested the parts of plants which they knew to have been used to treat similar symptoms. This is how they came to test compounds from the bark of the Pacific yew tree. The bark was known to have strong effects on the body. The tests showed that something in the bark stopped the growth of cancerous tumors. The drug Taxol was derived from the compounds found in the yew tree.

Natural medicines are much more than simple folk cures. Many powerful medicines are based on compounds found in nature. But these compounds can be limited in supply. They also may have harmful side effects. Organic chemists must find ways to make these compounds safer and produce them in greater amounts.

Modeling the Molecule

To make a compound, a chemist must know what its molecule looks like, atom by atom. Many useful drugs have structures that contain many atoms arranged in complicated ways. The chemist must know exactly how many atoms of each kind are in the molecule and how they are arranged. One atom in the wrong place might mean that the drug won't work the way it should.

To study the structures of molecules, chemists use a method called spectroscopy. Spectroscopy is a process that shows how the molecules of a compound respond to certain forms of radiation. Three important types of spectroscopy are

• NMR (nuclear magnetic resonance) spectroscopy, which allows chemists to identify small groups of atoms within larger molecules

• IR (infrared) spectroscopy, which shows the presence of certain types of bonds in molecules

• X-ray studies, which show details such as how much space there is between atoms and what the overall physical shapes of molecules are

Chemists put all this information together to determine the structure of a molecule. They might even build a plastic model of the molecule.

Assembling the Puzzle

Once chemists know the structure of the molecule, they must figure out how to make it. They must determine the starting substances and the specific sequence of chemical reactions that will produce that molecule. It is a lot like doing a jigsaw puzzle. You know what the final picture looks like, but you still have to fit together all the pieces. In this case, however, the chemists may not even be sure what the little pieces look like.

Organic chemists often prefer to complete the process backward. They look at a model of the complete molecule and then figure out how they might build one just like it. How do chemists know what kinds of reactions might produce a certain molecule? Chemists have classified chemical reactions into different types. They determine how combinations of reactions will put the various kinds of atoms into their correct places in the molecule. Chemists may need to combine dozens of reactions to get the molecule they want.

Testing the Medicine

Once chemists have produced the desired drug molecule, the synthetic compound must be carefully tested. They need to make sure it works like the natural substance does. The sequence of reactions must also be tested. They need to make sure they produce the same compound when larger amounts of chemicals are used.

SCIENTIFIC AMERICAN FRONTIERS

View the "Endangered Wonder Drug" segment of your *Scientific American Frontiers* video to see how modern medicines can be developed from chemical compounds found in nature.

IN THIS SCENE FROM THE VIDEO ▶

A researcher works with a substance found in bark.

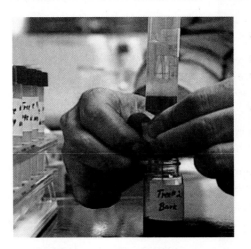

SAVING LIVES THROUGH NATURE AND CHEMISTRY
Medicines from plants have been used by different cultures around the world for thousands of years. The ephedra plant contains the raw material for many decongestants, which help shrink swollen nasal passages. It was used by the Chinese more than 5000 years ago. Today, the bark of the Pacific yew tree is being used as the source of the anticancer drug Taxol. A large amount of bark from the tree, however, is needed to make just one dose of the drug, and very few Pacific yew trees are available. Chemists, therefore, are trying to make this medicine in the laboratory.

Once a potential new drug is found in nature, it may take several years, or even decades, to figure out how to produce the drug synthetically and test it for safety. Only a small percentage of drugs tested ever goes to market. The drugs must undergo several stages of testing on both animals and humans. Today, chemists routinely search the seas and the forests for marine organisms and rare plants that might have the power to fight cancer, heart disease, or viruses.

Chemists often use computers to make models of drug molecules. Computers allow the chemists to see how the drug molecules will interact with other molecules.

UNANSWERED Questions

The search for new chemical compounds that can be used to treat human illnesses raises many questions. Scientists need to find ways to investigate, produce, and test new, more powerful drugs.

- How might scientists more quickly test the safety and effectiveness of new medicines?

- Can easily synthesized compounds be just as effective as natural medicines?

- Might the processes that produce these drugs in nature be duplicated in a lab?

- Can we discover other new sources of medicines in the natural world?

UNIT PROJECTS

As you study this unit, work alone or with a group on one of these projects.

Medicines Around You (8.3.f)

Present a report about a plant in your region that has medicinal properties.

- Collect samples of a plant that has medicinal properties.

- Bring your plant samples into your classroom. Prepare and present a report about the plant and the way it is used in medicine.

Model Medicine (8.3.f)

Build a scale model of a molecule that is used to treat a certain illness.

- Using the Internet or an encyclopedia, determine the structure of a compound that interests you.

- Using foam balls, toothpicks, water colors, string, and other materials, construct a model of the molecule. Describe your model to the class.

Remedies (8.6.c)

Write a news report about a popular herbal remedy, such as Saint John's Wort.

- To learn more about the herbal remedy, try interviewing a personal fitness trainer or an employee of a health-food store.

- Deliver a news report to the class telling of the advantages of the remedy and warning of its potential dangers.

CAREER CENTER
CLASSZONE.COM

Learn more about careers in chemistry.

CHAPTER

8 Chemical Bonds and Compounds

the BIG idea

The properties of compounds depend on their atoms and chemical bonds.

How do these skydivers stay together? How is this similar to the way atoms stay together?

Key Concepts

SECTION

1 Elements combine to form compounds.
Learn the difference between elements and compounds. Learn how to write and name chemical compounds.

SECTION

2 Chemical bonds hold compounds together.
Learn about the different types of chemical bonds.

SECTION

3 Substances' properties depend on their bonds.
Learn how bonds give compounds certain properties.

California ClassZone

CLASSZONE.COM

Chapter 8 online resources: Content Review, two Visualizations, two Resource Centers, Math Tutorial, Test Practice

EXPLORE (the BIG idea)

The Shape of Things

> **8.3.c** Students know atoms and molecules form solids by building up repeating patterns, such as the crystal structure of NaCl or long-chain polymers.

Pour some salt onto dark paper. Look at the grains through a hand lens. Try to observe a single grain. Look at several different grains individually. Note anything you find interesting about each grain. Draw pictures of the grains to help you remember your observations.

Observe and Think What do you notice about the salt grains? What do you think might affect the way the grains look?

Internet Activity: Bonding

> **8.3.d** Students know the states of matter (solid, liquid, gas) depend on molecular motion.

Go to **ClassZone.com** and watch the animation showing ionic and covalent bonding. Observe the differences in the two types of bonding. Note in particular how the electrons are arranged around the atoms. Count the number of electrons around each atom. Pay attention to the signs and arrows.

Observe and Think What's the difference between an ionic and a covalent bond? Explain how covalent bonding can have different characteristics.

NSTA
scilinks.org
SCiLINKS

Compounds Code: MDL023

Getting Ready to Learn

◀ CONCEPT REVIEW

- Electrons occupy a cloud around an atom's nucleus.
- Atoms form ions by losing or gaining electrons.

◀ VOCABULARY REVIEW

element p. 144

compound p. 145

electron p. 201

CONTENT REVIEW
CLASSZONE.COM

Review concepts and vocabulary.

▶ TAKING NOTES

MAIN IDEA AND DETAIL NOTES

Make a two-column chart. Write the main ideas, such as those in the blue headings, in the column on the left. Write details about each of those main ideas in the column on the right.

VOCABULARY STRATEGY

Place each vocabulary term at the center of a **description wheel** diagram. Write some words describing it on the spokes.

See the Note-Taking Handbook on pages R45–R51.

SCIENCE NOTEBOOK

MAIN IDEAS	DETAIL NOTES
Atoms combine in predictable numbers.	• Each compound has a specific ratio of atoms. • A ratio is a comparison between two quantities.
Writing chemical formulas	• Find symbols on the periodic table. • Note ratio of atoms with subscripts.

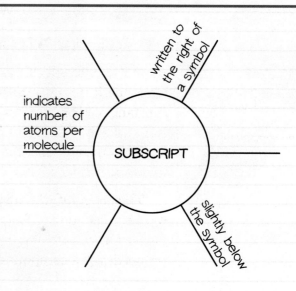

indicates number of atoms per molecule

written to the right of a symbol

SUBSCRIPT

slightly below the symbol

Elements combine to form compounds.

CALIFORNIA
Content Standards

8.3.b Students know that compounds are formed by combining two or more different elements and that compounds have properties that are different from their constituent elements.

8.5.a Students know reactant atoms and molecules interact to form products with different chemical properties.

BEFORE, you learned

• Atoms make up everything on Earth
• Atoms form compounds

NOW, you will learn

• How compounds differ from the elements that make them
• How a chemical formula represents the ratio of atoms in a compound
• How the same atoms can form different compounds

VOCABULARY

chemical formula p. 245
subscript p. 245

EXPLORE Compounds (8.3.b)

How are compounds different from elements?

PROCEDURE

① Examine the lump of carbon, the beaker of water, and the sugar. Record your observations of each.

② Light the candle. Pour some sugar into a test tube and heat it over the candle for several minutes. Record your observations.

MATERIALS

• carbon
• water
• sugar
• test tube
• test-tube holder
• candle
• matches

WHAT DO YOU THINK?

• The sugar is made up of atoms of the same elements that are in the carbon and water. How are sugar, carbon, and water different from one another?
• Does heating the sugar give you any clue that sugar contains more than one element?

Compounds have different properties from the elements that make them.

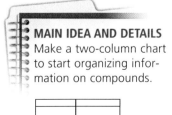

MAIN IDEA AND DETAILS
Make a two-column chart to start organizing information on compounds.

All of the different substances around you are not elements. In fact, while there are just over 100 elements, there are millions of different substances. Most substances are compounds. A compound is a substance made of atoms of two or more different elements. Just as 26 letters in the alphabet can form thousands of words, about 100 elements in the periodic table form millions of compounds.

The atoms of different elements are held together in compounds by chemical bonds. Chemical bonds can hold atoms together in large networks or in small groups. Chemical bonds help determine the properties of a compound.

The properties of a compound depend on which atoms of which elements the compound contains. Properties also depend on how the atoms are arranged. Atoms of carbon and hydrogen, for example, can combine to form many thousands of different compounds. These compounds include natural gas, parts of automobile gasoline, the hard waxes in candles, and many plastics. Each of these compounds has a certain number of carbon and hydrogen atoms arranged in a specific way.

The properties of compounds are often very different from the properties of the elements that make them. For example, water is made from two atoms of hydrogen bonded to one atom of oxygen. At room temperature, hydrogen and oxygen are both colorless, odorless gases. They remain gases down to extremely low temperatures. Water, however, is a liquid at temperatures up to 100°C (212°F) and a solid below 0°C (32°F). Sugar is a compound composed of atoms of carbon, hydrogen, and oxygen. Its properties, however, are unlike those of carbon, hydrogen, or oxygen.

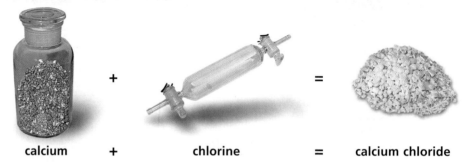

calcium   +   chlorine   =   calcium chloride

The picture above shows what happens when the elements calcium and chlorine combine to form the compound calcium chloride. Calcium is a soft, silvery metallic solid. Chlorine is a greenish-yellow gas that is extremely reactive and poisonous to humans. Calcium chloride, however, is a nonpoisonous white solid. People who live in cold climates often use calcium chloride to melt the ice on streets in the wintertime.

 CHECK YOUR READING   How do the properties of a compound compare with the properties of the elements that make it?

Atoms combine in predictable numbers.

A given compound always contains atoms of elements in a specific ratio. For example, the compound ammonia always has three hydrogen atoms for every nitrogen atom. This is a 3 to 1 ratio of hydrogen to nitrogen. This same 3:1 ratio holds for every sample of ammonia, under all physical conditions. A substance with a different ratio of hydrogen to nitrogen atoms is not ammonia. For example, hydrazoic acid also contains atoms of hydrogen and nitrogen but in a ratio of one hydrogen atom to three nitrogen atoms, or 1:3.

INVESTIGATE Element Ratios

How can you model a compound?

PROCEDURE

1. Collect a number of nuts and bolts. The nuts represent hydrogen atoms. The bolts represent carbon atoms.

2. Connect the nuts to the bolts to model the compound methane. Methane contains four hydrogen atoms attached to one carbon atom. Make as many of these models as you can.

3. Count the nuts and bolts left over.

WHAT DO YOU THINK?

- What ratio of nuts to bolts did you use to make a model of a methane atom?

- How many methane models did you make? Why couldn't you make more?

CHALLENGE The compound ammonia has one nitrogen atom and three hydrogen atoms. How would you use the nuts and bolts to model this compound?

SKILL FOCUS
Modeling (8.3.b)

MATERIAL
- nuts and bolts
- Modeling Compounds Datasheet

TIME
20 minutes

Chemical Formulas

Remember that atoms of elements can be represented by their chemical symbols, as given in the periodic table. A **chemical formula** uses these chemical symbols to represent the atoms of the elements and their ratios in a chemical compound.

Carbon dioxide is a compound consisting of one atom of carbon attached by chemical bonds to two atoms of oxygen. Here is how you would write the chemical formula for carbon dioxide:

- Find the symbols for carbon (C) and oxygen (O) on the periodic table. Write these symbols side by side.

- To show that there are two oxygen atoms for every carbon atom, place the subscript *2* to the right of the oxygen atom's symbol. A **subscript** is a number written to the right of a chemical symbol and slightly below it.

- Because there is only one atom of carbon in carbon dioxide, you need no subscript for carbon. The subscript 1 is never used. The chemical formula for carbon dioxide is, therefore,

$$CO_2$$

The chemical formula shows one carbon atom bonded to two oxygen atoms.

VOCABULARY
Remember to create a description wheel diagram for *chemical formula* and other vocabulary words.

READING TiP

The word *subscript* comes from the prefix *sub-*, which means "under," and the Latin word *scriptum,* which means "written." A subscript is something written under something else.

Chemical Formulas

Chemical formulas show the ratios of atoms in a chemical compound.

Compound Name	Atoms	Atomic Ratio	Chemical Formula
Hydrogen chloride	H Cl	1:1	HCl
Water	H H O	2:1	H_2O
Ammonia	N H H H	1:3	NH_3
Methane	C H H H H	1:4	CH_4
Propane	C C C H H H H H H H H	3:8	C_3H_8

 How many more hydrogen atoms does propane have than methane?

 RESOURCE CENTER
CLASSZONE.COM

Find out more about chemical formulas.

The chart above shows the names, atoms, ratios, and chemical formulas for several chemical compounds. The subscripts for each compound show the number of atoms that combine to make that compound. Notice how hydrogen combines with different atoms in different ratios. Notice that methane and propane are made of atoms of the same elements, carbon and hydrogen, only in different ratios. This example shows why it's important to pay attention to ratios when writing chemical formulas.

CHECK YOUR READING Why is the ratio of atoms in a chemical formula so important?

Same Elements, Different Compounds

Even before chemists began writing chemical formulas, they realized that different compounds could be composed of atoms of the same elements. Nitrogen and oxygen, for example, form several compounds. One compound has one atom of nitrogen attached to one atom of oxygen; this compound's formula is NO. A second compound has one atom of nitrogen attached to two atoms of oxygen, so its formula is NO_2. A third compound has two nitrogen atoms attached to one oxygen atom, so its formula is N_2O. The properties of these compounds are different, even though they are made of atoms of the same elements.

water (H₂O) hydrogen peroxide (H₂O₂)

There are other examples of atoms of the same elements forming different compounds. The photographs above show two bottles filled with clear, colorless liquids. You might use the liquid in the first bottle to cool off after a soccer game. The bottle contains water, which is a compound made from two atoms of hydrogen and one atom of oxygen (H_2O). You could not survive for long without water.

You would not like to drink the liquid in the second bottle. This bottle also contains a compound of hydrogen and oxygen, hydrogen peroxide. But hydrogen peroxide has two hydrogen and two oxygen atoms (H_2O_2). Hydrogen peroxide is commonly used to kill bacteria on skin. One way to tell these two compounds apart is to test them using a potato. A drop of hydrogen peroxide on a raw potato will bubble; a drop of water on the potato will not.

The difference between the two compounds is greater than just the labels. The hydrogen peroxide that you buy at a drugstore is a mixture of hydrogen peroxide and water. In its concentrated form, hydrogen peroxide is a thick, syrupy liquid that boils at 150°C (302°F). Hydrogen peroxide can even be used as a fuel. What a difference one oxygen atom can make!

CHECK YOUR READING What are the chemical formulas for water and hydrogen peroxide?

Review

KEY CONCEPTS

1. How do the properties of compounds often compare with the properties of the elements that make them? (8.3.b)

2. How many atoms are in the compound represented by the formula $C_{12}H_{22}O_{11}$? (8.3.b)

3. How can millions of compounds be made from the atoms of about 100 elements? (8.3.b)

CRITICAL THINKING

4. **Apply** If a chemical formula has no subscripts, what can you conclude about the ratio of the atoms in it?

5. **Infer** Would two compounds made of nitrogen and oxygen always be identical? Explain why or why not.

CHALLENGE

6. **Analyze** A chemist analyzes two compounds and finds that they both contain only carbon and oxygen. The two compounds, however, have different properties. How can two compounds made from the same elements be different?

MATH TUTORIAL
CLASSZONE.COM
Click on Math Tutorial
for more help with ratios.

Math 7.NS.1.2
Science 8.5.a

A good strikeout-to-walk ratio for a baseball pitcher is 2:1. This means that for every two strikeouts achieved, the pitcher only allows one walk.

SKILL: CALCULATING RATIOS

Regarding Ratios

No pitcher gets a batter out every time. Sometimes even the worst pitchers have spectacular games. If you're a fan of professional baseball, you've probably seen the quality of certain players rated by using a ratio. A ratio is a comparison of two quantities. For a major league baseball pitcher, for example, one ratio you might hear reported is the number of strikeouts to the number of walks during a season. Chemical formulas are also ratios—ratios that compare the numbers of atoms in a compound.

Example

Consider the chemical formula for the compound glucose:

$$C_6H_{12}O_6$$

From this formula you can write several ratios. To find the ratio of carbon atoms to hydrogen atoms, for instance, do the following:

(1) Find the number of each kind of atom by noting the subscripts.

6 carbon, 12 hydrogen

(2) Write the first number on the left and the second on the right, and place a colon between them.

6:12

(3) Reduce the ratio by dividing each side by the largest number that goes into each evenly, in this case 6.

1:2

ANSWER The ratio of carbon to hydrogen in glucose is 1:2.

Use the table below to answer the following questions.

Compounds and Formulas	
Compound Name	**Chemical Formula**
Carbon dioxide	CO_2
Methane	CH_4
Sulfuric acid	H_2SO_4
Glucose	$C_6H_{12}O_6$
Formic acid	CH_2O_2

1. In carbon dioxide, what is the ratio of carbon to oxygen?

2. What is the ratio of carbon to hydrogen in methane?

3. In sulfuric acid, what is the ratio of hydrogen to sulfur? the ratio of sulfur to oxygen?

CHALLENGE What two chemical compounds in the table have the same ratio of carbon atoms to oxygen atoms?

8.2 Chemical bonds hold compounds together.

CALIFORNIA
Content Standards

8.3.b Students know that compounds are formed by combining two or more different elements and that compounds have properties that are different from their constituent elements.

8.3.c Students know atoms and molecules form solids by building up repeating patterns, such as the crystal structure of NaCl or long-chain polymers.

VOCABULARY

ionic bond p. 250
covalent bond p. 252
molecule p. 253
polar covalent bond p. 253

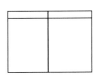

MAIN IDEA AND DETAILS
Make a two-column chart to organize information on chemical bonds.

◀ BEFORE, you learned

- Elements combine to form compounds
- Electrons are located in a cloud around the nucleus
- Atoms can lose or gain electrons to form ions

▶ NOW, you will learn

- How electrons are involved in chemical bonding
- About the different types of chemical bonds
- How chemical bonds affect structure

THINK ABOUT

How do you keep things together?

Think about the different ways the workers at this construction site connect materials. They may use nails, screws, or even glue, depending on the materials they wish to keep together. Why would they choose the method they do? What factors do you think about when you join two objects?

Chemical bonds between atoms involve electrons.

Water is a compound of hydrogen and oxygen. The air you breathe, however, contains oxygen gas, a small amount of hydrogen gas, and water vapor. How can hydrogen and oxygen be water sometimes and at other times not? The answer is by forming chemical bonds.

Chemical bonds are the "glue" that holds the atoms of elements together in compounds. Chemical bonds are what make compounds more than just mixtures of atoms.

Remember that an atom has a positively charged nucleus surrounded by a cloud of electrons. Chemical bonds form when the electrons in the electron clouds around two atoms interact. How the electron clouds interact determines the kind of chemical bond that is formed. Chemical bonds have a great effect on the chemical and physical properties of compounds. Chemical bonds also influence how different substances interact. You'll learn more about how substances interact in a later chapter.

Atoms can transfer electrons.

REMINDER

Remember that the elements in columns of the periodic table show similar chemical properties.

Ions are formed when atoms gain or lose electrons. Gaining electrons changes an atom into a negative ion. Losing electrons changes an atom into a positive ion. Individual atoms often do not form ions by themselves. Instead, ions typically form in pairs when one atom transfers one or more electrons to another atom.

An element's location on the periodic table can give a clue as to the type of ions the atoms of that element will form. The illustration to the left shows the characteristic ions formed by several groups. Notice that all metals lose electrons to form positive ions. Group 1 metals commonly lose only one electron to form ions with a single positive charge. Group 2 metals commonly lose two electrons to form ions with two positive charges. Other metals, like the transition metals, also always form positive ions, but the number of electrons they may lose varies.

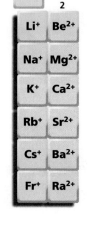
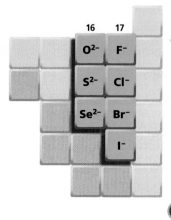

Nonmetals form ions by gaining electrons. Group 17 nonmetals, for example, gain one electron to form ions with a 1− charge. The nonmetals in Group 16 gain two electrons to form ions with a 2− charge. The noble gases do not normally gain or lose electrons and so do not normally form ions.

CHECK YOUR READING What type of ions do metals form?

Ionic Bonds

What happens when an atom of an element from Group 1, like sodium, comes near an atom of an element from Group 17, like chlorine? Sodium is likely to lose an electron to form a positive ion. Chlorine is likely to gain an electron to form a negative ion. An electron, therefore, moves from the sodium atom to the chlorine atom.

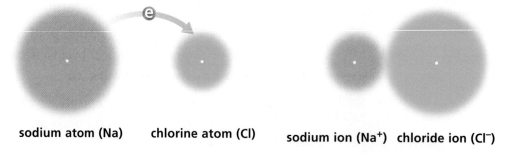

sodium atom (Na)   chlorine atom (Cl)   sodium ion (Na^+) chloride ion (Cl^-)

Remember that particles with opposite electrical charges attract one another. When the ions are created, therefore, they are drawn toward one another by electrical attraction. This force of attraction between positive and negative ions is called an **ionic bond.**

Electrical forces act in all directions. Each ion, therefore, attracts all other nearby ions with the opposite charge. The next illustration shows how this all-around attraction produces a network of sodium and chloride ions known as a sodium chloride crystal.

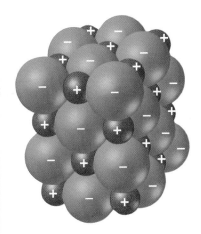

Notice how each positive ion is surrounded by six negative ions. Each negative ion is surrounded by six positive ions. This regular arrangement gives the sodium chloride crystal its characteristic cubic shape. You can see this crystal shape when you look at table salt crystals through a magnifying glass.

Ionic bonds form between all nearby ions of opposite charge. These bonds make ionic compounds very stable and their crystals very strong. Sodium chloride crystals have a cubic shape. Other ionic compounds form crystals with different regular patterns. The shape of the crystals of an ionic compound depends, in part, on the ratio of positive and negative ions and the sizes of the ions.

The cubic shape of sodium chloride crystals is a result of how the ions form crystals.

Names of Ionic Compounds

The name of an ionic compound is based on the names of the ions it is made of. The name for a positive ion is the same as the name of the atom from which it is formed. The name of a negative ion is formed by dropping the last part of the name of the atom and adding the suffix *-ide*. To name an ionic compound, the name of the positive ion is placed first, followed by the name of the negative ion. For example, the chemical name for table salt is sodium chloride. *Sodium* is the positive sodium ion and *chloride* is the negative ion formed from chlorine.

Therefore, to name the compound with the chemical formula BaI_2

- First, take the name of the positive metal element: barium.
- Second, take the name of the negative, nonmetal element, iodine, and give it the ending *-ide:* iodide.
- Third, combine the two names: barium iodide.

Similarly, the name for KBr is potassium bromide, and the name for MgF_2 is magnesium fluoride.

Atoms can share electrons.

In general, ionic bonds form between metals and nonmetals. The metal loses the electron, so the nonmetal gains the electrons. Another way in which atoms can bond together is by sharing electrons. Nonmetal atoms usually form bonds with each other by sharing electrons.

Covalent Bonds

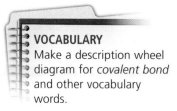

VOCABULARY
Make a description wheel diagram for *covalent bond* and other vocabulary words.

A pair of shared electrons between two atoms is called a **covalent bond.** In forming a covalent bond, neither atom gains or loses an electron, so no ions are formed. The shared electrons are attracted to both positively charged nuclei. The illustrations below show a covalent bond between two iodine atoms. In the first illustration, notice how the electron clouds overlap. A covalent bond also is often represented as a line between the two atoms, as in the second illustration.

Iodine (I₂)

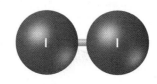

electron cloud model   ball-and-stick model

The number of covalent bonds that an atom can form depends on the number of electrons that it has available for sharing. For example, atoms of the halogen group and hydrogen can contribute only one electron to a covalent bond. These atoms, therefore, can form only one covalent bond. Atoms of Group 16 elements can form two covalent bonds. Atoms of the elements of Group 15 can form three bonds. Carbon and silicon in Group 14 can form four bonds. For example, in methane (CH_4), carbon forms four covalent bonds with four hydrogen atoms, as shown below.

READING TiP

To help yourself remember that a covalent bond involves a sharing of electrons, remember that the prefix *co-* means "partner."

Methane (CH₄)

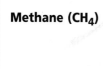

ball-and-stick model   space-filling model

We need not always show the lines representing the covalent bonds between the atoms. The space-filling model still shows the general shape of the bonded atoms, but occupies far less space on the page. Scientists use different atomic models for different purposes.

Each carbon-hydrogen bond in methane is a single bond because one pair of electrons is shared between the atoms. Sometimes atoms may share more than one pair of electrons with another atom. For example, the carbon atom in carbon dioxide (CO_2) forms double bonds with each of the oxygen atoms. A double bond consists of four (two pairs of) shared electrons. Two nitrogen atoms form a triple bond, meaning that they share six (three pairs of) electrons.

Remember that each line in the model stands for a covalent bond—one shared pair of electrons.

A group of atoms held together by covalent bonds is called a **molecule.** A molecule can contain from two to many thousand atoms. Most molecules contain the atoms of two or more elements. For example, water (H_2O), ammonia (NH_3), and methane (CH_4) are all compounds made up of molecules. However, some molecules contain atoms of only one element. The following elements exist as two-atom molecules: H_2, N_2, O_2, F_2, Cl_2, Br_2, and I_2.

 What is a molecule?

Polar Covalent Bonds

In an iodine molecule, both atoms are exactly the same. The shared electrons therefore are attracted equally to both nuclei. If the two atoms in a covalent bond are very different, however, the electrons have a stronger attraction to one nucleus than to the other. A covalent bond in which the electrons are shared unequally is called a **polar covalent bond.** The word *polar* refers to anything that has two extremes, such as a magnet with its two opposite poles.

To remind yourself that polar covalent bonds have opposite partial charges, remember that Earth has both a North Pole and a South Pole.

Water (H_2O)

ball-and-stick model

space-filling model

In a water molecule (H_2O), the oxygen atom attracts electrons far more strongly than the hydrogen atoms do. The oxygen nucleus has eight protons, and the hydrogen nucleus has only one proton. The oxygen atom pulls the shared electrons more strongly toward it. In a water molecule, therefore, the oxygen side has a slightly negative charge, and the hydrogen side has a slightly positive charge.

Examine how electrons move in a polar covalent molecule.

Comparing Bonds

Near San Francisco Bay in California, salt is mined from salt water. The salt is harvested as the water evaporates into the air, leaving the salt behind. All types of chemical bonds are involved.

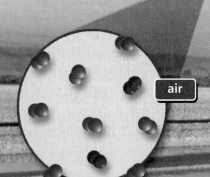
air

salt

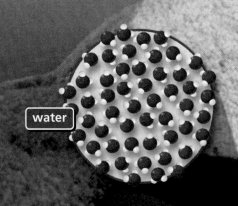
water

Ionic Bonds (salt)

Sodium Chloride (NaCl)
A complete transfer of electrons produces the ionic bonds that hold sodium chloride (table salt) crystals together.

Covalent Bonds (air)

Nitrogen (N_2) and Oxygen (O_2)
Some molecules in air contain multiple covalent bonds. Nitrogen has triple bonds. Oxygen has double bonds.

Polar Covalent Bonds (water)

Water (H_2O)
The covalent bonds in water are very polar because oxygen attracts electrons far more strongly than hydrogen does.

READING VISUALS   Atoms of which element are shown both in the air and in the water?

Chemical bonds give all materials their structures.

The substances around you have many different properties. The crystal structure and molecules that make up these substances are responsible for many of these properties. For example, crystals bend rays of light and metals shine. Medications can affect certain diseases in the body because their atoms are arranged in specific ways.

Ionic Compounds

Most ionic compounds have a regular crystal structure. Remember how the size, shape, and ratio of the sodium ions and chloride ions give the sodium chloride crystal its shape. Other ionic compounds, such as calcium chloride, have different but equally regular structures. One result of such rigid structures is that, when enough force is applied to the crystal, it shatters rather than bends.

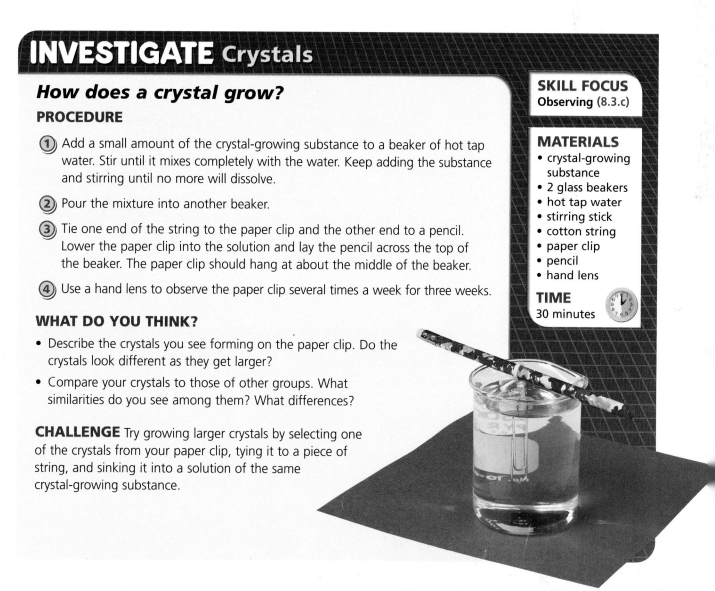

INVESTIGATE Crystals

How does a crystal grow?

PROCEDURE

1. Add a small amount of the crystal-growing substance to a beaker of hot tap water. Stir until it mixes completely with the water. Keep adding the substance and stirring until no more will dissolve.

2. Pour the mixture into another beaker.

3. Tie one end of the string to the paper clip and the other end to a pencil. Lower the paper clip into the solution and lay the pencil across the top of the beaker. The paper clip should hang at about the middle of the beaker.

4. Use a hand lens to observe the paper clip several times a week for three weeks.

WHAT DO YOU THINK?

- Describe the crystals you see forming on the paper clip. Do the crystals look different as they get larger?

- Compare your crystals to those of other groups. What similarities do you see among them? What differences?

CHALLENGE Try growing larger crystals by selecting one of the crystals from your paper clip, tying it to a piece of string, and sinking it into a solution of the same crystal-growing substance.

SKILL FOCUS
Observing (8.3.c)

MATERIALS
- crystal-growing substance
- 2 glass beakers
- hot tap water
- stirring stick
- cotton string
- paper clip
- pencil
- hand lens

TIME
30 minutes

Covalent Compounds

Unlike ionic compounds, covalent compounds come in individual molecules. Chemical bonds give each molecule a specific, three-dimensional shape called its molecular structure. Molecular structure can influence how a specific substance feels and how well it bonds with other substances.

READING TiP

To help yourself appreciate the differences among these structures, try making three-dimensional models of them.

A few basic molecular structures are shown below. Molecules can have a simple linear shape, such as iodine. Or they can be bent, such as a water molecule (H_2O). The atoms in an ammonia molecule (NH_3) form a pyramid. Methane (CH_4) molecules even have a slightly more complex shape. A molecule's shape can be extremely complex. Some molecules contain thousands of atoms. You will learn more about some very complex molecules in a later chapter.

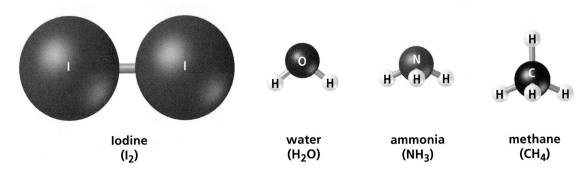

| Iodine (I_2) | water (H_2O) | ammonia (NH_3) | methane (CH_4) |

Molecular shape can affect many properties of compounds. For example, some scientists think we detect scents because molecules with certain shapes fit into certain smell receptors in the nose. Molecules with similar shapes, therefore, should have similar smells. Molecular structure also determines how our bodies respond to certain drugs. Some drugs work because molecules with certain shapes can fit into specific receptors in body cells.

8.2 Review

KEY CONCEPTS

1. What part of an atom is involved in chemical bonding? (8.3.a)

2. How are ionic bonds and covalent bonds different? (8.3.a)

3. Describe two ways that crystal and molecular structures affect the properties of ionic and covalent compounds. (8.3.c)

CRITICAL THINKING

4. **Analyze** Would you expect the bonds in ammonia to be polar covalent? Why or why not?

5. **Infer** What kind of bond would you expect atoms of strontium and iodine to form? Why? Write the formula and name the compound.

◑ CHALLENGE

6. **Conclude** Is the element silicon likely to form ionic or covalent bonds? Explain.

California Close-Up

The Man Who Saw Molecules

> 8.3.b Students know that compounds are formed by combining two or more different elements and that compounds have properties that are different from their constituent elements.

Linus Pauling was one of the great chemists of the 20th century. He was a professor of chemistry at the California Institute of Technology for 22 years. In 1939 he published a book about chemical bonding. In it, Pauling showed that properties such as the melting point or the boiling point of a substance depend on molecular structure. He showed how chemical bonding influences a molecule's structure.

It's in the Genes

Pauling discovered that oddly shaped molecules could cause disease. For three years, he researched a disease called sickle cell anemia. A protein called hemoglobin carries oxygen through the blood. Pauling found that in people with sickle cell anemia, these molecules have a different shape. In parts of the bloodstream where there is low oxygen, these differently shaped molecules cluster together. This creates cells with long rod shapes resembling a sickle. It becomes harder for the blood to circulate. These molecules also don't absorb oxygen, so part of the body is starved of oxygen and iron. Pauling had shown how a simple variation in molecular structure could be very important.

Normal red blood cells are round. In sickle cell anemia, red blood cells are crescent shaped.

Dangerous Chemistry

Pauling also studied how radiation affects humans. He determined that radiation changes the chemistry of the body. It damages human cells by changing the shapes of molecules inside the body. The effects of radiation could cause cancer and birth defects. Pauling gave speeches around the world, arguing against nuclear testing. Finally, in 1963 the United States, the Soviet Union, and Great Britain signed a limited test ban treaty. That year, Pauling was awarded the Nobel Peace Prize. He is the only person ever to receive two Nobel prizes as an individual.

WRITING ABOUT SCIENCE

Find out more about Linus Pauling's life and work. Then write him a thank-you letter. Describe one way his research improved your life or the lives of other people.

Linus Pauling held that vitamin C could prevent the common cold. Oranges are a good source of vitamin C.

Substances' properties depend on their bonds.

CALIFORNIA
Content Standards

8.3.c Students know atoms and molecules form solids by building up repeating patterns, such as the crystal structure of NaCl or long-chain polymers.

8.7.c Students know substances can be classified by their properties, including their melting temperature, density, hardness, and thermal and electrical conductivity.

VOCABULARY

metallic bond p. 258

BEFORE, you learned

- Chemical bonds hold the atoms of compounds together
- Chemical bonds involve the transfer or sharing of electrons
- Molecules have a structure

NOW, you will learn

- How metal atoms form chemical bonds with one another
- How ionic and covalent bonds influence substances' properties

---

EXPLORE Bonds in Metals (8.7.c)

What objects conduct electricity?

PROCEDURE

① Tape one end of a copper wire to one terminal of the battery. Attach the other end of the copper wire to the light bulb holder. Attach a second wire to the holder. Tape a third wire to the other terminal of the battery.

② Touch the ends of both wires to objects around the classroom. Notice if the bulb lights or not.

WHAT DO YOU THINK?
- Which objects make the bulb light?
- How are these objects similar?

MATERIALS
- masking tape
- 3 pieces of copper wire (15 cm)
- D cell (battery)
- light bulb and holder
- objects to test

Metals have unique bonds.

REMINDER

Chemical bonds involve the sharing of or transfer of electrons.

Metal atoms bond together by sharing their electrons with one another. The atoms share the electrons equally in all directions. The equal sharing allows the electrons to move easily among the atoms of the metal. This special type of bond is called a **metallic bond.**

The properties of metals are determined by metallic bonds. One common property of metals is that they are good conductors of electric current. The electrons in a metal flow through the material, carrying the electric current. The free movement of electrons among metal atoms also means that metals are good conductors of heat. Metals also typically have high melting points. Except for mercury, all metals are solids at room temperature.

Metallic Properties

Copper and other metals get their properties from metallic bonds.

The ability of electrons to move freely makes metals
- good conductors of electricity
- good conductors of heat
- easy to shape

copper wire

copper atom

electron

Two other properties of metals are that they are easily shaped by pounding and can be drawn into a wire. These properties are also explained by the nature of the metallic bond. In metallic compounds, atoms can slide past one another. It is as if the atoms are swimming in a pool of electrons. Pounding the metal simply moves these atoms into other positions. This property makes metals ideal for making coins.

CHECK YOUR READING What three properties do metals have because of metallic bonds?

Ionic and covalent bonds give compounds certain properties.

The properties of a compound depend on the chemical bonds that hold its atoms together. For example, you can be almost certain an ionic compound will be a solid at room temperature. Ionic compounds, in fact, usually have extremely high melting and boiling points. It takes a lot of energy to break all the bonds among all the ions in the crystal. The rigid crystal network also makes ionic compounds hard, brittle, and poor conductors of electricity. No moving electrical charges means no current will flow.

Ionic compounds, however, often dissolve easily in water. They separate into positive ions and negative ions. The separated ions can move freely. These solutions of ionic compounds are good conductors of electricity. Your body, in fact, uses ionic solutions to help transmit impulses between nerve and muscle cells. Exercise can rapidly use up these ionic solutions in the body, so sports drinks contain ionic

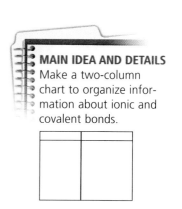

MAIN IDEA AND DETAILS Make a two-column chart to organize information about ionic and covalent bonds.

A hot pool in Yellowstone Park's Upper Geyser Basin. These pools are often characterized by their striking colors.

RESOURCE CENTER
CLASSZONE.COM

Find out more about the properties of ionic and covalent compounds.

compounds. These compounds, such as potassium chloride, replace the ions lost during physical activity.

Mineral hot springs, like those found in Yellowstone National Park, are another example of ionic solutions. Many of the ionic compounds dissolved in these hot springs contain the element sulfur. Sulfur can have an unpleasant odor. The white deposits around the pool come from the sulfur.

Covalent compounds have almost the opposite properties of ionic compounds. Melting or boiling a covalent compound does not require breaking chemical bonds. Therefore, covalent compounds often melt and boil at lower temperatures than ionic compounds. Unlike ionic compounds, molecules stay together when dissolved in water. Therefore, covalent compounds are poor conductors of electric charge. Table sugar, for example, does not conduct an electric current when in solution.

Bonds can make the same element look different.

Covalent bonds do not always form small individual molecules. This explains how the element carbon can exist in three very different forms—diamond, graphite, and fullerene. The properties of each depend on how the carbon atoms are bonded to each other.

Diamond is the hardest natural substance. This property makes diamond useful for cutting other substances. Diamonds are made entirely of carbon. Each carbon atom forms covalent bonds with four other carbon atoms. The pattern of linked atoms extends throughout the entire volume of a diamond crystal. This three-dimensional structure of carbon atoms gives diamonds their strength—diamonds do not break easily.

Another form of carbon is graphite. Graphite is the dark, slippery component of pencil "lead." Graphite has a different structure from diamond, although both are networks of interconnected atoms. Each carbon atom in graphite forms covalent bonds with three other atoms to form two-dimensional layers. These layers stack on top of one another like sheets of paper. The layers can slide past one another easily. Graphite feels slippery. It is used as a lubricant to reduce friction between metal parts of machines.

graphite

diamond

A third form of carbon, fullerene, contains large molecules. One type of fullerene, called buckminsterfullerene, has molecules shaped like a soccer ball. Scientists nicknamed it the "Buckyball" after architect R. Buckminster Fuller, the designer of the geodesic dome. In 1985 chemists made a fullerene molecule consisting of 60 carbon atoms. Since then, many similar molecules have been made, ranging from 20 to more than 100 atoms per molecule.

buckminsterfullerene

8.3 Review

KEY CONCEPTS

1. How do metal atoms bond together? (8.3.c)

2. Why do ionic compounds have high melting points? (8.3.c)

3. What are three forms of the element carbon? (8.7.c)

CRITICAL THINKING

4. **Apply** A compound known as cubic boron nitride has a structure similar to that of a diamond. What properties would you expect it to have?

5. **Infer** Sterling silver is a combination of silver and copper. How are the silver and copper atoms held together?

⚠ CHALLENGE

6. **Infer** Why might the water in mineral springs be a better conductor of electricity than drinking water?

CHAPTER INVESTIGATION

Chemical Bonds

OVERVIEW AND PURPOSE Chemists can identify the type of bonds in a substance by examining its properties. In this investigation you will examine the properties of different substances and use what you have learned about chemical bonds to identify the type of bond each substance contains. You will
- observe the structure of substances with a hand lens
- test the conductivity of substances
- determine the melting point of substances

▶ Problem

How can you determine the type of chemical bond a substance has?

▶ Hypothesize

Write three hypotheses in "if . . . , then . . . , because . . ." form to answer the problem question for each bond type—ionic, covalent, and metallic.

▶ Procedure

1. Create a data table similar to the one shown on the sample notebook page.

2. To build the conductivity tester, connect the first wire to one terminal of the battery and to one of the metal strips. Attach the second wire to the other terminal and to the lamp socket. Finally, connect the lamp socket to the third wire, and connect the other end of this wire to the second metal strip.

3. To make sure your tester works properly, touch the tips of the metal strips together. If the bulb lights, the tester is working properly. If not, check the connections carefully.

4. Get the following test compounds from your teacher: Epsom salts ($MgSO_4$), sugar ($C_{12}H_{22}O_{11}$), and iron filings (Fe). For each substance, put about 20 grams in a cup and label it.

MATERIALS
- 3 wire leads with alligator clips
- battery
- zinc and copper strips
- light bulb and socket
- test compounds
- 3 plastic cups
- distilled water
- beaker
- construction paper
- hand lens
- plastic spoon
- 3 test tubes
- test-tube rack
- candle
- wire test-tube holder

 8.7.c, 8.9.a, 8.9.b

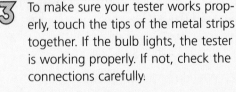

Content Standard
8.7.c Students know substances can be classified by their properties, including their melting temperature, density, hardness, and thermal and electrical conductivity.

Investigation Standard
8.9.b Evaluate the accuracy and reproducibility of data.

5 Test the conductivity of distilled water. Fill the beaker with 30 mL of water. Place the two metal strips into the water. Does the bulb light? Record your observations. Dry the strips completely.

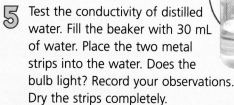

6 Place dry Epsom salts on dark paper. Observe them with a hand lens. Do you see any kind of patterns in the different grains? Put the salts between the metal strips. Can you get the bulb to light by bringing the strips closer together? Record your observations.

7 Add all but a small amount of the Epsom salts to the beaker of water. Stir well. Repeat the conductivity test. What happens when you put the metal strips into the solution? Record your results.

8 Rinse and dry the beaker. Repeat steps 6–7 with other test substances. Record your results.

9 Put the remainder of each test substance into its own clean, dry test tube. Label the tubes. Light the candle. Use a test tube holder to hold each compound over the candle flame for 2 minutes. Do you notice any signs of melting? Record your observations.

▶ Observe and Analyze ✎ Write It Up

1. **RECORD OBSERVATIONS** Be sure you have entered all your observations in your data table.

2. **CLASSIFY** Using the periodic table, find the elements these compounds contain. How might consulting the periodic table help you determine what type of bond exists in the compound?

▶ Conclude ✎ Write It Up

1. **INTERPRET** Review your recorded observations. Classify the compounds as having ionic, covalent, or metallic bonds. Fill in the last row of the data table with your conclusions.

2. **INFER** Compare your results with your hypotheses. Did your results support your hypotheses?

3. **EVALUATE** Describe possible limitations, errors, or places where errors might have occurred.

4. **APPLY** Electrocardiograms are graphs that show the electrical activity of the heart. When an electrocardiogram is made, a paste of sodium chloride is used to hold small metal discs on the patient's skin. What property of ionic compounds does this medical test make use of?

▶ INVESTIGATE Further

CHALLENGE To grow crystals, put about 60 grams of Epsom salts into a baby-food jar that is half full of hot water. Do the same using a second jar containing about 60 grams of sugar. Cover and shake the jars for a count of 60. Line two clean jar lids with dark paper. Brush or spoon a thin coating of each liquid over the paper. Let them stand in a warm place. After several days, observe the crystals that form, using a hand lens.

Chemical Bonds
Problem How can you determine the type of chemical bond a substance has?

Hypothesize

Observe and Analyze

Table 1: Properties of Bonds

Property	Epsom Salts $(MgSO_4)$	Sugar $(C_{12}H_{22}O_{11})$	Iron Filings (Fe)
Crystal structure			
Conductivity of solid			
Conductivity in water			
Melting			
Bond type			

Conclude

Chapter Review

the BIG idea

The properties of compounds depend on their atoms and chemical bonds.

 KEY CONCEPTS SUMMARY

1 Elements combine to form compounds.

- Compounds have different properties from the elements that made them.
- Atoms combine in predictable numbers.

 +  =

calcium (Ca) + chlorine (Cl₂) = calcium chloride (CaCl₂)

VOCABULARY
chemical formula p. 245
subscript p. 245

2 Chemical bonds hold compounds together.

- Chemical bonds between atoms involve electrons.
- Atoms can transfer electrons.
- Atoms can share electrons.
- Chemical bonds give all materials their structure.

ionic bond

covalent bond

VOCABULARY
ionic bond p. 250
covalent bond p. 252
molecule p. 253
polar covalent bond
  p. 253

3 Substances' properties depend on their bonds.

- Metals have unique bonds.
- Ionic and covalent bonds give compounds certain properties.
- Bonds can make the same element look different.

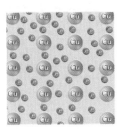

copper

diamond fragment

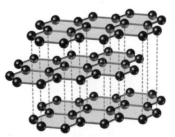

graphite fragment

VOCABULARY
metallic bond p. 258

Reviewing Vocabulary

Copy and complete the table below. Under each bond type, describe
- *how electrons are distributed*
- *how the compound is structured*
- *one of the properties of the compound containing this type of bond*

Some of the table has been filled out for you.

Ionic Bonds	Covalent Bonds	Metallic Bonds
1.	shared electron pair	**2.**
3.	**4.**	close-packed atoms in sea of electrons
have high melting points	**5.**	**6.**

Reviewing Key Concepts

Multiple Choice *Choose the letter of the best answer.*

7. Most substances are (8.7.c)
- **a.** elements
- **b.** compounds
- **c.** metals
- **d.** nonmetals

8. All compounds are made of (8.3.b)
- **a.** atoms of two or more elements
- **b.** two or more atoms of the same element
- **c.** atoms arranged in a crystal
- **d.** atoms joined by covalent bonds

9. The chemical formula for a compound having one barium (Ba) ion and two chloride (Cl) ions is (8.3.b)
- **a.** BCl
- **b.** BaCl
- **c.** $BaCl_2$
- **d.** Ba_2Cl_2

10. The 4 in the chemical formula CH_4 means there are (8.3.b)
- **a.** four carbon atoms to one hydrogen atom
- **b.** four carbon and four hydrogen atoms
- **c.** four hydrogen atoms to one carbon atom
- **d.** four total carbon CH combinations

11. The compound KBr has the name (8.3.b)
- **a.** potassium bromide
- **b.** potassium bromine
- **c.** bromide potassium
- **d.** bromine potassium

12. An atom becomes a positive ion when it (8.3.b)
- **a.** is attracted to all nearby atoms
- **b.** gains an electron from another atom
- **c.** loses an electron to another atom
- **d.** shares an electron with another atom

13. A polar covalent bond forms when two atoms (8.3.b)
- **a.** share one electron equally
- **b.** share two electrons equally
- **c.** share one electron unequally
- **d.** share two electrons unequally

14. Metallic bonds make many metals (8.3.c)
- **a.** poor conductors of heat
- **b.** liquid at room temperature
- **c.** difficult to shape
- **d.** good conductors of electricity

15. Three forms of carbon are (8.7.c)
- **a.** diamond, graphite, and salt
- **b.** diamond, graphite, and fullerene
- **c.** graphite, salt, and carbonate
- **d.** diamond, salt, and fullerene

Short Answer *Write a short answer to each question.*

16. Why does a mixture of sodium chloride and water conduct electricity but a sodium chloride crystal does not? (8.7.c)

17. Describe what makes diamond and graphite, two forms of the element carbon, so different. (8.7.c)

Thinking Critically

Use the illustration above to answer the next two questions.

18. **IDENTIFY** Write the chemical formula for the molecule pictured above. (8.3.b)

19. **ANALYZE** The nitrogen atom has a far greater attraction for electrons than hydrogen atoms. Copy the molecule pictured above and indicate which parts of the molecule have a slightly positive charge and which parts have a slightly negative charge. (8.3.b)

20. **PREDICT** The chemical formula for calcium chloride is $CaCl_2$. What would you predict the formula for magnesium chloride to be? [**Hint:** Find magnesium on the periodic table.] (8.3.b)

21. **INFER** When scientists make artificial diamonds, they sometimes subject graphite to very high temperatures and pressures. What do you think happens to change the graphite into diamond? (8.7.c)

22. **SYNTHESIZE** Why would seawater be a better conductor of electricity than river water? (8.7.c)

23. **ANALYZE** How does the nature of the metallic bond explain the observation that most metals can be drawn into a wire? (8.7.c)

24. **EVALUATE** Do you think the types of bonds you've studied occur on the planet Mars? Explain. (8.3.b)

25. **INFER** Why don't we use the term *ionic molecule?* (8.3.c)

Use the chemical formulas below and a periodic table to answer the next three questions.

Compound
I. K_2SO_4
II. CF_4
III. C_4H_{10}
IV. KCl

26. **APPLY** Name compound IV. Does this compound have ionic or covalent bonds? (8.3.c)

27. **ANALYZE** Name the elements in each compound. Tell how many atoms are in each compound. (8.3.b)

28. **CALCULATE** Express the ratio of atoms in compounds II, III, and IV. For compound I, express all three ratios. (8.3.b)

29. **APPLY** By 1800 Alessandro Volta had made the first electric battery. He placed pieces of cardboard soaked in saltwater in between alternating zinc and silver discs. What properties of the metals and the saltwater made them good materials for a battery? (8.5.a)

30. **PREDICT** What is the maximum number of covalent bonds that a hydrogen atom can form? Explain your answer. (8.3.b)

the BIG idea

31. **DRAW CONCLUSIONS** Look at the photograph on pages 240–241 again. Can you now recognize any similarities between how the skydivers stay together and how atoms stay together? (8.3.b)

32. **APPLY** Phosphorus can be a strange element. Pure phosphorus is sometimes white, black, or red. What can account for the differences in appearance? (8.7.c)

UNIT PROJECTS

If you are doing a unit project, make a folder for your project. Include in your folder a list of the resources you will need, the date on which the project is due, and a schedule to track your progress. Begin gathering data.

Standards-Based Assessment

Interpreting Tables

8.3.b, 8.3.c, 8.5.a, 8.7.c

The table below lists some of the characteristics of substances that contain different types of bonds. Use the table to answer the questions.

Bond Type	Usually Forms Between	Electrons	Properties	Examples
Ionic	an atom of a metal and an atom of a nonmetal	transferred between atoms	• high melting points • conducts electricity when in water	BaS, BaBr$_2$, Ca$_3$N$_2$, LiCl, ZnO
Covalent	atoms of nonmetallic elements	shared between atoms but often not equally	• low melting points • does not conduct electricity	C$_2$H$_6$, C, Cl$_2$, H$_2$, AsCl$_3$
Metallic	atoms of metallic elements	freely moving about the atoms	• high melting points • conducts electricity at all times • easily shaped	Ca, Fe, Na, Cu, Zn

1. Which of these compounds would you expect to have the highest melting point?
   a. C$_2$H$_6$
   b. Cl$_2$
   c. AsCl$_3$
   d. BaBr$_2$

2. Which substance is likely to be easily shaped?
   a. BaBr$_2$
   b. LiCl
   c. Na
   d. C

3. In the compound LiCl, electrons are
   a. shared equally
   b. shared but not equally
   c. transferred between atoms to form ions
   d. freely moving among the atoms

4. Which of the following is an ionic compound?
   a. C$_2$H$_6$
   b. Cl$_2$
   c. AsCl$_3$
   d. ZnO

5. Which of the following compounds has a low melting point?
   a. Cl$_2$
   b. ZnO
   c. Cu
   d. BaBr$_2$

6. A solid mass of which substance would conduct electricity?
   a. Ca$_3$N$_2$
   b. LiCl
   c. Cu
   d. AsCl$_3$

Extended Response

Answer the next two questions in detail.
Include some of the terms from the list in the box.
Underline each term you use in your answer.

share electron	transfer electron
freely moving electrons	charge
compound	chemical formula

7. Compare how electrons are involved in making the three main types of bonds: ionic, covalent, and metallic.

8. Just about 100 elements occur naturally. There are, however, millions of different materials. How can so few basic substances make so many different materials?

9

Chemical Reactions

the **BIG** idea

Chemical reactions form new substances by breaking and making chemical bonds.

What changes are happening in this chemical reaction?

Key Concepts

SECTION

1 **Chemical reactions alter arrangements of atoms.**
Learn how chemical reactions are identified and controlled.

SECTION

2 **The masses of reactants and products are equal.**
Learn how chemical equations show the conservation of mass.

SECTION

3 **Chemical reactions involve energy changes.**
Learn how energy is absorbed or released by chemical reactions.

California ClassZone

CLASSZONE.COM

Chapter 9 online resources: Content Review, two Visualizations, two Resource Centers, Math Tutorial, Test Practice

Changing Steel Wool

> **8.5.a** Students know reactant atoms and molecules interact to form products with different chemical properties.

Place a small lump of steel wool in a cup. Pour in enough vinegar to cover the steel wool. After five minutes, take the steel wool out of the vinegar. Shake the steel wool to remove any excess vinegar. Place the steel wool in a small plastic bottle, and cover the mouth of the bottle with a balloon. Observe the steel wool and balloon after one hour.

Observe and Think What happened to the steel wool and balloon? What might have caused this to occur?

Internet Activity: Reactions

> **8.5.b** Students know the idea of atoms explains the conservation of matter: In chemical reactions the number of atoms stays the same no matter how they are arranged, so their total mass stays the same.

Go to **ClassZone.com** to explore chemical reactions and chemical equations. Learn how a chemical equation can be balanced.

Observe and Think How do chemical equations show what happens during a chemical reaction? Describe the symbols used in chemical equations. How could you become better at balancing chemical equations?

NSTA
scilinks.org

SCiLINKS

Chemical Reactions **Code: MDL024**

Getting Ready to Learn

CONCEPT REVIEW

- Atoms combine to form compounds.
- Atoms gain or lose electrons when they form ionic bonds.
- Atoms share electrons in covalent bonds.

VOCABULARY REVIEW

chemical change p. 137

atom p. 154

electron p. 201

ionic bond p. 250

covalent bond p. 252

CONTENT REVIEW
CLASSZONE.COM

Review concepts and vocabulary.

TAKING NOTES

COMBINATION NOTES

To take notes about a new concept, first make an informal outline of the information. Then make a sketch of the concept and label it so you can study it later.

VOCABULARY STRATEGY

Write each new vocabulary term in the center of a **four square** diagram. Write notes in the squares around each term. Include a definition, some characteristics, and some examples of the term. If possible, write some things that are not examples of the term.

See the Note-Taking Handbook on pages R45–R51.

SCIENCE NOTEBOOK

NOTES

Chemical reactions
- cause chemical changes
- make new substances
- change reactants into products

Evidence of Chemical Reactions

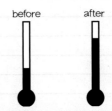

before   after

increase in temperature

Definition	Characteristics
substance present before a chemical reaction occurs	its bonds are broken during a reaction
REACTANT	
Examples	Nonexample
oxygen in a combustion reaction	carbon dioxide in a combustion reaction

9.1 Chemical reactions alter arrangements of atoms.

CALIFORNIA
Content Standards

8.5.a Students know reactant atoms and molecules interact to form products with different chemical properties.

8.5.c Students know chemical reactions usually liberate heat or absorb heat.

8.5.d Students know physical processes include freezing and boiling, in which a material changes form with no chemical reaction.

VOCABULARY

chemical reaction p. 271
reactant p. 273
product p. 273
precipitate p. 274
catalyst p. 278

BEFORE, you learned

- Atoms of one element differ from atoms of all other elements
- Chemical bonds hold compounds together
- Chemical bonds may be ionic or covalent

NOW, you will learn

- About chemical changes and how they occur
- About three types of chemical reactions
- How the rate of a chemical reaction can be changed

EXPLORE Chemical Changes (8.5.a)

How can you identify a chemical change?

PROCEDURE

① Pour about 3 cm (1 in.) of vinegar into the bowl. Add a spoonful of salt. Stir until the salt dissolves.

② Put the pennies into the bowl. Wait two minutes, and then put the nail into the bowl.

③ Observe the nail after five minutes and record your observations.

WHAT DO YOU THINK?

- What did you see on the nail? Where do you think it came from?
- Did a new substance form? What evidence supports your conclusion?

MATERIALS
- vinegar
- clear bowl
- plastic spoon
- table salt
- 20 pennies
- large iron nail

Atoms interact in chemical reactions.

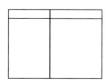

COMBINATION NOTES
Use combination notes to organize information about how atoms interact during chemical reactions.

You see substances change every day. Some changes are physical, such as when liquid water changes to water vapor during boiling. Other changes are chemical, such as when wood burns to form smoke and ash, or when rust forms on iron. During a chemical change, substances change into one or more different substances.

A **chemical reaction** produces new substances by changing the way in which atoms are arranged. In a chemical reaction, bonds between atoms are broken and new bonds form between different atoms. This breaking and forming of bonds takes place when particles of the original materials collide with one another. After a chemical reaction, the new arrangements of atoms form different substances.

Physical Changes

A change in the state of a substance is an example of a physical change. The substance may have some different properties after a physical change, but it is still the same substance. For example, you know that water can exist in three different physical states: the solid state (ice), the liquid state (water), and the gas state (water vapor). In each state it is still water. It is still H_2O molecules. As ice melts, the molecules of water move around more quickly. But the molecules do not change. As water vapor condenses, the molecules of water move more slowly. They are still the same molecules.

Substances can undergo different kinds of physical changes. For example, sugar dissolves in water but still tastes sweet. The molecules that make up sugar do not change when it dissolves. The pressure of helium changes when it is pumped from a high-pressure tank into a balloon. The gas still remains helium.

CHECK YOUR READING What happens to a substance when it undergoes a physical change?

When water changes from a liquid to a solid, it undergoes a physical change.

Ice is composed of water molecules that are locked together.

Liquid water is composed of molecules that move freely past each other.

Chemical Changes

Water can also undergo a chemical change. Water molecules can be broken down into hydrogen and oxygen molecules by a chemical reaction called electrolysis. When an electric current is passed through liquid water (H_2O), it changes the water into two gases—hydrogen and oxygen. The molecules of water break apart into individual atoms. These atoms then recombine into hydrogen molecules (H_2) and oxygen molecules (O_2). The original material (water) changes into different substances through a chemical reaction.

Hydrogen and oxygen are used as rocket fuel for the space shuttle. During liftoff, liquid hydrogen and liquid oxygen are combined in a reaction that is the opposite of electrolysis. This reaction produces water and a large amount of energy that helps push the shuttle into orbit.

 CHECK YOUR READING How does a chemical change differ from a physical change?

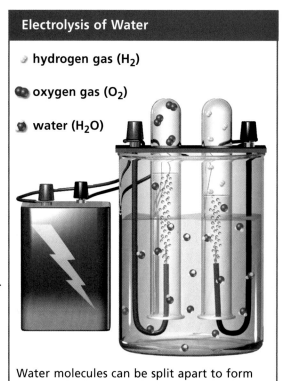

Electrolysis of Water

- hydrogen gas (H_2)
- oxygen gas (O_2)
- water (H_2O)

Water molecules can be split apart to form separate hydrogen and oxygen molecules.

Reactants and Products

Reactants are the substances present at the beginning of a chemical reaction. In the burning of natural gas, for example, methane (CH_4) and oxygen (O_2) are the reactants in the chemical reaction. **Products** are the substances formed by a chemical reaction. In the burning of natural gas, carbon dioxide (CO_2) and water (H_2O) are the products formed by the reaction. Reactants and products can be elements or compounds, depending on the reaction taking place.

During a chemical reaction, bonds between atoms in the reactants are broken and new bonds are formed in the products. When natural gas is burned, bonds between the carbon and hydrogen atoms in methane are broken. Bonds between the oxygen atoms in oxygen molecules are broken. New bonds are formed between carbon and oxygen in carbon dioxide gas and between hydrogen and oxygen in water vapor.

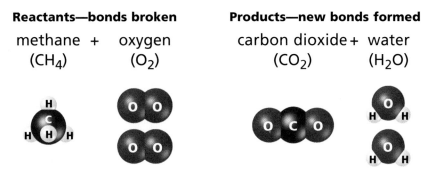

Reactants—bonds broken	Products—new bonds formed
methane + oxygen	carbon dioxide + water
(CH_4) (O_2)	(CO_2) (H_2O)

 CHECK YOUR READING What must happen for reactants to be changed into products?

Evidence of Chemical Reactions

Some chemical changes are easy to observe. The products formed by the rearrangement of atoms look different than the reactants. Other changes are not easy to see but can be detected in other ways.

Color Change Substances often change color during a chemical reaction. For example, when gray iron rusts, the product that forms is brown, as shown in the photograph below.

Formation of a Precipitate Many chemical reactions form products that exist in a different physical state from the reactants. A solid product called a **precipitate** may form when chemicals in two liquids react, as shown in the photograph below. Seashells are often formed this way when a sea creature releases a liquid that reacts with seawater.

VOCABULARY
Remember to use a four square diagram for *precipitate* and other vocabulary terms.

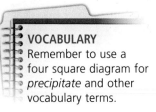

Color Change

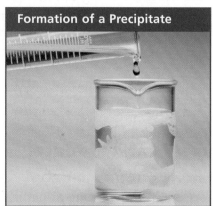
Formation of a Precipitate

Formation of a Gas Chemical reactions may produce a gas, like that formed when antacid pills are mixed with stomach acid. The photograph below shows an example in which carbon dioxide gas is produced by a chemical reaction.

Temperature Change Most chemical reactions involve a temperature change. Sometimes you can recognize the change when you see a flame. Notice the burning of the metal magnesium in the photograph. Other temperature changes are not immediately obvious. If you touch concrete before it hardens, you may notice that it feels warm. This warmth is due to a chemical reaction.

Formation of a Gas

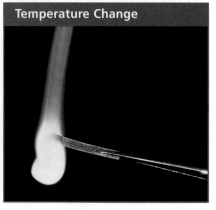
Temperature Change

Chemical reactions can be classified.

Scientists classify chemical reactions in several ways. All reactions form new products. The ways these products are made, however, can differ.

Synthesis In a synthesis reaction, a new compound is formed by the combination of simpler reactants. For example, nitrogen dioxide (NO_2), a part of smog, forms when nitrogen and oxygen combine in the air.

READING **TiP**

Synthesis means "making a substance from simpler substances."

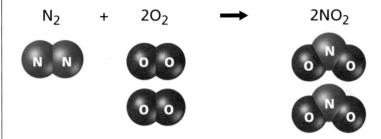

$$N_2 \quad + \quad 2O_2 \quad \longrightarrow \quad 2NO_2$$

Decomposition In a decomposition reaction, a reactant breaks down into simpler products. The products could be elements or other compounds. Decomposition reactions can be thought of as being the reverse of synthesis reactions. For example, water can be decomposed into its elements—hydrogen and oxygen.

READING **TiP**

Decomposition means "separation into parts."

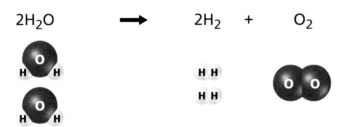

$$2H_2O \quad \longrightarrow \quad 2H_2 \quad + \quad O_2$$

Combustion In a combustion reaction, one reactant is always oxygen. Another reactant often contains carbon and hydrogen. The carbon and hydrogen atoms combine with oxygen, producing carbon dioxide and water. The burning of methane is a combustion reaction.

READING **TiP**

Combustion is the process of burning with oxygen.

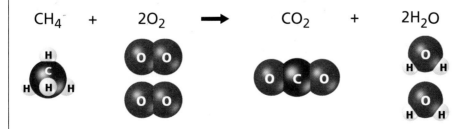

$$CH_4 \quad + \quad 2O_2 \quad \longrightarrow \quad CO_2 \quad + \quad 2H_2O$$

CHECK YOUR READING — How are synthesis reactions different from decomposition reactions?

The rates of chemical reactions can vary.

Most chemical reactions take place when particles of reactants collide with enough force to react. Chemical reactions can occur at different rates. Striking a match causes a very quick chemical reaction. The rusting of an iron nail may take months. However, the rate of a reaction can be changed. For instance, a nail can be made to rust more quickly. Concentration, surface area, and temperature are physical factors that can change the rate of a chemical reaction. A catalyst is a chemical factor that can greatly affect the rate of a chemical reaction.

VISUALIZATION
CLASSZONE.COM

Observe how changing the concentration of a reactant can change the rate of a reaction.

Concentration

Concentration is a measure of the number of particles present in a certain volume. A high concentration of reactants means a large number of particles that can collide and react. Turning up the gas stove increases the concentration of methane molecules that can combine with oxygen in the air. The result is a bigger flame and a faster combustion reaction.

Surface Area

Suppose one of the reactants in a chemical reaction is a single large piece of material. Particles of the second reactant cannot get inside the large piece. They can react only with particles on the surface. To make the reaction go faster, the large piece of material could be broken into smaller pieces before the reaction starts.

INVESTIGATE Chemical Reactions

How can the rate of a reaction be changed?

PROCEDURE

1. Place a whole seltzer tablet in one cup. Crush the second tablet and place it in the second cup.

2. At the same time, fill both cups halfway with water.

3. Time how long the tablet in each cup fizzes.

WHAT DO YOU THINK?

- How long did the whole tablet fizz? What about the crushed tablet?

- How are these results related to the rate of a chemical reaction? Explain.

CHALLENGE How might your results be related to collisions between particles during a chemical reaction?

SKILL FOCUS
Inferring (8.5.a)

MATERIALS
- 2 seltzer tablets
- 2 plastic cups
- tap water
- stopwatch

TIME
15 minutes

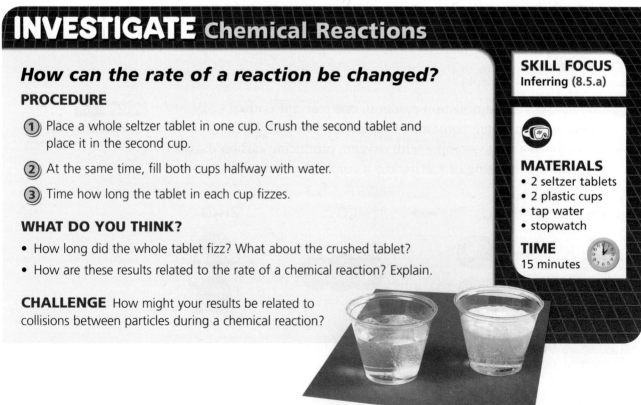

Breaking a large piece of material into smaller parts increases the surface area of the material. All of the inner material has no surface when it is inside a larger piece. Each time the large piece is broken, however, more surfaces are exposed. The amount of material does not change. Breaking it into smaller parts, however, increases its surface area. Increasing the surface area increases the rate of the reaction.

 CHECK YOUR READING Why does a reaction proceed faster when the reactants have greater surface areas?

Temperature

The rate of a reaction can be increased by making the particles move faster. The result is that more collisions take place per second and occur with greater force. The most common way to make the particles move faster is to add energy to the reactants. Adding energy raises their temperature.

▼ **REMINDER**
Temperature is the average amount of kinetic energy of the particles in a substance.

You may think of reaction rates as you cook. Many chemical reactions during cooking go very slowly, or do not take place at all, unless heat energy is added to the reactants. Too much heat may make a reaction go too fast, and so burn the food. Chemical reactions, however, can also slow or stop by decreasing the temperature of the reactants. Again, think about cooking. The reactions that take place during cooking can be stopped by removing the food from the heat source.

Particles and Reaction Rates		
Changes in Reactants	**Normal Reaction Rate**	**Increased Reaction Rate**
Concentration An increase in concentration of the reactants increases the number of particles that can interact.		
Surface area An increase in the surface area of the reactants increases the number of particles that can interact.		
Temperature Adding energy makes particles move faster and increases temperature. The increase in motion allows reactants to collide and react more frequently.		

Catalysts

RESOURCE CENTER
CLASSZONE.COM

Learn more about catalysts and how they work in living things.

The rate of a reaction can be changed chemically by adding a catalyst. A **catalyst** is a substance that increases the rate of a chemical reaction but is not itself consumed in the reaction. This means that after the reaction is complete, the catalyst remains unchanged. Catalysts are very important for many industrial and biological reactions. In fact, many chemical reactions would proceed slowly or not take place at all without catalysts.

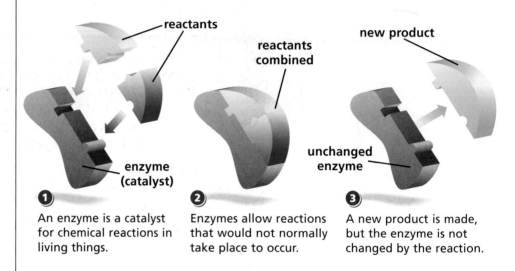

① An enzyme is a catalyst for chemical reactions in living things.

② Enzymes allow reactions that would not normally take place to occur.

③ A new product is made, but the enzyme is not changed by the reaction.

In living things, catalysts called enzymes are absolutely necessary for life. Without them, many important reactions could not take place within your body. In fact, in 2003, scientists reported that they had discovered the slowest known chemical reaction in living things. This reaction would normally take one trillion years. Enzymes, though, allow the reaction to occur in 0.01 seconds.

CHECK YOUR READING Why are catalysts important in chemical reactions?

9.1 Review

KEY CONCEPTS

1. How do physical changes differ from chemical changes? Explain. (8.5.d)

2. Describe four types of evidence of a chemical reaction. (8.5.c)

3. Describe the ways in which the rate of a chemical reaction can be changed. (8.5.a)

CRITICAL THINKING

4. **Synthesize** What evidence shows that the burning of methane is a chemical reaction?

5. **Compare** What about combustion reactions makes them different from either synthesis or decomposition reactions?

⬥ CHALLENGE

6. **Apply** How might the chewing of food be related to the rate of a chemical reaction—digestion—that occurs in your body? Explain.

MATH in SCIENCE

Before | After

The reactants in the iodine clock reaction produce a sudden color change several seconds after the reactants are mixed.

The Iodine Clock

Can a chemical reaction be timed? In the iodine clock reaction, a sudden color change indicates that the reaction has occurred. The length of time that passes before the color changes depends on the concentration ratios of the reactants. As shown in the graph below, the greater the concentration of the reactants, the faster the reaction.

Example

Suppose you are given an unknown iodine concentration to test in the iodine clock reaction. What is the concentration ratio of the iodine if it takes 40 seconds for the color change to occur?

(1) Find 40 seconds on the *x*-axis of the graph below and follow the vertical line up to the plotted data.

(2) Draw a horizontal line from that point on the curve to the *y*-axis to find the iodine concentration ratio in your sample.

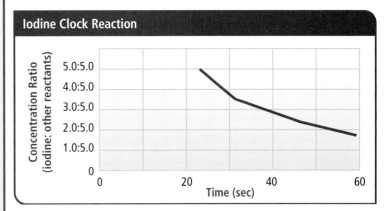

Iodine Clock Reaction

ANSWER The unknown concentration ratio is approximately 3.0:5.0.

Answer the following questions using the information in the graph above.

1. Approximately how long will it take for the reaction to occur if the concentration ratio is 4.0:5.0? 2.0:5.0?

2. Suppose you could extend the curve on the graph. If the reaction took 70 seconds to occur, what would be the approximate iodine concentration ratio?

CHALLENGE Using the following concentration ratios and times for another reactant, draw a reaction rate graph similar to the one shown above.
Concentration Ratios = 5.0:5.0, 4.0:5.0, 3.0:5.0, 2.0:5.0
Times = 24 sec, 25 sec, 43 sec, 68 sec

9.2 The masses of reactants and products are equal.

CALIFORNIA
Content Standard

8.5.b Students know the idea of atoms explains the conservation of matter: In chemical reactions the number of atoms stays the same no matter how they are arranged, so their total mass stays the same.

BEFORE, you learned

- Chemical reactions turn reactants into products by rearranging atoms
- Chemical reactions can be observed and identified
- The rate of chemical reactions can be changed

NOW, you will learn

- About the law of conservation of mass
- How a chemical equation represents a chemical reaction
- How to balance a simple chemical equation

VOCABULARY

law of conservation of mass p. 281
coefficient p. 284

THINK ABOUT

What happens to burning matter?

You have probably watched a fire burn in a fireplace, a campfire, or a candle flame. It looks as if the wood or candle disappears over time, leaving a small pile of ashes or wax when the fire has finished burning. But does matter really disappear? Combustion is a chemical reaction, and chemical reactions involve rearrangements of atoms. The atoms do not disappear, so where do they go?

Careful observations led to the discovery of the conservation of mass.

COMBINATION NOTES
Take notes on the conservation of mass using combination notes.

The ashes left over from a wood fire contain less mass than the wood. In many other chemical reactions, mass also appears to decrease. That is, the mass of the products appears to be less than the mass of the reactants. In other reactions, the products appear to gain mass. For example, plants grow through a complex series of reactions, but where does their extra mass come from? Does it come from the air or soil? How could one know?

During the 1780s the French chemist Antoine Lavoisier (luh-VWAH-zee-ay) showed that matter can never be created or destroyed in a chemical reaction. Lavoisier made very careful measurements in his experiments. He showed that reactions that seem to gain or lose mass actually involved the release of gases into the air. These gases could not be seen, but their masses could be measured.

An example of Lavoisier's work is his study of the heating of the metal mercury. In this reaction, the reddish-orange product formed has more mass than the original metal. Lavoisier placed some mercury in a jar, sealed the jar, and recorded the total mass of the setup. After the mercury had been heated in the jar, the total mass of the jar and its contents had not changed.

Lavoisier showed that the air left in the jar would no longer support burning—a candle flame was snuffed out by this air. He concluded that a gas in the air, which he called oxygen, had combined with the mercury to form the new product.

Lavoisier conducted many experiments of this type. He found in all cases that the mass of the reactants is equal to the mass of the products. His conclusion, called the **law of conservation of mass,** states that in a chemical reaction, atoms are neither created nor destroyed. All atoms present in the reactants are also present in the products.

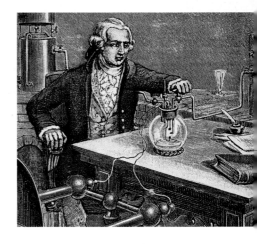

Lavoisier carefully measured both the reactants and the products of chemical reactions.

 CHECK YOUR READING How did Lavoisier investigate the conservation of mass?

INVESTIGATE Conservation of Mass

Why is it important to measure the masses of reactants and products?

PROCEDURE

(1) Measure 2 tsp of baking soda. Use a funnel to put the baking soda in a balloon.

(2) Pour 2 tsp of vinegar into the plastic bottle.

(3) Secure the balloon over the mouth of the bottle with the balloon hanging to the side of the bottle. Find and record the mass of the experimental setup.

(4) Lift the balloon so that the baking soda drops into the bottle. Observe for five minutes, and then find and record the mass of the setup again.

WHAT DO YOU THINK?

- Did the mass of the experimental setup change?
- How do your observations demonstrate the conservation of mass?

CHALLENGE What do you think you would have observed if you had not used the balloon? Explain.

SKILL FOCUS
Measuring (8.5.b)

MATERIALS
- teaspoon
- baking soda
- funnel
- balloon
- vinegar
- plastic bottle
- balance

TIME
35 minutes

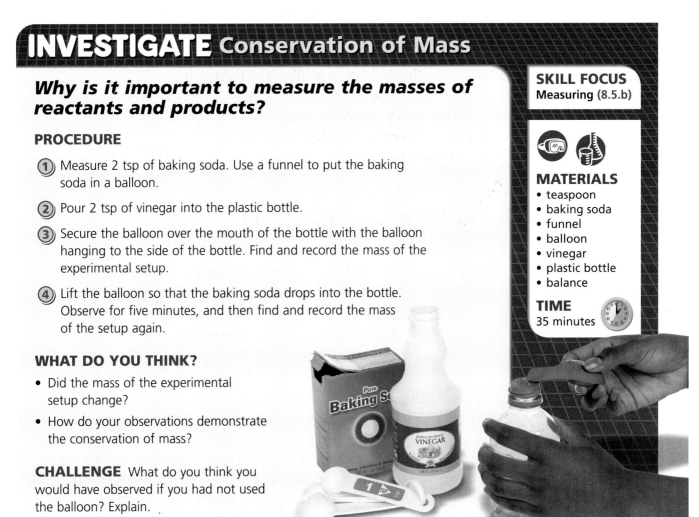

Chemical reactions can be described by chemical equations.

The law of conservation of mass states that in a chemical reaction, the total mass of reactants is equal to the total mass of products. For example, the mass of sodium plus the mass of chlorine that reacts with the sodium equals the mass of the product sodium chloride. Because atoms are only rearranged in a chemical reaction, there must be the same number of sodium atoms and chlorine atoms in both the reactants and products.

Chemical equations represent how atoms are rearranged in a chemical reaction. The atoms in the reactants are shown on the left side of the equation. The atoms in the products are shown on the right side of the equation. No atoms are created or destroyed. The number of atoms of each different element, therefore, must be the same on each side of the equation.

 CHECK YOUR READING How does a chemical equation show the conservation of mass?

In order to write a chemical equation, the information that you need to know is

- the reactants and products in the reaction
- the atomic symbols and chemical formulas of the reactants and products in the reaction
- the direction of the reaction

Carbon dioxide is a gas that animals exhale.

The following equation describes the formation of carbon dioxide from carbon and oxygen. In words, this equation says "Carbon reacts with oxygen to yield carbon dioxide." Notice that instead of an equal sign, an arrow appears between the reactants and the products. The arrow shows which way the reaction proceeds—from reactants on the left to the product or the products on the right.

reactants	direction of reaction	product
$C + O_2$	$\longrightarrow$	CO_2

Remember, the numbers below the chemical formulas for oxygen and carbon dioxide are called subscripts. A subscript indicates the number of atoms of an element in a molecule. You can see in the equation above that the oxygen molecule has two oxygen atoms, and the carbon dioxide molecule also has two oxygen atoms. If the chemical formula of a reactant or product does not have a subscript, it means that only one atom of each element is present in the molecule.

Chemical equations must be balanced.

Remember, chemical reactions follow the law of conservation of mass. Chemical equations show this conservation, or equality, in terms of atoms. The same number of atoms of each element must appear on both sides of a chemical equation. However, simply writing down the chemical formulas of reactants and products does not always result in equal numbers of atoms. You have to balance the equation to make the number of atoms equal on each side of an equation.

Balancing Chemical Equations

To learn how to balance an equation, look at the example of the combustion of natural gas, which is mostly methane (CH_4). The reactants are methane and oxygen. The products are carbon dioxide and water. You can write this reaction as the following equation.

REMINDER

Oxygen is always a reactant in a combustion reaction.

Unbalanced Equation

$$CH_4 \quad + \quad O_2 \quad \longrightarrow \quad CO_2 \quad + \quad H_2O$$

This equation is not balanced. There is one C on each side of the equation, so C is balanced. However, on the left side, H has a subscript of 4, which means there are four hydrogen atoms. On the right side, H has a subscript of 2, which means there are two hydrogen atoms. Also, there are two oxygen atoms on the left and three oxygen atoms on the right. Because of the conservation of mass, you know that hydrogen atoms do not disappear and oxygen atoms do not suddenly appear.

READING TiP

As you read how to balance the equation, look at the illustrations and count the atoms. The number of each type of atom is shown below the formula.

You can balance a chemical equation by changing the amounts of reactants or products represented.

- To balance H first, add another H_2O molecule on the right. Now, both C and H are balanced.

- There are now two oxygen atoms on the left side and four oxygen atoms on the right side. To balance O, add another O_2 molecule on the left.

Balanced Equation

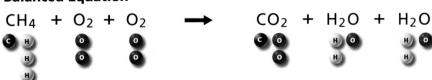

$$CH_4 + O_2 + O_2 \quad \longrightarrow \quad CO_2 + H_2O + H_2O$$

Using Coefficients to Balance Equations

The balanced equation for the combustion of methane shows that one molecule of methane reacts with two molecules of oxygen to produce one molecule of carbon dioxide and two molecules of water. The equation can be simplified by writing $2O_2$ instead of $O_2 + O_2$, and $2H_2O$ instead of $H_2O + H_2O$.

The numbers in front of the chemical formulas are called coefficients. **Coefficients** indicate how many molecules take part in the reaction. If there is no coefficient, then only one molecule of that type takes part in the reaction. The balanced equation, with coefficients, for the combustion of methane is shown below.

Balanced Equation with Coefficients

$$CH_4 \quad + \quad 2O_2 \quad \longrightarrow \quad CO_2 \quad + \quad 2H_2O$$

coefficient   subscript

Chemical formulas can have both coefficients and subscripts. In these cases, multiply the two numbers together to find the number of atoms involved in the reaction. For example, two water molecules $(2H_2O)$ contain $2 \cdot 2 = 4$ hydrogen atoms and $2 \cdot 1 = 2$ oxygen atoms. Remember, coefficients in a chemical equation indicate how many molecules of each type take part in the reaction.

Only coefficients can be changed in order to balance a chemical equation. Subscripts are part of the chemical formula for reactants or products and cannot be changed to balance an equation. Changing a subscript changes the substance represented by the formula.

For example, the equation for the combustion of methane cannot be balanced by changing the formula CO_2 to CO. The formula CO_2 represents carbon dioxide gas, which animals exhale when they breathe. The formula CO represents carbon monoxide gas, which is a very different compound from CO_2. Carbon monoxide gas is poisonous, and breathing too much of it can be fatal.

The combustion of methane (CH_4) is used to melt glass.

> **REMINDER**
> A subscript shows the number of atoms in a molecule. If a subscript is changed, the molecule represented by the formula is changed.

 CHECK YOUR READING Why are coefficients used to balance equations?

Balancing Equations with Coefficients

The steps below show how to balance the equation for the synthesis reaction between nitrogen (N_2) and hydrogen (H_2), which produces ammonia (NH_3).

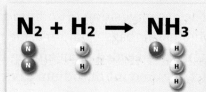

$$N_2 + H_2 \longrightarrow NH_3$$

1 **Count the atoms.** Neither N nor H is balanced. The reactants contain two atoms each of N and H, but the product contains one N atom and three H atoms.

$N_2 + H_2 \longrightarrow NH_3$	
N = 2	N = 1
H = 2	H = 3

Tip: Listing the number of atoms of each element makes it easy to see which elements must be balanced.

2 **Use a coefficient to add atoms to one side of the equation.** A coefficient of 2 on NH_3 balances the number of N atoms.

$N_2 + H_2 \longrightarrow 2\ NH_3$	
N = 2	N = 2
H = 2	H = 6

Tip: When adding coefficients, start with the reactant or product that contains the greatest number of different elements.

3 **Add a coefficient to another reactant or product.** Adding a coefficient of 3 to H_2 on the left side of the equation balances the number of H atoms on both sides. Now the equation is balanced.

$N_2 + 3\ H_2 \longrightarrow 2NH_3$	
N = 2	N = 2
H = 6	H = 6

Tip: Make sure that the coefficients in your balanced equation are the smallest whole numbers possible—that is, they have no common factor other than 1.

$$N_2 + 3H_2 \longrightarrow 2NH_3$$

APPLY
Balance the following equations.
1. $Hg + O_2 \longrightarrow HgO$
2. $Zn + HCl \longrightarrow ZnCl_2 + H_2$

The decomposition of sodium azide is used to inflate air bags in automobiles.

Using the Conservation of Mass

A balanced chemical equation shows that no matter how atoms are rearranged during a chemical reaction, the same number of atoms must be present before and after the reaction. The following example demonstrates the usefulness of chemical equations and the conservation of mass.

The decomposition of sodium azide (NaN_3) is used to inflate automobile air bags. Sodium azide is a solid, and the amount of sodium azide needed in an air bag fills only a small amount of space. In fact, the amount of sodium azide used in air bags is only about 130 grams—an amount that would fit in a large spoon. An inflated air bag, though, takes up much more space even though it contains the same number of atoms that entered the reaction. The reason is illustrated by the chemical equation for this reaction.

Balanced Equation

$$2NaN_3 \longrightarrow 2Na + 3N_2$$

According to the balanced equation shown above, three molecules of nitrogen gas are formed for every two molecules of sodium azide that decompose. Because the nitrogen is a gas, it fills a much greater volume than the original sodium azide. In fact, 67 liters of nitrogen gas are produced by the 130 grams of sodium azide in the reaction. This amount of nitrogen is enough to quickly inflate the air bag during a collision. The decomposition of sodium azide to sodium and nitrogen takes 0.03 seconds. But remember, just because the volume changed, it does not mean the mass changed. There was as much nitrogen and sodium before the reaction as there is after it.

▼ **REMINDER**

Decomposition means "breaking into parts".

△ **CHECK YOUR READING** Why must chemical equations be balanced?

9.2 Review

KEY CONCEPTS

1. State the law of conservation of mass. (8.5.b)

2. Write the chemical equation that shows sodium (Na) and chlorine (Cl_2) combining to form table salt (NaCl). (8.5.a)

3. Is the following equation balanced? Why or why not?

$CO \longrightarrow C + O_2$ (8.5.b)

CRITICAL THINKING

4. **Communicate** Describe Lavoisier's experiment with mercury. How does this experiment show the law of conservation of mass?

5. **Synthesize** Suppose a log's mass is 5 kg. After burning, the mass of the ash is 1 kg. Explain what may have happened to the other 4 kg of mass.

△ CHALLENGE

6. **Synthesize** Suppose a container holds 1000 hydrogen molecules (H_2) and 1000 oxygen molecules (O_2) that react to form water. How many water molecules will be in the container? Will anything else be in the container? If so, what?

Chemistry in Firefighting

A firefighter needs to know about chemical reactions. A fire is a combustion reaction that requires oxygen as a reactant. Firefighters, therefore, try to prevent oxygen from reaching the burning substances. Firefighters often use water or carbon dioxide for this purpose, but these materials make some types of fires more dangerous.

> 8.5.a Students know reactant atoms and molecules interact to form products with different chemical properties.

Grease Fires

Some fires can be extinguished by a chemical reaction. In kitchen grease fires, the chemicals that are used to fight the fire react with the grease. The reaction produces a foam that puts out the fire.

Metal Fires

Some fires involve metals such as magnesium. This metal burns at a very high temperature and reacts violently with water. Firefighters try to smother metal fires with a material such as sand.

Hazardous Reactions

Chemicals may react with water to form poisonous gases or acids. Firefighters might use a foam that extinguishes the fire, cools the area around the fire, and traps gases released by the fire. The symbols shown on the left are among several that show firefighters what chemical dangers may be present.

The fire shown above is a magnesium fire in Chicago in 1998. Firefighters used water to protect surrounding buildings, but dumped road salt on the burning magnesium.

EXPLORE

Build a carbon dioxide fire extinguisher.

1. Put 3 tsp of baking soda on a tissue and roll it into a tube. Tie the ends and middle of the tube with thread. Leave extra thread at one end of the tube.
2. Mold clay tightly around a straw.
3. Pour some vinegar into a bottle.
4. Hold the thread to suspend the tissue tube above the vinegar. Place the straw inside the bottle. Use the clay molded around the straw to hold the thread in place. Be sure that the straw is not touching the vinegar.
5. Shake and observe the fire extinguisher.

9.3 Chemical reactions involve energy changes.

CALIFORNIA
Content Standard

8.5.c Students know chemical reactions usually liberate heat or absorb heat.

◀ **BEFORE, you learned**

- Bonds are broken and made during chemical reactions
- Mass is conserved in all chemical reactions
- Chemical reactions are represented by balanced chemical equations

▶ **NOW, you will learn**

- About the energy in chemical bonds between atoms
- Why some chemical reactions release energy
- Why some chemical reactions absorb energy

VOCABULARY

bond energy p. 288
exothermic reaction p. 289
endothermic reaction p. 289
photosynthesis p. 292

EXPLORE Energy Changes (8.5.c)

How can you identify a transfer of energy?

PROCEDURE

(1) Pour 50 mL of hot tap water into the cup and place the thermometer in the cup.

(2) Wait 30 seconds, then record the temperature of the water.

(3) Measure 5 tsp of Epsom salts. Add the Epsom salts to the cup and immediately record the temperature while stirring the contents of the cup.

(4) Continue to record the temperature every 30 seconds for 2 minutes.

WHAT DO YOU THINK?

- What happened to the temperature after you added the Epsom salts?
- What do you think caused this change to occur?

MATERIALS

- graduated cylinder
- hot tap water
- plastic cup
- thermometer
- stopwatch
- plastic spoon
- Epsom salts

WATER

Chemical reactions release or absorb energy.

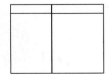

COMBINATION NOTES
Use combination notes to organize information on how chemical reactions absorb or release energy.

Chemical reactions involve breaking bonds in reactants and forming new bonds in products. Breaking bonds requires energy, and forming bonds releases energy. The energy associated with bonds is called **bond energy.** What happens to this energy during a chemical reaction?

Chemists have determined the bond energy for bonds between atoms. Breaking a bond between carbon and hydrogen requires a certain amount of energy. This amount of energy is different from the amount of energy needed to break a bond between carbon and oxygen, or between hydrogen and oxygen.

Energy is needed to break bonds in reactant molecules. Energy is released when bonds are formed in product molecules. By adding up the bond energies in the reactants and products, you can determine whether energy will be released or absorbed.

Sometimes more energy is released when products form than is needed to break the bonds in the reactants. Then energy is released during the reaction. A reaction in which energy is released is called an **exothermic reaction.**

Sometimes more energy is required to break the bonds in the reactants than is released when the products form. Then energy must be added to the reaction. That is, the reaction absorbs energy. A reaction in which energy is absorbed is called an **endothermic reaction.**

These types of energy changes can also be observed in different physical changes such as dissolving or changing state. The state change from a liquid to a solid, or freezing, releases energy—this is an exothermic process. The state change from a solid to a liquid, or melting, absorbs energy—this is an endothermic process.

How are exothermic and endothermic reactions different?

Exothermic reactions release energy.

Exothermic chemical reactions often produce an increase in temperature. In exothermic reactions, the bond energies of the reactants are less than the bond energies of the products. As a result, less energy is needed to break the bonds in the reactants than is released during the formation of the products. This energy difference between reactants and products is often released as heat. The release of heat causes a change in the temperature of the reaction mixture.

Even though energy is released by exothermic reactions, some energy must first be added to break bonds in the reactants. In exothermic reactions, the formation of bonds in the products releases more energy. Overall, more energy is released than is added.

Some reactions are highly exothermic. These reactions produce a great deal of heat and significantly raise the temperature of their surroundings. One example is the reaction of powdered aluminum metal with a type of iron oxide. This reaction is known as the thermite reaction. The equation for this reaction is

$$2Al + Fe_2O_3 \longrightarrow Al_2O_3 + 2Fe$$

This reaction releases enough heat to melt the iron that is produced. In fact, this reaction is used to weld iron rails together.

What is evidence for an exothermic chemical reaction?

The white clouds of water vapor are formed by the exothermic reaction between hydrogen and oxygen.

$$2H_2 + O_2 \longrightarrow 2H_2O$$

The thermite reaction releases enough heat to weld pieces of iron together.

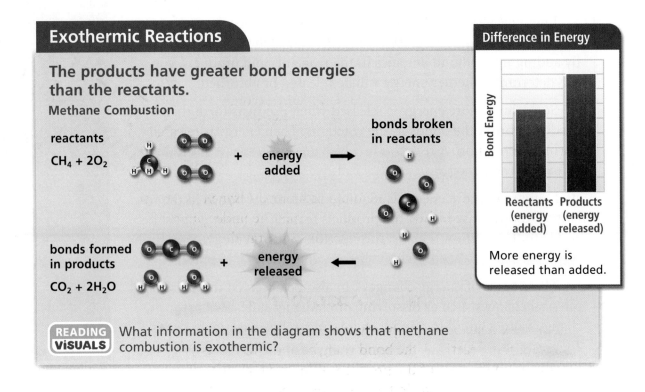

Exothermic Reactions

The products have greater bond energies than the reactants.

Methane Combustion

reactants

$CH_4 + 2O_2$

+ energy added →

bonds broken in reactants

bonds formed in products

$CO_2 + 2H_2O$

+ energy released ←

Difference in Energy

Bond Energy

Reactants (energy added) Products (energy released)

More energy is released than added.

READING VISUALS What information in the diagram shows that methane combustion is exothermic?

All common combustion reactions, such as the combustion of methane, are exothermic. To determine how energy changes in this reaction, the bond energies in the reactants—oxygen and methane—and in the products—carbon dioxide and water—can be added and compared. This process is illustrated by the diagram above. The difference in energy is released to the air as heat.

Some chemical reactions release excess energy as light instead of heat. For example, glow sticks work by a chemical reaction that releases energy as light. One of the reactants, a solution of hydrogen peroxide, is contained in a thin glass tube within the plastic stick. The rest of the stick is filled with a second chemical and a brightly colored dye. When you bend the stick, the glass tube inside it breaks and the two solutions mix. The result is a bright glow of light.

These cup coral polyps glow because of exothermic chemical reactions.

Exothermic chemical reactions also occur in living things. Some of these reactions release energy as heat, and others release energy as light. Fireflies light up due to a reaction that takes place between oxygen and a chemical called luciferin. This is a type of exothermic reaction. It does not happen only in fireflies. In fact, similar reactions are found in several different species of fish, squid, jellyfish, and shrimp.

CHECK YOUR READING In which ways might an exothermic reaction release energy?

The bombardier beetle, shown in the photograph on the right, uses natural exothermic reactions to defend itself. Although several chemical reactions are involved, the end result is the production of a hot, toxic spray. The most important reaction in the process is the decomposition of hydrogen peroxide into water and oxygen.

$$2H_2O_2 \longrightarrow 2H_2O + O_2$$

First, the hydrogen peroxide rapidly breaks down. Then a hot, toxic mixture is made by the reactions. Oxygen gas from the reaction in the equation above puts the mixture under pressure. After enough pressure builds up, the beetle can spray the mixture.

Endothermic reactions absorb energy.

Endothermic reactions often produce a decrease in temperature. In endothermic reactions, the bond energies of the reactants are greater than the bond energies of the products. As a result, more energy is needed to break the bonds in the reactants than is released during the formation of the products. The difference in energy is usually absorbed from the surroundings as heat. This often causes a decrease in the temperature of the reaction mixture.

All endothermic reactions absorb energy. However, they do not all absorb energy as heat. One example of this type of endothermic reaction is the decomposition of water by electrolysis. In this case, the energy that is absorbed is in the form of electrical energy. When the electric current is turned off, the reaction stops. The change in energy that occurs in this reaction is shown below.

READING TiP

The prefix *endo-* means "inside."

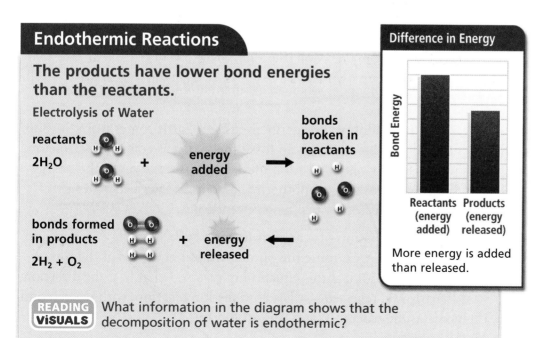

Endothermic Reactions

The products have lower bond energies than the reactants.

Electrolysis of Water

reactants

2H₂O

+ energy added →

bonds broken in reactants

bonds formed in products

2H₂ + O₂

+ energy released ←

Difference in Energy

Bond Energy

Reactants (energy added)   Products (energy released)

More energy is added than released.

READING VISUALS What information in the diagram shows that the decomposition of water is endothermic?

Probably the most important series of endothermic reactions on Earth is photosynthesis. Many steps occur in the process, but the overall chemical reaction is

$$6CO_2 + 6H_2O \longrightarrow C_6H_{12}O_6 + 6O_2$$

Unlike many other endothermic reactions, photosynthesis does not absorb energy as heat. Instead, during **photosynthesis,** plants absorb energy from sunlight to turn carbon dioxide and water into oxygen and glucose, which is a type of sugar molecule. The energy is stored in the glucose molecules, ready to be used when needed.

 How can you determine if a reaction is endothermic?

Exothermic and endothermic reactions work together to supply energy.

VISUALIZATION
CLASSZONE.COM
View examples of endothermic and exothermic reactions.

When you think about exothermic and endothermic reactions, consider energy to be part of the reaction. An exothermic reaction releases energy, so energy is on the product side of the chemical equation. An endothermic reaction absorbs energy, so energy is on the reactant side of the chemical equation.

Exothermic Reaction

Reactants $\longrightarrow$ Products + Energy

Endothermic Reaction

Reactants + Energy $\longrightarrow$ Products

As you can see in the general reactions above, exothermic and endothermic reactions have opposite energy changes. This means that if an exothermic chemical reaction proceeds in the opposite direction, it becomes an endothermic reaction that absorbs energy. Similarly, if an endothermic reaction proceeds in the opposite direction, it becomes an exothermic reaction that releases energy.

 What happens when an exothermic reaction is reversed?

CALIFORNIA Focus

The supply of energy generated from the relationship between exothermic and endothermic reactions in fossil fuels such as petroleum is in high demand in California. California ranks first in gasoline consumption in the United States, and fourth in oil production.

A large amount of the energy we use on Earth comes from the Sun. This energy includes energy in fossil fuels such as coal and petroleum, as well as energy obtained from food. In all of these cases, the energy in sunlight is stored by endothermic reactions. When the energy is needed, it is released by exothermic reactions.

This combination of reactions forms a cycle of energy storage and use. For example, examine the photosynthesis equation at the top of the page. If you look at this equation in reverse—that is, if the direction of the arrow is reversed—it is a combustion reaction, with oxygen and glucose as the reactants, and it is exothermic.

Cars and trucks release energy from fossil fuels through combustion, as shown here on the 101 Freeway near Encino, California.

Plants store energy through the endothermic reactions of photo-synthesis. Living things can release this energy through a series of exothermic reactions called respiration.

The energy stored in plants through photosynthesis can also be released in other ways. Consider energy from fossil fuels. Fossil fuels include petroleum, natural gas, and coal. These substances formed from fossilized materials, mainly plants. The materials had been under high pressures and temperatures for millions of years. When these plants were alive, they used photosynthesis to produce glucose and other molecules from carbon dioxide and water.

The energy stored in the bonds of these molecules remains, even though the molecules have changed over time. The burning of gaso-line in a car releases this energy, enabling the car's engine to work. Similarly, the burning of coal, or the burning of natural gas, releases the energy originally stored by the endothermic series of photosynthe-sis reactions.

CHECK YOUR READING How can endothermic and exothermic reactions work together?

9.3 Review

KEY CONCEPTS

1. What are the differences between exothermic and endothermic reactions? (8.5.c)

2. Is the combustion of methane an exothermic or endothermic reaction? Explain. (8.5.c)

3. Is photosynthesis an exothermic or endothermic reaction? Explain. (8.5.c)

CRITICAL THINKING

4. **Synthesize** Describe the connections between the processes of photosynthesis and combustion.

5. **Communicate** Explain how most energy used on Earth can be traced back to the Sun.

CHALLENGE

6. **Synthesize** Electrolysis of water is endothermic. What does this indicate about the bond energy in the reactants and products? What happens when this reaction is reversed?

CHAPTER INVESTIGATION

Exothermic or Endothermic?

OVERVIEW AND PURPOSE A clue that a chemical reaction has taken place is a transfer of energy, often in the form of heat or light. The chemical reaction used to demolish an old building, as shown in the photograph to the left, is a dramatic example of energy release by a reaction. In this investigation, you will use what you have learned about chemical reactions to
- measure and record temperature changes in two processes
- compare temperature changes during the processes in order to classify them as exothermic or endothermic

▶ Procedure

1. Make a data table like the one shown on the sample notebook page.

2. Work with a partner. One should keep track of time. The other should observe the thermometer and report the temperature.

PART 1

3. Pour 30 mL of hydrogen peroxide into a beaker. Put a thermometer into the beaker. Wait 2 minutes to allow the thermometer to reach the temperature of the hydrogen peroxide. During the time you are waiting, measure 1 g of yeast with the balance.

4. Record the starting temperature. Add the yeast to the beaker and immediately record the temperature while gently stirring the contents of the beaker. Continue to record the temperature every 30 seconds as you observe the process for 5 minutes.

step 4

MATERIALS

- graduated cylinder
- hydrogen peroxide
- 2 beakers
- 2 thermometers
- stopwatch
- measuring spoons
- yeast
- balance
- plastic spoon
- large plastic cup
- hot tap water
- vinegar
- baking soda

8.5.c, 8.9.b, 8.9.e

Content Standard
8.5.c Students know chemical reactions usually liberate heat or absorb heat.

Investigation Standard
8.9.e Construct appropriate graphs from data and develop quantitative statements about the relationships between variables.

PART 2

5 Make a hot water bath by filling a large plastic cup halfway with hot tap water.

6 Measure and pour 30 mL of vinegar into a small beaker. Set this beaker in the hot water bath and place a thermometer in the vinegar. Wait until the temperature of the vinegar rises to between 32 and 38°C (90 to 100°F). While waiting for the vinegar's temperature to increase, measure 1 g of baking soda.

step 6

7 Remove the beaker from the hot water bath. Record the starting temperature.

8 Add the baking soda to the vinegar and immediately record the temperature as you swirl the contents of the beaker. Continue to record the temperature every 30 seconds as you observe the reaction for 5 minutes.

▶ Observe and Analyze   Write It Up

1. **RECORD OBSERVATIONS** Remember to complete your data table.

2. **GRAPH** Use the information from your data table to graph your results. Make a double-line graph, plotting your data in a different color for each part of the investigation. Plot temperature in degrees Celsius on the vertical, or *y*-axis. Plot the time in minutes on the horizontal, or *x*-axis.

3. **ANALYZE DATA** Examine the graph. When did the temperature change the most in each part of the investigation? When did it change the least? Compare the temperature at the start of each process with the temperature after 5 minutes. How do the temperature changes compare?

▶ Conclude   Write It Up

1. **CLASSIFY** Is the mixture of hydrogen peroxide and yeast endothermic or exothermic? Is the reaction between vinegar and baking soda endothermic or exothermic? Provide evidence for your answers.

2. **EVALUATE** Did you have any difficulties obtaining accurate measurements? Describe possible limitations or sources of error.

3. **APPLY** What does the reaction between baking soda and vinegar tell you about their bond energies?

▶ INVESTIGATE Further

CHALLENGE Repeat Part 2, but instead of using the hot water bath, add the hot water directly to the vinegar before pouring in the baking soda. Does this change in procedure change the results of the experiment? Why might your observations have changed? Explain your answers.

Exothermic or Endothermic?

Observe and Analyze

Table 1. Temperature Measurements

Time (min)	Hydrogen Peroxide and Yeast Temperature (°C)	Vinegar and Baking Soda Temperature (°C)
0		
0.5		
1.0		
....		
5.0		

Conclude

the **BIG** idea

Chemical reactions form new substances by breaking and making chemical bonds.

CONTENT REVIEW
CLASSZONE.COM

KEY CONCEPTS SUMMARY

Chemical reactions alter arrangements of atoms.

- Chemical changes occur through chemical reactions.
- Evidence of a chemical reaction includes a color change, the formation of a precipitate, the formation of a gas, and a change in temperature.
- Chemical reactions change reactants into products.

VOCABULARY
chemical reaction p. 271
reactant p. 273
product p. 273
precipitate p. 274
catalyst p. 278

The masses of reactants and products are equal.

- Mass is conserved in chemical reactions.
- Chemical equations summarize chemical reactions.
- Balanced chemical equations show the conservation of mass.

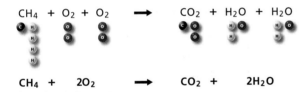

$$CH_4 + O_2 + O_2 \longrightarrow CO_2 + H_2O + H_2O$$

$$CH_4 + 2O_2 \longrightarrow CO_2 + 2H_2O$$

VOCABULARY
law of conservation of mass p. 281
coefficient p. 284

Chemical reactions involve energy changes.

- Different bonds contain different amounts of energy.
- In an exothermic reaction, more energy is released than added.
- In an endothermic reaction, more energy is added than released.

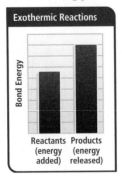
Exothermic Reactions

Bond Energy

Reactants (energy added) Products (energy released)

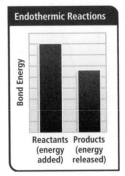
Endothermic Reactions

Bond Energy

Reactants (energy added) Products (energy released)

VOCABULARY
bond energy p. 288
exothermic reaction p. 289
endothermic reaction p. 289
photosynthesis p. 292

Reviewing Vocabulary

Describe how the vocabulary terms in the following pairs are related to each other. Explain the relationship in a one- or two-sentence answer.

1. reactant, product

2. law of conservation of mass, chemical reaction

3. endothermic, exothermic

4. photosynthesis, endothermic

Reviewing Key Concepts

Multiple Choice *Choose the letter of the best answer.*

5. During a chemical reaction, reactants always (8.5.a)
   a. become more complex
   b. require catalysts
   c. lose mass
   d. form products

6. The splitting of water molecules into hydrogen and oxygen molecules is an example of a (8.5.a)
   a. combustion reaction
   b. chemical change
   c. synthesis reaction
   d. physical change

7. Combustion reactions (8.5.a)
   a. destroy atoms   **c.** form precipitates
   b. require glucose   **d.** require oxygen

8. Which of the following will increase the rate of a reaction? (8.5.a)
   a. breaking solid reactants into smaller pieces
   b. removing a catalyst
   c. decreasing the temperature
   d. decreasing the concentration

9. What does a catalyst do in a chemical reaction? (8.5.a)
   a. It slows the reaction down.
   b. It speeds the reaction up.
   c. It becomes a product.
   d. It is a reactant.

10. During a chemical reaction, the total amount of mass present (8.5.c)
   a. increases
   b. decreases
   c. may increase or decrease
   d. does not change

11. Chemical equations show summaries of (8.5.a)
   a. physical changes
   b. changes of state
   c. chemical reactions
   d. changes in temperature

12. A chemical equation must (8.5.b)
   a. show energy   **c.** use subscripts
   b. be balanced   **d.** use coefficients

13. What type of reaction occurs if the reactants have a greater total bond energy than the products? (8.5.c)
   a. an endothermic reaction
   b. a synthesis reaction
   c. an exothermic reaction
   d. a decomposition reaction

14. Endothermic reactions always (8.5.c)
   a. absorb energy
   b. make more complex products
   c. release energy
   d. make less complex products

Short Answer *Write a short answer to each question.*

15. Describe the differences between physical and chemical changes. How can each be identified? (8.5.d)

16. Explain the difference between products and reactants in a chemical reaction. (8.5.a)

17. Indentify four ways a chemical change can be detected. (8.5.a)

18. When you balance a chemical equation, why can you change coefficients of reactants or products, but not subscripts? (8.5.b)

Thinking Critically

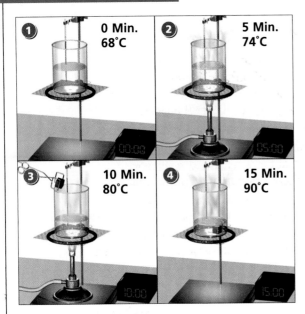

(1) 0 Min. 68°C   (2) 5 Min. 74°C

(3) 10 Min. 80°C   (4) 15 Min. 90°C

The series of illustrations above shows a chemical reaction at five-minute intervals. Use the information in the illustrations to answer the following six questions.

19. OBSERVE What happened to the temperature of the substance in the beaker from the beginning to the end of each five-minute interval? (8.5.c)

20. ANALYZE Does the reaction appear to continue in step 4? What evidence tells you?

21. CLASSIFY Is this an endothermic or exothermic reaction? Explain. (8.5.c)

22. INFER Suppose the metal cube placed in the beaker in step 3 is a catalyst. What effect did the metal have on the reaction? Why? (8.5.a)

23. PREDICT If the metal cube is a catalyst, how much of the metal cube will be left in the beaker when the reaction is completed? Explain. (8.5.a)

24. SYNTHESIZE Assume that the reaction shown is a decomposition reaction. Describe what happens to the reactants. (8.5.a)

Using Math Skills in Science

Answer the following ten questions based on the equations below.

Equation 1—HgO $\longrightarrow$ Hg + O$_2$

Equation 2—Al + O$_2$ $\longrightarrow$ Al$_2$O$_3$

Equation 3—S$_8$ + O$_2$ $\longrightarrow$ SO$_3$

25. Copy and balance equation 1. (8.5.b)

26. What coefficients, if any, did you add to equation 1 to balance it? (8.5.b)

27. How many Hg atoms take part in the reaction shown by equation 1 when it is balanced? (8.5.b)

28. Copy and balance equation 2. (8.5.b)

29. What coefficients, if any, did you add to equation 2 to balance it? (8.5.b)

30. How many O atoms take part in the reaction shown in equation 2 when it is balanced? (8.5.b)

31. Copy and balance equation 3. (8.5.b)

32. What coefficients, if any, did you add to equation 3 to balance it? (8.5.b)

33. How many S atoms take part in the reaction shown in equation 3 when it is balanced? (8.5.b)

34. How many O atoms take part in the reaction shown in equation 3 when it is balanced? (8.5.b)

the BIG idea

35. DRAW CONCLUSIONS Describe three chemical reactions you see each day. How do you know they are chemical reactions?

36. ANALYZE Look back at the photograph and question on pages 268 and 269. Answer the question in terms of the chapter's Big Idea.

UNIT PROJECTS

Check your schedule for your unit project. How are you doing? Be sure that you have placed data or notes from your research in your project folder.

Analyzing Theories

8.5.b

Answer the questions based on the information in the following passage.

During the 1700s, scientists thought that matter contained a substance called phlogiston. According to this theory, wood was made of phlogiston and ash. When wood burned, the phlogiston was released and the ash was left behind.

The ash that remained had less mass than the original wood. This decrease in mass was explained by the release of phlogiston. However, when substances such as phosphorus and mercury burned, the material that remained had more mass than the original substances. This increase in mass did not make sense to some scientists.

The scientists who supported the phlogiston theory said that the phlogiston in some substances had negative mass. So, when the substances burned, they released phlogiston and gained mass. Other scientists disagreed, and their research led to the discovery of a scientific law. Antoine Lavoisier carried out several experiments by burning metals in sealed containers. He showed that mass is never lost or gained in a chemical reaction.

1. What did the phlogiston theory successfully explain?
   a. the presence of ash in unburned wood
   b. the apparent gain of mass in some reactions
   c. the chemical makeup of the air
   d. the apparent decrease in mass in some situations

2. Why did some scientists disagree with the phlogiston theory?
   a. Burning a substance always produced an increase in mass.
   b. Burning a substance always produced a decrease in mass.
   c. Burning could produce either an increase or decrease in mass.
   d. Burning wood produced ash and phlogiston.

3. What law did Lavoisier's work establish?
   a. conservation of energy
   b. conservation of mass
   c. conservation of momentum
   d. conservation of resources

4. To carry out his experiments, what kind of equipment did Lavoisier need?
   a. devices to separate the different elements in the air
   b. machines that could separate wood from ash
   c. microscopes that could be used to study rust and ash
   d. balances that could measure mass very accurately

Extended Response

Answer the following questions in detail.
Include some of the terms from the list on the right.
Underline each term you use in your answers.

catalyst	coefficient	concentration
temperature	reaction	subscript
surface area		

5. Suppose you wanted to change the rate of a chemical reaction. What might you change in the reaction? Explain each factor.

6. Is the chemical equation shown below balanced? Why or why not? How are balanced chemical equations related to conservation of mass?

$$6CO_2 + 6H_2O \longrightarrow C_6H_{12}O_6 + O_2$$

TIMELINES in Science

UNDERSTANDING ATOMS AND BONDS

About 2500 years ago, Greek thinkers said that all matter consisted of extremely tiny particles called atoms. The sizes and shapes of different atoms, they said, were what determined the properties of a substance. This early atomic theory, however, was not widely accepted. Many at the time found these tiny, invisible particles difficult to accept.

The story of atoms and bonds is interesting. Scientists had to make predictions about things they couldn't see based on what they could see. The modern view of atoms and how they form chemical bonds is the result of scientists trying to make sense of the patterns in the world.

This timeline shows a few of the major events that led to our modern view of atoms and how they bind. The atomic theory was developed long before scientists ever saw an image of an atom. The atomic theory is a good theory because it explains many things. It explains how atoms form chemical bonds. It also explains how one element is different from another.

1661

Boyle Challenges Concept of the Four Elements

British chemist Robert Boyle says that more than four basic substances exist. Boyle also concludes that all matter is made of very tiny particles he calls corpuscles.

EVENTS

| 1600 | 1620 | 1640 | 1660 |

APPLICATIONS AND TECHNOLOGY

TECHNOLOGY

Collecting and Studying Gases

Throughout the 1600s, scientists tried to study gases. They had difficulty collecting them. English biologist Stephen Hales designed an apparatus to collect gases. The "pneumatic trough" was a breakthrough in chemistry. It allowed scientists to collect and study gases for the first time. It was later used by such chemists as Joseph Black, Henry Cavendish, and Joseph Priestley to study the gases that make up air. The work of these scientists showed that air was made of more than a single gas.

1808

John Dalton Says: "Bring Back the Atom"

English chemist John Dalton revives the ancient Greek idea that all matter is made of atoms. Dalton claims that each element has its own type of atom and that the atoms combine in fixed ratios with one another.

1808

Humphrey Davy Shocks Chemistry

English chemist Humphrey Davy applies an electric current to different materials. He discovers that many materials once thought to be elements break apart into even simpler materials. Davy succeeds in isolating the elements sodium, calcium, strontium, and barium.

1897

It's Smaller Than the Atom!

English physicist Joseph John Thomson discovers the electron—the first subatomic particle to be identified. Thomson concludes that these tiny particles have a negative charge. Thomson will later propose that atoms are made of a great many of these negative particles floating in a sea of positive charge. Thomson suggests that each atom resembles a dish of pudding with raisins in it. The electrons are the raisins and the pudding the positive charge in which they float.

| 1800 | 1820 | 1840 | 1860 | 1880 |

TECHNOLOGY

Chemistry and Electric Charge

In 1800 Italian physicist Alessandro Volta announced that he had produced an electric current from a pile, or battery, of alternating zinc and silver discs. Volta's invention was important for the study of atoms and elements in two ways. First, the fact that the contact of two different metals could produce an electric current suggested that electric charge must be part of matter. Second, the powerful electric current produced by the batteries enabled chemists to break apart many other substances, showing that there were more elements than previously thought.

1903
Atoms Release Energy

Polish-born French physicist Marie Curie and her husband, Pierre, have won the Nobel Prize for their isolation of the elements polonium and radium. These elements are unique because they release energy. Marie Curie names this trait radioactivity. They share the award with Henri Becquerel, who previously observed this trait with the element uranium.

1911
Atoms Have a Center

By aiming a stream of particles at a piece of gold foil, New Zealand-born physicist Ernest Rutherford finds that atoms are not like a dish of pudding filled with raisins, as J. J. Thomson had suggested. Atoms must have a dense center because many of the particles bounce back. He calls the atom's center its nucleus.

1913
Bohr Puts Electrons into Orbit

Building on the work of Rutherford, Danish physicist Niels Bohr claims that electrons move about the nucleus only in certain, well-defined orbits. Bohr also says that electrons can jump to different orbits and emit or absorb energy when doing so.

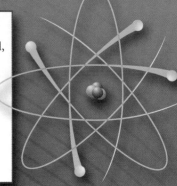

1919
Atoms Share a Common Bond

U.S. chemists G.N. Lewis and Irving Langmuir suggest that atoms of many elements form bonds by sharing pairs of electrons. Chemists now can explain how molecules can have certain structures.

1900   1905   1910   1915   1920   1940

APPLICATION

The Chemistry of Communication

The discovery of the electron resulted in more than a greater understanding of the atom. It also opened new ways of communicating. In 1906, U.S. inventor Lee De Forest made a device for detecting radio signals. He called it the audion. The audion worked by producing a beam of electrons inside a vacuum tube. The beam was then made to respond to radio signals that it received from an antenna. The audion helped pave the way for later devices such as the transistor.

1960s
Smaller Particles Discovered

By smashing atoms into one another, scientists discover that protons and neutrons are themselves composed of even smaller particles. In a bit of scientific humor, these smaller particles are named quarks, a nonsense word taken from a novel. Scientists detect these particles by observing the tracks they make in special detectors.

1980s

Tunneling to the Atomic Level

Scanning tunneling microscopes (STMs) allow scientists to interact with matter at the atomic level. Electrons on the tiny tip of an STM "tunnel" through the gap between the tip and target surface. By recording changes in the tunneling current, researchers get an accurate picture.

 RESOURCE CENTER
CLASSZONE.COM

Explore advances in atomic research.

1960   1980   2000

TECHNOLOGY

Particle Accelerators

Particle accelerators speed up charged particles by passing them through an electric field. By smashing subatomic particles into one another, scientists are able to learn what these particles are made of and what are the forces holding them together. The H1 particle detector in Hamburg, Germany, can accelerate protons to 800 billion volts and is used to study the quarks that make up protons.

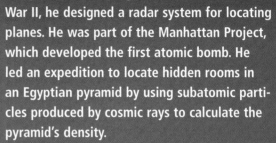

SPOTLIGHT on
LUIS ALVAREZ

Luis Alvarez (1911–1988) was an award-winning physicist with many interests. During World War II, he designed a radar system for locating planes. He was part of the Manhattan Project, which developed the first atomic bomb. He led an expedition to locate hidden rooms in an Egyptian pyramid by using subatomic particles produced by cosmic rays to calculate the pyramid's density.

In 1968 Alvarez was awarded the Nobel Prize in Physics for developing the liquid hydrogen bubble chamber, used to detect subatomic particles. His research group discovered more than 70 elementary particles, leading to a change in previously held nuclear theories.

ACTIVITIES

Explore a Model Atom

The discovery of the nucleus was one of the most important discoveries in human history. Rutherford's experiment, however, was a simple one that you can model. Take an aluminum pie plate and place a table tennis ball-sized piece of clay at its center. The clay represents a nucleus. Place the end of a grooved ruler at the edge of the plate. Hold the other end up to form a ramp. Roll a marble down the groove toward the clay. Move the ruler to different angles with each roll. Roll the marble 20 times. How many rolls out of 20 hit the clay ball? How do you think the results would be different if the atoms looked like pudding with raisins in it, as Thomson suggested?

Writing About Science

Suppose you are an atom. Choose one of the events on the timeline and describe it from the atom's point of view.

CHAPTER
10 Solutions

the BIG idea

When substances dissolve to form a solution, the properties of the mixture change.

Why might some substances dissolve in the seawater in this photograph, but others do not?

Key Concepts

SECTION

1 A solution is a type of mixture.
Learn how solutions differ from other types of mixtures.

SECTION

2 The amount of solute that dissolves can vary.
Learn how solutions can contain different amounts of dissolved substances.

SECTION

3 Solutions can be acidic, basic, or neutral.
Learn about acids and bases and where they are found.

 California ClassZone

CLASSZONE.COM

Chapter 10 online resources: Content Review, Visualization, Resource Center, Math Tutorial, Test Practice

EXPLORE (the BIG idea)

Does It Dissolve?

> **8.5.d** Students know physical processes include freezing and boiling, in which a material changes form with no chemical reaction.

Pour water into four small clear cups. Add a teaspoon of each of the following: in cup 1, powdered drink mix; in cup 2, vinegar; in cup 3, milk; in cup 4, sand. Stir briefly. Observe the contents of all four cups for five minutes.

Observe and Think Do all of the substances dissolve in water? How can you tell?

Acid Test

> **8.5.a** Students know reactant atoms and molecules interact to form products with different chemical properties.

Rub a radish on three blank index cards until the marks on the cards become dark pink. Use cotton swabs to wipe lemon juice onto the mark on the first card, tap water onto the mark on the second card, and soda water onto the mark on the third card. Observe the color of the radish mark on each index card.

Observe and Think What happened to the color on each index card? How might the three liquids that you tested differ?

NSTA
scilinks.org
SCI LINKS

Solutions Code: MDL025

Getting Ready to Learn

◀ CONCEPT REVIEW

- Matter can change from one physical state to another.
- A mixture is a blend of substances that do not react chemically.
- Particles can have electrical charges.

◀ VOCABULARY REVIEW

molecule p. 139

mixture p. 145

proton p. 201

ion p. 205

chemical reaction p. 271

CONTENT REVIEW
CLASSZONE.COM

Review concepts and vocabulary.

▶ TAKING NOTES

MIND MAP

Write each main idea, or blue heading, in an oval; then write details that relate to each other and to the main idea. Organize the details so that each line of the map has a note about one part of the main idea.

CHOOSE YOUR OWN STRATEGY

For each new vocabulary term, take notes by choosing one of the strategies from earlier chapters—**frame game**, **description wheel**, or **four square** diagram. You can also use other vocabulary strategies that you might already know.

See the Note-Taking Handbook on pages R45–R51.

SCIENCE NOTEBOOK

parts not easily separated or differentiated

substances dissolved in a solvent

(A solution is a type of mixture.)

can be solid, liquid, or gas

physical properties differ from solvent

Frame Game
example
example TERM example
example

Description Wheel
feature
feature TERM feature
feature

Four Square
definition | characteristics
TERM
examples | nonexamples

KEY CONCEPT

10.1 A solution is a type of mixture.

CALIFORNIA
Content Standards

8.5.b Students know the idea of atoms explains the conserva-tion of matter: In chemical reactions the number of atoms stays the same no matter how they are arranged, so their total mass stays the same.

8.5.d Students know physical processes include freezing and boiling, in which a material changes form with no chemical reaction.

8.5.e Students know how to determine whether a solution is acidic, basic, or neutral.

BEFORE, you learned

• Ionic or covalent bonds hold a compound together
• Chemical reactions produce chemical changes
• Chemical reactions alter the arrangements of atoms

NOW, you will learn

• How a solution differs from other types of mixtures
• About the parts of a solution
• How properties of solutions differ from properties of their separate components

VOCABULARY

solution p. 307
solvent p. 308
solute p. 308
suspension p. 309

VOCABULARY
Remember to use the strategy of your choice. You might use a four square diagram for *solution*.

EXPLORE Mixtures (8.5.d)

Which substances dissolve in water?

PROCEDURE

(1) Pour equal amounts of water into each cup.

(2) Pour one spoonful of table salt into one of the cups. Stir.

(3) Pour one spoonful of flour into the other cup. Stir.

(4) Record your observations.

WHAT DO YOU THINK?
• Did the salt dissolve? Did the flour dissolve?
• How can you tell?

MATERIALS
• tap water
• 2 clear plastic cups
• plastic spoon
• table salt
• flour

The parts of a solution are mixed evenly.

A mixture is a combination of substances, such as a fruit salad. The ingredients of any mixture can be physically separated from each other. They are not chemically changed—they are still the same sub-stances. Sometimes, however, a mixture is completely blended. Its ingredients cannot be identified as different substances. A **solution** is a type of mixture that is the same throughout. A solution can be physi-cally separated, but all portions of a solution have the same properties.

If you stir sand into a glass of water, you can identify the sand as a separate substance that falls to the bottom of the glass. Sand in water is a mixture that is not a solution. If you stir sugar into a glass of water, you cannot identify the sugar as a separate substance. Sugar in water is a common solution. Seawater, gasoline, and the liquid part of your blood are also solutions.

Solutes and Solvents

READING **TiP**

The words *solvent* and *solute* are both related to the Latin word *solvere,* which means "to loosen."

Like other mixtures, a solution has definite parts. A **solvent** is a substance that dissolves a solute. A **solute** (SAHL-yoot) is a substance that is dissolved to make a solution. When a solute dissolves, it separates into individual particles. It is not possible to identify the solute and solvent as different substances in a solution.

In a solution of table salt and water, the salt is the solute and the water is the solvent. In the cells of your body, substances such as calcium ions and sugar are solutes, and water is the solvent. Water is the most common and important solvent. Other substances can also be solvents. For example, if you have ever used an oil-based paint you know that water will not clean the paintbrushes. Instead, a solvent like turpentine must be used.

 CHECK YOUR READING What is the difference between a solute and a solvent?

Types of Solutions

You probably think of solutions as solids dissolved in liquids. However, solutes, solvents, and solutions can be gases, liquids, or solids. For example, oxygen, a gas, is dissolved in seawater. The bubbles in carbonated drinks come from the release of carbon dioxide gas that was dissolved in the drink.

In some solutions, both the solute and the solvent are in the same physical state. Vinegar, for example, is a solution of acetic acid in water. In a solution of two liquids, it may be difficult to say which substance is the solute and which is the solvent. In general, the substance present in the greater amount is the solvent. In vinegar, water is the solvent and acetic acid is the solute.

Bronze is a solid solution. Tin is the solute and copper is the solvent. Solid solutions are not formed as solids. Instead, the solvent metal is heated until it melts and becomes a liquid. Then the solute is added, and the substances are thoroughly mixed together. When the mixture cools, it is a solid solution.

Solutions made of combinations of gases are also common. The air you breathe is a solution. Nitrogen makes up the largest portion of air, so it is the solvent. Other gases present, such as oxygen and carbon dioxide, are solutes.

 CHECK YOUR READING When substances in a solution are in the same physical state, which is the solvent?

Gas Solution
Air is oxygen and other gases dissolved in nitrogen.

Solid Solution
Bronze consists of tin dissolved in copper.

Liquid Solution
Water often contains many dissolved substances.

INVESTIGATE Solutions

How can you separate the parts of a solution?

PROCEDURE

① Draw a solid black circular region 6 cm in diameter around the point of the filter.

② Place the filter, point up, over the top of the bottle.

③ Squeeze several drops of water onto the point of the filter.

④ Observe the filter once every minute for 10 minutes. Record your observations.

WHAT DO YOU THINK?

• What happened to the ink on the filter?

• Identify, in general, the solutes and the solution in this investigation.

CHALLENGE Relate your observations of the ink and water on the coffee filter to the properties of solutions.

SKILL FOCUS
Observing (8.7.c)

MATERIALS
• black marker
• coffee filter
• plastic bottle
• eyedropper
• tap water
• stopwatch

TIME
15 minutes

Suspensions

When you add flour to water, the mixture turns cloudy. This mixture is not a solution but a suspension. In a **suspension,** the particles are larger than those found in a solution. Instead of dissolving, these larger particles turn the liquid cloudy. Sometimes you can separate the parts of a suspension by filtering the mixture.

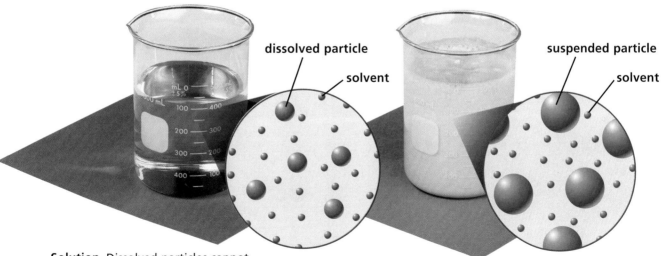

dissolved particle

solvent

suspended particle

solvent

Solution Dissolved particles cannot be identified as a substance different from the solvent.

Suspension Particles that do not dissolve make a suspension look cloudy.

Solvent and solute particles interact.

The parts of a solution can be physically separated. They are not changed into new substances. However, individual particles of solute and solvent do interact. When a solid dissolves in a liquid, the particles of the solute are surrounded by particles of the liquid. The solute particles become evenly distributed throughout the solvent.

The way in which a solid compound dissolves in a liquid depends on the type of bonds in the compound. Ionic compounds, such as table salt (NaCl), split apart into individual ions. When table salt dissolves in water, the sodium and chloride ions separate. Each ion is surrounded by water molecules. When a covalent compound, such as table sugar ($C_{12}H_{22}O_{11}$), dissolves, each solute molecule becomes surrounded by solvent molecules. The processes that take place when ionic and covalent compounds dissolve are shown below.

How Solutes Dissolve

Ionic compounds separate into ions. Covalent compounds separate into individual molecules.

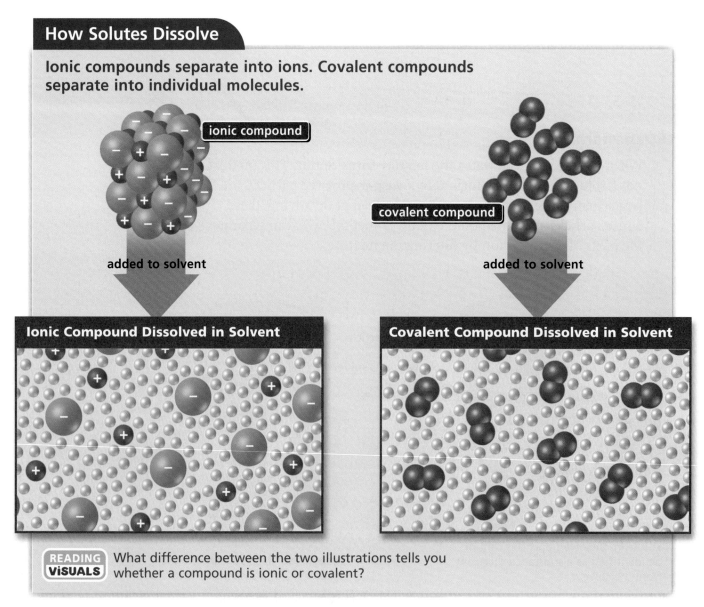

ionic compound

covalent compound

added to solvent

added to solvent

Ionic Compound Dissolved in Solvent

Covalent Compound Dissolved in Solvent

READING VISUALS   What difference between the two illustrations tells you whether a compound is ionic or covalent?

Properties of solvents change in solutions.

In every solution, solutes change the physical properties of a solvent. Therefore, a solution's physical properties differ from the physical properties of the pure solvent. The amount of solute determines how much the physical properties of the solvent are changed.

Lowering the Freezing Point

The freezing point is the temperature at which a liquid becomes a solid. The freezing point of a liquid solvent decreases—becomes lower—when a solute is dissolved in it. For example, pure water freezes at 0°C (32°F) under normal conditions. When a solute is dissolved in water, the resulting solution has a freezing point below 0°C.

▼ REMINDER

In temperature measurements, *C* stands for "Celsius" and *F* stands for "Fahrenheit."

Lowering the freezing point of water can be very useful in winter. Road crews spread salt on streets and highways during snowstorms. Salt lowers the freezing point of water. When snow mixes with salt on the roads, a saltwater solution that does not freeze at 0°C is formed. The more salt that is used, the lower the freezing point of the solution.

Salt can dissolve in the small amount of water usually on the surface of ice. Salt can, therefore, melt ice on the roads. However, there is a limit to salt's effectiveness. This is because there is a limit to how much salt will dissolve. No matter how much salt is used, once the temperature goes below –21°C (–6°F), the melted ice will freeze again.

△ CHECK YOUR READING How does the freezing point of a solvent change when a solute is dissolved in it?

Making ice cream also depends on lowering the freezing point of a solvent. Most hand-cranked ice cream makers hold the liquid ice cream ingredients in a canister. The canister is surrounded by a mixture of salt and ice. The salt added to the ice lowers the freezing point. This causes the ice to melt—absorbing heat from its surroundings, including the ice cream ingredients. The ice cream mix is chilled while being constantly stirred. As a result, tiny ice crystals form all at once in the ice cream mixture. If this weren't the case, only a few crystals would form and grow larger as the mix freezes. This whole process helps to make ice cream that is smooth and creamy.

Adding salt to lower the freezing point of ice helps to make ice cream.

311

Raising the Boiling Point

The boiling point of a liquid is the temperature at which the liquid forms bubbles and becomes a gas. Under normal conditions, a substance cannot exist as a liquid at a temperature greater than its boiling point. However, the boiling point of a solution is higher than the boiling point of the pure solvent. Therefore, a solution can remain a liquid at a higher temperature than its pure solvent.

For example, the boiling point of pure water is 100°C (212°F) under normal conditions. Saltwater, however, can be a liquid at temperatures above 100°C. Salt raises the boiling point of water. The amount of salt in the water determines how much the boiling point is increased. The more solute that is dissolved in a solution, the greater the increase in boiling point.

APPLY Why might the addition of antifreeze to the water in this car's radiator have prevented the car from overheating?

 CHECK YOUR READING How does the boiling point of a solution depend on the amount of solute in it?

A solute lowers the freezing point and raises the boiling point of the solvent in the solution. The result is that the solute extends the temperature range in which the solvent remains a liquid. One place where extending this range is useful is in a car's radiator. Antifreeze, which is mostly a chemical called ethylene glycol, is often added to the water in the radiator. This solution prevents the water from freezing in the winter and also keeps it from boiling in the summer.

10.1 Review

KEY CONCEPTS

1. How is a solution different from other mixtures? (8.5.d)

2. Describe the two parts of a solution. How can you tell them apart? (8.5.d)

3. How does the boiling point of a solvent change when a solute is dissolved in it? How does the freezing point change? (8.5.d)

CRITICAL THINKING

4. **Contrast** Contrast the way in which an ionic compound, such as table salt, dissolves with the way in which a covalent compound, such as sugar, dissolves.

5. **Infer** Pure water freezes at 0°C and boils at 100°C. Would tap water likely freeze and boil at those exact temperatures? Why or why not?

⬢ CHALLENGE

6. **Synthesize** People often sprinkle salt on icy driveways and sidewalks. Would a substance like flour have a similar effect on the ice? Explain.

MATH TUTORIAL
CLASSZONE.COM
Click on Math Tutorial for more help understanding percents.

Math 7.N.S.1.3
Science 8.5.e

The Mixtures in Alloys

An alloy is a mixture of a metal with other substances. Because even a small change in the percentages of materials in an alloy can change its properties, alloys are made according to strict specifications. For example, steel is an alloy of iron and carbon. Steel that contains 0.6 percent carbon by mass is used in steel beams. Steel that contains 1.0 percent carbon by mass, which makes it harder, is used to make tools and springs. How can the percentages of materials in an alloy be calculated?

Example

Calculate the percentage of nickel in an alloy if a small portion of the alloy has 10 atoms, 3 of which are nickel.

(1) Convert the number of atoms into a fraction.

3 of 10 atoms in the alloy are nickel $= \dfrac{3}{10}$

(2) To calculate a percentage, first find an equivalent fraction that has a denominator of 100. Use x as the numerator.

$$\dfrac{3}{10} = \dfrac{x}{100}$$

(3) Convert the fraction into a percentage by using cross products

$$3 \cdot 100 = 10 \cdot x$$
$$300 = 10x$$
$$30 = x$$

ANSWER The percentage of nickel atoms in the alloy is 30%.

Answer the following questions.

1. A sample of an alloy contains 4 iron atoms, 3 zinc atoms, 2 aluminum atoms, and 1 copper atom.

  a. What percentage of the alloy is aluminum by number of atoms?

  b. What percentage is zinc by number of atoms?

2. A sample of an alloy contains 12 titanium atoms, 4 niobium atoms, and 4 aluminum atoms.

  a. What percentage of the alloy is titanium by number of atoms?

  b. What percentage is niobium by number of atoms?

CHALLENGE Suppose there is an alloy in which 2 of every 3 atoms are silver atoms, 1 of every 4 atoms is a copper atom, and 1 of every 12 atoms is a tin atom. What are the percentages of each metal in the alloy by number of atoms?

The steel in girders like these contains iron and 0.6 percent carbon by mass.

10.2

KEY CONCEPT

The amount of solute that dissolves can vary.

CALIFORNIA
Content Standard

8.5.d Students know physical processes include freezing and boiling, in which a material changes form with no chemical reaction.

8.5.e Students know how to determine whether a solution is acidic, basic, or neutral.

VOCABULARY

concentration p. 314
dilute p. 315
saturated p. 315
solubility p. 316

◁ BEFORE, you learned

- Solutions are a type of mixture
- A solution is made when a solute is dissolved in a solvent
- Solutes change the properties of solvents

▷ NOW, you will learn

- About the concentration of a solution
- How a solute's solubility can be changed
- How solubility depends on molecular structure

EXPLORE Solutions and Temperature (8.5.d)

How does temperature affect a solution?

PROCEDURE

① Pour cold soda water into one cup and warm soda water into another cup. Record your observations.

② After 5 minutes, observe both cups of soda water. Record your observations.

WHAT DO YOU THINK?
- Which solution bubbled more at first?
- Which solution bubbled for a longer period of time?

MATERIALS
- soda water
- 2 clear plastic cups

A solution with a high concentration contains a large amount of solute.

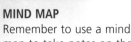

MIND MAP
Remember to use a mind map to take notes on the concentration of a solution.

Think of water from the ocean and water from a well. Water from the ocean tastes salty. Water from a well does not. The well water does contain salt, but in a concentration so low that you cannot taste it. A solution's **concentration** depends on the amount of solute dissolved in a solvent at a particular temperature. A solution with only a small amount of dissolved solute, such as the salt dissolved in well water, has a low concentration. As more solute is dissolved, the concentration gets higher.

You may have used a powdered mix to make lemonade. You can change the concentration of the drink by varying the amount of mix you put into a certain amount of water. Two scoops of mix in a pitcher of water makes the lemonade stronger than just one scoop. The lemonade with two scoops of mix has a higher concentration of the mix than the lemonade made with one scoop.

Degrees of Concentration

A solution that has a low concentration of solute is called a **dilute** solution. Salt dissolved in the drinking water from a well is a dilute solution. The concentration of a solution can be even further reduced, or diluted, by adding more solvent. On the other hand, as more solute is added to a solution, the solution becomes more concentrated. A concentrated solution has a large amount of solute.

READING TIP

The word *dilute* can be used as either an adjective or a verb. A dilute solution has a low concentration of solute. To dilute a solution is to add more solvent to it, thus lowering the concentration of the solution.

Dilute

solvent

solute

Less solute is dissolved in a dilute solution.

Concentrated

More solute is dissolved in a concentrated solution.

There is a limit to how much solute a solvent can dissolve. For example, if you keep adding sugar to a glass of iced tea, eventually no more sugar will dissolve. The tea will contain as much dissolved sugar as it can hold at that temperature. This solution is called a **saturated** solution. It contains the maximum amount of solute that can be dissolved in the solvent at a given temperature. If a solution contains less solute than this maximum amount, it is an unsaturated solution.

 CHECK YOUR READING How are the terms *dilute* and *saturated* related to the concept of concentration?

Supersaturated Solutions

Sometimes, a solution contains more dissolved solute than is normally possible. This type of solution is said to be supersaturated. A saturated solution can become supersaturated if more solute is added while the temperature is raised. Then if this solution is slowly cooled, the solute can remain dissolved. This type of solution is very unstable, though. If the solution is disturbed, or one crystal of solute is added, the extra solute will quickly become solid and form a precipitate. This process is shown in the photographs on the top of page 316.

VISUALIZATION
CLASSZONE.COM
Explore supersaturated solutions and precipitation.

A supersaturated solution contains more dissolved solute than is normally possible.

After a crystal of solute is added, or the solution is disturbed, a precipitate forms.

One example of a supersaturated solution is a chemical heat pack. The pack contains sodium acetate and water. It contains more sodium acetate than can normally dissolve at room temperature. When the pack is heated in a microwave oven, all of the sodium acetate dissolves. The solution inside the pack is supersaturated. The heat pack is activated by bending it. Bending disturbs the solution. The sodium acetate solidifies and releases a large amount of heat over a long period of time.

Solubility

The **solubility** (SAHL-yuh-BIHL-ih-tee) of a substance is the amount of that substance that will dissolve in a certain amount of solvent at a given temperature. For example, consider household ammonia used for cleaning. This ammonia is not pure ammonia. It is a solution of ammonia in water.

A large amount of ammonia can dissolve in water. Ammonia, therefore, is said to have a high solubility in water. However, other substances do not dissolve in such large amounts in water. Only a small amount of carbon dioxide will dissolve in water. Carbon dioxide, therefore, has a low solubility in water. Oils do not dissolve at all in water, so oils are said to be insoluble in water.

The amount of solute needed to make a saturated solution depends on the solubility of a solute in a particular solvent.

- If the solute is highly soluble, a saturated solution will be very concentrated.
- If the solute has a low solubility, the saturated solution will be dilute.

In other words, a saturated solution can be either dilute or concentrated, depending on the solubility of a solute in a particular solvent.

CHECK YOUR READING How does solubility affect a solution?

The solubility of a solute can be changed.

The solubility of a solute can be changed in two ways. Raising the temperature is one way. For example, most solids are more soluble at higher temperatures. Another way to change solubility when the solute is a gas is to change the pressure. The solubility of gases in a liquid solvent increases at high pressure.

Temperature and Solubility

An increase in temperature has two effects on most solid solutes. They dissolve more quickly, and a greater amount of the solid dissolves in a given amount of solvent. Most solids are more soluble at higher temperatures, and they dissolve faster.

> **REMINDER**
> An increase in temperature means an increase in particle movement.

The opposite is true of all gases. An increase in temperature makes a gas less soluble in water. You can see this by warming tap water in a pan. As the water approaches its boiling point, any air that is dissolved in the water comes out of solution. The air forms tiny bubbles that rise to the surface.

CHECK YOUR READING What effect does temperature have on most solid solutes? on gaseous solutes?

INVESTIGATE Solubility

How can you change solubility?

Use what you know about solubility to design an experiment that shows how a change in temperature can change the amount of table salt that will dissolve in water.

DESIGN —YOUR OWN— EXPERIMENT

PROCEDURE

1. Use the materials in the list to identify the relationship between temperature and solubility.

2. Write your procedure, identifying the constants and variables.

3. Perform your experiment and record your results.

WHAT DO YOU THINK?

- Which variable did you change? What were your constants? Why?

- How do your results demonstrate the effect of temperature on solubility?

SKILL FOCUS
Designing experiments (8.5.e)

MATERIALS
- clear plastic cups
- thermometer
- tap water
- table salt
- balance
- plastic spoon
- hot-water bath
- cold-water bath

TIME
20 minutes

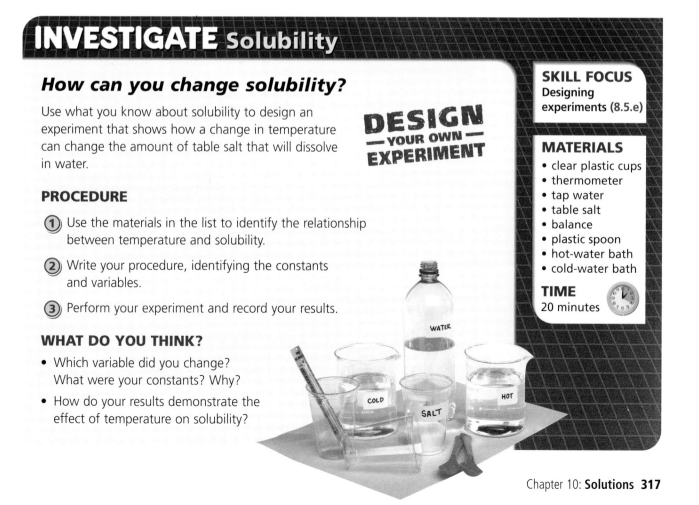

Think back to the earlier discussion of supersaturated solutions. One way in which a solution can become supersaturated is through a change in temperature. For example, suppose that a solution is saturated at 50°C (122°F), and is then allowed to cool slowly. The solid is less soluble in the cooler solution, but the excess solute may not form a precipitate. As a result, the solution contains more of the dissolved solute than would be possible under normal conditions because of the change in temperature.

Temperature and Solubility		
Solute	Increased Temperature	Decreased Temperature
Solid	increase in solubility	decrease in solubility
Gas	decrease in solubility	increase in solubility

A change in temperature can produce changes in solutions in the environment. For example, a factory located on the shore of a lake may use the lake water as a coolant. The factory might then return the heated water to the lake. The temperature of the lake's water increases. The increase in temperature, however, decreases the solubility of oxygen in the lake water. As a result, less oxygen will remain dissolved in the water. A decrease in the oxygen concentration can harm plant and animal life in the lake.

Changing Temperature Changes Solubility

More sugar dissolves in hot water than in cold water.

Solubility of Table Sugar (in 100 g H_2O)

Amount Dissolved (g) vs. Temperature (°C)

The solubility of most solids increases with a rise in temperature.

READING VISUALS About how much sugar will dissolve in 100 g of water at 70°C?

Pressure and Solubility

A change in pressure does not usually change the solubility of solid or liquid solutes. However, the solubility of any gas increases at higher pressures and decreases at lower pressures.

Manufacturers of carbonated beverages, such as soda, add carbon dioxide gas at a pressure slightly greater than normal air pressure. When you open the can or bottle, the pressure decreases. The carbon dioxide bubbles out of solution with a fizz.

Another example is shown in the photograph on the right. When a diver's tank contains regular air, about 79 percent of the air is nitrogen. People breathe air like this all the time without any problem. However, the pressure underwater is much greater than on Earth's surface. The higher pressure increases the solubility of nitrogen in the diver's blood.

When a diver heads up to the surface too fast, the pressure decreases, and so does the solubility of the nitrogen. The nitrogen comes out of solution, forming bubbles in the diver's blood vessels. These bubbles can cause a painful and sometimes fatal condition called the bends.

Divers can avoid the bends in two ways. They can rise to the surface very slowly, so that nitrogen bubbles stay small and pass through the bloodstream more easily. They can also breathe a different mixture of gases. Some professional divers breathe a mixture of oxygen and nitrogen that contains only about 66 percent nitrogen. For very deep dives, the mixture can also include helium because helium is less soluble in blood than nitrogen.

CHECK YOUR READING How does pressure affect the solubility of solids? of gases?

INFER If these divers are breathing regular air, why might they be looking at their depth gauges?

Pressure and Solubility		
Solute	Increased Pressure	Decreased Pressure
Solid	no effect on solubility	no effect on solubility
Gas	increase in solubility	decrease in solubility

Solubility depends on molecular structure.

Everyone knows that oil and water do not mix. When a tanker spills oil near shore, the oil floats on the water and pollutes the beaches. Why do oil and water not mix? The answer involves their different molecular structures.

When a substance dissolves, its molecules or ions separate from one another and become evenly mixed with molecules of the solvent. Recall that water contains polar covalent bonds. As a result, water molecules have a negative region and a positive region. Water molecules are said to be polar. The molecules of an oil are nonpolar— the molecules do not have positive and negative regions. This difference makes oil insoluble in water.

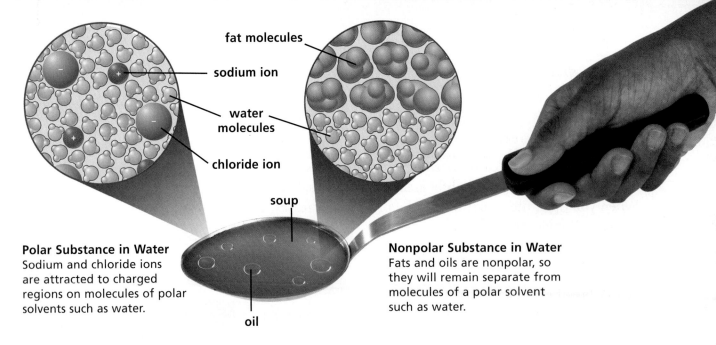

fat molecules

sodium ion

water molecules

chloride ion

soup

Polar Substance in Water
Sodium and chloride ions are attracted to charged regions on molecules of polar solvents such as water.

oil

Nonpolar Substance in Water
Fats and oils are nonpolar, so they will remain separate from molecules of a polar solvent such as water.

Because water is polar and oil is nonpolar, their molecules are not attracted to each other. The molecules of a polar solvent like water are attracted to other polar molecules, such as those of sugar. This explains why sugar has such a high solubility in water. Ionic compounds, such as sodium chloride, are also highly soluble in water. Because water molecules are polar, they interact with the sodium and chloride ions. In general, polar solvents dissolve polar solutes, and nonpolar solvents dissolve nonpolar solutes. This concept is often expressed as "Like dissolves like."

So many substances dissolve in water that it is sometimes called the universal solvent. Water is considered to be essential for life because it can carry just about anything the body needs to take in or needs to get rid of.

 CHECK YOUR READING   Why will a nonpolar substance not dissolve in a polar substance?

10.2 Review

KEY CONCEPTS

1. How can a solution be made more concentrated? less concentrated?

2. What two factors can change the solubility of a gas?

3. Are nonpolar compounds highly soluble in water? Why or why not? (8.5.d)

CRITICAL THINKING

4. **Predict** Suppose you stir sugar into ice water. Some sugar remains on the bottom of the glass. After the glass sits out for an hour, you stir it again. What will happen? Why?

5. **Infer** A powder dissolves easily in water but not in oil. Are the molecules in the powder probably polar or nonpolar? Explain.

CHALLENGE

6. **Synthesize** If mixing a substance with water forms a suspension, does the substance have a high or a low solubility in water? Explain.

California Close-Up

SOLUTIONS

The Problem with Solutions

> 8.3.c Students know atoms and molecules form solids by building up repeating patterns, such as the crystal structure of NaCl or long-chain polymers.

Solutes may be invisible in solution. This can be a problem when it comes to drinking water. Keeping harmful chemicals out of drinking water is a big concern of the California Department of Health Services (CDHS). Two chemicals that currently concern CDHS are MTBE and the perchlorates. In the body the structures of these very soluble molecules can interfere with important chemical reactions.

MTBE

MTBE (Methyl tertiary-butyl ether) is added to gasoline to stop the release of harmful substances in car exhausts. California gasoline producers used it to meet demands for a less-polluting fuel. Scientists now think MTBE may be a cause of cancer.

MTBE enters the environment through leaks in underground tanks or gasoline pipelines. Once in the soil, MTBE quickly mixes with the groundwater supply. Its solubility makes it very difficult to remove. The shape of the molecule, however, may cause it to interfere with the chemical bonds of substances in the cells of living things. This is the reason scientists suspect it may cause cancer. California banned all use of MTBE in gasoline in January of 2004.

Contamination from MTBE can come from leaky gas pipes. Proper maintenance of these pipes is important.

Perchlorates

A class of chemicals called perchlorates is a problem for the same reason: perchlorates are also soluble in water. Water-quality experts found these chemicals in wells in southern California. They also found some in water from the Colorado River, which flows to Los Angeles. The perchlorates had flowed from factories in Nevada.

Perchlorates are used to make rocket fuel and explosives. In the human body, they block the absorption of iodide in the thyroid. The thyroid regulates hormones. When it doesn't work properly, important chemical reactions cannot occur. This is harmful to babies as they develop. In adults, the thyroid controls metabolism and other functions. CDHS is currently working on regulations to curb the use of perchlorates.

WRITING ABOUT SCIENCE

Write a letter to CDHS in support of their drinking-water regulations. In your letter, explain why certain molecules can be dangerous to the body. Describe why getting these molecules out of the water supply can be difficult.

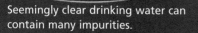

Seemingly clear drinking water can contain many impurities.

10.3 Solutions can be acidic, basic, or neutral.

CALIFORNIA
Content Standard

8.5.e Students know how to determine whether a solution is acidic, basic, or neutral.

BEFORE, you learned

- Substances dissolved in solutions can break apart into ions
- Concentration is the amount of a substance dissolved in a solution
- Water is a common solvent

NOW, you will learn

- What acids and bases are
- How to determine if a solution is acidic or basic
- How acids and bases react with each other

VOCABULARY

acid p. 323
base p. 323
pH p. 326
neutral p. 326

EXPLORE Acids and Bases (8.5.e)

What happens when an antacid mixes with an acid?

PROCEDURE

1. Fill the cup halfway with vinegar.

2. Observe the vinegar in the cup. Record your observations.

3. Crush two antacid tablets and place them in the vinegar.

4. Observe the contents of the cup for 5 minutes. Record your observations.

WHAT DO YOU THINK?

- What did you observe before adding the antacid tablets?
- What happened after you added the tablets?

MATERIALS

- clear plastic cup
- vinegar
- 2 antacid tablets

Acids and bases have distinct properties.

Many solutions have certain properties that make us call them acids or bases. Acids are found in many foods, such as orange juice, tomatoes, and vinegar. They taste slightly sour when dissolved in water and produce a burning or itchy feeling on the skin. Strong acids should never be tasted or touched. These solutions are used in manufacturing and are dangerous chemicals.

Bases are the chemical opposite of acids. They tend to taste bitter rather than sour and often feel slippery to the touch. Bases are also found in common products around the home, including soap, ammonia, and antacids. Strong bases, like the lye used for unclogging drains, are also dangerous chemicals.

> **READING TiP**
>
> The prefix ant- means "against," so an antacid is a substance that works against an acid.

Acids, Bases, and Ions

Generally, a compound that is an acid or a base acts as an acid or a base only when it is dissolved in water. In a water-based solution, these compounds produce ions. Recall that an ion is a charged particle. For example, if a hydrogen atom, which consists of one proton and one electron, loses its electron, it becomes a hydrogen ion. The hydrogen ion is simply a proton and has a positive charge.

An **acid** can be defined as a substance that can donate a hydrogen ion—that is, a proton—to another substance. The diagram below shows what happens when the compound hydrogen chloride (HCl) is dissolved in water. The compound separates into hydrogen ions (H^+) and chloride ions (Cl^-). Hydrogen ions are free to react with other substances, so the solution is an acid. When hydrogen chloride is dissolved in water, the solution is called hydrochloric acid.

Acid

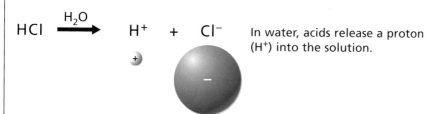

In water, acids release a proton (H^+) into the solution.

READING TiP

The H_2O above the arrow means the substance on the left is added to water and the substances on the right are dissolved in the water.

A **base** can be defined as a substance that can accept a hydrogen ion from another substance. The diagram below shows what happens when the compound sodium hydroxide (NaOH) is dissolved in water. The compound separates into sodium ions (Na^+) and hydroxide ions (OH^-). The hydroxide ions are free to accept protons from other substances, so the solution is a base. The solution that results when NaOH is dissolved in water is called sodium hydroxide.

Base

NaOH $\xrightarrow{H_2O}$ Na$^+$ + OH$^-$

In water, many bases release a hydroxide ion (OH^-), which can accept a proton.

On the atomic level, the difference between acids and bases is that acids donate protons and bases accept protons. When a proton—a hydrogen ion—from an acid is accepted by a hydroxide ion from a base, the two ions join together and form a molecule of water. This simple transfer of protons between substances is involved in a great many useful and important chemical reactions.

RESOURCE CENTER
CLASSZONE.COM

Find out more about acids and bases.

CHECK YOUR READING How are protons related to acids and bases?

Characteristics of Acids

As you read earlier, acids in foods taste sour and produce a burning or prickling feeling on the skin. However, tasting or touching an unknown chemical is extremely dangerous. Other methods are needed to tell whether a solution is an acid.

One safe way to test for an acid is to place a few drops of a solution on a compound that contains a carbonate (CO_3). For example, limestone is a rock that contains calcium carbonate ($CaCO_3$). When an acid touches a piece of limestone, a reaction occurs that produces carbon dioxide gas.

Acids also react with most metals. The reaction produces hydrogen gas, which you can see as bubbles in the photograph on the right. Such a reaction is characteristic of acids.

The feature of acids most often used to identify them is their ability to change the colors of certain compounds known as acid-base indicators. One common indicator is litmus, which is often prepared on slips of paper. When a drop of an acid is placed on litmus paper, the paper turns red.

Acids react with some metals, such as zinc, and release hydrogen gas.

$$2HCl + Zn \longrightarrow H_2 + ZnCl_2$$

CHECK YOUR READING What are three safe methods to test for an acid?

Characteristics of Bases

Bases also have certain common characteristics. Mild bases in foods taste bitter and feel slippery. However tasting and touching are not safe ways of testing whether a solution is a base. In fact, some strong bases can burn the skin as badly as strong acids.

Bases feel soapy or slippery because they react with acidic molecules in your skin called fatty acids. In fact, this is exactly how soap is made. Mixing a base—usually sodium hydroxide—with fatty acids produces soap. So, when a base touches your skin, the combination of the base with your own fatty acids actually makes a small amount of soap.

Like acids, bases change the colors of acid-base indicators, but the colors they produce are different. Bases turn litmus paper blue. A base will counteract the effect that an acid has on an acid-base indicator. You might put a few drops of acid on litmus paper to make it turn red. If you put a few drops of a base on the red litmus paper, the litmus paper will change colors again.

CHECK YOUR READING How do the characteristics of bases differ from those of acids?

Bases are found in many cleaning agents, including soap.

The strengths of acids and bases can be measured.

Battery fluid and many juices contain acids. Many people drink some type of juice every morning. You would not want to drink, or even touch, the liquid in a car battery. Similarly, you probably wash your hands with soap several times a day, but you would not want to touch the liquid used to unclog drains. Both soap and drain cleaners are bases. Clearly, some acids and bases are stronger than others.

MIND MAP

Remember to use a mind map to take notes about acid and base strength.

Acid and Base Strength

Strong acids break apart completely into ions. For example, hydrogen chloride (HCl) dissolves in water to form hydrochloric acid. It breaks down into hydrogen ions and chloride ions. No hydrogen chloride remains in the solution. Because all of the hydrogen chloride forms separate ions, hydrochloric acid is a strong acid.

A weak acid does not form many ions in solution. Acetic acid ($HC_2H_3O_2$) is the acid in vinegar. When it dissolves in water, only about 1 percent of the acetic acid breaks up into hydrogen ions and acetate ions. The other 99 percent of the acetic acid remains unchanged. Therefore, acetic acid is a weak acid.

CALIFORNIA Focus

The most acid place on Earth is thought to be Iron Mountain Mine near Redding. Abandoned now, the mine's waters have been measured as having negative pH values.

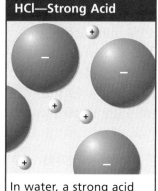

HCl—Strong Acid

In water, a strong acid dissolves completely into ions.

$HC_2H_3O_2$—Weak Acid

In water, a weak acid forms only a small number of ions.

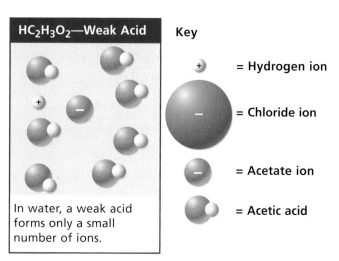

Key

⊕ = Hydrogen ion

⊖ = Chloride ion

= Acetate ion

= Acetic acid

Bases also can be strong or weak. When sodium hydroxide (NaOH) dissolves in water, it forms sodium ions (Na^+) and hydroxide ions (OH^-). None of the original NaOH remains in the solution, so sodium hydroxide is a strong base. However, when ammonia (NH_3) dissolves in water, only about 1 percent of the ammonia reacts with water to form OH^- ions.

$$NH_3 + H_2O \longrightarrow NH_4^+ + OH^-$$

The other 99 percent of the ammonia remains unchanged, so ammonia is a weak base. The ions formed when NaOH or NH_3 is dissolved in water are shown on the top of page 326.

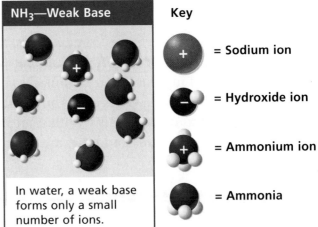

Sodium Hydroxide

NaOH—Strong Base

In water, a strong base dissolves completely into ions.

Ammonia

NH₃—Weak Base

In water, a weak base forms only a small number of ions.

Key

 = Sodium ion

= Hydroxide ion

= Ammonium ion

= Ammonia

READING TiP

Look at the reaction on the bottom of page 325 for help with the illustration of NH_3 in water.

The strength of an acid or base is not the same as its concentration. Dilute hydrochloric acid is still strong and can burn holes in your clothing. Dilute acetic acid cannot. The strengths of acids and bases depend on the percentage of the substance that forms ions.

CHECK YOUR READING What determines acid and base strength?

Measuring Acidity

The strip of universal indicator paper in the bottom front of the photograph shows a nearly neutral pH.

The acidity of a solution depends on the concentration of H^+ ions in the solution. This concentration is often measured on the **pH** scale. In this scale, a high H^+ concentration is shown by a low number. A low H^+ concentration is shown by a high number. The numbers of the pH scale usually range from 0 to 14. However numbers outside this range are possible. The middle number, 7, represents a neutral solution. A **neutral** substance is neither an acid nor a base. Pure water has a pH of 7.

Numbers below 7 indicate acidic solutions. A concentrated strong acid has a low pH value. The pH of concentrated hydrochloric acid, for example, is less than 0. Numbers above 7 indicate a basic solution. A concentrated strong base has a high pH value. The pH of concentrated sodium hydroxide, for example, is greater than 14. The illustration on page 327 shows the pH values of some common acids and bases.

Today, electronic pH meters are commonly used to measure pH. A probe is placed in a solution, and the pH value is indicated by the meter. An older method of measuring pH is to use an acid-base indicator. You read earlier that acids turn litmus paper red and bases turn litmus paper blue. Other acid-base indicators show a variety of colors at different pH values.

CHECK YOUR READING Is the pH of a base higher or lower than the pH of an acid?

Common Acids and Bases

Dilute acids and bases are found in many common products.

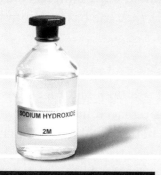

sodium hydroxide (NaOH)—pH > 14

Concentrated NaOH has a pH greater than 14 because it has a very low H^+ concentration. Drain openers usually contain concentrated NaOH.

milk—pH 6.5

Milk contains molecules called fatty acids, which make milk slightly acidic.

lemon—pH 2

Lemons and other types of citrus fruit contain citric acid.

low H^+ concentration

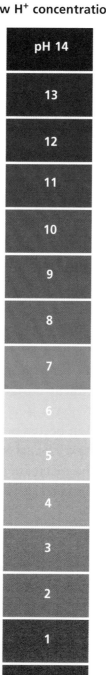

| pH 14 |
| 13 |
| 12 |
| 11 |
| 10 |
| 9 |
| 8 |
| 7 |
| 6 |
| 5 |
| 4 |
| 3 |
| 2 |
| 1 |
| pH 0 |

high H^+ concentration

soap—pH 10

Soap is commonly made by mixing fats with NaOH. There is a relatively low concentration of NaOH in soap.

pure water (H₂O)—pH 7

In pure water, the H^+ concentration is equal to the OH^- concentration. Pure water has a pH of 7 and is neutral.

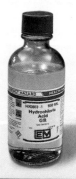

hydrochloric acid (HCl)—pH < 0

Concentrated HCl has a pH lower than 0 because it has a very high H^+ concentration. HCl is used in many processes, including refining sugar from sugar cane.

READING VISUALS Where are the strong acids on the chart? Where are the strong bases? How does the concentration of hydrogen ions change?

Acid-base reactions have many uses.

READING TiP

The salt produced by a neutralization reaction is not necessarily table salt.

Acids donate hydrogen ions. Bases accept hydrogen ions. Acids and bases, therefore, react with one another. For example, consider the reaction of hydrochloric acid (HCl) with the base sodium hydroxide (NaOH).

$$HCl + NaOH \longrightarrow NaCl + H_2O$$

Look closely at the products of the reaction. Hydrogen has replaced sodium to make water. Sodium has replaced hydrogen to make sodium chloride, which you know better as table salt. In chemistry, the term *salt* usually refers to the product of such an acid-base reaction. Both water and sodium chloride are neither acidic or basic; they are neutral. Therefore, an acid-base reaction is called a neutralization (NOO-truh-lih-ZAY-shuhn) reaction. Acid-base reactions are occuring all around you.

This Inuit artist is examining one of his etchings as it comes off the press. The damp paper readily takes up the ink. The ink is in the grooves cut by the acid.

Acidic Arts

Many people enjoy the unique look achieved by using an acid to etch lines into metal. Artists like the method because it offers a way to reproduce a single drawing many times. First, the artist places a film of wax over a copper or iron plate. The artist then scratches the design directly into the wax, exposing the metal in those spots. When an acid is applied to the surface of the plate, a reaction occurs between it and the exposed metal, but not the wax. The artist then scrapes off the wax. The lines left in the metal are filled with ink. Now, the artist can impress the image on sheets of paper.

A Neutral Environment

You've likely heard about or seen the destructive effects of acid rain. Too strong of either an acid or base certainly can have disastrous effects. Monitoring the levels of acids and bases in the environment is a job of a surprising number of people, not just scientists with pieces of litmus paper.

Testing the pH of the water in a swimming pool is crucial to keeping the water comfortable for swimmers.

The pH level of swimming pool water must be managed closely. Not only does a nearly neutral pH increase the comfort of the swimmers, it also ensures enough chlorine is available to kill harmful microorganisms. Farmers and even home gardeners will use a pH meter to test the acidity of a soil. Some plants grow better than others in slightly acidic or basic soils.

Stomaching Acid

Perhaps nowhere can the imbalance between acids and bases cause more pain than in the stomach. The digestive enzymes need to be at a pH of about 1 to 3 to work effectively. Some food we eat may be acidic. Some may be basic. Acid-base reactions in the stomach work to keep the digestive juices at a pH that is best suited for digestion.

We usually treat an "upset" stomach by taking antacid tables. The idea is to get the stomach solution back to regular acid levels. But these tablets can do too good a job. They may neutralize stomach acids so effectively that enzymes may be unable to digest foods properly. Calcium especially needs a specific pH to be absorbed by the stomach effectively. By too freely ingesting antacid tables, it's possible we could prevent the stomach from maintaining proper pH levels. The result is we could not digest food as effectively.

When selecting foods, try to seek a balance between acidic and basic food. This will ensure the proper functioning of enzymes in the stomach. Many traditional pairings, such as rice with beans, may very likely have become associated with one another because they were an acid and a base.

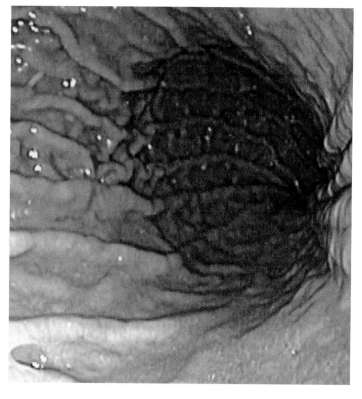

Digestive enzymes need to be acidic to work best. Notice the mucus lining of the stomach. This prevents the stomach acids from eating away at tissues.

 At what pH should stomach acids be?

10.3 Review

KEY CONCEPTS

1. Use the concept of ions to explain the difference between an acid and a base. (8.5.e)

2. How do the properties of an acid differ from the properties of a base? (8.5.e)

3. What happens when an acid and a base react with each other? (8.5.e)

CRITICAL THINKING

4. **Infer** When an acid reacts with a metal, such as zinc, what is released? Where does that product come from?

5. **Infer** Suppose that you have 1 L of an acid solution with a pH of 2. You add 1 L of pure water. What happens to the pH of the solution? Explain.

CHALLENGE

6. **Synthesize** Suppose that equal amounts of solutions of HCl and NaOH with the same concentration are mixed together. What will the pH of the new solution be? What are the products of this reaction?

CHAPTER INVESTIGATION

Acids and Bases

OVERVIEW AND PURPOSE Acids and bases are very common. For example, the limestone formations in the cave shown on the left are made of a substance that is a base when it is dissolved in water. In this activity you will use what you have learned about solutions, acids, and bases to

- test various household substances and place them in categories according to their pH values
- investigate the properties of common acids and bases

▶ Procedure

1. Make a data table like the one shown on the sample notebook page.

2. Set out 7 cups in your work area. Collect the substances that you will be testing: baking soda, fruit juice, shampoo, soda water, table salt, laundry detergent, and vinegar.

3. Label each cup. Be sure to wear goggles when pouring the substances that you will be testing. Pour 30 mL of each liquid substance into a separate cup. Dissolve 1 tsp of each solid substance in 30 mL of distilled water in a separate cup. To avoid contaminating the test solutions, wash and dry your measuring tools and hands between measurements.

MATERIALS
- plastic cups
- baking soda
- fruit juice
- shampoo
- soda water
- table salt
- detergent powder
- vinegar
- masking tape
- marking pen
- measuring spoons
- graduated cylinder
- distilled water
- paper towels
- pH indicator paper

8.5.e, 8.9.b, 8.9.c

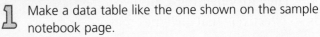

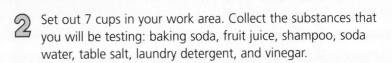

Content Standard
8.5.e Students know how to determine whether a solution is acidic, basic, or neutral.

Investigation Standard
8.9.c Distinguish between variable and controlled parameters in a test.

4 Dip a piece of indicator paper into each solution. Compare the color of the test strip with the colors in the chart included in the package. Record the indicator color and the approximate pH number for each solution.

Step 4

SHAMPOO

5 After you have tested all of the solutions, arrange the cups in order of their pH values.

▶ Observe and Analyze
Write It Up

1. **RECORD DATA** Check to be sure that your data table is complete.

2. **ANALYZE DATA** What color range did the substances show when tested with the indicator paper? What do your results tell you about the pH of each substance you tested?

3. **CLASSIFY** Look for patterns in the pH values. Use your test results to place each household substance in one of three groups—acids, bases, or neutral.

4. **MODEL** Draw a diagram of the pH scale from 0 to 14. Use arrows and labels to show where the substances you tested fall on this scale.

▶ Conclude
Write It Up

1. **GENERALIZE** What general conclusions can you draw about the hydrogen ion concentration in many acids and bases found in the home? Are the hydrogen ion concentrations very high or very low? How do you know?

2. **EVALUATE** What limitations or difficulties did you experience in interpreting the results of your tests or other observations?

3. **APPLY** Antacid tablets react with stomach acid containing hydrochloric acid. What is this type of reaction called? What are the products of this type of reaction?

▶ INVESTIGATE Further

CHALLENGE Repeat the experiment, changing one variable. You might change the concentrations of the solutions you are testing or see what happens when you mix an acidic solution with a basic solution. Get your teacher's approval of your plan before proceeding. How does changing one particular variable affect the pH of the solutions?

SALT

SODA WATER

Acids and Bases
Observe and Analyze

Table 1. Acid-Base Test Results

Substance	Indicator Color	pH	Group
baking soda			
juice			
shampoo			
soda water			
table salt			

Conclude

10 Chapter Review

the BIG idea

When substances dissolve to form a solution, the properties of the mixture change.

CONTENT REVIEW
CLASSZONE.COM

KEY CONCEPTS SUMMARY

1 A solution is a type of mixture.

- A solution is a mixture in which one or more solutes are dissolved in a solvent.
- A solution is a homogeneous mixture.

Ionic compound dissolved in solvent

VOCABULARY
solution p. 307
solvent p. 308
solute p. 308
suspension p. 309

2 The amount of solute that dissolves can vary.

- The amount of dissolved solute determines a solution's concentration.
- The more soluble a substance is, the more of it will dissolve in a solution.

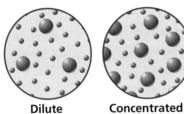

Dilute   Concentrated

VOCABULARY
concentration p. 314
dilute p. 315
saturated p. 315
solubility p. 316

3 Solutions can be acidic, basic, or neutral.

- Acids donate protons (H+) in solutions, and bases accept protons in solutions.
- Acidity is measured by the H+ concentration on the pH scale.

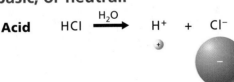

Acid $HCl \xrightarrow{H_2O} H^+ + Cl^-$

Base $NaOH \xrightarrow{H_2O} Na^+ + OH^-$

VOCABULARY
acid p. 323
base p. 323
pH p. 326
neutral p. 326

Reviewing Vocabulary

Draw a diagram similar to the example shown below to connect and organize the concepts of related vocabulary terms. After you have completed your diagram, explain in two or three sentences why you organized the terms in that way. Underline each of the terms in your explanation.

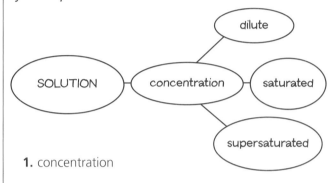

1. concentration

2. acid

3. base

4. neutral

5. pH

Latin Roots *Several of the vocabulary terms in this chapter come from the Latin word* solvere, *which means "to loosen." Describe how each of the following terms is related to the Latin word.*

6. solution

7. solute

8. solvent

9. solubility

Reviewing Key Concepts

Multiple Choice *Choose the letter of the best answer.*

10. What makes a solution different from other types of mixtures?
    a. Its parts can be separated.
    b. It is the same throughout.
    c. Its parts can be seen.
    d. It is a liquid.

11. When a solute is dissolved in a solvent, the solvent's (8.5.d)
    a. boiling point decreases
    b. boiling point decreases and its freezing point increases
    c. freezing point increases
    d. freezing point decreases and its boiling point increases

12. When a compound held together by ionic bonds dissolves, the compound (8.3.b)
    a. releases molecules into the solution
    b. forms a suspension
    c. releases ions into the solution
    d. becomes nonpolar

13. Water is called the universal solvent because it (8.7.c)
    a. dissolves many substances
    b. dissolves very dense substances
    c. has no charged regions
    d. is nonpolar

14. How does an increase in temperature affect the solubility of solids and gases? (8.7.c)
    a. It increases solubility of most solids and decreases the solubility of gases.
    b. It decreases solubility of most solids and gases.
    c. It increases solubility of gases and decreases the solubility of most solids.
    d. It increases solubility of both solids and gases.

15. A solution with a very high H^+ concentration has a (8.5.e)
    a. very high pH   c. pH close to 5
    b. very low pH   d. pH close to 7

16. Why are oils insoluble in water? (8.5.e)
    a. They are acids.   c. They are bases.
    b. They are polar.   d. They are nonpolar.

Short Answer *Write a short answer to each question.*

17. Describe the reaction that occurs when a strong acid reacts with a strong base. (8.5.e)

18. What is a buffer and where might you find an example of one?

Thinking Critically

The illustration below shows the results of pH tests of four different solutions. Assume the solutions are made with strong acids or strong bases. Use the diagram to answer the next four questions.

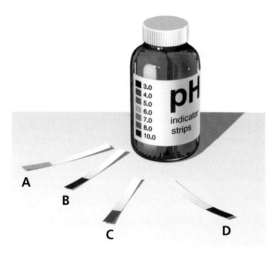

19. OBSERVE Which of the indicator strips show an acidic solution? Which show a basic solution? (8.5.e)

20. INFER Which strip of indicator paper detected the highest concentration of H$^+$ ions? How do you know? (8.5.e)

21. PREDICT What would happen if you mixed together equal amounts of the solutions that produced the results of strip B and strip D? (8.5.e)

22. INFER Suppose you mix together equal amounts of the solutions that produced the results of strip C and strip D, then test the pH of this new solution. What color will the indicator paper be? Explain. (8.5.e)

23. CAUSE AND EFFECT Suppose that you place a beaker containing a solution in a refrigerator. An hour later there is a white solid on the bottom of the beaker. What happened? Why?

24. INFER Suppose you run wind sprints for physical education class. What would happen to the pH level of your blood? Why? Explain. (8.5.e)

Using Math Skills in Science

Use the graph below to answer the next three questions.

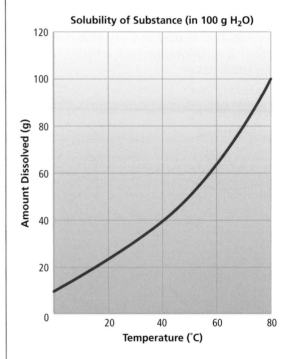

25. What happens to the solubility of the substance as the temperature increases? decreases? (8.9.e)

26. Approximately how many grams of the substance dissolve at 20°C? 60°C? (8.9.e)

27. Is the substance a solid or a gas? Explain. (8.9.e)

the BIG idea

28. APPLY Look back at pages 304–305. Think about the answer you gave to the question about the photograph. How has your understanding of solutions and their properties changed? (8.7.c)

29. COMPARE Describe the similarities and differences between solutions of table salt (NaCl) in water and sugar in water. Do both solutes have similar effects on the properties of the solvent? Explain. (8.7.c)

UNIT PROJECTS

Check your schedule for your unit project. How are you doing? Be sure that you have placed data or notes from your research in your project folder.

Standards-Based Assessment

Interpreting Graphs

8.5.e, 8.9.e

Use the information in the paragraph and the graph to answer the questions.

Acid rain is an environmental concern in the United States and in other countries. Acid rain is produced when the burning of fuels releases certain chemicals into the air. These chemicals can react with water vapor in Earth's atmosphere to form acids. The acids then fall back to the ground in either rain or snow. The acids can damage plants, animals, and buildings. Normally, rain has a pH of about 5.6, which is slightly acidic. But rain in some areas of the United States has a pH that is lower than 4.0. The graph shows the pH of water in several lakes.

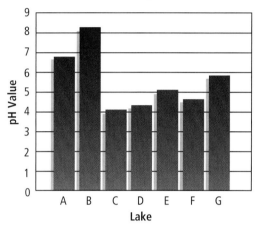

Lake Water pH Values

1. Which lake is the most acidic?
   - **a.** Lake A
   - **b.** Lake B
   - **c.** Lake C
   - **d.** Lake D

2. Which lake is the least acidic?
   - **a.** Lake A
   - **b.** Lake B
   - **c.** Lake C
   - **d.** Lake D

3. Which lake has water the closest to neutral?
   - **a.** Lake A
   - **b.** Lake B
   - **c.** Lake E
   - **d.** Lake G

4. Lakes that form on a bed of limestone are less likely to suffer from high acidity. The limestone reacts with acids to neutralize them. Which of the following lakes is most likely to have a limestone bed?
   - **a.** Lake C
   - **b.** Lake D
   - **c.** Lake F
   - **d.** Lake G

5. Lake trout are fish that live in many freshwater lakes. When the pH of the water in a lake drops below 5.5, this species of fish can no longer reproduce, because its eggs cannot hatch. Which of the following statements is most likely true?
   - **a.** Lake trout have probably stopped reproducing in all the lakes.
   - **b.** In terms of reproducing, lake trout are not in danger in any of the lakes.
   - **c.** Lake trout will probably be able to reproduce in lakes A, B, and G but not in the others.
   - **d.** Lake trout have probably stopped reproducing only in lakes C, D, and F.

Extended Response

Answer the following two questions in detail. Include some of the terms from the list in the box. Underline each term you use in your answers.

| concentration | solute | solubility |
| polar | solution | solvent |

6. Suppose you are trying to make two solutions. One contains water and salt. The other contains water and oil. What do you think will happen in both cases? How might charges on particles affect your results?

7. Explain why some substances dissolve more easily than others. How can this characteristic of a solute be changed by changing the temperature or pressure of a solution?

CHAPTER

11 Chemistry of Living Systems

the BIG idea

Carbon and other elements are essential to living things.

What chemistry important for living things is shown in this picture?

Key Concepts

SECTION

1 Living things depend on chemical processes.
Learn about some of the chemical processes that occur in living things.

SECTION

2 Carbon-based molecules have many structures.
Learn why carbon forms many different compounds.

SECTION

3 Carbon-based molecules are life's building blocks.
Learn about the four main types of carbon-based molecules in living things.

California ClassZone

CLASSZONE.COM

Chapter 11 online resources: Content Review, Visualization, three Resource Centers, Math Tutorial, Test Practice

EXPLORE (the BIG idea)

Sweet Crackers

> 8.6.c Students know that living organisms have many different kinds of molecules, including small ones, such as water and salt, and very large ones, such as carbohydrates, fats, proteins, and DNA.

Eat an unsalted cracker, but chew it for a long time. Keep the cracker in your mouth for a few minutes before you swallow it.

Observe and Think What happened to the taste of the cracker during the time it was in your mouth? What does the change in taste tell you about the molecules in the cracker?

Internet Activity: Polymers

> 8.6.c Students know that living organisms have many different kinds of molecules, including small ones, such as water and salt, and very large ones, such as carbohydrates, fats, proteins, and DNA.

Visit **ClassZone.com** to explore the Polymer Resource Center. Discover some of the common polymers that you use every day. Investigate how a change in a polymer's structure can make a very different material.

Observe and Think
What things around you might be polymers? How might the variety of polymers be related to the way in which carbon atoms bond to each other?

NSTA scilinks.org SCiLINKS

Organic Compounds **Code: MDL026**

Getting Ready to Learn

◀ CONCEPT REVIEW

- Atoms share electrons when they form covalent bonds.
- Some atoms can form multiple bonds with another atom.
- Chemical reactions alter the arrangement of atoms.

◀ VOCABULARY REVIEW

electron p. 201

covalent bond p. 252

chemical reaction p. 271

catalyst p. 278

CONTENT REVIEW
CLASSZONE.COM
Review concepts and vocabulary.

▶ TAKING NOTES

SUPPORTING MAIN IDEAS

Make a chart to show main ideas and the information that supports them. Copy each blue heading. Below each heading, add supporting information, such as reasons, explanations, and examples.

VOCABULARY STRATEGY

Think about a vocabulary term as a **magnet word** diagram. Write the other terms or ideas related to that term around it.

See the Note-Taking Handbook on pages R45–R51.

SCIENCE NOTEBOOK

About 25 common elements make up living things.

Carbon, hydrogen, oxygen, nitrogen, phosphorus, and sulfur are the six most common elements in living things.

The common elements make up the structures of cells and provide nourishment for the body.

Other elements are only present in small amounts in the body.

study of substances and processes in living things

BIOCHEMISTRY

elements, ions, acids, and bases

chemistry of life

living things are like chemical laboratories

11.1
Living things depend on chemical processes.

CALIFORNIA
Content Standards

8.6.b Students know that living organisms are made of molecules consisting largely of carbon, hydrogen, nitrogen, oxygen, phosphorus, and sulfur.

8.6.c Students know that living organisms have many different kinds of molecules, including small ones, such as water and salt, and very large ones, such as carbohydrates, fats, proteins, and DNA.

BEFORE, you learned

• Elements combine to form compounds
• Chemical reactions turn reactants into products by rearranging atoms

NOW, you will learn

• About the elements that make up living things
• How some simple compounds are important to living things

VOCABULARY

biochemistry p. 339

EXPLORE Elements in Bones (8.6.b)

What makes bones strong?

PROCEDURE

① Examine a bone from a chicken. Be sure the bone is dry and free of any meat. Record how the bone appears to you.

② Place the bone into a jar with white vinegar. Be sure the vinegar completely covers the bone.

③ Allow the bone to sit for three days to a week. Refresh the vinegar every two days.

④ Examine the bone again. Compare the way the bone feels now to the way it felt before.

MATERIALS
• chicken bone
• white vinegar
• jar

WHAT DO YOU THINK?
• How does the bone feel different from before?
• What do you think happened to the bone in the vinegar?

Living things have the same chemistry as nonliving things.

READING TiP

The prefix *bio-* is from the Greek word *bios* which means "for life." The word *chemistry* comes from an Arabic word possibly meaning "that which is poured."

Chemical reactions happen everywhere, including in living things. Living things, in fact, are a lot like chemical laboratories. For example, exothermic reactions provide us with the energy we need to carry out daily activities. Ions in our cells allow electric impulses to stimulate our nerves. In the stomach, acids break foods apart.

Everything you learned in previous chapters about elements, ions, acids, and bases doesn't just apply in the chemistry laboratory. It is important for understanding all life on Earth. **Biochemistry** is the study of the substances and processes occurring in living organisms.

About 25 common elements make up living things.

Close to 100 elements occur naturally. Of these, 25 are found in living things. As you can see in the pie graph at the left, about 97 percent of your body's mass consists of just four major elements—oxygen, carbon, hydrogen, and nitrogen.

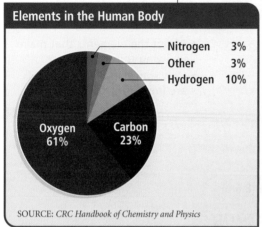

Elements in the Human Body

Nitrogen 3%
Other 3%
Hydrogen 10%
Oxygen 61%
Carbon 23%

SOURCE: *CRC Handbook of Chemistry and Physics*

Major Elements

The six most common elements in living things are carbon, hydrogen, oxygen, nitrogen, phosphorus, and sulfur. Atoms of these elements combine and form thousands of large molecules. These large molecules make up the structures of cells and carry out many processes essential to life.

Later in this chapter you will learn about the properties of carbon atoms that allow them to form a huge number of different large molecules. Carbon molecules can be long chains or rings of atoms. Some are even a combination of chains and rings. We call life on Earth carbon-based because of carbon's essential role.

Other Elements

Other elements are also important to the proper functioning of organisms. These elements include sodium, chlorine, fluorine, potassium, calcium, iron, and magnesium. The illustration on page 341 presents an overview of some important functions of these elements. The following are only three examples.

- Sodium (Na^+) and potassium (K^+) ions play a key role in the transmission of nerve impulses between your brain and all parts of the body.

- Calcium (Ca^{2+}) ions are essential for muscle contractions and the clotting of blood.

- Fluorine forms a salt with calcium. This salt makes the teeth stronger.

There are even some very important elements that are present in only small amounts. They may seem insignificant. They are not. For example, iron makes up only about 0.004 percent of your body mass, but you couldn't live without it. Oxygen from the air you breathe binds to the iron in the hemoglobin molecules in your blood. The blood carries this oxygen to body cells, where it is used in cellular respiration.

CHECK YOUR READING Why is life on Earth called carbon-based?

Elements and the Human Body

Atoms of various elements play many important roles in your body. Whether you are working out or even taking a nap, there is an incredible amount of chemistry going on inside of you.

The combination of **fluorine** with **calcium** produces a salt with a very strong crystal structure. This provides protection for the teeth.

Sulfur is an important part of the molecules that make up hair and fingernails.

Iron is the central atom in the molecule hemoglobin. Hemoglobin carries oxygen in the blood.

Sodium ions regulate the amount of fluid in the blood.

Chlorine atoms combine with hydrogen atoms in the stomach to create hydrochloric acid. Hydrochloric acid helps digest food.

Calcium makes bones and teeth hard and resistant to wear.

Potassium ions play a role in the transmission of nerve impulses.

Molecules containing elements of **carbon, hydrogen, oxygen, nitrogen, phosphorus,** and **sulfur** make up the structures in cells and provide nourishment for the body. You will learn more about these molecules in the last section of this chapter.

Magnesium plays an important role in muscle contractions.

Molecules containing **phosphorus** are important for energy transfer in cells. Some phosphorus is involved in almost every biochemical reaction in the body.

READING VISUALS Atoms of which element play an important role in muscle contractions?

Water and salt are very important to living things.

The human body relies on many compounds. Many of these have very complicated molecular structures. However, two of the most important compounds, water and salt, have very simple chemical structures. They are important because of the types of bonds they contain.

Water

Remember that polar covalent bonds are what hold a water molecule together. These bonds make water an excellent solvent. Our body cells contain mostly water, so many substances can dissolve inside cells. This allows many chemical reactions to take place there as well. Substances can easily pass in solution from the outside of the cell to the inside of the cell. Blood, too, is mostly water and therefore can easily transport nutrients throughout the body.

Sweat and urine are, likewise, mostly water. Waste products from the body can easily dissolve in them. The waste products can then leave the body when the sweat and urine do. Water is important to just about every function of the body.

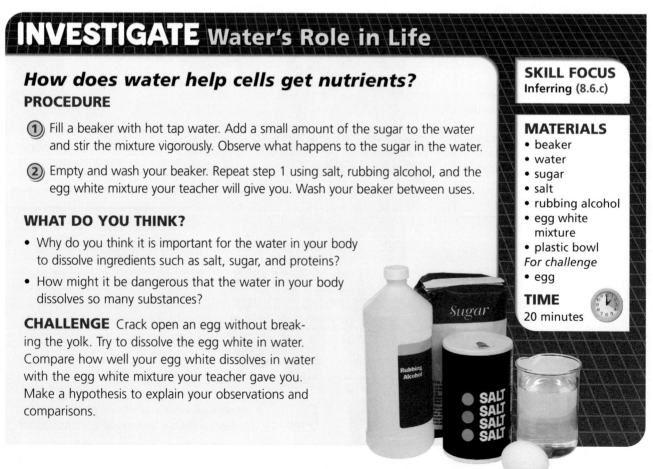

INVESTIGATE Water's Role in Life

How does water help cells get nutrients?

PROCEDURE

1. Fill a beaker with hot tap water. Add a small amount of the sugar to the water and stir the mixture vigorously. Observe what happens to the sugar in the water.

2. Empty and wash your beaker. Repeat step 1 using salt, rubbing alcohol, and the egg white mixture your teacher will give you. Wash your beaker between uses.

WHAT DO YOU THINK?

- Why do you think it is important for the water in your body to dissolve ingredients such as salt, sugar, and proteins?

- How might it be dangerous that the water in your body dissolves so many substances?

CHALLENGE Crack open an egg without breaking the yolk. Try to dissolve the egg white in water. Compare how well your egg white dissolves in water with the egg white mixture your teacher gave you. Make a hypothesis to explain your observations and comparisons.

SKILL FOCUS
Inferring (8.6.c)

MATERIALS
- beaker
- water
- sugar
- salt
- rubbing alcohol
- egg white mixture
- plastic bowl
For challenge
- egg

TIME
20 minutes

Salt

Salt (NaCl) is another useful compound for the body. Like water, salt also is important because of the type of bonding it contains—ionic. Remember, when ionic compounds dissolve in water, they separate into positive and negative ions. These ions are in solution in the blood and cells.

Salt separates into positive sodium (Na$^+$) and negative chloride (Cl$^-$) ions. Recall that separated ions allow a solution to conduct an electric current. This is how the body sends nerve impulses. If you touch a hot stove, for example, nerve cells in your skin sense the heat. Sodium ions (Na$^+$) in the fluid surrounding the nerve cells get pumped into the nerves. At the same time, potassium (K$^+$) ions get pumped out of the nerves. This allows an impulse to be conducted through the nerves to the muscles of your arm.

Sodium ions also help to keep the amount of water constant in the cells of body tissues. They do this by regulating the amount of water that passes in and out of the cells. Too much water in cells could cause them to burst. Not enough water could dry out the cells or prevent chemical reactions from taking place.

Chloride ions help our bodies digest food. They combine with hydrogen to make hydrochloric acid (HCl). Hydrochloric acid plays a role in food digestion.

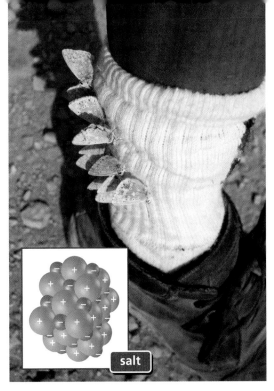

salt

These butterflies are enjoying a tasty snack from this hiker's sock. Butterflies need both water and salt, and they can get both from the sweat absorbed by the sock.

 CHECK YOUR READING What are two functions of sodium ions in the body?

11.1 Review

KEY CONCEPTS

1. List the six most common elements that make up living things. (8.6.b)
2. What property of water makes it so useful in living things? (8.6.c)
3. How does salt help conduct nerve impulses? (8.6.c)

CRITICAL THINKING

4. **Classify** Describe an example of water's use as a solvent, and one of its uses as a transporter.
5. **Infer** Do you think the body can get too much water? What might be the effects?

⬤ CHALLENGE

6. **Analyze** If the fluid inside nerve cells contained pure water instead of a solution of ions, would nerve impulses be able to travel through the body? Explain.

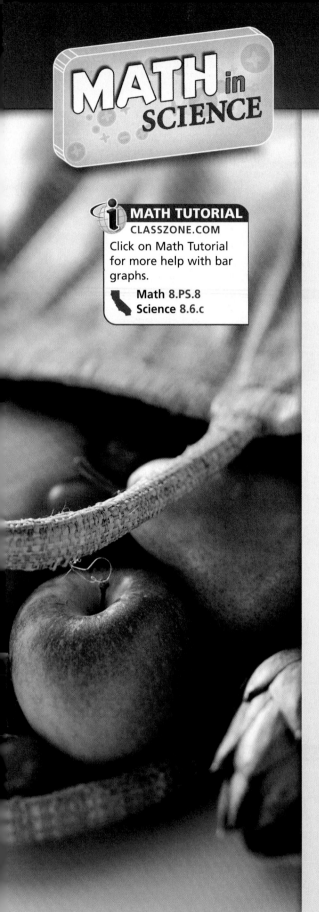

SKILL: MAKING BAR GRAPHS

Graphing Good Food

People need to eat different types of foods to have a healthy diet. Different amounts of each type of organic molecule are recommended for different groups of people. In general, grains, vegetables, and fruits contain sugars and starches. Dairy products, meats, and beans contain proteins and fats. The table on the right shows dietary recommendations. The information could also be shown in a bar graph.

Recommended Servings

Food Group	Young Children	Teen Girls	Teen Boys
Grains	5	6	7
Vegetables	3	5	6
Fruits	3	3	6
Dairy	2	3	3
Meats, beans	2	2	3

SOURCE: U.S. Department of Agriculture

Example

Create a bar graph that shows the dietary recommendation of grains for each group.

(1) Use the height of the bar to indicate the numerical value of a piece of data.

(2) Show the number of servings on the vertical axis. Label each group of bars on the horizontal axis.

(3) Use a different color for each group.

ANSWER

■ Young Children
■ Teen Girls
■ Teen Boys

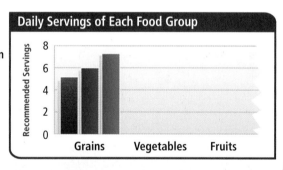

Daily Servings of Each Food Group

Use the Recommended Servings table above to answer the following questions.

1. Copy and complete the bar graph to show the dietary recommendations for the other four food groups.

2. Which group has the tallest bars on the graph? the shortest?

CHALLENGE Choose one group of people and make a pie graph showing recommendations for them. (**Hint:** First convert the numbers of servings into fractions of the whole diet.)

KEY CONCEPT

11.2 Carbon-based molecules have many structures.

VOCABULARY

organic compound p. 345
inorganic compound p. 346
polymer p.348
isomer p. 350

BEFORE, you learned

- A few basic elements make up all living things
- Atoms of one element differ from atoms of other elements
- Life on Earth is based on carbon

NOW, you will learn

- About the importance of carbon in living things
- Why carbon can form many different compounds
- About different structures of carbon-based molecules

VOCABULARY
Remember to make a magnet word diagram for *organic compound* and for other vocabulary terms.

THINK ABOUT

Where can you find carbon?

The wood of a pencil consists of carbon-based molecules. These molecules are considered to be organic. The graphite in the center of the pencil is also made of carbon. In fact, graphite is pure carbon, but it is not considered to be organic. What makes the carbon in wood different from the carbon in graphite?

Living and nonliving things contain carbon.

In the previous section, you learned that life on Earth is based on carbon. Carbon may not be the most abundant element in living things, but it certainly is the most important.

At one time, scientists thought that the chemical reactions that took place inside of living things could not occur outside of them. The carbon molecules were so complex, scientists thought they must have been made in some unknown ways. They therefore called compounds based on carbon **organic compounds.** Notice the similarity between the words *organic* and *organism.* Here on earth, living things contain carbon.

Of course, scientists eventually realized that the reactions occurring inside the body could occur outside it as well. They even found they could make some of the very complex carbon compounds found in the body. They learned that carbon's importance in living things comes from its ability to bond with other atoms in different ways. As you will see in this section, carbon is an atomic acrobat.

Organic Compound

Sugar, shown here as cubes, is organic and contains carbon atoms. It is made by plants from inorganic substances.

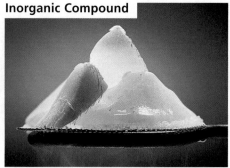

Inorganic Compound

Carbon dioxide, shown here as dry ice, is inorganic even though it contains carbon atoms. It is used by plants to make sugars.

Of course, this does not mean that all substances made from carbon are found in living things. For example, in a previous section you learned about diamond and graphite. These are made entirely of carbon but are not considered to be organic. The same is true of some compounds, such as hydrogen cyanide (HCN), calcium carbonate ($CaCO_3$), and carbon dioxide (CO_2). These carbon-containing compounds and all compounds without carbon are called **inorganic compounds.**

READING TiP

The prefix *in-* means "not," so *inorganic* means "not organic."

Carbon forms many different compounds.

SUPPORTING MAIN IDEAS
Make a chart about how carbon forms many different compounds.

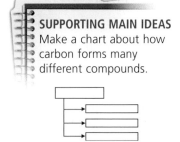

Millions of different carbon-based molecules exist. Consider the number of molecules that are needed to make up living things. Think of all of the processes that occur in living things. Carbon-based molecules are vital for all of them. The large variety of carbon-based molecules is a result of the number of bonds that each carbon atom forms in a molecule. It also is a result of a carbon atom's ability to form bonds with atoms of many different elements. In compounds, carbon atoms always share four pairs of electrons in four covalent bonds. This means that one carbon atom can form single bonds with up to four other atoms. Carbon atoms can also form multiple bonds with other atoms including other carbon atoms. Different ways of showing carbon-based molecules are shown below and on page 349.

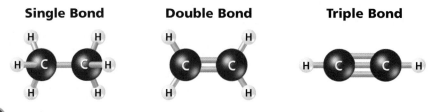

Single Bond   **Double Bond**   **Triple Bond**

CHECK YOUR READING   How many bonds can one carbon atom form?

As you can see, two carbon atoms can form single, double, or even triple bonds with one another. The compounds have different numbers of hydrogen atoms. They also have different numbers of bonds between their carbon atoms. Count the bonds for each carbon atom. Each carbon atom makes a total of four bonds.

Organic molecules are often shown in a simplified way. Instead of models that place all of a molecule's atoms and bonds, structural formulas—such as those shown below—can be used.

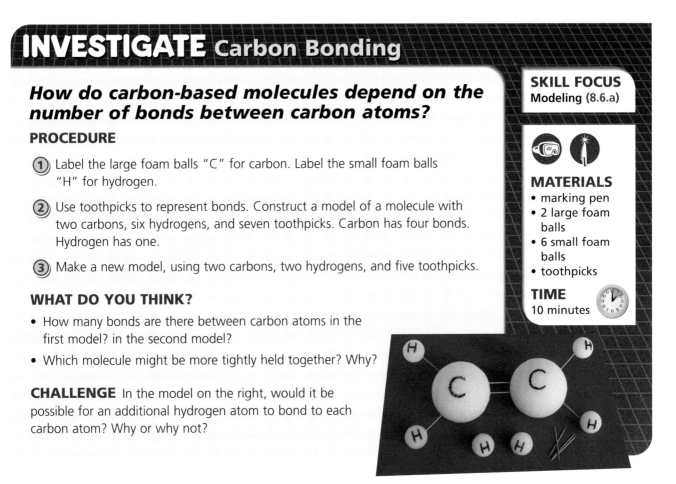

REMINDER

One pair of electrons is shared in a single covalent bond.

Full Structural Formulas

$$H-\underset{\underset{H}{|}}{\overset{\overset{H}{|}}{C}}-\underset{\underset{H}{|}}{\overset{\overset{H}{|}}{C}}-H \qquad \underset{\underset{H}{|}}{\overset{\overset{H}{|}}{C}}=\underset{\underset{H}{|}}{\overset{\overset{H}{|}}{C}} \qquad H-C\equiv C-H$$

Simplified Structural Formulas

$$CH_3-CH_3 \qquad CH_2=CH_2 \qquad CH\equiv CH$$

Carbon-based molecules can have many different structures. One important structure has molecules shaped like long chains. Another structure has molecules shaped like rings.

INVESTIGATE Carbon Bonding

How do carbon-based molecules depend on the number of bonds between carbon atoms?

PROCEDURE

1. Label the large foam balls "C" for carbon. Label the small foam balls "H" for hydrogen.

2. Use toothpicks to represent bonds. Construct a model of a molecule with two carbons, six hydrogens, and seven toothpicks. Carbon has four bonds. Hydrogen has one.

3. Make a new model, using two carbons, two hydrogens, and five toothpicks.

WHAT DO YOU THINK?

• How many bonds are there between carbon atoms in the first model? in the second model?

• Which molecule might be more tightly held together? Why?

CHALLENGE In the model on the right, would it be possible for an additional hydrogen atom to bond to each carbon atom? Why or why not?

SKILL FOCUS
Modeling (8.6.a)

MATERIALS
• marking pen
• 2 large foam balls
• 6 small foam balls
• toothpicks

TIME
10 minutes

SIMULATION
CLASSZONE.COM

Observe and rotate three-dimensional models of carbon-based molecules.

Long-Chain Polymers

Unlike atoms of other elements, carbon atoms can bond to each other to form very long chains. One carbon chain might contain hundreds of carbon atoms. A carbon chain can be straight or branched.

Straight Chain

$$CH_3 - CH_2 - CH_2 - CH_2 - CH_2 - CH_3$$

Branched Chain

In a branched carbon chain, other carbon atoms, or even other carbon chains, can bond to carbon atoms in the main carbon chain. Straight chains and branched chains are both results of carbon's ability to form four bonds. Notice how the CH_2 units repeat. A very large carbon-based molecule made of repeating units is called a **polymer.** Each unit of a polymer is known as a monomer. A polymer can be thousands of atoms long.

CHECK YOUR READING How is it possible for carbon atoms to form both straight and branched chains?

Carbon Rings

Carbon-based molecules also can be shaped like rings. Carbon rings containing five or six carbon atoms are the most common ones.

One of the most important carbon-based ring molecules is benzene (BEHN–ZEEN). Benzene contains six carbon atoms and six hydrogen atoms. Benzene has alternating single and double bonds between carbon atoms, as shown below. The benzene molecule is often shown as a circle inside a hexagon. Remember, a hexagon is a six-sided figure.

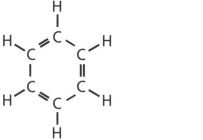

Benzene Ring   **Simplified Benzene Ring**

Many compounds are based on benzene's ring structure. These carbon-based molecules often have very strong smells, or aromas. They are called aromatic compounds. One aromatic compound that contains a benzene ring is a molecule called vanillin. Vanillin is the molecule that gives vanilla its strong smell.

Carbon Chains and Carbon Rings

Carbon-based molecules shaped like chains or rings are found in the world around you.

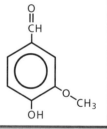

Carbon Chains

One of the carbon chains in the diesel fuel for this locomotive has the formula $C_{15}H_{32}$. It contains 13 CH_2 groups between the CH_3 groups that are on each end of the molecule. This molecule can be written as $CH_3(CH_2)_{13}CH_3$.

$$CH_3 - CH_2 - CH_2 - CH_2 - CH_2 - CH_2 - CH_2 - CH_2 - CH_2 - CH_2 - CH_2 - CH_2 - CH_2 - CH_2 - CH_3$$

Carbon Rings

Vanilla ice cream gets its flavor from vanilla, which is also used to enhance other flavors. The molecule that gives vanilla its strong smell is based on the benzene carbon ring.

Carbon Chains and Rings

The molecules in polystyrene, which make up this foam container, contain carbon rings attached to a long carbon chain. The dashed lines at both ends of the structural formula tell you that the molecule continues in both directions.

$$---CH_2 - CH - CH_2 - CH - CH_2 - CH---$$

Isomers

READING TiP

The prefix *iso-* means "equal," and the suffix *-mer* means "part."

There is another reason why there are so many carbon-based molecules. Carbon can form different molecules with the same atoms. The atoms in these molecules are in different places. The molecules have different structures. Because the atoms are arranged differently, they are actually two different substances. Compounds that contain the same atoms, but in different places, are called **isomers.**

The formulas below show a pair of isomers, butane and isobutane. Both molecules contain four carbon atoms and ten hydrogen atoms. However, butane molecules are straight chains of carbon atoms. Isobutane molecules are branched chains of carbon atoms. Even though both butane and isobutane contain the same atoms, the structures of the molecules are different, so they are isomers. These two isomers are very similar and are often mixed with one another. Isobutane, however, does have a slightly lower boiling point than regular butane.

Butane

$$CH_3 - CH_2 - CH_2 - CH_3$$

Butane contains four carbon atoms and ten hydrogen atoms. It has a straight chain structure.

Isobutane

$$CH_3$$
$$|$$
$$CH_3 - CH - CH_3$$

Isobutane also contains four carbon atoms and ten hydrogen atoms. It has a branched chain structure.

Some carbon-based molecules can shift from one isomer to another. For example, isomers of a molecule called retinal are necessary for your eyesight. When light strikes retinal, its structure changes from one isomer to another. The new isomer of retinal starts a process that sends a signal from the eye to the brain. After the retinal isomer gives the signal, the molecule shifts back to its original structure.

 CHECK YOUR READING If two substances are isomers of each other, how are they the same? different?

11.2 Review

KEY CONCEPTS

1. Why were carbon-based compounds first called organic? How has the understanding of organic compounds changed? (8.6.b)

2. How is the way in which carbon atoms bond to each other important for the number of carbon-based compounds? (8.6.a)

3. Describe three structures of carbon-based molecules. (8.6.a)

CRITICAL THINKING

4. **Infer** Could the last carbon atom in a carbon chain make bonds with four hydrogen atoms? Why or why not?

5. **Synthesize** Do you think molecules based on carbon rings can have isomers? Why or why not?

CHALLENGE

6. **Communicate** A molecule called naphthalene consists of ten carbon atoms and eight hydrogen atoms in two linked benzene rings. Draw a diagram of a molecule that could be naphthalene. Be sure to include the atoms and the bonds between the atoms.

California Close-Up

This scene shows how it may have looked when an animal was caught in the tar.

Shrink-Wrapped Carnivores!

> **8.6.b** Students know that living organisms are made of molecules consisting largely of carbon, hydrogen, nitrogen, oxygen, phosphorus, and sulfur.

About 40,000 years ago, something happened near Rancho La Brea in southern California. Oil from deep in Earth's crust seeped to the surface. There it sat in pools. Under the heat of the Sun, parts of the mixture evaporated. This left a sticky, gooey tar. Animals that walked on the tar became trapped. Unable to move, they eventually were covered over for thousands of years.

Digging Up Bones

The La Brea Tar Pits, in Los Angeles, are famous all over the world. Here, scientists found the bones of extinct elephants, camels, early horses, and saber-toothed cats. The bones have been preserved almost perfectly.

When animals die and their bodies are exposed to water and air, they decompose. The body parts are broken down into individual elements. Bones are usually the last parts of the body to decompose. If the bones are in wet, acidic soils, they dissolve completely. Bacteria in the soil also help decompose bones. The complex molecules that once made up the bones break down into carbon, hydrogen, nitrogen, calcium, magnesium, and other elements.

Stuck in the Muck

In the La Brea Tar Pits, however, the animals were trapped in a pit of tar. The tar seeped into every pore. It sealed the bones from any chemicals, water, acids, and bacteria. The bones did not decompose into individual elements such as calcium and carbon. It's almost as if the bones were wrapped in a thick, tight coating of plastic.

Excavation still goes on at the La Brea Tar Pits. Mounds and mounds of gooey tar need to be sifted through.

The black thighbone of a saber-toothed cat sticks out of the tar. Bones of this mammal are the type most commonly found in the La Brea Tar Pits.

WRITING ABOUT SCIENCE

Suppose a local politician is trying to stop the exploration of the La Brea Tar Pits. The politician claims nothing more can be learned from the bones found there. Write a letter explaining why the fossils in the La Brea Tar Pits are valuable for understanding the past.

11.3 Carbon-based molecules are life's building blocks.

CALIFORNIA Content Standards

8.6.a Students know that carbon, because of its ability to combine in many ways with itself and other elements, has a central role in the chemistry of living organisms.

8.6.c Students know that living organisms have many different kinds of molecules, including small ones, such as water and salt, and very large ones, such as carbohydrates, fats, proteins, and DNA.

VOCABULARY

carbohydrate p. 353
lipid p. 354
protein p. 356
enzyme p. 357
nucleic acid p. 359

BEFORE, you learned

- Carbon is the basis of life on Earth
- Carbon atoms can form multiple bonds
- Carbon can form molecules shaped like chains or rings

NOW, you will learn

- About the functions of carbohydrates and lipids in living things
- About structures and functions of proteins
- How nucleic acids carry instructions for building proteins

EXPLORE Carbon in Food (8.6.a)

How can you see the carbon in food?

PROCEDURE

① Place the candle in the pie plate and light the candle.

② Use the tongs to hold each food sample in the candle flame for 20 seconds. Record your observations.

WHAT DO YOU THINK?

- What changes did you observe in the samples?
- What type of chemical reaction might have caused these changes?

MATERIALS

- aluminum pie plate
- candle
- wooden matches
- tongs
- small marshmallow
- piece of carrot

Carbon-based molecules have many functions in living things.

You depend on carbon-based molecules for all of the activities in your life. For example, when you play softball, you need energy to swing the bat and run the bases. Carbon-based molecules are the source of the chemical energy your muscle cells need. Carbon-based molecules make up your muscle cells. They provide those cells with the ability to contract and relax. Carbon-based molecules carry oxygen to your muscle cells so that your muscles can work properly. Carbon-based molecules even provide the information for building new molecules.

The many carbon-based molecules in all living things have certain similarities. They all contain carbon and elements such as hydrogen, oxygen, nitrogen, sulfur, and phosphorus. Many of the molecules are also very large molecules called macromolecules. However, these molecules have different structures and different functions.

READING TIP

The prefix *macro-* means "large," so a macromolecule is a large molecule.

Living things contain four major types of carbon-based molecules.

The organic molecules in living things fall into four major groups—carbohydrates, lipids, proteins, and nucleic acids. You may already be familiar with these types of molecules and their functions.

Carbohydrates include sugars and starches. They are found in foods such as bread and pasta. Many lipids are fats or oils. Proteins are necessary for many functions in the body, including the formation of muscle tissue. Nucleic acids are the molecules that carry the genetic code for all living things. As you read about each of these types of molecules, try to see how its function depends on its molecular structure.

Carbohydrates

Carbohydrates (KAHR-boh-HY-DRAYTZ) include sugars, starches, and cellulose. They contain atoms of three elements—carbon, hydrogen, and oxygen. They serve two main functions. Carbohydrates are a source of chemical energy for cells in many living things. They are also part of the structural materials of plants.

One important carbohydrate is the sugar glucose. It has the chemical formula $C_6H_{12}O_6$. Cells in both plants and animals break down glucose for energy. In plants, glucose molecules also can join together to form more complex carbohydrates, such as starch and cellulose. Starch is a macromolecule that consists of many glucose molecules, or units, bonded together. Many foods, such as pasta, contain starch. When starch is broken back down into individual glucose molecules, those glucose molecules can be used as an energy source by cells.

> **Modeling Glucose**
>
> The glucose molecule can be represented by a hexagon. The red O shows that an oxygen atom is in the ring.

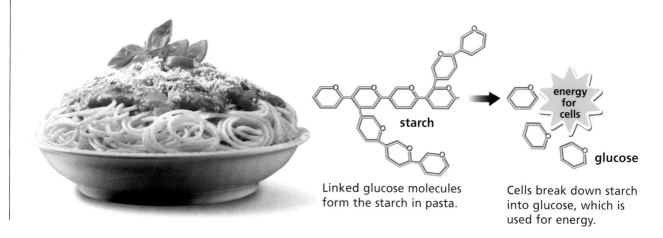

Linked glucose molecules form the starch in pasta.

starch → **energy for cells**

glucose

Cells break down starch into glucose, which is used for energy.

Moss Leaf Cells

Plants make their own glucose through a process called photosynthesis. You read about this chemical reaction earlier. Some of the glucose made during photosynthesis is used to make complex carbohydrate molecules. These molecules form a plant's structure.

Cellulose

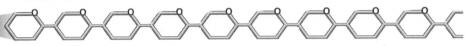

Cellulose is a long chain-like molecule that forms part of a plant's structure.

Unlike animal cells, plant cells have a cell wall. A cell wall is a tough, protective layer outside the cell membrane. Cellulose (SEHL-yuh-LOHS) is a macromolecule found in plant cell walls. The cell wall is a large part of vegetables such as lettuce and celery. The illustration shows moss leaf cells with their cell walls, and a diagram of part of a cellulose molecule.

Cellulose and starch are both carbohydrates made up of glucose molecules, but the glucose molecules that make up these larger macromolecules are linked in different ways. Because of their different structures, starch and cellulose have different functions. In fact, this difference in structure also prevents your body from breaking down and using cellulose as it would starch.

 CHECK YOUR READING What are some functions of carbohydrates in animals? in plants?

Lipids

VOCABULARY
Make a magnet word diagram for *lipid* and for other vocabulary terms.

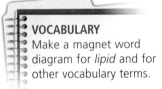

Lipids include fats and oils. They are used mainly for energy and as structural materials in living things. Like carbohydrates, most lipids are made of carbon, hydrogen, and oxygen. Even though lipids and carbohydrates have many similarities, they have different structures and properties.

Animals store chemical energy in fat. Plants store chemical energy in oils, such as olive oil and peanut oil. Fats and oils store energy very efficiently. One gram of fat contains about twice as much energy as one gram of carbohydrate or protein. Molecules of fats and oils contain three linked carbon chains called fatty acids. The illustration below shows the general structure of a fatty acid.

Modeling Fatty Acids

The carbon chains in lipids are called fatty acids. A carbon atom is at each bend of the zig-zag model above. The break in the middle of the chain shows that some carbon atoms have been left out.

You may have heard the terms *saturated* and *unsaturated* in relation to fats. If all of the bonds between carbon atoms in the fatty acids are single bonds, the lipid is a saturated fat. If one or more of these bonds is a double bond, the lipid is an unsaturated fat. Most animal fats are saturated, and most oils from plants are unsaturated. Diets high in saturated fats have been linked to heart disease. Lipids in the butter in the photograph on the right are saturated fats.

Fat Structure

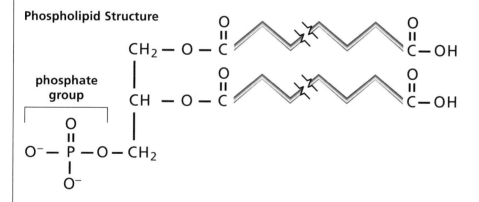

Fats in butter contain three fatty acids and are used for energy. Butter contains saturated fats.

> **CHECK YOUR READING** What is the difference between a saturated fat and an unsaturated fat?

Some lipids are important parts of cell structure. Some structural lipids contain the element phosphorus. They are called phospholipids. Phospholipids are an important part of cell membranes. The nerve cell in the photograph is one example.

Phospholipid Structure

phosphate group

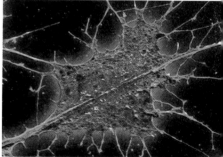

Some lipids in this nerve cell's membrane have two fatty acids and one phosphate group. These lipids are called phospholipids.

Another lipid involved in cell structure is cholesterol. It is a part of cell membranes. Cholesterol has other functions as well. It is needed to make hormones. Hormones, such as adrenaline, are chemical messengers in the body.

Your body makes some of the cholesterol that it needs, but it also uses cholesterol from foods you eat. Cholesterol is found in many foods that come from animals, such as meat and eggs. Even some plant products, such as coconut oil, can increase the amount of cholesterol in your body. Although you need cholesterol, eating too much of it can lead to heart disease.

INVESTIGATE Organic Molecules

Where can you find organic molecules?

PROCEDURE

1. Place a dropper of cornstarch solution into one jar lid and a dropper of liquid gelatin into a second jar lid.

2. Add a drop of iodine solution to the cornstarch sample and to the gelatin sample.

3. Examine the jar lids after one minute. Record your observations.

4. Using the remaining two jar lids, repeat steps 2 and 3 with the bread and the tofu instead of the cornstarch and gelatin.

WHAT DO YOU THINK?

- What changes occurred after the addition of iodine to the cornstarch and to the gelatin?

- Iodine can be used to detect the presence of starches. What carbon-based molecules might be in the bread and tofu? How do you know?

CHALLENGE Suppose you tested a piece of pepperoni pizza with iodine. Which ingredients (crust, sauce, cheese, pepperoni) would likely contain starch?

Proteins

Proteins are macromolecules that are made of smaller molecules called amino acids. Proteins, like carbohydrates and lipids, contain carbon, hydrogen, and oxygen. However, proteins differ from carbohydrates and lipids in that they also contain nitrogen, sulfur, and other elements. Carbohydrates and lipids are used primarily for energy and structure. Proteins, however, have many different functions.

Think of a protein as being like a word. Amino acids are the letters in that word. The meaning of a word depends on the order of letters in the word. For example, rearranging the letters in the word *eat* makes different words with different meanings like *tea* and *ate*. Similarly, proteins depend on the order of their amino acids.

Linked Amino Acids

tyrosine   lysine   cysteine   serine   leucine

Just as 26 letters of the alphabet make up all words in the English language, 20 amino acids make up all of the proteins in your body. The structure of a protein is determined by the order of its amino acids. If two amino acids change places, the entire protein changes.

The function of a protein depends on its structure. There are at least 100,000 proteins in your body, each with a different structure that gives it a specific function. Some proteins are structural materials. Some control chemical reactions. Others transport substances within cells and through the body. Still others are a part of the immune system, which protects you from infections.

 CHECK YOUR READING How does the function of a protein depend on its structure?

Proteins that are part of the structure of living things are often shaped like coils. One coil-shaped protein, keratin, is part of human hair as shown on the left below. Proteins called actin and myosin are coil-shaped proteins that help your muscles contract.

Other types of proteins have coiled regions but curl up into shapes like balls. One example is hemoglobin, shown on the right below. Hemoglobin is a transport protein that carries oxygen in the blood.

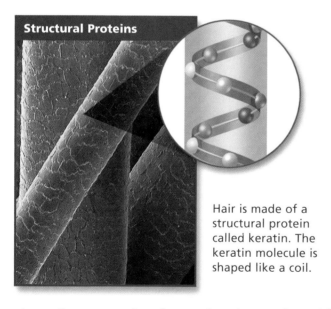

Structural Proteins

Hair is made of a structural protein called keratin. The keratin molecule is shaped like a coil.

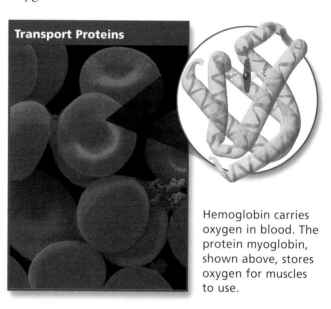

Transport Proteins

Hemoglobin carries oxygen in blood. The protein myoglobin, shown above, stores oxygen for muscles to use.

Some proteins that curl up into a shape like a ball are enzymes. An **enzyme** (EHN-zym) is a catalyst for a chemical reaction in living things. Catalysts speed up the rate of chemical reactions. Enzymes are necessary for many chemical reactions in your body. Without enzymes, these reactions would occur too slowly to keep you alive.

It is important to have proteins in your diet so that your body can make its own proteins. Proteins in foods such as meats, soybeans, and nuts are broken down into amino acids by your body. These amino acids are then used by your cells to make new proteins.

Nucleic Acid Structure and Function

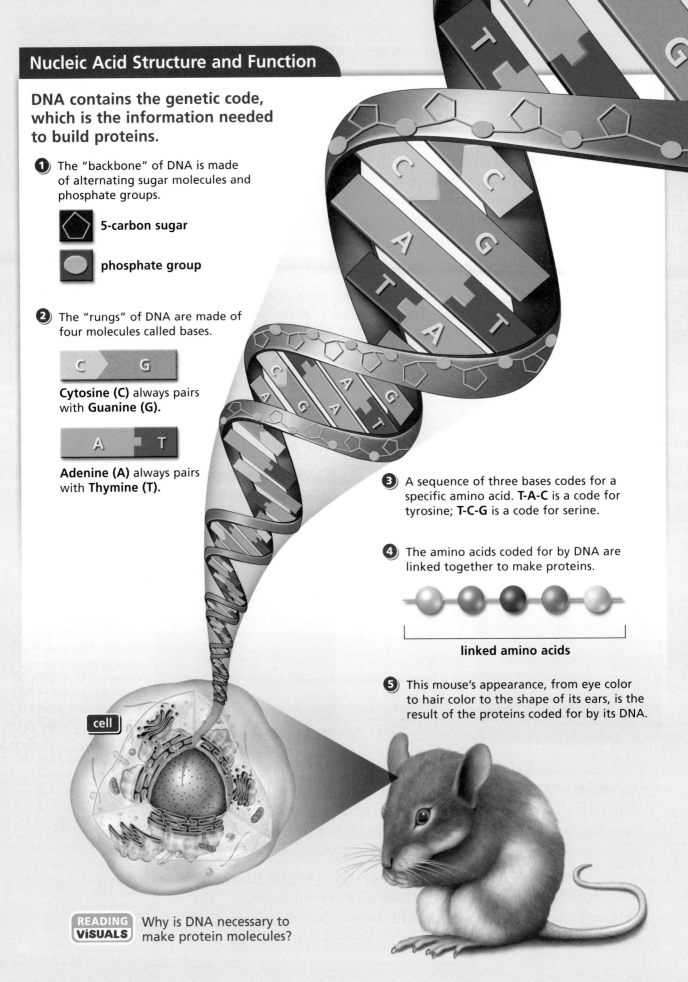

DNA contains the genetic code, which is the information needed to build proteins.

1 The "backbone" of DNA is made of alternating sugar molecules and phosphate groups.

- ⬠ **5-carbon sugar**
- ⬭ **phosphate group**

2 The "rungs" of DNA are made of four molecules called bases.

C ▸ G

Cytosine (C) always pairs with **Guanine (G)**.

A ▸ T

Adenine (A) always pairs with **Thymine (T)**.

3 A sequence of three bases codes for a specific amino acid. **T-A-C** is a code for tyrosine; **T-C-G** is a code for serine.

4 The amino acids coded for by DNA are linked together to make proteins.

linked amino acids

5 This mouse's appearance, from eye color to hair color to the shape of its ears, is the result of the proteins coded for by its DNA.

cell

READING VISUALS Why is DNA necessary to make protein molecules?

Nucleic Acids

Nucleic acids (noo-KLEE-ihk AS-ihdz) are huge, complex carbon-based molecules. They contain the information that cells use to make proteins. These macromolecules are made of carbon, hydrogen, and oxygen, as well as nitrogen and phosphorus. Each of the cells in your body contains a complete set of nucleic acids. This means that each cell has all of the instructions necessary for making any protein in your body.

The illustration on page 358 shows part of a nucleic acid molecule called DNA, which looks like a twisted ladder. The sides of the ladder are made of sugar molecules and phosphate groups. Each rung of the ladder is composed of two nitrogen-containing molecules called bases. DNA has four types of bases, represented by the letters A, C, T, and G. The order of the bases in a DNA molecule is the way in which DNA stores the instructions for making proteins. How do just four molecules—A, C, T, and G—carry all of this important information?

READING TiP
The *NA* in *DNA* stands for "nucleic acid." The *D* stands for "deoxyribose," which is the type of sugar in the molecule.

Recall that a protein is composed of amino acids that have to be linked in a certain order. Each of the 20 amino acids is represented by a particular series of three DNA bases. For example, the sequence T–A–C corresponds to, or is a code for, the amino acid tyrosine. There are 64 different three-base sequences in DNA, each of which has a specific meaning. This genetic code works in the same way in every living thing on Earth. It provides a complete set of instructions for linking amino acids in the right order to make each specific protein molecule. The DNA code is only one part of making proteins, though. Other types of nucleic acids, called RNA, are responsible for reading the code and assembling a protein with the correct amino acids.

RESOURCE CENTER
CLASSZONE.COM

Find out more about carbohydrates, lipids, proteins, and nucleic acids.

CHECK YOUR READING How many different types of bases make up the genetic code in DNA?

11.3 Review

KEY CONCEPTS

1. How does the function of a lipid depend on its structure? (8.3.c)

2. What determines the structure of a protein? (8.3.a)

3. What role does DNA perform in the making of proteins? (8.3.c)

CRITICAL THINKING

4. **Synthesize** Give two examples of carbon-based molecules in living things that are based on a chain structure. Explain.

5. **Compare and Contrast** How are carbohydrates and lipids similar? How are they different?

⬙ CHALLENGE

6. **Infer** Suppose the order of bases in a DNA molecule is changed. What do you think will happen to the structure of the protein that is coded for by that region of DNA? Why?

CHAPTER INVESTIGATION

Extract and Observe DNA

OVERVIEW AND PURPOSE Nucleic acids contain the information needed to make proteins. DNA is the nucleic acid found in the body that carries the code to make all proteins the body needs. In this activity, you will work with several simple chemicals that can break down the membranes of a cell. You will

- extract DNA from the cells in raw wheat germ
- examine properties of the extracted DNA

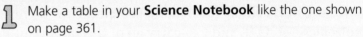

▶ Procedure

1. Make a table in your **Science Notebook** like the one shown on page 361.

2. Place a small scoop of wheat germ in a test tube. The wheat germ should be about 1 cm high in the test tube.

3. Add enough distilled water to wet and cover all of the wheat germ in the test tube. Add 3 grams of meat tenderizer.

4. Add 25–30 drops of detergent solution to the test tube.

5. For 3 minutes, gently swirl the test tube contents by rotating your wrist while holding the tube. Try not to make bubbles.

step 5

6. Add 25–30 drops of the salt solution to the test tube, and swirl for 1 more minute.

7. Hold the test tube tilted at an angle. Slowly add alcohol so that it runs down the inside of the test tube and forms a separate layer on top of the material already in the tube. Add enough alcohol to double the total volume. Let the test tube stand for 2 minutes.

step 7

MATERIALS

- raw wheat germ
- scoop
- test tube
- warm distilled water
- detergent solution
- salt solution
- cold ethyl or isopropyl alcohol
- meat tenderizer
- bent paper clip
- test tube rack

8.6.c, 8.9.c

Content Standard
8.6.c Students know that living organisms have many different kinds of molecules, including small ones, such as water and salt, and very large ones, such as carbohydrates, fats, proteins, and DNA.

Investigation Standard
8.9.c Distinguish between variable and controlled parameters in a test.

8. Watch for stringy, cloudy material to rise up from the bottom layer into the alcohol layer. This is the DNA.

9. Use the bent paper clip to remove some DNA. Be careful to probe only the alcohol layer and not disturb the material at the bottom of the test tube.

step 9

10. Wash your hands after working with the chemicals.

▶ Observe and Analyze
Write It Up

1. **OBSERVE** How do your observations of the DNA you just extracted compare with what you know about DNA? Record these comparisons in your notebook in a table similar to the one shown.

2. **INFER** What type of organism is wheat? Where is the DNA located in a wheat germ cell?

3. **INFER** What do you think was the purpose of using detergent in this experiment? **Hint:** How does soap work on greasy dishes?

4. **IDENTIFY VARIABLES** Why might you have not obtained the DNA sample? What could you try changing to see if you would get better results? Think: Are you certain your chemicals are pure?

▶ Conclude
Write It Up

1. **INFER** If you had used cooked or toasted wheat germ in this experiment, you would not have gotten good results. Why do you think this is the case?

2. **INFER** Would this experiment work with cells from other organisms, such as bananas, onions, or cells from the inside of your mouth? Why or why not?

3. **INFER** Would DNA from a single cell be visible to the naked eye?

4. **APPLY** The procedure that you performed today is used by many people to obtain DNA for further study. Give some examples of how DNA information is used in the world today.

▶ INVESTIGATE Further

CHALLENGE Repeat the experiment replacing the alcohol with water in step 7. Compare the results with the results you obtained using alcohol.

Extract and Observe DNA

Table 1. Properties and Observations

Properties of DNA	Observations

Chapter Review

the BIG idea

Carbon and other elements are essential to living things.

CONTENT REVIEW
CLASSZONE.COM

KEY CONCEPTS SUMMARY

 Living things depend on chemical processes.

- Living things have the same chemistry as nonliving things.
- About 25 common elements make up living things.
- Water and salt are very important to living things.

Elements in the Human Body

Nitrogen 3%
Other 3%
Hydrogen 10%
Oxygen 61%
Carbon 23%

VOCABULARY
biochemistry
p. 339

---

2 **Carbon-based molecules have many structures.**

Carbon forms a large number of different compounds because of the number of bonds it can make with other atoms.

Single Bond

Double Bond

Triple Bond

Carbon can form chains and rings.

Hexane

$CH_3 - CH_2 - CH_2 - CH_2 - CH_2 - CH_3$

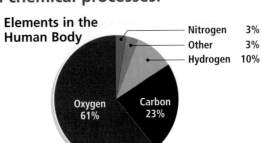

Vanillin

VOCABULARY
organic compound
 p. 345
inorganic compound
 p. 346
polymer p. 348
isomer p. 350

---

3 **Carbon-based molecules are life's building blocks.**

There are four main types of carbon-based molecules in living things.

Carbon-Based Molecules			
Carbohydrates	**Lipids**	**Proteins**	**Nucleic Acids**
• sugars and starches • energy for cells • plant cell walls	• fats and oils • energy for cells • cell membranes	• strings of amino acids • used for structure, transport, immune system, enzymes	• DNA and RNA • genetic code • code for amino acids

VOCABULARY
carbohydrate p. 353
lipid p. 354
protein p. 356
enzyme p. 357
nucleic acid p. 359

Reviewing Vocabulary

Copy and complete the chart below. Fill in the blanks with the missing term, example, or function. See the example in the chart.

Term	Example	Function
inorganic compound	*carbon dioxide*	*used by plants to make glucose*
1. organic compound	glucose	
2. carbohydrate	sugar	
3.	fat	stores chemical energy
4.	keratin	found in hair and feathers
5. nucleic acid		instructions for proteins

Greek Origins *Describe how each of the following terms is related to one or more of the following Greek prefixes or suffixes.*

iso- means "equal"   *mono-* means "one"
-mer means "part"   *poly-* means "many"

6. isomer

7. polymer

8. monomer

9. polyunsaturated

Reviewing Key Concepts

Multiple Choice *Choose the letter of the best answer.*

10. Which element is the most abundant in human beings? (8.6.b)
   a. sulfur
   b. oxygen
   c. carbon
   d. hydrogen

11. What is a role for sodium ions (Na^+) in our bodies? (8.6.c)
   a. to control digestion
   b. to send nerve impulses
   c. to serve as protein building blocks
   d. to store chemical energy

12. All life on Earth is based on atoms of which element? (8.6.b)
   a. oxygen
   b. nitrogen
   c. carbon
   d. hydrogen

13. One reason that carbon atoms can form large numbers of compounds is that a carbon atom forms (8.6.a)
   a. two bonds with a hydrogen atom
   b. four bonds in its compounds
   c. ionic bonds in its compounds
   d. bonds with up to five hydrogen atoms

14. Which of the following is not found in living things? (8.6.c)
   a. proteins   **c.** lipids
   b. petroleum   **d.** carbohydrates

15. What functions do carbohydrates and lipids perform in living things? (8.6.c)
   a. They provide energy and instructions.
   b. They provide water and oxygen.
   c. They provide water and immunity.
   d. They provide energy and structure.

16. The molecules that carry instructions to make other molecules are called (8.6.c)
   a. nucleic acids   **c.** carbohydrates
   b. proteins   **d.** lipids

Short Answer *Write a short answer to each question.*

17. Explain how carbon's ability to form isomers is related to the large number of carbon-based molecules that exist. (8.6.a)

18. Describe the function of potassium ions in living things. (8.6.b)

Thinking Critically

The following illustration models linked amino acids. Use the illustration to answer the next four questions.

19. **SYNTHESIZE** Why can the model shown by the illustration be considered to be a polymer? (8.6.c)

20. **CONCLUDE** What would cause the amino acids in the illustration to be placed in that particular order? Explain. (8.6.c)

21. **APPLY** If the order of amino acids shown in the illustration changes, would the protein formed likely still have the same function? Why or why not? (8.6.c)

22. **PREDICT** Suppose the protein formed by the amino acids has a coiled shape. What might be the general function of that protein? What if the protein is coiled but also curls up into a ball? (8.6.c)

23. **COMPARE AND CONTRAST** Copy and complete the chart below. Provide two similarities and two differences for each pair of items.

Items	Similarities	Differences
starch/ cellulose	both carbohydrates; both polymers	starch used for energy, cellulose for structure; starch molecule branched, cellulose molecule straight
carbon chains/ carbon rings		
proteins/lipids		
glucose/ amino acids		

Using Math Skills in Science

The following nutrition label shows the calories and the amount of fat, carbohydrates, and protein in a type of cracker. Use the information on the label to answer the following three questions.

Nutrition Facts

Servings Per Container   about 15

Amount Per Serving

Calories	150
Total Fat	6g
Total Carbohydrates	20g
Protein	2g

24. Fats contain about twice as many calories per gram as carbohydrates and proteins. Assume that all of the calories on the label come from the carbohydrates, fats, and proteins. About how many calories come from each substance? (8.6.c)

25. Make a pie chart that compares the number of calories from carbohydrates, fats, and proteins contained in this food. (8.6.c)

26. Adult athletes are recommended to eat a diet that provides 15 percent of its calories from protein, 30 percent from fats, and 55 percent from carbohydrates. Does this food have the recommended balance of nutrients? Why or why not? (8.6.c)

the BIG idea

27. **DRAW CONCLUSIONS** Look at the photograph on pages 336–337. Identify three elements and three compounds in the photograph. Explain how chemistry is important in the scene.

28. **SYNTHESIZE** Write two or more paragraphs describing important molecules in living systems. (8.6.c)

UNIT PROJECTS

Evaluate all the data, results, and information from your project folder. Prepare to present your project.

Interpreting Tables

8.3.b, 8.3.c

Petroleum products are used in everything from fuels to road pavement. They come from the remains of organic material buried for millions of years beneath the Earth's surface. During that time, carbon molecules of varying chain lengths formed. The following table contains information about the uses and the properties of a few of these petroleum products.

Use the information in the table to answer questions 1–5.

Characteristics of Petroleum Products		
Product	Number of Carbon Atoms per Polymer Molecule	Boiling Point (°C)
Natural gas	1 to 4	lower than 20
Gasoline	5 to 12	35 to 220
Kerosene	12 to 16	200 to 315
Jet fuel	12 to 16	200 to 315
Diesel fuel	15 to 18	250 to 375
Heating oil	15 to 18	250 to 375
Lubricating oil	16 to 20	350 and higher
Asphalt	More than 25	600 and higher

SOURCE: *Mortimer, Chemistry, 6th edition*

1. Which petroleum product has the lowest boiling point?

  a. diesel fuel   **c.** kerosene

  b. gasoline   **d.** natural gas

2. Which petroleum product has the highest boiling point?

  a. asphalt   **c.** jet fuel

  b. heating oil   **d.** kerosene

3. Petroleum is heated and turned into gas. The gas rises in a tower. The lightest gases, those with the fewest carbon atoms, rise highest. The heaviest gases, those with the most carbon atoms, stay lowest. Which of the following products would be found lowest in the tower?

  a. diesel fuel   **c.** lubricating oil

  b. kerosene   **d.** natural gas

4. Petroleum is split into fractions. Each fraction includes all the products that have the same boiling point. Which of the following pairs of products are in the same fraction?

  a. gasoline and natural gas   **c.** lubricating oil and diesel fuel

  b. jet fuel and kerosene   **d.** natural gas and asphalt

5. What would you expect the boiling point of a petroleum product that contains 22 carbon atoms to be?

  a. 100°C   **c.** 500°C

  b. 300°C   **d.** 700°C

Extended Response

Answer the following two questions in detail. Include some of the terms from the list in the box at right. Underline each term that you use in your answers.

atoms	carbon chains	carbon rings
molecules	properties	structure
function	monomer	

6. Why is carbon able to form so many different types of compounds? What are two possible structures for carbon compounds?

7. Carbohydrates, lipids, and proteins are all carbon-based molecules. How are they similar? How are they different?

Space Science

comet

UNIVERSE

electromagnetic
radiation

telescope

Contents Overview

DANGER
from the Sky

How can astronomers find out whether a large object from space is going to strike our planet?

California Content Standards

8.4.e Students know the appearance, general composition, relative position and size, and motion of objects in the solar system, including planets, planetary satellites, comets, and asteroids.

SCIENTIFIC AMERICAN FRONTIERS

View the video segment "Big Dish" to learn how astronomers use the largest radio telescope on Earth.

The streak of light in the photograph above was produced by a tiny particle from space burning up in Earth's atmosphere. The photograph at left is of Barringer Crater in Arizona.

Collisions in Space

In the summer of 1994, telescopes all over the world were aimed at Jupiter. For the first time in history, astronomers had warning of a collision in space. Jupiter's gravity had split a comet into more than 20 large pieces. As the rocky objects collided with Jupiter's atmosphere, they exploded.

Astronomers have found evidence of impacts closer to home. The craters that cover much of the Moon's surface were caused by collisions with space objects billions of years ago. In 1953 an astronomer caught on film the bright flash of an object hitting the Moon. Other solid bodies in space also have impact craters. Little evidence of impacts remains on Earth because its surface is always changing. Fewer than 200 craters are still visible.

Earth's atmosphere protects us from collisions with small objects, which burn up in the air. However, when a large object strikes Earth, the atmosphere can spread the effects of the impact far beyond the crater. A large collision may throw dust high into the air, where it can be carried around the globe. The dust can block sunlight for months and sharply lower global temperatures.

About 65 million years ago, a large space object struck Earth. The dust from this collision can be found around the world in a layer of rock that was forming at the time. At about the same time, most species of organisms died out, including the dinosaurs. Many scientists think that the collision caused this global destruction.

The Risk of a Major Collision

When will the next space object hit Earth? A collision is probably occurring as you read this sentence. Tiny particles hit Earth's atmosphere all the time. Some of these particles have enough mass to make it through the atmosphere. Objects that reach Earth's surface are called meteorites. Most meteorites splash harmlessly into the ocean or hit areas with few or no people. Every few years a meteorite damages a home or other property. However, there is no known case of a person being killed by a meteorite.

Collisions that cause widespread damage happen less often because the solar system contains fewer large objects. In 1908 a large object from space exploded above a remote region of Russia. The explosion knocked down trees across an area more than half the size of Rhode Island. Even this impact was small compared with major collisions that affect the entire world. Such collisions happen on average about twice every million years. Events that kill off many species occur even less often.

Tracking Asteroids

Although Earth probably won't have a major collision with a space object anytime soon, the danger is too great to ignore. Scientists are using telescopes to find large, rocky space objects called asteroids. After locating an asteroid, they use computer models to predict its path centuries into the future. Scientists expect that they will soon have found almost all of the asteroids that could cause destruction on Earth.

Locating objects that may threaten life on Earth is just the first step. Scientists also want to

View the "Big Dish" segment of your *Scientific American Frontiers* video to learn how astronomers are using the giant Arecibo radio telescope to explore the universe.

IN THIS SCENE FROM THE VIDEO ▶

You see a close-up of the Arecibo telescope's dome and one of its antennas.

EXPLORING ASTEROIDS Asteroids crashing into Earth may seem like the subject of a science fiction movie. Yet asteroids pose a real danger to humans. Some asteroids could cause widespread destruction if they struck our planet.

Astronomers are tracking these asteroids to determine how close they will pass to Earth in the future.

Asteroids are too faint to be viewed clearly with optical telescopes on Earth. However, radio telescopes can provide detailed images of asteroids. Inside the dome of the Arecibo telescope is the world's most powerful radar transmitter. The transmitter can bounce a beam of radio waves off the telescope's dish to reach an asteroid millions of miles away. The telescope picks up returning signals, which are converted into images.

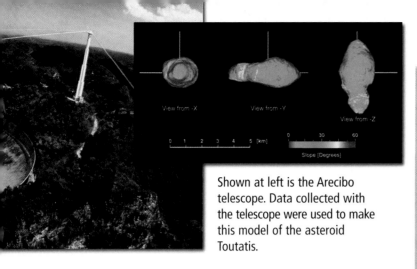

Shown at left is the Arecibo telescope. Data collected with the telescope were used to make this model of the asteroid Toutatis.

learn about the characteristics of asteroids. The Arecibo telescope in Puerto Rico is an important tool for studying asteroids. Arecibo is the largest radio dish in the world. It allows scientists to determine the motions and shapes of asteroids. Computer models and tests with real materials provide information about the mass, materials, and structure of each asteroid.

If scientists ever find an asteroid headed toward Earth, these studies may help us change the asteroid's course safely. Remember the comet that struck Jupiter in many pieces? If an asteroid broke apart before reaching Earth, pieces hitting different locations could cause more damage than a single impact. Before using a bomb or laser to change the course of an asteroid, governments must make sure that the asteroid will not break apart. Fortunately, scientists would have decades to study a dangerous asteroid and figure out what action to take.

UNANSWERED Questions

Scientists are learning about the risk of asteroids colliding with Earth. The more we learn about collisions in space, the more questions we have.

- What methods can be used to change the course of an asteroid that threatens Earth?

- How can we make sure that an asteroid will not break apart because of our efforts to change its course?

- How many smaller but still dangerous objects may be headed toward Earth?

UNIT PROJECTS

As you study this unit, work alone or with a group on one of these projects.

Observe the Sky (8.4.e)

Choose a space object or part of the distant sky to observe over a month. Keep a journal of what you see and think.

- Pay special attention to any changes relative to other objects in the sky.

- Look up information or construct tools to help you observe.

- Copy your best drawings for a display board. Explain your observations.

Multimedia Presentation (8.4)

The Arecibo telescope is not used only for studying asteroids. Prepare a multimedia presentation on other research that is being carried out with the giant radio telescope.

- Find information about the research from Internet sites and other sources.

- Prepare both audio and visual components for your presentation.

Map a Space Object (8.4.e)

Use a large potato to represent a newly explored space object. Draw lines of latitude and longitude. Then identify features, and make a flat map.

- Use roller-ball pens to mark poles, an equator, and lines of longitude and latitude. Try not to pierce the potato's skin.

- Do the potato's eyes seem like craters or volcanoes? Decide how to name the different types of features.

- Make a flat map of the space object.

CAREER CENTER
CLASSZONE.COM

Learn about careers in astronomy.

Earth, Moon, and Sun

the **BIG** idea

Earth and the Moon move in predictable ways as they orbit the Sun.

Key Concepts

SECTION

1 **Some space objects are visible to the human eye.**
Learn about views of space from Earth and about the arrangement of the universe.

SECTION

2 **Earth rotates on a tilted axis and orbits the Sun.**
Learn what causes day and night and why there are seasons.

SECTION

3 **The Moon is Earth's natural satellite.**
Learn about the structure and motion of Earth's Moon.

SECTION

4 **Positions of the Sun and Moon affect Earth.**
Learn about phases of the Moon, eclipses, and tides.

California ClassZone

CLASSZONE.COM
Chapter 12 online resources: Content Review, two Visualizations, two Resource Centers, Math Tutorial, Test Practice

What would you see if you looked at the Moon with a telescope?

Why Does the Sun Appear to Move Around Earth?

> **8.4.e** Students know the appearance, general composition, relative position and size, and motion of objects in the solar system, including planets, planetary satellites, comets, and asteroids.

Stand in front of a floor lamp, and turn around slowly. Notice how the lamp moves within your field of vision.

Observe and Think
Why did the lamp seem to move?

What Makes the Moon Bright?

> **8.4.d** Students know that stars are the source of light for all bright objects in outer space and that the Moon and planets shine by reflected sunlight, not by their own light.

On a day when you see the Moon in the sky, compare it with a round object. Hold the object in line with the Moon. Make sure that your hand does not block the sunlight. Notice the part of the object that is bright.

Observe and Think
How does the sunlight on the object compare with the light on the Moon?

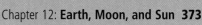

NSTA
scilinks.org
SCI
LINKS

The Moon **Code: MDL058**

Getting Ready to Learn

◀ CONCEPT REVIEW

- The sky seems to turn as Earth rotates.
- The motions of nearby space objects are visible from Earth.
- Light and other radiation carry information about space.

◀ VOCABULARY REVIEW

force p. 41

gravity p. 71

mass *see glossary*

CONTENT REVIEW
CLASSZONE.COM

Review concepts and vocabulary.

▶ TAKING NOTES

COMBINATION NOTES

To take notes about a new concept, first make an informal outline of the information. Then make a sketch of the concept and label it so you can study it later.

VOCABULARY STRATEGY

Write each new vocabulary term in the center of a **frame game** diagram. Decide what information to frame the term with. Use examples, descriptions, pictures, or sentences in which the term is used in context. You can change the frame to fit each term.

See the Note-Taking Handbook on pages R45–R51.

SCIENCE NOTEBOOK

NOTES

Constellations
- A group of stars that form a pattern in the sky.
  - Sky is divided into 88 areas named for constellations.
  - Ancient Greeks named constellations after animals and imaginary beings.
- Stars in constellations are not close together.
  - Stars in constellations appear close together when viewed from Earth.

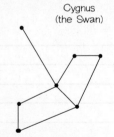

Cygnus (the Swan)

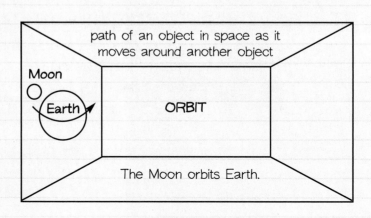

path of an object in space as it moves around another object

Moon

Earth

ORBIT

The Moon orbits Earth.

12.1

Some space objects are visible to the human eye.

CALIFORNIA
Content Standard

8.2.g Students know the role of gravity in forming and maintaining the shapes of planets, stars, and the solar system.

8.4.e Students know the appearance, general composition, relative position and size, and motion of objects in the solar system, including planets, planetary satellites, comets, and asteroids.

VOCABULARY

orbit p. 376
solar system p. 376
galaxy p. 376
universe p. 376
constellation p. 378

◀ BEFORE, you learned

- Earth is one of nine planets that orbit the Sun
- The Moon orbits Earth
- Earth turns on its axis every 24 hours

▶ NOW, you will learn

- How the universe is arranged
- How stars form patterns in the sky
- How the motions of bodies in space appear from Earth

EXPLORE Distance (8.4.e)

How far is the Moon from Earth?

PROCEDURE

1. Tie one end of the string around the middle of the tennis ball. The tennis ball will represent Earth.

2. Wrap the string 9.5 times around the tennis ball, and make a mark on the string at that point. Wrap the aluminum foil into a ball around the mark. The foil ball will represent the Moon.

3. Stretch out the string to put the model Moon and Earth at the right distance compared to their sizes.

WHAT DO YOU THINK?

- How does the scale model compare with your previous idea of the distance between Earth and the Moon?
- How many Earths do you estimate would fit between Earth and the Moon?

MATERIALS

- tennis ball
- aluminum foil (5 cm strip)
- string (250 cm)
- felt marker

We see patterns in the universe.

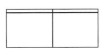

COMBINATION NOTES
Remember to take notes and make diagrams when you read about new ideas and terms.

For most of history, people had very limited knowledge of space. They saw planets and stars as points of light in the night sky. However, they did not know how far those bodies were from Earth or from each other. Early observers made guesses about planets and stars on the basis of their appearance and the ways they seemed to move in the sky. Different peoples around the world connected the patterns they saw in the sky with stories about imaginary beings.

We still have much to learn about the universe. Within the last few hundred years, however, new tools and scientific theories have greatly increased our knowledge. In this chapter you will learn about the arrangement of planets and stars. You will also learn about the ways in which astronomers explore and study space.

Arrangement of the Universe

If you look up at the sky on a clear night, you will see only a tiny fraction of the planets and stars that exist. The number of objects in the universe and the distances between them are greater than most people can imagine. Yet these objects are not spread around randomly. Gravity causes objects in space to be grouped together in different ways.

The images on page 377 show some basic structures in the universe. Like a camera lens zooming out, the images provide views of space at different levels of size.

The images on page 377

1 Earth Our planet's diameter is about 13,000 kilometers (8000 mi). This is almost four times the diameter of the Moon, which orbits Earth. An **orbit** is the path of an object in space as it moves around another object because of gravity.

2 Solar System Earth and eight other major planets orbit the Sun. The Sun, the planets, and various smaller bodies make up the **solar system.** The Sun is about 100 times greater in diameter than Earth. You could fit more than 4000 bodies the size of the Sun between the Sun and the solar system's outermost planet at its average distance from the Sun. The Sun is one of countless stars in space. Astronomers have detected planets orbiting some of these other stars.

3 The Milky Way Our solar system and the stars you can see with your bare eyes are part of a galaxy called the Milky Way. A **galaxy** is a group of millions or billions of stars held together by their own gravity. Most stars in the Milky Way are so far away that our galaxy appears to us as a hazy band of light.

4 The Universe The **universe** is everything—space and all the matter and energy in it. The Milky Way is just one of many billions of galaxies in the universe. These galaxies extend in all directions.

Astronomers study space at each of these different levels. Some focus on planets in the solar system. Other astronomers study distant galaxies. To learn how the universe formed, astronomers even study the smallest particles that make up all matter.

READING TiP

The word *orbit* can be a noun or a verb.

READING TiP

It is often hard to imagine what distances in space are like. If the solar system were the size of a penny, the length of the Milky Way would be roughly the length of California.

CHECK YOUR READING What is the relationship between the solar system and the Milky Way?

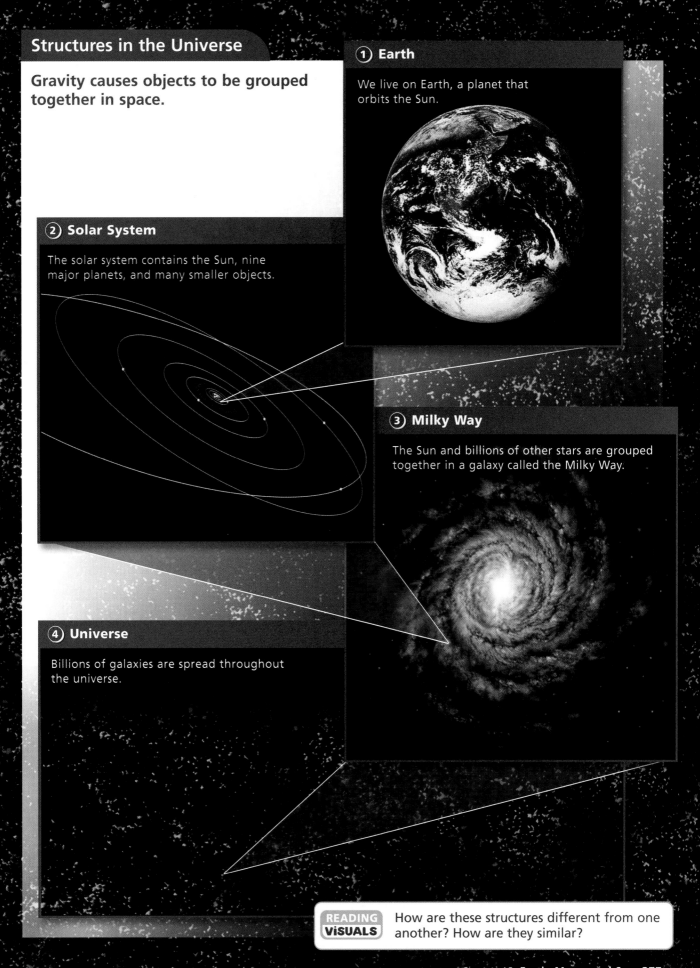

Structures in the Universe

Gravity causes objects to be grouped together in space.

① Earth

We live on Earth, a planet that orbits the Sun.

② Solar System

The solar system contains the Sun, nine major planets, and many smaller objects.

③ Milky Way

The Sun and billions of other stars are grouped together in a galaxy called the Milky Way.

④ Universe

Billions of galaxies are spread throughout the universe.

READING VISUALS How are these structures different from one another? How are they similar?

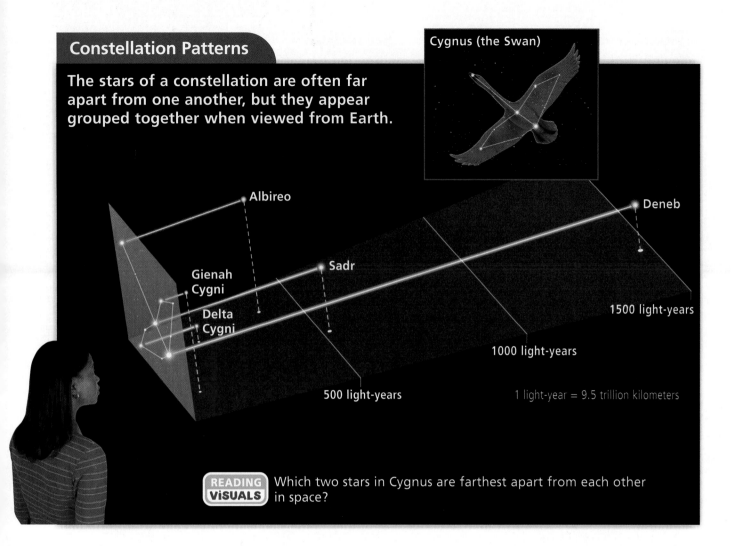

Constellation Patterns

The stars of a constellation are often far apart from one another, but they appear grouped together when viewed from Earth.

Cygnus (the Swan)

Albireo

Deneb

Gienah Cygni

Sadr

Delta Cygni

1500 light-years

1000 light-years

500 light-years

1 light-year = 9.5 trillion kilometers

READING VISUALS Which two stars in Cygnus are farthest apart from each other in space?

Constellations

VISUALIZATION
CLASSZONE.COM

View images of the night sky taken throughout the year.

If you want to find a particular place in the United States, it helps to know the name of the state it is in. Astronomers use a similar system to describe the locations of objects in the sky. They have divided the sky into 88 areas named for the constellations.

A **constellation** is a group of stars that form a pattern in the sky. In the constellation Cygnus, for example, a group of bright stars form the shape of a flying swan. Any other objects in that area of the sky, such as galaxies, are said to be located in Cygnus, even if they are not parts of the swan pattern. The ancient Greeks named many of the constellations for animals and imaginary beings.

Unlike the planets in the solar system, the stars in a constellation are usually not really close to each other. They seem to be grouped together when viewed from Earth. But as the illustration above shows, you would not see the same pattern in the stars if you viewed them from another angle.

CHECK YOUR READING What relationship exists among the stars in a constellation?

The sky seems to turn as Earth rotates.

You cannot see all of the constellations at once, because Earth blocks half of space from your view. However, you can see a parade of constellations each night as Earth rotates. As some constellations slowly come into view over the eastern horizon, others pass high in the sky above you, and still others set at the western horizon. Throughout the ages, many peoples have observed these changes and used them to help in navigation and measuring time.

If you extended the North Pole into space, it would point almost exactly to a star called Polaris, or the North Star. If you were standing at the North Pole, Polaris would be directly over your head. As Earth rotates through the night, the stars close to Polaris seem to move in circles around it. Although not the brightest star in the sky, Polaris is fairly bright and easy to find. You can use Polaris to figure out direction and location.

The stars in this image were photographed over several hours to show how they move across the night sky. The person was photographed just once.

 CHECK YOUR READING What causes constellations to change positions during the night?

INVESTIGATE Constellation Positions

How does time of day affect the positions of constellations?

PROCEDURE

1. Cut out both diagrams on the Constellation Wheel Sheet and assemble them as shown.

2. Rotate the wheel so that the current month is aligned with 9 P.M. Observe the positions of the constellations.

3. Align the current month with other times to determine how the positions of the constellations change during the night.

WHAT DO YOU THINK?

- How do the positions of the constellations change during the night?

- In which direction does the northern sky seem to turn?

CHALLENGE Earth's rotation makes the sky seem to turn. What does the model tell you about the direction of Earth's rotation?

SKILL FOCUS
Analyzing (8.4.e)

MATERIALS
- Constellation Wheel Sheet
- scissors
- brass fastener

TIME
20 minutes

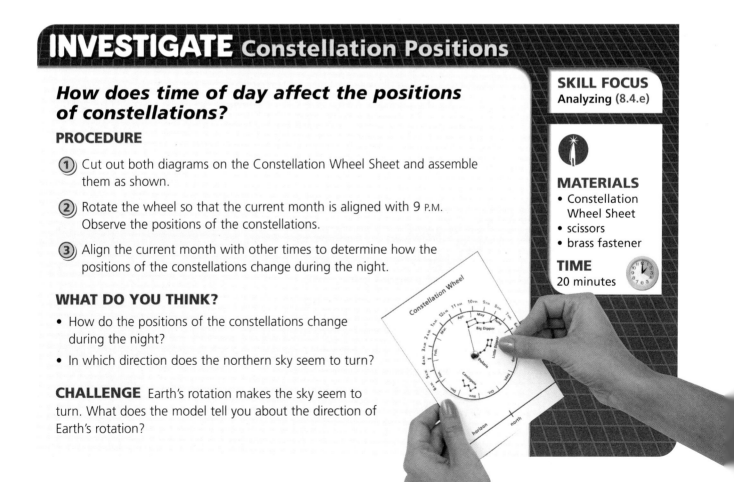

The movements of planets and other nearby objects are visible from Earth.

A jet plane travels at a greater speed and altitude than a bird. Yet if a bird and a plane flew overhead at the same time, you might think that the bird was faster. You would have this impression because the farther away a moving object is from you, the less it seems to move.

Stars are always moving, but they are so far away that you cannot see their movements. Observers have seen the same constellation patterns for thousands of years. Only over a much longer period does the motion of stars gradually change constellation patterns.

By contrast, the Moon moves across the star background a distance equal to its width every hour as it orbits Earth. The Moon is our closest neighbor. The planets are farther away, but you can see their gradual movements among the constellations over a period of weeks or months.

Planet comes from a Greek word that means "wanderer." Ancient Greek astronomers used this term because they noticed that planets move among the constellations. It is easiest to see the movements of Venus and Mars, the two planets closest to Earth. They change their positions in the sky from night to night.

The apparent movement of the sky led early astronomers to believe that Earth was at the center of the universe. Later astronomers discovered that Earth and the other planets orbit the Sun. The time-line on pages 446–449 introduces some of the astronomers who helped discover how planets really move in the solar system.

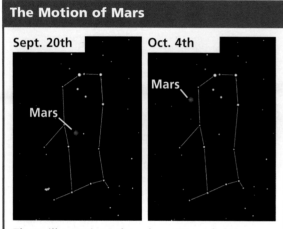

The Motion of Mars

Sept. 20th | Oct. 4th

Mars | Mars

These illustrations show how Mars changes positions in the constellation Gemini over a period of two weeks.

12.1 Review

KEY CONCEPTS

1. What are the basic structures in which objects are grouped together in space? (8.2.g)
2. What is an orbit? (8.2.g)
3. How does Earth's rotation affect our view of stars? (8.2.g)

CRITICAL THINKING

4. **Compare and Contrast** How is the grouping of stars in a constellation different from the grouping of planets in the solar system?

5. **Apply** The planet Jupiter is farther than Mars from Earth. Which planet seems to move faster when viewed from Earth? Explain.

○ CHALLENGE

6. **Predict** Suppose that you are standing at the North Pole on a dark night. If you keep turning clockwise at the same speed as Earth's rotation, how would your movement affect your view of the stars?

12.2 Earth rotates on a tilted axis and orbits the Sun.

CALIFORNIA
Content Standards

8.4.d Students know that stars are the source of light for all bright objects in outer space and that the Moon and planets shine by reflected sunlight, not by their own light.

8.4.e Students know the appearance, general composition, relative position and size, and motion of objects in the solar system, including planets, planetary satellites, comets, and asteroids.

BEFORE, you learned

- Stars seem to rise, cross the sky, and set because Earth turns
- The Sun is very large and far from Earth
- Earth orbits the Sun

NOW, you will learn

- Why Earth has day and night
- How the changing angles of sunlight produce seasons

VOCABULARY

axis of rotation p. 382
revolution p. 383
season p. 384
equinox p. 384
solstice p. 384

THINK ABOUT

When is sunset?

Suppose you were watching the Sun set. Would someone in New York be watching the Sun set at the same time? What about people in Africa? When the Sun sets in California, it is already dark in New York. For people in Africa, it is already past midnight.

Earth's rotation causes day and night.

When astronauts explored the Moon, they felt the Moon's gravity pulling them down. Their usual "down"—Earth—was up in the Moon's sky.

As you read this book, it is easy to tell which way is down. But is down in the same direction for a person on the other side of Earth? If you both pointed down, you would be pointing toward each other. Earth's gravity pulls objects toward the center of Earth. No matter where you stand on Earth, the direction of down will be toward Earth's center. There is no bottom or top. Up is out toward space, and down is toward the center of the planet.

As Earth turns, so do you. You keep the same position with respect to what is below your feet, but the view above your head changes.

 CHECK YOUR READING In what direction does gravity pull objects near Earth?

The directions north, south, east, and west are based on the way the planet rotates, or turns. Earth rotates around an imaginary line running through its center called an **axis of rotation.** The ends of the axis are the north and south poles. Any location on the surface moves from west to east as Earth turns. If you extend your right thumb and pretend its tip is the North Pole, then your fingers curve the way Earth rotates.

At any one time, about half of Earth is in sunlight and half is dark. However, Earth turns on its axis in 24 hours, so locations move through the light and darkness in that time. When a location is in sunlight, it is daytime there. When a location is in the middle of the sunlit side, it is noon. When a location is in darkness, it is night there, and when the location is in the middle of the unlit side, it is midnight.

The globe and the flat map show the progress of daylight across Earth in two ways. This location is experiencing sunrise.

noon

night moves westward

midnight

○ **CHECK YOUR READING** If it is noon at one location, what time is it at a location directly on the other side of Earth?

INVESTIGATE Rotation

What causes day and night?

In this model the lamp represents the Sun, and your head represents Earth. The North Pole is at the top of your head. You will need to imagine locations on your head as if your head were a globe.

PROCEDURE

1. Face the lamp and hold your hands to your face as shown in the photograph. Your hands mark the horizon. For a person located at your nose, the Sun would be high in the sky. It would be noon.

2. Face away from the lamp. Determine what time it would be at your nose.

3. Turn to your left until you see the lamp along your left hand.

4. Continue turning to the left, through noon, until you just stop seeing the lamp.

WHAT DO YOU THINK?

- What times was it at your nose in steps 2, 3, and 4?
- When you face the lamp, what time is it at your right ear?

CHALLENGE How can a cloud be bright even when it is dark on the ground?

SKILL FOCUS
Making models
(8.4.e)

MATERIALS
lamp

TIME
15 minutes

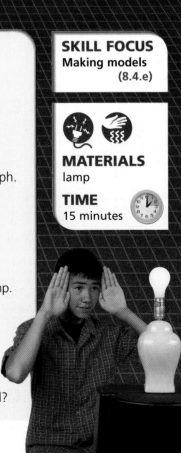

Earth's tilted axis and orbit cause seasons.

Just as gravity causes objects near Earth to be pulled toward Earth's center, it also causes Earth and other objects near the Sun to be pulled toward the Sun's center. Fortunately, Earth does not move straight into the Sun. Earth moves sideways, at nearly a right angle to the Sun's direction. Without the Sun's gravitational pull, Earth would keep moving in a straight line out into deep space. However, the Sun's pull changes Earth's path from a straight line to a round orbit about 300 million kilometers (200,000,000 mi) across.

Just as a day is the time it takes Earth to rotate once on its axis, a year is the time it takes Earth to orbit the Sun once. In astronomy, a **revolution** is the motion of one object around another. The word *revolution* can also mean the time it takes an object to go around once.

Earth's rotation and orbit do not quite line up. If they did, Earth's equator would be in the same plane as Earth's orbit, like a tiny hoop and a huge hoop lying on the same tabletop. Instead, Earth rotates at about a 23° angle, or tilt, from this lined-up position.

READING TiP

Use the second vowel in *rotate* and *revolve* to help you remember that an object rot**a**tes on its own **axis**, but rev**o**lves around another **object**.

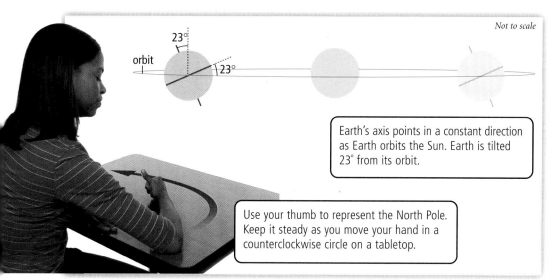

Not to scale

Earth's axis points in a constant direction as Earth orbits the Sun. Earth is tilted 23° from its orbit.

Use your thumb to represent the North Pole. Keep it steady as you move your hand in a counterclockwise circle on a tabletop.

As Earth moves, its axis always points in the same direction in space. You could model Earth's orbit by moving your right fist in a circle on a desktop. You would need to point your thumb toward your left shoulder and keep it pointing that way while moving your hand around the desktop.

Earth's orbit is not quite a perfect circle. In January, Earth is about 5 million kilometers closer to the Sun than it is in July. You may be surprised to learn that this distance makes only a tiny difference in temperatures on Earth. However, the combination of Earth's motion around the Sun with the tilt of Earth's axis does cause important changes of temperature. Turn the page to find out how.

July
153,000,000 km
148,000,000 km
January *Not to scale*

Earth's orbit is almost a circle. Earth's distance from the Sun varies by only about 5,000,000 km—about 3%—during a year.

Seasonal Patterns

Most locations on Earth experience **seasons,** patterns of temperature changes and other weather trends over the course of a year. Near the equator, the temperatures are almost the same year-round. Near the poles, there are very large changes in temperatures from winter to summer. The temperature changes occur because the amount of sunlight at each location changes during the year. The changes in the amount of sunlight are due to the tilt of Earth's axis.

Look at the diagram on page 385 to see how the constant direction of Earth's tilted axis affects the pattern of sunlight on Earth at different times of the year. As Earth travels around the Sun, the area of sunlight in each hemisphere changes. At an **equinox** (EE-kwuh-NAHKS), sunlight shines equally on the northern and southern hemispheres. Half of each hemisphere is lit, and half is in darkness. As Earth moves along its orbit, the light shifts more into one hemisphere than the other. At a **solstice** (SAHL-stihs), the area of sunlight is at a maximum in one hemisphere and a minimum in the other hemisphere. Equinoxes and solstices happen on or around the 21st days of certain months of the year.

1 **September Equinox** When Earth is in this position, sunlight shines equally on the two hemispheres. You can see in the diagram that the North Pole is at the border between light and dark. The September equinox marks the beginning of autumn in the Northern Hemisphere and of spring in the Southern Hemisphere.

2 **December Solstice** Three months later, Earth has traveled a quarter of the way around the Sun, but its axis still points in the same direction into space. The North Pole seems to lean away from the direction of the Sun. The solstice occurs when the pole leans as far away from the Sun as it will during the year. You can see that the North Pole is in complete darkness. At the same time, the opposite is true in the Southern Hemisphere. The South Pole seems to lean toward the Sun and is in sunlight. It is the Southern Hemisphere's summer solstice and the Northern Hemisphere's winter solstice.

3 **March Equinox** After another quarter of its orbit, Earth reaches another equinox. Half of each hemisphere is lit, and the sunlight is centered on the equator. You can see that the poles are again at the border between day and night.

4 **June Solstice** This position is opposite the December solstice. Earth's axis still points in the same direction, but now the North Pole seems to lean toward the Sun and is in sunlight. The June solstice marks the beginning of summer in the Northern Hemisphere. In contrast, it is the winter solstice in the Southern Hemisphere.

 CHECK YOUR READING In what month does winter begin in the Southern Hemisphere?

VOCABULARY
Remember to put each new term into a frame game diagram.

READING TiP
Equinox means "equal night"—daylight and night-time are equal in length.

READING TiP
The positions and lighting can be hard to imagine, so you might use a model as well as the diagram on the next page to help you understand.

Seasons

Earth's orbit and steady, tilted axis produce seasons.

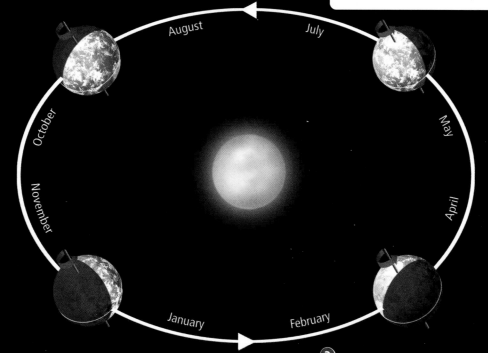

① September Equinox Half of the sunlight is in each hemisphere. The strongest sunlight is on the equator.

④ June Solstice More than half of the Northern Hemisphere is in sunlight. The strongest sunlight is north of the equator, so the Northern Hemisphere grows warmer.

August · July · October · May · November · April · January · February

Not to scale

② December Solstice Less than half of the Northern Hemisphere is in sunlight. The strongest sunlight is south of the equator, so the Southern Hemisphere grows warmer.

③ March Equinox Half of the sunlight is in each hemisphere. The strongest sunlight is on the equator.

View from the Sun

If you could stand on the Sun and look at Earth, you would see different parts of Earth at different times of year.

fall — spring
❶ September Equinox

winter — summer
❷ December Solstice

spring — fall
❸ March Equinox

summer — winter
❹ June Solstice

The equinoxes and solstices mark the beginnings of seasons in the two hemispheres. Warmer seasons occur when more of a hemisphere is in sunlight.

READING VISUALS Look at the poles to help you see how each hemisphere is lit. When is the South Pole completely in sunlight?

Angles of Sunlight

RESOURCE CENTER
CLASSZONE.COM

Learn more about seasons.

You have seen that seasons change as sunlight shifts between hemispheres during the year. On the ground, you notice the effects of seasons because the angle of sunlight and the length of daylight change over the year. The effects are greatest at locations far from the equator. You may have noticed that sunshine seems barely warm just before sunset, when the Sun is low in the sky. At noon the sunshine seems much hotter. The angle of light affects the temperature.

When the Sun is high in the sky, sunlight strikes the ground at close to a right angle. The energy of sunlight is concentrated. Shadows are short. You may get a sunburn quickly when the Sun is at a high angle. When the Sun is low in the sky, sunlight strikes the ground at a slant. The light is spread over a greater area, so it is less concentrated and produces long shadows. Slanted light warms the ground less.

Near the equator, the noonday Sun is almost overhead every day, so the ground is warmed strongly year-round. In the middle latitudes, the noon Sun is high in the sky only during part of the year. In winter the noon Sun is low and warms the ground less strongly.

 CHECK YOUR READING   How are temperatures throughout the year affected by the angles of sunlight?

Sun Height and Shadows

Winter Solstice, 12 P.M.

Winter shadows are long because sunlight is spread out. The Sun appears low in the sky even at noon.

location on Earth

Spring Equinox, 12 P.M.

Spring and fall shadows are of medium length, and the noon Sun appears higher in the sky.

Summer Solstice, 12 P.M.

Summer shadows are short because the light is concentrated in a small area. The noon Sun appears high in the sky.

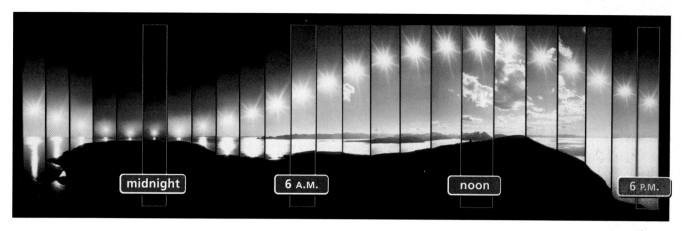

Lengths of Days

Seasonal temperatures depend on the amount of daylight, too. In Sacramento, for example, the summer Sun heats the ground for about 15 hours a day, but in winter there may be only 9 hours of sunlight each day. The farther you get from the equator, the more extreme the changes in day length become. As you near one of the poles, summer daylight may last for 20 hours or more.

Very close to the poles, the Sun does not set at all for six months at a time. It can be seen shining near the horizon at midnight. Tourists often travel far north just to experience the midnight Sun. At locations near a pole, the Sun sets on an equinox and then does not rise again for six months. Astronomers go to the South Pole in March to take advantage of the long winter night, which allows them to study objects in the sky without the interruption of daylight.

Very near the equator, the periods of daylight and darkness are almost equal year-round—each about 12 hours long. Visitors who are used to hot weather during long summer days might be surprised when a hot, sunny day ends suddenly at 6 P.M. At locations away from the equator, daylight lasts 12 hours only around the time of an equinox.

Near the pole in the summer, the Sun stays above the horizon, so there is no night. This series of photographs was taken over the course of a day.

12.2 Review

KEY CONCEPTS

1. What causes day and night? (8.4.e)

2. What happens to Earth's axis of rotation as Earth orbits the Sun? (8.4.e)

3. How do the areas of sunlight in the two hemispheres change over the year? (8.4.e)

CRITICAL THINKING

4. **Apply** If you wanted to enjoy longer periods of daylight in the summertime, would you head closer to the equator or farther from it? Why?

5. **Compare and Contrast** How do the average temperatures and the seasonal changes at the equator differ from those at the poles?

⬤ CHALLENGE

6. **Infer** If Earth's axis were tilted so much that the North Pole sometimes pointed straight at the Sun, how would the hours of daylight be affected at your location?

CHAPTER INVESTIGATION

Modeling Seasons

OVERVIEW AND PURPOSE Why is the weather in North America so much colder in January than in July? You might be surprised to learn that it has nothing to do with Earth's distance from the Sun. In fact, Earth is closest to the Sun in January. In this lab, you will model the cause of seasons as you
- orient a light source at different angles to a surface
- determine how the angles of sunlight at a location change as Earth orbits the Sun

▶ Problem
Write It Up

How does the angle of light affect the amount of solar energy a location receives at different times of year?

▶ Hypothesize
Write It Up

After performing step 3, write a hypothesis to explain how the angles of sunlight affect the amounts of solar energy your location receives at different times of year. Your hypothesis should take the form of an "If . . . , then . . . , because . . ." statement.

▶ Procedure

MATERIALS
- flashlight
- meter stick
- protractor
- globe
- stack of books
- sticky note

8.4.e, 8.9.a, 8.9.b

1. Set up the globe, books, and flashlight as shown in the photograph. Point the globe's North Pole to the right. This position represents solstice A.

2. Measure the distance between the books and the globe. Record this measurement in your notebook.

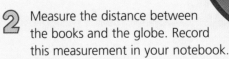
solstice A

3. Find your location on the globe. Place a folded sticky note onto the globe at your location as shown in the photograph. Rotate the globe on its axis until the note faces toward the flashlight.

light

steps 2–3

Content Standard
8.4.e Students know the appearance, general composition, relative position and size, and motion of objects in the solar system, including planets, planetary satellites, comets, and asteroids.

Investigation Standard
8.9.a Plan and conduct a scientific investigation to test a hypothesis.

4 The flashlight beam represents noonday sunlight at your location. Use the protractor to estimate the angle of the light on the surface. Also record how bright the light appears to be on the note.

5 Move the globe to the left side of the table and the flashlight and books to the right side of the table.

solstice B

6 Use the meter stick to position the globe so that it is the same distance from the books that you measured in step 2.

7 Point the North Pole to the right as shown in the photograph. This is solstice B.

8 Repeat step 4 for solstice B.

▶ Observe and Analyze
Write It Up

1. RECORD Draw the setup of your materials in each part of the investigation. Organize your notes.

2. COMPARE Compare the angles of light in steps 4 and 8. In which position was the angle of light closer to 90°?

3. EVALUATE At which angle did the light on the sticky note seem brightest?

▶ Conclude
Write It Up

1. EVALUATE How did the angle of sunlight at your location differ at the two times of year? At which position is sunlight more concentrated at your location?

2. SYNTHESIZE At which solstice did the sticky note receive more energy from the flashlight? Explain your reasoning.

3. APPLY The amount of solar energy at a location affects temperature. Which solstice—A or B—represents the summer solstice at your location?

4. INTERPRET Do your results support your hypothesis? Explain why or why not.

▶ INVESTIGATE Further

CHALLENGE What happens in the other hemisphere at the two times of year? Use the model to find out.

Modeling Seasons

Problem How does the angle of light affect the amount of solar energy a location receives at different times of year?

Hypothesize

Observe and Analyze

Distance between globe and books: _____ cm.

Table 1. Solstices A and B

	Solstice A	Solstice B
Drawing		
Angle of light (°)		
Observations		

The Moon is Earth's natural satellite.

CALIFORNIA
Content Standard

8.4.e Students know the appearance, general composition, relative position and size, and motion of objects in the solar system, including planets, planetary satellites, comets, and asteroids.

BEFORE, you learned

- Earth turns as it orbits the Sun
- The day side of Earth is the part in sunlight
- The Moon is the closest body to Earth

NOW, you will learn

- How the Moon moves
- What the Moon's dark-colored and light-colored features are
- About the inside structure of the Moon

VOCABULARY

mare p. 391

EXPLORE The Moon's Motion (8.4.e)

How much does the Moon turn?

PROCEDURE

1. Draw a circle to represent the Moon's orbit with Earth at the center. The compass represents the Moon.

2. Move the compass around the circle. Keep the side of the compass marked *E* always facing Earth.

3. Observe the positions of the *E* and the compass needle at several positions on the circle.

WHAT DO YOU THINK?
What does the model tell you about the Moon's motion?

MATERIALS
- paper
- magnetic compass

The Moon rotates as it orbits Earth.

When you look at the disk of the Moon, you may notice darker and lighter areas. Perhaps you have imagined them as features of a face or some other pattern. People around the world have told stories about the animals, people, and objects they have imagined while looking at the light and dark areas of the Moon. As you will read in this chapter, these areas tell a story to scientists as well.

The pull of gravity keeps the Moon, Earth's natural satellite, in orbit around Earth. Even though the Moon is Earth's closest neighbor in space, it is far away compared to the sizes of Earth and the Moon.

The Moon's diameter is about 1/4 Earth's diameter, and the Moon is about 30 Earth diameters away.

Earth   Moon

The distance between Earth and the Moon is roughly 380,000 kilometers (240,000 mi) —about a hundred times the distance between New York and Los Angeles. If a jet airliner could travel in space, it would take about 20 days to cover a distance that huge. Astronauts, whose spaceships traveled much faster than jets, needed about 3 days to reach the Moon.

You always see the same pattern of dark-colored and light-colored features on the Moon. Only this one side of the Moon can be seen from Earth. The reason is that the Moon, like many other moons in the solar system, always keeps one side turned toward its planet. This means that the Moon turns once on its own axis each time it orbits Earth.

 Why do you see only one side of the Moon?

The Moon's craters show its history.

The half of the Moon's surface that constantly faces Earth is called the near side. The half that faces away from Earth is called the far side. Much of the Moon's surface is light-colored. Within the light-colored areas are many small, round features. There are also dark-colored features, some of which cover large areas. Much of the near side of the Moon is covered with these dark-colored features. In contrast, the far side is mostly light-colored with just a few of the darker features.

Just as on Earth, features on the Moon are given names to make it easier to discuss them. The names of the larger surface features on the Moon are in the Latin language, because centuries ago scientists from many different countries used Latin to communicate with one another. Early astronomers thought that the dark areas might be bodies of water, so they used the Latin word for "sea." Today, a dark area on the Moon is still called a lunar **mare** (MAH-ray). The plural form is *maria* (MAH-ree-uh).

The maria are not bodies of water, however. All of the features that can be seen on the Moon are different types of solid or broken rock. The Moon has no air, no oceans, no clouds, and no life.

Moon

The side of the Moon that constantly faces Earth has large, dark areas called maria.

Mass 1% of Earth's mass
Diameter 27% of Earth's diameter
**Average distance
   from Earth** 380,000 km
Orbits in 27.3 Earth days
Rotates in 27.3 Earth days

READING TiP

Lunar means "having to do with the Moon." The word comes from *luna*, the Latin word for the Moon.

Craters and Maria

The light-colored areas of the Moon are higher—at greater altitudes—than the maria, so they are called the lunar highlands. The ground of the lunar highlands is rocky, and some places are covered with a powder made of finely broken rock.

The highlands have many round features, called impact craters, that formed when small objects from space hit the Moon's surface. Long ago, such collisions happened more often than they do today. Many impact craters marked the surfaces of the Moon, Earth, and other bodies in space. On Earth, however, most craters have been worn away by water and wind. On the dry, airless Moon, impact craters from a long time ago are still visible.

Long ago, some of the largest craters filled with molten rock, or lava, that came from beneath the Moon's surface. The lava filled the lowest areas and then cooled, forming the large, flat plains called maria. Smaller impacts have continued to occur, so the dark plains of the maria do contain some craters. Most of the large maria are on the near side of the Moon. However, the widest and deepest basin on the Moon is on the far side, near the Moon's south pole.

 CHECK YOUR READING How did the maria form? List the steps.

Lunar Map

Light-colored highlands and dark maria form a familiar pattern on the near side of the Moon and a very different pattern on the far side.

Near Side

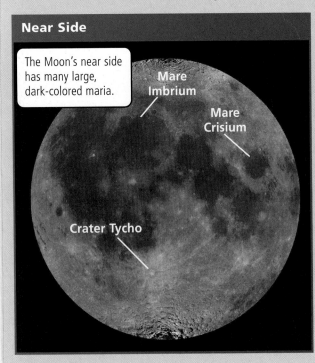

The Moon's near side has many large, dark-colored maria.

Mare Imbrium

Mare Crisium

Crater Tycho

Far Side

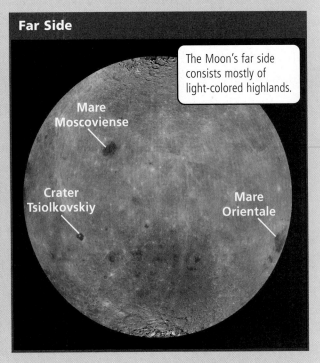

The Moon's far side consists mostly of light-colored highlands.

Mare Moscoviense

Crater Tsiolkovskiy

Mare Orientale

INVESTIGATE Moon Features

How did the Moon's features form?

In this model, you will use a paper towel to represent the Moon's surface and gelatin to represent molten rock from inside the Moon.

PROCEDURE

1. Pour about 1 cm of partly cooled liquid gelatin into the cup.

2. Hold the paper towel by bringing its corners together. Push the towel into the cup until the center of the towel touches the bottom of the cup. Open the towel slightly.

3. Place the cup in the bowl of ice, and allow the gelatin time to solidify.

WHAT DO YOU THINK?

- What part of the towel did the gelatin affect?
- When you look down into the cup, what can the smooth areas tell you about heights?

CHALLENGE Early astronomers thought there might be oceans on the Moon. How does your model lava resemble an ocean?

Moon Rocks

Moon rocks have different ages. Some of the surface rock of the Moon is about 4.5 billion years old—as old as the Moon itself. This very old rock is found in the lunar highlands. The rock in the maria is younger because it formed from lava that solidified later, 3.8–3.1 billion years ago. These two main types of rock and their broken pieces cover most of the Moon's surface. Astronauts explored the Moon and brought back samples of as many different types of material as they could.

Impacts from space objects leave craters, and they also break the surface material into smaller pieces. This breaking of material is called weathering, even though it is not caused by wind and water. Weathered material on the Moon forms a type of dry, lifeless soil. The lunar soil is more than 15 meters (50 ft) deep in some places. Impacts can also toss lunar soil into different places, compact it into new rocks, or melt it and turn it into a glassy type of rock.

The dark-colored rock that formed from lava is called basalt (buh-SAWLT). Lunar basalt is similar to the rock deep beneath Earth's oceans. The basalt of the lunar maria covers large areas but is often only a few hundred meters in depth. However, the basalt can be several kilometers deep at the center of a mare, a depth similar to that of Earth's oceans.

Almost 400 kg (weighing more than 800 lb) of Moon rocks and soil were collected and brought back to Earth by astronauts.

highland rock

basalt

The Moon has layers.

COMBINATION NOTES
Remember to take notes and make diagrams when you read about new ideas and terms.

Scientists on Earth have analyzed the lunar rocks and soil to determine their ages and materials. These results told scientists a story about how the Moon changed over time. During an early stage of the Moon's history, impacts happened often and left craters of many different sizes. That stage ended about 3.8 billion years ago, and impacts have happened much less often since then. The highland rocks and soil come from the original surface and impacts. Shortly after the impacts slowed, lava flooded the low-lying areas and formed the maria. Then the flooding stopped. During the last 3 billion years, the Moon has gained new impact craters from time to time but has remained mostly unchanged.

Structure

Scientists have used information from lunar rocks and other measurements to figure out what is inside the Moon. Beneath its thin coating of crushed rock, the Moon has three layers—a crust, a mantle, and a core. As on Earth, the crust is the outermost layer. It averages about 70 kilometers (about 40 mi) thick and contains the least dense type of rock.

The Moon's interior resembles Earth's interior in several ways.

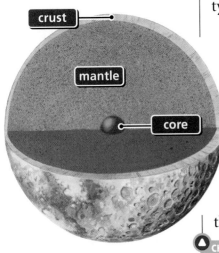

Beneath the crust is a thick mantle that makes up most of the Moon's volume. The mantle is made of dense types of rock that include the elements iron and magnesium. The basalt on the lunar surface contains these same elements, so scientists infer that the material of the basalt came from the mantle.

In the middle of the Moon is a small core, approximately 700 kilometers (400 mi) across. Although dense, it makes up only a tiny fraction of the Moon's mass. Scientists have less information about the core than the mantle because material from the core did not reach the Moon's surface. The core seems to consist of iron and other metals.

 CHECK YOUR READING What are your own questions about the Moon?

Formation

Scientists develop models to help them understand their observations, such as the observed similarities and differences between Earth and the Moon. The two objects have similar structures and are made of similar materials. However, the materials are in different proportions. The Moon has more materials like Earth's crust and mantle and less material like Earth's core.

Scientists have used these facts to develop models of how the Moon formed. A widely accepted model involves a giant collision, in which an early version of Earth was hit by a smaller space body.

Formation of the Moon

Collision	Re-Forming	Earth and Moon

An early version of Earth is struck by a slightly smaller space body.	The many pieces pull each other into orbits. Most of the material forms a new version of Earth.	The Moon forms from material that orbits the new version of Earth.

Much of the material from both bodies, especially the cores, combined to form a new version of Earth. The energy of the collision also threw material out, away from Earth. Bits of material from the crusts and mantles of both bodies went into orbit around the new Earth. Much of this orbiting material clumped together and became the Moon. Computer simulations of these events show that the Moon may have formed quickly—perhaps within just one year.

Evidence from fossils and rocks on Earth show that, whether the Moon formed from a giant collision or in some other way, it was once much closer to Earth than it is today. The Moon has been moving slowly away from Earth. It now moves 3.8 centimeters (1.5 in.) farther from Earth each year. However, this change is so slow that you will not notice any difference in your lifetime.

12.3 Review

KEY CONCEPTS

1. How many times does the Moon rotate on its axis during one trip around Earth? (8.4.e)

2. What are the dark spots and the light areas on the Moon called? (8.4.e)

3. Describe the Moon's layers. (8.4.e)

CRITICAL THINKING

4. **Compare and Contrast** How are the Moon's dark-colored areas different from its light-colored areas?

5. **Draw Conclusions** How have the Moon rocks that astronauts brought back to Earth helped scientists understand the history of the Moon?

⬥ CHALLENGE

6. **Analyze** Scientists use indirect methods to learn about the cores of Earth and the Moon. Imagine you have several Styrofoam balls, some with steel balls hidden inside. Without breaking a ball open, how might you tell whether it contains a steel ball?

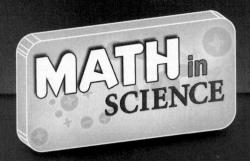

Graphing Sunlight

The location of the Moon and the Sun in the sky depend on your location on Earth and when you look. In summer, the noon Sun is at a greater angle above the horizon—closer to 90°—than it is in winter. In summer, the Sun rises earlier and sets later than in winter. Longer days and steeper angles of sunlight combine to make summer days much warmer than winter days. Plot the data for Washington, D.C. (latitude 39° N) to see the changing patterns of sunlight.

MATH TUTORIAL

CLASSZONE.COM

Click on Math Tutorial for more help with line graphs.

Math 7.SD.1.2
Science 8.4.e, 8.9.e

Washington, D.C.

Month	Sunlight Each Day (h)	Angle of Sun at Noon (°)
Jan.	9.9	31.4
Feb.	11.0	40.8
Mar.	12.2	51.6
Apr.	13.5	63.2
May	14.5	71.4
June	14.9	74.6
July	14.5	71.4
Aug.	13.5	63.0
Sept.	12.2	51.6
Oct.	11.0	40.2
Nov.	9.9	31.1
Dec.	9.5	27.7

This is a series of images of the Sun photographed at exactly the same time of day every few days over most of a year. The bottom of the photograph is from just one of the days and includes a stone circle calendar.

Example

You can make a double line graph to see patterns in the data. Use a colored pencil to label the second *y*-axis.

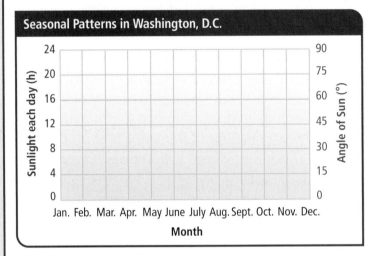

(1) Copy all three graph axes onto graph paper.

(2) Use the *y*-axis on the left to plot the data for the hours of daylight. Draw line segments to connect the points.

(3) Use the *y*-axis on the right and a colored pencil to plot the data for the angle of the Sun. Draw line segments to connect the points.

Answer the following questions.

1. During which time period do days get shorter?

2. About how many degrees higher in the sky is the noon Sun in June than in December? About how many more hours of sunlight are there each day in June than in December?

3. Does the angle of the Sun change more quickly between June and July or between September and October? How can you tell?

CHALLENGE Copy the axes again, then graph the data your teacher gives you for a location near the North Pole. Use your graphs to compare daylight patterns at the two latitudes.

Positions of the Sun and Moon affect Earth.

CALIFORNIA
Content Standards

8.4.d Students know that stars are the source of light for all bright objects in outer space and that the Moon and planets shine by reflected sunlight, not by their own light.

8.4.e Students know the appearance, general composition, relative position and size, and motion of objects in the solar system, including planets, planetary satellites, comets, and asteroids.

VOCABULARY

eclipse p. 401
umbra p. 401
penumbra p. 401

◀ BEFORE, you learned

- The Moon orbits Earth
- Sunlight shines on Earth and the Moon

▶ NOW, you will learn

- Why the Moon has phases
- What causes eclipses
- Why Earth's oceans have tides

THINK ABOUT

Have you seen the Moon in daylight?

Many people think that the Moon is visible only at night. This idea is not surprising, because the Moon is the brightest object in the sky at night. In the daytime the Moon is only as bright as a tiny, thin cloud. It is easy to miss, even in a cloudless blue sky. You can see the Moon sometimes in the daytime, sometimes at night, often at both times, and sometimes not at all. Why does the Moon sometimes disappear from view?

Phases are different views of the Moon's sunlit half.

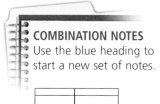

COMBINATION NOTES
Use the blue heading to start a new set of notes.

What you see as moonlight is really light from the Sun reflected by the Moon's surface. At any time, sunlight shines on half of the Moon's surface. Areas where sunlight does not reach look dark, just as the night side of Earth looks dark from space. As the Moon turns on its axis, areas on the surface move into and out of sunlight.

When you look at the Moon, you see a bright shape that is the lit part of the near side of the Moon. The unlit part is hard to see. Lunar phases are the patterns of lit and unlit portions of the Moon that you see from Earth. It takes about a month for the Moon to orbit Earth and go through all the phases.

 CHECK YOUR READING Why do you sometimes see only part of the near side of the Moon?

VISUALIZATION
CLASSZONE.COM

Explore lunar phases.

The Moon's position in its monthly orbit determines how it appears from Earth. The diagram on page 399 shows how the positions of the Moon, the Sun, and Earth affect the shapes you see in the sky.

Waxing Moon

First Week The cycle begins with a new moon. From Earth, the Moon and the Sun are in the same direction. If you face a new moon, you face the Sun. Your face and the far side of the Moon are in sunlight. The near side of the Moon is unlit, so you do not see it. During a new moon, there appears to be no Moon.

As the Moon moves along its orbit, sunlight begins falling on the near side. You see a thin crescent shape. During the first week, the Moon keeps moving farther around, so more of the near side becomes lit. You see thicker crescents as the Moon waxes, or grows.

Second Week When half of the near side of the Moon is in sunlight, the Moon has completed one-quarter of its cycle. The phase is called the first quarter, even though you might describe the shape as a half-moon. You can see in the diagram that the Moon is 90 degrees—at a right angle—from the Sun. If you face the first-quarter moon when it is high in the sky, sunlight will shine on the right side of your head and the right side of the Moon.

You see more of the Moon as it moves along its orbit during the second week. The phase is called gibbous (GIHB-uhs) when the near side is more than half lit but not fully lit. The Moon is still waxing, so the phases during the second week are called waxing gibbous moons.

 Why does the Moon sometimes seem to have a crescent shape?

Waning Moon

Third Week Halfway through its cycle, the whole near side of the Moon is in sunlight—a full moon. You might think of it as the second quarter. Viewed from Earth, the Moon and the Sun are in opposite directions. If you face a full moon at sunset, sunlight from behind you lights the back of your head and the near side of the Moon.

As the Moon continues around during the third week, less and less of the near side is in sunlight. The Moon seems to shrink, or wane, so these phases are called waning gibbous moons.

Fourth Week When the near side is again only half in sunlight, the Moon is three-quarters of the way through its cycle. The phase is called the third quarter. The Moon is again 90 degrees from the Sun. If you face the third-quarter moon when it is high in the sky, sunlight will shine on the left side of your head and the left side of the Moon.

READING TiP

Use the black dashed lines at each position in the diagram on page 399 to determine what part of the Moon is visible from Earth.

READING TiP

Crescent and *gibbous* describe the shape, while *waxing* and *waning* describe the changes— growing or shrinking.

The appearance of the Moon depends on the positions of the Sun, Moon, and Earth.

If you could watch the Moon from high above its pole, you would always see half the Moon in sunlight and half in darkness.

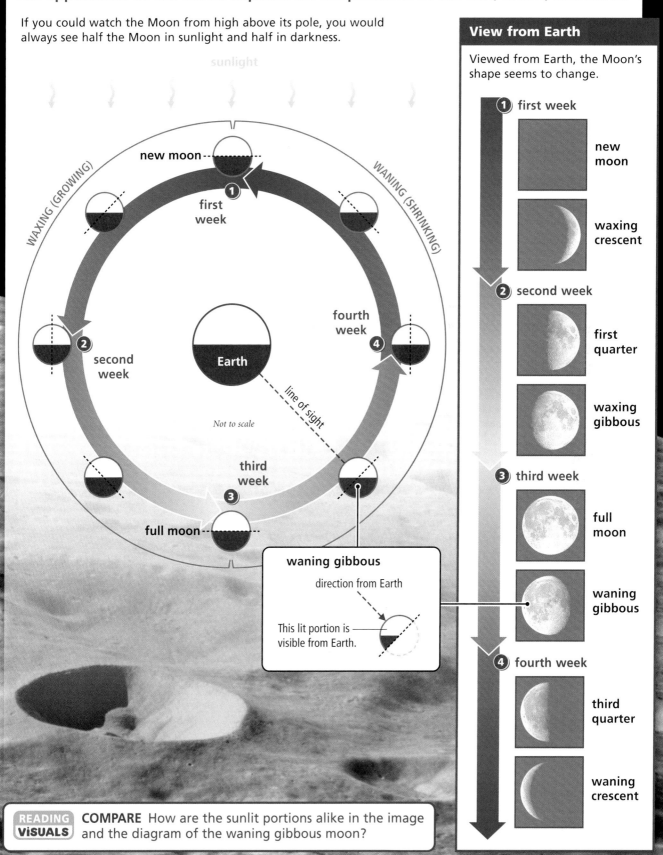

sunlight

WAXING (GROWING)

WANING (SHRINKING)

new moon

first week

①

second week

②

Earth

Not to scale

line of sight

fourth week

④

third week

③

full moon

waning gibbous

direction from Earth

This lit portion is visible from Earth.

View from Earth

Viewed from Earth, the Moon's shape seems to change.

① **first week**

new moon

waxing crescent

② **second week**

first quarter

waxing gibbous

③ **third week**

full moon

waning gibbous

④ **fourth week**

third quarter

waning crescent

READING VISUALS **COMPARE** How are the sunlit portions alike in the image and the diagram of the waning gibbous moon?

As the Moon continues to move around Earth during the fourth week, less and less of the near side is in sunlight. The waning crescent moon grows thinner and thinner. At the end of the fourth week, the near side is again unlit, and the new moon begins a new cycle.

Crescent and Gibbous Moons

Think through the waxing lunar phases again. The Moon waxes from new to crescent to gibbous during the first half of its cycle. Then it wanes from full to gibbous to crescent during the second half of its cycle.

The amount of the Moon that you see from Earth depends on the angle between the Moon and the Sun. When this angle is small, you see only a small amount of the Moon. Crescent moons occur when the Moon appears close to the Sun in the sky. As a result, they are visible most often in the daytime or around the time of sunrise or sunset. When the angle between the Sun and the Moon is large, you see a large amount of the Moon. Gibbous and full moons appear far from the Sun in the sky. You may see them in the daytime, but you are more likely to notice them at night.

 CHECK YOUR READING What shape does the Moon appear to be when it is at a small angle to the Sun?

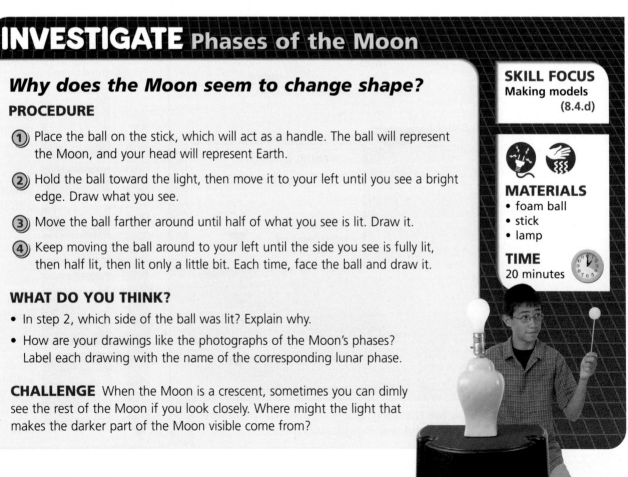

INVESTIGATE Phases of the Moon

Why does the Moon seem to change shape?

PROCEDURE

1. Place the ball on the stick, which will act as a handle. The ball will represent the Moon, and your head will represent Earth.

2. Hold the ball toward the light, then move it to your left until you see a bright edge. Draw what you see.

3. Move the ball farther around until half of what you see is lit. Draw it.

4. Keep moving the ball around to your left until the side you see is fully lit, then half lit, then lit only a little bit. Each time, face the ball and draw it.

WHAT DO YOU THINK?

- In step 2, which side of the ball was lit? Explain why.
- How are your drawings like the photographs of the Moon's phases? Label each drawing with the name of the corresponding lunar phase.

CHALLENGE When the Moon is a crescent, sometimes you can dimly see the rest of the Moon if you look closely. Where might the light that makes the darker part of the Moon visible come from?

SKILL FOCUS
Making models
(8.4.d)

MATERIALS
- foam ball
- stick
- lamp

TIME
20 minutes

Shadows in space cause eclipses.

Sunlight streams past Earth and the Moon, lighting one side of each body. Beyond each body is a long, thin cone of darkness where no sunlight reaches—a shadow in space. The two bodies are far apart, so they usually miss each other's shadow as the Moon orbits Earth. However, if the Moon, the Sun, and Earth line up exactly, a shadow crosses Earth or the Moon. An **eclipse** occurs when a shadow makes the Sun or the Moon seem to grow dark. In a lunar eclipse, the Moon darkens. In a solar eclipse, the Sun seems to darken.

VOCABULARY
Remember to record vocabulary terms.

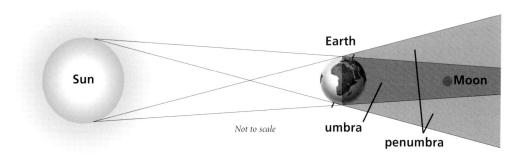

Sun

Earth

Moon

Not to scale

umbra

penumbra

Lunar Eclipses

The Moon becomes dark during a lunar eclipse because it passes through Earth's shadow. There are two parts of Earth's shadow, as you can see in the diagram above. The **umbra** is the darkest part. Around it is a spreading cone of lighter shadow called the **penumbra.**

Just before a lunar eclipse, sunlight streaming past Earth produces a full moon. Then the Moon moves into Earth's penumbra and becomes slightly less bright. As the Moon moves into the umbra, Earth's dark shadow seems to creep across and cover the Moon. The entire Moon can be in darkness because the Moon is small enough to fit entirely within Earth's umbra. After an hour or more, the Moon moves slowly back into the sunlight that is streaming past Earth.

A total lunar eclipse occurs when the Moon passes completely into Earth's umbra. If the Moon misses part or all of the umbra, part of the Moon stays light and the eclipse is called a partial lunar eclipse.

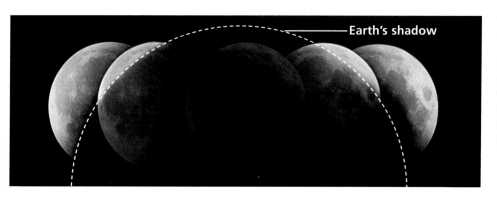

Earth's shadow

The Moon starts getting dark on one side as it passes into Earth's umbra. Even when the Moon is completely within Earth's umbra, some red sunlight, bent by Earth's atmosphere, may still reach the Moon.

Solar Eclipses

In a solar eclipse, the Sun seems to darken because the Moon's shadow falls onto part of Earth. Imagine that you are in the path of a solar eclipse. At first, you see a normal day. You cannot see the dark Moon moving toward the Sun. Then part of the Sun seems to disappear as the Moon moves in front of it. You are in the Moon's penumbra. After several hours of growing darkness, the Moon covers the Sun's disk completely. The sky becomes as dark as night, and you may see constellations. In place of the Sun is a black disk—the new moon— surrounded by a pale glow. You are in the Moon's umbra, the darkest part of the shadow, experiencing a total solar eclipse. After perhaps a minute, the Sun's bright surface starts to appear again.

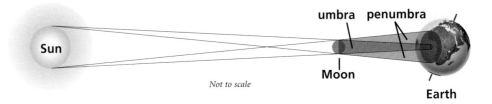

Not to scale

A solar eclipse occurs when the Moon passes directly between Earth and the Sun. As you can see in the diagram above, the side of the Moon that faces Earth is unlit, so solar eclipses occur only during new moons.

If you could watch a solar eclipse from space, it might seem more like a lunar eclipse. You would see the Moon's penumbra, with the dark umbra in the center, move across Earth's daylight side. However, the Moon is smaller than Earth, so it casts a smaller shadow. As you can see in the diagram above, the Moon's umbra covers only a fraction of Earth's surface at a time.

June 21, 2001, Eclipse

total eclipse

This time-lapse photograph shows the Sun's path. The new moon is not visible. When the Sun is directly behind the Moon, the sky is dark enough for you to see the Sun's corona around the Moon.

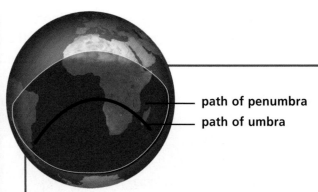

path of penumbra
path of umbra

Path of June 21, 2001, Eclipse Only locations along the thin central path of the shadow experience a total eclipse. Other locations experience a partial eclipse.

Only locations in the path of the Moon's shadow experience a solar eclipse. Some people travel thousands of miles to be in the thin path of the Moon's umbra so that they can experience a total solar eclipse. Locations near the path of the umbra get an eclipse that is less than total. If only the penumbra moves over your location, you experience a partial solar eclipse. The Moon covers just part of the Sun.

Bright light from the Sun's disk can damage your eyes if you look directly at it. The Sun is unsafe to look at even when the Moon covers most of the Sun's disk. If you have the chance to experience a solar eclipse, use a safe method to view the Sun.

 CHECK YOUR READING Where is the Moon during a solar eclipse? Find a way to remember the difference between the two types of eclipses.

COMBINATION NOTES
Remember to make notes about new ideas.

The Moon's gravity causes tides on Earth.

If you have spent time near an ocean, you may have experienced the usual pattern of tides. At first, you might see dry sand that slopes down to the ocean. Then, waves creep higher and higher onto the sand. The average water level rises slowly for about 6 hours. The highest level is called high tide. Then the water level slowly drops for about 6 hours. The lowest level is called low tide. Then the water level rises and falls again. The entire pattern—two high tides and two low tides—takes a little more than 24 hours.

CHECK YOUR READING How many high tides do you expect per day?

In areas with tides, the water generally reaches its lowest level twice a day and its highest level twice a day.

Tides occur because the Moon's gravity changes the shape of Earth's oceans. The Moon pulls on different parts of Earth with different amounts of force. It pulls hardest on the side of Earth nearest it, a little less hard on the center of Earth, and even less hard on the farthest side of Earth. If Earth were flexible, it would be pulled into a football shape. Earth's crust is hard enough to resist being pulled into a different shape, but Earth's oceans do change shape.

Cause of Tides

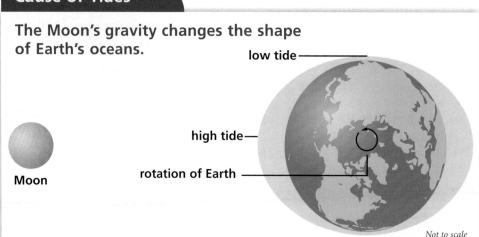

The Moon's gravity changes the shape of Earth's oceans.

low tide

high tide

rotation of Earth

Moon

Not to scale

The diagram above shows what would happen if Earth were covered with a thick layer of water. The Moon's pull produces a bulge of thicker ocean water on the side of Earth nearest the Moon. Another bulge of water is produced on the side of Earth farthest from the Moon because the Moon pulls the center of Earth away from that side. The layer of water is thinnest in the middle, between the bulges.

A location moves past different thicknesses of water as Earth turns on its axis. As a result, the water level there rises and falls. The thickest water produces the highest level, which is high tide. A quarter of a rotation—6 hours—later, the location has moved to the thinnest layer of water, or low tide. Another high tide and low tide complete the cycle. Because the Moon is orbiting while Earth is turning, the cycle takes a little longer than the 24 hours in a day.

 Why does a cycle of tides take about 24 hours?

12.4 Review

KEY CONCEPTS

1. When the Moon is full, where is it in its orbit around Earth? (8.4.e)

2. Where is the Moon in its orbit at the time of a solar eclipse? (8.4.e)

3. If it is high tide where you are, is the tide high or low on the side of Earth directly opposite you? (8.4.e)

CRITICAL THINKING

4. **Apply** If you were on the Moon's near side during a new moon, how much of the side of Earth facing you would be sunlit?

5. **Predict** If Earth did not turn, how would the pattern of tides be affected?

◐ CHALLENGE

6. **Predict** Would we see lunar phases if the Moon did not rotate while it orbits Earth?

A View of Space

> 8.4.a Students know galaxies are clusters of billions of stars and may have different shapes.

In 1904 George Ellery Hale decided to build a telescope near Los Angeles. He chose Mt. Wilson because it was remote and the skies were clear most of the year. Hale used mules to haul tons of parts up the mountain. In 1917 at 3 A.M. on a clear California night, he finally looked through the completed telescope. He saw the clearest view any human had ever had of our galaxy. A new era of astronomical discovery had begun.

Years of Discovery

Until the mid-1950s, Mt. Wilson had the two largest telescopes in the world. With these telescopes, astronomers and students studied the universe. At Mt. Wilson, Edwin Hubble found a way to measure the distances of cloudlike structures in the night sky. He discovered these structures were much too far away to be in the Milky Way. They were, instead, other galaxies similar to our own Milky Way. In the late 1920s, Hubble concluded that these other galaxies are moving away from ours. Hubble's observations and conclusions were revolutionary. His work provided the first pieces of evidence showing that the universe originated as a single point and is expanding.

Edwin Hubble explored the universe through Mt. Wilson's 100-inch telescope.

The Hooker 100-inch telescope is named after John D. Hooker. It was the largest telescope in the world from 1917 to 1948.

Changing Times

By the end of World War II, Los Angeles was a large city. Light from the city made certain types of observations difficult. Astronomers call this problem light pollution. To see into deep space, scientists use more remote observatories in Chile and Hawaii. They also use the Hubble telescope, an orbiting telescope named after Edwin Hubble. However, the observatory at Mt. Wilson is still used to study the Sun and closer planets. The telescopes there are also used for types of astronomy that light pollution affects much less.

WRITE ABOUT SCIENCE

Choose one of these scientists to learn more about: George Ellery Hale, Edwin Hubble, Harlow Shapely, Walter Baade, Olin Wilson. Write a paper that tells what the scientist discovered. Describe how the Mt. Wilson Observatory helped the atronomer in his work.

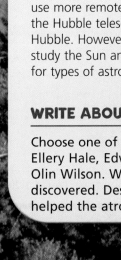

Chapter Review

the BIG idea

Earth and the Moon move in predictable ways as they orbit the Sun.

CONTENT REVIEW
CLASSZONE.COM

◀ KEY CONCEPTS SUMMARY

---

1 Some space objects are visible to the human eye.

- Gravity causes objects in space to be grouped together in different ways.
- Stars form patterns in the sky.
- The sky seems to turn as Earth rotates.

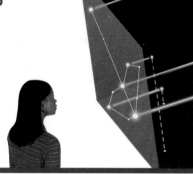

VOCABULARY
orbit p. 376
solar system p. 376
galaxy p. 376
universe p. 376
constellation p. 378

---

2 Earth rotates on a tilted axis and orbits the Sun.

Earth's rotation in sunlight causes day and night.

The changing angle of sunlight on Earth causes seasons.

VOCABULARY
axis of rotation p. 382
revolution p. 383
season p. 384
equinox p. 384
solstice p. 384

---

3 The Moon is Earth's natural satellite.

Dark-colored maria formed from lava-filled craters.

Light-colored highlands are old and cratered.

The Moon's near side always faces Earth.

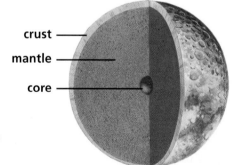

crust
mantle
core

VOCABULARY
mare p. 391

---

4 Positions of the Sun and Moon affect Earth.

Lunar phases are different views of the Moon's sunlit half.

The Moon's gravity causes tides as Earth turns.

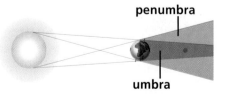

penumbra
umbra

Shadows cause eclipses.

VOCABULARY
eclipse p. 401
umbra p. 401
penumbra p. 401

Reviewing Vocabulary

Use words and diagrams to show the relationship between the terms in each the following pairs. Underline the two terms in each answer.

1. revolution, rotation

2. revolution, season

3. solstice, equinox

4. mare, impact crater

5. eclipse, umbra

6. umbra, penumbra

Reviewing Key Concepts

Multiple Choice *Choose the letter of the best answer.*

7. How long does it take Earth to turn once on its axis of rotation? (8.4.e)
   - **a.** an hour
   - **b.** a day
   - **c.** a month
   - **d.** a year

8. How long does it take Earth to orbit the Sun? (8.4.e)
   - **a.** an hour
   - **b.** a day
   - **c.** a month
   - **d.** a year

9. About how long does it take the Moon to revolve once around Earth? (8.4.e)
   - **a.** an hour
   - **b.** a day
   - **c.** a month
   - **d.** a year

10. It is hotter in summer than in winter because in Summer (8.4.e)
    - **a.** Earth gets closer to the Sun
    - **b.** sunlight strikes the ground at higher angles
    - **c.** Earth turns faster
    - **d.** Earth revolves around the Sun more times

11. Examples of basic structures in the universe include (8.2.g)
    - **a.** the Milky Way
    - **b.** Earth
    - **c.** the solar system
    - **d.** all of the above

12. The lunar highlands have more impact craters than the maria, so scientists know that the highlands (8.4.e)
    - **a.** are older than the maria
    - **b.** are younger than the maria
    - **c.** are flatter than the maria
    - **d.** are darker than the maria

13. Why is just one side of the Moon visible from Earth? (8.4.e)
    - **a.** The Moon does not rotate on its axis as it orbits Earth.
    - **b.** The Moon rotates once in the same amount of time that it orbits.
    - **c.** Half of the Moon is always unlit by the Sun.
    - **d.** Half of the Moon does not reflect light.

14. Why does the Moon seem to change shape from week to week? (8.4.e)
    - **a.** Clouds block part of the Moon.
    - **b.** The Moon moves through Earth's shadow.
    - **c.** The Moon is lit in different ways.
    - **d.** Different amounts of the dark-colored side of the Moon face Earth.

15. Which phase of the Moon comes right after a full moon? (8.4.e)
    - **a.** new moon
    - **b.** waning crescent
    - **c.** waxing gibbous
    - **d.** waning gibbous

16. How many times greater is the Sun's diameter compared to Earth's? (8.2.g)
    - **a.** 10 times
    - **b.** 100 times
    - **c.** 1,000 times
    - **d.** 100,000,000 times

Short Answer *Write a short answer to each question.*

17. What motion produces two high tides in a day? Explain your answer. (8.4.e)

18. How are the structure of the Moon and the structure of Earth similar? (8.4.e)

Thinking Critically

Use the lunar map below to answer the next four questions.

Near Side

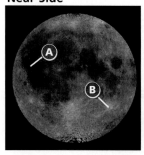

Far Side

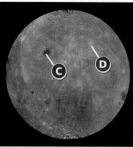

19. **APPLY** Which points are at higher elevations? Explain how you know. (8.4.e)

20. **COMPARE** During a first-quarter moon, will point A, point B, both, or neither be in sunlight? **Hint:** Use the diagram on page 401. (8.4.e)

21. **INFER** During a total lunar eclipse, which points will be in darkness? (8.4.e)

22. **INFER** During a total solar eclipse, the Moon is new. Which points will be in darkness? (8.4.e)

23. **CONNECT** Use your knowledge of the motions of Earth and the Moon to determine how long it takes the Moon to travel once around the Sun. (8.4.e)

24. **ANALYZE** Types of rock containing iron and magnesium are found in the mantle of the Moon and on the Moon's surface. What do scientists conclude from this? (8.4.e)

25. **APPLY** If it is noon for you, what time is it for someone directly on the opposite side of Earth? (8.4.e)

26. **CLASSIFY** If you look out a window at night and see stars, what galaxy would those stars be from? (8.4.a)

27. **APPLY** If it is the winter solstice in San Jose, what solstice or equinox is it in Sydney, Australia, in the Southern Hemisphere? (8.4.e)

28. **PREDICT** If Earth stayed exactly the same distance from the Sun throughout the year, would the seasons be different? Explain what you think would happen. (8.4.e)

29. **PREDICT** If Earth's axis were not tilted with respect to the orbit, would the seasons be different? Explain what you think would happen. (8.4.e)

30. **PROVIDE EXAMPLES** How do the positions of the Sun and the Moon affect what people do? Give three examples of the ways that people's jobs or other activities are affected by the positions of the Sun, the Moon, or both. (8.4.e)

31. **PREDICT** Which shape of the Moon are you most likely to see during the daytime? **Hint:** Compare the directions of the Sun and Moon from Earth in the diagram on page 399. (8.4.e)

32. **CLASSIFY** What are three different types of objects that astronomers study? (8.2.g)

— South Pole

33. **ANALYZE** The photograph above shows the side of Earth in sunlight at a particular time. The location of the South Pole is indicated. Was the photograph taken in March, in June, in September, or in December? (8.4.e)

the BIG idea

34. **APPLY** Look again at the photograph on pages 372–373. Now that you have finished the chapter, how would you change your response to the question on the photograph? (8.4.e)

35. **SYNTHESIZE** If you were an astronaut in the middle of the near side of the Moon during a full moon, how would the ground around you look? How would Earth, high in your sky, look? Describe what is in sunlight and what is in darkness. (8.4.e)

UNIT PROJECTS

If you are doing a unit project, make a folder for your project. Include in your folder a list of the resources you will need, the date on which your project is due, and a schedule to track your progress. Begin gathering data.

Analyzing a Diagram

The sketches show the phases of the Moon one week apart. The diagram shows the Moon's orbit around Earth. Use the diagram and the sketches to answer the questions below.

8.4.e

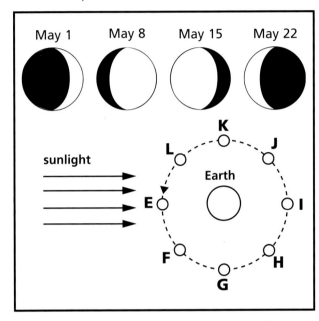

1. At which letter on the diagram might a full moon occur?

a. E

b. G

c. I

d. J

2. Which letter on the diagram shows the position of the Moon on May 8?

a. E

b. F

c. G

d. H

3. Approximately when was the Moon full?

a. May 4

b. May 11

c. May 18

d. May 29

4. At which letter on the diagram might a solar eclipse occur?

a. E

b. H

c. I

d. L

5. How much of the sunlit part of the Moon was visible from Earth on May 8?

a. None of the sunlit part was visible.

b. About one-quarter of the sunlit part was visible.

c. About three-quarters of the sunlit part was visible.

d. All of the sunlit part was visible.

6. Which of these sketches show Earth's shadow on the Moon?

a. those for May 1 and May 22

b. those for May 8 and May 15

c. all 4 of them

d. none of them

7. Which factor is most directly responsible for determining how often a full moon appears?

a. the size of the Moon

b. the size of Earth

c. how quickly the Moon orbits Earth

d. how quickly the Moon turns on its axis

Extended Response

Answer the two questions below in detail. A diagram may help you to answer.

8. The Moon was once much closer to Earth. What effect do you think that this distance had on eclipses?

9. What do you think would happen to tides on Earth if Earth eventually stopped rotating? Why?

Our Solar System

the BIG idea

Planets and other objects form a system around our Sun.

Key Concepts

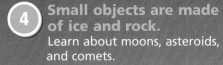 **California ClassZone**

CLASSZONE.COM

Chapter 13 online resources: Content Review, Visualization, two Resource Centers, Math Tutorial, Test Practice

This image shows Jupiter with one of its large moons. How big are these objects compared with Earth?

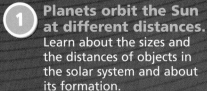

EXPLORE (the BIG idea)

How Big Is Jupiter?

> 8.4.e Students know the appearance, general composition, relative position and size, and motion of objects in the solar system, including planets, planetary satellites, comets, and asteroids.

Measure 1.4 mL of water (about 22 drops) into an empty 2L bottle to represent Earth. Use a full 2L bottle to represent Jupiter. Lift each one.

Observe and Think How massive is Jupiter compared with Earth? Using this scale, you would need more than nine hundred 2L bottles to represent the Sun. How big is the Sun compared with Jupiter?

Internet Activity: Spacing

> 8.4.e Students know the appearance, general composition, relative position and size, and motion of objects in the solar system, including planets, planetary satellites, comets, and asteroids.

Go to **ClassZone.com** to take a virtual spaceflight through the solar system. Examine distances between planets as your virtual spaceship travels at a constant speed.

Observe and Think What do you notice about the relative distances of the planets?

NSTA *SCi*LINKS
scilinks.org
The Solar System **Code: MDL059**

Getting Ready to Learn

CONCEPT REVIEW

- The planets we see are much closer than the stars in constellations.
- The Sun, the planets, and smaller bodies make up the solar system.
- Scientists observe different types of electromagnetic radiation from space objects.

VOCABULARY REVIEW

orbit p. 376

solar system p. 376

axis of rotation p. 382

CONTENT REVIEW
CLASSZONE.COM

Review concepts and vocabulary.

TAKING NOTES

MAIN IDEA AND DETAILS

Make a two-column chart. Write **main ideas,** such as those in the blue headings, in the column on the left. Write **details** about each of those main ideas in the column on the right.

VOCABULARY STRATEGY

Draw a **word triangle** diagram for each new vocabulary term. In the bottom row write and define the term. In the middle row, use the term correctly in a sentence. At the top, draw a small picture to help you remember the term.

See the Note-Taking Handbook on pages R45–R51.

SCIENCE NOTEBOOK

MAIN IDEAS	DETAIL NOTES
1. Planets have different sizes and distances.	1. Objects in the solar system • Sun • planets • moons • comets and asteroids 2.

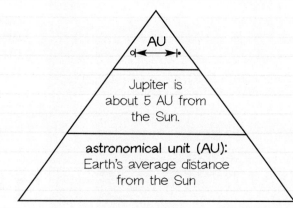

AU

Jupiter is about 5 AU from the Sun.

astronomical unit (AU): Earth's average distance from the Sun

13.1 Planets orbit the Sun at different distances.

CALIFORNIA
Content Standards

8.2.g Students know the role of gravity in forming and maintaining the shapes of planets, stars, and the solar system.

8.4.d Students know that stars are the source of light for all bright objects in outer space and that the Moon and planets shine by reflected sunlight, not by their own light.

8.4.e Students know the appearance, general composition, relative position and size, and motion of objects in the solar system, including planets, planetary satellites, comets, and asteroids.

BEFORE, you learned

- Earth orbits the Sun
- The Moon is Earth's natural satellite
- The Moon's features tell us about its history

NOW, you will learn

- What types of objects are in the solar system
- About sizes and distances in the solar system
- How the solar system formed

EXPLORE Planet Formation (8.4.e)

How do planets form?

PROCEDURE

1. Fill the bowl about halfway with water.
2. Stir the water quickly, using a circular motion, and then remove the spoon.
3. Sprinkle wax pieces onto the swirling water.

WHAT DO YOU THINK?

- In what direction did the wax move?
- What else happened to the wax?

MATERIALS
- bowl
- water
- spoon
- wax pieces

VOCABULARY

astronomical unit (AU) p. 415

ellipse p. 415

MAIN IDEA AND DETAILS
Put sizes and distances in the solar system into a chart.

Planets have different sizes and distances.

You may have seen some planets in the sky without realizing it. They are so far from Earth that they appear as tiny dots of light in the darkened sky. If you have seen something that looks like a very bright star in the western sky in the early evening, you have probably seen the planet Venus. Even if you live in a city, you may have seen Mars, Jupiter, or Saturn but thought that you were seeing a star. Mercury is much more difficult to see. You need a telescope to see three of the planets in our solar system—Uranus, Neptune, and Pluto.

Like the Moon, planets can be seen because they reflect sunlight. Planets do not give off visible light of their own. Sunlight is also reflected by moons and other objects in space, called comets and asteroids. However, these objects are usually too far away and not bright enough to see without a telescope.

 CHECK YOUR READING Why do planets look bright?

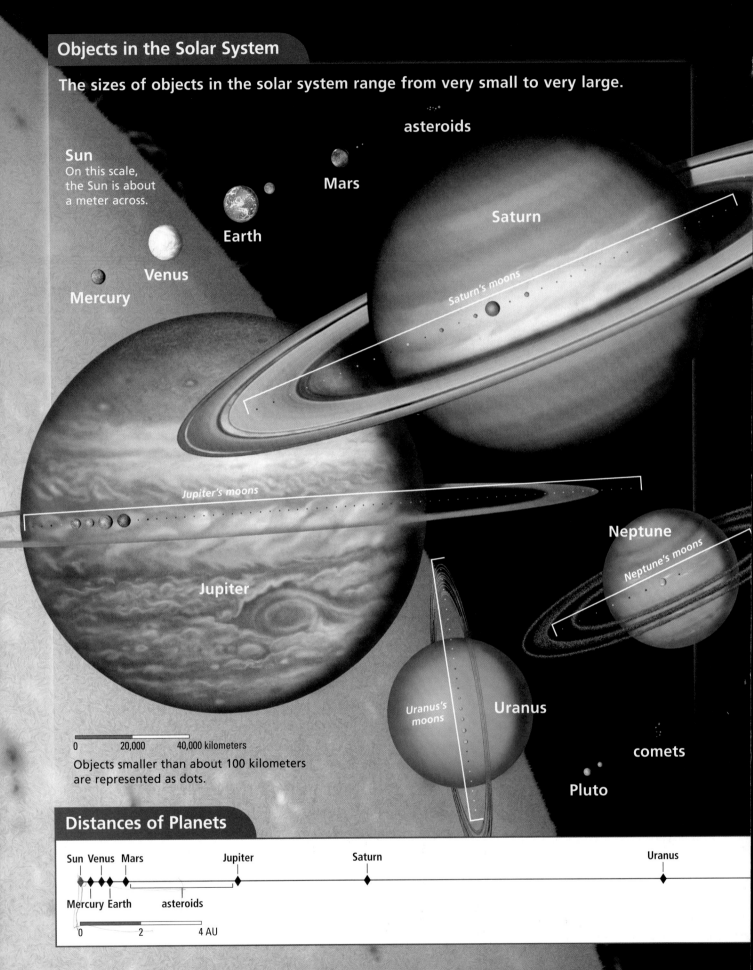

Objects in the Solar System

The sizes of objects in the solar system range from very small to very large.

asteroids

Sun
On this scale,
the Sun is about
a meter across.

Mars

Earth

Saturn

Saturn's moons

Venus

Mercury

Jupiter's moons

Neptune

Neptune's moons

Jupiter

Uranus's
moons

Uranus

0   20,000   40,000 kilometers

Objects smaller than about 100 kilometers
are represented as dots.

comets

Pluto

Distances of Planets

| Sun | Venus | Mars | | Jupiter | | Saturn | | Uranus |

Mercury Earth   asteroids

0   2   4 AU

Objects in the solar system have very different sizes. An asteroid may be as small as a mountain, perhaps 1/1000 Earth's diameter. In contrast, the largest planets are about 10 Earth diameters across. The Sun's diameter is about 100 times Earth's. If the planets were the sizes shown on page 414, the Sun would be about a meter across.

Distances

The distances between most objects in space are huge in comparison with the objects' diameters. If Earth and the Sun were the sizes shown on page 414, they would be more than 100 meters from each other.

Astronomers understand huge distances by comparing them with something more familiar. One **astronomical unit,** or AU, is Earth's average distance from the Sun. An AU is about 150 million kilometers (93 million mi). Mercury is less than 0.5 AU from the Sun, Jupiter is about 5 AU from the Sun, and Pluto gets nearly 50 AU from the Sun at times. You can use the diagram at the bottom of pages 414–415 to compare these distances. However, the planets are not arranged in a straight line—they move around the Sun.

You can see that the planets are spaced unevenly. The first four planets are relatively close together and close to the Sun. They define a region called the inner solar system. Farther from the Sun is the outer solar system, where the planets are much more spread out.

VOCABULARY
Draw word triangles in your notebook for new terms.

 CHECK YOUR READING What are the two regions of the solar system?

Orbits

More than 99 percent of all the mass in the solar system is in the Sun. The gravitational pull of this huge mass causes planets and most other objects in the solar system to move around, or orbit, the Sun.

The shape of each orbit is an **ellipse**—a flattened circle or oval. A circle is a special type of ellipse, just as a square is a special type of rectangle. Most of the planets' orbits are very nearly circles. Only one planet—Pluto—has an orbit that looks a little flattened instead of round.

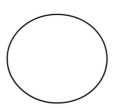

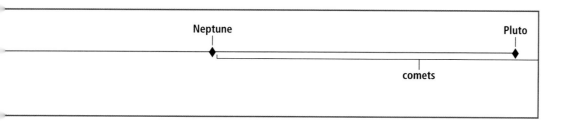

Neptune

Pluto

comets

INVESTIGATE Distances

How far apart are the planets?

PROCEDURE

1. Mark one sheet from the end of the roll of paper as the location of the Sun. Mark an *X* and write the word *Sun* with dots rather than lines.

2. Use the Distance Table data sheet to mark the distances for the rest of the solar system. Count sheets and estimate tenths of a sheet as necessary. Re-roll or fold the paper neatly.

3. Go to a space where you can unroll the paper. Compare the distances of planets as you walk along the paper and back again.

WHAT DO YOU THINK?

• How does the distance between Earth and Mars compare with the distance between Saturn and Uranus?

• How would you use the spacing to sort the planets into groups?

CHALLENGE It took two years for the *Voyager 2* spacecraft to travel from Earth to Jupiter. About how long do you think it took for *Voyager 2* to travel from Jupiter to Neptune?

SKILL FOCUS
Using models
(8.4.c)

MATERIALS
• roll of toilet paper
• felt-tipped pen
• Distance Table

TIME
30 minutes

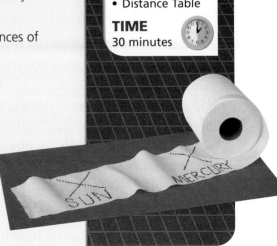

The solar system formed from a swirling cloud of gas and dust.

MAIN IDEA AND DETAILS
Remember to take notes about how the solar system formed.

The planets orbit the Sun in similar ways. Their paths are almost in a flat plane, like the rings of a target. They all orbit the Sun in the same direction—counterclockwise as seen from above Earth's North Pole. Most of the planets rotate on their axes in this direction, too. Many other objects in the solar system also orbit and rotate in this same direction. These similar motions have given scientists clues about how the solar system formed.

According to the best scientific model, the solar system formed out of a huge cloud of different gases and specks of dust. The cloud flattened into a disk of whirling material. Most of the mass fell to the center and became a star—the Sun. At the same time, tiny bits of dust and frozen gases in the disk stuck together into clumps. The clumps stuck together and became larger. Large clumps became planets. They moved in the same direction that the flat disk was turning.

Not all the clumps grew big enough to be called planets. However, many of these objects still orbit the Sun the same way that planets orbit. Some of the objects close to the Sun are like rocks or mountains in space and are called asteroids. Other objects, farther from the Sun, are more like enormous snowballs or icebergs. They are called comets.

Formation of the Solar System

The Sun and other objects formed out of material in a flat disk.

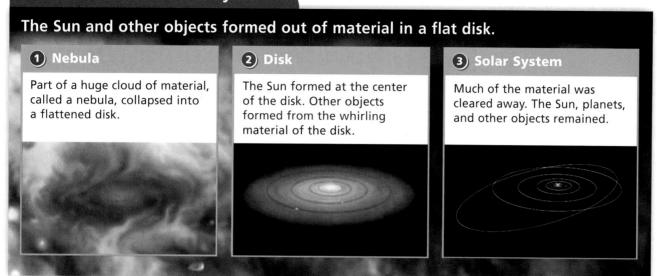

1 Nebula
Part of a huge cloud of material, called a nebula, collapsed into a flattened disk.

2 Disk
The Sun formed at the center of the disk. Other objects formed from the whirling material of the disk.

3 Solar System
Much of the material was cleared away. The Sun, planets, and other objects remained.

Some objects orbit planets instead of orbiting the Sun directly, so they are considered moons. You will read more about asteroids, comets, and moons in Section 13.4.

You can tell a little bit about the size of an object in space from its shape. Lumpy objects are usually much smaller than round objects. As a space object starts to form, the clumps come together from many directions and produce an uneven shape. The gravity of each part affects every other part. The pieces pull each other closer together. When an object has enough mass, this pulling becomes strong enough to make the object round. Any parts that would stick far out are pulled in toward the center until the object becomes a sphere.

CHECK YOUR READING Why do planets and large moons have a spherical shape?

13.1 Review

KEY CONCEPTS

1. What are the types of space objects in the solar system? (8.4.e)

2. Why is the unit of measurement used for the distances of planets from the Sun different from the unit used for their sizes? (8.4.e)

3. How did planets and other objects in the solar system form out of material in a disk? (8.2.g)

CRITICAL THINKING

4. **Analyze** Why do the planets all orbit in one direction?

5. **Infer** Which of the two moons below has more mass? Explain why you think so.

CHALLENGE

6. **Apply** Could you model all the sizes of objects in the solar system by using sports balls? Explain why or why not.

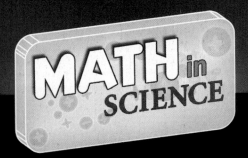

MATH TUTORIAL
CLASSZONE.COM
Click on Math Tutorial for more help with the percent equation.
Math 7.MR.1.1
Science 8.2.g

How Much Would You Weigh on Other Worlds?

When astronauts walked on the Moon, they felt much lighter than they felt when they were on Earth. Neil Armstrong's total mass—about 160 kilograms with space suit and backpack—did not change. However, the Moon did not pull as hard on him as Earth did, so he weighed less on the Moon. At the surface, the Moon's gravitational pull is only 17% of Earth's gravitational pull. You can use percentages to calculate Neil Armstrong's weight on the Moon.

Example

On Earth, with his heavy space suit and backpack, Neil Armstrong weighed about 1600 newtons (360 lb). To calculate his weight on the Moon, find 17% of 1600 newtons.

Of means "multiply."	17% of 1600 N = 17% × 1600 N
Change the percent to a decimal fraction.	= 0.17 × 1600 N
Simplify.	= 272 N

ANSWER With his suit and backpack, Neil Armstrong weighed about 270 newtons on the Moon.

Use the percentages in the table to answer the following questions.

1. A backpack weighs 60 newtons (13 lb) on Earth. **(a)** How much would it weigh on Jupiter? **(b)** How much would it weigh on Jupiter's moon Io?

2. **(a)** How much would a student weighing 500 newtons (110 lb) on Earth weigh on Saturn? **(b)** on Venus?

3. On which planet or moon would you be lightest?

CHALLENGE A pencil weighs 0.3 newtons (1 oz) on Earth. How much would it weigh on the Moon? If an astronaut let go of the pencil on the Moon, would the pencil fall? Explain.

Percent of Weight on Earth	
Planet or Moon	**%**
Mercury	38
Venus	91
Earth	100
Moon (Earth)	17
Mars	38
Jupiter	236
Io (Jupiter)	18
Europa (Jupiter)	13
Ganymede (Jupiter)	15
Callisto (Jupiter)	13
Saturn	92
Titan (Saturn)	14
Uranus	89
Neptune	112
Triton (Neptune)	8.0
Pluto	6.7
Charon (Pluto)	2.8

This picture of Buzz Aldrin on the Moon was taken by Neil Armstrong, who can be seen reflected in Aldrin's helmet.

13.2 The inner solar system has rocky planets.

BEFORE, you learned

- Planets are closer together in the inner solar system than in the outer solar system
- Planets formed along with the Sun
- Gravity made planets round

NOW, you will learn

- How four processes change the surfaces of solid planets
- How atmospheres form and then affect planets
- What the planets closest to the Sun are like

VOCABULARY

terrestrial planet p. 419
tectonics p. 420
volcanism p. 420

EXPLORE Surfaces (8.4.e)

How does a planet's mantle affect its surface?

PROCEDURE

1. Dampen a paper towel and place it on top of two blocks to model a crust and a mantle.

2. Move one block. Try different amounts of motion and different directions.

WHAT DO YOU THINK?

- What happened to the paper towel?
- What landforms like this have you seen?

MATERIALS

- 2 blocks
- paper towel
- newspaper

The terrestrial planets have rocky crusts.

Scientists study Earth to learn about other planets. They also study other planets to learn more about Earth. The **terrestrial planets** are Mercury, Venus, Earth, and Mars—the four planets closest to the Sun. They all have rocky crusts and dense mantles and cores. Their insides, surfaces, and atmospheres formed in similar ways and follow similar patterns. One planet—Earth—can be used as a model to understand the others. In fact, the term *terrestrial* comes from *terra*, the Latin word for Earth.

Earth

Most of Earth's rocky surface is hidden by water. More details about Earth and other planets are listed in the Appendix at the back of this book.

Mass 6×10^{24} kg
Diameter 12,800 km
Average distance from Sun 1 AU

Orbits in 365 days
Rotates in 24 hours

Processes and Surface Features

All terrestrial planets have layers. Each planet gained energy from the collisions that formed it. This energy heated and melted the planet's materials. The heaviest materials were metals, which sank to the center and formed a core. Lighter rock formed a mantle around the core. The lightest rock rose to the surface and cooled into a crust.

Four types of processes then shaped each planet's rocky crust. The processes acted to different extents on each planet, depending on how much the crust and inside of the planet cooled.

READING TiP

Compare what you read about each type of feature with the pictures and diagrams on page 421.

❶ Tectonics Earth's crust is split into large pieces called tectonic plates. These plates are moved by Earth's hot mantle. Mountains, valleys, and other features form as the plates move together, apart, or along each other. The crusts of other terrestrial planets are not split into plates but can be twisted, wrinkled up, or stretched out by the mantle. **Tectonics** is the processes of change in a crust due to the motion of hot material underneath. As a planet cools, the crust gets stiffer and the mantle may stop moving, so this process stops.

❷ Volcanism A second process, called **volcanism,** occurs when molten rock moves from a planet's hot interior onto its surface. The molten rock is called lava when it reaches the surface through an opening called a volcano. On Earth, lava often builds up into mountains. Volcanoes are found on Earth, Venus, and Mars. Lava can also flow onto large areas and cool into flat plains like the lunar maria. When the inside of a planet cools enough, no more molten rock reaches the surface.

❸ Weathering and Erosion You have read about weathering on Earth and the Moon. Weather or small impacts break down rocks. The broken material is moved by a group of processes called erosion. The material may form dunes, new layers of rock, or other features. On Earth, water is important for weathering and erosion. However, similar things happen even without water. Wind can carry sand grains that batter at rocks and form new features. Even on a planet without air, rock breaks down from being heated in the daylight and cooled at night. The material is pulled downhill by gravity.

RESOURCE CENTER
CLASSZONE.COM

Find out more about impact craters on Earth and other space objects.

❹ Impact Cratering A small object sometimes hits a planet's surface so fast that it causes an explosion. The resulting impact crater is often ten times larger than the object that produced it. On Earth, most craters have been erased by other processes. Impact craters are easier to find on other planets. If a planet or part of a planet is completely covered with impact craters, then the other processes have not changed the surface much in billions of years.

 CHECK YOUR READING What processes affect the surfaces of terrestrial planets?

Features of Rocky Planets

The processes that shape features on a planet's surface can be divided into four types. The features can tell you different things about the planet.

① Tectonics

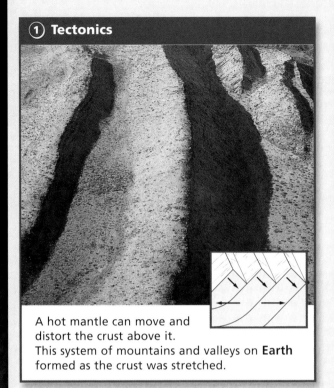

A hot mantle can move and distort the crust above it.
This system of mountains and valleys on **Earth** formed as the crust was stretched.

② Volcanism

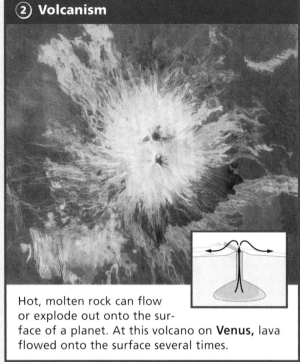

Hot, molten rock can flow or explode out onto the surface of a planet. At this volcano on **Venus,** lava flowed onto the surface several times.

③ Weathering and Erosion

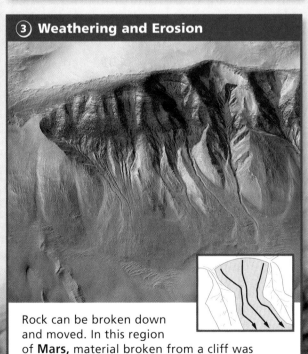

Rock can be broken down and moved. In this region of **Mars,** material broken from a cliff was moved by erosion into new slopes and dunes.

④ Impact Cratering

A small space object can hit a planet's surface and leave a crater. Because the other processes on **Mercury** are weak, newer craters can be seen on a background of older, more eroded craters.

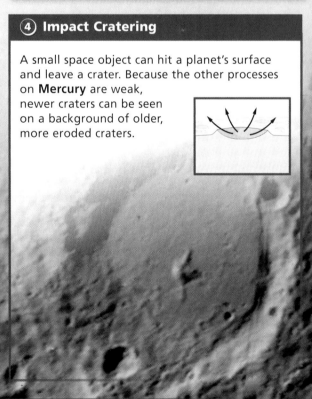

READING VISUALS Which two processes happen because of hot material beneath the surface?

How do the layers inside of planets form?

In this model, the materials you use represent different rocks and metals that make up the solid planets.

PROCEDURE

1. Put pieces of gelatin into the container until it is about one-quarter full.

2. Mix in a spoonful each of sand and wax. Use the spoon to break the gelatin into small pieces as you mix. Remove the spoon.

3. Place the container in a bowl of hot tap water (about 70°C) and observe what happens as the gelatin melts.

WHAT DO YOU THINK?

- What happened to each of the materials when the gelatin melted?
- How do the results resemble the core, mantle, and crust of Earth and other planets?

CHALLENGE How might you improve this model?

MATERIALS
- container
- spoon
- firm gelatin
- sand
- wax pieces
- bowl of hot tap water

TIME
40 minutes

Atmospheres

Atmospheres on terrestrial planets mainly formed from gases that poured out of volcanoes. If a planet's gravity is strong enough, it pulls the gases in and keeps them near the surface. If a planet's gravity is too weak, the gases expand into outer space and are lost.

Venus, Earth, and Mars each had gravity strong enough to hold heavy gases such as carbon dioxide. However, the lightest gases—hydrogen and helium—escaped into outer space. The atmospheres of Venus and Mars are mostly carbon dioxide.

An atmosphere can move energy from warmer places to cooler places. This movement of heat energy makes temperatures more uniform between a planet's day side and its night side and between its equator and its poles. An atmosphere can also make a planet's whole surface warmer by slowing the loss of energy from the surface.

After Earth formed, its atmosphere of carbon dioxide kept the surface warm enough for water to be liquid. Oceans covered most of Earth's surface. The oceans changed the gases of the atmosphere, and living organisms caused even more changes. Earth's atmosphere is now mostly nitrogen with some oxygen.

 Why is the solid Earth surrounded by gases?

Craters cover the surface of Mercury.

Mercury, like the Moon, has smooth plains and many craters. The processes at work on Earth also affected Mercury.

Tectonics Long, high cliffs stretch across Mercury's surface. Scientists think that Mercury's huge core of iron shrank when it cooled long ago. The crust wrinkled up, forming cliffs, as the planet got a little smaller.

Volcanism Parts of the surface were covered with lava long ago. Large, smooth plains formed. The plains are similar to lunar maria.

Weathering and Erosion Small impacts and temperature changes have broken rock. Gravity has moved broken material downhill.

Impact Cratering Round features cover much of the surface. These craters show that the other processes have not changed Mercury's surface very much for a long time.

Mercury has the longest cycle of day and night of the terrestrial planets—three months of daylight and three months of darkness. There is no atmosphere to move energy from the hot areas to the cold areas. In the long daytime, it can get hotter than 420°C (about 800°F)—hot enough to melt lead. During the long, cold night, the temperature can drop lower than –170°C (about –280°F).

—no data

Mercury

This map of Mercury was made from many images taken by one spacecraft. The blank patches show areas that were not mapped by the spacecraft.

Mass 6% of Earth's mass

Diameter 38% of Earth's diameter

Average distance from Sun 0.39 AU

Orbits in 88 Earth days

Rotates in 59 Earth days

CHECK YOUR READING How is Mercury similar to the Moon?

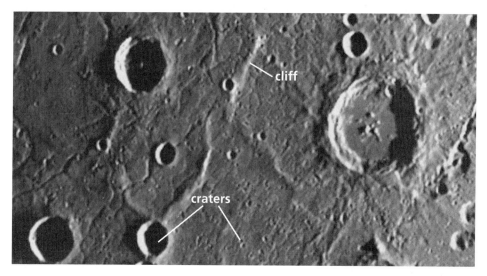
craters
cliff

Craters of all sizes cover Mercury's surface, but there are also flat lava plains and cliffs from long ago.

Volcanoes shape the surface of Venus.

The planet Venus is only a little smaller than Earth and orbits a little closer to the Sun. As a result, Venus is sometimes called Earth's sister planet. However, Venus is different from Earth in important ways.

Venus takes about eight months to turn just once on its axis. Unlike most other planets, Venus rotates and orbits in opposite directions. The rotation and orbit together produce very long days and nights—two months of daylight followed by two months of darkness.

The atmosphere of Venus is very dense. Air pressure on Venus is 90 times that on Earth. Venus's atmosphere is mostly carbon dioxide. This gas slows the loss of energy and makes the surface very hot. The ground temperature on Venus is about 470°C (about 870°F). The atmosphere of Venus moves energy around so well that the long nights are as hot as the days and the poles are as hot as the equator. In addition, there are droplets of sulfuric acid, a corrosive chemical, in the atmosphere. These droplets form thick white clouds that completely cover the planet and hide the surface.

Like Mercury, Venus is affected by the same four types of processes that change Earth's surface. Scientists think that tectonics and volcanism may still be changing Venus's surface today.

Tectonics Patterns of cracks and cliffs have formed as movements of the hot mantle have stretched, wrinkled, and twisted the surface.

Volcanism Most of the surface of Venus has been covered with lava in the last billion years or so. Volcanoes and flat lava plains are found all over the surface.

Thick clouds make it impossible to see Venus's surface in visible light. This inset shows a map of Venus that scientists made using radio waves.

Venus

Venus is nearly the size of Earth but has a thicker atmosphere and is much hotter than Earth. The surface is rocky, as you can see in the image below.

Mass 82% of Earth's mass
Diameter 95% of Earth's diameter
Average distance from Sun 0.72 AU

Orbits in 225 Earth days
Rotates in 243 Earth days

weathered and eroded rock

spacecraft

Weathering and Erosion Venus is too hot to have liquid water, and the winds do not seem to move much material. Erosion may be slower on Venus than on Earth.

Impact Cratering Round craters mark the surface here and there. Older craters have been erased by the other processes. Also, Venus's thick atmosphere protects the surface from small impacts.

 CHECK YOUR READING Why is Venus not covered with craters?

Erosion changes the appearance of Mars.

Mars is relatively small, with a diameter about half that of Earth. The orange color of some of the surface comes from molecules of iron and oxygen—rust. Mars has two tiny moons. They were probably once asteroids that were pulled into orbit around Mars.

Surface of Mars

The same processes that affect the other terrestrial planets affect Mars.

Tectonics Valleys and raised areas formed on Mars as the mantle moved. One huge system of valleys, called Valles Marineris, is long enough to stretch across the United States.

Volcanism Most of the northern hemisphere has smooth plains of cooled lava. Several volcanoes are higher than any mountain on Earth. The lava must have built up in the same spot for a long time, so scientists have inferred that the crust of Mars has cooled more than Earth's crust. On Earth, the tectonic plates move, so chains of smaller volcanoes form instead of single larger volcanoes.

Weathering and Erosion Fast winds carry sand that breaks down rocks. Wind and gravity move the broken material, forming new features such as sand dunes. There are also landforms that look like the results of gigantic flash floods that happened long ago.

Impact Cratering Round craters cover much of the southern hemisphere of Mars. Many craters are very old and eroded. A few impact craters on the volcanoes make scientists think that the volcanoes have not released lava for a long time.

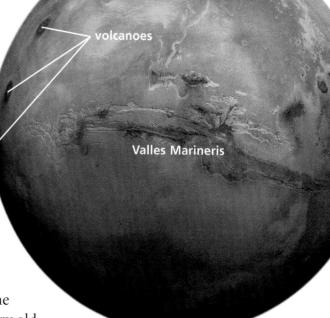

Mars

The atmosphere of Mars is thin but causes weathering and erosion.

Mass 11% of Earth's mass
Diameter 53% of Earth's diameter
Average distance from Sun 1.5 AU
Orbits in 1.9 Earth years
Rotates in 25 hours

volcanoes

Valles Marineris

red dust carried by wind

distant hills

weathered and eroded rock

The sky of Mars is made red by dust that the wind picks up and carries to new places.

Gases and Water on Mars

The atmosphere of Mars is mostly carbon dioxide. The air pressure is only about 1 percent of the air pressure on Earth. The gas is not dense enough to keep the surface warm or to move much energy from cold areas to warmer areas. Therefore, temperatures may reach almost 20°C (about 60°F) in the daytime and −90°C (−130°F) at night. The large differences in temperature produce fast winds. The winds cause gigantic dust storms that sometimes cover most of the planet.

Like Earth, Mars has polar caps that grow in winter and shrink in summer. However, the changing polar caps of Mars are made mostly of frozen carbon dioxide—dry ice. The carbon dioxide of the atmosphere can also form clouds, fog, and frost on the ground.

There is no liquid water on the surface of Mars today. Any water would quickly evaporate or freeze. However, there were floods in the past, and there is still frozen water in the ground and in one polar cap. Water is important for life and will also be needed to make rocket fuel if humans are ever to make trips to Mars and back.

 CHECK YOUR READING In what ways is Mars different from Earth?

13.2 Review

KEY CONCEPTS

1. What are the four types of processes that shape planets' surfaces? For each, give one example of a feature that the process can produce. (8.4.e)

2. How can an atmosphere affect the temperature of a planet's surface? (8.4.e)

3. Which terrestrial planet has the oldest, least-changing surface? (8.4.e)

CRITICAL THINKING

4. **Compare and Contrast** Make a chart with columns for the four types of processes and for an atmosphere. Fill out a row for each planet.

5. **Apply** If a planet had a surface with craters but no other features, what could you say about the inside of the planet?

CHALLENGE

6. **Infer** Describe how a hot mantle can affect a planet's atmosphere. **Hint**: Which of the four processes is involved?

What Shapes the Surface of Mars?

> 8.4.e Students know the appearance, general composition, relative position and size, and motion of objects in the solar system, including planets, planetary satellites, comets, and asteroids.

Many features on Mars, when seen close up, look a lot like features found on Earth. Astronomers use their knowledge of the four types of processes that affect the terrestrial planets to hypothesize about the features on Mars. Using what you know about the processes, make your own hypotheses to explain the features in the image to the left.

▶ Results of Research

- Small objects hit the surface, producing craters.
- Volcanoes erupt, creating mountains and flows of lava.
- The mantle moves the crust, producing mountains and valleys.
- Wind, water, and gravity move material on the surface, eroding some places and building up others.

▶ Observations

- Dark, raised triangles point roughly east.
- Patterns of light stripes run mostly north-south between the dark hills.
- The features are inside a huge impact crater.

dark hills

light stripes

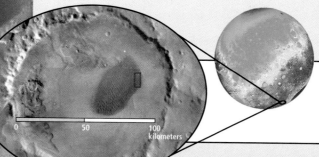

The large image shows details of the area in the red rectangle.

0   50   100
kilometers

The black oval on the globe shows the location of the crater.

0   0.5   1.0 kilometers

▶ Form a Hypothesis

On Your Own Consider one or more processes that might produce the hills and stripes seen in the image at left.

As a Group With a small group discuss possible hypotheses to explain the formation of these features. See if the group can agree on which one is most reasonable.

CHALLENGE Create a model that you can use to test your hypothesis. What will you use to represent the surface of Mars and the forces acting on it?

The outer solar system has four giant planets.

CALIFORNIA Content Standard

8.4.e Students know the appearance, general composition, relative position and size, and motion of objects in the solar system, including planets, planetary satellites, comets, and asteroids.

◀ **BEFORE, you learned**

- Planets formed along with the Sun
- Vast distances separate planets
- The gravity of a terrestrial planet may be strong enough to hold the heavier gases

▶ **NOW, you will learn**

- About the four giant planets in the solar system
- What the atmospheres of giant planets are like
- About the rings of giant planets

VOCABULARY

gas giant p. 428
ring p. 431

THINK ABOUT

What is Jupiter like inside?

Most of Jupiter's huge mass is hidden below layers of clouds. Scientists learn about Jupiter by studying its gravity, its magnetic field, its motions, and its radiation. Scientists also use data from other space bodies to make models, from which they make predictions. Then they observe Jupiter to test their predictions. What might it be like under Jupiter's clouds?

VOCABULARY
Remember to draw a word triangle diagram when you read a new term.

The gas giants have very deep atmospheres.

You have already read about the four rocky planets in the inner solar system, close to the Sun. Beyond Mars stretches the outer solar system, where the four largest planets slowly orbit the Sun. The **gas giants**— Jupiter, Saturn, Uranus (YUR-uh-nuhs), and Neptune—are made mainly of hydrogen, helium, and other gases.

When you think of gases, you probably think of Earth's air, which is not very dense. However, the giant planets are so large and have such large amounts of these gases that they have a lot of mass. The huge gravitational force from such a large mass is enough to pull the gas particles close together and make the atmosphere very dense. Inside the giant planets, the gases become more dense than water. The outermost parts are less dense and more like Earth's atmosphere.

 Why are the gas giants dense inside?

The atmosphere of a giant planet is very deep. Imagine traveling into one. At first, the atmosphere is thin and very cold. There may be a haze of gases. A little lower is a layer of clouds that reflect sunlight, just like clouds on Earth. There are strong winds and other weather patterns. Lower down, it is warmer and there are layers of clouds of different materials. As you go farther, the atmosphere gradually becomes dense enough to call a liquid. It also gets thousands of degrees hotter as you get closer to the center of the planet. The materials around you become more and more dense until they are solid. Scientists think that each of the four gas giants has a solid core, larger than Earth, deep in its center.

Interior of a Giant Planet

Jupiter

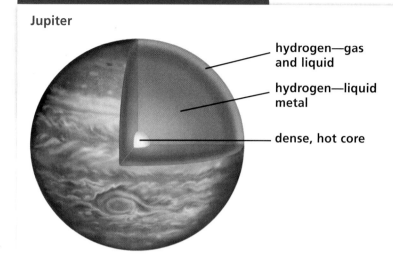

hydrogen—gas and liquid

hydrogen—liquid metal

dense, hot core

Jupiter is a world of storms and clouds.

Jupiter is the largest planet in the solar system. It is more than 10 times larger than Earth in diameter and more than 1200 times larger in volume. A jet plane that could circle Earth in about 2 days would take 23 days to circle Jupiter. If you could weigh the planets on a cosmic scale, all the other planets put together would weigh less than half as much as Jupiter.

Jupiter is more than five times farther from the Sun than Earth is. It moves more slowly through space than Earth and has a greater distance to travel in each orbit. Jupiter takes 12 Earth years to go once around the Sun.

Even though it is big, Jupiter takes less than 10 hours to turn once on its axis. This fast rotation produces fast winds and stormy weather. Like Earth, Jupiter has bands of winds that blow eastward and westward, but Jupiter has many more bands than Earth does.

Jupiter

Jupiter's colorful stripes are produced by clouds at different levels in Jupiter's deep atmosphere.

Mass 318 Earth masses
Diameter 11 Earth diameters
Average distance from Sun 5.2 AU
Orbits in 12 Earth years
Rotates in 9.9 hours

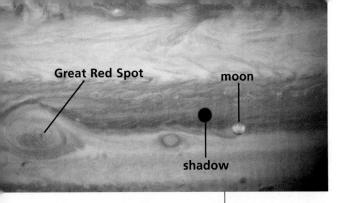

Great Red Spot

moon

shadow

This image shows one of Jupiter's moons casting a shadow on Jupiter. If you were in that shadow, you would experience a solar eclipse.

Stripes of cold clouds form along the bands. The clouds look white because they are made of crystals that reflect sunlight. The crystals in these high white clouds are frozen ammonia rather than frozen water, as on Earth. Between Jupiter's white bands of clouds, you can see down to the next layer. The lower clouds are brown or red and made of different chemicals. Sometimes there are clear patches in the brown clouds, where the next layer of bluish clouds shows through.

CHECK YOUR READING What are Jupiter's white stripes?

Storms can form between bands of winds that blow in opposite directions. Because Jupiter has no land to slow the storms, they can last for a long time. The largest of these storms is the Great Red Spot, which is twice as wide as Earth and at least 100 years old. Its clouds rise even higher than the white ammonia-ice clouds. Scientists are trying to find out which chemicals produce the spot's reddish color.

Saturn has large rings.

REMINDER

Density is the amount of mass in a given volume. An object of low density can still have a great total mass if it has a large volume.

The sixth planet from the Sun is Saturn. Saturn is only a little smaller than Jupiter, but its mass is less than one-third that of Jupiter. Because there is less mass, the gravitational pull is weaker, so the gas particles can spread out more. As a result, Saturn has a much lower density than Jupiter. The storms and stripes of clouds form deeper in Saturn's atmosphere than in Jupiter's, so the details are harder to see.

Saturn

Saturn has an average density less than that of liquid water on Earth. The diameter of Saturn's ring system is almost as great as the distance from Earth to the Moon.

Mass 95 Earth masses   **Orbits in** 29 Earth years
Diameter 9 Earth diameters   **Rotates in** 11 hours
Average distance from Sun 9.5 AU

Saturn was the first planet known to have rings. A planetary **ring** is a wide, flat zone of small particles that orbit a planet. All four gas giants have rings around their equators. Saturn's rings are made of chunks of water ice the size of a building or smaller. Larger chunks, considered to be tiny moons, orbit within the rings. Saturn's main rings are very bright. The outermost ring is three times as wide as the planet, but it is usually too faint to see. Saturn's rings have bright and dark stripes that change over time.

You can use Saturn's rings to see the planet's seasons. Like Earth's axis of rotation, Saturn's axis is tilted. The angle is 27 degrees. When the image on this page was taken, sunlight shone more on the northern hemisphere, so the north side of the rings was bright. The shadow of the rings fell on the southern hemisphere. Winter started in Saturn's northern hemisphere in May 2003 and will last more than seven Earth years. Saturn is almost ten times farther from the Sun than Earth is, so Saturn takes almost 30 Earth years to go around the Sun once.

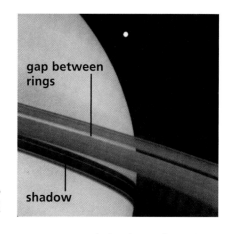

gap between rings

shadow

Sunlight shines from the upper right of this image. The rings cast shadows on Saturn's clouds.

INVESTIGATE Giant Planets

Why do Saturn's rings seem to change size?

PROCEDURE

1. Poke the stick through the plate and cut off the plate's rim. Shape the clay onto both sides of the plate to make a model of a planet with rings.

2. Model Saturn's orbit for your partner. Stand between your partner and the classroom clock. Point one end of the stick at the clock. Hold the model at the same height as your partner's eyes. Have your partner watch the model with just one eye open.

3. Move one step counterclockwise around your partner and point the stick at the clock again. Make sure the model is as high as your partner's eyes. Your partner may need to turn to see the model.

4. Continue taking steps around your partner and pointing the stick at the clock until you have moved the model all the way around your partner.

5. Switch roles with your partner and repeat steps 2, 3, and 4.

WHAT DO YOU THINK?

- How did your view of the rings change as the model planet changed position?
- How many times per orbit do the rings seem to vanish?

CHALLENGE How do Saturn's axis and orbit compare with those of Earth?

SKILL FOCUS
Observing (8.4.e)

MATERIALS
- ice-cream stick
- disposable plate
- scissors
- clay

TIME
20 minutes

Uranus and Neptune are extremely cold.

The seventh and eighth planets from the Sun are Uranus and Neptune. These planets are similar in size—both have diameters roughly one-third that of Jupiter. Unlike Jupiter and Saturn, Uranus and Neptune are only about 15 percent hydrogen and helium. Most of the mass of each planet is made up of heavier gases, such as methane, ammonia, and water. As a result, Uranus and Neptune are more dense than Jupiter.

Uranus looks blue-green, and Neptune appears deep blue. The color comes from methane gas, which absorbs certain colors of light. Each planet has methane gas above a layer of white clouds. Sunlight passes through the gas, reflects off the clouds, then passes through the gas again on its way out. The gas absorbs the red, orange, and yellow parts of sunlight, so each planet's bluish color comes from the remaining green, blue, and violet light that passes back out of the atmosphere.

Uranus is a smooth blue-green in visible light. The small infrared image shows that the pole facing the Sun is warmer than the equator.

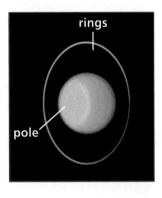

Uranus

Uranus is about twice Saturn's distance from the Sun. The farther a planet is from the Sun, the more slowly it moves along its orbit. The greater distance also results in a larger orbit, so it takes Uranus 84 Earth years to travel around the Sun.

Like the other gas giants, Uranus has a system of rings and moons around its equator. The ring particles and moons orbit Uranus in the same direction as the planet's spin. Unlike the other planets, Uranus has an axis of rotation that is almost in the plane of its orbit. As a result, Uranus seems to spin on its side. During a solstice, one pole of Uranus points almost straight toward the Sun.

Some scientists think that there was a large collision early in Uranus's history. The result left the planet and its system spinning at an unusual angle.

Uranus

Each pole of Uranus experiences more than 40 years of sunlight and then more than 40 years of darkness as the planet orbits the Sun.

Mass 15 Earth masses
Diameter 4 Earth diameters
Average distance from Sun 19 AU
Orbits in 84 Earth years
Rotates in 17 hours

Neptune

Neptune orbits about 10 AU farther from the Sun than Uranus, so you would expect it to be colder. However, Neptune has about the same outside temperature as Uranus because it is hotter inside.

Uranus is usually one smooth color, but light and dark areas often appear on Neptune. Clouds of methane ice crystals can form high enough in the atmosphere of Neptune to look white.

Storm systems can appear in darker shades of blue than the rest of the planet. One storm, seen during the flyby of the *Voyager 2* spacecraft in 1989, was named the Great Dark Spot. Unlike the huge storm on Jupiter, the Great Dark Spot did not stay at the same latitude. It moved toward Neptune's equator. The winds there may have broken up the storm. Images of Neptune obtained a few years later with the Hubble Space Telescope showed no sign of the Great Dark Spot.

CHECK YOUR READING What are the white patches often seen on Neptune?

Neptune

Neptune has a large moon that orbits in a direction opposite to Neptune's rotation. Scientists think a giant collision might have occurred in Neptune's past.

Mass 17 Earth masses
Diameter 4 Earth diameters
Average distance from Sun 30 AU
Orbits in 164 Earth years
Rotates in 16 hours

High clouds cast shadows on the layer below.

cloud

shadow

13.3 Review

KEY CONCEPTS

1. Which planet has a greater mass than all the other planets put together? (8.4.e)

2. What do you see instead of a solid surface when you look at an image of a giant planet? (8.4.e)

3. Which planets have rings? (8.4.e)

CRITICAL THINKING

4. **Compare and Contrast** Why do Jupiter and Saturn show a lot of white, while Uranus and Neptune are more blue in color?

5. **Analyze** Most of Saturn is much less dense than most of Earth. Yet Saturn's mass is much greater than Earth's mass. How can this be so?

CHALLENGE

6. **Apply** If Uranus had areas of ice crystals high in its atmosphere, how would its appearance change?

KEY CONCEPT

13.4 Small objects are made of ice and rock.

CALIFORNIA
Content Standard

8.4.e Students know the appearance, general composition, relative position and size, and motion of objects in the solar system, including planets, planetary satellites, comets, and asteroids.

VOCABULARY

asteroid p. 437
comet p. 438
meteor p. 439
meteorite p. 439

BEFORE, you learned

- Smaller bodies formed with the Sun and planets
- Planets in the inner solar system consist of rock and metal
- The outer solar system is cold

NOW, you will learn

- About Pluto and the moons of the giant planets
- How asteroids and comets are similar and different
- What happens when tiny objects hit Earth's atmosphere

THINK ABOUT

Do small space bodies experience erosion?

Very small bodies in space often have potato-like shapes. Some are covered with dust, boulders, and craters. Solar radiation can break down material directly or by heating and cooling a surface. Broken material can slide downhill, even on a small asteroid. What other processes do you think might act on small and medium-sized bodies in space?

Pluto and most objects in the outer solar system are made of ice and rock.

READING TIP

The name of Earth's satellite is the Moon, but the word *moon* is also used to refer to other satellites.

The materials in a space body depend on where it formed. The disk of material that became the solar system was cold around the outside and hottest in the center, where the Sun was forming. Far from the center, chemicals such as carbon dioxide, ammonia, and water were frozen solid. These ices became part of the material that formed bodies in the outer solar system. Bodies that formed near the center of the solar system are made mostly of rock and metal. Bodies that formed far from the center are mostly ice with some rock and a little metal.

Some of the bodies had enough mass to become rounded. Some even melted and formed cores, mantles, and crusts. Many of these bodies have mountains and valleys, volcanoes, and even winds and clouds. The processes at work on Earth also affect other space bodies.

 CHECK YOUR READING   What do the proportions of ice, rock, and metal show about a space object?

Pluto and Charon

Many space bodies of ice and rock orbit the Sun at the distance of Neptune and beyond. Since 1992, scientists have been using sophisticated equipment to find and study these bodies. However, one body has been known since 1930. Because Pluto was discovered decades before the other objects, it is considered one of the nine major planets.

Pluto is the smallest of the nine planets. It is smaller than the Moon. Pluto's mass is less than 0.3 percent of Earth's mass, so its gravitational pull is weak. However, Pluto is round and probably has a core, mantle, and crust. Pluto also has a thin atmosphere. No spacecraft has passed close to Pluto, so scientists do not have clear images of the planet's surface.

CHECK YOUR READING Why do scientists know less about Pluto than about other planets?

Pluto's moon, Charon, has a diameter half that of Pluto and a mass about 15 percent of Pluto's. Because Pluto and Charon orbit each other, they are sometimes called a double planet. Just as the Moon always has the same side facing Earth, Pluto and Charon always keep the same sides turned toward each other.

Pluto and Charon also move together around the Sun. Pluto's path around the Sun is not as round as the orbits of the rest of the planets, so its distance from the Sun changes a lot as it orbits. Pluto gets closer to the Sun than Neptune's distance of 30 AU. At the other side of its orbit, Pluto is about 50 AU from the Sun. Pluto's orbit is at an angle with respect to Neptune's, as you can see in the diagram below, so the two paths do not cross and the planets will not collide.

Pluto

This map of Pluto's surface shows only bright and dark areas because Pluto is very distant from Earth and no spacecraft has been close enough to see Pluto's surface in detail.

Mass 0.2% Earth's mass
Diameter 18% Earth's diameter
Average distance from Sun 40 AU
Orbits in 248 Earth years
Rotates in 6 Earth days

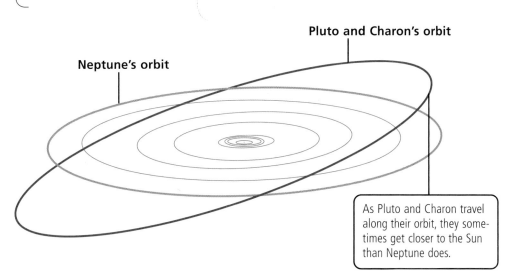

Neptune's orbit

Pluto and Charon's orbit

As Pluto and Charon travel along their orbit, they sometimes get closer to the Sun than Neptune does.

Moons of Gas Giants

RESOURCE CENTER
CLASSZONE.COM

Learn more about the different moons of giant planets.

Each giant planet has a system of moons. Six of the moons are larger than Pluto. Their features are formed by the same processes that shape the terrestrial planets. Saturn's largest moon, Titan, has a dense atmosphere of nitrogen, as Earth does, although a haze hides Titan's surface. Neptune's largest moon, Triton, has a thin atmosphere and ice volcanoes. Jupiter has four large moons—Io, Europa, Ganymede, and Callisto. Io (EYE-oh) is dotted with volcanoes, which continue to erupt, so Io has few impact craters. Europa (yu-ROH-puh) has long ridges where the crust has been pushed and pulled by the material beneath it. The outer two moons have craters over most of their surfaces.

The other moons of the gas giants are all smaller than Pluto, with diameters ranging from about 1600 kilometers (1000 mi) down to just a few kilometers. The smallest moons have irregular shapes, and some may be bodies that were captured into orbit.

CHECK YOUR READING What processes are at work on the largest moons?

Some Moons of Gas Giants

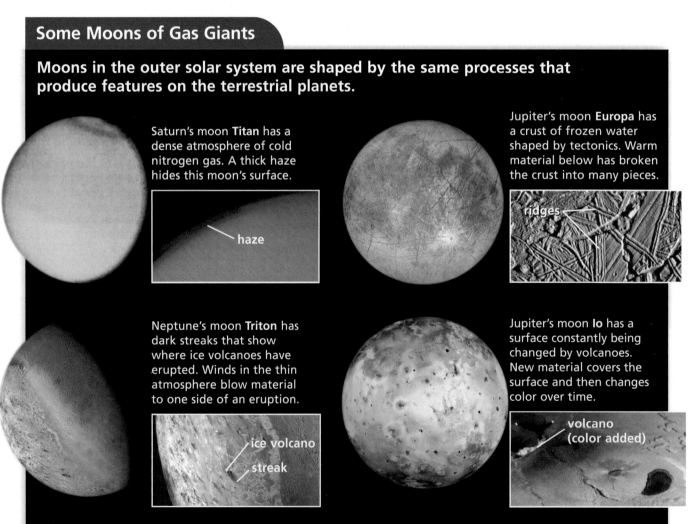

Moons in the outer solar system are shaped by the same processes that produce features on the terrestrial planets.

Saturn's moon **Titan** has a dense atmosphere of cold nitrogen gas. A thick haze hides this moon's surface.

haze

Jupiter's moon **Europa** has a crust of frozen water shaped by tectonics. Warm material below has broken the crust into many pieces.

ridges

Neptune's moon **Triton** has dark streaks that show where ice volcanoes have erupted. Winds in the thin atmosphere blow material to one side of an eruption.

ice volcano
streak

Jupiter's moon **Io** has a surface constantly being changed by volcanoes. New material covers the surface and then changes color over time.

volcano (color added)

READING VISUALS Which images show volcanoes?

Asteroids and comets orbit the Sun.

Objects called asteroids and comets formed along with the Sun, planets, and moons. These objects still orbit the Sun at different distances. Most of the objects are much smaller than planets and had too little mass to become round. The objects that formed far from the Sun are made mostly of ice, with some rock and metal. The objects that formed closer to the Sun, where it was warmer, have little or no ice.

MAIN IDEA AND DETAILS
Remember to take notes to help you study later.

Asteroids

Small, solid, rocky bodies that orbit close to the Sun are called **asteroids.** They range from almost 1000 kilometers (600 mi) in diameter down to a kilometer or less. Except for the largest, their gravity is too weak to pull them into round spheres. Therefore, most asteroids have irregular shapes. Some asteroids are the broken pieces of larger, rounded asteroids.

Most asteroids have paths that keep them between the orbits of Mars and Jupiter. This huge region is called the asteroid belt, and contains more than 10,000 asteroids. However, the asteroids are so far apart that spacecraft from Earth have passed completely through the belt without danger of collision. The mass of all the asteroids put together is estimated to be less than the mass of our Moon.

The surfaces of asteroids are covered with craters, broken rock, and dust. Even though asteroids are far apart, smaller objects do hit them from time to time. Impacts from very long ago are still visible because most asteroids are not massive enough to have formed cores, mantles, and crusts. Therefore, they do not have volcanism or tectonics to erase the craters. Most asteroids do not have atmospheres, so their surfaces change only when impacts happen or when gravity pulls material downhill.

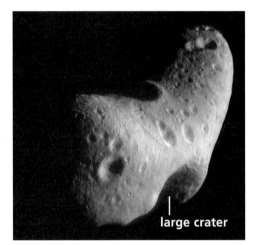

large crater

This asteroid is small compared with a planet, but it is large compared with a person. The large crater at the bottom is about the size of a small city.

 CHECK YOUR READING Why do asteroids have craters?

Some asteroids have collided with Earth in the past. The collisions left impact craters, some of which can still be seen today. Scientists have found evidence that an asteroid 10 kilometers (6 mi) in diameter hit Earth 65 million years ago. A cloud of dust from the collision spread around the world and probably affected surface temperatures. Many forms of life, including dinosaurs, died off at about that time, and the impact may have been part or all of the reason. Today astronomers are working to study all asteroids larger than 1 kilometer (0.6 mi) in diameter to determine whether any could hit Earth.

CALIFORNIA
Focus

The Jet Propulsion Laboratory, located at the California Institute of Technology, launched the Stardust spacecraft into Wild 2 comet in 2004 to collect dust samples from the comet for analysis and testing.

Comets

Sometimes, a fuzzy spot appears in the night sky. It grows from night to night as it changes position against the background stars. The fuzzy spot is a cloud of material, called a coma (KOH-muh), around a small space object. An object that produces a coma is called a **comet.** A comet without its coma is a small, icy object that is difficult to see even with a powerful telescope. Scientists use the number of comets that have become visible to infer that vast numbers of comets exist.

Comets formed far from the Sun, so they are made of different ices as well as rock and some metal. Their orbits are usually more oval than the paths of planets. A comet's orbit may carry it from regions far beyond Pluto's orbit to the inner solar system.

When a comet gets close to the Sun, solar radiation warms the surface and turns some of the ice into gas. A coma forms as the gas moves outward, often carrying dust with it. High-speed particles and radiation from the Sun push this material into one or more tails that can stretch for millions of kilometers. A comet's tails point away from the Sun no matter which way the comet is moving. The coma and tails look bright because sunlight shines on them, even though they may be less dense than Earth's atmosphere.

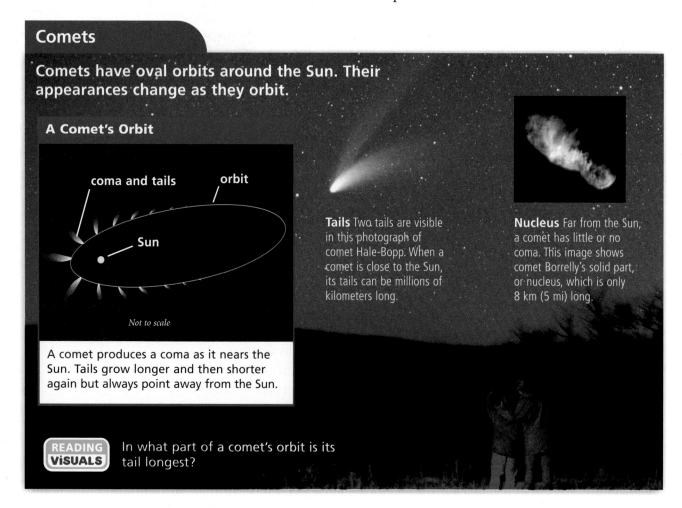

Comets

Comets have oval orbits around the Sun. Their appearances change as they orbit.

A Comet's Orbit

coma and tails

orbit

Sun

Not to scale

A comet produces a coma as it nears the Sun. Tails grow longer and then shorter again but always point away from the Sun.

Tails Two tails are visible in this photograph of comet Hale-Bopp. When a comet is close to the Sun, its tails can be millions of kilometers long.

Nucleus Far from the Sun, a comet has little or no coma. This image shows comet Borrelly's solid part, or nucleus, which is only 8 km (5 mi) long.

READING VISUALS In what part of a comet's orbit is its tail longest?

Most comets are too faint to be noticed easily from Earth. Many years can go by between appearances of bright comets, such as the one in the photograph on page 438.

 CHECK YOUR READING What makes a comet visible?

Meteors and Meteorites

Earth collides constantly with particles in space. Earth orbits the Sun at about 100,000 kilometers per hour (70,000 mi/h), so these particles enter Earth's thin upper atmosphere at very high speeds. The particles and the air around them become hot enough to glow, producing brief streaks of light called **meteors.** You may be able to see a few meteors per hour on a clear, dark night. Several times during the year, Earth passes through a stream of orbiting particles left by a comet. In the resulting meteor shower, you can see many meteors per hour.

A meteor produced by a particle from a comet may last less than a second. Bits of rock or metal from asteroids may produce brighter, longer-lasting meteors. Rarely, a very bright meteor, called a fireball, lights up the sky for several seconds.

An object with greater mass, perhaps 10 grams or more, may not be destroyed by Earth's atmosphere. A **meteorite** is a space object that reaches Earth's surface. The outside of a meteorite is usually smooth from melting, but the inside may still be frozen. Most meteorites come from the asteroid belt, but a few are rocky fragments that have been blasted into space from the Moon and Mars.

This piece of iron is part of a huge meteorite. The energy of the impact melted the metal and changed its shape.

 CHECK YOUR READING What is the difference between a meteor and a meteorite?

13.4 Review

KEY CONCEPTS

1. How are Pluto and most moons of the gas giant planets similar? (8.4.e)
2. List two differences between asteroids and comets. (8.4.e)
3. What causes meteors? (8.4.e)

CRITICAL THINKING

4. **Apply** Of the four types of processes that shape terrestrial worlds, which also shape the surfaces of moons of giant planets?
5. **Compare and Contrast** How is a comet different from a meteor?

⬥ CHALLENGE

6. **Predict** What do you think Pluto would look like if its orbit brought it close to the Sun?

CHAPTER INVESTIGATION

Exploring Impact Craters

OVERVIEW AND PURPOSE Nearly 50,000 years ago, an asteroid plummeted through Earth's atmosphere and exploded near what is now Winslow, Arizona. The photograph at left shows the resulting impact crater, which is about 1.2 kilometers (0.7 mi) wide. Most of the other craters on Earth have been erased. However, some planets and most moons in the solar system have surfaces that are covered with craters. In this investigation you will

- use solid objects to make craters in a flour surface
- determine how one variable affects the resulting crater

Problem

How does one characteristic of an impact or a colliding object affect the resulting crater?

Hypothesize

Complete steps 1–5 before writing your problem statement and hypothesis. Once you have identified a variable to test, write a hypothesis to explain how changing this variable will affect the crater. Your hypothesis should take the form of an "If . . . , then . . . , because . . ." statement.

Procedure

1. Place the container on newspapers and add flour to a depth of 2–4 cm. Stir the flour to break up any lumps, and then smooth the surface with a ruler. Sprinkle the top with colored powder.

2. Drop an object into the flour from waist height, then carefully remove it without disturbing the flour. Use the diagram to identify the various parts of the impact crater you made.

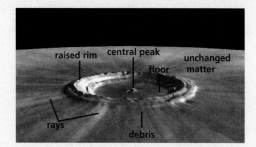

raised rim   central peak   unchanged matter
floor
rays   debris

3. To help you design your experiment, try several cratering methods. Make each new crater in a different location in the container. If your container becomes too full of craters, stir the flour, smooth it, and sprinkle on more colored powder.

Content Standard
8.4.e Students know the appearance, general composition, relative position and size, and motion of objects in the solar system, including planets, planetary satellites, comets, and asteroids.

Investigation Standard
8.9.c Distinguish between variable and controlled parameters in a test.

4. Design an experiment to test the effects of a variable. Choose just one variable to change—the height, the size or mass of the object, or perhaps the fluffiness of the flour. Determine how much you need to change your variable in order to get results different enough to see.

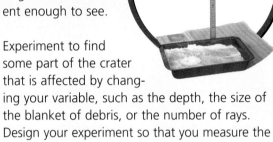

5. Experiment to find some part of the crater that is affected by changing your variable, such as the depth, the size of the blanket of debris, or the number of rays. Design your experiment so that you measure the part of the crater that changes the most.

6. Write a specific problem statement by completing the question, How does _____ affect _____? Write a hypothesis to answer your problem statement.

7. Perform your experiment. Do not change any factors except your chosen variable.

8. Make several trials for each value of your variable, because there are some factors you cannot control.

9. Record measurements and other observations and make drawings as you go along.

▶ Observe and Analyze   [Write It Up]

1. **RECORD** Use a diagram to show how you measure the craters. Organize your data into a table. Include spaces for averages.

2. **IDENTIFY VARIABLES** List the variables and constants. The independent variable is the factor that you changed. The dependent variable is affected by this change. Use these definitions when you graph your results.

3. **CALCULATE** Determine averages by adding all of your measurements at each value of your independent variable, then dividing the sum by the number of measurements.

4. **GRAPH** Make a line graph of your average results. Place the independent variable on the horizontal axis and the dependent variable on the vertical axis. Why should you use a line graph instead of a bar graph for these data?

▶ Conclude   [Write It Up]

1. **ANALYZE** Answer your problem statement. Do your data support your hypothesis?

2. **EVALUATE** Did you identify a trend in your results? Is your experiment a failure if you did not identify a trend? Why or why not?

3. **IDENTIFY LIMITS** How would you modify the design of your experiment now that you have seen the results?

4. **APPLY** What do you think would happen if a colliding object hit water instead of land?

▶ INVESTIGATE Further

CHALLENGE How do the craters in this model differ from real impact craters? Design, but do not attempt, an experiment to simulate the cratering process more realistically.

Exploring Impact Craters
Problem How does _____ affect _____?
Hypothesize
Observe and Analyze
Table 1. Data and Averages

Conclude

13 Chapter Review

the BIG idea

Planets and other objects form a system around our Sun.

CONTENT REVIEW
CLASSZONE.COM

KEY CONCEPTS SUMMARY

1 Planets orbit the Sun at different distances.

The planets have different sizes and distances from the Sun. The solar system formed from a disk of dust and gas. Massive objects became round.

inner solar system	outer solar system
Mercury, Venus, Earth, Mars, asteroids	Jupiter, Saturn, Uranus, Neptune, Pluto, comets

VOCABULARY
astronomical unit (AU) p. 415
ellipse p. 415

2 The inner solar system has rocky planets.

- The terrestrial planets are round and have layers.
- Atmospheres came from volcanoes and impacts.
- Four processes produce surface features.

   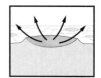

tectonics   volcanism   weathering and erosion   impact cratering

VOCABULARY
terrestrial planet p. 419
tectonics p. 420
volcanism p. 420

3 The outer solar system has four giant planets.

- The gas giants have very dense, deep atmospheres with layers of clouds.
- All four giant planets have ring systems.

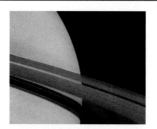

Close-up of Saturn's rings

VOCABULARY
gas giant p. 428
ring p. 431

4 Small objects are made of ice and rock.

- Objects in the inner solar system are rocky.
- Pluto and most other objects in the outer solar system are made of ice and rock.
- Rocky asteroids and icy comets orbit the Sun and produce tiny fragments that may become meteors.

The asteroid Eros

VOCABULARY
asteroid p. 437
comet p. 438
meteor p. 439
meteorite p. 439

Reviewing Vocabulary

Make a Venn diagram for each pair of terms. Put an important similarity in the overlapping part. Use the rest of the diagram to show important differences.

Example:

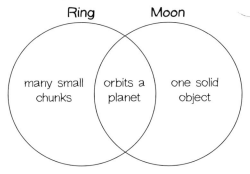

Ring   Moon

many small chunks | orbits a planet | one solid object

1. terrestrial planet, gas giant

2. volcanism, impact cratering

3. erosion, tectonics

4. asteroid, comet

5. meteor, meteorite

6. comet, meteor

Reviewing Key Concepts

Multiple Choice *Choose the letter of the best answer.*

7. Even though orbits are ellipses, what shape is a typical planet's orbit most like? (8.2.g)

  a. a short rectangle

  b. an egg-shape with a pointy end

  c. a long, narrow oval

  d. a circle

8. How is a moon different from a planet? (8.4.e)

  a. A moon is smaller than any planet.

  b. A moon is less massive than any planet.

  c. A moon is in orbit around a planet.

  d. A moon is unable to have an atmosphere.

9. Which of these appears in Earth's atmosphere? (8.4.e)

  a. a moon   **c.** a meteor

  b. an asteroid   **d.** a comet

10. How did planets and other objects in the solar system form? (8.2.g)

  a. After the Sun formed, it threw off hot pieces that spun and cooled.

  b. The Sun captured objects that formed in other places in the galaxy.

  c. Two stars collided, and the broken pieces went into orbit around the Sun.

  d. Material in a disk formed large clumps as the Sun formed in the center of the disk.

11. Which process occurs only when a small space object interacts with a larger space body? (8.4.e)

  a. tectonics   **c.** erosion

  b. volcanism   **d.** impact cratering

12. Which processes occur because a planet or another space body is hot inside? (8.4.e)

  a. tectonics and volcanism

  b. volcanism and erosion

  c. erosion and impact cratering

  d. impact cratering and tectonics

13. What do all four gas giants have that terrestrial planets do not have? (8.4.e)

  a. atmospheres   **c.** moons

  b. solid surfaces   **d.** rings

14. What are the white stripes of Jupiter and the white spots of Neptune? (8.4.e)

  a. clouds high in the atmosphere

  b. smoke from volcanoes

  c. continents and islands

  d. holes in the atmosphere

Short Answer *Write a short answer to each question.*

15. The solid part of a comet is small in comparison with a planet. However, sometimes a comet appears to be larger than the Sun. What makes it seem so large? (8.4.e)

16. Why do all nine major planets orbit the Sun in the same direction? (8.4.e)

Thinking Critically

Use the image of Jupiter's moon Ganymede to answer the next five questions.

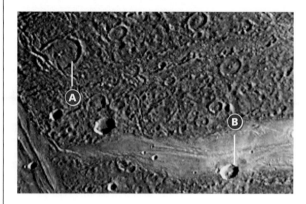

17. OBSERVE Which crater, A or B, is more eroded? Explain why you think so. (8.4.e)

18. COMPARE AND CONTRAST Describe the differences between the surface in the upper half of the image and the long, triangular area near the bottom of the image. (8.4.e)

19. INFER Explain which area of the surface, the smooth part or the heavily cratered part, is probably older. (8.4.e)

20. APPLY The lighter area was produced by tectonic processes and may have been covered with molten material. What can you infer about the inside of this moon? (8.4.e)

21. SEQUENCE A crack runs through part of crater A. Explain how you can tell whether the crack or the crater formed first. **Hint:** Think about what would have happened if the other feature had formed first. (8.4.e)

22. PREDICT Suppose the Moon were hotter inside. How might its surface be different? (8.4.e)

23. IDENTIFY CAUSE Mercury's surface is not as hot as Venus's, even though Mercury is closer to the Sun. In addition, the night side of Mercury gets very cold, while the night side of Venus is about as hot as the day side. Why are the temperature patterns on these two planets so different? (8.4.e)

24. EVALUATE Would it be easier to design a lander mission for the surface of Venus or the surface of Mercury? Explain your reasoning. (8.4.e)

25. INFER Some comets orbit in a direction opposite to that of the planets. Why might this make some scientists wonder if they formed with the rest of the solar system? (8.4.e)

26. HYPOTHESIZE Scientists calculate the mass of a planet from the effects of its gravity on other objects, such as moons. However, Mercury and Venus have no moons. What other objects in space could have been used to determine the planets' masses? (8.4.e)

27. COMPARE AND CONTRAST Images of Earth from space show white clouds above darker land and water. In what ways are they like and unlike images of Jupiter? (8.4.e)

Earth   **Jupiter**

28. ANALYZE Scientists sometimes use round numbers to compare quantities. For example, a scientist might say that the Sun's diameter is about 100 times Earth's diameter, even though she knows that the precise value is 109 times. Why might she use such an approximation? (8.4.e)

the BIG idea

29. APPLY Look back at pages 410–411. Think about the answer you gave to the question about the large image of a planet and moon. How would you answer this question differently now? (8.4.e)

30. SYNTHESIZE Ice is generally less dense than rock, which is generally less dense than metal. Use what you know about materials in the solar system to estimate whether a moon of Mars, a moon of Uranus, or the planet Mercury should be the least dense. (8.4.e)

UNIT PROJECTS

Check your schedule for your unit project. How are you doing? Be sure that you have placed data or notes from your research in your project folder.

Interpreting a Passage

8.4.e

Read the following passage. Then answer the questions that follow.

Life in Extreme Environments

Could living organisms survive in the crushing, hot atmosphere of Venus? Could they thrive on a waterless asteroid or get their energy from tides in the dark ocean that might be beneath the surface of Europa? Scientists are looking for answers to these questions right here on Earth. They study extremophiles, which are life forms that can survive in extreme environments—very high or low temperatures or other difficult conditions. These environments have conditions similar to those on other planets, and those on moons, asteroids, and comets.

Scientists have found tiny organisms that grow in the scalding water of hot vents on the ocean floor, deep inside rock, and in miniature ponds within glaciers. Scientists have also found organisms that were dormant because they were frozen solid for thousands of years but that were still capable of living and growing after warming up. By studying extremophiles, scientists learn more about the conditions needed to support life.

Choose from the following four environments to answer each of the next three questions.

- the dark ocean that might be underneath Europa's surface
- the flood channels on Mars, which have been dry and frozen for a long time
- the very hot, high-pressure environment of Venus
- the dry rock of an asteroid that alternately heats and cools

1. Some organisms survive deep underwater, where photosynthesis does not occur because little or no sunlight reaches those depths. Which environment can these organisms teach about?
   a. under Europa's surface   **c.** Venus
   b. Martian flood channels   **d.** an asteroid

2. Some organisms survive in very deep cracks in rocks, where they are protected from changing temperatures. Where else might scientists look for these types of organisms?
   a. under Europa's surface   **c.** Venus
   b. Martian flood channels   **d.** an asteroid

3. Where might scientists look for tiny organisms that are dormant but that might revive if given warmth and water?
   a. under Europa's surface   **c.** Venus
   b. Martian flood channels   **d.** an asteroid

4. Where, outside Earth, should scientists look for tiny ponds of water within solid ice?
   a. the other terrestrial planets
   b. the gas giants
   c. small space objects in the inner solar system
   d. small space objects in the outer solar system

Extended Response

Answer the two questions in detail.

5. A class was given a sample of ordinary dormant, dry yeast that had been exposed to an extreme environment. Describe ways the students might test the yeast to see if it remained undamaged, or even survived, the conditions.

6. Imagine that scientists have found extremophiles in clouds of frozen water crystals high in Earth's atmosphere. How might this discovery affect a search for organisms on the gas giants?

📞 8.2.g, 8.4.a, 8.4.b, 8.4.e

THE STORY OF ASTRONOMY

Around the year A.D. 140, an astronomer named Ptolemy wrote down his ideas about the motion of bodies in space. Ptolemy shared the view of many Greek astronomers that the Sun, the Moon, and the planets orbit Earth in perfect circles. The Greeks had observed that planets sometimes seem to reverse direction in their motion across the sky. Ptolemy explained that the backward movements are smaller orbits within the larger orbits. For 1400 years, Europeans accepted this Earth-centered model. In the mid-1500s, however, astronomers began to challenge and then reject Ptolemy's ideas.

The timeline shows a few events in the history of astronomy. Scientists have developed special tools and procedures to study objects in the sky. The boxes below the timeline show how technology has led to new knowledge about space and how that knowledge has been applied.

1543

Sun Takes Center Stage

Nicolaus Copernicus, a Polish astronomer, proposes that the planets orbit the Sun rather than Earth. His Sun-centered model shocks many because it conflicts with the traditional belief that Earth is the center of the universe.

EVENTS

| 1500 | 1520 | 1540 | 1560 |

APPLICATIONS AND TECHNOLOGY

APPLICATION

Navigating by Sunlight and Starlight

For thousands of years, sailors studied the sky to find their way at sea. Because the Sun and stars move in predictable ways, sailors used them to navigate across water. During the 1400s, sailors began to use a device called a mariner's astrolabe to observe the positions of the Sun and stars. Later devices allowed sailors to make more accurate measurements.

This mariner's astrolabe was made in the 1600s.

1609
Scientist Pinpoints Planet Paths

German astronomer Johannes Kepler concludes that the orbits of planets are not circles but ellipses, or flattened circles. Kepler, formerly the assistant of Tycho Brahe, reached his conclusion by studying Brahe's careful observations of the motions of planets.

1863
Stars and Earth Share Elements

English astronomer William Huggins announces that stars are made of hydrogen and other elements found on Earth. Astronomers had traditionally believed that stars were made of a unique substance. Huggins identified the elements in stars by studying their spectra.

1687
Laws of Gravity Revealed

English scientist Isaac Newton explains that gravity causes planets to orbit the Sun. His three laws of motion explain how objects interact on Earth as well as in space.

| 1600 | 1620 | 1640 | 1660 | 1680 | 1860 |

TECHNOLOGY

Viewing Space

The telescope was probably invented in the early 1600s, when an eyeglass maker attached lenses to both ends of a tube. Soon afterward, Italian scientist Galileo Galilei copied the invention and used it to look at objects in space. Galileo's telescope allowed him to study features never seen before, such as mountains on the Moon. Most astronomers now use telescopes that gather visible light with mirrors rather than lenses. There are also special telescopes that gather other forms of electromagnetic radiation.

1912

Cycles of Stars Are Key to Distances

Certain types of stars, called Cepheid variables, get brighter and then dimmer in a regular cycle. Astronomer Henrietta Leavitt finds that brighter stars have longer cycles. This discovery will allow the distances to these stars to be calculated.

1916

Time, Space, and Mass Are Connected

The general theory of relativity expands Newton's theory of gravitation. Albert Einstein shows that mass affects time and space. According to this theory, gravity will affect the light we receive from objects in space.

1929

Big Is Getting Bigger

Edwin Hubble has already used Cepheid variables to show that some objects in the sky are actually distant galaxies. Now he finds that galaxies are generally moving apart, at rates that increase with distance. Many astronomers conclude that the universe is expanding.

1880   1900   1920   1940   1960

TECHNOLOGY

Colliding Particles Give Details About the Start of the Universe

Scientists think that all matter and energy was in an extremely hot, dense state and then exploded rapidly in an event called the big bang. Some scientists are attempting to re-create some of the conditions that existed during the first billionth of a second after the big bang. They use devices called particle accelerators to make tiny particles move almost at the speed of light. When the particles crash into each other, they produce different types of particles and radiation. Scientists use what they learn from the particles and the radiation to develop models of conditions at the beginning of the universe.

1998

Fast Is Getting Faster

Two groups of astronomers studying exploding stars called supernovae come to the same remarkable conclusion. Not only is the universe expanding, but the rate of expansion is increasing. In the diagram below, the rate of expansion is shown by the distances between rings and between galaxies.

The expanding universe

Present

Expansion slows down | Expansion speeds up

Big Bang

Farthest supernova

~15 billion years

RESOURCE CENTER
CLASSZONE.COM
Learn more about current advances in astronomy.

1980   2000

TECHNOLOGY

Measuring the Big Bang

In 1965 two researchers noticed radio waves that came from all directions instead of from just one direction, like a signal from a space object. They inferred that the radiation was left over from the big bang. In 1989 and again in 2001, NASA launched spacecraft to study the radiation. Data gathered using these telescopes in space are still being used to test different models of the big bang, including the arrangement of matter in the universe. In this map of the sky, red and yellow show the areas that were hottest after the big bang.

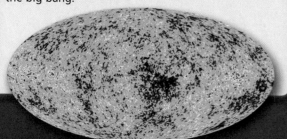

SPOTLIGHT on
NEIL deGRASSE TYSON

Astrophysicist Neil deGrasse Tyson has taken on many roles: research scientist, museum director, magazine columnist, book author, and public television host. All are connected by his interest in stars and the origins of the universe. In 2001 and 2004 he served on presidential commissions on the future of U.S. space exploration.

Tyson's recent research is in star formation, exploding stars, dwarf galaxies, and the Milky Way's mysterious "bulge." His work is based on data from the Hubble Space Telescope and telescopes in California, Arizona, New Mexico, and Chile. In 2000 the International Astronomical Union recognized Tyson's accomplishments by naming an asteroid "13123 Tyson."

ACTIVITIES

Reliving History

Some early astronomers observed the Moon in order to develop and test their ideas about space. For two weeks or more, make frequent observations of the Moon and keep your notes, sketches, and thoughts in a notebook. You might look for the Moon at a certain time each day or night or perhaps record the direction in which the Moon sets. A newspaper may list the times of moonrise and moonset for your location.

Compare your observations and thoughts with those of other students. You might also find out what people in other cultures thought of the patterns of change they saw in the Moon.

Writing About Science

Choose one of these famous astronomers and research his or her story. Write a biographical profile or an imaginary interview with that person.

Stars, Galaxies, and the Universe

the **BIG** idea

Our Sun is one of billions of stars in one of billions of galaxies in the universe.

What could be present in the light and dark areas in this galaxy?

Key Concepts

SECTION

1 **The Sun is our local star.**
Learn how the Sun produces energy and about the Sun's layers and features.

SECTION

2 **Stars change over their life cycles.**
Learn how stars form and change.

SECTION

3 **Galaxies have different sizes and shapes.**
Learn how galaxies are classified.

SECTION

4 **The universe is expanding.**
Learn about the formation and expansion of the universe.

California ClassZone

CLASSZONE.COM

Chapter 14 online resources:
Visualization, Simulation,
three Resource Centers,
Math Tutorial, Test Practice

EXPLORE (the BIG idea)

How Can Stars Differ?

> **8.4.b** Students know that the Sun is one of many stars in the Milky Way galaxy and that stars may differ in size, temperature, and color.

Look at the sky at night and find three stars that differ in appearance. For example, you might try to find stars of different brightnesses or colors. Try to identify the locations of these stars, using the star maps in the Appendix at the back of this book.

Observe and Think
How did the characteristics of the stars differ? How were they the same?

Internet Activity: Galaxy Shapes

> **8.4.a** Students know galaxies are clusters of billions of stars and may have different shapes.

Go to **ClassZone.com** to explore the different shapes of galaxies in the universe. Describe the different shapes you see.

Observe and Think
How do the types of galaxies differ from one another?

The Sun Code: MDL060

Getting Ready to Learn

◀ CONCEPT REVIEW

- Electromagnetic radiation carries information about space.
- Our solar system is in the Milky Way galaxy.
- A galaxy is a group of millions or billions of stars.

◀ VOCABULARY REVIEW

solar system p. 376

galaxy p. 376

universe p. 376

See Glossary for definitions.
electromagnetic radiation, wavelength

CONTENT REVIEW
CLASSZONE.COM

Review concepts and vocabulary.

▶ TAKING NOTES

CHOOSE YOUR OWN STRATEGY

Take notes using one or both of the strategies from earlier chapters—**combination notes** or **main idea and details.** Feel free to mix and match the strategies, or use an entirely different note-taking strategy.

VOCABULARY STRATEGY

Place each vocabulary term at the center of a **description wheel** diagram. Write some words describing it on the spokes.

See the Note-Taking Handbook on pages R45–R51.

SCIENCE NOTEBOOK

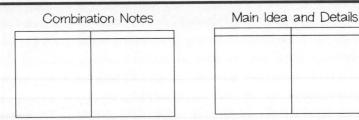

Combination Notes

Main Idea and Details

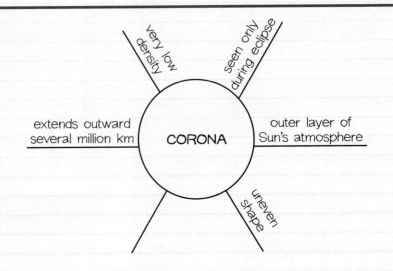

very low density

seen only during eclipse

extends outward several million km

CORONA

outer layer of Sun's atmosphere

uneven shape

14.1
KEY CONCEPT
The Sun is our local star.

CALIFORNIA
Content Standards

8.4.b Students know that the Sun is one of many stars in the Milky Way galaxy and that stars may differ in size, temperature, and color.

8.4.d Students know that stars are the source of light for all bright objects in outer space and that the Moon and planets shine by reflected sunlight, not by their own light.

VOCABULARY

fusion p. 454
convection p. 454
corona p. 454
sunspot p. 456
solar wind p. 457

BEFORE, you learned

- There are different wavelengths of electromagnetic radiation
- The Sun provides light in the solar system

NOW, you will learn

- How the Sun produces energy
- How energy flows through the Sun's layers
- About solar features and solar wind

EXPLORE Solar Atmosphere (8.4.d)

How can blocking light reveal dim features?

PROCEDURE

(1) Unbend the paper clip and use it to make a tiny hole in the center of the card.

(2) Turn on the lamp, and briefly try to read the writing on the bulb.

(3) Close one eye, and hold the card in front of your other eye. Through the hole, try to read the writing on the bulb.

WHAT DO YOU THINK?

- How did looking through the hole affect your view of the writing?
- How might a solar eclipse affect your view of the Sun's dim outermost layer?

MATERIALS

- small paper clip
- index card
- lamp with 45-watt bulb

MAIN IDEA AND DETAILS
You could record information about the Sun by using a main idea and details table.

The Sun produces energy from hydrogen.

The Sun is the only star in our solar system. Astronomers have been able to study the Sun in more detail than other stars because it is much closer to Earth. As a result, they have learned a great deal about its size and composition and the way it produces energy.

The Sun is far larger than any of the planets. It contains 99.9 percent of the mass of the entire solar system. For comparison, imagine that Earth had the mass of a sparrow; then the Sun would have the mass of an elephant.

The Sun consists mostly of hydrogen gas. Energy is produced when hydrogen in the Sun's interior turns into helium. This energy is the source of light and warmth that make life possible on Earth.

Energy flows through the Sun's layers.

Although the Sun is made entirely of gas, it does have a structure. Energy produced in the center of the Sun flows out through the Sun's layers in different forms, including visible light.

The Sun's Interior

The Sun's interior generally becomes cooler and less dense as you move away from the center.

REMINDER

Remember that radiation is energy that travels across distances as electromagnetic waves.

1 Core The center of the Sun, called the core, is made of very dense gas. Temperatures reach about 15 million degrees Celsius. Under these extreme conditions, some hydrogen particles collide and combine to form helium in a process called **fusion.** The process releases energy that travels through the core by radiation.

2 Radiative Zone Energy from the core moves by radiation through a thick layer called the radiative zone. Although this layer is very hot and dense, conditions in the radiative zone are not extreme enough for fusion to occur.

3 Convection Zone In the convection zone, energy moves mainly by convection. **Convection** is the transfer of energy from place to place by the motion of heated gas or liquid. Rising currents of hot gas in the convection zone carry energy toward the Sun's surface.

 CHECK YOUR READING Where does the Sun's energy come from?

The Sun's Atmosphere

SIMULATION
CLASSZONE.COM

View the Sun at different wavelengths.

The Sun's outer layers are called its atmosphere. These layers are much less dense than the interior. The atmosphere generally becomes hotter and less dense as you move outward.

4 Photosphere Visible light moves by radiation out into space from the photosphere. It takes about eight minutes for the light to reach Earth. Since the photosphere is the layer you see in photographs of the Sun, it is often called the Sun's surface. Convection currents beneath the photosphere cause it to have a bumpy texture.

5 Chromosphere The chromosphere is the thin middle layer of the Sun's atmosphere. It gives off a pinkish light.

6 Corona The Sun's outermost layer is called the **corona.** The corona, which varies in shape, extends outward several million kilometers. Both the chromosphere and the corona are much hotter than the photosphere. However, they have such low densities that you can see their light only during a total eclipse of the Sun, when the Moon blocks the much brighter light from the photosphere.

Layers of the Sun

Energy produced by fusion in the Sun's core flows out through its layers.

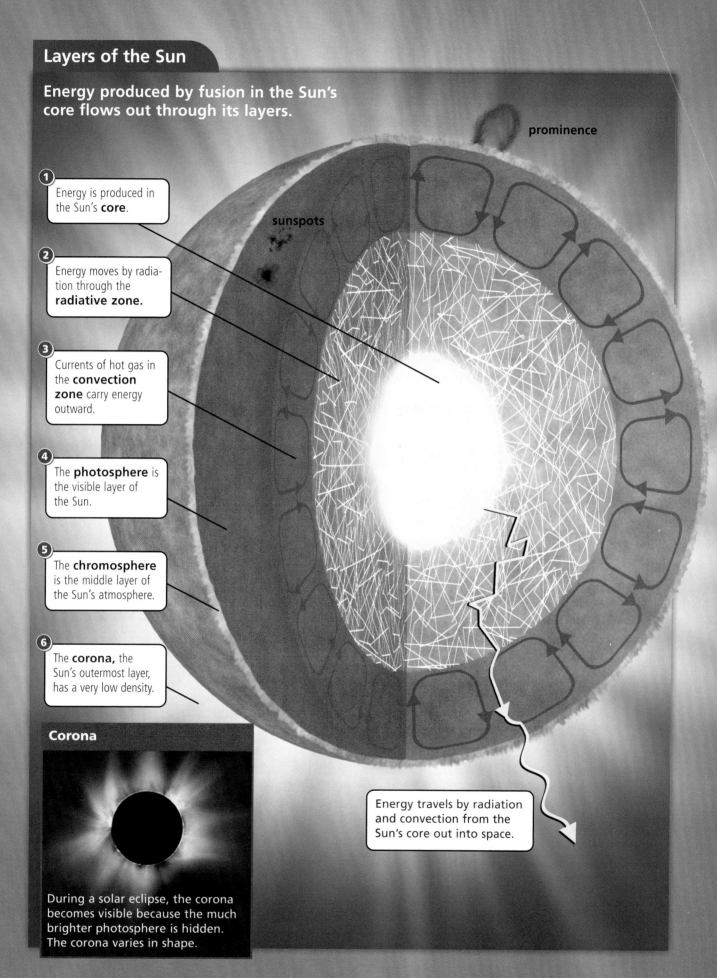

① Energy is produced in the Sun's **core**.

② Energy moves by radiation through the **radiative zone.**

③ Currents of hot gas in the **convection zone** carry energy outward.

④ The **photosphere** is the visible layer of the Sun.

⑤ The **chromosphere** is the middle layer of the Sun's atmosphere.

⑥ The **corona,** the Sun's outermost layer, has a very low density.

prominence

sunspots

Energy travels by radiation and convection from the Sun's core out into space.

Corona

During a solar eclipse, the corona becomes visible because the much brighter photosphere is hidden. The corona varies in shape.

Features on the Sun

Astronomers have observed features on the Sun that vary over time. Near the Sun's surface there are regions of magnetic force called magnetic fields. These magnetic fields get twisted into different positions as the Sun rotates. Features appear on the surface in areas where strong magnetic fields are located.

Sunspots are spots on the photosphere that are cooler than surrounding areas. Although they appear dark, sunspots are actually bright. They only seem dim because the rest of the photosphere is so much brighter.

Sunspot activity follows a pattern that lasts about 11 years. At the peak of the cycle, dozens of sunspots may appear. During periods of low activity, there may not be any sunspots.

Sunspots move across the Sun's surface as it rotates. Astronomers first realized that the Sun rotates when they noticed this movement. Because the Sun is not solid, some parts rotate faster than others.

Other solar features include flares and prominences (PRAHM-uh-nuhn-sihz). Flares are eruptions of hot gas from the Sun's surface. They usually occur near sunspots. Prominences are huge loops of glowing gas that extend into the corona. They occur where magnetic fields connecting sunspots soar into the outer atmosphere.

CHECK YOUR READING How are sunspots different from other areas of the photosphere?

CALIFORNIA Focus

In the 1960s, an astronomer at Mt. Wilson discovered that the Sun vibrated with a 5-minute cycle. Mt. Wilson's 60-foot Solar Tower is still used today to study these vibrations, called solar quakes.

Solar Features

Features on the Sun appear in areas where a magnetic field is strong.

Sunspots

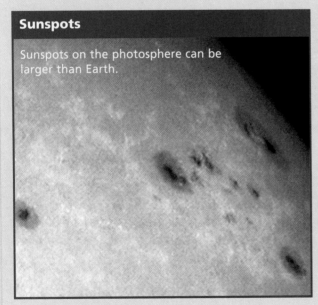

Sunspots on the photosphere can be larger than Earth.

Prominences

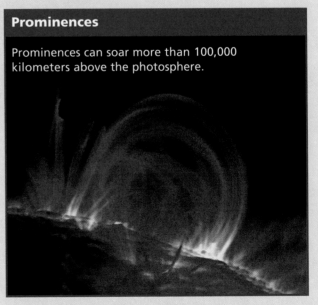

Prominences can soar more than 100,000 kilometers above the photosphere.

Solar Wind

Material in the Sun's corona is continually streaming out into space. The electrically charged particles that flow out in all directions from the corona are called the **solar wind.** The solar wind extends throughout our solar system.

This circular green aurora occurred over Alaska when particles from the solar wind entered the atmosphere.

Most of the solar wind flowing toward Earth is safely guided around the planet by Earth's magnetic field. When solar-wind particles do enter the upper atmosphere, they release energy, which can produce beautiful patterns of glowing light in the sky. Such displays of light are called auroras (uh-RAWR-uhz), or the northern and southern lights. Auroras often occur near the poles.

Earth's atmosphere usually prevents charged particles from reaching the surface. However, during the peak of the sunspot cycle, flares and other kinds of solar activity release strong bursts of charged particles into the solar wind. These bursts, called magnetic storms, can disrupt electric-power delivery across large regions by causing surges in power lines. They can also interfere with radio communication.

Magnetic storms are much more harmful above the protective layers of Earth's atmosphere. Bursts of particles in the solar wind can damage or destroy orbiting satellites. The solar wind also poses a danger to astronauts during space flights.

 CHECK YOUR READING What causes auroras to form?

14.1 Review

KEY CONCEPTS

1. How does the Sun produce energy? (8.4.b)
2. How does energy move from the Sun's core to the photosphere? (8.4.b)
3. How does the solar wind normally affect Earth? (8.4.b)

CRITICAL THINKING

4. **Analyze** Why is the core the only layer of the Sun where energy is produced?
5. **Compare and Contrast** Make a diagram comparing sunspots, flares, and prominences.

⬥ CHALLENGE

6. **Infer** A communications satellite stops working while in orbit, and a surge in an electric power line causes blackouts in cities across a large region. What probably happened in the Sun's atmosphere shortly before these events?

CHAPTER INVESTIGATION

Temperature, Brightness, and Color

OVERVIEW AND PURPOSE Think of the metal heating surface on a hot plate. How can you tell whether the hot plate is fully heated? Is the metal surface brighter or dimmer than when it is just starting to get warm? Does the color of the surface change as the hot plate gets hotter? You may already have an idea of how temperature, brightness, and color are related—at least when it comes to heated metal. Do the same relationships apply to electric lights? to stars? This investigation is designed to help you find out. You will

- construct a wax photometer to compare the brightnesses and colors of different light sources
- determine how the temperature of a light source affects its brightness and color

▶ Problem
Write It Up

How are brightness and color related to temperature?

▶ Hypothesize
Write It Up

Write a hypothesis to explain how brightness and color are related to temperature. Your hypothesis should take the form of an "If . . . , then . . . , because . . ." statement.

▶ Procedure

1. An instrument called a photometer makes it easier to compare the brightnesses and colors of different light sources. Assemble the wax photometer as shown on page 459. The aluminum foil between the wax blocks should be folded so that the shiny side faces out on both sides. Use the photometer assembly datasheet as a guide.

2. Hold the photometer so that you can see both blocks. Bring it to different locations in the classroom, and observe how the brightnesses and colors of the blocks change as the two sides of the photometer are exposed to different light conditions.

3. Tape a piece of copper wire to each end of a battery, and connect the wires to a light-bulb holder. The battery will provide electricity to heat up the wire inside a light bulb.

MATERIALS

- 2 paraffin blocks
- aluminum foil
- 2 rubber bands
- photometer assembly datasheet
- 2 light-bulb holders
- 2 miniature light bulbs
- 3 AA batteries
- 4 pieces of uninsulated copper wire 15 cm long
- masking tape

for Challenge:
- incandescent lamp
- dimmer switch

8.4.b, 8.9.a

step 3

Content Standard
8.4.b Students know that the Sun is one of many stars in the Milky Way galaxy and that stars may differ in size, temperature, and color.

Investigation Standard
8.9.a Plan and conduct a scientific investigation to test a hypothesis.

4 Tape the negative terminal, or flat end, of one battery to the positive terminal of another battery. Tape a piece of copper wire to each end, and connect the wires to a light-bulb holder. Because two batteries will provide electricity to the bulb in this holder, the wire in the bulb will be hotter than the wire in the bulb powered by one battery.

step 4

5 With the room darkened, insert a bulb into each light-bulb holder. If the bulb connected to two batteries does not light up, you may need to press the two batteries together with your fingers.

6 Place the photometer halfway between the two light bulbs. Compare the brightnesses of the two light sources. Record your observations in your **Science Notebook.**

7 Move the photometer closer to the cooler bulb until both sides of the photometer are equally bright. Compare the colors of the two light sources. Record your observations in your **Science Notebook**. To avoid draining the batteries, remove the bulbs from the holders when you have completed this step.

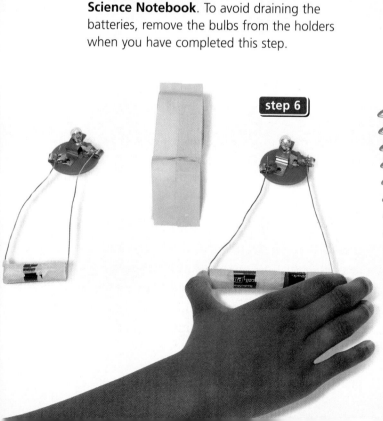
step 6

▶ Observe and Analyze
Write It Up

1. **RECORD OBSERVATIONS** Draw the setup of your photometer and light sources. Be sure your data table is complete with descriptions of brightness and color.

2. **IDENTIFY** Identify the variables in this experiment. List them in your **Science Notebook.**

▶ Conclude
Write It Up

1. **INTERPRET** Answer the question in the problem. Compare your results with your hypothesis.

2. **ANALYZE** How does distance affect your perception of the brightness of an object?

3. **APPLY** Judging by the results of the investigation, would you expect a red star or a yellow star to be hotter? Explain why.

▶ INVESTIGATE Further

CHALLENGE Connect an incandescent lamp to a dimmer switch. Write a procedure to show how you would use a photometer to show the relationship between the color and the temperature of the bulb as it fades from brightest to dimmest. Then carry out your procedure.

Temperature, Brightness, and Color
Observe and Analyze
Table 1. Properties of Light from Two Sources

	Cooler Bulb (one battery)	Warmer Bulb (two batteries)
Brightness		
Color		

14.2 Stars change over their life cycles.

CALIFORNIA
Content Standards

8.4.b Students know that the Sun is one of many stars in the Milky Way galaxy and that stars may differ in size, temperature, and color.

8.4.c Students know how to use astronomical units and light years as measures of distances between the Sun, stars, and Earth.

8.4.d Students know that stars are the source of light for all bright objects in outer space and that the Moon and planets shine by reflected sunlight, not by their own light.

BEFORE, you learned

- The Sun is our local star
- The other stars are outside our solar system
- There are huge distances between objects in the universe

NOW, you will learn

- How stars are classified
- How stars form and change

VOCABULARY

light-year p. 460
parallax p. 461
nebula p. 463
main sequence p. 464
neutron star p. 464
black hole p. 464

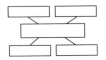

MAIN IDEA WEB
A main idea web would be a good choice for taking notes about the characteristics of stars.

EXPLORE Characteristics of Stars (8.4.b)

How does distance affect brightness?

PROCEDURE

1. In a darkened room, shine a flashlight onto a dark surface from 30 cm away while your partner shines a flashlight onto the surface from the same distance. Observe the two spots of light.

2. Move one of the flashlights back 15 cm and then another 15 cm. Compare the two spots of light each time you move the flashlight.

MATERIALS
- 2 flashlights
- meter stick
- dark surface

WHAT DO YOU THINK?
- How did distance affect the brightness of the light on the dark surface?
- How does the distance of a star from Earth affect our view of it?

We classify stars by their characteristics.

Like our Sun, all stars are huge balls of glowing gas that produce or have produced energy by fusion. However, stars differ in size, brightness, and temperature. Some stars are smaller, fainter, and cooler than the Sun. Others are much bigger, brighter, and hotter.

Stars look like small points of light because they are very far away. At most, only a few thousand can be seen without a telescope. To describe the distances between stars, astronomers often use a unit called the light-year. A **light-year** is the distance light travels in one year, which is about 9.5 trillion kilometers (6 trillion mi). Outside the solar system, the star closest to Earth is about 4 light-years away.

Brightness and Distance

If you look at stars, you will probably notice that some appear to be brighter than others. The amount of light a star gives off and its distance from Earth determine how bright it appears to an observer. A star that gives off a huge amount of light can appear faint if it is far away. On the other hand, a star that gives off much less light can appear bright if it is closer to Earth. Therefore, to determine the true brightness of a star, astronomers must measure its distance from Earth.

One way astronomers measure distance is by using **parallax,** which is the apparent shift in the position of an object when viewed from different locations. Look at an object with your right eye closed. Now quickly open it and close your left eye. The object will seem to move slightly because you are viewing it from a different angle. The same kind of shift occurs when astronomers view stars from different locations.

To measure the parallax of a star, astronomers plot the star's position in the sky from opposite sides of Earth's orbit around the Sun. They then use the apparent shift in position and the diameter of Earth's orbit to calculate the star's distance.

 CHECK YOUR READING What factors affect how bright a star appears from Earth?

INVESTIGATE Parallax

How does the distance of an object affect parallax?

PROCEDURE

1. Stand 1 m away from a classmate. Have the classmate hold up a meter stick at eye level.

2. With your left eye closed, hold a capped pen up close to your face. Look at the pen with your right eye, and line it up with the zero mark on the meter stick. Then open your left eye and quickly close your right eye. Observe how many centimeters the pen seems to move. Record your observation.

3. Repeat step 2 with the pen held at arm's length and then with the pen held at half your arm's length. Record your observation each time.

WHAT DO YOU THINK?

- How many centimeters did the pen appear to move each time you observed it?

- How is parallax affected when you change the distance of the pen from you?

CHALLENGE How could you use this method to estimate distances that you cannot measure directly?

SKILL FOCUS
Measuring (8.4.c)

MATERIALS
- meter stick
- capped pen

TIME
10 minutes

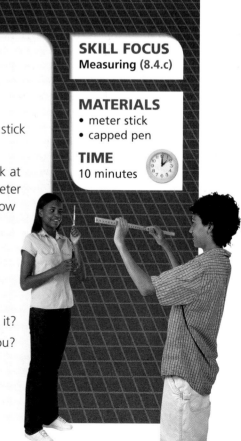

Size

It is hard to get a sense of how large stars are from viewing them in the sky. Even the Sun, which is much closer than any other star, is far larger than its appearance suggests. The diameter of the Sun is about 100 times greater than that of Earth. A jet plane flying 800 kilometers per hour (500 mi/h) would travel around Earth's equator in about two days. If you could travel around the Sun's equator at the same speed, the trip would take more than seven months.

Some stars are much larger than the Sun. Giant and supergiant stars range from ten to hundreds of times larger. A supergiant called Betelgeuse (BEET-uhl-JOOZ) is more than 600 times greater in diameter than the Sun. If Betelgeuse replaced the Sun, it would fill space in our solar system well beyond Earth's orbit. Because giant and supergiant stars have such huge surface areas to give off light, they are very bright. Betelgeuse is one of the brightest stars in the sky, even though it is 522 light-years away.

There are also stars much smaller than the Sun. Stars called white dwarfs are about 100 times smaller in diameter than the Sun, or roughly the size of Earth. White dwarfs cannot be seen without a telescope.

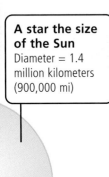

A star the size of the Sun
Diameter = 1.4 million kilometers (900,000 mi)

White dwarf
1/100 the Sun's diameter

Giant star
10–100 times the Sun's diameter

Supergiant star
100–1000 times the Sun's diameter

Color and Temperature

If you observe stars closely, you may notice that they vary slightly in color. Most stars look white. However, a few appear slightly blue or red. The differences in color are due to differences in temperature.

You can see how temperature affects color by heating up metal. For example, if you turn on a toaster, the metal coils inside will start to glow a dull red. As they get hotter, the coils will turn a brighter orange. The illustration on page 463 shows changes in the color of a metal bar as it heats up.

Like the color of heated metal, the color of a star indicates its temperature. Astronomers group stars into classes by color and surface temperature. The chart on page 463 lists the color and temperature range of each class of star. The coolest stars are red. The hottest stars are blue-white. Our Sun—a yellow, G-class star—has a surface temperature of about 6000°C.

Stars of every class give off light that is made up of a range of colors. Astronomers can spread a star's light into a spectrum to learn about the star's composition. The colors and lines in a spectrum reveal which gases are present in the star's outer layers.

CHECK YOUR READING How does a star's temperature affect its appearance?

Color and Temperature

Objects that radiate light change color as they heat up.

Classification of Stars		
Class	**Color**	**Surface Temperature (°C)**
O	blue-white	above 25,000
B	blue-white	10,000–25,000
A	white	7500–10,000
F	yellow-white	6000–7500
G	yellow	5000–6000
K	orange	3500–5000
M	red	below 3500

Stars are classified according to their colors and temperatures. The Sun is a G-class star.

When heated to about 1500°C, a steel bar gives off white light.

At about 1200°C the metal gives off yellow light.

A steel bar glows red when heated to about 600°C.

Stars have life cycles.

Although stars last for very long periods, they are not permanent. Stars are not alive, but they go through stages similar to birth, maturity, and death. The different stages a star goes through depend on the mass of the star. Higher-mass stars develop more quickly than lower-mass stars. Higher-mass stars also have different end stages than lower-mass stars.

Stars form inside a cloud of gas and dust called a **nebula** (NEHB-yuh-luh). Gravity pulls gas and dust closer together in some regions of a nebula. As the matter contracts, it forms a hot, dense sphere. The sphere becomes a star if its center grows hot and dense enough for fusion to occur.

When a star dies, its matter does not disappear. Some of it may form a nebula or move into an existing one. There, the matter may eventually become part of new stars.

CHECK YOUR READING How is gravity involved in the formation of stars?

Colors have been added to this photograph of the Omega Nebula in order to bring out details.

Stages in the Life Cycles of Stars

The diagram on page 465 shows the stages that stars go through in their life cycles. Notice that the length of a cycle and the way a star changes depend on the mass of the star at its formation.

RESOURCE CENTER
CLASSZONE.COM

Learn more about life cycles of stars.

Lower-Mass Stars The stage in which stars produce energy through the fusion of hydrogen into helium is called the **main sequence.** Because they use their fuel slowly, lower-mass stars can remain in the main-sequence stage for billions of years. The Sun has been a main-sequence star for 4.6 billion years and will remain one for about another 5 billion years. When a lower-mass star runs out of hydrogen, it expands into a giant star, in which helium fuses into carbon. Over time a giant star sheds its outer layers and becomes a white dwarf. A white dwarf is simply the dead core of a giant star. Although no fusion occurs in white dwarfs, they remain hot for billions of years.

Higher-Mass Stars Stars more than eight times as massive as our Sun spend much less time in the main-sequence stage because they use their fuel rapidly. After millions of years, a higher-mass star expands to become a supergiant star. In the core of a supergiant, fusion produces heavier and heavier elements. When an iron core forms, fusion stops and gravity causes the core to collapse. Then part of the core bounces outward, and the star erupts in an explosion called a supernova.

For a brief period, a supernova can give off as much light as a galaxy. The outer layers of the exploded star shoot out into space, carrying with them heavy elements that formed inside the star. Eventually this matter may become part of new stars and planets.

Neutron Stars and Black Holes

A pulsar emits beams of radio waves as it spins rapidly. The pulsar seems to pulse as the beams rotate toward and away from Earth.

The collapsed core of a supergiant star may form an extremely dense body called a **neutron star.** Neutron stars measure only about 20 kilometers (12 mi) in diameter, but their masses are one to three times that of the Sun.

Neutron stars emit little visible light. However, they strongly emit other forms of radiation, such as x-rays. Some neutron stars emit beams of radio waves as they spin. These stars are called pulsars because they seem to pulse as the beams rotate.

Sometimes a supernova leaves behind a core with a mass more than three times that of the Sun. In such a case, the core does not end up as a neutron star. Instead, it collapses even further, forming an invisible object called a **black hole.** The gravity of a black hole is so strong that no form of radiation can escape from it.

 CHECK YOUR READING   How do lower-mass stars differ from higher-mass stars after the main-sequence stage?

Life Cycles of Stars

A star forms inside a cloud of gas and dust called a nebula.
The life cycle of a star depends on its mass.

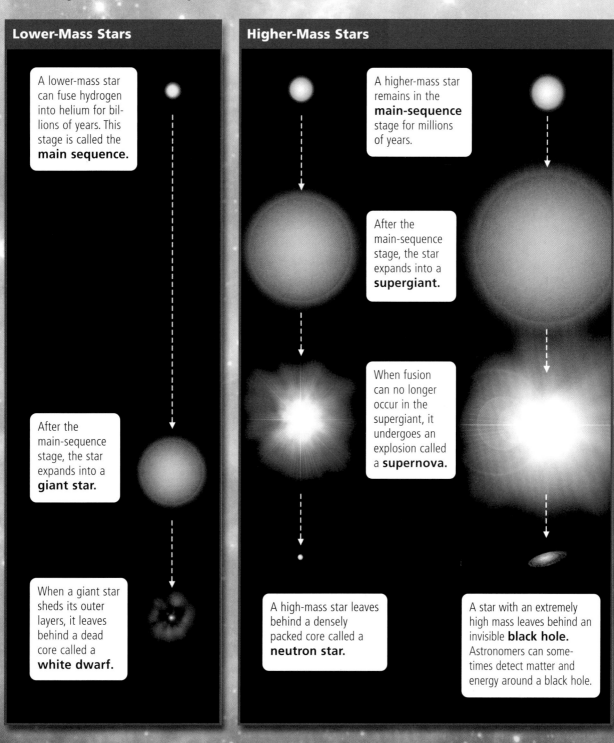

Lower-Mass Stars

A lower-mass star can fuse hydrogen into helium for billions of years. This stage is called the **main sequence.**

After the main-sequence stage, the star expands into a **giant star.**

When a giant star sheds its outer layers, it leaves behind a dead core called a **white dwarf.**

Higher-Mass Stars

A higher-mass star remains in the **main-sequence** stage for millions of years.

After the main-sequence stage, the star expands into a **supergiant.**

When fusion can no longer occur in the supergiant, it undergoes an explosion called a **supernova.**

A high-mass star leaves behind a densely packed core called a **neutron star.**

A star with an extremely high mass leaves behind an invisible **black hole.** Astronomers can sometimes detect matter and energy around a black hole.

READING VISUALS How do the stars shown in this illustration differ in the main-sequence stage of their life cycles?

Star Systems

Unlike our Sun, most stars do not exist alone. Instead, they are grouped with one or more companion stars. The stars are held together by the force of gravity between them. A binary star system consists of two stars that orbit each other. A multiple star system consists of more than two stars.

In many star systems, the stars are too close together to be seen individually. However, astronomers have developed ways of detecting such systems. For example, in a binary star system, one of the stars may orbit in front of the other when viewed from Earth. The star that orbits in front will briefly block some of the other star's light, providing a clue that more than one star is present. The illustration at right shows a binary star system that can be detected this way. Sometimes astronomers can also figure out whether a star is really a star system by studying its spectrum.

Star systems are an important source of information about star masses. Astronomers cannot measure the mass of a star directly. However, they can figure out a star's mass by observing the effect of the star's gravity on a companion star.

Binary Star System

Some binary star systems appear to dim briefly when one star orbits in front of the other and blocks some of its light.

When neither star is in front of the other, the star system appears to give off more light.

 CHECK YOUR READING Why are star systems important to astronomers?

14.2 Review

KEY CONCEPTS

1. Why must astronomers figure out a star's distance to calculate its actual brightness? (8.4.c)

2. How are color and temperature related in stars? (8.4.b)

3. How does a star's mass affect its life cycle? (8.4.b)

CRITICAL THINKING

4. **Analyze** Some of the brightest stars are red supergiants. How can stars with cooler red surfaces be so bright?

5. **Infer** Will the Sun eventually become a black hole? Why or why not?

⬤ CHALLENGE

6. **Infer** At what stage in the life cycle of the Sun will it be impossible for life to exist on Earth? Explain.

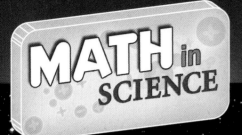

Brightness and Temperature of Stars

A star's brightness, or luminosity, depends on the star's surface temperature and size. If two stars have the same surface temperature, the larger star will be more luminous. The Hertzsprung-Russell (H-R) diagram below is a scatter plot that shows the relative temperatures and luminosities of various stars.

MATH TUTORIAL
CLASSZONE.COM
Click on Math Tutorial for more help with scatter plots.

Math 7.SD.1.2, 8.PS.8
Science 8.4.b

Example

Describe the surface temperature and luminosity of Spica.

(1) Surface temperature: Without drawing on the graph, imagine a line extending from Spica down to the temperature axis. Spica is one of the hottest stars.

(2) Luminosity: Imagine a line extending from Spica across to the luminosity axis. Spica has a high luminosity.

ANSWER Spica is one of the hottest and most luminous stars.

Hertzsprung-Russell (H-R) Diagram

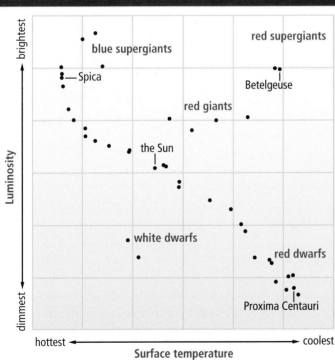

Use the diagram to answer the questions.

1. Describe the surface temperature and luminosity of Proxima Centauri.

2. Compare the surface temperature and luminosity of the Sun with the surface temperature and luminosity of Betelgeuse.

3. Compare the surface temperature and luminosity of the red dwarfs with the surface temperature and luminosity of the blue supergiants.

CHALLENGE When an old red giant star loses its outer atmosphere, all that remains is the very hot core of the star. Because the core is small, it does not give off much light. What kind of star does the red giant star become after it loses its outer atmosphere? How can you tell from the diagram?

14.3 Galaxies have different sizes and shapes.

CALIFORNIA
Content Standard

8.4.a Students know galaxies are clusters of billions of stars and may have different shapes.

BEFORE, you learned

- Our solar system is part of a galaxy called the Milky Way
- Stars change over their life cycles

NOW, you will learn

- About the size and shape of the Milky Way
- How galaxies are classified
- About the centers of galaxies

VOCABULARY

quasar p. 471

EXPLORE The Milky Way (8.4.a)

Why does the Milky Way look hazy?

PROCEDURE

1. Use a white gel pen to make 50 small dots close together on a piece of black paper.

2. Tape the paper to a wall, and move slowly away from it until you have difficulty seeing the individual dots.

WHAT DO YOU THINK?

- At what distance did the dots become hazy?
- Why might some of the stars in the Milky Way appear hazy from Earth?

MATERIALS

- white gel pen
- black paper
- tape

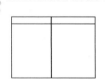

COMBINATION NOTES
You could record information about the Milky Way in a combination notes table.

Our solar system lies within the Milky Way galaxy.

The Sun lies within a galaxy called the Milky Way. Remember that a galaxy is a huge grouping of stars, gas, and dust held together by gravity. Without a telescope, you can only see nearby stars clearly. Those stars are a tiny fraction of the several hundred billion in the Milky Way.

The Milky Way is shaped like a disk with a bulge in the center. Because Earth is inside the disk, you have an edge-on view of part of the galaxy. On a dark night, the galaxy appears as a band of blended starlight. The Milky Way got its name from the hazy, or milky, appearance of this band of stars. You cannot see the center of the galaxy because it is hidden by dust.

 Why can't we see all of the Milky Way from Earth?

The Milky Way

When you look at the Milky Way, it appears as a band of hazy light.

Illustration of Side View

disk   Sun's location   bulge

The Milky Way is about 100,000 light-years in diameter.

The disk of the Milky Way measures more than 100,000 light-years in diameter. The bulge of densely packed stars at the center is located about 26,000 light-years from the Sun. A large but very faint layer of stars surrounds the disk and bulge. In addition to stars, the Milky Way contains clouds of gas and dust called nebulae.

The stars and nebulae in the Milky Way orbit the galaxy's center at very high speeds. However, the galaxy is so large that the Sun takes about 250 million years to complete one orbit.

INVESTIGATE Galaxy Shapes

How can you classify galaxies according to shape?

PROCEDURE

1. Cut out the photographs of galaxies on the Galaxy Photo Sheet.

2. Sort the galaxies into different groups according to their shapes. You may need a group for galaxies that do not fit in other groups.

WHAT DO YOU THINK?

• How many groups did you sort the galaxies into?

• Describe each group briefly, and list which galaxies you put in each group.

CHALLENGE What is the connection between the apparent shape of a galaxy and the galaxy's relationship to the viewer? **Hint:** Think about how an edge-on view of a compact disc differs from a view of it lying flat on a table.

SKILL FOCUS
Classifying (8.4.a)

MATERIALS
• Galaxy Photo Sheet
• scissors

TIME
15 minutes

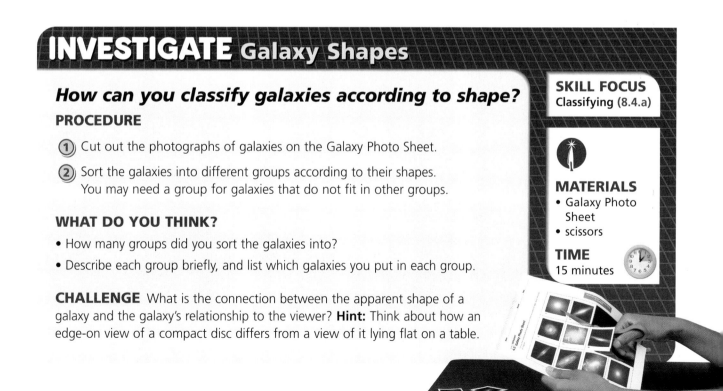

Galaxies vary in appearance.

Learn more about galaxies.

Galaxies differ greatly in size. Some contain as few as a hundred million stars, but the biggest have more than a trillion stars. Galaxies also vary in shape. Astronomers have classified galaxies into three main types based on their shape.

 What are two ways in which galaxies can differ from one another?

Types of Galaxies

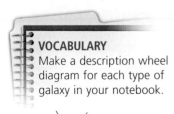

VOCABULARY
Make a description wheel diagram for each type of galaxy in your notebook.

The three main types of galaxies are spiral, elliptical, and irregular. Most galaxies are either spiral or elliptical.

Spiral galaxies have arms of stars, gas, and dust that curve away from the center of the galaxy in a spiral pattern. The Milky Way is a spiral galaxy. Like the Milky Way, other spiral galaxies are disk-shaped and have a central bulge. Most of the stars in the disk and the bulge are old stars. However, the dense spiral arms within the disk contain many young, bright stars.

Elliptical galaxies are shaped like spheres or eggs. Unlike spiral galaxies, elliptical galaxies have almost no dust or gas between stars, and all of their stars are old.

Irregular galaxies are faint galaxies without a definite shape. They are smaller than the other types of galaxies and have many fewer stars.

Galaxies sometimes collide with other galaxies. These collisions can cause changes in their shapes. The Extreme Science feature on page 472 describes such collisions.

Spiral Galaxy

Elliptical Galaxy

Irregular Galaxy

Centers of Galaxies

Most large galaxies seem to have supermassive black holes at their centers. The mass of a supermassive black hole can be millions or even billions of times greater than that of the Sun. At the center of the Milky Way, for example, is a black hole with a mass about three million times that of the Sun.

Like all black holes, a supermassive black hole is invisible. Astronomers can identify the presence of a black hole by the behavior of matter around it. The gravity of a supermassive black hole is so strong that it draws in a huge whirlpool of gas from nearby stars. As gases are pulled toward the black hole, they become compressed and extremely hot, so they give off very bright light. The motions of stars orbiting the black hole can also reveal its presence.

Evidence of a Supermassive Black Hole

disk of gas swirling around the black hole

gas being drawn into the black hole

If the center of a galaxy is very bright, it may look like a star from a great distance. The very bright centers of some distant galaxies are called **quasars.** *Quasar* is a shortened form of *quasi-stellar,* which means "seeming like a star." The galaxy surrounding a quasar is often hard to see because the quasar is so much brighter than it.

 CHECK YOUR READING How can astronomers detect the presence of a supermassive black hole at the center of a galaxy?

14.3 Review

KEY CONCEPTS

1. What is the shape of the Milky Way? (8.4.a)

2. Why does the Milky Way look like a hazy band of stars in the sky? (8.4.a)

3. What keeps the stars in galaxies from moving apart? (8.4.a)

CRITICAL THINKING

4. **Compare and Contrast** Make a diagram showing similarities and differences among the three main types of galaxies.

5. **Infer** How might our view of the Milky Way be different if the Sun were located inside the central bulge?

CHALLENGE

6. **Predict** If two spiral galaxies collide, what might eventually happen to the supermassive black holes at their centers?

EXTREME SCIENCE

ASTRONOMY AND THE UNIVERSE

> 8.4.a Students know galaxies are clusters of billions of stars and may have different shapes.

When Galaxies Collide

A small galaxy is moving through our galaxy, the Milky Way, right now!

- The small galaxy may be destroyed by the collision, but the Milky Way is not in danger.
- The same galaxy seems to have moved through the Milky Way ten times before.
- Other galaxies may also be moving through the Milky Way.

Not to Worry!

Galaxies containing many billions of stars are colliding all the time. What are the chances that their stars will crash into one another? The chances are very small, because there is so much empty space between stars.

Galactic Cannibals

When galaxies collide, a larger galaxy can "eat up" a smaller one.

- The stars of the smaller galaxy become part of the larger one.
- The collision of two spiral galaxies may form a new elliptical galaxy.

Bent Out of Shape

Sometimes galaxies pass very close to each other without actually colliding. In these near misses, gravity can produce some interesting new shapes. For example, the Tadpole Galaxy (left) has a long tail of dust and gas pulled out by the gravity of a passing galaxy.

Model Galaxies

Astronomers use computer simulations to predict how the stars and gas in galaxies are affected by a collision. To understand galaxy collisions better, they then compare the simulations with images of actual galaxies.

EXPLORE

1. **PREDICT** Draw the shape of the new galaxy that the two in the photograph on the left might form.

2. **CHALLENGE** Look at online images and simulations of galaxy collisions. Make a chart showing how these collisions can differ.

RESOURCE CENTER
CLASSZONE.COM
Find out more about galaxy collisions.

Come back in a few billion years and you may see that these two spiral galaxies have become one elliptical galaxy.

14.4 The universe is expanding.

◁ BEFORE, you learned

- Galaxies contain millions or billions of stars
- Electromagnetic radiation carries information about space

▷ NOW, you will learn

- How galaxies are moving apart in the universe
- What scientists are discovering about the development of the universe

VOCABULARY

Doppler effect p. 474
big bang p. 476

EXPLORE Large Numbers (8.4.a)

How much is a billion?

PROCEDURE

MATERIALS
- book
- ruler
- calculator

1. Guess how thick a billion-page book would be. Write down your guess.

2. Count how many sheets of paper in a book add up to a millimeter in thickness. Multiply by 2 to calculate the number of pages.

3. Then divide 1 billion (1,000,000,000) by that number to determine how many millimeters thick the book would be. Divide your result by 1,000,000 to convert to kilometers.

WHAT DO YOU THINK?
- How thick would a billion-page book be?
- How close was your guess?

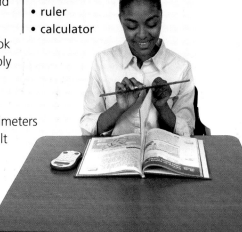

Galaxies are moving farther apart in the universe.

COMBINATION NOTES
You could record information about the expansion of the universe in a combination notes table.

The universe is unbelievably huge. It consists of all space, energy, and matter. The Milky Way is just one of about 100 billion galaxies. These galaxies occur in groups that together form superclusters. Between the superclusters are huge areas of nearly empty space.

Because the universe is so huge, you might think that the most distant regions of the universe are very different from space near Earth. Astronomers study the spectra of light from stars and galaxies. From those, they have determined that the same elements are found throughout the universe. Scientific observations also indicate that the same physical forces and processes operate everywhere.

Looking Back in Time

When we look far out into space, we see galaxies by the light they gave off long ago. This light has traveled millions or even billions of years before reaching telescopes on Earth. The Andromeda Galaxy, for example, is the closest large galaxy. The light of its stars takes over 2 million years to reach Earth. When we view this galaxy through a telescope, we are seeing what happened in it 2 million years ago. To see what is happening there now, we would have to wait 2 million years for the light to arrive.

Light from the Andromeda Galaxy takes 2 million years to reach Earth.

As astronomers look at galaxies farther and farther away, they see how the universe looked at different times in the past. These views are like photographs in an album that show someone at various stages of life. Astronomers can see how the universe has developed over billions of years.

CHECK YOUR READING Why can astronomers learn about the past by looking at distant galaxies?

The Motion of Galaxies

Have you ever noticed that the sound of an ambulance siren changes as it travels toward and then away from you? The pitch of the siren seems to be higher as the ambulance approaches. As the ambulance passes you and starts moving away, the pitch of the siren seems to get lower. The shifting pitch of the siren is an example of the Doppler effect. The **Doppler effect** is a change in the observed wavelength or frequency of a wave that occurs when the source of the wave or the observer is moving.

The Doppler effect occurs with light as well as sound. If a galaxy is moving toward Earth, the light we receive will seem compressed to shorter wavelengths. This change is called a blue shift because the light shifts toward the blue end of the spectrum. If a galaxy is moving away from Earth, the light we receive will seem stretched to longer wavelengths. This change is called a red shift because the light shifts toward the red end of the spectrum.

In the early 1900s, astronomers discovered that light from distant galaxies is stretched to longer wavelengths. This fact indicates that the galaxies are moving apart. By analyzing the spectra of galaxies, astronomers also discovered that the galaxies are moving apart faster the farther away they are. These observations led astronomers to conclude that the universe has been expanding throughout its history.

Evidence of an Expanding Universe

The Doppler effect can show how galaxies are moving in relation to Earth.

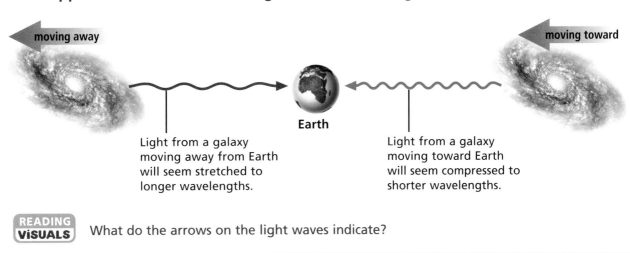

moving away

moving toward

Earth

Light from a galaxy moving away from Earth will seem stretched to longer wavelengths.

Light from a galaxy moving toward Earth will seem compressed to shorter wavelengths.

READING VISUALS What do the arrows on the light waves indicate?

The illustration of raisin-bread dough rising will help you imagine this expansion. Suppose you were a raisin. You would observe that all the other raisins are moving away from you as the dough expands. The raisins are being moved apart by the expanding dough. Furthermore, you would observe that distant raisins are moving away faster than nearby raisins. They move away faster because there is more dough expanding between you and those raisins.

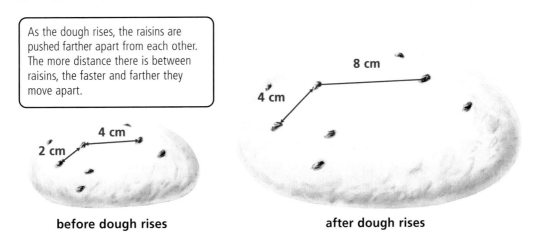

As the dough rises, the raisins are pushed farther apart from each other. The more distance there is between raisins, the faster and farther they move apart.

4 cm

8 cm

2 cm

4 cm

before dough rises

after dough rises

Like the dough that expands and moves raisins apart, space in the universe is expanding and moving galaxies apart. The universe does not expand into anything, since there is nothing outside the universe. Rather, the universe itself is expanding.

CHECK YOUR READING How are galaxies moving in relation to each other?

INVESTIGATE Galaxies

How does the universe expand?

PROCEDURE

1 Spread the cut rubber band against the ruler without stretching it. Mark off every centimeter for 6 centimeters.

2 Align the first mark on the rubber band with the 1-centimeter mark on the ruler and hold it in place tightly. Stretch the rubber band so that the second mark is next to the 3-centimeter mark on the ruler.

3 Observe how many centimeters each mark has moved from its original location against the ruler.

WHAT DO YOU THINK?

• How far did each mark on the rubber band move from its original location?

• What does this activity demonstrate about the expansion of the universe?

CHALLENGE How could you calculate the rates at which the marks moved when you stretched the rubber band?

SKILL FOCUS
Measuring (8.4)

MATERIALS
• thick rubber band cut open
• ballpoint pen
• ruler

TIME
20 minutes

Scientists are investigating the origin of the universe.

After astronomers learned that galaxies are moving apart, they developed new ideas about the origin of the universe. They concluded that all matter was once merged together and then the universe suddenly began to expand. The evidence for this scientific theory is so strong that almost all astronomers now accept it.

The **big bang** is the moment in time when the universe started to expand. Astronomers have calculated that this event happened about 14 billion years ago. One phase of expansion may have been very rapid. In a tiny fraction of a second, the universe may have expanded from a size much smaller than a speck of dust to the size of our solar system.

VOCABULARY
Add a description wheel diagram for *big bang* in your notebook.

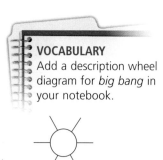

Evidence of the Big Bang

Evidence for the big bang comes from various sources. One important source of evidence is microwave radiation. Astronomers predicted in 1948 that the universe would still be filled with microwaves emitted shortly after the big bang. In 1965 researchers detected this kind of radiation streaming through space in all directions.

Besides the presence of microwave radiation and the motions of galaxies, scientists have found other evidence of the big bang by observing space. For example, images of very distant galaxies provide information about the universe's development. Additional evidence of the big bang has come from experiments and computer models.

Development of the Universe

Immediately after the big bang, the universe was incredibly dense and hot—much hotter than the core of the Sun. Matter and energy behaved very differently than they do under present conditions. As the universe rapidly expanded, it went through a series of changes.

Scientists do not fully understand what conditions were like in the early universe. However, they are gaining a clearer picture of how the universe developed. One way that scientists are learning about this development is by performing experiments in particle accelerators. These huge machines expose matter to extreme conditions.

Scientists have found that the earliest stages in the universe's development occurred in a tiny fraction of a second. However, it took about 300,000 years for the first elements to form. Stars, planets, and galaxies began to appear within the next billion years. Some evidence suggests that the first stars formed only a few hundred million years after the big bang.

This Hubble telescope image of very distant galaxies has helped scientists learn what the universe was like about 13 billion years ago.

CHECK YOUR READING What happened to the universe shortly after the big bang?

 **Review**

KEY CONCEPTS

1. How are distant regions of the universe similar to space near Earth? (8.4)

2. What does the Doppler effect indicate about the motion of galaxies? (8.4.e)

3. How do scientists explain the origin of the universe? (8.4)

CRITICAL THINKING

4. **Apply** If a star 100 light-years from Earth is beginning to expand into a giant star, how long will it take for astronomers to observe this development? Explain.

5. **Analyze** Why do scientists need to perform experiments to learn about the earliest stages of the universe?

○ CHALLENGE

6. **Infer** Galaxy A and galaxy B both give off light that appears stretched to longer wavelengths. The light from galaxy B is stretched to even longer wavelengths than the light from galaxy A. What can you infer from these data?

Chapter Review

14

the BIG idea

Our Sun is one of billions of stars in one of billions of galaxies in the universe.

CONTENT REVIEW
CLASSZONE.COM

◀ KEY CONCEPTS SUMMARY

1️⃣ The Sun is our local star.

The Sun produces energy from hydrogen. Energy flows through the Sun's layers. Features appear on the Sun's surface.

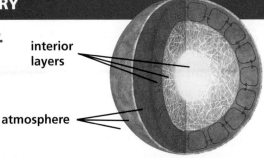

interior layers

atmosphere

VOCABULARY
fusion p. 454
convection p. 454
corona p. 454
sunspot p. 456
solar wind p. 457

2️⃣ Stars change over their life cycles.

Stars vary in brightness, size, color, and temperature. The development of a star depends on the mass of the star. Most stars are grouped with one or more companion stars.

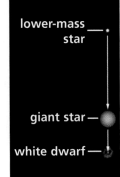

lower-mass star

giant star

white dwarf

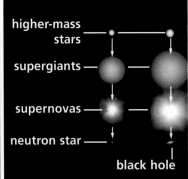

higher-mass stars

supergiants

supernovas

neutron star

black hole

VOCABULARY
light-year p. 460
parallax p. 461
nebula p. 463
main sequence p. 464
neutron star p. 464
black hole p. 464

3️⃣ Galaxies have different sizes and shapes.

Our galaxy, the Milky Way, is a spiral galaxy. Galaxies can also be elliptical or irregular. Irregular galaxies have no definite shape.

Spiral Galaxy

Elliptical Galaxy

Irregular Galaxy

VOCABULARY
quasar p. 471

4️⃣ The universe is expanding.

Galaxies are moving farther apart in the universe. Scientists are investigating the origin and development of the universe.

VOCABULARY
Doppler effect p. 474
big bang p. 476

Reviewing Vocabulary

Make a frame for each of the vocabulary words listed below. Write the word in the center. Decide what information to frame it with. Use definitions, examples, descriptions, parts, or pictures. An example is shown below.

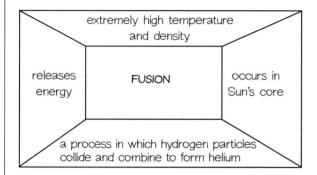

extremely high temperature and density

releases energy

FUSION

occurs in Sun's core

a process in which hydrogen particles collide and combine to form helium

1. convection

2. corona

3. sunspot

4. solar wind

5. nebula

6. black hole

7. Doppler effect

8. big bang

Reviewing Key Concepts

Multiple Choice *Choose the letter of the best answer.*

9. Which layer do you usually see in photographs of the Sun? (8.4.b)
   a. convection zone   **c.** chromosphere
   b. photosphere   **d.** corona

10. Which statement is true of sunspots? (8.4.b)
   a. They are permanent features on the Sun's surface.
   b. They are caused by solar wind.
   c. They are where fusion occurs.
   d. They are cooler than surrounding areas.

11. Which unit is usually used to describe the distances of stars? (8.4.c)
   a. astronomical units **c.** kilometers
   b. light-years   **d.** miles

12. Which example best shows the relationship between color and temperature? (8.4.b)
   a. A rainbow forms when sunlight strikes raindrops.
   b. A flashlight beam looks red when passed through a red plastic filter.
   c. A chemical light-stick glows a yellow-green color.
   d. A metal rod in a fireplace changes in color from red to orange.

13. How do lower-mass stars differ from higher-mass stars? (8.4.b)
   a. They develop more quickly.
   b. They develop more slowly.
   c. They end up as black holes.
   d. They have too little mass to produce energy.

14. Which term describes the Milky Way? (8.4.a)
   a. spiral galaxy   **c.** irregular galaxy
   b. elliptical galaxy   **d.** quasar

15. The Doppler effect is used to determine (8.4)
   a. the number of stars in a galaxy
   b. the number of galaxies in the universe
   c. the size of the universe
   d. whether a galaxy is moving toward or away from Earth

16. What is the big bang? (8.4)
   a. the collision of galaxies
   b. the formation of the solar system
   c. the beginning of the universe's expansion
   d. the time when stars began to form

Short Answer *Write a short answer to each question.*

17. Why can't we see the Sun's corona under normal conditions? (8.4.b)

18. How do astronomers use parallax to calculate a star's distance? (8.4.c)

19. Where do heavy elements, such as iron, come from? (8.4.e)

20. How can astronomers tell whether a black hole exists in the center of a galaxy? (8.4.a)

Thinking Critically

The table below shows the distances of some galaxies and the speeds at which they are moving away from the Milky Way. Use the table to answer the next three questions.

Galaxy	Distance (million light-years)	Speed (kilometers per second)
NGC 7793	14	241
NGC 6946	22	336
NGC 2903	31	472
NGC 6744	42	663

21. COMPARE AND CONTRAST How do the speed and distance of NGC 7793 compare with the speed and distance of NGC 2903? (8.4.a)

22. ANALYZE What general pattern do you see in these data? (8.4.a)

23. APPLY What would you estimate to be the speed of a galaxy located 60 million light-years away? **Hint:** Notice the pattern between the first and third rows and the second and fourth rows in the chart. (8.4.a)

24. INFER Why might the solar wind have a stronger effect on inner planets than on outer planets in the solar system? (8.4.e)

25. PREDICT The core of a particular star consists almost entirely of helium. What will soon happen to this star? (8.4.e)

26. ANALYZE Planets shine by reflected light. Why do some planets in our solar system appear brighter than stars, even though the stars give off their own light? (8.4.d)

27. IDENTIFY CAUSE A star dims for a brief period every three days. What could be causing it to dim? (8.4.d)

28. COMPARE AND CONTRAST Describe the similarities and differences between the life cycles of lower-mass stars and higher-mass stars. (8.4.b)

29. EVALUATE If you wanted to study a neutron star, would you use a visible-light telescope or an x-ray telescope? Explain why. (8.4.b)

30. INFER Suppose that astronomers find evidence of iron and other heavy elements in a galaxy. On the basis of this evidence, what can you assume has already occurred in that galaxy? (8.4.a)

31. ANALYZE Why did the discovery that galaxies are moving farther apart help scientists conclude that all matter was once merged together? (8.4.a)

32. PREDICT What changes do you predict will happen in the universe over the next 10 billion years? (8.4)

33. COMPARE AND CONTRAST The photographs above show a spiral galaxy and an elliptical galaxy. What similarities and differences do you see in these two types of galaxies? (8.4.a)

the BIG idea

34. INFER Look again at the photograph on pages 450–451. Now that you have finished the chapter, how would you change your response to the question on the photograph? What else might be present? (8.4.e)

35. SYNTHESIZE Think of a question that you still have about the universe. What information would you need to answer the question? How might you obtain this information?

UNIT PROJECTS

Evaluate all the data, results, and information in your project folder. Prepare to present your project.

Standards-Based Assessment

Analyzing a Chart

8.4.b, 8.4.c

Use the chart and diagram to answer the next six questions.

Classification of Stars

Class	Color	Surface Temperature (°C)
O	blue-white	above 25,000
B	blue-white	10,000–25,000
A	white	7500–10,000
F	yellow-white	6000–7500
G	yellow	5000–6000
K	orange	3500–5000
M	red	below 3500

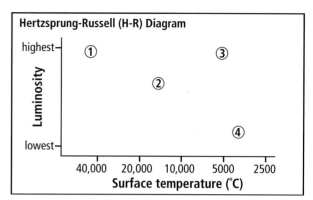

1. Which class of star has the lowest surface temperature?
   - **a.** O
   - **b.** B
   - **c.** G
   - **d.** M

2. Which class of star has the highest surface temperature?
   - **a.** O
   - **b.** B
   - **c.** G
   - **d.** M

3. What would be the color of a star with a surface temperature of 8000°C?
   - **a.** blue-white
   - **b.** white
   - **c.** orange
   - **d.** red

4. Toward the end of their life cycles, very massive stars expand in size, and their surface temperature becomes lower. Which of the following is an example of this change?
   - **a.** A white star becomes a blue-white star.
   - **b.** A blue-white star becomes a red star.
   - **c.** A red star becomes a blue-white star.
   - **d.** A yellow star becomes a yellow-white star.

5. The H-R diagram above shows the surface temperatures and luminosities, or true brightnesses, of four stars. Which of the stars is a type O?
   - **a.** 1
   - **b.** 2
   - **c.** 3
   - **d.** 4

6. Which two stars on the H-R diagram have the most similar surface temperatures?
   - **a.** 1 and 2
   - **b.** 1 and 3
   - **c.** 2 and 3
   - **d.** 3 and 4

Extended Response

Answer the two questions below in detail.

7. Why is looking at a star in the night sky like seeing back into time?

8. How could you use two flashlights to demonstrate the concept that the apparent brightness of a star is affected by its distance from Earth? You can include a diagram as part of your answer.

Student Resource Handbooks

Scientific Thinking Handbook

SCIENTIFIC THINKING HANDBOOK

Making Observations

An **observation** is an act of noting and recording an event, characteristic, behavior, or anything else detected with an instrument or with the senses.

Observations allow you to make informed hypotheses and to gather data for experiments. Careful observations often lead to ideas for new experiments. There are two categories of observations:

- **Quantitative observations** can be expressed in numbers and include records of time, temperature, mass, distance, and volume.

- **Qualitative observations** include descriptions of sights, sounds, smells, and textures.

EXAMPLE

A student dissolved 30 grams of Epsom salts in water, poured the solution into a dish, and let the dish sit out uncovered overnight. The next day, she made the following observations of the Epsom salt crystals that grew in the dish.

> To determine the mass, the student found the mass of the dish before and after growing the crystals and then used subtraction to find the difference.

> The student measured several crystals and calculated the mean length. (To learn how to calculate the mean of a data set, see page R36.)

Table 1. Observations of Epsom Salt Crystals

Quantitative Observations	Qualitative Observations
• mass = 30 g	• Crystals are clear.
• mean crystal length = 0.5 cm	• Crystals are long, thin, and rectangular.
• longest crystal length = 2 cm	• White crust has formed around edge of dish.

> Photographs or sketches are useful for recording qualitative observations.

 Epsom salt crystals

MORE ABOUT OBSERVING

- Make quantitative observations whenever possible. That way, others will know exactly what you observed and be able to compare their results with yours.

- It is always a good idea to make qualitative observations too. You never know when you might observe something unexpected.

Predicting and Hypothesizing

A **prediction** is an expectation of what will be observed or what will happen. A **hypothesis** is a tentative explanation for an observation or scientific problem that can be tested by further investigation.

EXAMPLE

Suppose you have made two paper airplanes and you wonder why one of them tends to glide farther than the other one.

1. Start by asking a question.

2. Make an educated guess. After examination, you notice that the wings of the airplane that flies farther are slightly larger than the wings of the other airplane.

3. Write a prediction based upon your educated guess, in the form of an "If . . . , then . . ." statement. Write the independent variable after the word *if*, and the dependent variable after the word *then*.

4. To make a hypothesis, explain why you think what you predicted will occur. Write the explanation after the word *because*.

1. Why does one of the paper airplanes glide farther than the other?

2. The size of an airplane's wings may affect how far the airplane will glide.

3. Prediction: If I make a paper airplane with larger wings, then the airplane will glide farther.

To read about independent and dependent variables, see page R30.

4. Hypothesis: If I make a paper airplane with larger wings, then the airplane will glide farther, because the additional surface area of the wing will produce more lift.

Notice that the part of the hypothesis after *because* adds an explanation of why the airplane will glide farther.

MORE ABOUT HYPOTHESES

- The results of an experiment cannot prove that a hypothesis is correct. Rather, the results either support or do not support the hypothesis.

- Valuable information is gained even when your hypothesis is not supported by your results. For example, it would be an important discovery to find that wing size is not related to how far an airplane glides.

- In science, a hypothesis is supported only after many scientists have conducted many experiments and produced consistent results.

Inferring

An **inference** is a logical conclusion drawn from the available evidence and prior knowledge. Inferences are often made from observations.

EXAMPLE

A student observing a set of acorns noticed something unexpected about one of them. He noticed a white, soft-bodied insect eating its way out of the acorn.

The student recorded these observations.

Observations

- There is a hole in the acorn, about 0.5 cm in diameter, where the insect crawled out.
- There is a second hole, which is about the size of a pinhole, on the other side of the acorn.
- The inside of the acorn is hollow.

Here are some inferences that can be made on the basis of the observations.

Inferences

- The insect formed from the material inside the acorn, grew to its present size, and ate its way out of the acorn.
- The insect crawled through the smaller hole, ate the inside of the acorn, grew to its present size, and ate its way out of the acorn.
- An egg was laid in the acorn through the smaller hole. The egg hatched into a larva that ate the inside of the acorn, grew to its present size, and ate its way out of the acorn.

When you make inferences, be sure to look at all of the evidence available and combine it with what you already know.

MORE ABOUT INFERENCES

Inferences depend both on observations and on the knowledge of the people making the inferences. Ancient people who did not know that organisms are produced only by similar organisms might have made an inference like the first one. A student today might look at the same observations and make the second inference. A third student might have knowledge about this particular insect and know that it is never small enough to fit through the smaller hole, leading her to the third inference.

Identifying Cause and Effect

In a **cause-and-effect relationship,** one event or characteristic is the result of another. Usually an effect follows its cause in time.

There are many examples of cause-and-effect relationships in everyday life.

Cause	Effect
Turn off a light.	Room gets dark.
Drop a glass.	Glass breaks.
Blow a whistle.	Sound is heard.

Scientists must be careful not to infer a cause-and-effect relationship just because one event happens after another event. When one event occurs after another, you cannot infer a cause-and-effect relationship on the basis of that information alone. You also cannot conclude that one event caused another if there are alternative ways to explain the second event. A scientist must demonstrate through experimentation or continued observation that an event was truly caused by another event.

EXAMPLE

Make an Observation

Suppose you have a few plants growing outside. When the weather starts getting colder, you bring one of the plants indoors. You notice that the plant you brought indoors is growing faster than the others are growing. You cannot conclude from your observation that the change in temperature was the cause of the increased plant growth, because there are alternative explanations for the observation. Some possible explanations are given below.

- The humidity indoors caused the plant to grow faster.

- The level of sunlight indoors caused the plant to grow faster.

- The indoor plant's being noticed more often and watered more often than the outdoor plants caused it to grow faster.

- The plant that was brought indoors was healthier than the other plants to begin with.

To determine which of these factors, if any, caused the indoor plant to grow faster than the outdoor plants, you would need to design and conduct an experiment.

See pages R28–R35 for information about designing experiments.

Recognizing Bias

Television, newspapers, and the Internet are full of experts claiming to have scientific evidence to back up their claims. How do you know whether the claims are really backed up by good science?

Bias is a slanted point of view, or personal prejudice. The goal of scientists is to be as objective as possible and to base their findings on facts instead of opinions. However, bias often affects the conclusions of researchers, and it is important to learn to recognize bias.

When scientific results are reported, you should consider the source of the information as well as the information itself. It is important to critically analyze the information that you see and read.

SOURCES OF BIAS

There are several ways in which a report of scientific information may be biased. Here are some questions that you can ask yourself:

1. **Who is sponsoring the research?**

   Sometimes, the results of an investigation are biased because an organization paying for the research is looking for a specific answer. This type of bias can affect how data are gathered and interpreted.

2. **Is the research sample large enough?**

   Sometimes research does not include enough data. The larger the sample size, the more likely that the results are accurate, assuming a truly random sample.

3. **In a survey, who is answering the questions?**

   The results of a survey or poll can be biased. The people taking part in the survey may have been specifically chosen because of how they would answer. They may have the same ideas or lifestyles. A survey or poll should make use of a random sample of people.

4. **Are the people who take part in a survey biased?**

   People who take part in surveys sometimes try to answer the questions the way they think the researcher wants them to answer. Also, in surveys or polls that ask for personal information, people may be unwilling to answer questions truthfully.

SCIENTIFIC BIAS

It is also important to realize that scientists have their own biases because of the types of research they do and because of their scientific viewpoints. Two scientists may look at the same set of data and come to completely different conclusions because of these biases. However, such disagreements are not necessarily bad. In fact, a critical analysis of disagreements is often responsible for moving science forward.

Identifying Faulty Reasoning

Faulty reasoning is wrong or incorrect thinking. It leads to mistakes and to wrong conclusions. Scientists are careful not to draw unreasonable conclusions from experimental data. Without such caution, the results of scientific investigations may be misleading.

EXAMPLE

Scientists try to make generalizations based on their data to explain as much about nature as possible. If only a small sample of data is looked at, however, a conclusion may be faulty. Suppose a scientist has studied the effects of the El Niño and La Niña weather patterns on flood damage in California from 1989 to 1995. The scientist organized the data in the bar graph below.

The scientist drew the following conclusions:

1. The La Niña weather pattern has no effect on flooding in California.

2. When neither weather pattern occurs, there is almost no flood damage.

3. A weak or moderate El Niño produces a small or moderate amount of flooding.

4. A strong El Niño produces a lot of flooding.

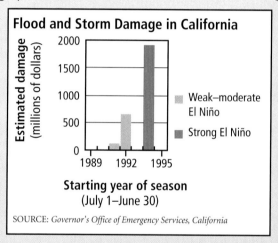

SOURCE: *Governor's Office of Emergency Services, California*

For the six-year period of the scientist's investigation, these conclusions may seem to be reasonable. However, a six-year study of weather patterns may be too small of a sample for the conclusions to be supported. Consider the following graph, which shows information that was gathered from 1949 to 1997.

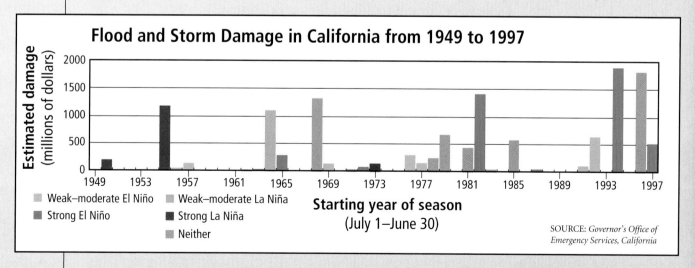

SOURCE: *Governor's Office of Emergency Services, California*

The only one of the conclusions that all of this information supports is number 3: a weak or moderate El Niño produces a small or moderate amount of flooding. By collecting more data, scientists can be more certain of their conclusions and can avoid faulty reasoning.

Analyzing Statements

To **analyze** a statement is to examine its parts carefully. Scientific findings are often reported through media such as television or the Internet. A report that is made public often focuses on only a small part of research. As a result, it is important to question the sources of information.

Evaluate Media Claims

To **evaluate** a statement is to judge it on the basis of criteria you've established. Sometimes evaluating means deciding whether a statement is true.

Reports of scientific research and findings in the media may be misleading or incomplete. When you are exposed to this information, you should ask yourself some questions so that you can make informed judgments about the information.

1. **Does the information come from a credible source?**

   Suppose you learn about a new product and it is stated that scientific evidence proves that the product works. A report from a respected news source may be more believable than an advertisement paid for by the product's manufacturer.

2. **How much evidence supports the claim?**

   Often, it may seem that there is new evidence every day of something in the world that either causes or cures an illness. However, information that is the result of several years of work by several different scientists is more credible than an advertisement that does not even cite the subjects of the experiment.

3. **How much information is being presented?**

   Science cannot solve all questions, and scientific experiments often have flaws. A report that discusses problems in a scientific study may be more believable than a report that addresses only positive experimental findings.

4. **Is scientific evidence being presented by a specific source?**

   Sometimes scientific findings are reported by people who are called experts or leaders in a scientific field. But if their names are not given or their scientific credentials are not reported, their statements may be less credible than those of recognized experts.

Differentiate Between Fact and Opinion

Sometimes information is presented as a fact when it may be an opinion. When scientific conclusions are reported, it is important to recognize whether they are based on solid evidence. Again, you may find it helpful to ask yourself some questions.

1. **What is the difference between a fact and an opinion?**

   A **fact** is a piece of information that can be strictly defined and proved true. An **opinion** is a statement that expresses a belief, value, or feeling. An opinion cannot be proved true or false. For example, a person's age is a fact, but if someone is asked how old they feel, it is impossible to prove the person's answer to be true or false.

2. **Can opinions be measured?**

   Yes, opinions can be measured. In fact, surveys often ask for people's opinions on a topic. But there is no way to know whether or not an opinion is the truth.

HOW TO DIFFERENTIATE FACT FROM OPINION

Human Activities and the Environment

Opinions

Notice words or phrases that express beliefs or feelings. The words *unfortunately* and *careless* show that opinions are being expressed.

Unfortunately, human use of fossil fuels is one of the most significant developments of the past few centuries. Humans rely on fossil fuels, a non-renewable energy resource, for more than 90 percent of their energy needs.

This careless misuse of our planet's resources has resulted in pollution, global warming, and the destruction of fragile ecosystems. For example, oil pipelines carry more than one million barrels of oil each day across tundra regions. Transporting oil across such areas can only result in oil spills that poison the land for decades.

Facts

Statements that contain statistics tend to be facts. Writers often use facts to support their opinions.

Opinion

Look for statements that speculate about events. These statements are opinions, because they cannot be proved.

Safety Rules

Before you work in the laboratory, read these safety rules twice. Ask your teacher to explain any rules that you do not completely understand. Refer to these rules later on if you have questions about safety in the science classroom.

Directions

- Read all directions and make sure that you understand them before starting an investigation or lab activity. If you do not understand how to do a procedure or how to use a piece of equipment, ask your teacher.
- Do not begin any investigation or touch any equipment until your teacher has told you to start.
- Never experiment on your own. If you want to try a procedure that the directions do not call for, ask your teacher for permission first.
- If you are hurt or injured in any way, tell your teacher immediately.

Dress Code

goggles

apron

gloves

- Wear goggles when
  — using glassware, sharp objects, or chemicals
  — heating an object
  — working with anything that can easily fly up into the air and hurt someone's eye
- Tie back long hair or hair that hangs in front of your eyes.
- Remove any article of clothing—such as a loose sweater or a scarf—that hangs down and may touch a flame, chemical, or piece of equipment.
- Observe all safety icons calling for the wearing of eye protection, gloves, and aprons.

Heating and Fire Safety

fire safety

heating safety

- Keep your work area neat, clean, and free of extra materials.
- Never reach over a flame or heat source.
- Point objects being heated away from you and others.
- Never heat a substance or an object in a closed container.
- Never touch an object that has been heated. If you are unsure whether something is hot, treat it as though it is. Use oven mitts, clamps, tongs, or a test-tube holder.
- Know where the fire extinguisher and fire blanket are kept in your classroom.
- Do not throw hot substances into the trash. Wait for them to cool or use the container your teacher puts out for disposal.

Electrical Safety

electrical safety

- Never use lamps or other electrical equipment with frayed cords.
- Make sure no cord is lying on the floor where someone can trip over it.
- Do not let a cord hang over the side of a counter or table so that the equipment can easily be pulled or knocked to the floor.
- Never let cords hang into sinks or other places where water can be found.
- Never try to fix electrical problems. Inform your teacher of any problems immediately.
- Unplug an electrical cord by pulling on the plug, not the cord.

Chemical Safety

chemical safety

poison

fumes

- If you spill a chemical or get one on your skin or in your eyes, tell your teacher right away.
- Never touch, taste, or sniff any chemicals in the lab. If you need to determine odor, waft. Wafting consists of holding the chemical in its container 15 centimeters (6 in.) away from your nose, and using your fingers to bring fumes from the container to your nose.
- Keep lids on all chemicals you are not using.
- Never put unused chemicals back into the original containers. Throw away extra chemicals where your teacher tells you to.
- Pour chemicals over a sink or your work area, not over the floor.
- If you get a chemical in your eye, use the eyewash right away.
- Always wash your hands after handling chemicals, plants, or soil.

Wafting

Glassware and Sharp-Object Safety

sharp objects

- If you break glassware, tell your teacher right away.
- Do not use broken or chipped glassware. Give these to your teacher.
- Use knives and other cutting instruments carefully. Always wear eye protection and cut away from you.

Animal Safety

- Never hurt an animal.
- Touch animals only when necessary. Follow your teacher's instructions for handling animals.
- Always wash your hands after working with animals.

Cleanup

disposal

- Follow your teacher's instructions for throwing away or putting away supplies.
- Clean your work area and pick up anything that has dropped to the floor.
- Wash your hands.

Using Lab Equipment

Different experiments require different types of equipment. But even though experiments differ, the ways in which the equipment is used are the same.

Beakers

- Use beakers for holding and pouring liquids.
- Do not use a beaker to measure the volume of a liquid. Use a graduated cylinder instead. (See page R16.)
- Use a beaker that holds about twice as much liquid as you need. For example, if you need 100 milliliters of water, you should use a 200- or 250-milliliter beaker.

Test Tubes

- Use test tubes to hold small amounts of substances.
- Do not use a test tube to measure the volume of a liquid.
- Use a test tube when heating a substance over a flame. Aim the mouth of the tube away from yourself and other people.
- Liquids easily spill or splash from test tubes, so it is important to use only small amounts of liquids.

Test-Tube Holder

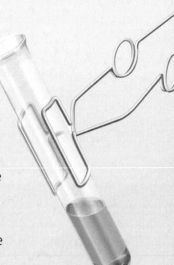

- Use a test-tube holder when heating a substance in a test tube.
- Use a test-tube holder if the substance in a test tube is dangerous to touch.
- Make sure the test-tube holder tightly grips the test tube so that the test tube will not slide out of the holder.
- Make sure that the test-tube holder is above the surface of the substance in the test tube so that you can observe the substance.

Test-Tube Rack

- Use a test-tube rack to organize test tubes before, during, and after an experiment.

- Use a test-tube rack to keep test tubes upright so that they do not fall over and spill their contents.

- Use a test-tube rack that is the correct size for the test tubes that you are using. If the rack is too small, a test tube may become stuck. If the rack is too large, a test tube may lean over, and some of its contents may spill or splash.

Forceps

- Use forceps when you need to pick up or hold a very small object that should not be touched with your hands.

- Do not use forceps to hold anything over a flame, because forceps are not long enough to keep your hand safely away from the flame. Plastic forceps will melt, and metal forceps will conduct heat and burn your hand.

Hot Plate

- Use a hot plate when a substance needs to be kept warmer than room temperature for a long period of time.

- Use a hot plate instead of a Bunsen burner or a candle when you need to carefully control temperature.

- Do not use a hot plate when a substance needs to be burned in an experiment.

- Always use "hot hands" safety mitts or oven mitts when handling anything that has been heated on a hot plate.

Microscope

Scientists use microscopes to see very small objects that cannot easily be seen with the eye alone. A microscope magnifies the image of an object so that small details may be observed. A microscope that you may use can magnify an object 400 times—the object will appear 400 times larger than its actual size.

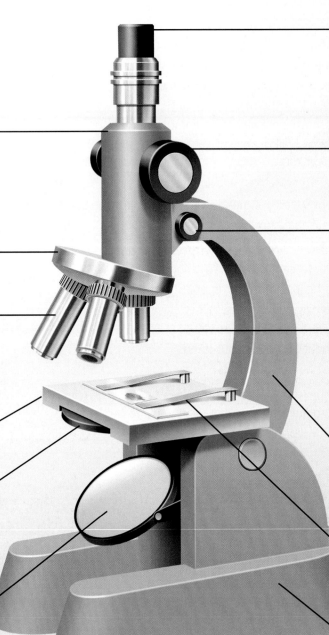

Body The body separates the lens in the eyepiece from the objective lenses below.

Nosepiece The nosepiece holds the objective lenses above the stage and rotates so that all lenses may be used.

High-Power Objective Lens This is the largest lens on the nosepiece. It magnifies an image approximately 40 times.

Stage The stage supports the object being viewed.

Diaphragm The diaphragm is used to adjust the amount of light passing through the slide and into an objective lens.

Mirror or Light Source Some microscopes use light that is reflected through the stage by a mirror. Other microscopes have their own light sources.

Eyepiece Objects are viewed through the eyepiece. The eyepiece contains a lens that commonly magnifies an image 10 times.

Coarse Adjustment This knob is used to focus the image of an object when it is viewed through the low-power lens.

Fine Adjustment This knob is used to focus the image of an object when it is viewed through the high-power lens.

Low-Power Objective Lens This is the smallest lens on the nosepiece. It magnifies an image approximately 10 times.

Arm The arm supports the body above the stage. Always carry a microscope by the arm and base.

Stage Clip The stage clip holds a slide in place on the stage.

Base The base supports the microscope.

VIEWING AN OBJECT

1. Use the coarse adjustment knob to raise the body tube.
2. Adjust the diaphragm so that you can see a bright circle of light through the eyepiece.
3. Place the object or slide on the stage. Be sure that it is centered over the hole in the stage.
4. Turn the nosepiece to click the low-power lens into place.
5. Using the coarse adjustment knob, slowly lower the lens and focus on the specimen being viewed. Be sure not to touch the slide or object with the lens.
6. When switching from the low-power lens to the high-power lens, first raise the body tube with the coarse adjustment knob so that the high-power lens will not hit the slide.
7. Turn the nosepiece to click the high-power lens into place.
8. Use the fine adjustment knob to focus on the specimen being viewed. Again, be sure not to touch the slide or object with the lens.

MAKING A SLIDE, OR WET MOUNT

1 Place the specimen in the center of a clean slide.

2 Place a drop of water on the specimen.

3 Place a cover slip on the slide. Put one edge of the cover slip into the drop of water and slowly lower it over the specimen.

4 Remove any air bubbles from under the cover slip by gently tapping the cover slip.

5 Dry any excess water before placing the slide on the microscope stage for viewing.

Spring Scale (Force Meter)

- Use a spring scale to measure a force pulling on the scale.

- Use a spring scale to measure the force of gravity exerted on an object by Earth.

- To measure a force accurately, a spring scale must be zeroed before it is used. The scale is zeroed when no weight is attached and the indicator is positioned at zero.

- Do not attach a weight that is either too heavy or too light to a spring scale. A weight that is too heavy could break the scale or exert too great a force for the scale to measure. A weight that is too light may not exert enough force to be measured accurately.

Graduated Cylinder

- Use a graduated cylinder to measure the volume of a liquid.

- Be sure that the graduated cylinder is on a flat surface so that your measurement will be accurate.

- When reading the scale on a graduated cylinder, be sure to have your eyes at the level of the surface of the liquid.

- The surface of the liquid will be curved in the graduated cylinder. Read the volume of the liquid at the bottom of the curve, or meniscus (muh-NIHS-kuhs).

- You can use a graduated cylinder to find the volume of a solid object by measuring the increase in a liquid's level after you add the object to the cylinder.

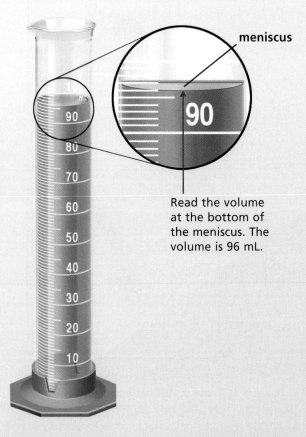

meniscus

Read the volume at the bottom of the meniscus. The volume is 96 mL.

Metric Rulers

- Use metric rulers or meter sticks to measure objects' lengths.

- Do not measure an object from the end of a metric ruler or meter stick, because the end is often imperfect. Instead, measure from the 1-centimeter mark, but remember to subtract a centimeter from the apparent measurement.

- Estimate any lengths that extend between marked units. For example, if a meter stick shows centimeters but not millimeters, you can estimate the length that an object extends between centimeter marks to measure it to the nearest millimeter.

- **Controlling Variables** If you are taking repeated measurements, always measure from the same point each time. For example, if you're measuring how high two different balls bounce when dropped from the same height, measure both bounces at the same point on the balls—either the top or the bottom. Do not measure at the top of one ball and the bottom of the other.

EXAMPLE

How to Measure a Leaf

1. Lay a ruler flat on top of the leaf so that the 1-centimeter mark lines up with one end. Make sure the ruler and the leaf do not move between the time you line them up and the time you take the measurement.

2. Look straight down on the ruler so that you can see exactly how the marks line up with the other end of the leaf.

3. Estimate the length by which the leaf extends beyond a marking. For example, the leaf below extends about halfway between the 4.2-centimeter and 4.3-centimeter marks, so the apparent measurement is about 4.25 centimeters.

4. Remember to subtract 1 centimeter from your apparent measurement, since you started at the 1-centimeter mark on the ruler and not at the end. The leaf is about 3.25 centimeters long (4.25 cm – 1 cm = 3.25 cm).

Triple-Beam Balance

This balance has a pan and three beams with sliding masses, called riders. At one end of the beams is a pointer that indicates whether the mass on the pan is equal to the masses shown on the beams.

1. Make sure the balance is zeroed before measuring the mass of an object. The balance is zeroed if the pointer is at zero when nothing is on the pan and the riders are at their zero points. Use the adjustment knob at the base of the balance to zero it.

2. Place the object to be measured on the pan.

3. Move the riders one notch at a time away from the pan. Begin with the largest rider. If moving the largest rider one notch brings the pointer below zero, begin measuring the mass of the object with the next smaller rider.

4. Change the positions of the riders until they balance the mass on the pan and the pointer is at zero. Then add the readings from the three beams to determine the mass of the object.

300 g	position of largest rider
90 g	position of middle rider
+ 3 g	position of smallest rider
393 g	mass of beaker

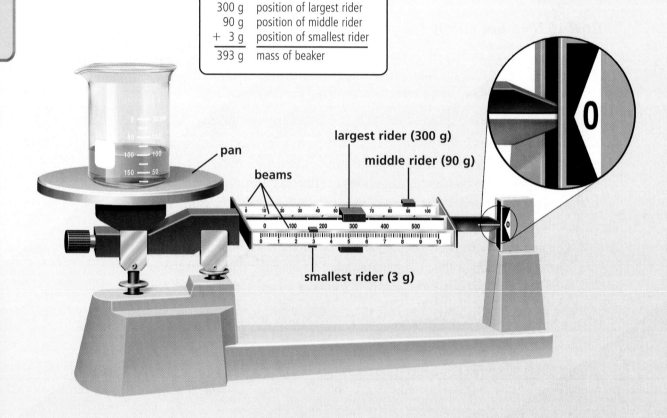

pan

beams

largest rider (300 g)

middle rider (90 g)

smallest rider (3 g)

Double-Pan Balance

This type of balance has two pans. Between the pans is a pointer that indicates whether the masses on the pans are equal.

1. Make sure the balance is zeroed before measuring the mass of an object. The balance is zeroed if the pointer is at zero when there is nothing on either of the pans. Many double-pan balances have sliding knobs that can be used to zero them.

2. Place the object to be measured on one of the pans.

3. Begin adding standard masses to the other pan. Begin with the largest standard mass. If this adds too much mass to the balance, begin measuring the mass of the object with the next smaller standard mass.

4. Add standard masses until the masses on both pans are balanced and the pointer is at zero. Then add the standard masses together to determine the mass of the object being measured.

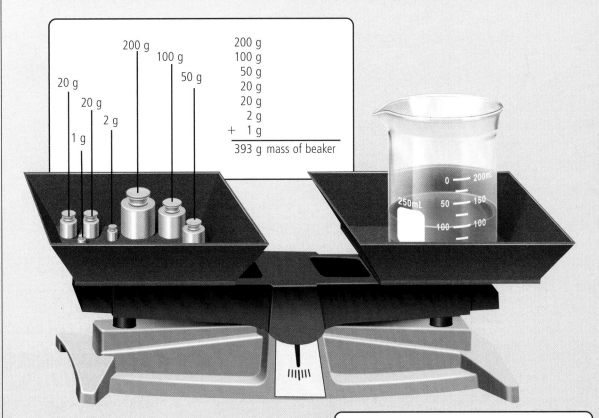

	200 g
	100 g
	50 g
	20 g
	20 g
	2 g
+	1 g

393 g mass of beaker

Never place chemicals or liquids directly on a pan. Instead, use the following procedure:

1. Determine the mass of an empty container, such as a beaker.

2. Pour the substance into the container, and measure the total mass of the substance and the container.

3. Subtract the mass of the empty container from the total mass to find the mass of the substance.

The Metric System and SI Units

Scientists use International System (SI) units for measurements of distance, volume, mass, and temperature. The International System is based on multiples of ten and the metric system of measurement.

Basic SI Units		
Property	**Name**	**Symbol**
length	meter	m
volume	liter	L
mass	kilogram	kg
temperature	kelvin	K

SI Prefixes		
Prefix	**Symbol**	**Multiple of 10**
kilo-	k	1000
hecto-	h	100
deca-	da	10
deci-	d	$0.1 \left(\frac{1}{10}\right)$
centi-	c	$0.01 \left(\frac{1}{100}\right)$
milli-	m	$0.001 \left(\frac{1}{1000}\right)$

Changing Metric Units

You can change from one unit to another in the metric system by multiplying or dividing by a power of 10.

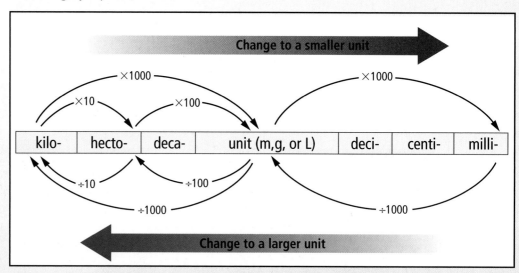

Example

Change 0.64 liters to milliliters.

(1) Decide whether to multiply or divide.

(2) Select the power of 10.

ANSWER 0.64 L = 640 mL

Change to a smaller unit by multiplying.

L ———— × 1000 ———→ mL

0.64 × 1000 = 640.

Example

Change 23.6 grams to kilograms.

(1) Decide whether to multiply or divide.

(2) Select the power of 10.

ANSWER 23.6 g = 0.0236 kg

Change to a larger unit by dividing.

kg ←——— ÷ 1000 ———— g

23.6 ÷ 1000 = 0.0236

Temperature Conversions

Even though the kelvin is the SI base unit of temperature, the degree Celsius will be the unit you use most often in your science studies. The formulas below show the relationships between temperatures in degrees Fahrenheit (°F), degrees Celsius (°C), and kelvins (K).

$$°C = \frac{5}{9}(°F - 32)$$

$$°F = \frac{9}{5}°C + 32$$

$$K = °C + 273$$

See page R42 for help with using formulas.

Examples of Temperature Conversions		
Condition	Degrees Celsius	Degrees Fahrenheit
Freezing point of water	0	32
Cool day	10	50
Mild day	20	68
Warm day	30	86
Normal body temperature	37	98.6
Very hot day	40	104
Boiling point of water	100	212

Converting Between SI and U.S. Customary Units

Use the chart below when you need to convert between SI units and U.S. customary units.

SI Unit	From SI to U.S. Customary			From U.S. Customary to SI		
Length	When you know	multiply by	to find	When you know	multiply by	to find
kilometer (km) = 1000 m	kilometers	0.62	miles	miles	1.61	kilometers
meter (m) = 100 cm	meters	3.28	feet	feet	0.3048	meters
centimeter (cm) = 10 mm	centimeters	0.39	inches	inches	2.54	centimeters
millimeter (mm) = 0.1 cm	millimeters	0.04	inches	inches	25.4	millimeters
Area	When you know	multiply by	to find	When you know	multiply by	to find
square kilometer (km²)	square kilometers	0.39	square miles	square miles	2.59	square kilometers
square meter (m²)	square meters	1.2	square yards	square yards	0.84	square meters
square centimeter (cm²)	square centimeters	0.155	square inches	square inches	6.45	square centimeters
Volume	When you know	multiply by	to find	When you know	multiply by	to find
liter (L) = 1000 mL	liters	1.06	quarts	quarts	0.95	liters
	liters	0.26	gallons	gallons	3.79	liters
	liters	4.23	cups	cups	0.24	liters
	liters	2.12	pints	pints	0.47	liters
milliliter (mL) = 0.001 L	milliliters	0.20	teaspoons	teaspoons	4.93	milliliters
	milliliters	0.07	tablespoons	tablespoons	14.79	milliliters
	milliliters	0.03	fluid ounces	fluid ounces	29.57	milliliters
Mass	When you know	multiply by	to find	When you know	multiply by	to find
kilogram (kg) = 1000 g	kilograms	2.2	pounds	pounds	0.45	kilograms
gram (g) = 1000 mg	grams	0.035	ounces	ounces	28.35	grams

LAB HANDBOOK

Precision and Accuracy

When you do an experiment, it is important that your methods, observations, and data be both precise and accurate.

low precision

precision, but not accuracy

precision and accuracy

Precision

In science, **precision** is the exactness and consistency of measurements. For example, measurements made with a ruler that has both centimeter and millimeter markings would be more precise than measurements made with a ruler that has only centimeter markings. Another indicator of precision is the care taken to make sure that methods and observations are as exact and consistent as possible. Every time a particular experiment is done, the same procedure should be used. Precision is necessary because experiments are repeated several times and if the procedure changes, the results will change.

EXAMPLE

Suppose you are measuring temperatures over a two-week period. Your precision will be greater if you measure each temperature at the same place, at the same time of day, and with the same thermometer than if you change any of these factors from one day to the next.

Accuracy

In science, it is possible to be precise but not accurate. **Accuracy** depends on the difference between a measurement and an actual value. The smaller the difference, the more accurate the measurement.

EXAMPLE

Suppose you look at a stream and estimate that it is about 1 meter wide at a particular place. You decide to check your estimate by measuring the stream with a meter stick, and you determine that the stream is 1.32 meters wide. However, because it is hard to measure the width of a stream with a meter stick, it turns out that you didn't do a very good job. The stream is actually 1.14 meters wide. Therefore, even though your estimate was less precise than your measurement, your estimate was actually more accurate.

Making Data Tables and Graphs

Data tables and graphs are useful tools for both recording and communicating scientific data.

Making Data Tables

You can use a **data table** to organize and record the measurements that you make. Some examples of information that might be recorded in data tables are frequencies, times, and amounts.

EXAMPLE

Suppose you are investigating photosynthesis in two elodea plants. One sits in direct sunlight, and the other sits in a dimly lit room. You measure the rate of photosynthesis by counting the number of bubbles in the jar every ten minutes.

1. Title and number your data table.
2. Decide how you will organize the table into columns and rows.
3. Any units, such as seconds or degrees, should be included in column headings, not in the individual cells.

Table 1. Number of Bubbles from Elodea

Time (min)	Sunlight	Dim Light
0	0	0
10	15	5
20	25	8
30	32	7
40	41	10
50	47	9
60	42	9

Always number and title data tables.

The data in the table above could also be organized in a different way.

Table 1. Number of Bubbles from Elodea

Light Condition	Time (min)						
	0	10	20	30	40	50	60
Sunlight	0	15	25	32	41	47	42
Dim light	0	5	8	7	10	9	9

Put units in column heading.

Making Line Graphs

You can use a **line graph** to show a relationship between variables. Line graphs are particularly useful for showing changes in variables over time.

EXAMPLE

Suppose you are interested in graphing temperature data that you collected over the course of a day.

Table 1. Outside Temperature During the Day on March 7

	Time of Day						
	7:00 A.M.	9:00 A.M.	11:00 A.M.	1:00 P.M.	3:00 P.M.	5:00 P.M.	7:00 P.M.
Temp (°C)	8	9	11	14	12	10	6

1. Use the vertical axis of your line graph for the variable that you are measuring—temperature.

2. Choose scales for both the horizontal axis and the vertical axis of the graph. You should have two points more than you need on the vertical axis, and the horizontal axis should be long enough for all of the data points to fit.

3. Draw and label each axis.

4. Graph each value. First find the appropriate point on the scale of the horizontal axis. Imagine a line that rises vertically from that place on the scale. Then find the corresponding value on the vertical axis, and imagine a line that moves horizontally from that value. The point where these two imaginary lines intersect is where the value should be plotted.

5. Connect the points with straight lines.

Be sure to add a number and a title to your graph.

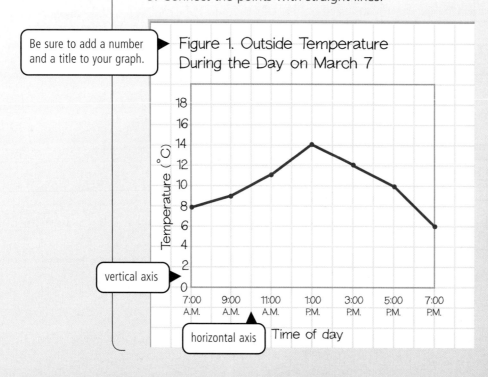

Figure 1. Outside Temperature During the Day on March 7

vertical axis

horizontal axis

LAB HANDBOOK

Making Circle Graphs

You can use a **circle graph,** sometimes called a pie chart, to represent data as parts of a circle. Circle graphs are used only when the data can be expressed as percentages of a whole. The entire circle shown in a circle graph is equal to 100 percent of the data.

EXAMPLE

Suppose you identified the species of each mature tree growing in a small wooded area. You organized your data in a table, but you also want to show the data in a circle graph.

1. To begin, find the total number of mature trees.

    56 + 34 + 22 + 10 + 28 = 150

2. To find the degree measure for each sector of the circle, write a fraction comparing the number of each tree species with the total number of trees. Then multiply the fraction by 360°.

    Oak: $\frac{56}{150} \times 360° = 134.4°$

3. Draw a circle. Use a protractor to draw the angle for each sector of the graph.

4. Color and label each sector of the graph.

5. Give the graph a number and title.

Table 1. Tree Species in Wooded Area

Species	Number of Specimens
Oak	56
Maple	34
Birch	22
Willow	10
Pine	28

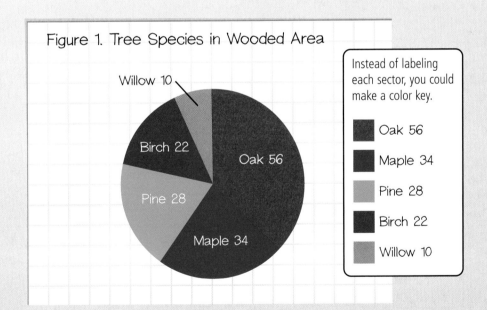

Figure 1. Tree Species in Wooded Area

Willow 10
Birch 22
Oak 56
Pine 28
Maple 34

Instead of labeling each sector, you could make a color key.

Oak 56
Maple 34
Pine 28
Birch 22
Willow 10

Bar Graph

A **bar graph** is a type of graph in which the lengths of the bars are used to represent and compare data. A numerical scale is used to determine the lengths of the bars.

EXAMPLE

To determine the effect of water on seed sprouting, three cups were filled with sand, and ten seeds were planted in each. Different amounts of water were added to each cup over a three-day period.

Table 1. Effect of Water on Seed Sprouting

Daily Amount of Water (mL)	Number of Seeds That Sprouted After 3 Days in Sand
0	1
10	4
20	8

1. Choose a numerical scale. The greatest value is 8, so the end of the scale should have a value greater than 8, such as 10. Use equal increments along the scale, such as increments of 2.

2. Draw and label the axes. Mark intervals on the vertical axis according to the scale you chose.

3. Draw a bar for each data value. Use the scale to decide how long to make each bar.

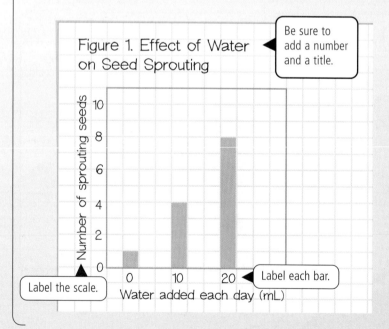

Figure 1. Effect of Water on Seed Sprouting

Be sure to add a number and a title.

Number of sprouting seeds

Water added each day (mL)

Label the scale.

Label each bar.

Double Bar Graph

A **double bar graph** is a bar graph that shows two sets of data. The two bars for each measurement are drawn next to each other.

EXAMPLE

The seed-sprouting experiment was done using both sand and potting soil. The data for sand and potting soil can be plotted on one graph.

1. Draw one set of bars, using the data for sand, as shown below.
2. Draw bars for the potting-soil data next to the bars for the sand data. Shade them a different color. Add a key.

Table 2. Effect of Water and Soil on Seed Sprouting

Daily Amount of Water (mL)	Number of Seeds That Sprouted After 3 Days in Sand	Number of Seeds That Sprouted After 3 Days in Potting Soil
0	1	2
10	4	5
20	8	9

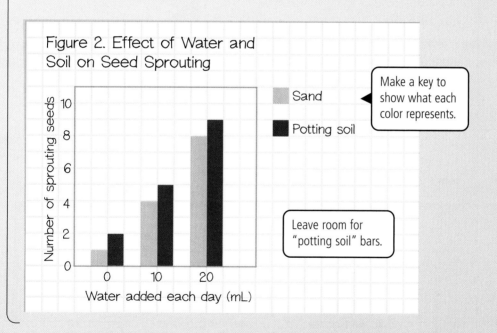

Figure 2. Effect of Water and Soil on Seed Sprouting

Make a key to show what each color represents.

Leave room for "potting soil" bars.

Designing an Experiment

Use this section when designing or conducting an experiment.

Determining a Purpose

You can find a purpose for an experiment by doing research, by examining the results of a previous experiment, or by observing the world around you. An **experiment** is an organized procedure to study something under controlled conditions.

1. Write the purpose of your experiment as a question or problem that you want to investigate.

2. Write down research questions and begin searching for information that will help you design an experiment. Consult the library, the Internet, and other people as you conduct your research.

> Don't forget to learn as much as possible about your topic before you begin.

EXAMPLE

Middle school students observed an odor near the lake by their school. They also noticed that the water on the side of the lake near the school was greener than the water on the other side of the lake. The students did some research to learn more about their observations. They discovered that the odor and green color in the lake

came from algae. They also discovered that a new fertilizer was being used on a field nearby. The students inferred that the use of the fertilizer might be related to the presence of the algae and designed a controlled experiment to find out whether they were right.

Problem

How does fertilizer affect the presence of algae in a lake?

Research Questions

- Have other experiments been done on this problem? If so, what did those experiments show?
- What kind of fertilizer is used on the field? How much?
- How do algae grow?
- How do people measure algae?
- Can fertilizer and algae be used safely in a lab? How?

> **Research**
> As you research, you may find a topic that is more interesting to you than your original topic, or learn that a procedure you wanted to use is not practical or safe. It is OK to change your purpose as you research.

LAB HANDBOOK

Writing a Hypothesis

A **hypothesis** is a tentative explanation for an observation or scientific problem that can be tested by further investigation. You can write your hypothesis in the form of an "If . . . , then . . . , because . . ." statement.

> Hypothesis
>
> If the amount of fertilizer in lake water is increased, then the amount of algae will also increase, because fertilizers provide nutrients that algae need to grow.

Hypotheses
For help with hypotheses, refer to page R3.

Determining Materials

Make a list of all the materials you will need to do your experiment. Be specific, especially if someone else is helping you obtain the materials. Try to think of everything you will need.

> Materials
> • 1 large jar or container
> • 4 identical smaller containers
> • rubber gloves that also cover the arms
> • sample of fertilizer-and-water solution
> • eyedropper
> • clear plastic wrap
> • scissors
> • masking tape
> • marker
> • ruler

Determining Variables and Constants

EXPERIMENTAL GROUP AND CONTROL GROUP

An experiment to determine how two factors are related always has two groups—a control group and an experimental group.

1. Design an experimental group. Include as many trials as possible in the experimental group in order to obtain reliable results.

2. Design a control group that is the same as the experimental group in every way possible, except for the factor you wish to test.

Experimental Group: two containers of lake water with one drop of fertilizer solution added to each

Control Group: two containers of lake water with no fertilizer solution added

Go back to your materials list and make sure you have enough items listed to cover both your experimental group and your control group.

VARIABLES AND CONSTANTS

Identify the variables and constants in your experiment. In a controlled experiment, a **variable** is any factor that can change. **Constants,** or controlled parameters, are all of the factors that are the same in both the experimental group and the control group.

Hypothesis
If the amount of fertilizer in lake water is increased, then the amount of algae will also increase, because fertilizers provide nutrients that algae need to grow.

1. Read your hypothesis. The **independent variable** is the factor that you wish to test and that is manipulated or changed so that it can be tested. The independent variable is expressed in your hypothesis after the word *if*. Identify the independent variable in your laboratory report.

2. The **dependent variable** is the factor that you measure to gather results. It is expressed in your hypothesis after the word *then*. Identify the dependent variable in your laboratory report.

Table 1. Variables and Constants in Algae Experiment

Independent Variable	Dependent Variable	Constants
Amount of fertilizer in lake water	Amount of algae that grow	• Where the lake water is obtained • Type of container used • Light and temperature conditions where water will be stored

Set up your experiment so that you will test only one variable.

MEASURING THE DEPENDENT VARIABLE

Before starting your experiment, you need to define how you will measure the dependent variable. An **operational definition** is a description of the one particular way in which you will measure the dependent variable.

Your operational definition is important for several reasons. First, in any experiment there are several ways in which a dependent variable can be measured. Second, the procedure of the experiment depends on how you decide to measure the dependent variable. Third, your operational definition makes it possible for other people to evaluate and build on your experiment.

EXAMPLE 1

An operational definition of a dependent variable can be qualitative. That is, your measurement of the dependent variable can simply be an observation of whether a change occurs as a result of a change in the independent variable. This type of operational definition can be thought of as a "yes or no" measurement.

Table 2. Qualitative Operational Definition of Algae Growth

Independent Variable	Dependent Variable	Operational Definition
Amount of fertilizer in lake water	Amount of algae that grow	Algae grow in lake water

A qualitative measurement of a dependent variable is often easy to make and record. However, this type of information does not provide a great deal of detail in your experimental results.

EXAMPLE 2

An operational definition of a dependent variable can be quantitative. That is, your measurement of the dependent variable can be a number that shows how much change occurs as a result of a change in the independent variable.

Table 3. Quantitative Operational Definition of Algae Growth

Independent Variable	Dependent Variable	Operational Definition
Amount of fertilizer in lake water	Amount of algae that grow	Diameter of largest algal growth (in mm)

A quantitative measurement of a dependent variable can be more difficult to make and analyze than a qualitative measurement. However, this type of data provides much more information about your experiment and is often more useful.

Writing a Procedure

Write each step of your procedure. Start each step with a verb, or action word, and keep the steps short. Your procedure should be clear enough for someone else to use as instructions for repeating your experiment.

If necessary, go back to your materials list and add any materials that you left out.

Procedure

1. Put on your gloves. Use the large container to obtain a sample of lake water.

2. Divide the sample of lake water equally among the four smaller containers.

Controlling Variables
The same amount of fertilizer solution must be added to two of the four containers.

3. Use the eyedropper to add one drop of fertilizer solution to two of the containers.

4. Use the masking tape and the marker to label the containers with your initials, the date, and the identifiers "Jar 1 with Fertilizer," "Jar 2 with Fertilizer," "Jar 1 without Fertilizer," and "Jar 2 without Fertilizer."

5. Cover the containers with clear plastic wrap. Use the scissors to punch ten holes in each of the covers.

Controlling Variables
All four containers must receive the same amount of light.

6. Place all four containers on a window ledge. Make sure that they all receive the same amount of light.

7. Observe the containers every day for one week.

8. Use the ruler to measure the diameter of the largest clump of algae in each container, and record your measurements daily.

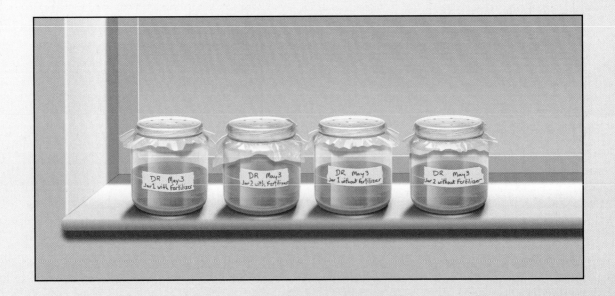

Recording Observations

Once you have obtained all of your materials and your procedure has been approved, you can begin making experimental observations. Gather both quantitative and qualitative data. If something goes wrong during your procedure, make sure you record that too.

> **Observations**
> For help with making qualitative and quantitative observations, refer to page R2.

> For more examples of data tables, see page R23.

Table 4. Fertilizer and Algae Growth

Date and Time	Experimental Group		Control Group		Observations
	Jar 1 with Fertilizer (diameter of algae in mm)	Jar 2 with Fertilizer (diameter of algae in mm)	Jar 1 without Fertilizer (diameter of algae in mm)	Jar 2 without Fertilizer (diameter of algae in mm)	
5/3 4:00 P.M.	0	0	0	0	condensation in all containers
5/4 4:00 P.M.	0	3	0	0	tiny green blobs in jar 2 with fertilizer
5/5 4:15 P.M.	4	5	0	3	green blobs in jars 1 and 2 with fertilizer and jar 2 without fertilizer
5/6 4:00 P.M.	5	6	0	4	water light green in jar 2 with fertilizer
5/7 4:00 P.M.	8	10	0	6	water light green in jars 1 and 2 with fertilizer and in jar 2 without fertilizer
5/8 3:30 P.M.	10	18	0	6	cover off jar 2 with fertilizer
5/9 3:30 P.M.	14	23	0	8	drew sketches of each container

> Notice that on the sixth day, the observer found that the cover was off one of the containers. It is important to record observations of unintended factors because they might affect the results of the experiment.

> Use technology, such as a microscope, to help you make observations when possible.

Drawings of Samples Viewed Under Microscope on 5/9 at 100x

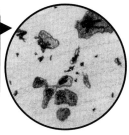

Jar 1 with Fertilizer

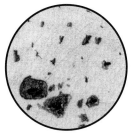

Jar 2 with Fertilizer

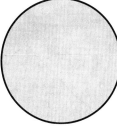

Jar 1 without Fertilizer

Jar 2 without Fertilizer

Summarizing Results

To summarize your data, look at all of your observations together. Look for meaningful ways to present your observations. For example, you might average your data or make a graph to look for patterns. When possible, use spreadsheet software to help you analyze and present your data. The two graphs below show the same data.

EXAMPLE 1

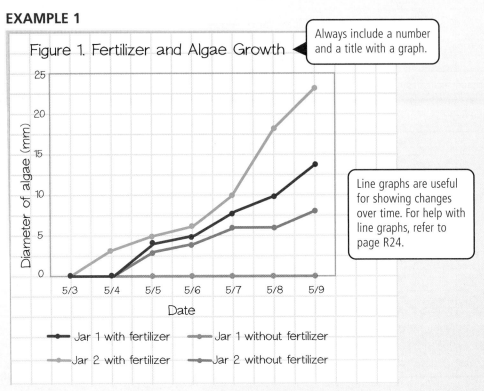

Figure 1. Fertilizer and Algae Growth

Always include a number and a title with a graph.

Line graphs are useful for showing changes over time. For help with line graphs, refer to page R24.

Bar graphs are useful for comparing different data sets. This bar graph has four bars for each day. Another way to present the data would be to calculate averages for the tests and the controls, and to show one test bar and one control bar for each day.

EXAMPLE 2

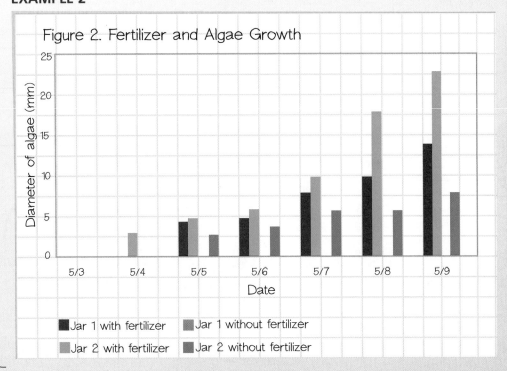

Figure 2. Fertilizer and Algae Growth

Drawing Conclusions

RESULTS AND INFERENCES

To draw conclusions from your experiment, first write your results. Then compare your results with your hypothesis. Do your results support your hypothesis? Be careful not to make inferences about factors that you did not test.

> For help with making inferences, see page R4.

Results and Inferences

The results of my experiment show that more algae grew in lake water to which fertilizer had been added than in lake water to which no fertilizer had been added. My hypothesis was supported. I infer that it is possible that the growth of algae in the lake was caused by the fertilizer used on the field.

> Notice that you cannot conclude from this experiment that the presence of algae in the lake was due only to the fertilizer.

QUESTIONS FOR FURTHER RESEARCH

Write a list of questions for further research and investigation. Your ideas may lead you to new experiments and discoveries.

Questions for Further Research

- What is the connection between the amount of fertilizer and algae growth?
- How do different brands of fertilizer affect algae growth?
- How would algae growth in the lake be affected if no fertilizer were used on the field?
- How do algae affect the lake and the other life in and around it?
- How does fertilizer affect the lake and the life in and around it?
- If fertilizer is getting into the lake, how is it getting there?

Math Handbook

Describing a Set of Data

Means, medians, modes, and ranges are important math tools for describing data sets such as the following widths of fossilized clamshells.

13 mm   25 mm   14 mm   21 mm   16 mm   23 mm   14 mm

Mean

The **mean** of a data set is the sum of the values divided by the number of values.

> **Example**
>
> To find the mean of the clamshell data, add the values and then divide the sum by the number of values.
>
> $$\frac{13 \text{ mm} + 25 \text{ mm} + 14 \text{ mm} + 21 \text{ mm} + 16 \text{ mm} + 23 \text{ mm} + 14 \text{ mm}}{7} = \frac{126 \text{ mm}}{7} = 18 \text{ mm}$$
>
> **ANSWER** The mean is 18 mm.

Median

The **median** of a data set is the middle value when the values are written in numerical order. If a data set has an even number of values, the median is the mean of the two middle values.

> **Example**
>
> To find the median of the clamshell data, arrange the values in order from least to greatest. The median is the middle value.
>
> 13 mm   14 mm   14 mm   16 mm   21 mm   23 mm   25 mm
>
> **ANSWER** The median is 16 mm.

Mode

The **mode** of a data set is the value that occurs most often.

> ### Example
>
> To find the mode of the clamshell data, arrange the values in order from least to greatest and determine the value that occurs most often.
>
> 13 mm 14 mm 14 mm 16 mm 21 mm 23 mm 25 mm
>
> **ANSWER** The mode is 14 mm.

A data set can have more than one mode or no mode. For example, the following data set has modes of 2 mm and 4 mm:

2 mm 2 mm 3 mm 4 mm 4 mm

The data set below has no mode, because no value occurs more often than any other.

2 mm 3 mm 4 mm 5 mm

Range

The **range** of a data set is the difference between the greatest value and the least value.

> ### Example
>
> To find the range of the clamshell data, arrange the values in order from least to greatest.
>
> 13 mm 14 mm 14 mm 16 mm 21 mm 23 mm 25 mm
>
> Subtract the least value from the greatest value.
>
> 13 mm is the least value.
> 25 mm is the greatest value.
>
> 25 mm − 13 mm = 12 mm
>
> **ANSWER** The range is 12 mm.

Using Ratios, Rates, and Proportions

You can use ratios and rates to compare values in data sets. You can use proportions to find unknown values.

Ratios

A **ratio** uses division to compare two values. The ratio of a value a to a nonzero value b can be written as $\frac{a}{b}$.

Example

The height of one plant is 8 centimeters. The height of another plant is 6 centimeters. To find the ratio of the height of the first plant to the height of the second plant, write a fraction and simplify it.

$$\frac{8 \text{ cm}}{6 \text{ cm}} = \frac{4 \times \overset{1}{\cancel{2}}}{3 \times \underset{1}{\cancel{2}}} = \frac{4}{3}$$

ANSWER The ratio of the plant heights is $\frac{4}{3}$.

You can also write the ratio $\frac{a}{b}$ as "a to b" or as $a:b$. For example, you can write the ratio of the plant heights as "4 to 3" or as $4:3$.

Rates

A **rate** is a ratio of two values expressed in different units. A unit rate is a rate with a denominator of 1 unit.

Example

A plant grew 6 centimeters in 2 days. The plant's rate of growth was $\frac{6 \text{ cm}}{2 \text{ days}}$. To describe the plant's growth in centimeters per day, write a unit rate.

Divide numerator and denominator by 2: $\quad \dfrac{6 \text{ cm}}{2 \text{ days}} = \dfrac{6 \text{ cm} \div 2}{2 \text{ days} \div 2}$

> You divide 2 days by 2 to get 1 day, so divide 6 cm by 2 also.

Simplify: $\quad = \dfrac{3 \text{ cm}}{1 \text{ day}}$

ANSWER The plant's rate of growth is 3 centimeters per day.

MATH HANDBOOK

Proportions

A **proportion** is an equation stating that two ratios are equivalent. To solve for an unknown value in a proportion, you can use cross products.

Example

If a plant grew 6 centimeters in 2 days, how many centimeters would it grow in 3 days (if its rate of growth is constant)?

Write a proportion: $\dfrac{6 \text{ cm}}{2 \text{ days}} = \dfrac{x}{3 \text{ days}}$

Set cross products: $6 \text{ cm} \cdot 3 = 2x$

Multiply 6 and 3: $18 \text{ cm} = 2x$

Divide each side by 2: $\dfrac{18 \text{ cm}}{2} = \dfrac{2x}{2}$

Simplify: $9 \text{ cm} = x$

ANSWER The plant would grow 9 centimeters in 3 days.

Using Decimals, Fractions, and Percents

Decimals, fractions, and percentages are all ways of recording and representing data.

Decimals

A **decimal** is a number that is written in the base-ten place value system, in which a decimal point separates the ones and tenths digits. The values of each place is ten times that of the place to its right.

Example

A caterpillar traveled from point *A* to point *C* along the path shown.

A ——— 36.9 cm ——— B ——— 52.4 cm ——— C

ADDING DECIMALS To find the total distance traveled by the caterpillar, add the distance from *A* to *B* and the distance from *B* to *C*. Begin by lining up the decimal points. Then add the figures as you would whole numbers and bring down the decimal point.

$$
\begin{array}{r}
36.9 \text{ cm} \\
+\ 52.4 \text{ cm} \\
\hline
89.3 \text{ cm}
\end{array}
$$

ANSWER The caterpillar traveled a total distance of 89.3 centimeters.

Example continued

SUBTRACTING DECIMALS To find how much farther the caterpillar traveled on the second leg of the journey, subtract the distance from *A* to *B* from the distance from *B* to *C*.

$$
\begin{array}{r}
52.4 \text{ cm} \\
-\ 36.9 \text{ cm} \\
\hline
15.5 \text{ cm}
\end{array}
$$

ANSWER The caterpillar traveled 15.5 centimeters farther on the second leg of the journey.

Example

A caterpillar is traveling from point *D* to point *F* along the path shown. The caterpillar travels at a speed of 9.6 centimeters per minute.

D ————— E ———— 33.6 cm ———— F

MULTIPLYING DECIMALS You can multiply decimals as you would whole numbers. The number of decimal places in the product is equal to the sum of the number of decimal places in the factors.

For instance, suppose it takes the caterpillar 1.5 minutes to go from *D* to *E*. To find the distance from *D* to *E*, multiply the caterpillar's speed by the time it took.

$$
\begin{array}{rl}
9.6 & \quad 1 \text{ decimal place} \\
\times\ 1.5 & +1 \text{ decimal place} \\
\hline
480 & \\
96\ \ & \\
\hline
14.40 & \quad 2 \text{ decimal places}
\end{array}
$$

Align as shown.

ANSWER The distance from *D* to *E* is 14.4 centimeters.

DIVIDING DECIMALS When you divide by a decimal, move the decimal points the same number of places in the divisor and the dividend to make the divisor a whole number.

For instance, to find the time it will take the caterpillar to travel from *E* to *F*, divide the distance from *E* to *F* by the caterpillar's speed.

$$
9.6\overline{)33.6}
$$

Move each decimal point one place to the right.

$$
\begin{array}{r}
3.5 \\
96\overline{)336.}\ \ \\
\underline{288}\ \ \ \\
480 \\
\underline{480} \\
0
\end{array}
$$

Line up decimal points.

ANSWER The caterpillar will travel from *E* to *F* in 3.5 minutes.

Fractions

A **fraction** is a number in the form $\frac{a}{b}$, where b is not equal to 0. A fraction is in **simplest form** if its numerator and denominator have a greatest common factor (GCF) of 1. To simplify a fraction, divide its numerator and denominator by their GCF.

Example

A caterpillar is 40 millimeters long. The head of the caterpillar is 6 millimeters long. To compare the length of the caterpillar's head with the caterpillar's total length, you can write and simplify a fraction that expresses the ratio of the two lengths.

Write the ratio of the two lengths: $\dfrac{\text{Length of head}}{\text{Total length}} = \dfrac{6 \text{ mm}}{40 \text{ mm}}$

Write numerator and denominator as products of numbers and the GCF: $= \dfrac{3 \times 2}{20 \times 2}$

Divide numerator and denominator by the GCF: $= \dfrac{3 \times \cancel{2}^{1}}{20 \times \cancel{2}_{1}}$

Simplify: $= \dfrac{3}{20}$

ANSWER In simplest form, the ratio of the lengths is $\dfrac{3}{20}$.

Percents

A **percent** is a ratio that compares a number to 100. The word *percent* means "per hundred" or "out of 100." The symbol for *percent* is %.

For instance, suppose 43 out of 100 caterpillars are female. You can represent this ratio as a percent, a decimal, or a fraction.

Percent	Decimal	Fraction
43%	0.43	$\dfrac{43}{100}$

Example

In the preceding example, the ratio of the length of the caterpillar's head to the caterpillar's total length is $\dfrac{3}{20}$. To write this ratio as a percent, write an equivalent fraction that has a denominator of 100.

Multiply numerator and denominator by 5: $\dfrac{3}{20} = \dfrac{3 \times 5}{20 \times 5}$

$= \dfrac{15}{100}$

Write as a percent: $= 15\%$

ANSWER The caterpillar's head represents 15 percent of its total length.

Using Formulas

A **formula** is an equation that shows the general relationship between two or more quantities.

The term *variable* is also used in science to refer to a factor that can change during an experiment.

In science, a formula often has a word form and a symbolic form. The formula below expresses Ohm's law.

Word Form

$$\text{Current} = \frac{\text{voltage}}{\text{resistance}}$$

Symbolic Form

$$I = \frac{V}{R}$$

In this formula, I, V, and R are variables. A mathematical **variable** is a symbol or letter that is used to represent one or more numbers.

Example

Suppose that you measure a voltage of 1.5 volts and a resistance of 15 ohms. You can use the formula for Ohm's law to find the current in amperes.

Write the formula for Ohm's law: $\quad I = \dfrac{V}{R}$

Substitute 1.5 volts for V and 15 ohms for R: $\quad I = \dfrac{1.5 \text{ volts}}{15 \text{ ohms}}$

Simplify: $\quad I = 0.1 \text{ amp}$

ANSWER The current is 0.1 ampere.

If you know the values of all variables but one in a formula, you can solve for the value of the unknown variable. For instance, Ohm's law can be used to find a voltage if you know the current and the resistance.

Example

Suppose that you know that a current is 0.2 amperes and the resistance is 18 ohms. Use the formula for Ohm's law to find the voltage in volts.

Write the formula for Ohm's law: $\quad I = \dfrac{V}{R}$

Substitute 0.2 amp for I and 18 ohms for R: $\quad 0.2 \text{ amp} = \dfrac{V}{18 \text{ ohms}}$

Multiply both sides by 18 ohms: $\quad 0.2 \text{ amp} \cdot 18 \text{ ohms} = V$

Simplify: $\quad 3.6 \text{ volts} = V$

ANSWER The voltage is 3.6 volts.

Finding Areas

The area of a figure is the amount of surface the figure covers.

Area is measured in square units, such as square meters (m^2) or square centimeters (cm^2). Formulas for the areas of three common geometric figures are shown below.

Area = (side length)^2
$A = s^2$

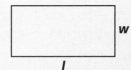

Area = length × width
$A = lw$

Area = $\frac{1}{2}$ × base × height
$A = \frac{1}{2} bh$

Example

Each face of a halite crystal is a square like the one shown. You can find the area of the square by using the steps below.

3 mm

3 mm

Write the formula for the area of a square: $A = s^2$

Substitute 3 mm for s: $= (3 \text{ mm})^2$

Simplify: $= 9 \text{ mm}^2$

ANSWER The area of the square is 9 square millimeters.

Finding Volumes

The volume of a solid is the amount of space contained by the solid.

Volume is measured in cubic units, such as cubic meters (m^3) or cubic centimeters (cm^3). The volume of a rectangular prism is given by the formula shown below.

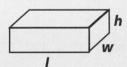

Volume = length × width × height
$V = lwh$

Example

A topaz crystal is a rectangular prism like the one shown. You can find the volume of the prism by using the steps below.

10 mm

12 mm

20 mm

Write the formula for the volume of a rectangular prism: $V = lwh$

Substitute dimensions: $= 20 \text{ mm} \times 12 \text{ mm} \times 10 \text{ mm}$

Simplify: $= 2400 \text{ mm}^3$

ANSWER The volume of the rectangular prism is 2400 cubic millimeters.

Using Significant Figures

The **significant figures** in a decimal are the digits that are warranted by the accuracy of a measuring device.

When you perform a calculation with measurements, the number of significant figures to include in the result depends in part on the number of significant figures in the measurements. When you multiply or divide measurements, your answer should have only as many significant figures as the measurement with the fewest significant figures.

Example

Using a balance and a graduated cylinder filled with water, you determined that a marble has a mass of 8.0 grams and a volume of 3.5 cubic centimeters. To calculate the density of the marble, divide the mass by the volume.

Write the formula for density: $\text{Density} = \dfrac{\text{mass}}{\text{Volume}}$

Substitute measurements: $= \dfrac{8.0 \text{ g}}{3.5 \text{ cm}^3}$

Use a calculator to divide: $\approx 2.285714286 \text{ g/cm}^3$

ANSWER Because the mass and the volume have two significant figures each, give the density to two significant figures. The marble has a density of 2.3 grams per cubic centimeter.

Using Scientific Notation

Scientific notation is a shorthand way to write very large or very small numbers. For example, 73,500,000,000,000,000,000,000 kg is the mass of the Moon. In scientific notation, it is 7.35×10^{22} kg.

Example

You can convert from standard form to scientific notation.

Standard Form	Scientific Notation
720,000	7.2×10^5
5 decimal places left	Exponent is 5.
0.000291	2.91×10^{-4}
4 decimal places right	Exponent is −4.

You can convert from scientific notation to standard form.

Scientific Notation	Standard Form
4.63×10^7	46,300,000
Exponent is 7.	7 decimal places right
1.08×10^{-6}	0.00000108
Exponent is −6.	6 decimal places left

Note-Taking Handbook

Note-Taking Strategies

Taking notes as you read helps you understand the information. The notes you take can also be used as a study guide for later review. This handbook presents several ways to organize your notes.

Content Frame

1. Make a chart in which each column represents a category.
2. Give each column a heading.
3. Write details under the headings.

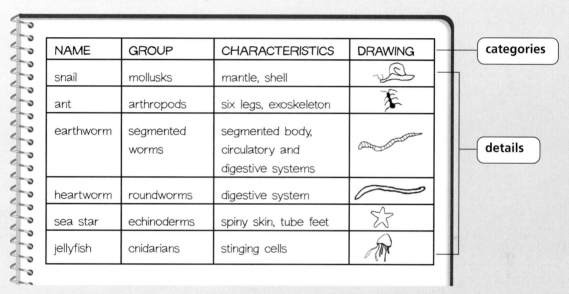

NAME	GROUP	CHARACTERISTICS	DRAWING
snail	mollusks	mantle, shell	
ant	arthropods	six legs, exoskeleton	
earthworm	segmented worms	segmented body, circulatory and digestive systems	
heartworm	roundworms	digestive system	
sea star	echinoderms	spiny skin, tube feet	
jellyfish	cnidarians	stinging cells	

categories

details

Combination Notes

1. For each new idea or concept, write an informal outline of the information.
2. Make a sketch to illustrate the concept, and label it.

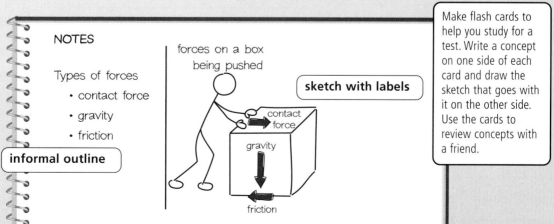

NOTES

Types of forces
- contact force
- gravity
- friction

informal outline

forces on a box being pushed

sketch with labels

contact force

gravity

friction

Make flash cards to help you study for a test. Write a concept on one side of each card and draw the sketch that goes with it on the other side. Use the cards to review concepts with a friend.

Main Idea and Detail Notes

1. In the left-hand column of a two-column chart, list main ideas. The blue headings express main ideas throughout this textbook.

2. In the right-hand column, write details that expand on each main idea.

You can shorten the headings in your chart. Be sure to use the most important words.

When studying for tests, cover up the detail notes column with a sheet of paper. Then use each main idea to form a question—such as "How does latitude affect climate?" Answer the question, and then uncover the detail notes column to check your answer.

MAIN IDEAS	DETAIL NOTES
1. Latitude affects climate.	1. Places close to the equator are usually warmer than places close to the poles.
main idea 1	1. Latitude has the same effect in both hemispheres.
2. Altitude affects climate.	2. Temperature decreases with altitude.
main idea 2	2. Altitude can overcome the effect of latitude on temperature.

details about main idea 1

details about main idea 2

Main Idea Web

1. Write a main idea in a box.
2. Add boxes around it with related vocabulary terms and important details.

You can find definitions near highlighted terms.

definition of *work*

Work is the use of force to move an object.

formula

Work = force · distance

main idea

Force is necessary to do work.

The joule is the unit used to measure work.

definition of *joule*

Work depends on the size of a force.

important detail

NOTE-TAKING HANDBOOK

Mind Map

1. Write a main idea in the center.

2. Add details that relate to one another and to the main idea.

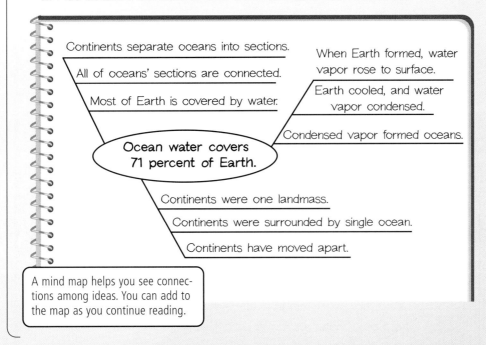

Continents separate oceans into sections.

All of oceans' sections are connected.

Most of Earth is covered by water.

When Earth formed, water vapor rose to surface.

Earth cooled, and water vapor condensed.

Condensed vapor formed oceans.

Ocean water covers 71 percent of Earth.

Continents were one landmass.

Continents were surrounded by single ocean.

Continents have moved apart.

A mind map helps you see connections among ideas. You can add to the map as you continue reading.

Supporting Main Ideas

1. Write a main idea in a box.

2. Add boxes underneath with information—such as reasons, explanations, and examples—that supports the main idea.

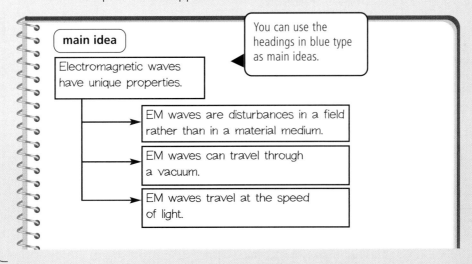

main idea

Electromagnetic waves have unique properties.

You can use the headings in blue type as main ideas.

EM waves are disturbances in a field rather than in a material medium.

EM waves can travel through a vacuum.

EM waves travel at the speed of light.

Outline

1. Copy the chapter title and headings from the book in the form of an outline.

2. Add notes that summarize in your own words what you read.

Cell Processes

1st key idea

I. Cells capture and release energy.

1st subpoint of I

A. All cells need energy.

2nd subpoint of I

B. Some cells capture light energy.

1st detail about B

1. Process of photosynthesis

2nd detail about B

2. Chloroplasts (site of photosynthesis)

3. Carbon dioxide and water as raw materials

4. Glucose and oxygen as products

C. All cells release energy.

1. Process of cellular respiration

2. Fermentation of sugar to carbon dioxide

3. Bacteria that carry out fermentation

II. Cells transport materials through membranes.

A. Some materials move by diffusion.

1. Particle movement from higher to lower concentrations

2. Movement of water through membrane (osmosis)

B. Some transport requires energy.

1. Active transport

2. Examples of active transport

Correct Outline Form
Include a title.

Arrange key ideas, subpoints, and details as shown.

Indent the divisions of the outline as shown.

Use the same grammatical form for items of the same rank. For example, if A is a sentence, B must also be a sentence.

You must have at least two main ideas or subpoints. That is, every A must be followed by a B, and every 1 must be followed by a 2.

Concept Map

1. Write an important concept in a large oval.

2. Add details related to the concept in smaller ovals.

3. Write linking words on arrows that connect the ovals.

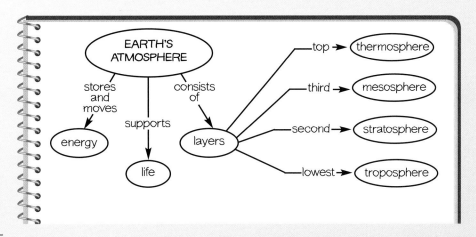

The main ideas or concepts can often be found in the blue headings. An example is "The atmosphere stores and moves energy." Use nouns from these concepts in the ovals, and use the verb or verbs on the lines.

Venn Diagram

1. Draw two overlapping circles, one for each item that you are comparing.

2. In the overlapping section, list the characteristics that are shared by both items.

3. In the outer sections, list the characteristics that are peculiar to each item.

4. Write a summary that describes the information in the Venn diagram.

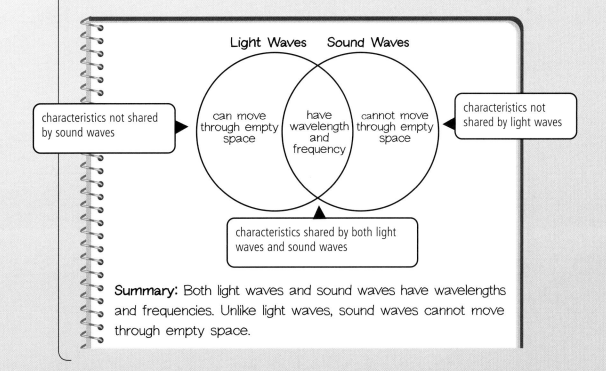

Summary: Both light waves and sound waves have wavelengths and frequencies. Unlike light waves, sound waves cannot move through empty space.

Vocabulary Strategies

Important terms are highlighted in this book. A definition of each term can be found in the sentence or paragraph where the term appears. You can also find definitions in the Glossary. Taking notes about vocabulary terms helps you understand and remember what you read.

Description Wheel

1. Write a term inside a circle.
2. Write words that describe the term on "spokes" attached to the circle.

When studying for a test with a friend, read the phrases on the spokes one at a time until your friend identifies the correct term.

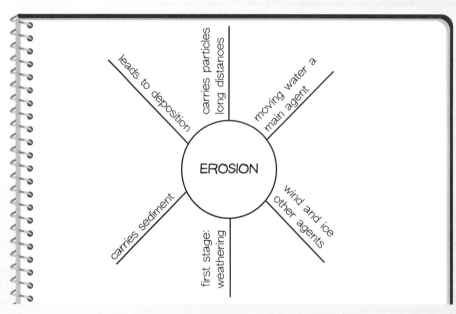

Four Square

1. Write a term in the center.
2. Write details in the four areas around the term.

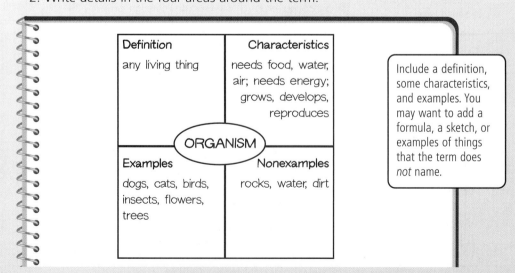

Include a definition, some characteristics, and examples. You may want to add a formula, a sketch, or examples of things that the term does *not* name.

NOTE-TAKING HANDBOOK

Frame Game

1. Write a term in the center.
2. Frame the term with details.

> Include examples, descriptions, sketches, or sentences that use the term in context. Change the frame to fit each new term.

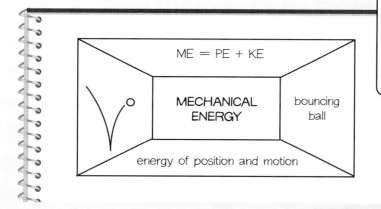

$ME = PE + KE$

MECHANICAL ENERGY

bouncing ball

energy of position and motion

Magnet Word

1. Write a term on the magnet.
2. On the lines, add details related to the term.

> You can also use phrases or sentences on the lines.

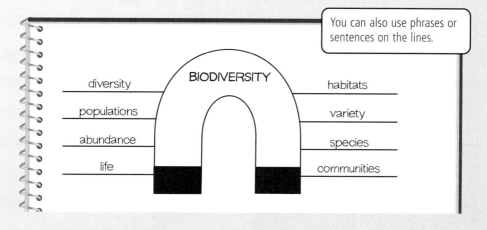

BIODIVERSITY

diversity

populations

abundance

life

habitats

variety

species

communities

Word Triangle

1. Write a term and its definition in the bottom section.
2. In the middle section, write a sentence in which the term is used correctly.
3. In the top section, draw a small picture to illustrate the term.

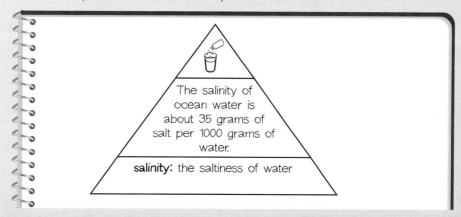

The salinity of ocean water is about 35 grams of salt per 1000 grams of water.

salinity: the saltiness of water

Appendix

The Periodic Table of the Elements

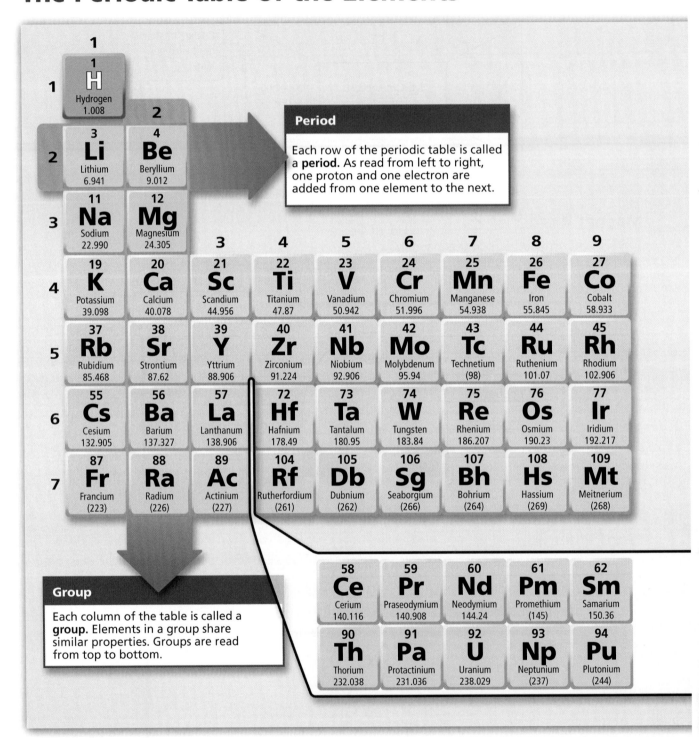

Period

Each row of the periodic table is called a **period.** As read from left to right, one proton and one electron are added from one element to the next.

Group

Each column of the table is called a **group.** Elements in a group share similar properties. Groups are read from top to bottom.

1

1	
1	
H	
Hydrogen	
1.008	

2

2		
3	4	
Li	**Be**	
Lithium	Beryllium	
6.941	9.012	

11	12
Na	**Mg**
Sodium	Magnesium
22.990	24.305

3 **4** **5** **6** **7** **8** **9**

3	4	5	6	7	8	9
19 **K** Potassium 39.098	20 **Ca** Calcium 40.078	21 **Sc** Scandium 44.956	22 **Ti** Titanium 47.87	23 **V** Vanadium 50.942	24 **Cr** Chromium 51.996	25 **Mn** Manganese 54.938
37 **Rb** Rubidium 85.468	38 **Sr** Strontium 87.62	39 **Y** Yttrium 88.906	40 **Zr** Zirconium 91.224	41 **Nb** Niobium 92.906	42 **Mo** Molybdenum 95.94	43 **Tc** Technetium (98)
55 **Cs** Cesium 132.905	56 **Ba** Barium 137.327	57 **La** Lanthanum 138.906	72 **Hf** Hafnium 178.49	73 **Ta** Tantalum 180.95	74 **W** Tungsten 183.84	75 **Re** Rhenium 186.207
87 **Fr** Francium (223)	88 **Ra** Radium (226)	89 **Ac** Actinium (227)	104 **Rf** Rutherfordium (261)	105 **Db** Dubnium (262)	106 **Sg** Seaborgium (266)	107 **Bh** Bohrium (264)

Iron 26 **Fe** 55.845, Cobalt 27 **Co** 58.933

Ruthenium 44 **Ru** 101.07, Rhodium 45 **Rh** 102.906

Osmium 76 **Os** 190.23, Iridium 77 **Ir** 192.217

Hassium 108 **Hs** (269), Meitnerium 109 **Mt** (268)

58	59	60	61	62
Ce	**Pr**	**Nd**	**Pm**	**Sm**
Cerium	Praseodymium	Neodymium	Promethium	Samarium
140.116	140.908	144.24	(145)	150.36
90	91	92	93	94
Th	**Pa**	**U**	**Np**	**Pu**
Thorium	Protactinium	Uranium	Neptunium	Plutonium
232.038	231.036	238.029	(237)	(244)

 Metal Metalloid Nonmetal **Fe** Solid **Hg** Liquid   ◯ Gas

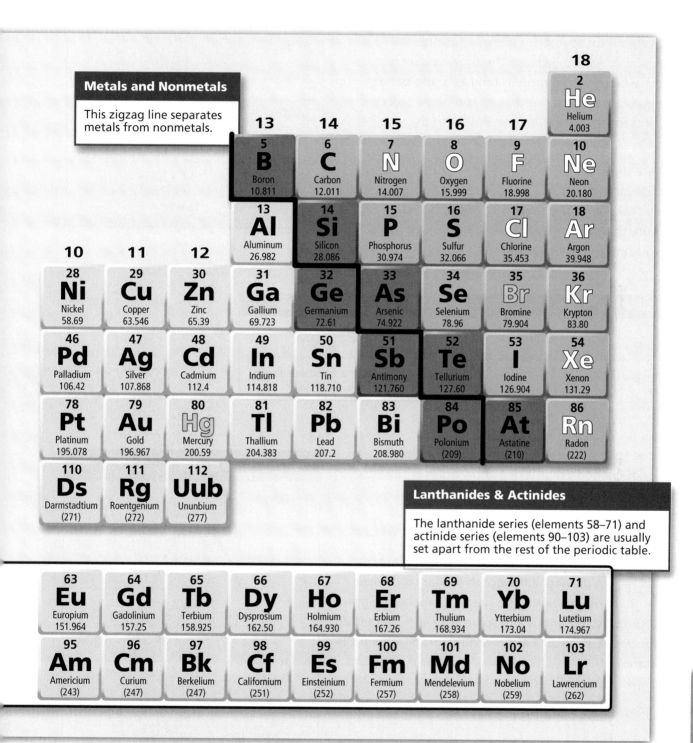

Metals and Nonmetals

This zigzag line separates metals from nonmetals.

18

| 2 **He** Helium 4.003 |

13	**14**	**15**	**16**	**17**
5 **B** Boron 10.811	6 **C** Carbon 12.011	7 **N** Nitrogen 14.007	8 **O** Oxygen 15.999	9 **F** Fluorine 18.998	10 **Ne** Neon 20.180

| 13 **Al** Aluminum 26.982 | 14 **Si** Silicon 28.086 | 15 **P** Phosphorus 30.974 | 16 **S** Sulfur 32.066 | 17 **Cl** Chlorine 35.453 | 18 **Ar** Argon 39.948 |

10	**11**	**12**

| 28 **Ni** Nickel 58.69 | 29 **Cu** Copper 63.546 | 30 **Zn** Zinc 65.39 | 31 **Ga** Gallium 69.723 | 32 **Ge** Germanium 72.61 | 33 **As** Arsenic 74.922 | 34 **Se** Selenium 78.96 | 35 **Br** Bromine 79.904 | 36 **Kr** Krypton 83.80 |

| 46 **Pd** Palladium 106.42 | 47 **Ag** Silver 107.868 | 48 **Cd** Cadmium 112.4 | 49 **In** Indium 114.818 | 50 **Sn** Tin 118.710 | 51 **Sb** Antimony 121.760 | 52 **Te** Tellurium 127.60 | 53 **I** Iodine 126.904 | 54 **Xe** Xenon 131.29 |

| 78 **Pt** Platinum 195.078 | 79 **Au** Gold 196.967 | 80 **Hg** Mercury 200.59 | 81 **Tl** Thallium 204.383 | 82 **Pb** Lead 207.2 | 83 **Bi** Bismuth 208.980 | 84 **Po** Polonium (209) | 85 **At** Astatine (210) | 86 **Rn** Radon (222) |

| 110 **Ds** Darmstadtium (271) | 111 **Rg** Roentgenium (272) | 112 **Uub** Ununbium (277) |

Lanthanides & Actinides

The lanthanide series (elements 58–71) and actinide series (elements 90–103) are usually set apart from the rest of the periodic table.

| 63 **Eu** Europium 151.964 | 64 **Gd** Gadolinium 157.25 | 65 **Tb** Terbium 158.925 | 66 **Dy** Dysprosium 162.50 | 67 **Ho** Holmium 164.930 | 68 **Er** Erbium 167.26 | 69 **Tm** Thulium 168.934 | 70 **Yb** Ytterbium 173.04 | 71 **Lu** Lutetium 174.967 |

| 95 **Am** Americium (243) | 96 **Cm** Curium (247) | 97 **Bk** Berkelium (247) | 98 **Cf** Californium (251) | 99 **Es** Einsteinium (252) | 100 **Fm** Fermium (257) | 101 **Md** Mendelevium (258) | 102 **No** Nobelium (259) | 103 **Lr** Lawrencium (262) |

Atomic Number number of protons in the nucleus of the element

1 **H** Hydrogen 1.008

Symbol Each element has a symbol. The symbol's color represents the element's state at room temperature.

Name

Atomic Mass average mass of isotopes of this element

Understanding Graphs of Motion

When an object travels at a constant speed, it travels the same distance each second. You can see this by rearranging the formula for speed, $S = d/t$, as a formula for distance: $d = St$. As you increase the time, you increase the distance by the same ratio as long as S, the speed, remains constant. A distance-time graph of an object with a constant speed would look similar to the one shown here.

Compare the distance formula to the equation for a straight line on a graph: $y = kx$, where k is a constant and the slope of the line. The slope of a line is found by dividing the change in y by the change in x. In other words, you find the rise over the run.

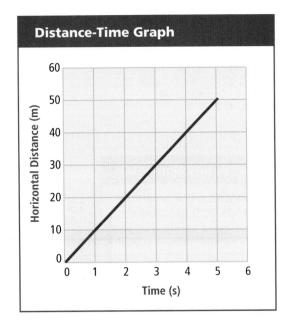

Distance-Time Graph

Vertical Value	Horizontal Value	Slope	Finding Slope
y	x	k	change in y divided by change in x
d (distance)	t (time)	S (speed)	change in distance divided by change in time

If the speed remains constant (the slope of the line does not change), then a line showing how distance changes with time will be a straight line and have a slope equal to the speed.

If the speed is changing, the line will be curved. An object thrown straight up into the air, for example, would have a distance-time graph similar to the one shown here on the right. The graph is labeled Height-Time Graph to show it is a graph of the vertical motion of the object. It is still a distance-time graph—height is a distance.

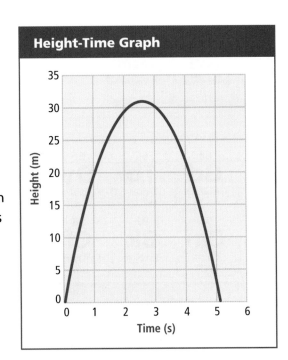

Height-Time Graph

Notice that the line showing the motion is not straight—the speed changes as the object moves. Notice also that after the object reaches its highest point, the height decreases again. If a distance-time graph has a line or curve that goes down toward the *x*-axis, that means the object is moving closer to its original position instead of moving farther away.

Motion in Two Dimensions

What if you threw a ball into the air so that it had both a horizontal speed and a vertical speed? How could you show its motion? You might show both the distance-time graph of the horizontal motion and the distance-time graph of the vertical motion. You can always treat the horizontal motion separately from the vertical motion. Notice here that the horizontal speed is constant, while the vertical speed is changing. This is because gravity acts to change the vertical speed of the ball as it moves through the air. There is no force acting to change the horizontal speed.

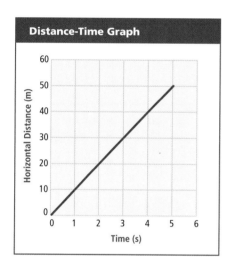

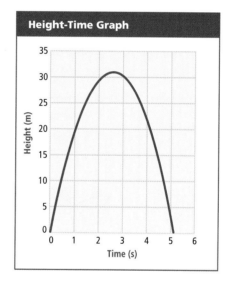

Another way to show motion in two dimensions is to show a graph of the ball's horizontal motion compared to its height. In the graph on the right, each point represents the position of the ball at half-second intervals. The line shows the path of the ball in the air. Unlike a distance-time graph, this graph does not give you direct information about the speed of the ball.

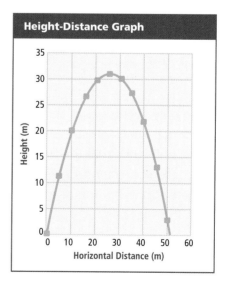

Momentum

A moving object has a property that is called momentum (moh-MEHN-tuhm). Momentum is a measure of mass in motion; the momentum of an object is the product of its mass and its velocity. Momentum is similar to inertia.

To calculate an object's momentum, you can use the following formula:

$$\textbf{momentum} = \textbf{mass} \cdot \textbf{velocity}$$
$$p = mv$$

In this formula, p stands for momentum, m for mass, and v for velocity. Momentum is usually measured in units of kilogram meters per second, or kg · m/s. Momentum, like acceleration and force, is a vector. The direction of momentum is the same as the direction of the velocity.

During a collision between two objects, each object exerts a force on the other. The colliding objects make up a system—a collection of objects that affect one another. As the two objects collide, the velocity and momentum of each object change. However, as no other forces are acting on the objects, the total momentum of the system is unchanged. The principle of conservation of momentum states that the total momentum of a system before a collision is the same as the total momentum after a collision, as long as no outside forces are acting on the system.

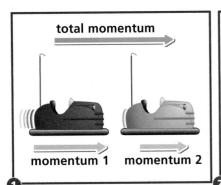

① Before the collision The momentum of the first car is greater than the momentum of the second car. Their combined momentum is the total momentum of the system.

② During the collision The forces on the two cars are equal and opposite, as described by Newton's third law. Momentum is transferred from one car to the other during the collision.

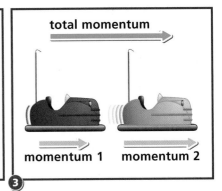

③ After the collision The momentum lost by one car was gained by the other car. The total momentum of the system remains the same as it was before the collision.

Collisions are not the only events in which momentum is conserved. For example, if you throw a ball while you are standing on in-line skates, the forward momentum of the ball will equal the backward change in your momentum. In fact, momentum is conserved whenever the only forces acting on objects are action/reaction force pairs. Conservation of momentum is really just another way of looking at Newton's third law.

Characteristics of Planets

Some data about the planets and Earth's satellite, the Moon, are listed below. Some data, such as the tilt of Mercury and the mass of Pluto, are not known as well as other data. One astronomical unit (AU) is Earth's average distance from the Sun, or 149,597,870 kilometers. For comparison, Earth's mass is 5.97×10^{24} kilograms, and Earth's diameter is 12,756 kilometers.

Eccentricity is a measure of how flattened an ellipse is. An ellipse with an eccentricity of 0 is a circle. An ellipse with an eccentricity of 1 is completely flat.

Venus, Uranus, and Pluto rotate backward compared to Earth. If you use your left thumb as one of these planets' north pole, your fingers curve in the direction the planet turns.

Characteristics of Planets

Characteristic	Mercury	Venus	Earth	Mars	Jupiter	Saturn	Uranus	Neptune	Pluto	Moon
Mean distance from Sun (AU)	0.387	0.723	1.00	1.52	5.20	9.55	19.2	30.1	39.5	
Period of revolution (Earth years)	0.241 (88 Earth days)	0.615 (225 Earth days)	1.00	1.88	11.9	29.4	83.7	164	248	0.075 (27.3 Earth days)
Eccentricity of orbit	0.206	0.007	0.017	0.093	0.048	0.056	0.046	0.009	0.249	0.055
Diameter (Earth = 1)	0.382	0.949	1.00	0.532	11.21	9.45	4.01	3.88	0.180	0.272
Volume (Earth = 1)	0.06	0.86	1.00	0.15	1320	760	63	58	0.006	0.02
Period of rotation	58.6 Earth days	243 Earth days	23.9 hours	24.6 hours	9.93 hours	10.7 hours	17.2 hours	16.1 hours	6.39 Earth days	27.3 Earth days
Tilt of axis (°) (from perpendicular to orbit)	0.1 (approximate)	2.6	23.45	25.19	3.12	26.73	82.14	29.56	60.4	6.67
Mass (Earth = 1)	0.0553	0.815	1.00	0.107	318	95.2	14.5	17.1	0.002	0.0123
Mean density (g/cm³)	5.4	5.2	5.5	3.9	1.3	0.7	1.3	1.6	2	3.3

Seasonal Star Maps

Your view of the night sky changes as Earth orbits the Sun. Some constellations appear throughout the year, but others can be seen only during certain seasons. And over the course of one night, the constellations appear to move across the sky as Earth rotates.

When you go outside to view stars, give your eyes time to adjust to the darkness. Avoid looking at bright lights. If you need to look toward a bright light, preserve your night vision in one eye by keeping it closed.

The star maps on pages R71–R74 show parts of the night sky in different seasons. If you are using a flashlight to view the maps, you should attach a piece of red balloon over the lens. The balloon will dim the light and also give it a red color, which affects night vision less than other colors. The following steps will help you use the maps:

1. Stand facing north. To find this direction, use a compass or turn clockwise 90° from the location where the Sun set.

2. The top map for each season shows some constellations that appear over the northern horizon at 10 P.M. During the night, the constellations rotate in a circle around Polaris, the North Star.

3. Now turn so that you stand facing south. The bottom map for the season shows some constellations that appear over the southern horizon at 10 P.M.

WINTER SKY to the NORTH, *January 15*

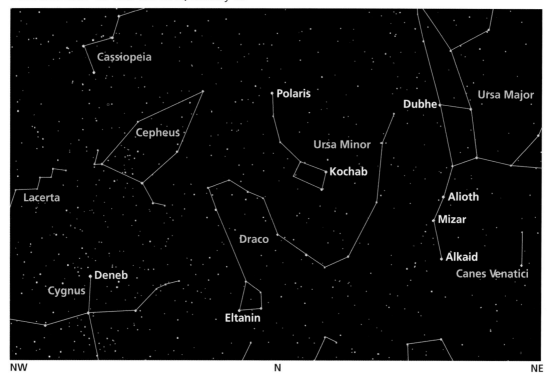

NW   N   NE

WINTER SKY to the SOUTH, *January 15*

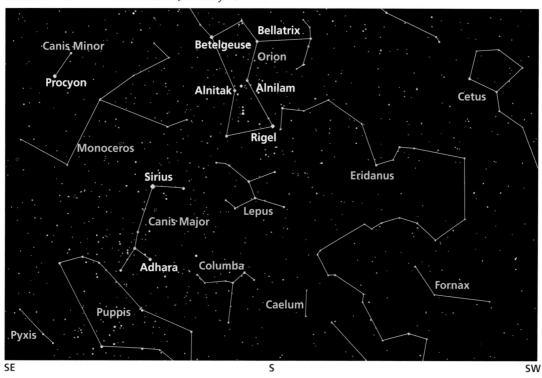

SE   S   SW

Seasonal Star Maps *continued*

SPRING SKY to the NORTH, *April 15*

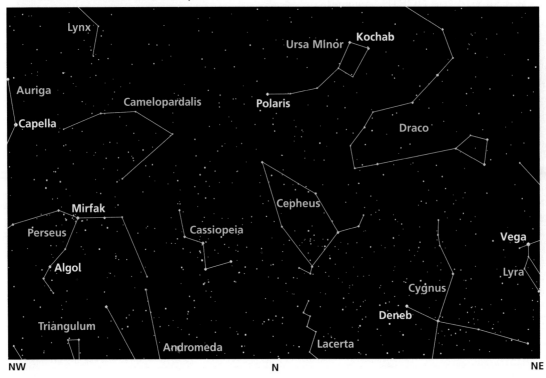

SPRING SKY to the SOUTH, *April 15*

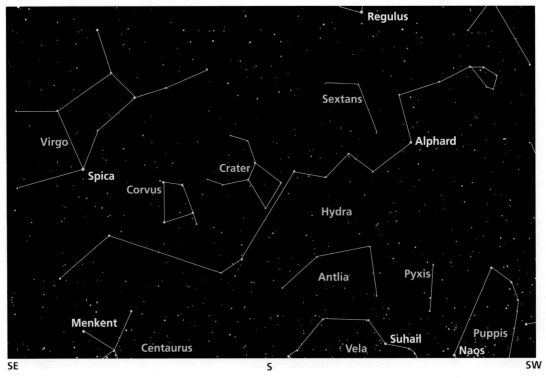

SUMMER SKY to the NORTH, *July 15*

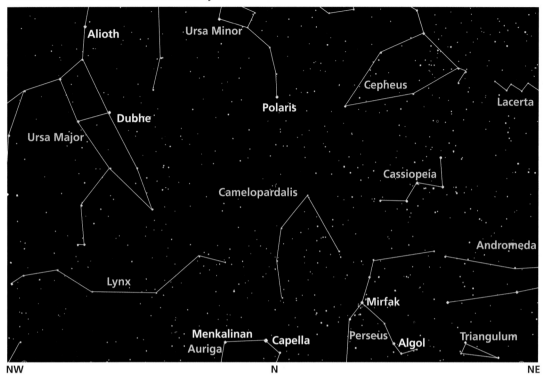

Alioth • Ursa Minor • Cepheus • Lacerta • Polaris • Dubhe • Ursa Major • Cassiopeia • Camelopardalis • Andromeda • Lynx • Mirfak • Menkalinan • Capella • Perseus • Algol • Triangulum • Auriga

NW • N • NE

SUMMER SKY to the SOUTH, *July 15*

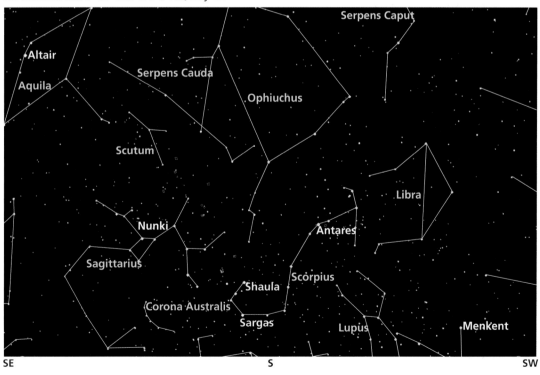

Serpens Caput • Altair • Serpens Cauda • Ophiuchus • Aquila • Scutum • Libra • Nunki • Antares • Sagittarius • Scorpius • Shaula • Corona Australis • Sargas • Lupus • Menkent

SE • S • SW

Seasonal Star Maps *continued*

AUTUMN SKY to the NORTH, *October 15*

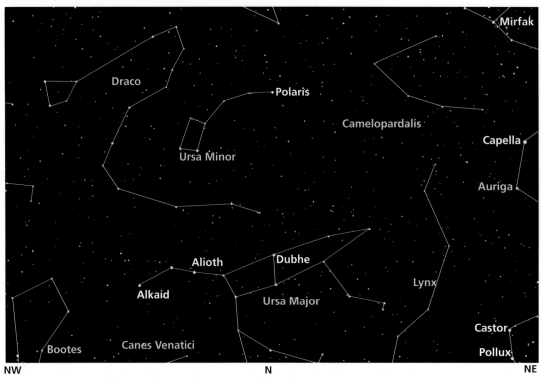

NW   N   NE

AUTUMN SKY to the SOUTH, *October 15*

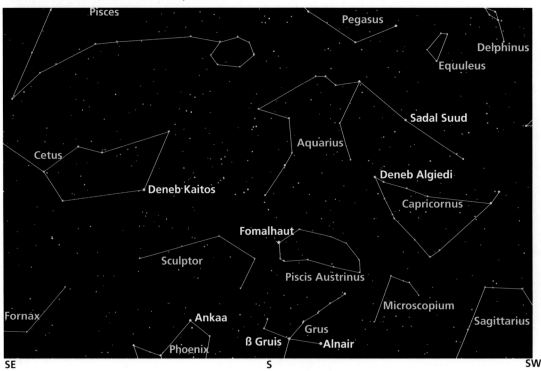

SE   S   SW

The Hertzsprung-Russell Diagram

The Hertzsprung-Russell (H-R) Diagram is a graph that shows stars plotted according to brightness and surface temperature. Most stars fall within a diagonal band called the main sequence. In the main-sequence stage of a star's life cycle, brightness is closely related to surface temperature. Red giant and red supergiant stars appear above the main sequence on the diagram. These stars are bright in relation to their surface temperatures because their huge surface areas give off a lot of light. Dim white dwarfs appear below the main sequence.

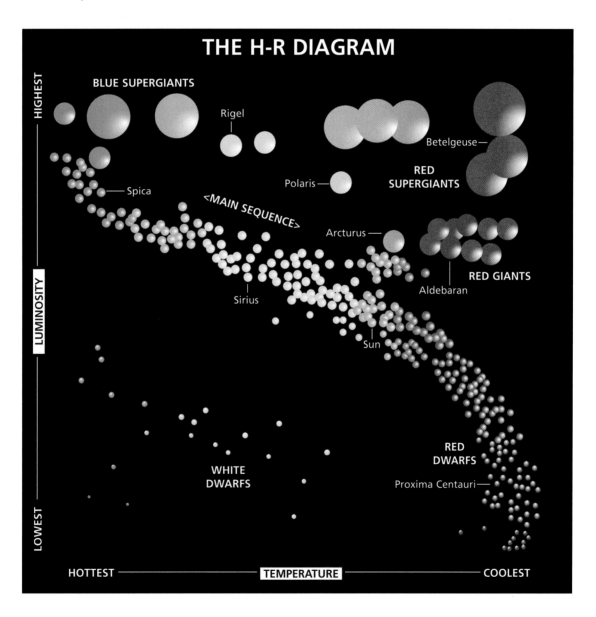

Physical Map of California

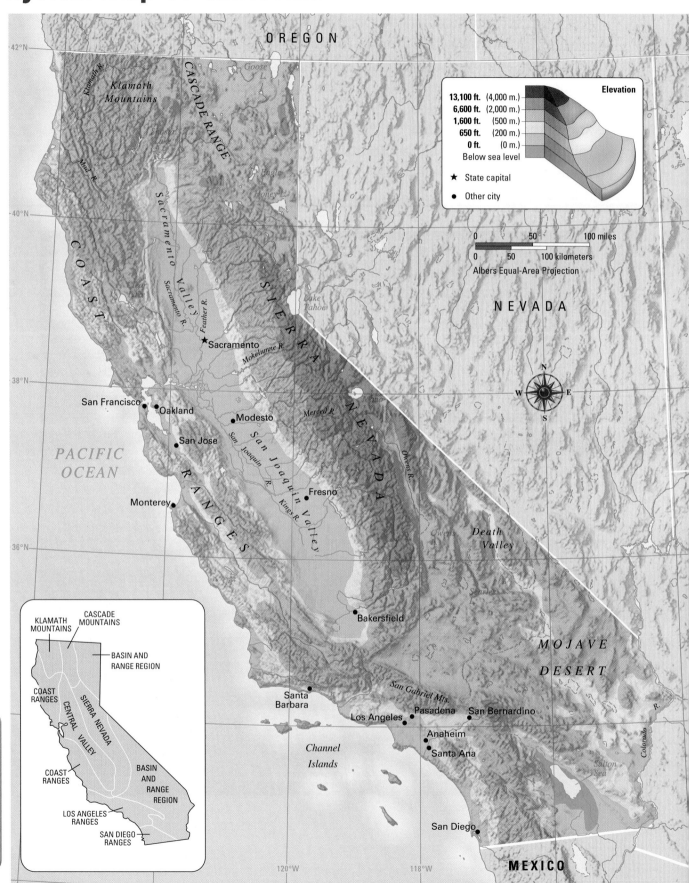

OREGON

Klamath R.

Klamath Mountains

CASCADE RANGE

Goose L.

Mad R.

Shasta Lake

Eagle L.

Honey L.

COAST

Sacramento Valley

Sacramento R.

Feather R.

★ Sacramento

Mokelumne R.

SIERRA

NEVADA

NEVADA

Elevation

13,100 ft. (4,000 m.)
6,600 ft. (2,000 m.)
1,600 ft. (500 m.)
650 ft. (200 m.)
0 ft. (0 m.)
Below sea level

★ State capital
● Other city

0   50   100 miles
0   50   100 kilometers
Albers Equal-Area Projection

Lake Tahoe

San Francisco ● Oakland
● Modesto
Merced R.

San Jose ●

San Joaquin R.

San Joaquin Valley

PACIFIC OCEAN

RANGES

Owens R.

Monterey ●

Kings R.

● Fresno

Owens

Death Valley

● Bakersfield

MOJAVE

DESERT

Santa Barbara ●

San Gabriel Mts.
Los Angeles ● Pasadena ● ● San Bernardino
● Anaheim
● Santa Ana

Channel Islands

Colorado R.

Salton Sea

● San Diego

120°W   118°W

MEXICO

KLAMATH MOUNTAINS
CASCADE MOUNTAINS
BASIN AND RANGE REGION
COAST RANGES
SIERRA NEVADA
CENTRAL VALLEY
COAST RANGES
BASIN AND RANGE REGION
LOS ANGELES RANGES
SAN DIEGO RANGES

Glossary

A

acceleration
The rate at which velocity changes over time. (p. 25)

    aceleración La razón a la cual la velocidad cambia con respecto al tiempo.

acid
A substance that can donate a proton to another substance and has a pH below 7. (p. 323)

    ácido Una sustancia que puede donar un protón a otra sustancia y que tiene un pH menor a 7.

adaptation
A characteristic, a behavior, or any inherited trait that makes a species able to survive and reproduce in a particular environment. (p. CA18)

    adaptación Una característica, un comportamiento o cualquier rasgo heredado que permite a una especie sobrevivir o reproducirse en un medio ambiente determinado.

air resistance
The fluid friction due to air. (p. 90)

    resistencia del aire La fricción fluida debida al aire.

asteroid
A small, solid, rocky body that orbits the Sun. Most asteroids orbit in a region between Mars and Jupiter called the asteroid belt. (p. 437)

    asteroide Un pequeño cuerpo sólido y rocoso que orbita alrededor del Sol. La mayoría de los asteroides orbitan en una región entre Marte y Júpiter denominada cinturón de asteroides.

astronomical unit AU
Earth's average distance from the Sun, which is approximately 150 million kilometers (93 million mi). (p. 415)

    unidad astronómica ua La distancia promedio de la Tierra al Sol, la cual es de aproximadamente 150 millones de kilómetros (93 millones de millas).

atmosphere (AT-muh-SFEER)
The outer layer of gases of a large body in space, such as a planet or star; the mixture of gases that surrounds the solid Earth; one of the four parts of the Earth system. (p. CA16)

atmósfera La capa externa de gases de un gran cuerpo que se encuentra en el espacio, como un planeta o una estrella; la mezcla de gases que rodea la Tierra sólida; una de las cuatro partes del sistema terrestre.

atom
The smallest particle of an element that has the chemical properties of that element. (p. 137)

    átomo La partícula más pequeña de un elemento que tiene las propiedades químicas de ese elemento.

atomic mass
The average mass of the atoms of an element. (p. 207)

    masa atómica La masa promedio de los átomos de un elemento.

atomic mass number
The total number of protons and neutrons in an atom's nucleus. (p. 202)

    número de masa atómica El número total de protones y neutrones que hay en el núcleo de un átomo.

atomic number
The number of protons in the nucleus of an atom. (p. 202)

    número atómico El número de protones en el núcleo de un átomo.

axis of rotation
An imaginary line about which a turning body, such as Earth, rotates. (p. 382)

    eje de rotación Una línea imaginaria alrededor de la cual gira un cuerpo, como lo hace la Tierra.

B

base
A substance that can accept a proton from another substance and has a pH above 7. (p. 323)

    base Una sustancia que puede aceptar un protón de otra sustancia y que tiene un pH superior a 7.

big bang
According to scientific theory, the moment in time when the universe started and began to expand. (p. 476)

    la gran explosión De acuerdo a la teoría científica, el momento en el tiempo en el cual el universo empezó a expandirse.

biochemistry
The study of the substances and processes occurring in living organisms. (p. 339)

bioquímica El estudio de sustancias y procesos que ocurren en organismos vivos.

biodiversity
The number and variety of living things found on Earth or within an ecosystem. (p. CA18)

biodiversidad La cantidad y variedad de organismos vivos que se encuentran en la Tierra o dentro de un ecosistema.

biosphere (BY-uh-SFEER)
All living organisms on Earth in the air, on the land, and in the waters; one of the four parts of the Earth system. (p. CA16)

biosfera Todos los organismos vivos de la Tierra, en el aire, en la tierra y en las aguas; una de las cuatro partes del sistema de la Tierra.

black hole
The final stage of an extremely massive star, which is invisible because its gravity prevents any form of radiation from escaping. (p. 464)

hoyo negro La etapa final de una estrella de enorme masa, la cual es invisible porque su gravedad evita que cualquier tipo de radiación escape.

boiling
A process by which a substance changes from its liquid state to its gas state. The liquid is heated to a specific temperature at which bubbles of vapor form within the liquid. (p. 184)

ebullición Un proceso mediante el cual una sustancia cambia de su estado líquido a su estado gaseoso se calienta el líquido a una determinada temperatura a la cual se forman burbujas de vapor dentro del líquido.

boiling point
The temperature at which a substance changes from its liquid state to its gas state through boiling. (p. 184)

punto de ebullición La temperatura a la cual una sustancia cambia de su estado líquido a su estado gaseoso mediante ebullición.

bond energy
The amount of energy in a chemical bond between atoms. (p. 288)

energía de enlace La cantidad de energía que hay en un enlace químico entre átomos.

buoyant force
The upward force on objects in a fluid; often called buoyancy. (p. 117)

fuerza flotante La fuerza hacia arriba que ejerce un fluido sobre un objeto inmerso en él, a menudo llamada flotación.

C

carbohydrate (KAHR-boh-HY-drayt)
A type of molecule made up of subunits of sugars and used for energy and structure. (p. 353)

carbohidrato Un tipo de molécula compuesta de unidades de azúcares y usada como fuente de energía y como material estructural.

catalyst
A substance that increases the rate of a chemical reaction but is not consumed in the reaction. (p. 278)

catalizador Una sustancia que aumenta el ritmo de la velocidad de una reacción química pero que no es consumida en la reacción.

cell
The smallest unit that is able to perform the basic functions of life. (p. CA18)

célula La unidad más pequeña capaz de realizar las funciones básicas de la vida.

centripetal force (sehn-TRIHP-ih-tuhl)
Any force that keeps an object moving in a circle. (p. 54)

fuerza centrípeta Cualquier fuerza que mantiene a un objeto moviéndose en forma circular.

chemical change
A change of one substance into another substance. (p. 154)

cambio químico La transformación de una sustancia a otra sustancia.

chemical formula
An expression that shows the number and types of atoms joined in a compound. (p. 245)

fórmula química Una expresión que muestra el número y los tipos de átomos unidos en un compuesto.

chemical property
A characteristic of a substance that describes how it can form a new substance. (p. 154)

propiedad química Una característica de una sustancia que describe como puede formar una nueva sustancia.

chemical reaction
The process by which chemical changes occur. In a chemical reaction, atoms are rearranged, and chemical bonds are broken and formed. (p. 271)

reacción química El proceso mediante el cual ocurren cambios químicos. En una reacción química, los átomos se reorganizan y los enlaces químicos se rompen y se vuelven a formar.

coefficient
The number before a chemical formula that indicates how many molecules are involved in a chemical reaction. (p. 284)

coeficiente El número anterior a una fórmula química que indica cuántas moléculas están involucradas en una reaccíon química.

comet
A body that produces a coma of gas and dust; a small, icy body that orbits the Sun. (p. 438)

cometa Un cuerpo que produce una coma de gas y polvo; un cuerpo pequeño y helado que se mueve en órbita alrededor del Sol.

compound
A substance made up of two or more different types of atoms bonded together. (p. 145)

compuesto Una sustancia formada por dos o más diferentes tipos de átomos enlazados.

compression
The process of pushing the particles of a material closer together. (p. 81)

compresión El proceso de empujar partículas materiales más cerca unos de otros.

concentration
The amount of solute dissolved in a solvent at a given temperature. (p. 314)

concentración La cantidad de soluto disuelta en un solvente a una temperature determinada.

condensation
The process by which a gas becomes a liquid. (p. 185)

condensación El proceso mediante el cual un gas se convierte en un líquido.

constellation
A group of stars that form a pattern in the sky. (p. 378)

constelación Un grupo de estrellas que forman un patrón en el cielo.

convection
The transfer of energy from place to place by the motion of heated gas or liquid; in Earth's mantle, convection is thought to transfer energy by the motion of solid rock, which when under great heat and pressure can move like a liquid. (p. 454)

convección La transferencia de energía de un lugar a otro por el movimiento de un líquido o gas calentado; se piensa que en el manto terrestre la convección transfiere energía mediante el movimiento de roca sólida, la cual puede moverse como un líquido cuando está muy caliente y bajo alta presión.

corona
The outer layer of the Sun's atmosphere. (p. 454)

corona La capa exterior de la atmósfera del Sol.

covalent bond
A pair of electrons shared by two atoms. (p. 252)

enlace covalente Un par de electrones compartidos por dos átomos.

cycle
n. A series of events or actions that repeat themselves regularly; a physical and/or chemical process in which one material continually changes locations and/or forms. Examples include the water cycle, the carbon cycle, and the rock cycle.

v. To move through a repeating series of events or actions.

ciclo *s.* Una serie de eventos o acciones que se repiten regularmente; un proceso físico y/o químico en el cual un material cambia continuamente de lugar y/o forma. Ejemplos: el ciclo del agua, el ciclo del carbono y el ciclo de las rocas.

D

data
Information gathered by observation or experimentation that can be used in calculating or reasoning. *Data* is a plural word; the singular is *datum.*

datos Información reunida mediante observación o experimentación y que se puede usar para calcular o para razonar.

density
A property of matter representing the mass per unit volume. (p. 105)

densidad Una propiedad de la materia que representa la masa por unidad de volumen.

dilute
adj. Having a low concentration of solute. (p. 315)

v. To add solvent in order to decrease the concentration of a solution.

diluido *adj.* Que tiene una baja concentración de soluto.

diluir *v.* Agregar solvente para disminuir la concentración de una solución.

Doppler effect

A change in the observed frequency of a wave, occurring when the source of the wave or the observer is moving. Changes in the frequency of light are often measured by observing changes in wavelength, whereas changes in the frequency of sound are often detected as changes in pitch. (p. 474)

efecto Doppler Un cambio en la frecuencia observada de una onda que ocurre cuando la fuente de la onda o el observador están en movimiento. Los cambios en la frecuencia de la luz a menudo se miden observando los cambios en la longitud de onda, mientras que los cambios en la frecuencia del sonido a menudo se detectan como cambios en el tono.

E

eclipse

An event during which one object in space casts a shadow onto another. On Earth, a lunar eclipse occurs when the Moon moves through Earth's shadow, and a solar eclipse occurs when the Moon's shadow crosses Earth. (p. 401)

eclipse Un evento durante el cual un objeto en el espacio proyecta una sombra sobre otro. En la Tierra, un eclipse lunar ocurre cuando la Luna se mueve a través de la sombra de la Tierra, y un eclipse solar ocurre cuando la sombra de la Luna cruza la Tierra.

elastic force

The force in an object that resists stretching or pressing. (p. 79)

fuerza elástica La fuerza en un objeto que resiste el estiraje o la presión.

electrical conductivity

A measure of how easily electric current passes through a particular substance. (p. 227)

conductividad eléctrica La capacidad de un medio de permitir el paso de la corriente eléctrica a su través.

electromagnetic radiation

Energy that travels across distances as certain types of waves. Types of electromagnetic radiation are radio waves, microwaves, infrared radiation, visible light, ultra violet radiation, x-rays, and gamma rays.

radiación electromagnética Energía que se transmite a través de la distancia por medio de ciertos tipos de ondas, tales como ondas de radio, microondas, luz infrarroja, luz visible, radiación ultravioleta, rayos X y rayos gamma.

electron

A negatively charged particle located outside an atom's nucleus. An electron is about 2000 times smaller than either a proton or a neutron. (p. 201)

electrón Una partícula con carga negativa localizada fuera del núcleo de un átomo. Un electrón es como aproximadamente 2000 veces más pequeño que un protón o un neutrón.

element

A substance that cannot be broken down into a simpler substance by ordinary chemical changes. An element consists of atoms of only one type. (p. 144)

elemento Una sustancia que no puede descomponerse en otra sustancia más simple por medio de cambios químicos normales. Un elemento consta de átomos de un solo tipo.

ellipse

An oval or flattened circle. (p. 415)

elipse Un óvalo o círculo aplanado.

endothermic reaction

A chemical reaction that absorbs energy. (p. 289)

reacción endotérmica Una reacción química que absorbe energía.

energy

The ability to do work or to cause a change. For example, the energy of a moving bowling ball knocks over pins; energy from food allows animals to move and to grow; and energy from the Sun heats Earth's surface and atmosphere, which causes air to move. (pp. CA14, CA16)

energía La capacidad para trabajar o causar un cambio. Por ejemplo, la energía de una bola de boliche en movimiento tumba los pinos; la energía proveniente de su alimento permite a los animales moverse y crecer; la energía del Sol calienta la superficie y la atmósfera de la Tierra, lo que ocasiona que el aire se mueva.

environment

Everything that surrounds a living thing. An environment is made up of both living and nonliving factors. (p. CA16)

medio ambiente Todo lo que rodea a un organismo vivo. Un medio ambiente está compuesto de factores vivos y factores sin vida.

enzyme

A type of protein that is a catalyst for chemical reactions in living things. (p. 357)

enzima Un tipo de proteína que es un catalizador de reacciones químicas en organismos vivos.

equinox (EE-kwuh-NAHKS)

In an orbit, a position and time in which sunlight shines equally on the Northern Hemisphere and the Southern Hemisphere; a time of year when daylight and darkness are nearly equal for most of Earth. (p. 384)

equinoccio En una órbita, la posición y el tiempo en los cuales la luz del Sol incide de la misma manera en el Hemisferio Norte y en el Hemisferio Sur; una época del año en la cual la luz del día y la oscuridad son casi iguales para la mayor parte de la Tierra.

evaporation
A process by which a substance changes from its liquid state to its gas state by random particle movement. Evaporation usually occurs at the surface of a liquid over a wide range of temperatures. (p. 183)

evaporación Un proceso mediante el cual una sustancia cambia de su estado líquido a su estado gaseoso por medio del movimiento aleatorio de las partículas. La evaporación normalmente ocurre en la superficie de un líquido en una amplia gama de temperaturas.

exothermic reaction
A chemical reaction that releases energy. (p. 289)

reacción exotérmica Una reacción química que libera energía.

experiment
An organized procedure to study something under controlled conditions. (p. CA21)

experimento Un procedimiento organizado para estudiar algo bajo condiciones controladas.

extinction
The permanent disappearance of a species. (p. CA18)

extinción La desaparición permanente de una especie.

F

fluid
A substance that can flow easily, such as a gas or a liquid. (p. 89)

fluido Una sustancia que fluye fácilmente, como por ejemplo un gas o un líquido.

force
A push or a pull; something that changes the motion of an object. (p. 41)

fuerza Un empuje o un jalón; algo que cambia el movimiento de un objeto.

freezing
The process by which a substance changes from its liquid state into its solid state. (p. 182)

congelación El proceso mediante el cual una sustancia cambia de su estado líquido a su estado sólido.

freezing point
The temperature at which a substance changes from its liquid state to its solid state through freezing. (p. 182)

punto de congelación La temperatura a la cual una sustancia cambia de su estado líquido a su estado sólido mediante congelación.

friction
A force that resists the motion between two surfaces in contact. (p. 86)

fricción Una fuerza que resiste el movimiento entre dos superficies en contacto.

fusion
A process in which particles of an element collide and combine to form a heavier element, such as the fusion of hydrogen into helium that occurs in the Sun's core. (p. 454)

fusión Un proceso en el cual las partículas de un elemento chocan y se combinan para formar un elemento más pesado, como la fusión de hidrógeno en helio que ocurre en el núcleo del Sol.

G

galaxy
Millions or billions of stars held together in a group by their own gravity. (p. 376)

galaxia Millones o miles de millones de estrellas unidas en un grupo por su propia gravedad.

gas
Matter with no definite volume and no definite shape. The molecules in a gas are very far apart, and the amount of space between them can change easily. (p. 166)

gas Materia sin volumen definido ni forma definida. Las moléculas en un gas están muy separadas unas de otras, y la cantidad de espacio entre ellas puede cambiar fácilmente.

gas giant
A large planet that consists mostly of gases in a dense form. The four large planets in the outer solar system—Jupiter, Saturn, Uranus, and Neptune—are gas giants. (p. 428)

gigante de gas Un planeta grande compuesto principalmente de gases en forma densa. Los cuatro planetas grandes en el sistema solar exterior—Júpiter, Saturno, Urano y Neptuno—son gigantes de gas.

geosphere (JEE-uh-SFEER)
All the features on Earth's surface—continents, islands, and seafloor—and everything below the surface—the inner and outer core and the mantle; one of the four parts of the Earth system. (p. CA16)

geosfera Todas las características de la superficie de la Tierra, es decir, continentes, islas y el fondo marino, y de todo bajo la superficie, es decir, el núcleo externo e interno y el manto; una de las cuatro partes del sistema de la Tierra.

gravity
The force that objects exert on each other because of their mass. (p. 71)

gravedad La fuerza que los objetos ejercen entre sí debido a su masa.

group
A vertical column in the periodic table of the elements. Elements in a group have similar properties. (p. 212)

grupo Una columna vertical en la tabla periódica de los elementos. Los elementos en un grupo tienen propiedades similares.

H

half-life
The amount of time it takes for half of the nuclei of a radioactive isotope to decay into atoms of another element. (p. 222)

vida media La cantidad de tiempo necesario para que se desintegren la mitad de los átomos de una muestra.

horizontal
Parallel to the horizon; level.

horizontal Paralelo al horizonte; nivelado.

hydrosphere (HY-druh-SFEER)
All water on Earth—in the atmosphere and in the oceans, lakes, glaciers, rivers, streams, and underground reservoirs; one of the four parts of the Earth system. (p. CA16)

hidrosfera Toda el agua de la Tierra: en la atmósfera y en los océanos, lagos, glaciares, ríos, arroyos y depósitos subterráneos; una de las cuatro partes del sistema de la Tierra.

hypothesis
A tentative explanation for an observation or phenomenon. A hypothesis is used to make testable predictions. (p. CA21)

hipótesis Una explicación provisional de una observación o de un fenómeno. Una hipótesis se usa para hacer predicciones que se pueden probar.

I, J

inertia (ih-NUR-shuh)
The resistance of an object to a change in the speed or the direction of its motion. (p. 46)

inercia La resistencia de un objeto al cambio de la velocidad o de la dirección de su movimiento.

inorganic compound
A compound that is not considered organic. All compounds that do not contain carbon are inorganic, as are some types of carbon-containing compounds. (p. 346)

compuesto inorgánico Un compuesto que no se considera orgánico. Todos los compuestos que no contienen carbono son inorgánicos, al igual que algunos tipos de compuestos que contienen carbono.

ion
An atom or group of atoms that has a positive or negative electric charge. (p. 204)

ión Un átomo o un grupo de átomos que tiene una carga eléctrica positiva o negativa.

ionic bond
The electrical attraction between a negative ion and a positive ion. (p. 250)

enlace iónico La atracción eléctrica entre un ión negativo y un ión positivo.

isomer
Any of two or more compounds that contain the same atoms but that have different structures. (p. 350)

isómero Cualquiera de dos o más compuestos que contienen los mismos átomos pero que tienen estructuras diferentes.

isotope
An atom of one element that has a different number of neutrons than another atom of the same element. (p. 202)

isótopo Un átomo de un elemento que tiene un número diferente de neutrones que otro átomo del mismo elemento.

K

kinetic energy (kuh-NEHT-ihk)
The energy of motion. A moving object has the most kinetic energy at the point where it moves the fastest.

energía cinética La energía de movimiento. Un objeto en movimiento tiene la mayor energía cinética en el punto en donde se mueve más rápidamente.

kinetic theory of matter (kuh-NEHT-ihk)
A theory stating that all matter is made of particles in motion. (p. 174)

> **teoría cinética de la materia** Una teoría que establece que toda materia está compuesta de partículas en movimiento.

L

law
In science, a rule or principle describing a physical relationship that always works in the same way under the same conditions. The law of conservation of energy is an example.

> **ley** En las ciencias, una regla o un principio que describe una relación física que siempre funciona de la misma manera bajo las mismas condiciones. La ley de la conservación de la energía es un ejemplo.

law of conservation of energy
A law stating that no matter how energy is transferred or transformed, it continues to exist in one form or another. (p. CA14)

> **ley de la conservación de la energía** Una ley que establece que no importa cómo se transfiere o transforma la energía, toda la energía sigue presente en alguna forma u otra.

law of conservation of mass
A law stating that atoms are not created or destroyed in a chemical reaction. (p. 281)

> **ley de la conservación de la masa** Una ley que establece que los átomos ni se crean ni se destruyen en una reacción química.

light-year
The distance light travels in one year, which is about 9.5 trillion kilometers (6 trillion mi). (p. 460)

> **año luz** La distancia que viaja la luz en un año, la cual es de casi 9.5 billones de kilómetros (6 billones de millas).

lipid
A type of molecule made up of subunits of fatty acids. Lipids are found in the fats, oils, and waxes used for structure and to store energy. (p. 354)

> **lípido** Un tipo de molécula compuesta de unidades de ácidos grasos. Los lípidos se encuentran en las grasas, los aceites y las ceras usadas como materiales estructurales y para almacenar energía.

liquid
Matter that has a definite volume but does not have a definite shape. The molecules in a liquid are close together but not bound to one another. (p. 166)

líquido Materia que tiene un volumen definido pero no tiene una forma definida. Las moléculas en un líquido están cerca unas de otras pero no están ligadas.

M

main sequence
The stage in which stars produce energy through the fusion of hydrogen into helium. (p. 464)

> **secuencia principal** La etapa en la cual las estrellas producen energía mediante la fusión de hidrógeno en helio.

mare (MAH-ray)
A large, dark plain of solidified lava on the Moon. The plural form of *mare* is *maria* (MAH-ree-uh). (p. 391)

> **mare** Una planicie grande y oscura de lava solidificada en la Luna. El plural de *mare* es *maría*.

mass
A measure of how much matter an object is made of. (p. 103)

> **masa** Una medida de la cantidad de materia de la que está compuesto un objeto.

matter
Anything that has mass and volume. Matter exists ordinarily as a solid, a liquid, or a gas. (p. CA12)

> **materia** Todo lo que tiene masa y volumen. Generalmente la materia existe como sólido, líquido o gas.

melting
The process by which a substance changes from its solid state to its liquid state. (p. 181)

> **fusión** El proceso mediante el cual una sustancia cambia de su estado sólido a su estado líquido.

melting point
The temperature at which a substance changes from its solid state to its liquid state through melting. (p. 181)

> **punto de fusión** La temperatura a la cual una sustancia cambia de su estado sólido a su estado líquido mediante fusión.

metal
An element that tends to be shiny, easily shaped, and a good conductor of electricity and heat. (p. 217)

> **metal** Un elemento que tiende a ser brilloso, fácilmente deformable moldeado y buen conductor de electricidad y calor.

metallic bond
A certain type of bond in which nuclei float in a sea of electrons. (p. 258)

    enlace metálico Cierto tipo de enlace en el cual los núcleos flotan en un mar de electrones.

metalloid
An element that has properties of both metals and non-metals. (p. 220)

    metaloide Un elemento que tiene propiedades de los metales así como de los no metales.

meteor
A brief streak of light produced by a small particle entering Earth's atmosphere at a high speed. (p. 439)

    meteoro Un breve rayo luminoso producido por una partícula pequeña que entra a la atmósfera de la Tierra a una alta velocidad.

meteorite
A small object from outer space that passes through Earth's atmosphere and reaches the surface. (p. 439)

    meteorito Un pequeño objeto del espacio exterior que pasa a través de la atmósfera de la Tierra y llega a la superficie.

meter m
The international standard unit of length, about 39.37 inches.

    metro La unidad estándar internacional de longitud, aproximadamente 39.37 pulgadas.

mixture
A combination of two or more substances that do not combine chemically but remain the same individual substances. Mixtures can be separated by physical means. (p. 145)

    mezcla Una combinación de dos o más sustancias que no se combinan químicamente sino que permanecen como sustancias individuales. Las mezclas se pueden separar por medios físicos.

molecule
A group of atoms that are held together by covalent bonds so that they move as a single unit. (pp. 139, 253)

    molécula Un grupo de átomos que están unidos mediante enlaces covalentes de tal manera que se mueven como una sola unidad.

motion
A change of position over time. (p. 12)

    movimiento Un cambio de posición a través del tiempo.

N

nebula (NEHB-yuh-luh)
A cloud of gas and dust in space. Stars form in nebulae. (p. 463)

    nebulosa Una nube de gas y polvo en el espacio. Las estrellas se forman en las nebulosas.

net force
The overall force acting on an object when all of the forces acting on it are combined. (p. 43)

    fuerza neta La fuerza resultante que actúa sobre un objeto cuando todas las fuerzas que actúan sobre él son combinadas.

neutral
Describing a solution that is neither an acid nor a base. A neutral solution has a pH of 7. (p. 326)

    neutro Que describe una solución que no es un ácido ni una base. Una solución neutra tiene un pH de 7.

neutron
A particle that has no electric charge and is located in an atom's nucleus. (p. 201)

    neutrón Una partícula que no tiene carga eléctrica y que se encuentra en el núcleo de un átomo.

neutron star
A dense core that may be left behind after a higher-mass star explodes in a supernova. (p. 464)

    estrella de neutrones Un núcleo denso que puede resultar después de que una estrella de mayor masa explota en una supernova.

Newton's first law
A scientific law stating that objects at rest remain at rest, and objects in motion remain in motion with the same velocity, unless acted on by an unbalanced force. (p. 45)

    primera ley de Newton Una ley científica que establece que los objetos en reposo permanecen en reposo, y que los objetos en movimiento permanecen en movimiento con la misma velocidad, a menos que actúe sobre ellos una fuerza no balanceada.

Newton's second law
A scientific law stating that the acceleration of an object increases with increased force and decreases with increased mass. (p. 50)

    segunda ley de Newton Una ley científica que establece que la aceleración de un objeto aumenta al incrementar la fuerza que actúa sobre él y disminuye al incrementar su masa.

Newton's third law

A scientific law stating that every time one object exerts a force on another object, the second object exerts a force that is equal in size and opposite in direction back on the first object. (p. 57)

tercera ley de Newton Una ley científica que establece que cada vez que un objeto ejerce una fuerza sobre otro objeto, el segundo objeto ejerce una fuerza de la misma magnitud y en dirección opuesta sobre el primer objeto.

nonmetal

An element that is not a metal and has properties generally opposite to those of a metal. (p. 219)

no metal Un elemento que no es un metal y que tiene propiedades generalmente opuestas a las de los metales.

nucleic acid (noo-KLEE-ihk)

A type of molecule, made up of subunits of nucleotides, that is part of the genetic material of a cell and is needed to make proteins. DNA and RNA are nucleic acids. (p. 359)

ácido nucleico Un tipo de molécula, compuesto de unidades de nucleótidos, que es parte del material genético de una célula y se necesita para producir proteínas. El ADN y el ARN son ácidos nucleicos.

nucleus

The central region of an atom, where most of the atom's mass is found in protons and neutrons. (p. 201)

núcleo La región central de un átomo donde se encuentra la mayor parte de la masa del átomo en forma de protones y neutrones.

orbit

n. The path of an object in space as it moves around another object due to gravity; for example, the Moon moves in an orbit around Earth. (pp. 74, 376)

v. To revolve around, or move in an orbit; for example, the Moon orbits Earth.

órbita *s.* La trayectoria de un objeto en el espacio a medida que se mueve alrededor de otro objeto debido a la gravedad; por ejemplo, la Luna se mueve en una órbita alrededor de la Tierra.

orbitar *v.* Girar alrededor de algo, o moverse en una órbita; por ejemplo, la Luna orbita la Tierra.

organic compound

A compound that is based on carbon. (p. 345)

compuesto orgánico Un compuesto basado en el carbono.

organism

An individual living thing, made up of one or many cells. (p. CA18)

organismo Un individuo vivo, compuesto de una o muchas células.

parallax

The apparent shift in the position of an object when viewed from different locations. (p. 461)

paralaje El cambio aparente en la posición de un objeto cuando se observa desde diferentes puntos.

particle

A very small piece of matter, such as an atom, molecule, or ion.

partícula Una cantidad muy pequeña de materia, como un átomo, una molécula o un ión.

pascal Pa

The unit used to measure pressure. One pascal is the pressure exerted by one newton of force on an area of one square meter, or one N/m^2. (p. 110)

pascal La unidad utilizada para medir presión. Un pascal es la presión ejercida por un newton de fuerza sobre un área de un metro cuadrado, o un N/m^2.

penumbra

A region of lighter shadow that may surround an umbra; for example, the spreading cone of lighter shadow cast by a space object. (p. 401)

penumbra Una región de sombra más tenue que puede rodear a una umbra; por ejemplo, la sombra más tenue cónica proyectada por un objeto espacial.

period

A horizontal row in the periodic table of the elements. Elements in a period have varying properties. (p. 212)

período Un renglón horizontal en la tabla periódica de los elementos. Los elementos en un período tienen distintas propiedades.

periodic table

A table of the elements, arranged by atomic number, that shows the patterns in their properties. (p. 208)

tabla periódica Una tabla de los elementos, organizada en base a número atómico, que muestra los patrones en sus propiedades.

pH

The concentration of hydrogen ions in a solution; a measurement of acidity. (p. 326)

pH La concentración de iones de hidrógeno en una solución;, una medida de acidez.

photosynthesis

In green plants, the endothermic process in which light is absorbed and used to change carbon dioxide and water into glucose and oxygen. (p. 292)

fotosíntesis En plantas verdes, el proceso endotérmico en el cual se absorbe luz y se usa para cambiar dióxido de carbono y agua a glucosa y oxígeno.

physical change

A change in a substance that does not change the substance into a different one. (p. 151)

cambio físico Un cambio en una sustancia que no transforma la sustancia a otra sustancia.

physical property

A characteristic of a substance that can be observed without changing the identity of the substance. (p. 149)

propiedad física Una característica de una sustancia que se puede observar sin cambiar la identidad de la sustancia.

polar covalent bond

The unequal sharing of electrons between two atoms that gives rise to negative and positive regions of electric charge. (p. 253)

enlace polar covalente El compartir electrones desigualmente entre dos átomos y que lleva a la formación de regiones de carga eléctrica positiva y regiones de carga eléctrica negativa.

polymer

A very large carbon-based molecule made of smaller, repeating units. (p. 348)

polímero Una molécula muy grande basada en el carbono compuesta de unidades más pequeñas que se repiten.

position

An object's location. (p. 9)

posición La ubicación de un objeto.

precipitate

n. A solid substance that forms as a result of a reaction between chemicals in two liquids. (p. 274)

v. To come out of solution.

precipitado *s.* Una sustancia sólida que se forma como resultado de la reacción entre sustancias químicas en dos líquidos.

precipitar *v.* Salir de solución.

pressure

A measure of how much force is acting on a certain area; how concentrated a force is. Pressure is equal to the force divided by area. (p. 110)

presión Una medida de cuánta fuerza actúa sobre cierta área; el nivel de concentración de la fuerza. La presión es igual a la fuerza dividida entre el área.

product

A substance formed by a chemical reaction. A product is made by the rearrangement of atoms and bonds in reactants. (p. 273)

producto Una sustancia formada por una reacción química. Un producto se hace mediante la reorganización de los átomos y los enlaces en los reactivos.

protein

One of many types of molecules made up of chains of amino acid subunits. Proteins control the chemical activity of a cell and support growth and repair. (p. 356)

proteína Uno de muchos tipos de moléculas formadas por cadenas de aminoácidos. Las proteínas controlan la actividad química de una célula y sustentan el crecimiento y la reparación.

proton

A positively charged particle located in an atom's nucleus. (p. 201)

protón Una partícula con cargada positivamente localizada en el núcleo de un átomo.

Q

quasar

The very bright center of a distant galaxy. (p. 471)

quásar El centro muy brillante de una galaxia distante.

R

radiation (RAY-dee-AY-shuhn)

Energy that travels across distances in the form of electromagnetic waves. (p. CA16)

radiación Energía que viaja a través de la distancia en forma de ondas electromagnéticas.

radioactivity

The process by which the nucleus of an atom of an element releases energy and particles. (p. 220)

radioactividad El proceso mediante el cual el núcleo de un átomo de un elemento libera energía y partículas.

reactant

A substance that is present at the beginning of a chemical reaction and is changed into a new substance. (p. 273)

reactivo Una sustancia que está presente en el comienzo de una reacción química y que se convierte en una nueva sustancia.

reactive
Likely to undergo a chemical change. (p. 216)

reactivo Que es probable que sufra un cambio químico.

reference point
A location with which another location is compared. (p. 10)

punto de referencia Una ubicación con la cual se compara otra ubicación.

revolution
The motion of one body around another, such as Earth in its orbit around the Sun; the time it takes an object to go around once. (p. 383)

revolución El movimiento de un cuerpo alrededor de otro, como la Tierra en su órbita alrededor del Sol; el tiempo que le toma a un objeto dar la vuelta una vez.

ring
In astronomy, a wide, flat zone of small particles that orbit around a planet's equator. (p. 431)

anillo En astronomía, una zona ancha y plana de pequeñas partículas que orbitan alrededor del ecuador de un planeta.

S

saturated
Containing the maximum amount of a solute that can be dissolved in a particular solvent at a given temperature and pressure. (p. 315)

saturado Que contiene la máxima cantidad de soluto que se puede disolver en un solvente en particular a determinada temperatura y presión.

season
One part of a pattern of temperature changes and other weather trends over the course of a year. Astronomical seasons are defined and caused by the position of Earth's axis relative to the direction of sunlight. (p. 384)

estación Una parte de un patrón de cambios de temperatura y otras tendencias meteorológicas en el curso de un año. Las estaciones astronómicas se definen y son causadas por la posición del eje de la Tierra en relación a la dirección de la luz del Sol.

second s
A unit of time equal to one-sixtieth of a minute.

segundo Una unidad de tiempo igual a una sesentava parte de un minuto.

solar system
The Sun and its family of orbiting planets, moons, and other objects. (p. 376)

sistema solar El Sol y su familia de planetas, lunas y otros objetos en órbita.

solar wind
A stream of electrically charged particles that flows out in all directions from the Sun's corona. (p. 457)

viento solar Una corriente de partículas eléctricamente cargadas que fluye hacia fuera de la corona del Sol en todas las direcciones.

solid
Matter that has a definite shape and a definite volume. The molecules in a solid are in fixed positions and are close together. (p. 166)

sólido La materia que tiene una forma definida y un volumen definido. Las moléculas en un sólido están en posiciones fijas y cercanas unas a otras.

solstice (SAHL-stihs)
In an orbit, a position and time during which one hemisphere gets its maximum area of sunlight, while the other hemisphere gets its minimum amount; the time of year when days are either longest or shortest, and the angle of sunlight reaches its maximum or minimum. (p. 384)

solsticio En una órbita, la posición y el tiempo durante los cuales un hemisferio obtiene su área máxima de luz del Sol, mientras que el otro hemisferio obtiene su cantidad mínima; la época del año en la cual los días son los más largos o los más cortos y el ángulo de la luz del Sol alcanza su máximo o su mínimo.

solubility
The amount of solute that dissolves in a certain amount of a solvent at a given temperature and pressure to produce a saturated solution. (p. 316)

solubilidad La cantidad de soluto que se disuelve en cierta cantidad de solvente a determinada temperatura y presión para producir una solución saturada.

solute
In a solution, a substance that is dissolved in a solvent. (p. 308)

soluto En una solución, una sustancia que se disuelve en un solvente.

solution
A mixture of two or more substances that is identical throughout; a homogeneous mixture. (p. 307)

solución Una mezcla de dos o más sustancias que es idéntica en su totalidad; una mezcla homogénea.

solvent
In a solution, the substance that dissolves a solute and makes up the largest percentage of a solution. (p. 308)

solvente En una solución, la sustancia que disuelve un soluto y que compone el porcentaje mayor de la una solución.

species
A group of living things that are so closely related that they can breed with one another and produce offspring that can breed as well. (p. CA18)

especie Un grupo de organismos que están tan estrechamente relacionados que pueden aparearse entre sí y producir crías que también pueden aparearse.

speed
A measure of how fast something moves through a particular distance over a definite time period. Speed is distance divided by time. (p. 16)

rapidez Una medida del desplazamiento de un objeto a lo largo de una distancia específica en un período de tiempo definido. La rapidez es la distancia dividida entre el tiempo.

states of matter
The different forms in which matter can exist. Three familiar states are solid, liquid, and gas. (p. 165)

estados de la materia Las diferentes formas en las cuales puede existir la materia. Los tres estados conocidos son sólido, líquido y gas.

sublimation
The process by which a substance changes directly from its solid state to its gas state without becoming a liquid first. (p. 183)

sublimación El proceso mediante el cual una sustancia cambia directamente de su estado sólido a su estado gaseoso sin convertirse primero en líquido.

subscript
A number written slightly below and to the right of a chemical symbol that shows how many atoms of an element are in a compound. (p. 245)

subíndice Un número que se escribe en la parte inferior a la derecha de un símbolo químico y que muestra cuantos átomos de un elemento están en un compuesto.

substance
Matter of a particular type. Elements, compounds, and mixtures are all substances.

sustancia La materia de cierto tipo. Los elementos, los compuestos y las mezclas son sustancias.

sunspot
A darker spot on the photosphere of the Sun. A sunspot appears dark because it is cooler than the surrounding area. (p. 456)

mancha solar Una mancha oscura en la fotosfera del Sol. Una mancha solar se ve oscura porque es más fría que el área que la rodea.

suspension
A mixture in which the different parts are identifiable as separate substances; a heterogeneous mixture. (p. 309)

suspensión Una mezcla en la cual las diferentes partes son identificables como sustancias distintas; una mezcla heterogénea.

system
A group of objects or phenomena that interact. A system can be as simple as a rope, a pulley, and a mass. It also can be as complex as the interaction of energy and matter in the four parts of the Earth system.

sistema Un grupo de objetos o fenómenos que interactúan. Un sistema puede ser algo tan sencillo como una cuerda, una polea y una masa. También puede ser algo tan complejo como la interacción de la energía y la materia en las cuatro partes del sistema de la Tierra.

T

technology
The use of scientific knowledge to solve problems or engineer new products, tools, or processes.

tecnología El uso de conocimientos científicos para resolver problemas o para diseñar nuevos productos, herramientas o procesos.

tectonics (tehk-TAHN-ihks)
The processes in which the motion of hot material under a crust changes the crust of a space body. Earth has a specific type of tectonics called plate tectonics. (p. 420)

tectónica Los procesos en los cuales el movimiento del material caliente bajo una corteza cambia la corteza de un cuerpo espacial. La Tierra tiene un tipo específico de tectónica denominado tectónica de placas.

temperature
A measure of the average amount of kinetic energy of the particles in an object. (p. 175)

temperatura Una medida de la cantidad promedio de energía cinética de las partículas en un objeto.

tension
The force that stretches an object. Tension also refers to the force transmitted through a stretched object. (p. 80)

tensión La fuerza que estira un objeto. La tensión se refiere también a la fuerza transmitida a través de un objeto estirado.

terrestrial planet
Earth or a planet similar to Earth that has a rocky surface. The four planets in the inner solar system—Mercury, Venus, Earth, and Mars—are terrestrial planets. (p. 419)

planeta terrestre La Tierra o un planeta parecido a la Tierra que tiene una superficie rocosa. Los cuatro planetas en el sistema solar interior—Mercurio, Venus, la Tierra y Marte—son planetas terrestres.

theory
In science, a set of widely accepted explanations of observations and phenomena. A theory is a well-tested explanation that is consistent with all available evidence.

teoría En las ciencias, un conjunto de explicaciones de observaciones y fenómenos que es ampliamente aceptado. Una teoría es una explicación bien probada que es consecuente con la evidencia disponible.

thermal conductivity
A measure of how easily thermal energy is transferred through a particular substance. (p. 227)

conductividad térmica La capacidad de los materiales para dejar pasar el calor.

thermometer
A device for measuring temperature. (p. 177)

termómetro Un aparato para medir la temperatura.

U

umbra
The dark, central region of a shadow, such as the cone of complete shadow cast by an object. (p. 401)

umbra La región central y oscura de una sombra, como la sombra completa cónica proyectada por un objeto.

universe
Space and all the matter and energy in it. (p. 376)

universo El espacio y toda la materia y energía que hay dentro de él.

V

variable
Any factor that can change in a controlled experiment, observation, or model.

variable Cualquier factor que puede cambiar en un experimento controlado, en una observación o en un modelo.

vector
A quantity that has both size and direction. (p. 22)

vector Una cantidad que tiene magnitud y dirección.

velocity
A speed in a specific direction. (p. 22)

velocidad Una rapidez en una dirección específica.

vertical
Straight up or down from a level surface.

vertical Que está dispuesto hacia arriba o hacia abajo de una superficie nivelada.

volcanism
The process of molten material moving from a space body's hot interior onto its surface. (p. 420)

vulcanismo El proceso del movimiento de material fundido del interior caliente de un cuerpo espacial a su superficie.

volume
An amount of three-dimensional space, often used to describe the space that an object takes up. (p. 103)

volumen Una cantidad de espacio tridimensional; a menudo se usa este término para describir el espacio que ocupa un objeto.

W, X, Y, Z

wavelength
The distance from one wave crest to the next crest; the distance from any part of one wave to the identical part of the next wave.

longitud de onda La distancia de una cresta de onda a la siguiente cresta; la distancia de cualquier parte de una onda a la parte idéntica de la siguiente onda.

weight
The force of gravity on an object. (p. 73)

peso La fuerza de la gravedad sobre un objeto.

Index

Note: The page numbers for definitions are printed in **boldface** type.
The page numbers for illustrations, maps, and charts are printed in *italic* type.

INDEX

I

INDEX

INDEX

INDEX

Mendeleev's, 208–209, *208*
metalloids, 220, *220*, 230, *230*
metals, 217–218, *217*, 226, *226*, 230, *230*
noble gases, 219, *219*, 226, *226*
nonmetals, 219, *219*, 226, 227, 230, *230*
organization of, 209, *209*, 210–211
physical properties and, 226–227
radioactive elements, 220–222, *220*
rare earth elements, 218, *218*
regions of, 216–220, *216*, 230, *230*
size of atoms and, 225
thermal conductivity and, 227
trends and patterns, 212–213, 224–228, 225, *225*, *226*, *228*
periods, in periodic table, 208, *210–211*, **212**, 212–213, *212*, 216, 225, *233*, *R52–R53*
perpetual-motion machine, 97, 98, *98*
Perrier, Carlo, 194
petroleum, CA25, 292, 307, 321
pH, **326**, *327*, 332
buffers, 329
neutralization and, 328–329
of stomach acid, 329
phases of the Moon, 398, *399*, 400, 406, *409*
phospholipids, 355, *355*
phosphorus (P), 206, *206*, 340, *340*, *341*, 345, 352, 355, 359
photosphere, 454, *455*, 456, *456*
photosynthesis, **292**, 292–293, 354
physical changes, *150*, **151**, 151–152, *153*, 158, *158*, 271, 272, *272*
change in state, 162, 180–185, *181*, *182*, *183*, *184*, *185*
Chapter Investigation, 156–157, *156*
in cooking process, 161
energy changes and, 289
physical laws, CA16
physical properties, **149**, 149–151, *150*, 158, *158*
chemical bonds and, 249
of groups of elements, 212
of metals, 258–259, *259*
periodic table and, 226
states of matter, 165–166, *167*, 168–171, *168*, *170*, *171*, 174, *174*
physical science, CA12, **CA13**, CA15, 206
physical states. *See* states of matter.
physics, **CA13**
planetary rings
of Saturn, 430, *430*, 431, *431*, *442*
of Uranus, 432, *432*
planetary satellites, 413, *414*. *See also* Moon of Earth.
Charon, 435, *435*
composition of, 410
formation of, 417
of gas giants, 431, *431*, 432, 436, *436*
of Jupiter, *430*
of Neptune, *433*
of Saturn, *431*
planets, *414*
cores of, 419, 429, *429*
crusts of, 419
distance from Sun, *414–415*, 415, *R57*
doubles, 435, *435*, 442, *442*
gas giants (outer solar system), *414*, 428–433, *428*, *429*, *430*, *431*, *432*, *433*, 436, *436*, 442

mantles of, 419
moons of, *414*, 417, *430*, 431, *431*, 432, 435, *435*, 436, *436*
movement of, 380, *380*
orbits of the Sun, 416, *419*, *423*, *424*, *425*, *429*, *430*, *432*, *432*, 433, *433*, 435, 446, *446*, 447
processes shaping surface of, 420, *421*, 423, *423*, 424
rings of, 430, *430*, 431, *431*, 432, *432*, *442*
role of gravity in formation of, 416, 477
rotation of, 416
sizes of, *414*
terrestrial (inner solar system), *414*, 419, *419*, *421*, 422, *423*, *424*, *425*, *426*, *427*, 434
plants, 292–293, 318
needs of, CA19
photosynthesis in, 354
storage of energy, 354
structural material of, 353, 354, *354*, *362*
plasmas, 171, *171*
plasma TV, 171
platinum (Pt), 200, 218
Pluto, 413, 435, *435*, 442
atmosphere of, 435
density of, *R57*
diameter of, *435*, *R57*
distance from the Sun, *414*, 415, *442*, *R57*
formation of, 434
gravity of, 435
layers of, 435
mass of, 435, *435*, *R57*
moon, 435
orbit of, 415, 435, *435*, *R57*
revolution of, *R57*
rotation of, *435*, R57, *R57*
size of, *414*, *R57*
tilt of axis, *R57*
Plutonium (Pu), 224
pneumatic trough, 300, *300*
point of reference, 34
poisons, 206
polar covalent bonds, **253**, 253, *254*, 319, 342
Polaris, 379, R58, *R63*
polar molecules, 319–320, *320*
pollution, CA25, 321, 329
polonium (Po), 220, *222*, 302
polystyrene, *349*
position, 6, **9**, 34, *34*
change in, 44–45, *45*
description of, 10, *10*
distance and, 11, *11*
distance-time graphs, 20, *21*, *30*, 37, *37*
of elements on periodic table, 216
motion and, 12, *12*
speed and, 16
velocity and, 23, 25
positive ions, 204, *204*, 250–251, *250*, *251*
of acids, 323, *323*, 325, *325*, 326, *326*, 328
of bases, 328
formation of, 226
in living things, 217, 343
in solution, 259
potassium (K), 206, *206*, 212, 213, 217, 340
praseodymium (Pr), 218
precipitate, 155, **274**, *274*, 296, *296*, 315–316, *316*

INDEX

T

X, Y, Z

Acknowledgments

Photography

Cover, i © David Sanger Photography/Alamy Images; **iii** Photograph of James Trefil by Evan Cantwell; **iii** Photograph of Donald Steely by Marni Stamm; **iii** Photograph of Linda Carnine by Amilcar Cifuentes; **iii** Photograph of Sam Miller by Samuel Miller; **iii** Photograph of Kenneth Cutler by Kenneth A. Cutler; **iii** Photograph of Rita Ann Calvo by Joseph Calvo; **iii** Photograph of Vicky Vachon by Redfern Photographics; **ix** © Mike Chew/Corbis; **v** Courtesy of Bernice Filerman; **v** © Mark Handwerker; **v** © Jack Castro; **v** © William M. Bruce; **v** Courtesy of Sandy Steinburg; **viii** © Arthur Tilley/Getty Images; **x** © Steve Allen/Brand X Pictures; **xii** From *General Chemistry* by P. W. Atkins, © 1988 by Peter Atkins. Used with permission of W. H. Freeman and Company; **xiii** © Gerald Nowak/Westend 61/Alamy Images; **xiv** NASA/JPL/University of Arizona; **xv** © IBM Almaden Research Center; **xv** David Malin Images/Anglo-Australian Observatory; **xx** Photograph by Sharon Hoogstraten; **xxi** Photograph by Sharon Hoogstraten; **CA11–CA12** © Larry Hamill/Age Fotostock America, Inc.; **CA13–CA14** © Fritz Poelking/Age Fotostock America, Inc.; **CA15–CA16** © AFLO Foto Agency; **CA17–CA18** © Georgette Douwma/Getty Images; **CA19** AP/Wide World Photos; **CA20** © David Parker/IMI/Univ. of Birmingham High, TC Consortium/Photo Researchers, Inc.; **CA21** *left* AP/Wide World Photos; **CA21** *right* Washington University Record; **CA22** *top* © Kim Steele/Getty Images; **CA22** *bottom* Reprinted with permission from S Zhou et al., SCIENCE 291:1944–47. Copyright 2001 AAAS; **CA23–CA24** © Mike Fiala/Getty Images; **CA24** *left* © Derek Trask/Corbis; **CA24** *right* AP/Wide World Photos

Unit 1

Divider, Unit Opener © Brett Froomer/Getty Images; **2, 3** NASA/JPL/Caltech; **4** *bottom* © The Chedd-Angier Production Company; **6–7** © Richard Cummins/Corbis; **7** *top right, center right* Photograph by Sharon Hoogstraten; **9** *right* © Corbis; **11** *top* Photograph by Sharon Hoogstraten; **12** *top* © Globus, Holway & Lobel/Corbis; **12** *bottom* © The Image Bank/Getty Images; **14** *top* © Georgina Bowater/Corbis; **14** *bottom* © SuperStock; **015** *top left* © Graham Wheatley/The Military Picture Library/Corbis; **16, 17** Photographs by Sharon Hoogstraten; **18** *top left* © Gunter Marx Photography/Corbis; **19** Photograph by Sharon Hoogstraten; **21** *bottom* © Tom Brakefield/Corbis; **22** *bottom* © David M. Dennis/Animals Animals; **23** *top* © Kelly-Mooney Photography/Corbis; **24** *left* © Gallo Images/Corbis; **25** *right* © 1986 Richard Megna/Fundamental Photographs, NYC; **27** Photograph by Sharon Hoogstraten; **28** *top left* © Royalty-Free/Corbis; **29** *bottom* NASA/JPL/Caltech; **30** © Robert Essel NYC/Corbis; **32** *top* © Mark Jenkinson/Corbis; **32** *bottom left* Photograph by Sharon Hoogstraten; **32** *bottom right* Photograph by Sharon Hoogstraten; **34** © Globus, Holway & Lobel/Corbis; **34** *center* Photograph by Sharon Hoogstraten; **36** © David M. Dennis/Animals Animals; **38–39** © Arthur Tilley/Getty Images; **39** Photograph by Sharon Hoogstraten; **41** Photograph by Sharon Hoogstraten; **42** © John Kelly/Getty Images; **43** *left* © AFP/Corbis; **43** *right* © Reuters NewMedia, Inc./Corbis; **44** © Michael Kevin Daly/Corbis; **45** *left* © Jim Cummins/Getty Images; **45** *right* © Piecework Productions/Getty Images; **46** Photograph by Sharon Hoogstraten; **47** © Jeffrey Lynch/Mendola, Ltd.; **47** © Jeffrey Lynch/Mendola, Ltd.; **47** © Jeffrey Lynch/Mendola, Ltd.; **48** *inset* © Bill Ross/Corbis; **48** *left* © Bill Ross/Corbis; **48** *right* Dr. Paula Messina/San Jose State University; **49, 50** Photographs by Sharon Hoogstraten; **52** AP/Wide World Photos; **53** NASA; **54** Photographs by Sharon Hoogstraten; **55** AP/Wide World Photos; **56** *bottom* John Lair, Jewish Hospital, University of Louisville and ABIOMED; **56** *top* Clare Hirn, Jewish Hospital, University of Louisville and ABIOMED; **57** © Danny Lehman/Corbis; **58, 59** Photographs by Sharon

Hoogstraten; **60** © Photodisc/Getty Images; **60** *background* © David C. Fritts/Animals Animals; **62** *top* Digital image © 1996 Corbis/Original image courtesy of NASA/Corbis; **62** *bottom left, bottom right, center right* Photographs by Sharon Hoogstraten; **64** *top* © Photodisc/Getty Images; **64** *bottom left, bottom right* Photograph by Sharon Hoogstraten; **65** © Photodisc/Getty Images; **66** Photographs by Sharon Hoogstraten; **68–69** © Mike Chew/Corbis; **69, 71** Photographs by Sharon Hoogstraten; **74** *Earth* NASA; **74** *Moon* © Photodisc/Getty Images; **74** *top left, top right* Photograph by Sharon Hoogstraten; **75** ball thrower photographs by Sharon Hoogstraten; **75** *background, top, bottom* NASA; **76** Photograph by Sharon Hoogstraten; **77, 78** NASA; **78** AP/Wide World Photos; **79** Photograph by Sharon Hoogstraten; **80** © Photonica/Getty Images; **81** Photographs by Sharon Hoogstraten; **82** © 2004 Flybar/SBI Enterprises, Inc.; **84** © Imageshop/Zefa/Alamy Images; **86** © John Beatty/Getty Images; **87, 88** Photograph by Sharon Hoogstraten; **89** *top* Photograph by Sharon Hoogstraten; **89** *bottom* © Al Francekevich/Corbis; **90** © Joe McBride/Getty Images; **91** *inset* © Michael S. Yamashita/Corbis; **91** © NatPhotos/Tony Sweet/Digital Vision; **92, 93** Photographs by Sharon Hoogstraten; **94** © Joe McBride/Getty Images; **94** *right* Photograph by Sharon Hoogstraten; **96** *top* © Erich Lessing/Art Resource, New York; **96** *bottom* © Dagli Orti/The Art Archive; **97** *top right* Sam Fogg Rare Books & Manuscripts; **97** *top left* © SPL/Photo Researchers, Inc.; **97** *bottom* © DK Images; **98** *top left* © Victoria & Albert Museum, London/Art Resource, New York; **98** *top right* Photo Franca Principe, Institute and Museum of the History of Science; **98** *bottom right* © DK Images; **98** *center right* © Scala/Art Resource, New York; **99** Courtesy Claudia Alexander/JPL; **99** *bottom* NASA; **99** *top* © Gerald L. Schad/Photo Researchers, Inc.; **100–101** NASA/Marshall Space Flight Center; **101, 103** Photographs by Sharon Hoogstraten; **104, 105** Photographs by Sharon Hoogstraten; **107** © Andrew Lambert Photography/Photo Researchers, Inc.; **107** © Lawrence Livermore National Laboratory/Photo Researchers, Inc.; **108–109** Photograph by Sharon Hoogstraten; **108** *top* © Stewart Cohen/Getty Images; **108** *bottom* Photograph by Sharon Hoogstraten; **109** Photographs by Sharon Hoogstraten; **110** © Earl Ripling/Solus Photography/Veer; **111** © Corbis/Royalty Free; **112** *bottom* Photograph by Sharon Hoogstraten; **113** © Ralph A. Clevenger/Corbis; **114** © Philip & Karen Smith/Getty Images; **115** © Brandon Cole/Visuals Unlimited; **116, 117** Photograph by Sharon Hoogstraten; **118** © Breitling/Corbis Sygma; **120** Photographs by Sharon Hoogstraten; **121** © Stephen Frink Collection/Alamy Images; **121** © Carol Buchanan/Alamy Images; **123** © George Matsumoto/MBARI; **123** © MBARI; **123** © MBARI/NOAA; **123** © MBARI; **123** © David French/MBARI 1996; **126** Photographs by Sharon Hoogstraten

Unit 2
Divider, Unit Opener © Scott T. Smith/Corbis; **130–131** NASA/JPL/Caltech; **132** © Babakin Space Center, The Planetary Society; **132** © The Chedd-Angier Production Company; **134–135** © David Leahy/Getty Images; **135** Photograph by Sharon Hoogstraten; **137** © Royalty-Free/Corbis; **138** Photograph by Sharon Hoogstraten; **139** © NatPhotos/Tony Sweet/Digital Vision; **140** © Charles D. Winters/Photo Researchers, Inc.; **140** © Andrew Syred/Photo Researchers, Inc.; **141** © Jake Rajs/Getty Images; **142** Courtesy IBM Archives; **143** Photograph by Sharon Hoogstraten; **144** *left* © James L. Amos/Corbis; **144** *right* © Omni Photo Communications, Inc./Index Stock; **145** © David R. Frazier Photolibrary, Inc./Alamy Images; **146** Photograph by Sharon Hoogstraten; **147** © Royalty-Free/Corbis; **148** © Nik Wheeler/Corbis; **149** Photograph by Sharon Hoogstraten; **150** *left* Photograph by Sharon Hoogstraten; **150** *right* © Dan Lim/Masterfile; **153** *top left* © Maryellen McGrath/Bruce Coleman Inc.; **153** *top center* © Jean-Bernard Vernier/Corbis; **153** *top right* © Angelo Cavalli/Getty Images; **153** *bottom* © Garry Black/Masterfile; **153** *inset* Photograph by Sharon Hoogstraten; **154** © Mark C. Burnett/Stock, Boston Inc./PictureQuest; **155** © J. Westrich/Masterfile; **156** © Robert M. Vera/Alamy Images; **158** *left* © James L. Amos/Corbis; **158** © Royalty-Free/Corbis; **158** *right* © Dan Lim/Masterfile; **158** © Mark C. Burnett/Stock, Boston

Inc./PictureQuest; **162–163** © Steve Allen/Brand X Pictures; **163, 165** Photographs by Sharon Hoogstraten; **168** © Robert F. Sisson/Getty Images; **169** Photograph by Sharon Hoogstraten; **171** © SPL/Photo Researchers, Inc.; **172** *top* © Doug Sokell/ Visuals Unlimited; **172** *bottom* © Wally Eberhart/Visuals Unlimited; **172** *background* © QT Luong/Terra Galleria Photography; **173** Photograph by Sharon Hoogstraten; **174** © Tracy Frankel/Getty Images; **175** Photographs by Sharon Hoogstraten; **176** © Daryl Benson/Masterfile; **176** *inset* © Spencer Grant/PhotoEdit; **177** Photograph by Sharon Hoogstraten; **178** *top* © Steve Vidler/SuperStock; **178** *bottom* © Chase Jarvis/Getty Images; **179** © FogStock/Alamy; **179** *inset* © Gordon Wiltsie/Getty Images; **180** © ImageState/Alamy; **181** © Bjanka Kadic/Alamy Images; **181** *right* © Peter Bowater/Alamy; **182** © Royalty-Free/Corbis; **183** © Winifred Wisniewski/Frank Lane Picture Agency/Corbis; **184** © A. Pasieka/Photo Researchers, Inc.; **185** © Sean Ellis/Getty Images; **186** *top* © Royalty-Free/Corbis; **186** *bottom* Photograph by Sharon Hoogstraten; **187, 188** Photograph by Sharon Hoogstraten; **190** © Winifred Wisniewski/Frank Lane Picture Agency/Corbis; **192** © Ted Kinsman/Photo Researchers, Inc.; **192** © Oxford Science Archive/Heritage-Image/The Image Works; **193** © Science Photo Library/Photo Researchers, Inc.; **193** © The Johns Hopkins University. Courtesy, American Institute of Physics, Emilio Segrè Visual Archives; **193** © SPL/Photo Researchers, Inc.; **194** © American Institute of Physics/Photo Researchers, Inc.; **194** © Mauro Fermariello/Photo Researchers, Inc.; **195** © Courtesy of University Archives, The Bancroft Library, University of California, Berkeley; **195** Illustration by Thomas Tegge, Lawrence Livermore National Laboratory; **196–197** © IBM Almaden Research Center; **197, 199** Photograph by Sharon Hoogstraten; **200** © Astrid and Hanns-Frieder Michler/Photo Researchers, Inc.; **200** © Andrew Lambert Photography/Photo Researchers, Inc.; **202** © Pascal Goetgheluck/Photo Researchers, Inc.; **203** Photograph by Sharon Hoogstraten; **206** © Cnri/Photo Researchers, Inc.; **207** Photograph by Sharon Hoogstraten; **208** *left* The Granger Collection, New York; **208** *right* The Granger Collection, New York; **214** *bottom* Photograph by Sharon Hoogstraten; **214** *top* © A. Hart-Davis/Photo Researchers, Inc.; **216** Photograph by Sharon Hoogstraten; **217** *center* © Rich Treptow/Visuals Unlimited; **217** *left* © Charles D. Winters/Photo Researchers, Inc.; **217** *right* © Corbis Images/PictureQuest; **218** © Peter Christopher/Masterfile; **219** © M. Gibbon/Robertstock.com; **220** © Superstock; **221** *top* © Simon Fraser/Photo Researchers, Inc.; **221** *bottom* Photograph by Sharon Hoogstraten; **223** © Alfred Pasieka/Photo Researchers, Inc.; **223** *inset* © John Walsh/Photo Researchers, Inc.; **225** © Goronwy Tudor Jones/University of Birmingham/Photo Researchers, Inc.; **226** © Andrew Lambert Photography/Photo Researchers, Inc.; **226** Courtesy, Red, Green & Blue Company, Ltd.; **228** © William Whitehurst/Corbis; **229** © Robert Holmes/Corbis; **229** © North Wind/Ancy Carter/North Wind Picture Archives; **229** AP/Wide World Photos

Unit 3
Divider, Unit Opener © Photodisc/Getty Images; **236–237** © David Cavagnaro/Peter Arnold, Inc.; **237** Joel Sartore/National Geographic Image Collection; **238** © The Chedd-Angier Production Company; **239** © Colin Cuthbert/Photo Researchers, Inc.; **240–241** © Digital Vision/PictureQuest; **241, 243** Photograph by Sharon Hoogstraten; **244** *left* © Rich Treptow/Visuals Unlimited; **244** *center* © E.R. Degginger/Color-Pic, Inc.; **244** *right* © E.R. Degginger/Color-Pic, Inc.; **245, 247** Photograph by Sharon Hoogstraten; **248** © Lawrence M. Sawyer/Photodisc/PictureQuest; **249** © IFA/eStock Photography (PQ price control)/PictureQuest; **251** © Runk and Schoenberger/Grant Heilman Photography, Inc.; **251–254** © Kevin Schafer/Corbis; **255** Photograph by Sharon Hoogstraten; **257** © Roger Ressmeyer/Corbis; **257** © Meckes/Ottawa/Photo Researchers, Inc.; **258** Photograph by Sharon Hoogstraten; **259** © David Wrobel/Visuals Unlimited; **260** © Rob Blakers/photolibrary/PictureQuest; **261** *left* © E.R. Degginger/ Robertstock.com; **261** *right* © C. Swartzell/Visuals Unlimited; **262** *bottom* Photograph by Sharon Hoogstraten; **262** *top* © David Young-Wolff/Getty Images; **263** Photograph by Sharon Hoogstraten; **264** *left* © Rich Treptow/Visuals Unlimited; **264** *center* © E.R.

Degginger/Color-Pic, Inc.; **264** *right* © E.R. Degginger/Color-Pic, Inc.; **268–269** From *General Chemistry* by P. W. Atkins, © 1988 by Peter Atkins. Used with permission of W. H. Freeman and Company; **269, 271** Photographs by Sharon Hoogstraten; **272** © Daryl Benson/Masterfile; **274** *top left* © Science VU/Visuals Unlimited; **274** *top right* © 1992 Richard Megna/Fundamental Photographs, NYC; **274** *bottom left* © E.R. Degginger/Color-Pic, Inc.; **274** *bottom right* © Larry Stepanowicz/Visuals Unlimited; **276** Photograph by Sharon Hoogstraten; **279** *inset* © Andrew Lambert Photography/Photo Researchers, Inc.; **279** © Corbis Images/PictureQuest; **280** © Wally Eberhart/Visuals Unlimited; **281** *top* The Granger Collection, New York; **281** *bottom* Photograph by Sharon Hoogstraten; **282** © William Ervin/Photo Researchers, Inc.; **284** © Maximilian Stock Ltd./Photo Researchers, Inc.; **286** © Index Stock; **287** *left, inset* Courtesy of Chicago Fire Department; **287** *bottom right* Photograph by Sharon Hoogstraten; **288** Photograph by Sharon Hoogstraten; **289** *top* NASA; **289** *bottom* © 1992 Richard Megna/Fundamental Photographs, NYC; **290** © Jeffrey L. Rotman/Corbis; **291** Thomas Eisner and Daniel Aneshansley, Cornell University; **293** © Mike Powell/Getty Images; **294** *bottom left, bottom right* Photograph by Sharon Hoogstraten; **294** *top* AP/Wide World Photos; **294** Photograph by Sharon Hoogstraten; **296** *top right* © 1992 Richard Megna/Fundamental Photographs, NYC; **300** From Hales, *Vegetable Statiks*; **301** *top* The Granger Collection, New York; **301** *bottom* Mary Evans Picture Library; **302** *top* AP/Wide World Photos; **302** *bottom* © DK Images; **303** Photographs © David Parker/Photo Researchers, Inc.; **304–305** © Stephen Frink/Index Stock; **305, 307** Photographs by Sharon Hoogstraten; **308** © Richard Cummins/Corbis; **309** Photographs by Sharon Hoogstraten; **311** Photograph by Sharon Hoogstraten; **312** *inset* © 2001 Kim Fennema/Visuals Unlimited; **312** © Peter & Georgina Bowater/Stock Connection/PictureQuest; **313** © IFA/eStock Photography (PQ price control)/PictureQuest; **314, 315** Photograph by Sharon Hoogstraten; **316** *left* © 1990 Richard Megna/Fundamental Photographs, NYC; **316** *right* © 1990 Richard Megna/Fundamental Photographs, NYC; **317, 318** Photographs by Sharon Hoogstraten; **319** © Stephen Frink/StephenFrink.com; **320** Photograph by Sharon Hoogstraten; **321** ©2005 Streano/Havens Photography; **322, 324, 326** Photograph by Sharon Hoogstraten; **327** *bottom right* © E.R. Degginger/Color-Pic, Inc.; **327** *center right* © Phil Degginger/Color-Pic, Inc.; **327** *top right* © Chuck Swartzell/Visuals Unlimited; **327** *top left* © Martyn F. Chillmaid/Photo Researchers; **327** *center left* © E.R. Degginger/Color-Pic, Inc.; **327** *bottom left* © Stockbyte; **328** © Sheila Terry/Photo Researchers, Inc.; **328** © Bryan and Cherry Alexander/Photo Researchers, Inc.; **328** © Swerve/Alamy Images; **329** © David M. Martin/Photo Researchers, Inc.; **330–331** Photograph by Sharon Hoogstraten; **330** © Runk and Schoenberger/Grant Heilman Photography, Inc.; **331** Photograph by Sharon Hoogstraten; **336–337** © Gerald Nowak/Westend 61/Alamy Images; **337** Photograph by Sharon Hoogstraten; **341** © Dennis MacDonald/Alamy Images; **343** © Dr. John Brackenbury/Photo Researchers, Inc.; **344** © Eising/StockFood; **345** Photograph by Sharon Hoogstraten; **346** *left* © E.R. Degginger/Color-Pic, Inc.; **346** *right* © Charles D. Winters/Photo Researchers, Inc.; **347** Photograph by Sharon Hoogstraten; **349** *top* © Claver Carroll/Age Fotostock America, Inc.; **349** *bottom right* Photograph by Sharon Hoogstraten; **349** *bottom left* © Fabio Cardoso/Age Fotostock America, Inc.; **351** © Peter Bennett/Ambient Images, Inc./Alamy Images; **351** © Soqui Ted/Corbis Sygma; **351** © Soqui Ted/Corbis Sygma; **352** Photograph by Sharon Hoogstraten; **353** © Marcialis/StockFood; **354** © John Durham/Photo Researchers, Inc.; **355** *bottom* © SPL/Photo Researchers, Inc.; **355** *top* © Meyer/StockFood; **356** Photograph by Sharon Hoogstraten; **357** *left* © Andrew Syred/Photo Researchers, Inc.; **357** *right* © SCIMAT 2000/Photo Researchers, Inc.; **360** *top left* © Ken Eward/Photo Researchers, Inc.; **360** Photograph by Ken O'Donoghue; **360, 361** Photographs by Frank Siteman; **367** Photos © David Nunuk/Photo Researchers, Inc.; **368–369** © Charles O'Rear/Corbis; **369** *top right* © D. Nunuk/Photo Researchers, Inc.; **370–371** *top* © David Parker/Photo Researchers, Inc.; **370** *bottom* © The Chedd-Angier Production Company; **371** *top center* NASA/JPL; **372-373** © Roger Ressmeyer/Corbis; **373, 375** Photographs by Sharon

ACKNOWLEDGMENTS

Inc.; **457** © Patrick J. Endres/Alaskaphotographics.com; **458** *top* © Dave Robertson/ Masterfile; **458** *bottom left, bottom right* Photographs by Sharon Hoogstraten; **459, 460, 461** Photographs by Sharon Hoogstraten; **463** *top left, center left, bottom left* © DK Images; **463** *bottom* NASA, ESA and J. Hester (ASU); **464** NASA/J. Hester et al./CXC/ASU; **465** *background* NASA/Hubble Heritage Team/AURA/STScI; **467** *background* © MPIA-HD, Birkle, Slawik/Photo Researchers, Inc.; **468** Photograph by Sharon Hoogstraten; **469** *top* © Allan Morton/Dennis Milon/SPL/Photo Researchers, Inc.; **469** *bottom* Photograph by Sharon Hoogstraten; **470** *bottom left* David Malin Images/Anglo-Australian Observatory; **470** *bottom center, bottom right* David Malin Images/Anglo-Australian Observatory; **471** Walter Jaffe/Leiden Observatory, Holland Ford/JHU/STScI, and NASA; **472** *left* NASA and Hubble Heritage Team (STScI); **472** *center* NASA, H. Ford (JHU), G. Illingworth (UCSC/LO), M. Clampin (STScI), G. Hartig (STScI), the ACS Science Team, and ESA; **473** Photograph by Sharon Hoogstraten; **474** Photograph by Jason Ware; **476** Photograph by Sharon Hoogstraten; **477** NASA/ESA/N. Benitez (JHU), T. Broadhurst (The Hebrew University), H. Ford (JHU), M. Clampin (STScI), G. Hartig (STScI), G. Illingworth (UCO/Lick Observatory), the AGS Science Team; **478** *spiral galaxy, elliptical galaxy, irregular galaxy* David Malin Images/Anglo-Australian Observatory; **478** *bottom* NASA/ESA/N. Benitez (JHU), T. Broadhurst (The Hebrew University), H. Ford (JHU), M. Clampin (STScI), G. Hartig (STScI), G. Illingworth (UCO/Lick Observatory), the AGS Science Team; **480** Photographs David Malin Images/Anglo-Australian Observatory

Illustrations and Maps

Accurate Art Incorporated **440**
Ampersand Design Group **15, 167, 287**
Julian Baum **395, 455 465 466 469 478**
Peter Bull **121, 385, 386**
Steve Cowden **386**
Stephen Durke **104, 139, 142, 144, 158, 168, 170, 201, 203, 204, 205, 230, 250, 251, 252, 253, 254, 256, 261, 264, 266, 272, 273, 275, 298, 334, 346, 356, 357, 358** *amino acid chain*, **362, 364, 378, 380, 406**
Patrick Gnan **358** *bottom right*
David A. Hardy **377, 414, 417** *top left, top center, top right* **429**
KO Studios **358** *top right*
Debbie Maizels **358** *bottom left*
MapQuest.com, Inc. **10, 402**
Tony Randazzo/American Artists Rep. Inc. **13**

The Periodic Table of the Elements

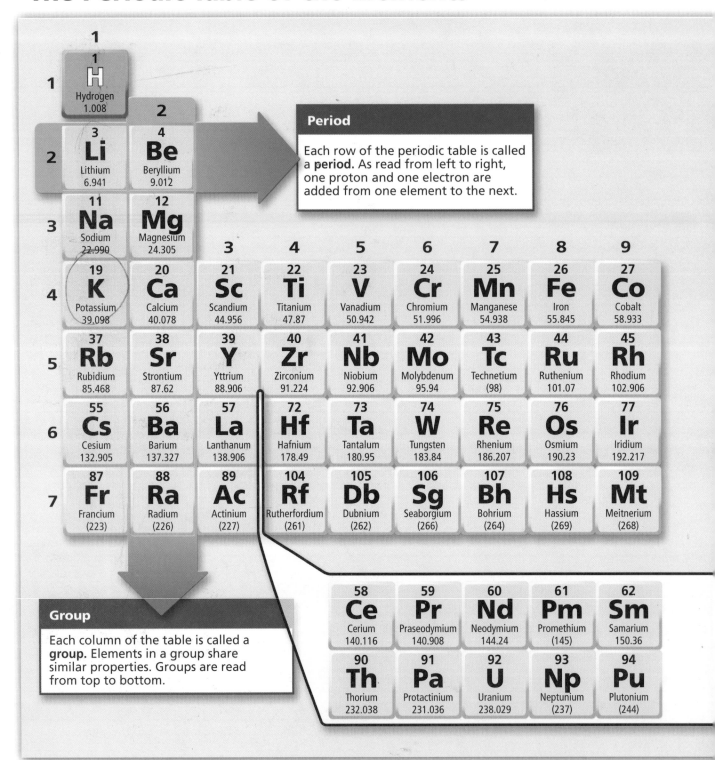

1								
1 **H** Hydrogen 1.008	**2**							
3 **Li** Lithium 6.941	**4** **Be** Beryllium 9.012							
11 **Na** Sodium 22.990	**12** **Mg** Magnesium 24.305	**3**	**4**	**5**	**6**	**7**	**8**	**9**
19 **K** Potassium 39.098	**20** **Ca** Calcium 40.078	**21** **Sc** Scandium 44.956	**22** **Ti** Titanium 47.87	**23** **V** Vanadium 50.942	**24** **Cr** Chromium 51.996	**25** **Mn** Manganese 54.938	**26** **Fe** Iron 55.845	**27** **Co** Cobalt 58.933
37 **Rb** Rubidium 85.468	**38** **Sr** Strontium 87.62	**39** **Y** Yttrium 88.906	**40** **Zr** Zirconium 91.224	**41** **Nb** Niobium 92.906	**42** **Mo** Molybdenum 95.94	**43** **Tc** Technetium (98)	**44** **Ru** Ruthenium 101.07	**45** **Rh** Rhodium 102.906
55 **Cs** Cesium 132.905	**56** **Ba** Barium 137.327	**57** **La** Lanthanum 138.906	**72** **Hf** Hafnium 178.49	**73** **Ta** Tantalum 180.95	**74** **W** Tungsten 183.84	**75** **Re** Rhenium 186.207	**76** **Os** Osmium 190.23	**77** **Ir** Iridium 192.217
87 **Fr** Francium (223)	**88** **Ra** Radium (226)	**89** **Ac** Actinium (227)	**104** **Rf** Rutherfordium (261)	**105** **Db** Dubnium (262)	**106** **Sg** Seaborgium (266)	**107** **Bh** Bohrium (264)	**108** **Hs** Hassium (269)	**109** **Mt** Meitnerium (268)

Period

Each row of the periodic table is called a **period**. As read from left to right, one proton and one electron are added from one element to the next.

Group

Each column of the table is called a **group**. Elements in a group share similar properties. Groups are read from top to bottom.

58	59	60	61	62
Ce Cerium 140.116	**Pr** Praseodymium 140.908	**Nd** Neodymium 144.24	**Pm** Promethium (145)	**Sm** Samarium 150.36
90 **Th** Thorium 232.038	**91** **Pa** Protactinium 231.036	**92** **U** Uranium 238.029	**93** **Np** Neptunium (237)	**94** **Pu** Plutonium (244)

 Metal Metalloid Nonmetal  **Fe** Solid **Hg** Liquid Gas